Abuse of Women: Legislation, Reporting, and Prevention

Abuse of Women: Legislation, Reporting, and Prevention

Joseph J. Costa

LexingtonBooks
D.C. Heath and Company
Lexington, Massachusetts
Toronto

Library of Congress Cataloging in Publication Data

Costa, Joseph J.
  Abuse of women.

  Bibliography: p.
  Includes index.
  1. Wife abuse—United States. 2. Abused wives—
Services for—United States. 3. Abused wives—
Services for—United States—Directories. I. Title.
HV6626.C67   1983   362.8'3   81-48512
ISBN 0-669-05374-0

Copyright © 1983 by D.C. Heath and Company

Published simultaneously in Canada

Printed in the United States of America

International Standard Book Number: 0-669-05374-0

Library of Congress Catalog Card Number: 81-48512

This effort, this work,
this life

for the greater honor and glory of God

Contents

Preface

The vast growth and development of this subject—abuse of women—in the past few years have brought to the public an awareness and a sharply honed interest of the highest priority. Likewise, the sources and resources have grown in leaps and bounds. The intent of this compilation is to put into some organized form the sources and resources that are available to women in need of this kind of information, service, and so forth and to make them aware that someone out there cares.

It is a very difficult task to assemble such information, knowing that as one is assembling same, changes are happening that make this effort outdated—for example, some resources are going out of existence, some are changing and developing to a different level, and some are combining their activities with others. Because of this aspect of growth and change, the readers must realize that this book cannot claim to be totally exhaustive, even though the attempt to that extent was made.

In all works of this nature, several people must be acknowledged for their support and efforts: Dr. Stephen R. Couch, sociologist, Schuylkill Campus, The Pennsylvania State University, for his moral support and writing and developing the introduction; Dr. Richard J. Gelles, for permission to reprint chapter 2; Karen Crist, editor, Center for Women Policy Studies, for permission to have several items reprinted, as well as for the availability of that organization's bibliographic resources; Fran Cable, Reference Department, Pattee Library, The Pennsylvania State University, for her assistance in establishing and completing the computerized literature search; Lorraine Stanton, library assistant, Schuylkill Campus, The Pennsylvania State University, for obtaining several resource items through the university's interlibrary loan and photoduplication services; Library Aides Diane Brower, Chris Dissinger, Joel Koch, and Debbie Pogash, for their assistance in this project in many ways; and Shenandoah Valley students Anne Ulicney, Regina Speaker, and Leslie Sienkiewicz for their services in proofreading.

Finally, a big thanks to my wife, Marie, for her efforts, time, inspiration, and motivation.

1

Research on Wife Abuse: A Scan of the Literature

Stephen R. Couch

Abuse of women by their husbands is not a new phenomenon. Evidence indicates that throughout most of recorded history wife abuse in one form or another has been a common and accepted practice in even some of the most advanced civilizations. Our society is no exception. Terry Davidson (1977, p.4) states that "it is a shock to read laws for the 1800s which regulate wifebeating: not criminalized it, but permitted it." To this day, cultural norms extolling the sanctity of the family and legitimizing husbands' rights as heads of household act to encourage wife abuse and to shield it from the attention of outsiders.

Consequently, wife abuse has suffered what Louis Dexter (1958) called selective inattention in the academic world. While marriage and the family have been subjects of intense interest among social scientists for many years, wife abuse was virtually ignored as an area of research until recently.

However, since 1970, the subject has been receiving significantly increased research attention. Due in large part to accomplishments of the women's movement, which has focused attention on all aspects of the degradation of women and has begun to effect a change in cultural norms supporting abuse, a large body of literature has developed that is beginning to erode our ignorance of the causes and consequences of wife abuse.

This chapter summarizes this body of literature—to determine what we know about wife abuse and what we still need to know. It is not a comprehensive review of the literature. Rather, it identifies the various strands of research that have developed, cites representative examples of each, and assesses what we know about wife abuse at this time.

Whatever conclusions are reached must remain tentative. Because of its nature, wife abuse is an elusive research topic, taking place behind closed doors and often unknown by anyone outside the immediate family involved. Most research has used small numbers of cases that have somehow come to the attention of social-service agencies or legal authorities. Therefore, generalizing findings to the entire population is full of difficulties. In addition, since most research has used data solicited from the victims of abuse, we have more-detailed information about the victims than about the abusers. Nevertheless, numerous suggestive conclusions have been reached thus far, and many of them hold consistently across different research studies.

Extent

It is extremely difficult to measure the extent of wife abuse in our society. Prescott and Letko (1977, p. 72) state that in 1973, nearly 15,000 complaints went to family court in New York State alone. They suggest that unreported cases might double or triple that total, pointing out that "most women will not make public the conflict in their marriages." Indeed, assault by relatives is estimated to be the most underreported crime covered by the National Crime Survey (Gaquin 1977–1978, p. 634). Even reported cases are often lost to the researcher since police use no uniform reporting procedures (Wisconsin Council 1980; Flynn 1977).

Nevertheless, it is becoming ever clearer that wife abuse is not a rare, isolated phenomenon but that it occurs in a strikingly large number of U.S. homes. In researching forty families suspected by social-service agencies of experiencing some form of family violence, Richard J. Gelles (1974) found that over one-half of the families reported at least one incident of spouse assault having occurred. Moreover, Gelles found that spouse assault was reported to have taken place in over one-third of a forty-family control sample used in the study. Murray A. Straus (1974) found that 16 percent of 385 college students sampled reported violence between their parents during the past year. On the basis of his research, John P. Flynn (1977) estimated that 10 percent of the families in and around Kalamazoo, Michigan, have experienced conjugal violence. After studying returns of a national sample of over two thousand families, Murray A. Straus (1980, pp. 11–12) reports: "Each year about sixteen out of every hundred American couples experience at least one incident in which either the husband or the wife uses physical force on the other." He goes on to state that in 6 percent of U.S. families a serious act of violence was involved, "such as kicking, punching, biting, hitting with an object, beating up the other, or using a knife or gun." Research is unanimous in concluding that the vast majority of cases of physical abuse is committed by the husband against his spouse.

Characteristics

Incidents of wife abuse most often occur at home, at night, and on weekends and holidays (Gelles 1974; Flynn 1977). The fact that there are no witnesses except perhaps the couple's children means that abuse can be easily kept secret and that community presence and response cannot act as an immediate restraint on the couple (Spiegel 1980). Numerous studies have exploded the myth that serious injuries seldom occur or that weapons are seldom used (for example, Carlson 1977; Flynn 1977). Multiple incidents in one family are not unusual either—if abuse happens once, it is likely to happen often (Bard and Zacker 1974; Carlson 1977; Flynn 1977; Gelles 1974).

People involved in spouse abuse often were abused by their parents and witnessed spouse abuse during childhood. This is true of both abusers (Carlson 1977; Flynn 1977) and abused (Gelles 1974; Wisconsin Council 1980). This suggests that a behavioral response pattern that legitimizes abuse and influences the ways in which both parties will behave toward one another is developed at an early age.

One interesting finding is that wife abuse often occurs when the educational level of the husband is lower than that of the wife (Gelles 1974; Carlson 1977). Researchers argue that this may create feelings of frustration and inferiority in the husband that contribute to his resorting to violence. In addition, the wife's education may make her more adept at verbal argument, leaving violence as the only recourse left for her husband if he is to win the altercation. The latter point receives support from Straus (1974) who found that rather than providing a safe outlet for family aggressions, verbal violence is more often linked with physical violence. Other studies have confirmed that physical violence is often preceded by verbal arguments (Flynn 1977; Gelles 1974).

Incidents of abuse are more likely to occur in families experiencing significant stress (Prescott and Letko 1977; Straus 1978; Flynn 1977). Problems dealing with family finances, employment, child rearing, or the marital relationship itself are consistently linked with cases of abuse. A picture emerges of pressures straining a marital relationship that, when combined with a history of family violence during childhood, is liable to lead to verbal and then physical abuse. Once the barrier has been broken, acts of abuse are likely to be repeated.

Regardless of early psychological studies and speculation to the contrary, women do not enjoy being abused (Wisconsin Council 1980). Many try to defend themselves against their husbands, only to find that the severity of the attack against them increases (Carlson 1977). A good number of abused women do seek outside help. Those who do are more likely to seek aid from the police or talk to a friend rather than to approach a social-service agency (Carlson 1977). Agency help is more likely to be sought if children are in the home (Prescott and Letko 1977) or if abuse is severe and recurrent (Gelles 1974). Abuse is also linked with separation and divorce that are both results of abuse and causes of further abuse (Gaquin 1977–1978; Carlson 1977; Flynn 1977). The added frustration and hostility created by the breakup of a marriage contributes to the pattern of family violence that continues to occur in significant numbers of cases well after the family is no longer a legal unit.

While evidence drawn from numerous studies suggests these characteristics, conflicting evidence concerns several other relationships. For example, statistics are inconclusive concerning whether men or women are more likely to become homicide victims as a result of fighting with a spouse (Wolfgang 1956; 1958; Breiter 1979; Flynn 1977). Conflicting evidence also exists concerning the social-class background of abusers and their spouses. Are they primarily persons from lower social classes or are they spread relatively evenly throughout the class spectrum (Bloch 1980; Carlson 1977; Flynn 1977; Straus 1980)? Another area of controversy deals with the role of alcohol in family violence. Opinion differs as to whether alcohol problems are significant causes of marital violence, or if they are contributing factors, or unrelated parallel problems, or relatively unrelated altogether (Carlson 1977; Flynn 1977; Bard and Zacker 1974).

These then, are some of the characteristics and controversies that emerge from literature on wife abuse. The bulk of the remainder of this chapter examines the research perspectives used to discover wife-abuse characteristics and attempts to use them to explain the causes of abuse.

Research Perspectives

There have been a number of stages in research on spouse abuse. The first stage has been called by some authors the blame-the-victim stage (Prescott and Letko 1977; Wisconsin Council 1980). Scholars argued that wives were to blame in some measure for their own abuse because of women's submissive nature, the masochistic pleasure received from being dominated, and so on.

Then, around 1970, attention shifted from blaming the victim to blaming the offender. Research began to focus on abusers and to explain abuse in terms of psychopathic deviance or character disorder of the perpetrators of abuse (Wisconsin Council 1980, pp. 1–2; Straus 1980, p. 9). Such a shift in focus provided a necessary corrective to earlier work by breaking down the myth that the abused were the causes of their own problem. However, like the earlier research, this work also emphasized the individual psychological aspects of the problem, ignoring social, cultural, and situational factors.

More-recent work has shifted away from psychological and pathological explanations and has focused instead on social and cultural reasons for conjugal violence. Even recent work by psychologists has been more concerned with the influence of social factors and transmission of cultural traits that cause abuse to take place. The remainder of this section of the chapter discusses some of this more-recent work.

In its more-extreme manifestations, the perspective that focuses on the social and cultural context of abuse has been called the societal-blame perspective (Wisconsin Council 1980)—that is, the structure and norms of society are seen as causing abuse by perpetuating male dominance. The sexist society encourages the maintenance of male dominance at all costs, with males resorting to physical violence when necessary (Wisconsin Council 1980; Straus 1980). Cultural values that teach and legitimize traditional sex roles are diffused throughout the society (Straus 1976; Gelles 1974) and are transmitted not only through face-to-face interaction with parents and peers but also through games, sports, literature, the media, and even fairy tales. As Gates (1978, p. 22) suggests, "What American girl, under the influence of a Disney production of these stories, has not dreamed of being a pure, pretty and pitiable victim?"

Linked with socialization to traditional sex roles is socialization to attitudes about the use of violence. Again, literature, the media, and sports are viewed as culprits (Wisconsin Council 1980), helping to socialize children to views of violence as normal and acceptable under a wide variety of circumstances (Wolfgang 1976). The fact that many spouses who are involved in the conjugal violence were abused as children and/or witnessed their parents engaged in spouse abuse is seen as a link between societal norms about sex roles and violence and specific internalized norms concerning behavior in marriage. Moreover, in this way, family violence becomes linked with love, justified in certain circumstances even (or especially) against a loved one (Straus 1980).

These cultural factors are perpetuated and reinforced by structural conditions. For example, women are economically vulnerable, experiencing financial and occupational constraints that often force dependence upon their husbands for financial support and that make protesting abuse or leaving home extremely difficult (Gelles 1977). Even when a woman does leave, she is unlikely to be able to remove herself entirely from her husband's presence and possible abuse, especially where children are involved and fathers are given visitation rights (Fields 1977–1978).

Other important structural problems lie within the male-dominated legal system. Our laws reflect what Goodman (1977, p. 141) calls "the attitude of the legislature, police and judge . . . that they are dealing not with a public crime, but with signs of a 'troubled marriage.'" Neither laws nor the criminal-justice system treat wife abusers harshly. The development of legal codes has consistently favored men (Shainess 1977, pp. 111–112). The police and courts do not encourage reporting of abuse cases (Gelles 1974). Policemen identify with the husbands and take abuse cases lightly (Martin 1978). Some operate on the basis of a so-called stitch rule whereby, unless injuries are serious enough to require a certain number of stitches, no one is arrested (Straus 1980).

Some observers argue that treatment in the courts is also biased against the victim. For example, prior to 1977, all abuse complaints in New York State were referred to family court, not criminal court. The abuser cannot be remanded to jail by family court for his original misbehavior but only for violating a court order. Since 1977, women in New York have had the option of having abuse cases handled by criminal court. Problems still exist, however. Even if the husband is arrested on an abuse complaint, he usually is released and given a future date for court appearance, allowing him to return home to the woman who lodged the complaint (Goodman 1977). These factors imply that the structure and operation of the legal system fail to operate as a deterrent to wife abuse and, in some cases, unwittingly encourage it.

In summary, then, those who argue from the social-and-cultural-context perspective see the problem of wife abuse as stemming from sexist institutions and cultural norms in our society that perpetuate male superiority and dominance and female inferiority and submissiveness and that justify the use of violence by husbands in a family setting. Wife abuse, then, appears to be a logical, understandable outcome of these societal conditions.

This approach is not without its critics. Among them are Dobash and Dobash (for example, 1976a and 1976b) who see this perspective as too general and therefore not really an explanation of how conjugal violence comes to occur. They urge the adoption of a context-specific approach that focuses on delineating the specific characteristics and causes of wife abuse as a particular form of behavior.

Others also have been concerned with the generality of much of the social-and-cultural-context work, asking why wife abuse is not nearly universal in our society if we are all socialized to sexist norms and dominated by sexist institutions. Insistence is placed on examining the specific mechanisms and conditions that result in some people engaging in or accepting abuse but not others. Shainess (1977) discusses the conditions under which various Freudian personality types may commit conjugal violence. She views people who are likely abusers to exhibit infantility and to have a low level of tolerance of frustration and of impulse control. While emphatically refuting the notion that women enjoy being beaten, she does argue that the personality of the wife contributes to the problem, since excessively submissive women are more likely to choose to marry overly dominant men. From a similar perspective, Bloch (1980) links wife abuse with characteristics such as authoritarianism, rigidity, low self-esteem, and a limited interpretive repertoire.

Evaluation of Research Perspectives

The study of wife abuse has advanced a long way from the time when the victims themselves were blamed for their fate and when internal personality disorders of the abused or abusers were advanced as the sole cause of the problem. These simple explanations have given way to more-fruitful attempts to develop multicausal models for the occurrence of abuse. This makes the study of this problem much more difficult and complex but promises to provide meaningful results that are well worth the effort.

The social-and-cultural-context perspective has called attention to the role of sexual inequality and institutionalized violence in creating conditions that breed family violence. It is absolutely necessary to ground all studies in this context. The work of proponents of this perspective has gone far in debunking the myth that most family abuse is psychologically pathological behavior, divorced from the influences of the mainstream of our society. Indeed, as many studies point out, we are all at least potential abusers or victims of some form of family violence.

At the same time, not all of us abuse or are abused. Blaming society's values and institutions is insufficient. Research must specify what conditions and personality types make abuse more likely to occur. While not falling back on solely psychological explanations, scholars should continue work on personality characteristics and situational factors that make abuse more or less likely and should attempt to link these characteristics with the social and cultural context in which they are produced. Indeed, a number of the proponents of the social-and-cultural-context approach recognize this, as chapter 2 by Richard Gelles indicates. Murray Straus (1980), while eschewing psychological explanations and arguing that abuse in the family is normal social behavior, points to many specific factors that influence the likelihood of abuse, like witnessing parental abuse as a child (which presumably influences the personality development of that child).

Reductionism in either direction, toward individual psychopathology or toward the culture or structure of society, should be avoided. What is needed is a synthesis that uses the growing social, cultural, situational, and psychological factors into a unified, grounded theory. Given the short life span of research in this field to date, it is premature to expect such a theory to have emerged. Yet good research, provocative analysis, and healthy controversy are taking place and should be preparing the way for a better understanding of wife abuse that can be used to help prevent and treat the problem more effectively.

Areas for Further Research

A number of areas involving the study of wife abuse are in need of further research. Additional studies are needed by which to verify the characteristics of abuser and abused that have emerged from studies done this far and to clear up areas in which evidence is conflicting. It would be extremely beneficial if information could be collected from large representative national samples of the population to supplement the work done with smaller samples of victims. Also it would be helpful (though difficult) to develop methodologies by which the abusers (as well as the victims) could be studied in depth, not in an attempt to return to seeing the problem as mainly pathological but to gain evidence from the other side of the problem and to attempt to understand the causes and consequences of abuse from the perspective of the perpetrator. This is not so we can justify abuse; but only if we understand it fully can we work to eliminate it.

Another area in which much work needs to be done is the cross-cultural study of wife abuse (Spiegel 1980; West 1980). We need to look both at subcultural variance in abuse within societies and at abuse (or lack of it) in different societies. Concerning the latter, a vast amount of data already exists in the form of anthropological enthnographies collected on various societies. Studying these data and collecting new cross-cultural material should help us to specify more precisely the social and cultural mechanisms that influence the scope and form of wife abuse.

Finally, to complement cross-cultural studies and large-scale surveys, additional research into the specific conditions that lead to abuse is necessary. We must attempt to discover why, within the same general social and cultural context, some couples experience abuse while others do not. Here, it is important to study nonabuse situations as well as their counterparts. for example, a study of couples that possess characteristics indicating a high probability of the occurrence of abuse, but that have not engaged in abuse, would help to uncover some important characteristics or conditions that have been overlooked or undervalued to this point.

Implications for Deterrence and Treatment

A detailed consideration of deterrence and treatment strategies is beyond the scope of this chapter. However, it may be helpful to point out some broad implications for those areas that are suggested by the research that has been done to date on wife abuse.

Two central problems concerning all attempts at deterrence and treatment are cultural values and social structures that reinforce the continuance of sexual inequality and the sanctity of the family unit and its private dwelling place. The former point has been discussed at some length. As for the latter, the legal, and especially cultural, inviolability of the family in our society inhibits attempts by public agencies to deal with wife abuse. Family business, even abuse, is too often considered to be a private, not a public, concern. Added to this is the belief that the family home is a private, shielded place in which abuse can take place in secret. A man's home may be his castle, but a woman's home too often is her dungeon. And yet, to open the home to easier public access and scrutiny would increase the potential of violations of individual human and constitutional rights.

Within this context deterrence and treatment strategies must be developed and implemented. In the long run, it appears that large-scale changes toward equality of the sexes and toward a less-violent and -stressful society are the only ways to reduce wife abuse significantly. Institutionalized inequality and violence appear to be the root causes of the problem. However, in the meantime, we must develop effective ways to deal with the symptoms.

The effort must be carried out on two fronts: (1) through the legal system and (2) through social-service agencies. In the first place, laws must be reformed so that abused women will gain adequate protection and legal recourse. Courts and law-enforcement officials should be educated to view abuse not only as a family problem but also as violent crime. Stricter laws and enforcement procedures will do little to deter initial acts of abuse since they are not by and large premeditated crimes. However, legal and enforcement reform would be likely to help deter repeated or secondary offenses and certainly would provide victims of abuse with added protection and recourse.

Social-service agencies can aid law-enforcement and court personnel in several ways. For example, agencies can educate them as to the nature of the problem and help to develop viable effective reforms. They can train police officers to deal compassionately and effectively with cases of domestic violence. Agency personnel might even accompany police responding to abuse complaints to offer their expertise and services.

In addition, it falls upon social-service organizations to provide education to the general public about wife abuse and to give counseling, shelter, and other aid to those involved. The content of such programs, and who should bear responsibility for administering them, are matters of debate within the field of social work. What is clear is that, to date, social-service programs have been inadequately funded and have had to spend much of their time fighting the old myths about wife abuse, myths that have been dispelled by research but that carry on in the minds of much of the public including many public officials. Researchers and social-service personnel alike should view the educating of the general public about wife abuse to be a major part of their professional function. Only then can treatment strategies become effective and can we move toward the time when wife abuse will only be a rare, pathological occurrence and not a horrible fact of life for thousands of families in the United States.

References

Bard, M., and Zacker, J. 1974. Assaultiveness and alcohol use in family disputes. *Criminology* 12:281–292.

Bloch, D.A. 1980. Discussion: violence in the family. In M.R. Green, ed., *Violence and the family*, pp. 32–36. Boulder, Colo.: Westview.

Breiter, T. 1979. Battered women. *Equal Opportunity Forum* (January):7.

Carlson, B.E. 1977. Battered women and their assailants. *Social Work* 22:455–460.

Davidson, T. 1977. Wifebeating: a recurring phenomenon throughout history. In M. Roy, ed., *Battered women: a psychosociological study of domestic violence*, pp. 2–23. New York: Van Nostrand Reinhold.

Dexter, L.A. 1958. A note on selective inattention in social science. *Social Problems* 6:176–182.

Dobash, R. Emerson, and Dobash, Russell P. 1976a. The importance of historical and contemporary contexts in understanding marital violence. Paper presented at the annual meeting of the American Sociological Association, New York.

———. 1976b. Love, honour and obey: institutional ideologies and the struggle for battered women. Paper presented at the annual meeting of the Society for the Study of Social Problems, New York.

Fields, M.D. 1977. Representing battered wives, or what to do until the police arrive. *Family Law Reporter* 3:4025–4029.

Flynn, J.P. 1977. Recent findings related to wife abuse. *Social Casework*:13–20.

Gaquin, D.A. 1977–1978. Spouse abuse: data from the national crime survey. *Victimology* 2:632–643.

Gates, M. 1978. Introduction. In J.R. Chapman and M. Gates, eds., *The victimization of women*, pp. 9–27. Beverly Hills, Calif.: Sage.

Gelles, R.J. 1977. No place to go: the social dynamics of marital violence. In M. Roy, ed., *Battered women: a psychosociological study of domestic violence*, pp. 46–62. New York: Van Nostrand Reinhold.

———. 1974. *The violent home*. Beverly Hills, Calif.: Sage.

Goodman, E.J. 1977. Legal solutions: equal protection under the law. In M. Roy, ed., *Battered women: a psychosociological study of domestic violence*, pp. 139–144. New York: Van Nostrand Reinhold.

Martin, D. 1978. Battered women: society's problem. In J.R. Chapman and M. Gates, eds., *The victimization of women*, pp. 130–133. Beverly Hills, Calif.: Sage.

Prescott, S., and Letko, C. 1977. Battered women: a social psychological perspective. In M. Roy, ed., *Battered women: a psychosociological study of domestic violence*, pp. 72–95. New York: Van Nostrand Reinhold.

Shainess, N. 1977. Psychological aspects of wifebeating. In M. Roy, ed., *Battered women: a psychosociological study of domestic violence*, pp. 111–119. New York: Van Nostrand Reinhold.

Spiegel, J.P. 1980. Ethnopsychiatric dimensions in family violence. In M.R. Green, ed., *Violence and the family*, pp. 79–89. Boulder, Colo.: Westview.

Straus, M.A. 1974. Levelling, civility and violence in the family. *Journal of Marriage and the Family* 34:13–29.

———. 1976. Sexual inequality, cultural norms, and wifebeating. *Victimology* 1:63–66.

———. 1980. A sociological perspective on the causes of family violence. In M.R. Green, ed., *Violence and the family*, pp. 7–31. Boulder, Colo.: Westview.

———. 1978. Stress and assault in a national sample of American families. Paper presented at the Colloquium on Stress and Crime, 5 December, National Institute of Law Enforcement and Criminal Justice, MITRE Corporation, Washington, D.C.

West, L.J. 1980. Discussion: violence in the family in perspective. In M.R. Green, ed., Violence and the family, pp. 90–104. Boulder, Colo.: Westview.

Wisconsin Council on Criminal Justice. 1980. *Violence against women: causes and prevention, a literature search and annotated bibliography*, 2d ed. Prepared by C.F. Wilson, Women's Education Resources, University of Wisconsin, K.F. Clarenbach, project director. In *Domestic violence*, monograph series, number 3, June 1980. Rockville, Md.: National Clearinghouse on Domestic Violence.

Wolfgang, M.E. 1956. Husband-wife homicides. *Journal of Social Therapy* 2:263–271.

———. 1958. *Patterns in criminal homicide*. Philadelphia: University of Pennsylvania Press.

2 Abused Wives: Why Do They Stay?

Richard J. Gelles

Why would a woman who has been physically abused by her husband remain with him? This question is one of the most frequently asked by both professionals and the lay public in the course of discussions of family violence, and one of the more difficult to adequately answer. The question itself derives from the elementary assumption that any reasonable individual, having been beaten and battered by another person, would avoid being victimized again (or at least avoid the attacker). Unfortunately, the answer to why women remain with their abusive husbands is not nearly as simple as the assumption that underlies the question. In the first place, the decision to either stay with an assaultive spouse or to seek intervention or dissolution of a marriage is not related solely to the extent or severity of the physical assault. Some spouses will suffer repeated severe beatings or even stabbings without so much as calling a neighbor, while others call the police after a coercive gesture from their husband. Secondly, the assumption that the victim would flee from a conjugal attacker overlooks the complex subjective meaning of intrafamilial violence, the nature of commitment and entrapment to the family as a social group, and the external constraint which limits a woman's ability to seek outside help. As has been reported elsewhere (Parnas, 1967; Gelles, 1974; Straus, 1974, 1975), violence between spouses is often viewed as normative and, in fact, mandated in family relations. Wives have reported that they believe that it is acceptable for a husband to beat his wife "every once and a while" (Parnas, 1967:952; Gelles, 1974:59–61).

This paper attempts to provide an answer to the question of why victims of conjugal violence stay with their husbands by focusing on various aspects of the family and family experience which distinguish between women who seek intervention or dissolution of a marriage as a response to violence and those women who suffer repeated beatings without seeking outside inter-

This chapter first appeared in the *Journal of Marriage and the Family* (November 1976): 659–669. Copyright 1976 by the National Council on Family Relations. Reprinted by permission. A revised version of a paper presented at the meetings of the Eastern Sociological Society, Boston, Massachusetts, March 26–28, 1976. This research was supported by NIMH grants MH 15521 and MH 24002. The research was conducted in 1973. I would like to thank Murray A. Straus, Howard Erlanger, Richard B. Pollnac, and Martha Mulligan for their comments and suggestions on the drafts of this paper.

vention.[1] We shall specifically analyze how previous experience with family violence affects the decision to seek intervention, and how the extent of violence, educational status, occupational status, number of children, and age of oldest child influence the wife's actions in responding to assaults from her husband. Finally, we shall discuss how external constraints lessen the likelihood of a woman seeking intervention in conjugal assaults.

Victims of Family Violence

Although no one has systematically attempted to answer the question of why an abused wife would stay with her husband, there has been some attention focused on women who attempt to seek intervention after being beaten by their husbands. Snell, Rosenwald, and Robey (1964) examined 12 clinical cases to determine why a wife takes her abusive husband to court. They begin by stating that the question answers itself (because he beats her!), but they go on to explain that the decision to seek legal assistance is the result of a change in the wife's behavior, not the husband's, since many wives report a history of marital violence when they did not seek assistance.

Truninger (1971) found that women attempt to dissolve a violent marriage only after a history of conflict and reconciliation. According to this analysis, a wife makes a decision to obtain a divorce from her abusive husband when she can no longer believe her husband's promises of no more violence nor forgive past episodes of violence. Truninger postulates that some of the reasons women *do not* break off relationships with abusive husbands are that: (1) they have negative self-concepts; (2) they believe their husbands will reform; (3) economic hardship; (4) they have children who need a father's economic support; (5) they doubt they can get along alone; (6) they believe divorcees are stigmatized; and (7) it is difficult for women with children to get work. Although this analysis attempts to explain why women remain with abusive husbands, the list does not specify which factors are the most salient in the wife's decision to either stay or seek help.

There are a number of other factors which help explain the wife's decision to stay or get help in cases of violence. Straus (1973) states that self-concept and role expectations of others often influence what is considered to be an intolerable level of violence by family members. Scanzoni's (1972) exchange model of family relations postulates that the ratio of rewards to punishments is defined subjectively by spouses and is the determining factor in deciding whether to stay married or not. The decision of whether or not to seek intervention or dissolution of a marriage may be partly based on the subjective definitions attached to the violence (punishment) and partly on the ratio of this punishment to other marital rewards (security, companionship, etc.).

Additional research on violence between husbands and wives suggests that severity of violence has an influence on the wife's actions (see O'Brien,

1971 and Levinger, 1966, for discussion of petitioners for divorce and their experience with violence). Research on victims of violence sheds little additional light on the actions of abused wives (Straus, 1975).[2]

Methodology

Data for this study were derived from interviews with members of 80 families. An unstructured informal interview procedure was employed to facilitate data collection on the sensitive topic of intrafamilial violence. Twenty families suspected of using violence were chosen from the files of a private social service agency. Another 20 families were selected by examining a police "blotter" to locate families in which the police had been summoned to break-up violent disputes. An additional 40 families were interviewed by selecting one neighboring family for each "agency" or "police" family.[3]

Strengths and Limitations of the Sample

The interviews were carried out in two cities in New Hampshire. The sampling procedure employed enhanced the likelihood of locating families in which violence had occurred, but it also meant that this sample was not representative of any larger populations.

Major limitations of this study are that it is exploratory in nature, the sample is small, and the representativeness of the sample is unknown. The small sample, the unknown representativeness, and the possible biases that enter into the study as a result of the sampling procedure all impinge on the generalizability of the findings presented in this paper.

There are, however, strengths in the study which tend to offset the limitations of sample design and sample size. First, this is a unique study. The area of spousal violence has long suffered from "selective inattention" (Dexter, 1958) on the part of both society and the research community. While some data have been gathered on the topic of family violence, most of the studies focus on one type of population—either petitioners for divorce (O'Brien, 1971; Levinger, 1966), patients of psychiatrists (Snell, Rosenwald, and Robey, 1964), or college students (Straus, 1974; Steinmetz, 1974). This study is one of the few which examine not only those in special circumstances (agency clients or those calling police), but also an equal number of families who had no contact with agencies of social service or control.[4] While the sample is obviously not representative, it is one of the closest yet to a study of violence in a cross-section of families.

A second strength of the methodology is that it yielded a population without a working class, lower class, or middle class bias. The sample ranged from families at the lowest regions of socioeconomic status, to middle class families in which one or both spouses had graduated from college and had a combined family income exceeding $25,000. (For a complete discussion of the social characteristics of the respondents and their families, see Gelles, 1974:205–215.

Although the methodology was not designed specifically to address the issue posed in this paper, it turned out to be particularly well suited for the proposed analysis. The sampling technique yielded wives who were divorced from violent husbands, wives who called the police, wives who were clients of a social service agency, and wives who had never sought any outside intervention.

The interviews with the 80 family members yielded 41 women who had been physically struck by their husbands during their marriage. Of these, nine women had been divorced or separated from their husbands; 13 had called on the police and were still married; eight sought counseling from a private social service agency (because of violence and other family problems); and 11 had sought no outside intervention.

Findings

We derived some ideas and predictions concerning factors which distinguished between beaten wives who obtained outside intervention and those who did not attempt to bring in outside resources or file for a divorce. These ideas are based on the interviews with the 41 members of violent families and on previous research on family violence. We utilized both quantitative and qualitative data obtained from the interviews to assess the effect of: (1) severity and frequency of violence; (2) experience and exposure to violence in one's family of orientation; (3) education and occupation of the wife, number of children, and age of oldest child; and (4) external constraint on the actions of the victimized wife.

Severity and Frequency of Violence

Common sense suggests that if violence is severe enough or frequent enough, a wife will eventually attempt to either flee from her abusive husband or to bring in some mediator to protect her from violence.

In order to analyze whether severity of violence influenced the reactions of the wife, we constructed a 10 point scale of violence severity (0=no violence; 1=pushed or shoved; 2=threw object; 3=slapped or bit; 4= punched or kicked; 5=pushed down; 6=hit with hard object; 7=choked; 8=stabbed; 9=shot)[5] This scale measured the most severe violence the wife had ever experienced as a victim.

Table 2-1 indicates that the more severe the violence, the more likely the wife is to seek outside assistance. An examination of wives' reactions to particular instances of violence reveals even more about the impact of violence severity on the actions of abused wives. Of the eight women who were either shot at (one), choked (six), or hit with a hard object (one), five had obtained divorces, two had called the police, and one had sought counseling from a social service agency. At the other extreme, of the nine women who had been pushed or shoved (eight), or had objects thrown at them (one), one had gotten a divorce, one had called the police, and seven had sought no assistance at all.

How frequently a wife is hit also influences her decision whether to remain with her husband, call the police, go to a social worker, or seek dissolution of the marriage. Only 42 percent of the woman who had been struck once in the marriage had sought some type of intervention, while 100 percent of the women who had been hit at least once a month and 83 percent of the women who had been struck at least once a week had either obtained a divorce or separation, called the police, or went to a social service agency. Frequency of violence is also related to what type of intervention a wife seeks. Women hit weekly to daily are most likely to call the police, while women hit less often (at least once a month) are more inclined to get a divorce or legal separation.

There are a number of plausible explanations as to why frequency of violence influences mode of intervention. Perhaps the more frequent the violence, the more a wife wants immediate protection, whereas victims of monthly violence gradually see less value in staying married to a husband who explodes occasionally. A possible explanation of the findings might be that women who were divorced or separated were ashamed to admit they tolerated violence as long as they did (for fear of being labeled "sado-masochists"). Also, it may be that victims of frequent violence are afraid of seeking a temporary or permanent separation. Victims of weekly violence may be terrorized by their violent husbands and view police intervention as more tolerable to their husbands than a divorce or separation. Finally, women who are struck frequently might feel that a separation or divorce

Table 2-1
Violence Severity by Intervention Mode

Intervention	Mean Violence Severity
No intervention	2.1
Divorced or separated	5.1
Called police	4.0
Went to agency	4.6
Total for all who sought intervention	4.6

F = 5.2 Statistically significant at the .01 level

might produce a radical or possible lethal reaction from an already violent husband.

Experience with and Exposure to Violence as a Child

Studies of murderers (Gillen, 1946; Guttmacher, 1960; Leon, 1969; Palmer, 1962; Tanay, 1969), child abusers (Bakan, 1971; Gelles, 1973; Gil, 1971; Kempe *et al.*, 1962; Steele and Pollock, 1974), and violent spouses (Gelles, 1974; Owens and Straus, 1975) support the assumption that the more an individual is exposed to violence as a child (both as an observer and a victim), the more he or she is violent as an adult. The explanation offered for this relationship is that the experience with violence as a victim and observer teaches the individual how to be violent and also to approve of the use of violence. In other words, exposure to violence provides a "role model" for violence (Singer, 1971). If experience with violence can provide a role model for the offender, then perhaps it can also provide a role model for the victim.

Women who observed spousal violence in their family of orientation were more likely to be victims of conjugal violence in their family of procreation. Of the 54 women who never saw their parents fight physically, 46 percent were victims of spousal violence, while 66 percent of the 12 women who observed their parents exchange blows were later victims of violent attacks. In addition, the more frequently a woman was struck by her parents, the more likely she was to grow up and be struck by her husband.[6]

There are two interrelated reasons why women who were exposed to or were victims of intrafamilial violence would be prone to be the victims of family violence as adults. It is possible that the more experience with violence a woman has, the more she is inclined to approve of the use of violence in the family. She may grow up with the expectation that husbands are "supposed" to hit wives, and this role expectation may in turn become the motivator for her husband to use violence on her. Another explanation of these findings integrates the subculture theory of violence (Wolfgang and Ferracuti, 1967) with the homogamy theory of mate selection (Centers, 1949; Ecklund, 1968; Hollingshead, 1950). Thus, it could be argued that women who grew up in surroundings which included and approved of family violence are more likely to marry a person who is prone to use violence.

Given the fact that being a victim of violence as a child or seeing one's parents physically fight makes a woman more vulnerable to becoming the victim of conjugal violence, does exposure and experience with violence as a child affect *the actions* of a beaten wife? There are two alternative predictions that could be made. First, the less a woman experienced violence in her family of orientation, the more likely she is to view intrafamilial violence as deviant, and thus, the more she is willing to seek intervention or a divorce when hit by her husband. On the other hand, exposure to violence may provide a role model for the woman as to what to do when attacked. Thus, the *more* violence she was exposed to, the more she will know about how to get outside help, and the more she will seek this help.

Being a victim of parental violence and frequency of victimization appear to have no bearing on the beaten wife's decision whether or not to seek outside intervention[7] (table 2–2). Those women who observed their parents engaged in physical fights were slightly more likely to obtain outside intervention after being hit by their husbands. For those women who did see their parents engage in conjugal violence, the predominant mode of intervention in their own family of procreation was a divorce or separation. There is no predominant mode of intervention chosen by those women who did not witness violence in their families of orientation.

Thus, neither of the alternative predictions is strongly supported by the data on experience and exposure to violence. There is the suggestion that exposure to conjugal violence makes women *less tolerant* of family violence and more desirous of ending a violent marriage. Along these lines, some of the women we interviewed stated that after they saw their parents fight they vowed that they would never stand for their own husbands hitting them. However, the data do not support the claim that this position is widespread among wives who witnessed violence as they grew up.

Education, Occupation, Number of Children,
Age of Children

Truninger (1971) has proposed that the stronger the commitment to marriage, the less a wife will seek legal action against a violent husband. We have modified this hypothesis by proposing that the fewer resources a wife

Table 2–2
Intervention Mode by Wife's Experience with Violence as a Child

	Type of Intervention			
Type of Experience as Child	Divorced or Separated	Called Police	Went to Agency	Total Seeking Intervention
A. Parents Violent to Respondent:				
None (N = 3)	33%	0%	66%	100%
Infrequent[a] (N = 13)	23%	38%	15%	76%
Frequent[b] (N = 17)	24%	35%	18%	77%
B. Parents Violent to Each Other:				
None observed (N = 25)	28%	28%	20%	76%
Observed (N = 8)	63%	13%	13%	89%

[a] less than 6 times a year
[b] from monthly to daily

has in a marriage, the fewer alternatives she has to her marriage; and the more "entrapped" she is in the marriage, the more reluctant she will be to seek outside intervention. Thus, we hypothesize that unemployed wives with low education will not do anything when beaten. It is difficult to predict what influence number of children and age of children have on the actions of the wife. Snell, Rosenwald, and Robey (1964) state that the presence of an older child motivates women to take their husbands to court.

Looking at the relationship between each variable and intervention, we see that the variable which best distinguishes wives who obtain assistance from those who remain with their husbands is holding a job. While only 25 percent of those wives who sought no help worked, 50 percent of the wives who called the police, went to a social service agency, or were separated or divorced from their husbands held jobs. This confirms our hypothesis that the more resources a wife has, the more she is able to support herself and her children, the more she will have a low threshold of violence and call outside agents or agencies to help her. Thus, the less dependent a wife is on her husband, the more likely she is to call for help in instances of violence. In addition to this resource dimension, wives reported that holding a job gave them a view of another world or culture. This new perspective made their own family problems seem less "normal" and more serious than they had felt when they were at home. This point is illustrated in the following excerpt from one of our interviews with a woman who was the client of a social service agency and who had been beaten by her husband when they were first married:

> Until I started being out in the public, to realize what was going on around me, I was so darned stupid and ignorant. I didn't know how the other half of the world lived. And when I started being a waitress I used to love to sit

Table 2–3
Education, Occupation, Number of Children, Age of Oldest Child by Intervention Mode

Intervention	Mean Education	Percentage Completed High School	Percentage Employed	Mean Number of Children	Mean Age of Oldest Child
No intervention (N = 11)	11.9	63	25	2.5	9.3
Divorced or separated (N = 9)	11.7	66	44	3.3	9.3
Called police (N = 13)	11	69	38	3	13
Went to agency (N = 8)	11.1	62	75	2.6	13.7
All intervention	11.3	67	50	3	12

Note: For those wives who are divorced or separated, some may have found employment *after* the divorce or separation. The data did not allow us to determine *when* the wife found employment.

there—when I wasn't busy—and watch the people—the mother and the father with their children—and see how they acted. And I started to feel like I was cheated . . . and it started to trouble me and I started to envy those people. So I said, "you know . . . am I supposed to live the way I'm living?"

Women who called the police or went to an agency often had teenage children. The data confirm the Snell, Rosenwald, and Robey (1964) finding that women who brought their husbands to court had teenage children. In some of our interviews, wives reported that they started calling the police when their son or daughter was old enough to get embroiled in the physical conflicts. In these cases, the wives wanted help to protect their children rather than themselves.

Neither education (measured by mean years of school completed and completed high school) nor number of children distinguishes between abused women seeking help and those staying with their husbands.

Combined Effects of Variables on Intervention

Up to this point we have examined the effects of the variables which we believed would be likely determinants of whether or not a wife sought intervention. This analysis, however, does not allow us to assess the effects of all these variables in explaining whether or not a wife would seek outside help in cases of conjugal violence. In order to examine the impact of all the variables together, we employed a step-wise multiple regression procedure which allowed us to see what proportion of the variance of intervention or particular intervention modalities is explained by combinations of the independent variables.[8]

Intervention: Table 2–4 reveals that the best predictor of whether or not a wife seeks intervention is violence severity in her family of procreation. Thus, women who seek intervention are strongly influenced by the level of violence in their family. The five variables entered into the regression analysis explain 32 percent of the variance in seeking intervention or not.

Divorced or Separated: The best predictor of whether or not a wife obtains a divorce or separation is the level of violence in her family of procreation. The combined effect of all the variables entered into the equation is the explanation of 14 percent of the variance in the dependent variable; however, the multiple R's are not statistically significant at the .05 level.

Called Police: We are able to explain 11 percent of the variance in this variable, but again, multiple R's are not statistically significant at the .05 level. Unlike separation or divorce, in which cases severity and extent of

Table 2-4
Stepwise Regression of Independent Variables and Intervention
and Intervention Modalities

		Multiple R	R^2	Beta
A.	Regression of intervention on:			
	Violence severity	.434[a]	.189	.365
	Completed high school	.488[a]	.238	.331
	Parental violence to respondent	.530[a]	.280	-.260
	Frequency of violence	.559[a]	.312	.221
	Wife's occupational status[c]	.570[a]	.324	-.136
B.	Regression of divorced or separated on:			
	Violence severity	.281	.080	.211
	Wife's education	.314	.099	.298
	Frequency of violence	.324	.105	.154
	Completed high school	.340	.115	-.136
	Wife's occupational status[c]	.347	.120	.089
	Violence between parents	.352	.124	-.027
	Number of children	.355	.126	.261
	Age of oldest child	.373	.140	.231
C.	Regression of called police on:			
	Wife's occupational status[c]	.195	.038	-.231
	Completed high school	.256	.065	.423
	Wife's education	.314	.099	-.245
	Parental violence to respondent	.319	.101	-.016
	Age of oldest child	.324	.105	-.233
	Number of children	.340	.115	.233
D.	Regression of went to agency on:			
	Parental violence to respondent	.326[b]	.106	-.191
	Age of oldest child	.350	.122	.480
	Number of children	.425[b]	.180	-.496
	Violence severity	.442	.196	.114

[a] statistically significant at the .01 level

[b] statistically significant at the .05 level

[c] Occupational Status measured using Bureau of Census status score (see Robinson, Athan-asiou, and Head, 1969:357).

violence in her family of procreation played major roles in the wife's actions, the calling of police is associated with the wife's occupational status and her education. Women with less occupational status and lower education are likely to call the police for help. This finding is consistent with the popular assumption that the poor man's social worker is the police officer.

Went to Agency: The best predictor of going to a social service agency is how much violence the wife experienced as a child. The less violence, the more likely she is to seek a social worker's help. In contrast to the previous dependent variables, age and number of children play a greater part in influencing a wife's decision to go to a social service agency. Almost 20 percent of the variance in seeking agency assistance is explained by the four variables included in the regression.

External Constraint

The fact that a woman would call the police or seek agency assistance after repeated incidents of conjugal violence does not necessarily mean that she will call the police again or continue going to an agency. One fact remained quite clear at the end of the eighty interviews: most agencies and most legal organizations are quite unprepared and unable to provide meaningful assistance to women who have been beaten by their husbands. With minor exceptions, such as the work done by Bard and his colleagues (1969; 1969; 1971), little formal training has been given to police in how to intercede in conjugal disputes. Truninger (1971) reports that the courts are often mired in mythology about family violence (*e.g.*, "violence fulfills the masochistic need of women victims"), and consequently the justice system is ineffective in dealing with marital violence. Field and Field (1973:225) echo these sentiments and state that unless the victim dies, the chances that the court system will deal seriously with the offender are slight. Women who are abused by their husbands must suffer grave injury in order to press legal charges. The California Penal Code states that a wife must be more injured than commonly allowed for battery to press charges against her husband (Calvert, 1974:89). As Field and Field (1973) state, there is an official acceptance of violence between "consenting" adults and the belief that this violence is a private affair. This attitude, held by police, the courts, and the citizenry, constrains many wives from either seeking initial help, or once obtaining help, continuing to use it.

Although social work agencies are not as "indifferent" about marital violence as the courts and police are (Field and Field, 1973:236), they are often unable to provide realistic answers for victims of violence because of the rather limited amount of knowledge in this area. The data on marital violence are so scanty that few policy or intervention strategies have been worked out for the use of social workers. Without a good knowledge of the causes and patterns of marital violence, many social workers have had to rely on stop-gap measures which never address the real problem of marital violence.

A final source of external constraint is the wife's fear that the myth of her peaceful family life will be exploded. Many women we spoke to would never think of calling the police, going to a social work agency, or filing for a divorce because those actions would rupture the carefully nurtured myth of their fine family life. One woman, who had been struck often and hard over a 30 year marriage said she would never call the police because she was afraid it would appear in the papers. Truninger (1971:264) supports these findings by stating that part of the reason why the courts are ineffective in dealing with marital violence is the strong social pressure on individuals to keep marital altercations private.

In summary, even if a woman wants to get help and protection from her husband, she all too frequently finds out that the agents and agencies she calls are ineffective or incapable of providing real assistance. During the course of the interviews, many wives who had sought intervention complained about the futility of such actions. One woman in particular had sought agency help, called the police, and finally filed for a divorce. However, none of these actions actually protected her, and her estranged husband almost strangled her one weekend morning.

The deficiencies of these external agencies and the pressure to cover-up family altercations are two powerful forces which keep women with their abusive husbands.

Conclusion

The purpose of this paper has been to address the important question of why victims of conjugal violence stay with their husbands. Our analysis of the variables which affect the decision to either stay with an abusive husband or to seek intervention uncovered three major factors which influence the actions of abused women. First, the less severe and the less frequent the violence, the more a woman will remain with her spouse and not seek outside aid. This finding is almost self-evident in that it posits that women seek intervention when they are severely abused. However, the problem is more complex, since severity and frequency of violence explain only part of the variance in abused wives' behavior. A second factor is how much violence a wife experienced as a child. The more she was struck by her parents, the more inclined she is to stay with her abusive husband. It appears that victimization as a child raises the wife's tolerance for violence as an adult. Lastly, educational and occupational factors are associated with staying with an abusive husband. Wives who do not seek intervention are less likely to have completed high school and more likely to be unemployed. We conclude that the fewer resources a woman has, the less power she has, and the more "entrapped" she is in her marriage, the more she suffers at the hands of her husband without calling for help outside the family.

Another factor which appears to influence the actions of a wife is external constraint in the form of police, agency, and court lack of understanding about marital violence.

Although we have presented some factors which partly explain why abused wives remain with their husbands, we have not provided a complete answer to the question this paper raises. The reason for this is that the factors influencing the reactions of an abused wife are tremendously complex. It is not simply how hard or how often a wife is hit, nor is it how much education or income she has. The decision of whether or not to seek intervention is the result of a complex interrelationship of factors, some of which have been identified in this paper.

Although we have provided tentative answers to the central question of this paper, a main underlying issue of this topic has not been addressed. Even though more than 75 percent of the women who had been struck had tried to get outside help, the end result of this intervention was not totally satisfactory. The outlook for women who are physically beaten and injured by their husbands is not good. For those who have few resources, no job, and no idea of how to get help, the picture is grim. But even the women who have the resources and desire to seek outside help often finding this help of little benefit.

Notes

1. While we would have liked to answer the same question for men who were struck by their wives, we interviewed too few men who had been hit by their wives to conduct any meaningful data analysis.

2. Since we are focusing on the reactions of victims of intrafamilial violence, we had hoped that some insight could be gained from the literature on "victimology." "Victimology" is defined by its proponents (see Drapkin and Viano, 1974; Von Hentig, 1948; and Schafer, 1968) as the scientific study of the criminal-victim relationship. However, the current work on these relationships does not focus specifically on factors which lead victims to sever relationships with offenders or to obtain outside intervention. Since victimologists' analyses of marital violence are typically limited to cases of homicide (see Wolfgang, 1957), there are few insights to be gained for the purposes of this paper from the study of the literature on the criminal-victim relationship.

3. For a complete discussion of the methodology, including an evaluation of the sampling procedure and instrument, see Gelles (1974:36–43).

4. Another study which examines a cross-section of families is Steinmetz' (1975) multimethod examination of 57 families randomly selected from New Castle County, Delaware. The sample size is small, but it is representative, if only of one county in Delaware.

5. For the purposes of this analysis, we viewed each higher point on the scale as more severe than the previous category of violence. In addition, we treated the scale as interval data in order to conduct a one-way Analysis of Variance. The scale was treated as an interval measure because this was the only possible way to assess the impact of violence severity on the wives.

6. Many individuals may find it difficult to label the use of physical force on children as "violence." This is because there are many powerful pro-use-of-physical-force-on-children norms in our society (Straus, 1975). If one defines violence as an act with the intent of physically injuring the victim, then physically punishing a child is violent. Note, a complete tabular presentation of these data is available from the author.

7. Although this study deals with 41 families in which the wife was a

victim of violence, table 2-2 presents only 33 such wives. The smaller number occurs because in some of the 41 families, we interviewed the husband and have no data on the wife's experience with violence. Some other women reported that they were brought up in foster homes or by one parent, and thus we have no "exposure to violence data" for these women.

8. In order to conduct this analysis the dependent variables (Intervention, Divorced or Separated, Called Police, and Went to an Agency) were transformed into "dummy variables." Each variable was treated as a dichotomy (*e.g.*, "Sought Intervention" or "Did Not Seek Intervention"). Certain ordinal variables (violence severity, completed high school, violence frequency, parental violence to respondent, and violence between parents) are treated as interval measures.

References

Baken, David. 1971. Slaughter of the Innocents: A Study of the Battered Child Phenomenon. Boston: Beacon Press.

Bard, Morton. 1969. "Family intervention police teams as a community mental health resource." The Journal of Criminal Law, Criminology, and Police Science 60 (June): 247–250.

Bard, Morton, and Bernard Berkowitz. 1969. "Family disturbance as a police function." In S. Cohen (Ed.), Law Enforcement Science and Technology II. Chicago: I.I.T. Research Institute.

Bard, Morton, and Joseph Zacher. 1971. "The prevention of family violence: Dilemmas of community intervention." Journal of Marriage and the Family 33 (November): 677–682.

Calvert, Robert. 1974. "Criminal and civil liability in husband-wife assaults." Pp. 88–90 in Suzanne K. Steinmetz and Murray A. Straus (Eds.), Violence in the Family. New York: Harper and Row.

Centers, Richard. 1949. "Marital selection and occupational strata." American Journal of Sociology 54 (May): 530–535.

Dexter, Louis A. 1958. "A note on selective inattention in social science." Social Problems 6 (Fall): 176–182.

Drapkin, Israel, and Emilio Viano (Eds.). 1974. Victimology. Lexington, Massachusetts: Lexington Books.

Ecklund, Bruce K. 1968. "Theories of mate selection." Eugenics Quarterly 15 (June): 71–84.

Field, Martha H., and Henry F. Field. 1973. "Marital violence and the criminal process: Neither justice nor peace." Social Service Review: 47 (June): 221–240.

Gelles, Richard J. 1973. "Child abuse as psychopathology: A sociological critique and reformulation." American Journal of Orthopsychiatry 43 (July): 611–621. 1974. The Violent Home: A Study of Physical Aggression Between Husbands and Wives. Beverly Hills: Sage Publications, Inc.

Gil, David G. 1971. "Violence against children." Journal of Marriage and the Family 33 (November): 637–648.

Gillen, John Lewis. 1946. The Wisconsin Prisoner: Studies in Crimogenesis. Madison: University of Wisconsin Press.

Guttmacher, Manfred. 1960. The Mind of the Murderer. New York: Farrar, Straus, and Cudahy.

Hollinshead, August B. 1950. "Cultural factors in the selection of mates." American Sociological Review 15 (October): 619–627.

Kempe, C. Henry, Frederic N. Silverman, Brandt F. Steele, William Droegemueller, and Henry K. Silver. 1962. "The battered child syndrome." Journal of the American Medical Association 181 (July 7): 17–24.

Leon, C.A. 1969. "Unusual patterns of crime during 'la Violencia' in Columbia." American Journal of Psychiatry 125 (May): 1564–1575.

Levinger, George. 1966. "Sources of marital dissatisfaction among applicants for divorce." American Journal of Orthopsychiatry 26 (October): 803–897. Pp. 126–132 in Paul H. Glasser and Louis N. Glasser (Eds.), Families in Crisis. New York: Harper and Row.

O'Brien, John E. 1971. "Violence in divorce prone families." Journal of Marriage and the Family 33 (November): 692–698.

Owens, David J., and Murray A. Straus. 1975. "Childhood violence and adult approval of violence." Aggressive Behavior 1 (2): 193–211.

Palmer, Stuart. 1962. The Psychology of Murder. New York: Thomas Y. Crowell Company.

Parnas, Raymond I. 1967. "The police response to domestic disturbance." Wisconsin Law Review 914 (Fall): 914–960.

Robinson, J. P., R. Athanasiou, and K. Head. 1969. Measures of Occupational Attitudes and Occupational Characteristics. Ann Arbor, Michigan: Survey Research Center.

Scanzoni, John H. 1972. Sexual Bargaining. Englewood Cliffs, New Jersey: Prentice-Hall.

Schafer, Stephen. 1968. The Victim and His Criminal: A Study in Functional Responsibility. New York: Random House.

Singer, Jerome. 1971. The Control of Aggression and Violence. New York: Academic Press.

Snell, John E., Richard J. Rosenwald, and Ames Robey. 1964. "The wifebeater's wife: A study of family interaction." Archives of General Psychiatry 11 (August): 107–113.

Steele, Brandt F., and Carl B. Pollock. 1974. "A psychiatric study of parents who abuse infants and small children." Pp. 89–134 in Ray E. Helfer and C. Henry Kempe (Eds.), The Battered Child. Chicago: University of Chicago Press.

Steinmetz, Suzanne K. 1974. "Occupational environment in relation to physical punishment and dogmatism." Pp. 166–172 in Suzanne K. Steinmetz and Murray A. Straus (Eds.), Violence in the Family. New York: Harper and Row. 1975. "Intra-familial patterns of conflict resolution: Husband/wife; parent/child; sibling/sibling." Unpublished doctoral dissertation, Case Western Reserve University.

Straus, Murray A. 1973. "A general systems theory approach to the development of a theory of violence between family members." Social Science Information 12 (June): 105–125. 1974. "Leveling, civility, and violence in the family." Journal of Marriage and the Family 36 (February): 13–30. 1975. "Cultural approval and structural necessity or intra-family assaults in sexist societies." Paper presented at the International Institute of Victimology, Bellagio, Italy, July.

Tanay, E. 1969. "Psychiatric study of homicide." American Journal of Psychiatry 125 (March): 1252–1258.

Truninger, Elizabeth. 1971. "Marital violence: The legal solutions." The Hastings Law Journal 23 (November): 259–276.

Von Hentig, Hans. 1948. The Criminal and His Victim: Studies in the Sociology of Crime. New Haven: Yale University Press.

Wolfgang, Marvin E. 1957. "Victim-precipitated criminal homicide." Journal of Criminal Law, Criminology and Police Science 48 (June): 1–11.

Wolfgang, Marvin E., and F. Ferracuti. 1967. The Subculture of Violence. London: Tavistock Publications.

3 Legal Help for Battered Women

Lisa G. Lerman

The Legal System

Each State has its own laws and its own court system. In every State there are two types of laws—civil laws and criminal laws. Civil and criminal laws are usually enforced in different courts. Below is a list of some important differences between civil and criminal cases.

Civil

Purpose: To settle disputes between individuals and to compensate for injuries.

Remedies: Court may order payment of money to an injured party, or may order a defendant to do or to stop doing certain acts.

Proof: Violation of the law must be proven by a "preponderance of evidence." It must be shown to be more likely than not that the act in question occurred.

Lawyers: Plaintiff (victim) hires a private attorney or goes to a legal services lawyer. The defendant (abuser) also must hire a private attorney or go to a legal services lawyer.

Criminal

Purpose: To punish acts which are disruptive of social order and to deter other similar acts.

Penalties: Conviction of a crime may result in a jail sentence, a fine, an order to pay money to the victim, or a term of probation during which certain conduct may be required or prohibited.

Proof: Violation of the law must be proven "beyond a reasonable doubt." This is a much higher standard than for a civil suit—more evidence is needed.

Lawyers: State hires prosecutors (district attorneys) to enforce criminal law. The prosecutor represents the State: this means that the prosecutor must act on behalf of both the victim and the community. *(In some places prosecution may occur even if the victim wants to drop charges. This is because the State has an interest in punishing a criminal even if the victim does not wish to do so.)* Defendant has a right to counsel if conviction could result in a jail sentence, and may have a public defender appointed to represent him.

Introduction

During the last few years, almost every State has made new legal remedies available to abused women. State laws have been passed which strengthen both civil protection and criminal penalties. Advocates for battered women are working with police, prosecutors, legal services lawyers, judges, and others to encourage active enforcement of these laws.

Until recently, family violence was largely ignored by policemen, lawyers, judges, and legislators. A victim of abuse could get a divorce based on her husband's cruelty, or she could get a piece of paper issued by the court warning her husband not to abuse her again. If the abuser disregarded the warning, the woman could only go back to the court for another piece of paper.

In many places the courts are still reluctant to intervene in family matters. Even where new laws have been passed, the remedies provided may not be effective because the law is not enforced. In most States, however, the courts provide some tools which a battered woman can use to change her situation. Through the courts she may terminate an abusive relationship, obtain financial support, or have the batterer evicted from a residence. She may get an order to compel the abuser to stop the violence which is enforceable by arrest. She may file assault charges against the abuser; if he is convicted he may be put in jail or ordered into a counseling program.

Availability of these tools varies from State to State. The following description of legal remedies for battered women does not explain which remedies are available in each State. Instead, it outlines the most effective of the recent developments in the laws affecting battered women, and describes some problems encountered in implementing the new laws.

Civil Remedies

Several forms of civil relief are available to battered women. These include:

Protection Orders

Temporary Protection Orders

Peace Bonds

Divorce or Separation

Child Custody and Visitation Rights

Alimony and Child Support

Money Damages for Personal Injury

Protection Order

What is a Protection Order? A protection order (also called a restraining order) is an order from a civil court to an abuser to require him to change his conduct. It can last for a period of up to 1 year. Depending on the State law, the court may order the respondent:

To refrain from abuse of any household member.

To leave the victim alone.

To move out of a residence shared with the victim even if the title or lease is in the abuser's name. The abuser may be required to make rent or mortgage payments even if he has been evicted.

To provide alternate housing for the victim.

To pay for the support of the victim and/or of minor children in her custody.

To attend a counseling program aimed to stop violence and/or alcohol or drug abuse. Both the abuser and the victim may be ordered to participate in counseling.

To pay the victim a sum of money for medical expenses, lost wages, moving expenses, property damage, court costs, or attorney's fees.

Also, temporary custody of minors may be awarded to the victim, and visitation rights of the abuser may be established.

Who Can Get a Protection Order? While rules differ from State to State, many States will issue a protection order on behalf of anyone abused by a spouse, former spouse, family member, household member, or former household member. Some States will only issue a protection order to a woman married to her abuser; in others, protection orders are available only to married women who have filed for separation or divorce.

How Can a Victim of Abuse Get a Protection Order? A protection order may be obtained by filing a petition in the court which has the authority to issue it. It is useful but not necessary for a victim to be represented by a lawyer when she files a petition. In some cities there are clinics which assist victims in writing their petitions.

When a petition is filed, the court schedules a hearing, usually within 2 weeks of the date of filing. The abuser is notified of the hearing and asked to appear. The hearing is before a judge or a magistrate; there is no jury. Both parties have an opportunity to testify as to why an order should or should not be issued.

Some form of protection order is available in nearly every State. To find out which court issues protection orders in a particular community, and where assistance in filing a petition can be obtained, a victim of abuse should call a local shelter, women's organization, legal services office, police department, or a clerk of a local court.

What Type of Abuse Must Be Shown to Get a Protection Order? "Abuse" for which a protection order is available may include:

An act causing physical injury, such as hitting, shoving, use of a weapon;

An attempt to cause physical injury, such as raising a fist, pointing a gun;

A threat to cause physical injury, such as saying "I'm going to beat you up";

Sexual abuse of a spouse or of her children.

How Are Protection Orders Enforced? Many States allow a police officer to make an arrest without first obtaining a warrant if he believes that a protection order has been violated or that a misdemeanor offense has been committed. In some places, warrantless arrest is allowed even if the officer did not witness the abuse and even if there are no visible injuries.

Violation of a protection order is either "contempt of court," or is a misdemeanor offense, punishable by a jail sentence (up to 6 months), a fine (up to $500), or both, or a term of probation. *(Contempt of court is the term used to describe any violation of a court order.)* An abuser released on probation may be required to attend counseling sessions, to avoid contact with the victim, to refrain from abuse, etc. The abuser must report to a probation officer, who is responsible for making sure that the abuser does what the order says.

Temporary Protection Order

A temporary protection order is an emergency order which may be issued within a few hours or a few days of the time it is requested. In most States, the temporary order is available to the same victims as a regular protection order; in most places the same relief is available under a temporary order, and the procedure for enforcement is the same. A temporary order is different from a protection order in the way it is obtained, the period of time it stays in effect, and the conduct or circumstances which must be proven to get one.

A temporary order:

May be issued *ex parte* (after a hearing at which the victim is present but not the abuser). This means the victim can obtain the order the same day that she files the petition.

May be available at night or on weekends from a magistrate's court when the civil or family court is closed.

Remains in effect until a full hearing can be held (usually within 2 weeks) or until the regular courts reopen the next weekday morning.

May be issued if "immediate and present danger of abuse" is shown. This usually includes visible injury or threat of serious physical injury.

Peace Bond

A peace bond is an order to an abuser to refrain from abuse and to deposit a sum of money with the court which is not refunded to the abuser if the order is violated. *(This procedure is similar to posting bail.)* In some States the peace bond is simply a warning to the abuser, and posting of bond is not required. This remedy has traditionally been used by the courts in lieu of measures with more "teeth."

Peace bonds are often ineffective, since the victim cannot get the abuser arrested when an order is violated. She must go back to court and request a hearing to determine whether the order has been violated. If she wins, the abuser will only lose the money he deposited.

Divorce and Separation

Many beaten women terminate their relationships with abusive husbands by filing for separation or divorce. While filing for divorce may not stop the violence, it can be an important step for a woman seeking to get away from an abusive relationship. Some abusers, however, become more violent when victims separate from them. It may be important for a victim to get a protection order when she starts divorce or separation proceedings. In some States divorce is granted if one party is shown to be at fault, and in those States "cruelty" is one ground for divorce.

When a separation or divorce is granted the court may grant custody of children to one parent and may decide a property settlement. One party may be ordered to provide financial support to his or her spouse and children, and property owned by either party may be awarded to the other or divided.

Personal Injury (Tort)

In some States a victim of domestic abuse may sue her mate to obtain a court order that he must pay for any injury to her or to her property. This type of lawsuit is like a criminal charge of assault and battery, false imprisonment, etc., except that it is brought by the victim and not by the State. This remedy has not yet been widely used, although battered women have won awards of money damages in at least a few cases.

A tort suit may be useful where the abuser has money or property and/or where there are large hospital bills, attorney fees, property damage, or lost wages. Damages may also be awarded for pain and suffering. Traditionally, husbands and wives were not allowed to sue each other, but the rule of interspousal immunity has been abolished in the majority of the States for intentional injuries. The disadvantages of this type of lawsuit are that it may take years to resolve, and attorney fees can be very high. Some lawyers will accept a contingency fee in tort cases. This means that if the lawsuit is successful, the lawyer will be paid a percentage (usually a third) of the money damages awarded. If the claim fails, the lawyer does not get paid.

Criminal Prosecution

Spouse abuse is a crime. Every State has laws prohibiting physical assault; these may be enforced against abusers where there has been physical violence or a threat of physical violence. Some States have enacted laws that make spouse abuse a separate criminal offense.

In the past, spouse abuse was treated as a family matter, and criminal law was rarely enforced against wife-beaters. Recently, however, several prosecutors' offices have initiated programs to increase prosecution of domestic abuse cases.

What Action May Be Prosecuted Under Criminal Law?

Conduct which may violate State criminal law and may be the basis of a criminal complaint includes:

Hitting, slapping, shoving, or other physical assault;

Sexual assault, rape, or attempted rape;

Harassment or threat of physical assault;

Any act causing the death of another;

Destruction of private property belonging to another;

Kidnapping or confining another against his or her will;

Violation of the terms of a protection order.

How Can A Battered Woman Get the State to File Criminal Charges?

There are two ways in which a criminal action against an abuser may be started:

When the police make an *arrest* after being called for assistance.

When the victim goes to the prosecutor's office or to an intake unit in criminal or family court to file a *private criminal complaint. (The prosecutor will be listed in the phone book in a section listing government offices. The office may be called the Office of the District Attorney, City Attorney, City Solicitor, Attorney General or United States Attorney.)*

Arrest. Each State has different rules on when police may make arrests. In many States police must obtain a warrant before making an arrest unless they have probable cause to believe a felony offense (a serious assault involving use of a weapon or causing severe injuries) has been committed, or unless they see a misdemeanor offense (a crime not serious enough to be a felony) committed.

In almost half the States, new laws allow police to make arrests without warrants in domestic violence cases, even if no weapons are used and there are no serious injuries. Some of these laws allow warrantless arrest only if a protection order has been violated.

If the police must obtain a warrant from a judge or magistrate before making an arrest, then the arrest cannot be made when the police are called to a residence. The police or the victim must go to the courthouse or police station to request a warrant, and must sometimes wait several hours for the request to be processed.

After an arrest is made a criminal charge is filed. In some places charges are filed by the police; in other places the police send a report to the prosecutor's office, and the prosecutor files charges.

Private Criminal Complaint. A victim of domestic abuse may file a criminal complaint if the police were not called after the abuse occurred, or if they were called but failed to appear or did not make an arrest. A complaint is a paper which describes the abusive incident. After a complaint is filed, the prosecutor's office will conduct an investigation and decide whether charges should be filed. If charges are filed, the court will issue a warrant for the arrest of the abuser or a summons directing him to appear in court on a certain date.

What Can a Prosecutor Do Besides File Criminal Charges?

In many cases it is inappropriate to file charges because the evidence is insufficient to make conviction likely or because the victim has no interest in prosecution. In these cases the prosecutor can take informal action to assist the victim in stopping the abuse. Below are examples of such informal action:

Information and Referral: The prosecutor can advise the victim of her legal and other options. After determining which of these options the victim wishes to pursue, the prosecutor can refer her to another legal or social service agency.

Warning Letter: The prosecutor can send a letter to the abuser to notify him that a complaint has been made that he has abused a member of his family, that such conduct is against the law, and that further violence will be prosecuted.

Meeting with Abuser: The prosecutor may request that the abuser come to the prosecutor's office to discuss the alleged misconduct. At the meeting he may be informed of the seriousness of the charges and of the potential consequences of further abuse.

What Can a Criminal Court Do After a Charge
Has Been Filed?

The arrest of the abuser and the filing of the criminal charge begins the process of prosecution. The next step is to hold an arraignment or bail hearing, at which the abuser may be required to submit a sum of money to the court to insure that he will reappear for his trial. Other conditions may be imposed on the abuser's pretrial release, such as participation in counseling, avoiding contact with the victim, or terminating the abuse. If the terms are violated, the abuser may be returned to custody until the prosecution is completed.

The filing of a criminal charge does not necessarily mean that there will be a trial. The charge may be disposed of in any of the following ways:

Pretrial Diversion, or Deferred Prosecution: Prosecution may be postponed after charges are filed in cases where injuries are not severe and the abuser is a first offender. The abuser makes an agreement with the prosecutor that during diversion he will attend counseling, avoid contact with the victim, move out of a shared residence, and/or cease the abuse. The prosecutor is responsible for making sure that the abuser complies with the agreement. If the abuser does so, then the charges will be dropped. If he violates the order, prosecution will be resumed.

Plea Bargaining: In most criminal cases the prosecutor, the defense attorney, and the defendant (the person charged with a crime) make a deal in which the defendant agrees to plead guilty to charges and the prosecutor agrees to request a less severe penalty than would be imposed if the defendant were convicted by a court. The process of making deals to avoid trial is called plea bargaining. Plea bargaining in spouse abuse cases usually results in a sentence of a period of probation. During probation the abuser may be required to attend counseling, to move out of a shared residence, to stay away from the victim, and/or to refrain from abuse. A probation officer is supposed to stay in touch with the abuser and make sure that he does not violate the court order. If the abuser violates the terms of probation, he may be put in jail without a trial since he has already agreed to his conviction by admitting guilt during the plea bargaining.

Trial: If the abuser pleads innocent, he will be tried on the offenses charged. If convicted, he may be jailed, fined, or placed on probation. Jail sentences are rarely imposed in domestic assault cases, and are seldom longer than 1 year. Where a victim of abuse is required to testify at a trial, she may be able to get help from either the prosecutor's office or from another agency. She may need someone to go to hearings with her, or to explain the court system to her. She may need child care while she goes to court. She may need assistance in getting housing, public benefits, a divorce, or a protection order. If no one in the prosecutor's office can help, then a local shelter or women's group can tell her where to go for help.

Choosing a Remedy

In many States, a battered woman can use any of the remedies described, or she may want to use more than one. For example, a protection order is often useful to a woman who files criminal charges against her husband. In deciding what action to take it is important to find out what the victim wants from the court. Most victims want to end the violence. Some may also want to punish the abuser, to get help for him, to end the relationship, or all of these. The remedy chosen must depend on which of the remedies available in the State best corresponds to the desires of the victim.

Information about the legal remedies available to battered women may be obtained from a local shelter or hotline, from a legal services office or the bar association, or from any victim/witness assistance program or women's organization. These will be listed in the yellow pages under attorneys, city government, women, human services, etc.

Legal action is only one of many options available to battered women. Other action in addition to or instead of getting help from the courts may be more successful. A victim of abuse may need immediate medical care. She may elect to spend time in a shelter or to stay with relatives or friends. She may eventually move to a new residence or a new city. She may wish to get help from a minister or a counselor in a mental health or family service agency. In the process of recovering from the trauma of a violent relationship, stopping the abuse is only the first step. A victim may need career counseling or job training. She may need public benefits from the welfare department, or the unemployment insurance board. She may need to apply for Aid to Families with Dependent Children or food stamps. Combined with other nonlegal assistance, the remedies provided by the courts may give a victim of abuse the strength to change or terminate a violent relationship.

4

State Legislation on Domestic Violence

Lisa G. Lerman, Leslie Landis,
and *Sharon Goldzweig*

Less than a decade ago few states had any laws aimed at reducing or preventing violence between family or household members. A battered woman[1] who sought legal protection from abuse had few options. If the woman was married, she could file for divorce, separation, or custody. In some states she could get an injunction ordering her husband not to abuse her while domestic relations proceedings were pending. Such orders were limited in scope and did not provide penalties for violation.

During the last five years, most states have passed extensive legislation on domestic violence. Most of the statutes create new civil and criminal legal remedies for persons abused by family or household members. Some laws specify the powers and duties of police and the courts who handle family violence cases. Some require agencies that offer services to violent families to keep records or write reports on family violence. Finally, and perhaps most important, some state legislatures have allocated funding for shelters and other services for violent families.

Forty-nine states and the District of Columbia have now enacted some type of legislation to protect battered women. Since July 1980, comprehensive protection order laws have been enacted in Georgia, Mississippi, Illinois, and Alabama, and introduced in Arkansas and New Jersey. There has been no recent action in South Dakota. The South Dakota legislature passed a protection order bill, but it was vetoed by the governor.

The rapid development of domestic violence law in the United States is the product of a broad network of community groups, legal service lawyers, shelter workers, and law enforcement officials working to make new services and legal options available to battered women. The initial efforts of this movement focused on setting up shelters and hotlines and developing a civil injunction by which battered women could obtain emergency protection without filing criminal charges. As experience was gained with the protection order laws, it became clear that injunctive relief is most effective when the statutes spell out specific procedures by which courts and law

This chapter first appeared in *Response to Violence in the Family* 4, no. 7 (September/October 1981) and is reprinted by permission of the Center for Women Policy Studies, 2000 P Street N.W., Suite 508, Washington, D.C. 20036.

enforcement agencies should issue and enforce orders, and when the laws make violation of a protection order a criminal offense. While new legislation cannot by itself change the response of courts, police, or social service agencies to the problem of family violence, it does furnish a tool that victims of abuse and their advocates can use to promote more effective court response and better services to violent families.

Using the Chart

The chart of state domestic violence laws on pages 48 to 56 may be used by persons drafting new state domestic violence legislation as a checklist of provisions that might be included. From the chart one can tell what legislation exists or is pending in each state and how many states have new laws on a certain subject. Although some sections of the chart are quite detailed, the statutes themselves must be consulted to determine what releif might be available to an individual. Therefore, a list of citations of the statutes charted is included on pages 48 to 56. Any listed provision may be located by matching the title of the section of the chart where the provision appears to the corresponding category in the right-hand column of the cite chart.

In most cases, a black dot on the chart indicates that a statute includes language similar to that listed on the chart. Statutory language varies widely; the provisions listed on the chart are an approximation of the most common statutory language. In some cases, marks on the chart reflect procedures being followed in a state that are not listed in the domestic violence law, but appear elsewhere in the state code. This is the case with most of the listed filing fees and fee waiver provisions.

Significant provisions which appear in only one or two statutes are listed in the footnotes to the chart. Each provision listed as a line on the chart appears in the statutes of three or more states. Where a dot and a footnote number appear on the chart, the statute includes the listed provision and another related provision. Where only a footnote number appears, the statute includes a provision different from but related to the listed provision.

The chart does not include all types of legislation that may benefit violent families, but focuses on recent legislation aimed at reducing or preventing mate abuse.[2] Legislation dealing only with physical or sexual abuse of children, or with elder abuse is not covered. However, much of the legislation on adult abuse may also be used to prevent subsequent child abuse or elder abuse.

New legislation on spousal rape is not charted; a survey of state rape laws has been published in the *Women's Rights Law Reporter*.[3]

Protection Order Laws

A protection order (also called a temporary restraining order or temporary injunction) is an injunction designed to prevent violence by one member of a household against another. The court may, depending on state law, order an abuser to move out of a residence shared with a victim, to refrain from abuse of or contact with the victim, to enter a counseling program, or to pay support, restitution, or attorney's fees. The court may award child custody and visitation rights or may restrict the use or disposition of personal property (see chart, Section IA).

Laws providing this type of protection have been passed in thirty-six states and the District of Columbia. Thirty-two of the protection order laws allow the court to evict an abuser from a residence shared with a victim of abuse. The eviction order is possibly the most important form of relief provided by the new legislation. It gives a victim of abuse an enforceable right to be safe in her home, and it establishes that the abuser rather than the victim should bear the burden of finding another residence. Many of the laws allow eviction even if the title or lease of the residence lists only the abuser's name. Some statutes allow eviction in such cases only if the abuser is found to have a legal obligation to support his wife and/or children.

The laws vary widely as to what relationship must exist between abuser and victim for protection to be available. Two statutes restrict elegibility to spouses; the others make relief available to other family or household members, and sometimes to former coresidents.[4]

Most of the statutes make eligibility for a protection order contingent on present and/or former cohabitation. A recent study of six hundred battered women found that 73 percent of the victims studied were single, divorced, or separated at the time the victim reported to a hospital after an abusive incident.[5] Under many of the current protection order laws, this group of victims would be ineligible for relief.

To get a full protection order (one issued after a hearing at which both parties are present), a victim must show, usually by a preponderance of evidence, that abuse has occurred, or that there has been some threatened or attempted abuse. Nine states also allow issuance of a protection order if it is shown that a child has been sexually abused (see chart, Section IB).

Few of the new laws make protection orders available based on a showing of harassment or psychological abuse. Coverage of such conduct would provide a remedy to persons who are kept prisoners in their homes, whose property is destroyed, or whose homes are broken into by boyfriends or former spouses.

The District of Columbia statute defines abuse to include any act committed against an eligible party that would be punishable as a criminal offense. This more general definition would allow issuance of protection orders not only for threatened or attempted assault, but also for burglary, larceny, kidnapping, harassment, or destruction of personal property. The rationale is that if an act may be the basis of a criminal prosecution, it is serious enough to justify issuance of a protection order.

The chart categorizes protection orders according to how quickly a court will respond after a petition is filed and how long the order may last. A full protection order may be issued only after the abuser is notified and a hearing is held at which both parties have an opportunity to testify. (If the abuser fails to appear at this hearing he is deemed to have waived his right to a hearing, so relief may be granted based on the victim's testimony.)

The less time it takes to obtain a protection order, the more effective it is likely to be. Thirty-five of the statutes provide for temporary protection orders, which are issued *ex parte* within a day or a few days after a petition is filed, following a hearing at which the victim but not the abuser is present. A temporary protection order lasts until the abuser receives notice and has an opportunity for a hearing on whether the order should be dissolved, at which time a full protection order may be issued.

A few of the laws allowing *ex parte* relief have been challenged as violating the due process clause of the fourteenth amendment, but so far such challenges have been unsuccessful.[6] The deferral of a hearing has been found permissible if there is a danger of irreparable harm unless relief is granted.

Since most abuse occurs at night, ten of the statutes provide for emergency protection orders, which may be issued at night or on weekends when the regular courts are not in session. The emergency order, often issued by a magistrate rather than a judge, lasts only until the next weekday morning when the victim must go to court to reapply for a temporary protection order.

In sixteen states, an abuser who violates a protection order may be prosecuted for a misdemeanor offense, and in twenty-four states for contempt of court. (Nine of these allow prosecution either for a misdemeanor or for contempt.) Thirteen of the statutes include explicit language allowing courts to impose a jail sentence of six months or more for violation of a protection order. The laws frequently allow imposition of a fine of $500 or more instead of or in addition to a jail sentence (see chart, Section IF). Imposition of a jail sentence in misdemeanor cases is relatively rare; more important to the enforcement of protection orders are the arrest power and other powers granted police in handling protection order violations (see "Police Intervention" below).

Each statute contains procedural rules on where, how, and by whom petitions may be filed, fees to be charged, when hearings must be held, and so on (see chart, Section IE). In many states, these procedures are not listed in a spouse abuse statute but may be found in the general rules of civil practice. Of particular importance are rules on fees for filing papers or delivery of orders to abusers. Provisions waiving filing fees, permitting victims to file without a lawyer, and requiring court clerks to assist victims in filing petitions are essential to ensure that protection orders will be available to victims of abuse who have no money or no access to their money.

Injunctions Pending Domestic Relations Proceedings

Before the new protection order laws were enacted, many state laws covering divorce and other domestic relations proceedings allowed courts to issue injunctions requiring payment of support, designating temporary custody, or prohibiting abuse until the court proceedings were finished. These injunctions were, and still are, available independent of allegations of abuse. In some states that have passed new protection order laws, the injunction pending divorce has been expanded and enforcement provisions have been added. However, injunctions pending divorce or other proceedings are the only form of civil injunction available in Idaho, Indiana, Michigan, New Jersey, New Mexico, Oklahoma, Rhode Island, South Carolina, South Dakota, Virginia, Washington, and Wyoming.

Criminal Law

Every state has laws imposing criminal penalties for assault, battery, burglary, and kidnapping. These laws could be enforced against persons who abuse their mates, but mate abuse has not traditionally been treated as a criminal matter.

To promote enforcement of criminal law against abusers, ten states have enacted legislation making spouse abuse a separate criminal offense. Like the protection order laws, these laws specify the relationships covered and the penalties that may be imposed for commission of the offense (see chart, Section IIIA). The intent of these statutes is to give direction to the enforcement of criminal law against abusive mates rather than to make any substantive change in the law. A specific criminal law also facilitates identification of family violence cases by statisticians or victim/witness services.

Some laws set out dispositions that may be used in place of a fine or jail sentence in domestic violence cases in which a criminal charge has been filed. Some allow a protection order prohibiting abuse of or contact with the victim; others allow the court to require the abuser to attend counseling.

In a few states, such as Washington, Ohio, and Illinois, criminal courts may issue broad protection orders similar to those generally available from civil courts.

The relief available may vary depending on the stage of the criminal process at which an order is issued. The court may impose requirements on an abuser as a condition of release, as a condition of deferred prosecution, or as a condition of probation after conviction. Violation of conditions of release could result in pretrial detention or setting of bail. Where prosecution is deferred pending compliance with a counseling or protection order, violation could result in later prosecution. Violation of terms of probation could result in revocation of probation and imposition of a jail sentence (see chart, Section IIIB).

The foregoing dispositional options, which are codified in many state laws, are also available in other jurisdictions as a matter of judicial discretion. Statutory authority is not necessary, for example, for a judge to order a defendant to stay away from the victim as a condition of release on bail. However, an explicit statute encourages judges to use particular options in cases in which the victim and offender are related.

Civil versus Criminal Relief

There are important differences between criminal and civil remedies created by the new legislation. The protection order laws generally offer broader, more flexible, and more immediate relief than can be obtained by filing a criminal charge. Also, the decision to file a protection order lies solely with a victim of abuse.

The passage of a new criminal statute does not guarantee a battered woman a new remedy, since the decision to file a charge is with the prosecutor, not with the victim. Criminal laws, however, may be more effective than civil relief in changing abusive behavior because there is a greater perceived or actual threat of punishment. If criminal penalties are available for violation of a protection order, the same type of leverage over the abuser may be possible in civil as in criminal cases.

Police Intervention

Twenty-seven of the recent state laws on domestic violence expand police power to arrest in domestic abuse cases. In twenty-one states, arrest without a warrant is permitted where a police officer has probable cause to believe that an abuser has committed a misdemeanor. In fourteen states, police may arrest without a warrant if they have probable cause to believe that an abuser has violated a protection order. (Eight states allow probable cause arrest in both cases.) Most of these arrest laws give police a discretionary power, but four state laws impose a duty to arrest where probable cause is present.

Almost half the states impose some duties on police responding to domestic disturbance calls, including transporting the victim to a hospital or shelter, informing her of her legal options, staying until she is no longer in danger, and so on. Many of the laws prescribing police duties or expanding arrest powers immunize law enforcement officials from suits for damages for any action taken in a good faith effort to enforce the law (see chart, Section IV).

Data Collection

Lack of adequate data on the nature and scope of family violence has hindered improvement of law enforcement response to the problem. Twenty-eight states have now passed laws that require agencies that assist violent families to either keep internal records of each case handled or to file reports on cases handled or on the general problem to another agency (see chart, Section V).

Funding

Thirty-seven states have appropriated funds for services to violent families. Such appropriations are made either by including a line item in the budget of a state agency or by passing a bill making a categorical appropriation. All appropriations must be approved by the state legislature. They may originate, however, in the governor's office as part of the proposed budget submitted each year to the legislature by the governor, or as a separate bill.

In fourteen states a new source of funding has been created by passage of legislation that imposes a surcharge on the marriage license. The money collected through the surcharge is distributed to shelters and other service organizations. In three states, the legislatures have appropriated funds in the state budgets in anticipation of income from the marriage license surcharge.

The funding legislation generally specifies whether funds are to be spent on shelters, on counseling services, on employment training, on legal advocacy, or on other services. In some states, the law suggests types of services to be funded while in other states a program must provide listed services in order to be eligible for funding.

The chart lists only statewide appropriations. In many states, other money for services to violent families is also available from city or county governments or from private sources. Nevertheless, the need for funding for shelters and other services to violent families is still largely unmet. Most shelters operate on a shoestring, provide only basic services, and must turn away a substantial percentage of the families which seek assistance.

Conclusion

The process of drafting and lobbying for new domestic violence legislation is difficult and time-consuming. Most of the existing legislation reflects a composite of what the drafters felt would benefit battered women and what was politically feasible in the state. Drafters should consider that setting up a commission to study the problem or to collect data on domestic violence may be easier politically than improving the available legal remedies, and that a protection order law may be less controversial than a funding bill.

In drafting legislation, advocates for battered women should consult with shelters and other groups around the state so that the bill submitted to the legislature will have widespread support. In addition, the legislative counsel's office at the state capitol should be asked to assist in tailoring legislation to fit the state code or court system. An expert on constitutional law should be asked to examine any drafts of bills for possible flaws.

A valuable resource on domestic violence law is a book titled *Adult Domestic Violence: Constitutional, Legislative, and Equitable Issues*, by Boylan and Taub. It is available from the National Clearinghouse for Legal Services, 500 N. Michigan Avenue, Suite 1940, Chicago, IL 60611, for $4.00. Order document #31673.

Notes

1. It is widely recognized that although some men are beaten by their mates, most adult victims are female. Therefore, victims of abuse are referred to as female and abusers as male for purposes of simplicity. Mate abuse is used instead of the more common term, spouse abuse, to include persons subject to violence by intimates, regardless of their marital status or living arrangements.

2. The chart does not list general criminal statutes (as distinguished from specific spouse abuse laws), crime victim compensation laws, public benefits laws, or divorce and custody laws. Neither does it list laws on immunity or waiver of immunity of spouses for damage suits for personal injury. The chart does not list every available remedy for battered women. For information on victim compensation, see Deborah Carrow, *Crime Victim* compensation (U.S. Department of Justice, National Institute of Justice, 1980).

3. Leigh Beinen, "Update of Rape II," *Women's Rights Law Reporter* (Spring 1980 Supp.).

4. Due to wide variations in statutory language and the possibility of several interpretations, charting the groups of victims covered by protection orders was difficult.

5. Evan Stark, Anne Flitcraft, *et al.*, *Battering in Medical Context* (a monograph prepared for the Office on Domestic Violence, Department of Health and Human Services). Another study of thirty battered women found that 69 percent of the women studied were single, separated, or divorced. Susan Malone Back, Ph.D. and Genet D'Arcy, *"Victims of Domestic Violence: Preliminary Study of Battered and Non-battered Female Psychiatric Patients"* (unpublished study, University of Colorado School of Medicine).

6. The only court that has published an opinion on the constitutionality of *ex parte* relief is the Pennsylvania Court of Common Pleas in which the Pennsylvania Protection From Abuse Act was upheld. Boyle v. Boyle, 5 *Family Law Reporter* 2916, Sept. 25, 1979. The Ohio protection order law was upheld against a constitutional challenge in Ohio v. Heyl. No. C79BR 120 (Hamilton County Municipal Court 1979).

KEY • - effective legislation; ○ - pending legislation; T- thousand; M - million; FY- fiscal year
Numbers beside dots or in lieu of dots refer to footnotes, except where a line on the chart refers to a time period or a sum of money.
A time period or a sum of money that is circled indicates pending legislation.

	Alabama	Alaska	Arizona	Arkansas	California	Colorado	Connecticut	Delaware	District of Columbia	Florida	Georgia	Hawaii	Idaho	Illinois	Indiana	Iowa	Kansas
I. PROTECTION ORDERS¹	•	•	•		•	•	•	•²	•	•	•	•		•		•	•
A. Court May Order:																	
1. Eviction of the abuser	•	•	•		•		•	•			•	•		•		•	•
(a) Allowed even if residence is in abuser's name	•				•			•						•			
2. Abuser to provide alternative housing for the victim	•										•			•		•	•
3. No further contact with the victim		•	•⁷		•			•	•				•		•		
4. No further abuse	•	•			•		•	•	•	•	•		•	•		•	•
5. No threat of abuse			•		•	•	•	•	•	•			•	•			
6. Abuser not to molest or disturb the peace of the victim							•	•	•			•		•			
7. No restrictions on the personal liberty of the victim							•	•	•					•			
8. Counseling for the abuser and/or the victim⁸					•		•	•						•¹⁰		•⁹	
9. Temporary support of spouse or minor children	•	•			•						•					•	•
10. Temporary child custody/visitation rights	•	•			•						•					•	•
11. Monetary compensation to the victim by the abuser		•			•									•			
12. Payment of the victim's court costs and/or attorney's fees by the abuser¹²	•		•		•		•				•			•			•
13. Temporary use or possession of personal property								•									•
14. No disposition of property								•						•			
15. Other terms may be set by the court¹³		•	•		•¹⁴	•	•¹⁴	•	•	•	•	•			•		
B. Abuse for Which a Protection Order is Available					17				16						17		
1. Physical abuse:																	
(a) of an adult	•	•	•		•	•	•	•	•	•	•	•			•	•	•
(b) of a child	•				•	•	•	•	•	•	•				•		
2. Threat of physical abuse	•	•	•		•	•		•	•	•				•		•	•
3. Attempt at physical abuse	•	•			•			•	•	•						•	•
4. Sexual abuse:																	
(a) of an adult							•	○									
(b) of a child							•	○									•
C. Who May Be Covered by a Protection Order (relationship to the abuser)			20														
1. Spouse	•	•	•		•	•	•	•	•	•	•	•		•		•	•
2. Minor child of one or both parties	•	•	•		•	•	•	•	•	•	•	•		•		•	•
3. Parent	•				•		•	•	•	•			•	•			
4. Household member related by blood or marriage²³	•		•		•	•	•	•	•	•	•	•	•	•		•	•
5. Person living as a spouse	•				•		•	•						•			
6. Unrelated household member		•			•		•		○			•		•		•	
7. Former spouse		•	•		•		•		○		•		•	•			•²⁷
8. Person formerly living as a spouse					•				○								
9. Former household member					•				○		•			•			•²⁷
D. Limits on Eligibility for a Protection Order																	
1. Protection order unavailable if the victim has filed for a separation or a divorce			•														
2. Eligibility unaffected if the victim leaves the residence to avoid abuse	•				•			•						•³⁰		•	
E. Procedural Provisions of the Protection Order Laws																	
1. In general																	
(a) Petition may be filed by:										31							
(i) Victim	•	•	•				•	•	○	•	•	•		•		•	•

I. Protection Orders

1. States marked on this line have laws providing for issuance of protection orders, usually by civil courts, independent of any action for divorce or separation. The section on procedure (IE) distinguishes full protection orders from temporary or emergency protection orders. The section that lists what a court may include in a protection order (IA) refers to protection orders issued after a full hearing. In some states, the same relief is available under temporary or emergency orders (which are issued *ex parte*) as under a full protection order. In other states, the available relief is more limited for temporary or emergency orders (see Section IE). The sections covering the types of abuse for which a protection order is available (IB) and who is eligible for a protection order (IC) include temporary and emergency orders in any references to protection orders.
2. The Delaware Family Court is empowered to act in any proceeding in which a member of a family alleges that some other member of the family is "imperiling the family relationship." The Division of Social Services or a licensed youth agency may also petition where it is alleged that the "conduct of a child, or his parents or custodians, or members of a family, imperils any family relationship or imperils the morals, health, maintenance or care of a child." Under this section, the court is empowered to "make such adjudications and dispositions as appear appropriate." This charted statute, together with the court's broad equitable powers, allows the court to issue protection orders similar to those available under the specific protection from abuse acts enacted in other states. In addition, the court may intervene before any physical abuse has taken place.
Ex parte hearings may be conducted on an emergency basis pursuant to court rule. An emergency hearing may be held if facts are set forth in affidavits or verified pleadings "upon which the court may conclude that unless the relief sought is granted prior to the hearing on the merits, substantial and irreparable harm will result." The charted statute for Delaware lists not only provisions expressly included in the law, but relief deemed to be available under the "imperiling" statute.
3. On the last day of the 1980 session, the South Dakota legislature passed a protection order bill similar to the Iowa law. The law was vetoed by the governor of South Dakota.
4. The Ohio law allows a court to prohibit a victim of abuse from allowing the abuser to enter a residence from which he has been evicted. This provision may be used only upon issuance of a second or subsequent protection order.
5. Under the Oregon protection order statute, eviction of an abuser is permitted only if minor children reside in the home. This is also true for an order pending divorce.
6. Under Maryland law, if the court determines that abuse has occurred it may as part of the relief granted under a protection order require the abuser to vacate the family home immediately and grant temporary possession of the home to the petitioner for up to 5 days. Any extensions to the order to vacate may not exceed a total period of 15 days.
7. Under Arizona law, "either or both parties may be restrained from coming near the residence, place of employment or school of the other party, or other specifically designated locations or persons on a showing that physical harm may otherwise result." Many of the statutes that allow no contact orders use similar language.
8. Some state laws allow the court to require that the abuser and/or victim attend counseling; other statutes allow the court to recommend counseling.
9. The Iowa law provides that where a counseling order is issued, the cost of counseling is to be paid by the abuser, or, if the abuser is indigent, by the abuser's county. A similar provision in North Dakota states that the costs of counseling are to be borne by the parties or by the county of residence for indigents.
10. Under New Hampshire and Illinois law, counseling may be recommended for the abuser only.
11. Missouri law allows assignment of income by the court.
12. Some of the statutes allow the court to order payment of court costs and attorneys' fees of the prevailing party by the other party.
13. "Other terms may be set by the court" means that the statute gives a judge discretion to add provisions to a protection order other than those listed in the law.
14. Under the laws of California and Connecticut, the court may prohibit the respondent from sexually abusing the victim.

	Louisiana	Maine	Maryland	Massachusetts	Michigan	Minnesota	Mississippi	Missouri	Montana	Nebraska	Nevada	New Hampshire	New Jersey	New Mexico	New York	North Carolina	North Dakota	Ohio	Oklahoma	Oregon	Pennsylvania	Rhode Island	South Carolina	South Dakota	Tennessee	Texas	Utah	Vermont	Virginia	Washington	West Virginia	Wisconsin	Wyoming
		•	•	•		•	•	•	•	•	•	•	•		○		•	•	•		•	•			3	•	•	•	•	•		•	•
		•	•[6]	•		•	•	•		•	•	•	•		○		•	•	•		•[4]		•[5]	•		•	•	•		•		•	•
		•					•					•	○		•		•		•		•			•		•		•				•	
		•		•			•						•		○		•	•	•		•			•		•						•	
		•	•	•		•	•	•	•	•	•	•			•		•	•	•		•			•		•	•	•	•		•		
		•		•			•			•	•	•			○		•	•	•		•			•		•							
		•		•							•				•		•	•								•						•	
										•		•			•												•						
		•	•			•	•				•[10]	○			•		•[9]	•						•									
		•		•		•	•	•[11]		•	•	•	○		•		•	•	•		•	•			•		•	•		•		•	•
		•	•	•		•	•	•		•	•	•	○		•		•	•	•		•	•			•		•		•		•	•	•
		•		•			•				•	•	○		•		•		•		•				•		•						•
		•	•	•		•	•	•			•	•	○		•		•	•		○					•		•		•				
		•					•				•	•			•				•		•				•		•					•	
							•		•																	•							
		•	•	•		•	•			•			•		•[15]				•		•				•		•	•	•	•		•	
															17										18								
		•	•	•		•	•	•		•	•	•	○		•		•	•	•		•	•			•		•	•		•		•	•
			•	•		•	•			•		•	○		•		•		•			•				•		•				•	•
		•	•	•		•	•	•		•	•	•	○		•		•	•	•		•	•			•		•		•			•	•
			•								•[19]	○								○								•					
												○								•						•		•					
						21					22														21								
		•	•	•		•	•	•		•	•	•	○		•	•	•	•		•	•			•		•	•		•		•	•
		•	•	•		•	•	•				•	○		•		•		•		•				•		•					•	•
		•	•			•	•	•				•	○		•		•	•	•		•				•		•		•			•	
		•	•	•[24]		•[24]	•	•		•	•	•	○		•			•		•				•[25]				•				
		•				•	•	•		•	•	•			•				•		•		•			•		•				•[26]
				•		•	•	•		•	•	•	○		•		•		•	○					•		•					
		•		•			•	•		•	•	•	○		•[27]	•	•	•		•	•[27]			•		•	•	•	•		•	•
							•								•				•		•				•		•				•	•
				•			•	•		•	•	•	○		•				•	○	•[27]				•		•					
						•	28			•									28					•	•		•	•				•[29]
		•[30]	•	•		•	•	•				•	○		•		•	•	•		•	•			•[30]		•	•	•	•		•	•
			•	•	○		•	•	•		•	•	•		○		•	•	•		•	•					•	•				•	•

15. A protection order in New York may order the parties, in addition to provisions listed, to give "proper attention to the care of the home," to refrain from actions that "make the home not a proper place for the child," or to participate in an "education program" for abusers which is similar to the program for those convicted of driving while intoxicated.

16. The protection order law in the District of Columbia allows issuance of an order for "any act, punishable as a criminal offense," against an eligible party.

17. Laws in New York and Illinois include harassment in the definition of abuse for which a protection order may be issued.

In California, temporary restraining orders are also available to persons who have suffered harassment. Harassment is defined as "a knowing and willful course of conduct directed at a specific person which seriously alarms, annoys, or harasses such person, and which serves no legitimate purpose. The course of conduct must be such as would cause a reasonable person to suffer substantial emotional distress, and must actually cause substantial emotional distress to the plaintiff. 'Course of conduct' is a pattern of conduct composed of a series of acts over a period of time, however short, evidencing a continuity of purpose. Constitutionally protected activity is not included within the meaning of 'course of conduct'"

18. New Hampshire law makes a protection order available for sexual abuse of an adult, but excludes spouses from relief under this provision.

19. Only spouses and former spouses are expressly covered by the Arizona protection order law, but the statute states that protection may be extended to other specifically designated persons at the discretion of the court.

21. Under the laws of Missouri and Tennessee, protection orders are available only if both the victim and the abuser are adults. The definitional section of the Tennessee law makes protection orders available to a broad group of victims, but an amendment at the end of the statute restricts availability of orders to currently married persons.

22. In Nevada and North Dakota, protection orders are available, in addition to parties listed, to any adult member of the abuser's family.

23. "Household members related by blood or marriage" is often stated in the law as "persons related by consanguinity or affinity," or in some states as "relatives." Consanguines include blood relatives and affines include spouses and inlaws. A few of the states listed do not require that persons in this category be co-residents.

24. In Massachusetts and Minnesota, "consanguines" but not "affines" are eligible for protection orders.

25. Under Texas law, no co-residency requirement is imposed on persons related by consanguinity or affinity. Texas law also covers foster parents and children.

26. Wisconsin law makes protection orders available to persons living as spouses only if they are of the opposite sex and have minor children in common.

27. The laws of Kansas and Pennsylvania allow issuance of protection orders to former spouses and former household members only if both parties still have legal access to the residence. An adult in Kansas may not obtain a protection order more than twice in a 12-month period. Kansas law allows issuance of protection orders to former household members only if they are related by blood or marriage.

New York law allows issuance of protection orders to former spouses only in conjunction with custody orders.

28. In Missouri, a protection order terminates, unless otherwise provided by law, upon the entry of a decree of dissolution of marriage or legal separation. Ohio law states that a protection order shall terminate no later than 60 days after the victim files for separation or divorce.

29. The protection order laws of Vermont and West Virginia state that orders are unavailable to victims of abuse who have filed for separation or divorce. However, both of these states have other legislation making protection orders available while proceedings for divorce or separation are pending (see Section II).

30. The Maine protection order law states, "The right to relief under this chapter shall not be affected by the plaintiff's use of reasonable force in response to abuse by the defendant." In Tennessee, eligibility for a protection order is unaffected by "use of such physical force against the respondent as is reasonably believed to be necessary to defend the petitioner or another from imminent physical injury or abuse." A similar provision is found in Illinois law.

	Alabama	Alaska	Arizona	Arkansas	California	Colorado	Connecticut	Delaware	District of Columbia	Florida	Georgia	Hawaii	Idaho	Illinois	Indiana	Iowa	Kansas
(ii) Parent of a minor victim	•				•				•					•			•
(iii) Adult member of the household for a minor	•										•			•			
(b) Filing for a protection order does not preclude other court action		•	•		•		•	•	o		•			•		•	•
(c) Protection order has no effect on legal title to real property	•								•					•		•	•
(d) Fee charged for filing a petition ($)			20		50-60	9-40			15		30	16		42		8	0
(e) Court may waive the filing fee for indigents		•	•		•				•					•[35]		•	
(f) Fee charged for delivery of a protection order to an abuser ($)					9[36]		10		0	0	12			11[36]			
(g) Victim may file a petition without a lawyer		•	•		•				•		•		•				
(h) Court clerk must assist the victim in filing a petition		•							•								
(i) Court must:																	
(i) Prepare forms useable by lay people		•	•		•				•		•		•				
(ii) Inform the victim of the availability of a protection order									•								
(iii) Inform the abuser of his right to obtain counsel	•	•							•							•	•
(iv) Give protection order petitions priority over other civil actions					•												
(j) Consent decree may be issued instead of a protection order	•				•				•			•				•	•
2. Full protection order procedure																	
(a) Maximum duration of full protection order (months)	12	1½	6		3		3		12		6	2		12		12	12[40]
(b) Maximum duration of eviction order if less than protection order (days)														30			
(c) Hearing must be held:																	
(i) Number of days after filing of a petition	10		10				14				10					10	10
(ii) Number of days after a temporary protection order is issued		10	10		15 or 20							15					
(d) Full protection order is renewable		•	•				•	•	•					•			•
(e) Full protection order is modifiable	•		•					•	•					•		•	•
3. Temporary protection order procedure																	
(a) Maximum duration of a temporary protection order (days)[43]					15-20						10			30	10		
(b) Hearing must be held within number of days after a petition is filed										20	1						
(c) Temporary protection order may be granted ex parte[43]	•	•	•		•		•	•	•	•	•			•		•	•
(d) Petition must list facts showing need for immediate relief[43]					•									•			•
(e) Must prove immediate danger of abuse to get an ex parte order	•	•	•		•		•	•	•					•		•	•
(f) Available relief is more limited than under a protection order														•			•
(g) Temporary protection order is renewable	•	•										•		•			•
(h) Temporary protection order lasts until full hearing is held					•												
(i) Full hearing must be held before a protection order is issued[45]		•										ʔ					
(j) Temporary protection order becomes full protection order unless the abuser requests a hearing[45]				•													
(k) No bond requirement					•											•	•
(l) Bond requirement waivable																	
4. Emergency protection order procedure																	
(a) Judge to issue emergency protection order at night and/or on weekends	•															•	•
(b) Emergency protection order lasts until the regular court opens (max. 72 hrs.)	•															•	•
(c) Upon expiration, the victim may petition for a temporary protection order	•															•	•
F. Enforcement of Full Protection Orders, Temporary Protection Orders, and Emergency Protection Orders									48								
1. Order issued to the abuser by the court	•				•				•		•			•		•	•
2. Order to be personally served on the abuser		•	•		•	•			•[49]					•			
3. Free copy of the order given to the victim	•				•[51]		•	•								•	•
4. Copy of the order sent to the local police by the court	•	•	•		•[52]	•			•			•		•		•	•
5. Penalties for violation of protection orders	•	•	•		•	•	•	•				•		•		•	•
(a) Misdemeanor			•		•	•			•			•		•			
(b) Contempt of court	•		•		•	•			•					•		•	•
(c) Maximum jail sentence (months)		55			6	6	(12)		24	6							
(d) Maximum fine ($)					500	500	(1000)		1000	300							

31. In the District of Columbia, only the Corporation Counsel may file protection order petitions. Victims of abuse have no private right of action except to seek temporary restraining orders as part of a divorce, custody, or other proceeding in family court. A pending amendment to the statute gives victims of abuse a private right of action.

32. In Minnesota and Pennsylvania, the laws allow any adult household member to file a petition on behalf of a child living in the residence.

33. Missouri law states, "No order entered pursuant to this act shall be *res judicata* to any other proceeding."

34. Under New York law, a victim of abuse may apply for relief in either family court or criminal court. Within 72 hours after filing a criminal charge or a petition for a protection order in family court, she may change her mind and switch from one court to the other. Petitioners are informed that the purpose of the family court proceeding is to keep the family intact, while the purpose of the criminal proceeding is prosecution.

35. In Maryland, Pennsylvania, and Illinois, if a person filing a petition alleges that she is indigent or unable to pay the filing fee, the fee is temporarily waived. At a later hearing it is determined if the fee should be waived or whether payment should be required. In Maryland, the abuser may be required to pay the filing fee for the victim.

36. In California, North Dakota, Vermont, and Illinois, the court may waive the fee for service of a protection order upon application by a victim of abuse to proceed *in forma pauperis*.

37. The Missouri statute declares that assistance provided to the victims by court clerks "shall not constitute the practice of law." In New York, legislation passed which gives indigent petitioners in family offense proceedings a right to court-appointed counsel.

38. Maine law provides that the address of the victim may be deleted from court papers.

39. New York requires that a summons issued to an abuser inform him of his right to be represented by a lawyer and of his right to have a court appoint a lawyer for him if he is indigent. New York law also gives indigent petitioners in family offense proceedings a right to court-appointed counsel.

40. A temporary support order is limited to 30 days in Kansas and 2 weeks in Pennsylvania.

41. Under Ohio law, if no *ex parte* protection order is requested, a petition will be heard on the same schedule as all other civil actions. If an *ex parte* order is requested, it must be heard on the same day. If an abuser is evicted on the basis of an *ex parte* hearing, a full hearing must be held within 3 days. If an eviction order is not issued, then a full hearing must be held within 10 days.

42. Under Minnesota law, a court referee may be appointed to take evidence and report it to the judge.

43. The provisions allowing *ex parte* eviction have been criticized as allowing a deprivation of property without notice and hearing in violation of the due process clause of the fourteenth amendment of the United States Constitution. In ruling on other statutes allowing injunction relief prior to notice and hearing, the Supreme

Table columns (state headings, left to right): Louisiana, Maine, Maryland, Massachusetts, Michigan, Minnesota, Mississippi, Missouri, Montana, Nebraska, Nevada, New Hampshire, New Jersey, New Mexico, New York, North Carolina, North Dakota, Ohio, Oklahoma, Oregon, Pennsylvania, Rhode Island, South Carolina, South Dakota, Tennessee, Texas, Utah, Vermont, Virginia, Washington, West Virginia, Wisconsin, Wyoming

(The body of this page is a large data matrix of dots and numbers aligned under the above state columns, with footnote markers; selected legible numeric rows include values such as 32, 33, 34, 35, 36, 37, 40, $0\text{-}69$, 34.50, $16\text{-}96$, 12.50, 11.50, $10\text{-}15$, $0\text{-}20$, $5\text{-}15$, 12, 30, and the bottom summary rows showing monetary/day figures such as 1000, 500, 5000, 250, 300, 2000, 50, etc.)

Court stated that deferral of a hearing on deprivation of property may be permissible if (1) the petition includes statements of specific facts that justify the requested relief; (2) notice and opportunity for a full hearing are given as soon as possible, preferably within a few days after the order is issued; and (3) the temporary injunction is issued by a judge. See *Mitchell v. Grant*, 416 U.S. 600 (1974). Drafting protection order laws that reflect these guidelines may minimize the risk that the laws will be found unconstitutional.

The case in which these guidelines were developed involved summary repossession of consumer goods on default of payments by the buyer. The court balanced the right of the buyer to notice and hearing before repossession against the seller's property interest. The balancing test used in *Mitchell* might be interpreted to find that a protection order is necessary to preserve the physical safety of the victim. (See p. 3, n. 6, *supra*).

44. In Vermont, an *ex parte* order prohibiting abuse of or interference with the personal liberty of the victim or minor children may be issued if the court finds that abuse has occurred. Vermont law allows issuance of a temporary custody order *ex parte* if the victim can show immediate danger of abuse of minor children. If she can show that she was forced to vacate her residence and is without shelter, the court may issue an *ex parte* eviction order.

45. Sections IE3i and IE3j distinguish two statutory alternatives for providing the abuser with "notice and the opportunity to be heard" required by the due process clause of the fourteenth amendment. Under some laws, a full hearing must be scheduled whenever a temporary protection order is issued. Other statutes require that the abuser be given notice when a temporary order is issued and have the opportunity to request a hearing. Under these laws, the temporary order becomes permanent unless the abuser requests that a full hearing be held.

46. In North Dakota and Pennsylvania, the relief that may be ordered on an emergency basis is more limited than that which may be ordered when a full protection order is issued. These provisions are parallel to those limiting relief available under a temporary protection order (see Section IE3f).

47. In Pennsylvania, emergency relief is available on weekends on a 24-hour basis, but emergency orders cannot be obtained on weeknights.

48. California law provides that the court may appoint counsel or the district attorney to represent the plaintiff in a proceeding to enforce the terms of a protection order. The defendant may be ordered to pay court costs and attorneys' fees incurred by the plaintiff or to reimburse the county for costs incurred if the plaintiff is represented by the district attorney.

49. In the District of Columbia, protection orders are served on the abuser by the U.S. Marshal, not by the D.C. Police.

50. Utah law makes a victim of abuse responsible for serving a protection order on her abuser.

51. In California, a free copy of a protection order is given to a victim of abuse only if the filing fee has been waived.

52. Under the laws of Oregon, Pennsylvania, and Utah, the victim rather than the court is required to deliver a copy of the protection order to the local police department. In California, both the victim and the court must deliver the order to the local

	Alabama	Alaska	Arizona	Arkansas	California	Colorado	Connecticut	Delaware	District of Columbia	Florida	Georgia	Hawaii	Idaho	Illinois	Indiana	Iowa	Kansas
II. INJUNCTIONS PENDING DOMESTIC RELATIONS PROCEEDINGS[56]																	
A. Order Restraining an Abuser is Available to a Victim Who Files for Divorce		•	•[57]		•[58]	•		•				•		•	•		•
B. Court May Order:																	
1. Eviction of the abuser			•		•	•		•						•	•		•
2. Abuser not to molest or disturb the peace of the victim			•[57]		•	•		•						•	•		•
3. No restriction on the liberty of the victim	•		•										•				
4. Support of a spouse or minor children	•	•			•	•	•	•	•	•	•	•	•	•	•		•
5. Child custody/visitation rights	•	•			•	•	•	•	•	•	•	•	•	•	•	•	•
6. No removal of children from the jurisdiction			•[57]		•									•	•		
7. Payment of court costs and/or attorney's fees of the victim by the abuser	•	•			•	•		•	•			•	•			•	•
8. Temporary use or possession of personal property			•		•	•		•							•	•	
9. No disposition of property	•		•[57]		•	•		•	•			•		•	•		•
10. Other terms may be set by the court					•	•		•						•			
C. Ex Parte Relief Available			•[57]		•	•		•						•	•		
D. Police Must Enforce Orders			•[57]		•	•		•									
E. Penalties May Be Imposed for Violation of Orders			•[57]		•	•		•									
III. CRIMINAL LAW																	
A. Statute Makes Domestic Violence a Separate Criminal Offense					•	•							•				
1. Charges include:																	
(a) Simple assault					•	•							•				
(b) Aggravated assault					•	•											
(c) Criminal trespass																	
2. Who may be charged (relationship to the abuser):																	
(a) Spouse					•[64]			•					•				
(b) Unmarried intimate								•									
(c) Former spouse								•									
3. Violation: felony					•	•											
4. Violation: misdemeanor					•	•		•									
5. Sentence upon conviction or guilty plea:																	
(a) Jail (maximum months)					36												
(b) Fine (maximum $)																	
B. Alternative Dispositions Authorized by State Law																	
1. Court may impose conditions on pretrial release, including:			•												•		
(a) Pretrial detention if the abuser is dangerous																	
(b) Protection order			•												•		
2. Deferred prosecution (diversion) program			•[72]		•[72]										•[72]		
(a) Arrest record expunged if abuser successfully completes diversion program								•							•[74]		
(b) Court may order mandatory counseling			•					•							•		
(c) Court may issue a protection order			•												•		
(d) Evidence from the program is not admissible if prosecution is resumed						•											
3. Court may impose conditions on probation, including:																	
(a) Mandatory counseling															•		
(b) Protection order															•		
C. Law Imposes Duties on the Court or the Prosecutor	•				•							○					

police.

53. Violation of a protection order in Maine is, in most cases, a misdemeanor. However, violation of provisions ordering counseling or payment of temporary support or compensation for injuries are punishable only as contempt of court.

54. The Texas protection order law states that violation of an *ex parte* protection order is punishable by up to 6 months in jail or a fine of $500 or both. Violation of a full protection order, also according to the civil law, is punishable by up to 12 months in jail or a $2000 fine or both. However, a proposed amendment to the crimnial code that was to accompany this new legislation was never voted on by the Texas legislature.

55. Alaska law provides that "a defendant convicted of assault in the third degree committed in violation of the provisions of [a protection order] . . . shall be sentenced to a minimum term of imprisonment of 10 days. The execution of sentence may not be suspended and probation or parole may not be granted until the minimum term of imprisonment has been served. Imposition of sentence may not be suspended, except upon condition that the defendant be imprisoned for no less than the minimum term of imprisonment provided in this section, and the minimum sentence provided for in this section may not be otherwise reduced."

II. Injunctions Pending Domestic Relations Proceedings

56. Many states allow some form of temporary injunctive relief during divorce, separation, or custody proceedings, whether or not abuse is alleged. All of these are listed on the chart because of their potential usefulness to battered women. Some of these laws include specific provisions for orders prohibiting abuse or evicting the abuser. These are listed under Section IIA.

57. Under Arizona law, an injunction is issued automatically against all parties to every divorce action. Such an injunction prohibits disposition of common property, prohibits molestation, harassment, assault, or disturbance of the peace of the other party or of any children of the parties, and prohibits removal of the children residing in Arizona without written consent of the parties or the court. These orders warn that violation is contempt of court and may subject the violator to arrest and prosecution for crimes committed in the course of violation of the order. Parties are encouraged to file the order with a local law enforcement agency. The statute provides for warrantless arrest for violation of the order based on probable cause and for imposition of conditions on release of persons arrested.

The orders listed above are issued in every divorce case regardless of allegations of violence. No application is necessary. Other orders pending divorce are available in Arizona upon application by a party.

58. In California, protection orders are available in some paternity proceedings as well as in domestic relations proceedings.

59. Under Massachusetts law, the court may order the husband or wife to vacate the marital home for a period of time not to exceed 90 days. The court may extend the period of time, after a hearing, if it finds that the health, safety, or welfare of the moving party or minor children would be endangered. The opposing party is given at least 3 days notice of such a hearing. However, if immediate danger can be demonstrated the court may enter a temporary order without notice and give the opposing party notice within 5 days and an opportunity to question the order's continuation.

III. Criminal Law

60. New York law provides that the family court and criminal court have concurrent jurisdiction over most family offenses. For first-degree assault, however, the criminal court has exclusive jurisdiction.

61. Pennsylvania law makes intimidation of a victim or witness of a crime a criminal offense. Depending on the method of intimidation used, the crime is either a third-degree felony or a second-degree misdemeanor. Protection orders for victims and witnesses may be issued on hearsay evidence. Compliance with this provision is made a condition of all pretrial releases

62. The criminal provisions charted for Massachusetts, New Hampshire, and Wisconsin were included in domestic violence legislation, but the laws are not specifically directed to spouse abuse. The Wisconsin law creates a "middle-level" battery, which is a class E felony. The laws in Massachusetts and New Hampshire make it a criminal trespass to enter or remain in defiance of the order of the owner or other authorized person.

63. Ohio law also allows former household members related by blood or marriage to be charged. Wyoming law criminalizes abuse or neglect of a disabled adult by a caretaker.

64. The spouse assault law of Arkansas refers to husbands rather than spouses.

	Louisiana	Maine	Maryland	Massachusetts	Michigan	Minnesota	Mississippi	Missouri	Montana	Nebraska	Nevada	New Hampshire	New Jersey	New Mexico	New York	North Carolina	North Dakota	Ohio	Oklahoma	Oregon	Pennsylvania	Rhode Island	South Carolina	South Dakota	Tennessee	Texas	Utah	Vermont	Virginia	Washington	West Virginia	Wisconsin	Wyoming

65. Under Ohio law, a first offense under the spouse assault law is a first-degree misdemeanor, punishable by a 6-month jail sentence or a $1,000 fine, or both. A subsequent offense is a fourth-degree felony, punishable by 5 years in jail or a $2,500 fine, or both. Wyoming law allows imprisonment for up to 5 years for second or subsequent offenses.

66. Under the laws of Massachusetts and New Hampshire, a convicted abuser may be ordered to compensate the victim for loss or injury resulting from the abuse.

67. Legislation in Ohio and Wisconsin allows a court to release a suspected abuser into the custody of a third party.

68. In Minnesota, post-arrest detention is allowed if the abuser is considered dangerous, but any person detained must be brought before a judge within 24 hours or else released. In New Hampshire, an abuser may be detained if he violates conditions of pretrial release, but a bail revocation hearing must be held within 24 hours.

69. Under North Carolina law, if a defendant in a domestic abuse case is charged with assault, threat of assault, criminal trespass, or violation of a protection order, then:

Upon a determination by the judicial official that the immediate release of the abuser is likely to result in intimidation of the alleged victim and upon a determination that the execution of an appearance bond . . . will not reasonably assure that such injury or intimidation will not occur, a judicial official may retain the defendant in custody for a reasonable period of time while determining the conditions of pretrial release.

70. Minnesota law prohibits an arresting officer from issuing a citation in lieu of arrest or detention to a person charged with assaulting a spouse or household member. Persons arrested for domestic violence are required by law to be released after arrest "unless it reasonably appears that detention is necessary to prevent bodily harm to the arrested person or another," or if the arrestee may not respond to a citation. Persons detained pursuant to this provision must be brought before a judge within 24 hours after arrest, excluding Sundays and holidays.

71. Protection orders available as a condition of release in Ohio are charted under the section on protection orders. There are a few significant differences between available civil and criminal protection orders in Ohio. Hearings must be held within 24 hours for a criminal temporary protection order, and the same day for a civil

temporary protection order. Also, the statute does not authorize eviction of abusers under a criminal order.

In other states, the injunctions available as a condition of release are separate from the civil protection order, which may be issued in an independent proceeding. Generally, the injunctive relief available from criminal court is more limited than relief provided by the civil protection order laws.

72. Arizona, California, and Wisconsin specify conditions that must be met before an abuser may be admitted to a deferred prosecution program. In Arizona, deferred prosecution is unavailable if the abuser has a prior criminal conviction or has in the past been unsatisfactorily terminated from a diversion program. An abuser cannot enter a diversion program without the consent and recommendation of the prosecutor and the victim. Diversion occurs after conviction but before adjudication of guilt is entered.

In California, deferred prosecution is available where the offense was charged as or reduced to a misdemeanor, where there has been no conviction of a violent crime within 3 years, where there has been no prior revocation of probation, and where the abuser has not previously participated in a diversion program. A 1980 amendment prohibits diversion of persons charged with assault with a deadly weapon or instrument upon a spouse or cohabitant.

If the defendant is eligible for diversion, the prosecutor must inform the defendant and his attorney of the existence of the diversion program and of the procedure for entry. The defendant must consent to participate and waive his right to a speedy trial. No admission of guilt is required. California law specifies that the abuser will be unsatisfactorily terminated from the program if he is convicted of another violent crime during the diversion period or if the prosecutor, the court, or the probation department finds that he is not participating in or benefiting from the program.

Wisconsin law requires that an abuser admitted to a diversion program consent to participate, waive his right to a speedy trial, and agree that the statute of limitations will be tolled during diversion (so that prosecution may be resumed if necessary). Abusers participating in diversion in Wisconsin must file monthly reports with prosecutors certifying compliance with conditions imposed.

In California, prosecution may be suspended for 6 to 24 months. In Wisconsin, prosecution may be suspended for up to 12 months.

While there is no deferred prosecution program in Illinois, the statute does

	Alabama	Alaska	Arizona	Arkansas	California	Colorado	Connecticut	Delaware	District of Columbia	Florida	Georgia	Hawaii	Idaho	Illinois	Indiana	Iowa	Kansas
IV. POLICE INTERVENTION																	
A. Warrantless Arrest:		•	•							•	•	•	•	•			
1. Permitted if probable cause that a misdemeanor or offense was committed		•	•							•	•	•	•	•			
2. Permitted if probable cause that a protection order was violated			•											•			
3. Arrest mandatory																	
4. Arrest discretionary		•	•							•	•	•	•	•			
5. Abuse need not occur in presence of the police		•	•							•		•	•	•			
B. Warrentless Arrest Allowed Only If:														85			
1. Physical evidence of abuse is visible										•							
2. Danger that the abuser would injure the victim or property unless arrested										•		•					
3. Police have verified the existence of an effective protection order																	
C. Police Department Must/May:																	
1. Establish procedure for informing officers on call of effective protection orders		•	•		•	•								•			
2. Develop and implement domestic violence training programs for officers		•												•			
D. Police Officer Must/May:89																	
1. Use all means necessary to prevent further abuse		•												•			
2. Enforce protection order		•	•		•	•			o					•		•	
3. Arrest the abuser where appropriate					•									•			
4. Transport the victim to a hospital					•							•		•			
5. Transport the victim to a shelter					•									•			
6. Inform the victim of her legal rights		•	•		•									•			
7. Stay until the victim is no longer in danger																	
8. Supervise eviction of the abuser, or his return home for personal property					•						•			•			•
9. Other duties											93			93			
E. Police Immune from Civil Liability for Good Faith Enforcement			•											•	•		
V. DATA COLLECTION AND REPORTING																	
A. Records Must be Kept on All Domestic Violence Cases by:																	
1. Police					•		•							•	•	•	
2. Social service agencies																	
3. Shelters	•																
4. Hospitals							•										
B. Statistical or Other Reports on Domestic Violence Must Be Prepared by:																	
1. State agency responsible for domestic violence services	•	•			•		•			•	•			•	•	•	
2. Police														•			
3. Shelters	•																
C. Personal Information Included in Reports is Confidential	•																
VI. FUNDING AND/OR SHELTER SERVICES	•	•	•		•		•	•		•		•		•	•	•	•
A. State Appropriations		•	•		•		•	•				•			•	•	•
1. Total amount appropriated ($)	2.5M 6M	548T			280T 500T		275T 325T	63T		212T (295T)				564T	50T	100T 100T	60T
2. Years covered	FY 80-81 81-82				FY 78-80		FY 79-80 80-81	FY 1981		FY 79-81 81-82				FY 82	FY 80-81	FY 79-80 80-81	FY 1981
B. Marriage License Surcharge	•				•					•				•	98		•99
1. Amount of surcharge ($)	5				8					5				10³⁶	10		5.60
2. Anticipatory appropriation ($)										880T FY 79-81							
3. Funds are collected and distributed statewide					103					•					•		•
C. Use of Funds Collected or Appropriated																	
1. Funds to be used for shelter services	•	•			•		•	•		•	•			•	•	•	•
2. Shelters to provide additional services104	•				•		•			•	•				•	•	
3. Funds to be used for other services		•105			•			•		•			•106		•		•
4. Maximum number of shelters to be funded																1	
5. Maximum amount per shelter per year ($)	75T									50T					50T		
6. Maximum percentage of shelter budget that may be supplied by state funds	50%									75%	75%				•	75%	
D. Other Provisions		109															
1. AFDC or other welfare funds available to shelter residents																•	
2. Shelter records confidential										•							
E. Shelter Legislation Without Appropriation												•					

establish a similar program termed supervision. When a defendant is placed on supervision the court enters an order for supervision for a specified period of time not to exceed 2 years, and defers further proceedings in the case until the conclusion of that period. The court sets reasonable conditions, some of which may include reporting to the court or a social service agency, undergoing counseling, attending or residing in a facility established for the instruction or residence of defendants on probation, and complying with the terms and conditions of an order of protection issued to the victim by the court. The court defers entering any judgement on the charges until the conclusion of the supervision. If the defendant successfully complies with all the conditions of supervision, the court will discharge the defendant and enter a judgement dismissing the charges. Discharge and dismissal upon successful conclusion of a disposition of supervision shall be deemed without an adjudication of guilt and shall not be termed a conviction for purposes of disqualification or disabilities imposed by laws upon conviction of a crime.

73. In Michigan, a person convicted of simple or aggravated assault against a spouse, former spouse, or present or former household member may be placed on probation prior to entry of a judgement of guilt and ordered to participate in counseling. If conditions of probation are fulfilled, proceedings are dismissed.

Column headers (states, left to right):

Kentucky · Louisiana · Maine · Maryland · Massachusetts · Michigan · Minnesota · Mississippi · Missouri · Montana · Nebraska · Nevada · New Hampshire · New Jersey · New Mexico · New York · North Carolina · North Dakota · Ohio · Oklahoma · Oregon · Pennsylvania · Rhode Island · South Carolina · South Dakota · Tennessee · Texas · Utah · Vermont · Virginia · Washington · West Virginia · Wisconsin · Wyoming

(Large matrix of entry markers by state, including footnote reference numbers 79–113 and appropriation/fiscal-year data; representative legible numeric rows below.)

	Maine	Maryland	Mass.	Michigan	Minnesota	...	New Jersey	New Mexico	New York	...	Ohio	Oklahoma	Oregon	Penn.	R.I.	S.C.	...	Texas	Utah	Vermont	...	Wash.	...	Wisc.	Wyo.
RT 261T	100T	176T	500T	2M	2.9M		280T		935T 100T	300T		265T 155T	2M	30T	50T		100T	79T	30T		1M		1M	576T
T 496T	150T			1.5M	3.7M		280T			300T		265T	1.5M	30T				166T 223T						
FY	FY	FY	FY	FY	FY		1980		FY	FY FY		FY	FY	FY	FY FY		1980	1979 FY			FY		FY FY	
79-80 79-80	80-81	1980	79-80	81-83			1981	81-83 81-82 79-80			1981	81-82 80-81					+	1980 81-82		79-81			80-81 81-82
31 80-81 80-81			80-81 81-83					80-81			1982	81-82 81-82			1981	1981							
15	15		14		5	13	5		19	10	20	8					102						15

74. In Illinois, after successful conclusion of a disposition of supervision the court enters a judgement dismissing the charges. Two years after discharge and dismissal a person may have his arrest record expunged.

75. Michigan law provides that when an abuser's arrest record is expunged, a nonpublic record is kept which is "furnished to a court or police agency for the purpose of showing that a defendant in a criminal action...has already once [participated in a diversion program]."

76. New Hampshire law requires that presentence investigation reports be prepared for all felony offenses, and upon the prosecutor's recommendation, for violent misdemeanor offenses, if there is reason to believe a similar offense was committed in the preceeding year. The period of probation is 3 years for a felony conviction and 1 year for a misdemeanor conviction.

77. New York law requires probation officials, law enforcement officials, and prosecutors to inform victims of abuse of their legal rights and states that "no official ...shall discourage or prevent any person who wishes to file a petition or sign a complaint from having access to any court for that purpose."

78. Of the statutes that impose duties on courts or prosecutors regarding prosecution of family violence cases, the Washington law is the most comprehensive. Under

Washington law. the police must send reports of domestic disturbance calls to the prosecutor if there is probable cause that an offense has been committed. Records must be coded to facilitate the identification of domestic violence cases. Prosecutors must notify victims of the decision to prosecute or not prosecute within 5 days after a report is received and must advise victims of private complaint procedures.

Courts may not dismiss criminal charges against abusers because of pending civil proceedings, they must not require that the victim have filed for divorce, and they may not require disclosure of the address of the victim. In addition, domestic violence actions must be identified on docket sheets.

IV. Police Intervention

79. Under Minnesota law, warrantless arrest had been allowed at a suspect's home or when the suspect was threatening to return if the officer has probable cause to believe that a misdemeanor assault occurred within the preceding 4 hours and there is evidence of physical abuse. An amendment was passed which removed the requirement for warrantless arrest that the suspect be present at the residence of the victim or threatening to return there.

80. Under Ohio law, if an officer has probable cause to believe abuse has occurred he or she may arrest a suspected abuser without a warrant if the victim or the parent of a minor victim signs a statement alleging that abuse occurred. This requirement is substituted for the common law rule that a police officer cannot make a warrantless arrest for a misdemeanor unless he or she sees the offense committed.

81. Under Michigan law, violation of an order issued during divorce or separate maintenance proceedings or violation of a peace bond justifies warrantless arrest.

82. North Carolina law requires police to make a warrantless arrest only if they have probable cause to believe an abuser has violated an eviction order.

83. Under Maine law, warrantless arrest is mandatory where the officer has probable cause to believe that an aggravated assault occurred. Warrantless arrest is mandatory for those violations of protection orders that constitute misdemeanors. Arrest without a warrant is not permitted for violation of those provisions of a protection order that are punishable only as contempt of court.

84. Oregon law mandates arrest of a suspected abuser where the officer has probable cause to believe that abuse has occurred or been threatened and where the victim does not object to the making of an arrest. Arrest is also mandatory where there is probable cause that a protection order has been violated; in such cases the duty to arrest is not conditioned on the consent of the victim. A pending amendment would delete the provision conditioning the duty to arrest on the non-objection of the victim.

85. In Hawaii, a police officer who has reasonable grounds to believe that recent physical harm to a spouse has occurred must order the abuser to leave the residence for a 3-hour cooling-off period. If the abuser refuses, the officer may make a warrantless arrest on a misdemeanor charge.

86. In Minnesota, warrantless arrest is allowed within 4 hours after an abusive incident. In New Hampshire, warrantless arrest is allowed within 6 hours of abuse. In Rhode Island, warrantless arrest is allowed within 24 hours of abuse.

87. An amendment to the Ohio law requires that each law enforcement agency keep an index of all protection orders sent to the agency, and keep records of the date and time that each order is delivered to a batterer.

88. In Nevada and Virginia, the state legislatures passed resolutions encouraging police departments to institute training programs on intervention in family violence cases.

89. Some statutes require that police provide certain services when responding to domestic calls. Others with less imperative language list services that police may provide to victims. Statutes that require rather than recommend certain types of assistance are easier to get enforced, because inaction by police then becomes a violation of law rather than a permissible exercise of discretion.

90. Utah law does not require that police transport victims to shelters or hospitals; rather, it requires police to make arrangements for the victims to obtain shelter and medical care. The law also provides that police may ask victims to sign written statements describing the alleged abuse.

91. Massachusetts laws require that the police give victims of abuse a written statement of their legal rights.

92. Under the laws of Maine and Missouri, police are required to respond to mate abuse as they would to any stranger crime. Missouri law, in addition, allows police to establish domestic crisis teams, consisting of police officers and domestic crisis workers, to intervene in domestic disputes.

93. Under the laws of Maryland, North Carolina, and Illinois, police must accompany a victim to her residence to pick up her children and personal property. In Georgia, and under pending legislation in New Jersey, the court may as part of a protection order direct that the police provide such assistance.

94. Under North Carolina law, law enforcement officers need not respond to multiple complaints from the same victim within 48 hours if they have "reasonable cause to believe that immediate assistance is not needed."

V. Data Collection and Reporting

95. Separate records on all domestic violence cases must be kept by the co New Hampshire and Washington. A New Jersey bill would require courts to records on domestic abuse and to report annually on the data collected to officials. The Mississippi law also makes professionals who report abuse or p pate in judicial proceedings immune from liability for good faith report testimony. Such action is declared not to constitute breach of confidentiali

96. Kentucky law provides that all persons who suspect abuse of an adu report such cases to a state agency, which is then required to investigate rep similar law in Wyoming applies only in cases of abuse or neglect of disabled

97. Under Minnesota law, persons reporting domestic violence cases are im from civil liability.

VI. Funding and/or Shelter Services

98. Indiana law imposes a surcharge on filing of an action for dissolution c riage rather than on the marriage license. Minnesota law imposes a $15. charge on both the filing of an action for dissolution of a marriage a filing for a marriage license. Illinois law imposes a $10.00 surcharge for a mc license and a $5.00 fee when filing for dissolution.

99. The marriage license surcharge passed by the Kansas legislature is to b to create a "Family and Children Trust Fund." A portion of the money deposit the fund is to be used for grants to shelters.

100. The marriage license surcharge in Michigan is used for a family coun service which is an arm of the circuit court. The law specifies that this pa "shall include counseling for domestic violence and child abuse."

101. Pending legislation in PA would impose an $8.00 surcharge on the m license. Separate legislation is pending which would impose a $10.00 persons convicted of crimes. The money from both bills would be used to f Office on Crime Victims, which would coordinate the services of and secure for family violence programs and other programs. Information charted under the section entitled "Use of funds collected or appropriated" refers no pending legislation but to legislation appropriations for family violence pro

102. Wisconsin law provides that where a fine is imposed as part of a pena crime involving domestic abuse, that a domestic abuse assessment, in the of 10% of the fine imposed, shall also be imposed. The money received is u funding programs providing services to battered women.

103. The marriage license surcharge laws in California, Michigan, Ohi Nevada provide that funds are to be collected and distributed by each coun groups of counties that elect to pool their funds.

104. Some legislation requires that state-funded shelters provide services to of abuse other than food and a place to sleep. Other required services may referral to or provision of psychological or employment counseling, medical services, public benefits counseling, child care, or abuser counseling. Son ters are required to maintain a 24-hour hotline or to develop material or training to educate the public about domestic violence. The states indicate chart impose various combinations of these duties on shelters that recei funds.

105. The 1980-81 apropriation figure includes a line item for a counseling p for male batterers. The 6M figure for 1981-82 is earmarked for capital improv and building of shelters.

106. The $212,000 appropriation listed for Hawaii is for programs providing to battered women and to abused children.

107. Minnesota law requires that a minimum of four shelters be funded usi funds appropriated.

108. Under authorization legislation which took effect in Michigan in Octob $55,000 is the maximum grant that may be made to any locality in 1 year. are made to two shelters in one town, the total may not exceed $55,000.

109. The laws of Alaska and Wisconsin exempt shelters from the requirem they obtain multiple dwelling licenses.

110. The laws of Minnesota and Washington include provisions that limit liability of shelters. Minnesota shelters, to qualify for state funds, must sho involvement with courts and law enforcement agencies.

111. New Jersey law requires shelters to provide bilingual services and p shelters from releasing minor children to a nonresident parent without order.

112. Ohio prohibits shelters from discriminating on the basis of race, religi or marital status.

113. The laws of Oregon and Washington provide that the addresses of shel to be kept secret.

Citations of State Domestic Violence Laws

Following is a list of citations of state statutes pertaining to domestic violence. Statutes that cannot be found in a law library may be obtained from the legislative counsel's office at the state capitol.

Citations for the statutes are listed alphabetically by state in the left-hand column. In the right-hand column entitled "Type of Provision," the statutes are categorized as follows:

Protection order is listed beside a statute that provides for civil injunctive relief for victims of abuse. Only statutes that make protection orders available independent of any other proceeding are listed.

Order pending divorce is listed beside a statute that provides for temporary injunctive relief during a divorce, separation, or custody proceeding.

Criminal law is listed beside a statute that creates a new substantive criminal offense for physical abuse of a family or household member or that provides new procedures for disposition of criminal charges in domestic violence cases, such as conditions on pretrial release, deferred prosecution, or conditions on probation. General criminal statutes that may be the basis of charges against abusive mates are not listed.

Police intervention is listed beside a statute that provides for warrantless arrest based on probable cause in domestic violence cases or that imposes duties on law enforcement officials handling disturbance calls.

Data collection and reporting is listed beside a statute that requires agencies that offer services to violent families to keep records on cases handled or to write statistical or other reports on family violence.

Funding and shelter services are listed beside a statute that appropriates funds for services to violent families or that establishes standards for operation of shelters for battered women.

In addition, citations are listed for some unusual statutes that are not included on the chart. The subject areas of these laws are listed in parentheses. The above categories also refer to sections of the Chart of State Legislation on Domestic Violence. More detailed information about each statute may be obtained by referring to the chart.

Citation	*Type of Provision*
Act No. 81-476, 1981 Ala. Acts, p. ___ , 1981	protection order
Act No. 81-813, 1981 Ala. Acts, p. ___ , 1981	funding, data collection, and reporting
ALASKA STAT. §§09.55.600 to 09.55.640, 12.55.135, 22.15.100(19)(enacted 1980)	protection order, police intervention
ALASKA STAT.§§09.55.200, 09.55.205(19)	injunctions pending domestic relations proceedings
ALASKA STAT. §§18.65.510, 18.65.520 (19)(enacted 1980)	police intervention

ALASKA STAT.§§18.69.010 to 18.69.080 (19)	funding and shelter services
Act No. 101, 1981 Alaska Sess. Laws, p. ___, 1981	funding and shelter services
ARIZ. REV. STAT. §§13.3601, 13.3602 (Supp. 1980) *as amended by* Chapter 244, 1981 Ariz. Legis. Serv., p. 796 (West 1981)	protection order, criminal law, police intervention
ARIZ. REV. STAT. §25-315(1956 and Supp. 1980) *as amended by* Chapter 244, 1981 Ariz. Legis. Serv., p. 796 (West 1981)	injunctions pending domestic relations proceedings
ARIZ. REV. STAT. §25-324(1956)	injunctions pending domestic relations proceedings
ARK. STAT. ANN. §§41.1653 to 41.1659 (enacted 1979)	criminal law
CAL.CIV. CODE §§4539, 5120(West 1970 & Supp. 1980)	protection order
CAL. CIV. PROC. CODE §527 (West 1970)	protection order
CAL. CIV. PROC. CODE §§540-543 & 545-553 (West Supp. 1981)	protection order
CAL. CIV. CODE §§4458, 4516, 7020, 4359, 4370, 4516 (West 1979 & Supp. 1981)	injunctions pending domestic relations proceedings
CAL. PENAL CODE §§273.5, 273.6, 1000.6 to 1000.11 (West Supp. 1980)	criminal law
CAL. GOV'T. CODE §§26840.6, 26840.7 (West 19)	funding and shelter services
CAL. WELF. & INST. CODE §§18290 to 18304 (West Supp. 1973-1979)	funding and shelter services
CAL. WELF. INST. CODE §§18230.5, 18980 to 18995 (West 19)	funding and shelter services
COLO. REV. STAT. §§13-6-104, 13-6-105 (1973 & Supp. 1979)	protection order
COLO. REV. STAT.§§14-10-108, 14-10-109 (1973)	injunctions pending domestic relations proceedings
COLO. REV. STAT.§16-3-401 (1973)	(peace bond)
CONN. GEN. STAT. ANN. §46b-38 (West Supp. 1980), *as repealed by Act of June 8, 1981,* Pub. Act No. 81-272, p. 721	protection order
Pub. Act No. 79-321, 1979 Conn. Legis. Serv., p. 346 (1979)	data collection and reporting

CONN. GEN. STAT. ANN. §§77-87, 78-36, 78-44 (West 19)	funding and shelter services
CONN. GEN. STAT. ANN., Pub. Act No. 79-506, p. 168, (West 1980 Appendix Pamph.)	funding and shelter services
DEL. CODE tit. 10§§902.92-(6), 925(15), 950(5)(1974 & Supp. 1978): Family Court Rules 140	protection order
DEL. CODE tit. 13§1509, 1510(Supp. 1980)	injunctions pending domestic relations proceedings
DEL. CODE tit. 13§1510(Supp. 1980)	police intervention— pending divorce
D.C. CODE §§16-1001 to 16-1006(1973)	protection order, criminal law
D.C. CODE §16-911(1973)	injunctions pending domestic relations proceedings— support, custody, attorney's fees, property
FLA. STAT. ANN. §741.30(West Supp. 1980)	protection order
FLA. STAT. ANN. §§409.607, 901.15(6)(West Supp. 1980)	police intervention
FLA. STAT. ANN. §§61.071 & 61.13(West 1969 & Supp. 1981)	injunctions pending domestic relations proceedings— support, custody
FLA. STAT. ANN. §409.606(West Supp. 1980)	data collection and reporting
FLA. STAT. ANN. §§409.602 to 409.605, 741.01(West Supp. 1980)	funding and shelter services
GA. H.B. 203(enacted 1981)	protection order
GA. S.B. 79(enacted 1981)	protection order, police intervention
GA. CODE ANN. §30-206(1980)	injunctions pending domestic relations proceedings— support, custody
GA. H.B. 203(enacted 1981)	funding and shelter services
HAW. REV. STAT. §§585-1 to 585-4(Supp. 1980)	protection order

HAW. REV. STAT. §§580-9 to 580-12(1976)	injunctions pending domestic relations proceedings
HAW. REV. STAT. §709-906(1976)*as amended by* Act 266, 1980 Haw. Sess. Laws, p. ___ , 1980 and *as amended by* Act 106, 1980 Haw. Sess. Laws, p. ___ , 1980	criminal law
HAW. REV. STAT. §709.906(1976) *as amended by* Act 266, 1980 Haw. Sess. Laws, p. ___ , 1980	police intervention
IDAHO CODE §32-704(1946 & Supp. 1979)	injunctions pending domestic relations proceedings— support, custody, attorney's fees
IDAHO CODE §19-603(1947 & Supp. 1979)	police intervention
ILL. H.B. 366 (enacted 1981)	protection order
ILL. ANN. STAT. ch. 40§§501, 602, 607 (Smith-Hurd 19)	injunctions pending domestic relations proceedings
ILL. ANN. STAT. ch. 85§507-a(Smith-Hurd 1979) *as amended by* H.B. 366(enacted 1981)	police intervention
ILL. ANN. STAT. ch. 38§206-5.1(Smith-Hurd Supp. 1980) *as amended by* H.B. 366	data collection
ILL. ANN. STAT. ch. 38§109-1(Smith-Hurd 19) *as amended by* H.B. 366	criminal law
ILL. ANN. STAT. ch. 38§1005-6-3(Smith-Hurd 19) *as amended by* H.B. 366	criminal law
ILL. H.B. 1619(enacted 1981)	funding and shelter services
IND. CODE ANN. §31-1-11.5-7(Burns Supp. 1979)	injunctions pending domestic relations proceedings
IND. CODE ANN. §§4-23-17.5 to 4-23-17.5-9 (Burns Supp. 1980)	funding and shelter services
IOWA CODE ANN. §236-1 to 236-8(West Supp. 1980)	protection order
IOWA CODE ANN. §236-11(West Supp. 1980)	police intervention

IOWA CODE ANN. §§236-9 & 236-10(West Supp. 1980)	data collection and reporting
IOWA CODE ANN. §598.11(West 1949 & Supp. 1980)	injunctions pending domestic relations proceedings— support, custody, attorney's fees
KAN. CIV. PRO. STAT. ANN. §§60-3101 to 60-3111(Vernon Supp. 1980)	protection order
KAN. CIV. PRO. STAT. ANN. §1607(Vernon 1967 & Supp. 1979)	injunctions pending domestic relations proceedings
KAN. STAT. ANN. §§23-108 to 23-110 & 23-112(Vernon 1974)	funding and shelter services
KY. REV. STAT. §403.710(Supp. 1980)	protection order
KY. REV. STAT. §§209.010, 209.020, 209.040 to 209.130(Supp. 1980)	protection order
KY. REV. STAT. §431.005(Supp. 1980)	police intervention
KY. REV. STAT. §403.160(Supp. 1980)	injunctions pending domestic relations proceedings— support, custody
KY. REV. STAT. §§209.010 to 209.030, 209.050, 209.130, 209.140(Supp. 1980)	data collection and reporting
Act 592, 1981 La. Sess. Law Serv. (West p. ___, 1981)	injunctions pending domestic relations proceedings
LA. REV. STAT. ANN. §§46:2121 to 46:2125 (West supp. 1980)	funding and shelter services
LA. SENATE RESOLUTION 21 (1977)	data collection and reporting
LA. REV. STAT. ANN. §46:2125(West Supp. 1980)	data collection and reporting
ME. REV. STAT. ANN. tit. 19§§761-770(1964 *as amended by* Chap. 420, Me. Legis. Serv., p. 836, 1981	protection order
ME. REV. STAT. ANN. tit. 19§§769, 770 (1964) *as amended by* Chap. 420, Me. Legis. Serv., p. 836, 1981	police intervention
ME. REV. STAT. ANN. tit. 17-A§15(1)(A) (5-a)(Supp. 1980)	police intervention

ME. REV. STAT. ANN. tit. 15§301(Supp. 1980-1981) *as amended by* Chap. 420, Me. Legis. Serv., p. 836, 1981	police intervention
ME. REV. STAT. ANN. tit. 15§301(Supp. 1980-1981) *as amended by* Chap. 420, Me. Legis. Serv., p. 836, 1981	criminal law
ME. REV. STAT. ANN. tit. 19§770(1964) *as amended by* Chap. 420 Me. Legis. Serv., p. 836, 1981	data collection and reporting
ME. REV. STAT. ANN. tit. 25§1544(1964 & Supp. 1980-1981)	data collection and reporting
ME. REV. STAT. ANN. tit. 22§8501(1964)	funding and shelter services
ME. REV. STAT. ANN. tit. 19§214(1964)	injunctions pending domestic relations proceedings
ME. REV. STAT. ANN. tit. 19§§693, 694, 722B(1964)	injunctions pending domestic relations proceedings
MD. CTS. & JUD. PROC. CODE ANN §§4-404, 4-501 to 4-506(Supp. 1980) *as amended by*	protection order
MD. ANN. CODE art. 88A §101 to 105(1979 Replacement Vol. & Supp. 1980)	funding and shelter services
MD. ANN. CODE art. 27 §11F(1980 Cum. Supp.)	criminal law, police intervention
MD. CTS. & JUD. PROC. CODE ANN. §§3-603 & 3-6A-06(1980 Replacement Vol. & Supp. 1980)	injunctions pending domestic relations proceedings
MD. HOUSE JOINT RESOLUTION NO. 32(1977)	data collection
MASS. GEN. LAWS ANN. ch. 209A§§1 to 7, ch. 208§34C(West Supp. 1980)	protection order
MASS. GEN. LAWS ANN. ch. 208§§17 to 20 & 34B, 34C(West 1954 & Supp. 1980)	injunctions pending domestic relations proceedings
MASS. GEN. LAWS ANN. ch. 276§§28, 42A (West 1972 & Supp. 1980)	criminal law, police intervention
MASS. GEN. LAWS ANN. ch 266§120(West Supp. 1970-1980)	criminal law
MASS. GEN. LAWS ANN. ch. 18§2(A)(14) (West Supp. 1974-1980)	funding and shelter services
MICH. COMP. LAWS ANN. §§552.15(West	injunctions pending

1967 & Supp. 1980)	domestic relations proceedings
MICH. COMP. LAWS ANN. §§764.15a, 769.4a, 772.13, 772.14a(West Supp. 1979)	criminal law, police intervention
MICH. COMP. LAWS ANN. §§28.251 to 28.257(West 1967 & Supp. 1980)	data collection and reporting
MICH. COMP. LAWS ANN. §§400.1501 to 400.1511(West 1980)	funding and shelter services
MICH. COMP. LAWS ANN. §§551.103, 551.331 to 551.344(West Supp. 1980)	funding and shelter services
MINN. STAT. ANN. §518B.01(Supp. 1980)	protection order
MINN. STAT. ANN. §§609.135(5), 629.72 (Supp. 1980)	criminal law
MINN. STAT. ANN. §629.341(Supp. 1980)	police intervention
MINN. STAT. ANN. §§241.62(5), 241.66 (Supp. 1980)	data collection and reporting
MINN. STAT. ANN. §§241.61 to 241.65, 256D.05(3)(Supp. 1980)	funding and shelter services
Chap. 360, 1981 Minn. Sess. Law Serv. (West, p. ___ , 1963, 1981)	funding and shelter services
Chap. 429, 1981 Miss. Laws. Advance Sheet No. 5, p. 31-36, 1981	protection order, data collection and reporting
MO. ANN. STAT. §§455.010 to 455.085 (Vernon Supp. 1980)	protection order, police intervention
MO. ANN. STAT. §452.315(1977)	injunctions pending domestic relations proceedings
MONT. CODE ANN. §§27-19-201 to 27-19-204, 27-19-301 to 27-19-307, 27-19-401 to 27-19-406(1979)	protection order
MONT. CODE ANN. §40-4-106(1979)	injunctions pending domestic relations proceedings
MONT. CODE ANN. §40-2-402(1979)	data collection and reporting
MONT. CODE ANN. §§40-2-402, 40-2-404, 40-2-405, 40-1-202(1979)	funding and shelter services
NEB. REV. STAT. §§42-901 to 42-903, 42-924 to 42-926 (1978)	protection order
NEB. REV. STAT. §42-927(1978)	police intervention
NEB. REV. STAT. §§42-904 to 42-923(1978)	funding and shelter services, data

	collection and reporting
NEB. REV. STAT. §§29-2219, 29-2262(1978)	criminal law
NEB. REV. STAT. §42.357(1978)	injunctions pending domestic relations proceedings
NEV. REV. STAT. §33.020(1979)	protection order
NEV. REV. STAT. §171.124(1979)	police intervention
NEV. REV. STAT. §§125-040 to 125-060, 125-200, 125-220, 125-230(1979)	injunctions pending domestic relations proceedings— support, custody, property
NEV. S.B. 371(enacted 1981)	funding and shelter services
N.H. REV. STAT. §§173-B:1 to 173-B:11 (Supp. 1979) *as amended by* Chap. 522, 522, 1981 N.W. Laws, p. ___ , 1981	protection order
N.H. REV. STAT. ANN. §458:16(Supp. 1979)	injunctions pending domestic relations proceedings
N.H. REV. STAT. ANN. §§597:7-a, 651:2VI, 651:4,I(Supp. 1979)	criminal law
N.H. REV. STAT. ANN. §635.2(Supp. 1979)	criminal law
N.H. REV. STAT. ANN. §594:10-1(Supp. 1979)	police intervention
N.H. REV. STAT. ANN. §106-B:14(Supp. 1979) *as amended by* Chap. 223, 1981 N.H. Laws, p. ___ , 1981	data collection and reporting
Chap. 223, 1981 N.H. Laws, p. ___ , 1981	funding and shelter services
N.J. STAT. ANN.§§30:14-1 to 30:14-14(West 1981)	funding and shelter services
N.J. STAT. ANN. §§40:55D-66.1, 40:55D-66.2(West Supp. 1980)	(shelter zoning law)
N.J. STAT. ANN. §§2A:34-23(West 1952 & Supp. 1980)	injunctions pending domestic relations proceedings— support, custody
Assembly Bill No. 1330(enacted 1981)	criminal law
N.M. STAT. ANN. §40-4-7(1978)	injunctions pending domestic relations

	proceedings—support, custody, attorney's fees
N.M. STAT. ANN. §31-1-7(Supp. 1978)	police intervention
Chap. 208, 1981 N.M. Laws, p. ___ ,1981	funding and shelter services
N.Y. FAM. CT. ACT §§155, 811, 813, 8917, 821, 822, 823, 824, 826, 827, 282, 834, 838, 843, 844, 845, 847(McKinney 1975 & Supp. 1976-1980)	protection order
N.Y. FAM. CT. ACT §168(McKinney 1975 & Supp. 1976-1980) *as amended by* Chap. 416 1981 N.Y. Laws, p. ___ , 1981.	protection order
N.Y. FAM. CT. ACT §812(McKinney 1975 & Supp. 1976-1980) *as amended by* Chap. 416 1981 N.Y. Laws, p. ___ , 1981	protection order
N.Y. FAM. CT. ACT §841(McKinney 1975 & Supp. 1976-1980) *as amended by* Chap. 416 1981 N.Y. Laws, p. ___ , 1981	protection order
N.Y. FAM. CT. ACT §§842, 846(McKinney 1975 & Supp. 1976-1980) *as amended by* Chap. 416, 1981 N.Y. laws, p. ___, 1981 and *as amended by* Chap. 965, 1981 N.Y. Laws, p. ___ , 1981	protection order
N.Y. FAM. CT. ACT §262(a)(ii)(McKinney 1975 & Supp. 1976-1980) *as amended by* Chap. 693, 1981 N.Y. Laws, p. ___ , 1981	protection order
N.Y. FAM. CT. ACT §§216, 818(McKinney 1975) *as amended by* Chap. 416, 1981 N.Y. Laws, p. ___ , 1981	protection order
N.Y. FAM. CT. ACT §655(McKinney Supp. 1976-1980)	injunctions pending domestic relations proceedings
N.Y. DOM. REL. LAWS §240(2)(McKinney Supp. 1980-1981)	injunctions pending domestic relations proceedings
N.Y. FAM. CT. ACT §§446, 551, 656 (McKinney1975) *as amended by* Chap. 416 and Chap. 965, 1981 N.Y. Laws, p. ___, 1981	injunctions pending domestic relations proceedings
N.Y. FAM. CT. ACT §759(McKinney 1975 & Supp. 1976-1980) *as amended by* Chap. 965 1981 N.Y. Laws, p. ___ , 1981	injunctions pending domestic relations proceedings
N.Y. FAM. CT. ACT §1056(McKinney 1975)	injunctions pending

as amended by Chap. 965, 1981 N.Y. Laws, p. ___ , 1981	domestic relations proceedings
N.Y. FAM. CT. ACT §§430,550,740, 1029 (McKinney 1975) *as amended by* Chap. 416, N.Y. Laws, p. ___ , 1981	injunctions pending domestic relations proceedings
N.Y. FAM. CT. ACT §655(McKinney Supp. 1976-1980) *as amended by* Chap. 416, N.Y. Laws, p. ___ , 1981	injunctions pending domestic relations proceedings
N.Y. FAM. CT. ACT §168(McKinney 1975 and Supp. 1976-1980) *as amended by* Chap. 416, 1981 N.Y. Laws, p. ___ ,1981	criminal law, police intervention
N.Y. FAM. CT. ACT §155(McKinney 1975 and Supp. 1976-1980)	criminal law, police intervention
N.Y. JUD. LAW. §§216 & 751(1)(McKinney Supp. 1980-1981)	criminal law, police intervention
N.Y. CRIM. PRO. LAW §100.07(McKinney Supp. 1980-1981)	criminal law, police intervention
N.Y. CRIM. PRO. LAW §170.55(McKinney Supp. 1972 to 1980)	criminal law, police intervention
N.Y. CRIM. PRO. LAW §§530.11, 530.12 (McKinney Supp. 1980-1981) *as amended by* Chap. 416, 1981 N.Y. Laws, p. ___ , 1981	criminal law, police intervention
N.Y. EXEC. ORDER NO. (Hugh L. Carey, Gov., May 17, 1979) 9 NYCRR §3.90	data collection and reporting
N.Y. SOC. SERV. LAW §2-31(a)-(b) (McKinney Supp. 1980-1981)	funding and shelter services
N.C. GEN. STAT. §§50B-1 to 50B-7(Supp. No. 5, 1979)	protection order, police intervention
N.C. GEN. STAT. §§50-13.5 & 50-16.6(1976 and Supp. 1979)	injunctions pending domestic relations proceedings
N.C. GEN. STAT. §§14-134.3, 15.A-401, 15A-534.1(1978, Supp. 1979)	criminal law
N.D. CENT. CODE §§14-07.1-01 to 14-07.1-08, 29-01-15(4)(Supp. 1979) *as amended by* N.D.S.B. 2339(enacted 1981)	protection order, police intervention
N.D. CENT. CODE §14-05-23(1971)	injunctions pending doemstic relations proceedings— support, custody, attorney's fees
N.D. CENT. CODE §§14-03-21, 14-03-22 (1971) *as amended by* N.D.H.B. 1313	funding and shelter services

OHIO REV. CODE ANN. §§1901.18, 1901.19, 1909.02, (Page Supp. 1980)	protection order
OHIO REV. CODE ANN. §2919.26(Page Supp. 1980) *as amended by* OHIO H.B. 920	protection order
OHIO REV. CODE ANN. §3113.31(Page 1980) *as amended by* OHIO H.B. 920)	protection order
OHIO REV. CODE ANN. §§2919.25, 2919.26, 2933.16(Page Supp. 1980) *as amended by* OHIO H.B. 920	criminal law
OHIO REV. CODE ANN. §§109.73, 109.77, 2935.03, 737.11(Page Supp. 1980)	police intervention
OHIO REV. CODE ANN. §3113.32(Page 1980)	data collection and reporting
OHIO REV. CODE ANN. §§3113.39(Page 1980) *as amended by* OHIO S.B. 382	data collection and reporting
OHIO REV. CODE ANN. §§3113.33 to 3113.39(Page 1980) *as amended by* OHIO H.B. 920	funding and shelter services
OKLA. STA. ANN. tit. 2§1276(West Supp. 1980)	injunctions pending domestic relations proceedings— support, custody, attorney's fees, property
Chap. 328, 1980 Okla. Sess. Laws, p. 945, 1981	funding and shelter services
Chap. 291, 1980 Okla. Sess. Laws, p. 714, 1980	(mental health facilities to provide services for victims of domestic violence
OR. REV. STAT. §§107.7, 133.055, 133.310 (1977)	protection order, criminal law, police intervention, data collection and reporting
OR. REV. STAT. §184.885, 184.890(1977)	funding and shelter services
OR. H.B. 2308(enacted 1981)	funding and shelter services
35 PA. CONS. STAT. ANN. §§ 10182 to 10190 (Purdon 1977 & Supp. 1979)	protection order

42 PA. CONS. STAT. ANN. R.C.P. RULES
    1901 to 1905(1981)   protection order
Act 187, 1980 Pa. Legis. Serv., p. 1031, 1980   criminal law
23 PA. STAT. ANN. §§403 and 502(Purdon   injunctions pending
    Supp.1980)   domestic relations
                                                proceedings
PA. H.B. 1414(enacted 1981)   funding and shelter
                                                services

R.I. GEN. LAWS §15-5-19(1969 & Supp. 1980) injunctions pending
                                                domestic relations
                                                proceedings

R.I. GEN. LAWS §11-5-9(Supp. 1980)   criminal law,
                                                police intervention

S.C. CODE §20-3-119(1976)   injunctions pending
                                                domestic relations
                                                proceedings

S.D. CODIFIED LAWS ANN. §§25-4-34,   injunctions pending
    25-4-38, 25-4-40(1976 & Supp. 1980)   domestic relations
                                                proceedings—
                                                support, custody

TENN. CODE ANN. §§36-1201 to 36-1215   protection order,
    (Supp. 1979)   police intervention
TENN. CODE ANN. §39-602(Cum. Supp.   criminal law
    1980)
TENN. CODE ANN. §39-601(Supp. 1980)   criminal law

TEX. FAM. CODE ANN. tit. 4§§71.01 to   protection order,
    71.19(Vernon Supp. 1980-1981)   police intervention,
                                                data collection and
                                                reporting
TEX. CODE CRIM. PROC. ANN. art. 14.03   police intervention
    (Vernon 1977) *as amended by* Chap. 422,
    1981 Tex. Sess. Law Serv., p. 1865, 1981
TEX. CODE CRIM. PROC. ANN. art. 6.01 to   criminal law,
    6.07(Vernon 1977 & Supp. 1980-1981)   police intervention
TEX. FAM. CODE ANN. tit. 1§7.4(Vernon   funding and shelter
    19   )   services
TEX. H.B. 1334(enacted 1981)   funding and shelter
                                                services
TEX. FAM. CODE ANN. tit. 1§§3.58, 3.59   injunctions pending
    (Vernon 1977 & Supp. 1979)   domestic relations
                                                proceedings—
                                                support

TEX. PENAL CODE ANN. tit. 5§§22.01(a), 22.02(a)(Vernon Supp. 1980-1981)	criminal law
UTAH CODE ANN. §§30-6-1 to 30-6-8(Supp. 1979)	protection order, police intervention
UTAH CODE ANN. §76-5-108(Supp. 1979)	criminal law
UTAH CODE ANN. §30.3-3(Second Replacement Vol. 3, 1953)	injunctions pending domestic relations proceedings— support, attorney's fees
UTAH CODE ANN. §30-6-9(Supp. 1979)	funding and shelter services
VT.STAT. ANN. tit. 15§§1101 to 1107(19)	protection order
VT. RULES OF CIV. PRO., RULE 80, (1971 & Supp. 1975)	injunctions pending domestic relations proceedings (custodial interference)
VT. STAT. ANN. tit. 13§2451(Supp. 1980)	
VA. CODE §20-103(1980 Replacement Vol.)	injunctions pending domestic relations proceedings
VA. CODE §16.1-279(L)(Cum. Supp. 1981)	(court may mandate counseling for a payment of shelter fees by abuser)
VA. HOUSE JOINT RESOLUTION 27 (19)	police intervention
VA. HOUSE JOINT RESOLUTION 31 (19)	funding and shelter services
VA. CODE §§63.1-319(1980 Replacement Vol.)	funding and shelter services
WASH. REV. CODE ANN. §26.09.060(Supp. 1981)	injunctions pending domestic relations proceedings
WASH. REV. CODE ANN. §§10.99.010 to 10.99.070(1980)	criminal law, police intervention data collection and reporting
WASH. REV. CODE §§70.123.010 to 70.123.900(Supp. 1981)	funding and shelter services
W. VA. CODE §§48.2A-1 to 48-2A-8(1980 Replacement Vol.)	protection order

W. VA. CODE §§48-2A-9, 48-2A-10(Supp.   protection order
1981)

W.VA. CODE §48-2-13(1980 Replacement   injunctions pending
Vol.)   domestic relations
                                                                proceedings

W. VA. CODE §§48-2C-1 to 48-2C-9, 48-1-24   data collection and
(Supp. 1981)   reporting, funding
                                                                and shelter
                                                                services

WIS. STAT. ANN. §§767.23(1), 767.23(m),   protection order
813.025(2)(a), 940.33(West Supp.
1980-1981)

WIS. STAT. ANN. §247.23(West 1957 & Supp.   injunctions pending
1979-1980)   domestic relations
                                                                proceedings

WIS. STAT. ANN. §§940.19, 971.37(West   criminal law
Supp. 1980-1981)

WIS. STAT. ANN. §165.85(4)(b)(West 1974)   police intervention

WIS. STAT. ANN. §§15.197(16), 20.435(8)(c),   funding and shelter
46.95, 50.01(1), 973, 05, 973.055(West Supp.   services
1980-1981)

WYO. STAT. ANN. §§20-2-106(c), 20-2-110   injunctions pending
(1977 Republished Ed.)   domestic relations
                                                                proceedings

Act 96, 1981 Wyo. Sess, Laws, p. ___ , 1981   data collection and
                                                                reporting, funding
                                                                and shelter services

Act 96, 1981 Wyo. Sess. Laws, p. ___ , 1981   criminal law

State Agencies Responsible for Services to Violent Families

State	Name	Purpose or Duties
Alabama	Office of Prosecution Services	Administers grants to shelters. Sets standards for shelters.
Alaska	Council on Domestic and Sexual Assault, Department of Health and Social Services	Administers grants to shelters. Sets standards for shelters. Provides, technical assistance to shelters.
California	Department of Social Services	Administers funds collected from marriage license surcharge, which are used for grants to shelters and for research. Serves as an information clearinghouse.

Connecticut	Department of Human Resources	Administers grants to shelters.
Florida	Department of Health and Rehabilitation Services	Administers grants to shelters. Sets standards for shelters. Provides technical assistance to shelters.
Georgia	Senate Study Committee on Domestic Violence	Studies the problem of family violence. A report will be submitted to the Senate in 1981.
Illinois	Department of Public Aid	Acts as liaison for Title XX program between state and Illinois Coalition Against Domestic Violence. The coalition awards grants to shelters, sets standards for shelters, and provides technical assistance to shelters.
Indiana	Domestic Violence and Treatment Council, Interdepartmental Board for the Coordination of Human Services Programs	Administers money collected from a surcharge on divorce actions. Recommends rules and regulations for shelters. Evaluates shelters yearly. Makes recommendations as to which shelters should receive grants. Conducts research. Will devise a uniform reporting system for law enforcement agencies.
Iowa	Department of Social Services	Administers one shelter pilot program.
Kansas	Advisory Committee to Division of Services to Children and Youth	Makes recommendations on disbursement of the Family and Children Trust Fund (funds collected from a marriage license surcharge). Money may be spent on prevention of problems of families and children, on grants for family abuse projects, and on evaluation of projects funded.
Kentucky	Department of Human Resources of Bureau for Social Services	Administers the Adult Protection Act.

Louisiana	Women's Advocacy Bureau, Department of Health and Human Resources	Develops shelter and other service programs. Establishes standards for these programs.
Maine	Department of Human Services	Administers state appropriations for shelters.
Massachusetts	Department of Public Welfare	Administers federal funds for domestic violence.
Michigan	Domestic Violence Treatment Board, Department of Social Services	Administers state domestic violence funds. Develops standards for shelters. Awards grants to shelters. Provides technical assistance to shelters. Assists state police in developing a uniform reporting system. Conducts research. Trains persons working in the domestic violence field.
Minnesota	Commission of Department of Corrections	Administers grants to at least four pilot shelter programs. Provides technical assistance to shelters. Awards grants to educational programs. The Commission is studying the possibility of instituting programs for abusers and has established two Crime Victim Crisis Centers. A nine-person Advisory Task Force will review requests for grants and will establish rules and regulations.
Montana	Department of Social and Rehabilitation Services	Administers grants (using funds collected from marriage license surcharge). Compiles domestic violence statistics. Conducts research.
Nebraska	Department of Public Welfare	Administers domestic violence programs that provide shelters and comprehensive services for victims, families, and abusers.
Nevada	Board of County Commissioners	Establishes Advisory Board. Awards grants to shelters and

		other organizations for services for victims of domestic violence.
New Hampshire	Welfare Division	Administers direct service grants. Works with the New Hampshire Coalition against Domestic Violence to provide technical assistance to shelters.
New Jersey	Advisory Council on Shelters for Victims of Domestic Violence, Commissioner of Department of Human Services	Establishes standards for shelters applying for services. Provides technical assistance to shelters on fund raising and training volunteers. Plans new programs and facilitates communication between existing programs.
New York	Governor's Task Force on Domestic Violence	Recommends legislation and administrative action on domestic violence.
North Dakota	Regional Human Service Centers, certified by State Health Department and Social Service Board	Provides assistance in domestic violence cases.
Ohio	Attorney General	Administers data collection of required police reporting. Distributes to shelters funds not allocated by counties from $10.00 marriage license fee. Prepares annual report on shelter funding.
	Department of Economic and Community Development, Division of Criminal Justice Services	Funds training and demonstration projects on domestic violence. Distributes LEAA funds for Ohio, which includes money for domestic violence services.
Oklahoma	Department of Mental Health	Administers grants to two domestic violence shelters.
Oregon	Department of Human Resources	Administers grants and contracts for domestic violence programs.
Texas	Department of	Contracts for shelter services

	Human Resources	using both state and federal funds.
Utah	Department of Social Services	Maintains comprehensive support services for victims of domestic violence using funds appropriated by state legislature.
Washington	Department of Social and Health Services	Administers grants to shelters. Sets standards for shelters and evaluates them every two years.
West Virginia	Governor's Committee on Crime, Delinquency, and Corrections	Administers grants to domestic violence programs.
Wisconsin	Council on Domestic Violence, Department of Health and Social Services	Reviews grant applications of shelters and makes recommendations.
Wyoming	Department of health and Social Services, Division of Public Assistance and Social Services	Administers grants. Maintains statistical data.

5

Government Services
for Battered Women

Abused Women's Aid in Crisis
G.P.O. Box 1699
New York, New York 10001
Dr. Doris Moss, executive director
(212) 686-3628
Founded: 1975. Staff: 9.

Abused Women's Aid in Crisis offers assistance to abused women and their families by providing onsite counseling to individuals and couples, telephone counseling, referrals to protective shelters, and advocacy and escort services through various agencies. The group conducts research projects, training seminars, and workshops. Although primarily active in the New York City area, Abused Women's Aid in Crisis serves as a national clearinghouse to provide information and referrals in answer to inquiries from across the United States.

ACTION (Agency for Volunteer Service)
806 Connecticut Avenue, N.W.
Washington, D.C. 20525

ACTION has been approached by Congresswoman Mikulski regarding the willingness of the agency to assume responsibility for a family violence program. ACTION's responsibility, among other things would be to:

> [E]stablish an office within the ACTION agency to be known as the National Volunteer Center for Community Action against Family Violence and to 1) develop and maintain an information clearinghouse, 2) establish a national toll free telephone number on problems of family violence and respond to requests for technical assistance, 3) provide technical assistance through the services of stipended volunteers.

The Office of Policy and Planning is exploring a program for implementation with the possibility of funding projects.

The programs in the field are providing assistance through volunteer services and small grants to assist in mobilizing volunteers in self-help projects. Many programs are in the area of assisting battered spouses and their children.

Those interested should write directly to ACTION for information on the VISTA, University Year of Action, Retired Senior Volunteer Program (RSVP), and minigrants.

Send for a list of ACTION's regional and state offices with addresses. All inquiries should be processed through the state office of the geographic area in which the requesting center is established.

RSVP has 250,000 senior volunteers serving with almost 700 projects throughout the country. RSVP volunteers could be assigned to a center for battered women, which would serve as a volunteer station. A list of all RSVPs is available from the Older Americans Volunteer Program Office, ACTION.

Center for Studies of Child and Family Mental Health
National Institute of Mental Health (NIMH)
Department of Health and Human Services
5600 Fishers Lane
Rockville, Maryland 20857
(301) 443-3556

The NIMH has funded the most widely known and quoted research studies in the field of family violence, including the works of Murray Straus, Richard Gelles, and Suzanne Steinmetz. These studies were funded by the Center for Studies of Crime and Delinquency.

The National Center for the Prevention and Control of Rape supports research in the legal, social, and medical aspects of rape; disseminates research-based information and training materials, and fosters communication through conferences, technical assistance, and a clearinghouse.

In the area of child abuse, the NIMH has a limited program coordinated through the National Center for Child Abuse and Neglect. The program focuses on mental-health aspects of this area of family violence and includes research grants on outcomes, intervention, and etiology (mainly from a mother-child-interaction view). Contracts have been awarded in the special areas of emotional abuse and adolescent abuse, as well as in the area of training mental-health professionals and nonprofessionals.

In the area of battered women or spouse abuse, the center has been providing consultation and technical assistance to shelters for battered women, to researchers, and to persons working with the media including radio, press, films, and so on.

Research grants are possible if the researcher is thoroughly familiar with research design and methods. An affiliation with a university is highly desirable.

Funds for direct services are available only to federally funded comprehensive community mental-health centers. The possibility for a shelter to become affiliated with a community mental-health center is limited.

Contracts are usually awarded to shelters for demonstration research. Different models of service delivery receive priority. Awards are also made for planning and holding conferences on spouse abuse, including writing up the proceedings. Such conferences should bring together twenty to twenty-five leaders in the field from the areas of research, training, and service delivery, including professional and grass-roots representatives.

The Center for Women Policy Studies
2000 P Street, N.W., Suite 508
Washington, D.C. 20036

The Center for Women Policy Studies is a nonprofit, tax-exempt corporation that works to educate both the public and policymakers about the need for change in the legal, social, and economic status of women.

The center was founded in 1972 as a feminist policy research center, with the belief that legal equality and economic independence for women continues to provide direction for the work of the center today.

Projects of the Center for Women Policy Studies are carried out by a staff of professionals who combine experience in economics, law, sociology, women's studies, social work, and public-policy development. Staff members work with an advisory board and with senior associates of the center.

Since its establishment, the center has chosen to focus its resources on four particular areas. First, the center has completed four major projects in the area of women's economic status: (1) women and credit, (2) implementation of the Equal Credit Opportunity Act, (3) the legal and economic impact of marriage, and (4) sex discrimination in the social security system. The Older Women's Program, launched by the center in mid-1980, focuses on the economic status of midlife and older women.

Second, one project, Women Employed in Corrections, examines the positions currently filled by women in the field of corrections and factors that limit women's roles and that affect their advancement and placement in the field. Another project, currently underway, examines the harassment of women in the work place. The project explores the nature, extent, and consequences of sexual harassment in employment.

Third, four projects have explored ways to improve the response of the criminal-justice system to victims of rape, family violence, and sexual assault. Another center project has focused on the female offender in the United States.

Fourth, in conjunction with work on family-violence and sexual-assault issues, the center has studied the response of health, mental-health, and social-welfare institutions and practitioners to the needs of women and their families in an effort to promote more-effective intervention and delivery of services.

In exploring these issues, both policy research and action research techniques are employed, often in sequential fashion. The results often have considerable impact on public policy. For example, in the area of women and credit, the center began its work in 1973 with a two-year study of the legal and economic barriers facing women seeking to obtain credit. One result of the study, which was supported by the Ford Foundation, was the compilation of source materials on women and credit into a bibliography. As a result of expertise developed in this area, center staff testified before a congressional committee and assisted the committee during mark-up of the bill that was eventually enacted into law as the 1974 Equal Credit Opportunity Act. Under contract with the Federal Reserve Board, the center later aided in the drafting of regulations to implement the Equal Credit Opportunity Act.

In the area of sexual assault, the center has been able to play an influential role in making the issue of rape a legitimate federal policy concern and in bringing about new legislation to support community-based rape-crisis services. Center activities in this area have also included a nationwide survey of new and promising programs for the treatment of rape victims and the development of operating guidelines for local social-service, medical, and criminal-justice programs.

Future directions for the center include exploration of new issues in the family-violence and sexual-assault field, expansion of the on-the-job-harassment project, further exploration into nontraditional employment issues, program development for female offenders, and further development of issues affecting older women to fill a critical lack of information in this area. Projects focusing on these activities are being developed by center staff, its board of directors, and its associates and advisers.

The work of the Center for Women Policy Studies is funded through grants, contracts, and donations from a wide variety of public- and private-sector sources. Among those institutions that have supported the center are the Ford Foundation, the Edna McConnell Clark Foundation, the New York Foundation, the Law Enforcement Assistance Administration, the Equal Employment Opportunity Commission, the U.S. Department of State, the Johnson Foundation, the U.S. Department of Health and Human Services, and several corporations.

Center for Women's Studies and Services
908 F Street
San Diego, California 92101
Carol Rowell, coordinator
Founded: 1969. Members: 900. Staff: 18. Local groups: 2.

The Center for Women's Studies and Services is a feminist organization founded to meet the unmet needs of female radical feminist services and programs and to advance the cause of women's rights. The center offers vocational counseling and job referral; assistance to women entering jobs traditionally held by men; feminist-oriented counseling on a one-to-one basis or in groups on pregnancy and abortion, alcoholism/crisis intervention, and other personal problems; information on and referral to other women's programs and organizations and to human-service agencies; information regarding educational programs and financial assistance; and assistance, counseling, and housing for battered women. Projects include a rape center, a young women's journalism project, and a high school women's manual. Its publications include *Storefront and Radical Feminist Counseling*, *Feminist Bulletin* (bimonthly), and *The Longest Revolution* (newspaper, bimonthly).

Community Services Administration (CSA)
1200 19th Street, N.W.
Washington, D.C. 20506
(202) 254-6110

Community action agencies (CAAs) are the primary grantees of the CSA. In thousands of communities across the United States, they provide advocacy and social-service delivery. When necessary, they make referrals of the poor and near-poor to other entities that can assist with their problems.

There are over 879 CAAs, covering over 2,293 of the 3,141 counties in the country. These counties contain 75 percent of the population and a similar percentage of the nation's poor.

Using the existing networks they have established in the communities they serve, CAAs would be capable of providing actual services, or appropriate referrals, to families or family members, in crisis situations.

Using its demonstration authority, CSA funded in 1978 pilot family crisis centers in five cities to be operated by CAAs. Each center will be open twenty-four hours a day and will provide services to an entire family in time of personal crisis. A major component and emphasis of the center will be its outreach activities by which families in need of immediate aid will be identified. Also, each center will house a team composed of a psychiatrist or psychologist, a family social worker, and a community person with psychological training who will provide intensive family counseling to these families and will see them through the emergency to the point where they can begin once again to handle their own lives. They will also receive services at the center such as medical care, emergency shelter and food, referral services to other agencies as well as many social services onsite—for example, food stamps, employment services, and welfare and SSI eligibility determination.

The family crisis centers will provide a unique approach to resolving family crises while using existing capabilities, services, and the networks established in the communities by the CAAs. Their goal will be to treat the problems faced by the total family that have caused one or more of its members to seek emergency assistance.

Demonstration Projects

The Office of Domestic Violence, the National Center on Child Abuse and Neglect, and HHS's Office of Planning Research and Evaluation/ Human Development Services are jointly funding three demonstration projects to provide services to children of battered spouses:

Harriet Tubman Woman's Shelter, Hennepin County Department of Community Services
30001 Oakland
Minneapolis, Minnesota 55414
Trudy Turnquist, director

This project focuses on the specific needs of a high-risk population of children who have been exposed to violence in their homes. The program's goal is to break the cycle of violence that has been passed from generation to generation by ensuring delivery of services to the children of abused women. The project will develop and implement linkages with community agencies to provide direct services to the children at the shelter.

Family Crisis Center, Child and Family Services of Knox County
2535 Magnolia Avenue
Knoxville, Tennessee 37914
Larry Feezel, director

This project focuses on treatment for both children and parents in abusive family relationships. The project utilizes family-systems therapy to address the interactions and interrelationships of all family members. The program will attempt to help abusive parents release frustration and anger in a nonviolent manner so that they may change their patterns of behavior. The entire family unit, including spouse, abuser, and children, will work together to modify and strengthen family life. Family units participating in the project are screened by the Tennessee Department of Human Resources.

Panel for Family Living, YWCA Women's Support Shelter
405 Broadway
Tacoma, Washington 98402
Carol Richards, director

This project is focused on the development of specific therapeutic child-care models for children who have been subjected to domestic violence. Time-limited modules for child-care activities that can be replicated in other shelter programs for battered women are being developed. Project goals are the development of basic survival and communication skills and positive nonviolent interactions between the parent and child.

Division of Special Treatment and Rehabilitation
National Institute on Alcohol Abuse and Alcoholism (NIAAA)
Department of Health, Education, and Welfare
5600 Fishers Lane
Rockville, Maryland 20857
(301) 443-6317

NIAAA legislation P.L. 91-616 and P.L. 94-371 do not specifically mandate the institute to support as a separate entity the provision of services for nonalcoholic family members (battered women, children, and so on) affected by alcoholism.

The institute's policy, however, does extend to include the provision of services for these populations in such cases where alcoholism is directly related to violence or neglect/abuse among family members.

Rationale for this policy stems from results of studies that indicate a definite correlation between battered wives, child neglect/abuse, and alcoholism. Children of alcoholic parents are, in most cases, negatively affected by parental alcoholism, and a high rate of juvenile delinquency, youth runaway problems, and wife abuse seems to exist in family alcoholism situations.

In order to qualify for grant support, program guidelines within the Division of Special Treatment and Rehabilitation require that all treatment programs place emphasis on involving and providing services for the so-called significant others affected by the alcohol problem.

Criminal-justice programs provide support for family services as a part of the treatment of persons convicted of and/or arrested for violence in the family as a result of alcoholism.

Program guidelines for women and youth place emphasis on intervention and treatment of alcohol abuse and alcoholism among these populations. However, if women and youth are among those suffering violence as a result of alcohol abuse and/or alcoholism and are considered high risk as a result of exposure to or involvement with alcohol abuse themselves, they would be eligible recipients for direct services.

Domestic Violence Resource Projects
National Clearinghouse on Domestic Violence
P.O. Box 2309
Rockville, Maryland 20852

Center for Women Policy Studies
2000 P Street, N.W. Suite 508
Washington, D.C. 20036

Office on Domestic Violence
400 6th Street, S.W.
Room 2044B
Washington, D.C. 20201
Attn: Ms. Jane Santos

For reference and referral services and published information on domestic violence, call (301) 251-5172.

For technical assistance, particularly with respect to legal issues, call (202) 872-1770

Feminist Alliance against Rape
P.O. Box 21033
Washington, D.C. 20009
Debra Friedman, production coordinator
Founded: 1974.

The alliance is dedicated to providing a forum for discussing and developing strategies to end rape. It publishes news, theoretical articles, and book and film reviews that deal with organizational problems of rape crisis centers, funding suggestions, law-reform efforts and significant legal cases, wife abuse, and issues related to self-defense. Its publications include *Aegis: Magazine on Ending Violence against Women* (bimonthly).

House of Ruth
459 Massachusetts Avenue, N.W.
Washington, D.C. 20001
Gwendolyn SidBerry, executive director
Founded: 1976. Staff: 20.

The House of Ruth is supported by individuals, churches, synagogues, service organizations, local businesses, and private foundations. Its goals are to provide shelter, on an emergency and temporary basis, for homeless and battered women and their children and to provide important support services and counseling, both individual and group. The center provides counseling and recreational and educational activities for children of abused women. It also provides a series of second-stage, or transitional, housing for former shelter residents.

International Council of Women
13, Rue Caumartin
F-75009 Paris, France
Dame Miriam Dell, president
Founded: 1888. Members: 72. Staff: 2.

National councils of women composed of national and local women's organizations of varying scope make up the International Council of Women.
From its inception, it has supported the ideas of international peace and
arbitration, equal legal status for women (including suffrage and rights of
citizenship, equal pay for equal work, equal moral standards, and equal
access to education), community development, and family and child welfare. The council carries out activities to encourage literacy among adult
women. It has consultative status with the Economic and Social Council of
the United Nations. Its publications include a triennial newsletter and triennial reports.

Law Enforcement Assistance Administration (LEAA)
U.S. Department of Justice
633 Indiana Avenue, N.W.
Washington, D.C. 20531
(202) 376-3550

Recent research of all projects funded by LEAA shows that it has spent
approximately $15 million on programs related to family crimes, with over
$8 million on that amount going to police crisis-intervention training. The
remaining funds have supported the Child Abuse Intervention Prescriptive
Package and several local child-abuse training efforts, runaway houses,
alcohol treatment programs, arbitration and mediation projects, and victim/
witness programs specifically designed to assist victims of domestic violence
and sexually abused children.

The LEAA Victim/Witness Assistance Program (V/WAP) focused its
efforts on victims of sensitive crimes that were defined as rape, sexual abuse
of children, and intrafamily violence. A grant was made to the Center for
Women Policy Studies in Washington, D.C., to establish a newsletter and a
clearinghouse to serve as mechanisms for information sharing among police,
prosecutors, social-service agencies, and medical facilities and for mental-
health response to victims of these crimes. These activities were part of a
larger technical assistance effort aimed at the many victim-assistance and
victim-advocacy programs funded by LEAA during the two previous years.
Through this grant, the center was able to assist several projects in improving their case management and their services related to these victims.

More recently another grant was made to the center to provide contin-
ued support for the newsletter and clearing as well as to provide technical
assistance to community groups interested in initiating and/or improving
services for sensitive-crime victims.

In addition to the grants made to the center, the V/WAP recently
funded four projects to assist battered women and has two grants under
review to assist children who have been sexually abused.

Based on the critical need for better programming in this area, violence in the home has become a LEAA priority for the future. Monies have been allocated to this program to support comprehensive programs addressing family violence. These programs would support not only shelters for battered women but also complementary components within the criminal-justice and social-service agencies, thereby providing several points of interaction at which these families could be helped.

Legal Services Corporation
133 15th Street, N.W.
Suite 700
Washington, D.C. 20005
(202) 376-5119

Women who need legal help in a civil matter but who cannot afford to hire a lawyer could contact the local legal-services program in their area to determine their eligibility for free legal assistance.

Legal-services programs operate in every state, as well as Puerto Rico, the Virgin Islands, and the Trust Territory of the Pacific Islands (Micronesia). The programs receive financial support from the Legal Services Corporation, a private, nonprofit organization created and funded by Congress to provide legal assistance to the poor and civil matters. The corporation receives an annual appropriation from Congress and distributes those federal funds through grants and contracts to legal-services programs that meet the requirements set forth in the Legal Services Corporation Act of 1974 (P.L. 93-355).

The corporation currently funds over 300 legal-assistance programs serving indigent clients in nearly 700 offices throughout the country. Each program is independently governed by a local board of directors that includes private attorneys and representatives of the client community. The board establishes program policy and priorities and sets forth financial eligibility standards in accordance with the broader framework of the Legal Services Corporation Act of 1974 and regulations promulgated by the corporation. Within the limitations of the federal statute, each program has broad authority to determine how it will conduct its operations. Because most programs do not have sufficient resources to meet all the needs of the eligible, the board may establish priorities by considering, among other factors, the availability of other sources of legal assistance in the locality.

A client's eligibility is determined primarily by family income, but other factors affecting a person's ability to pay for legal assistance are also taken into account, such as fixed debts and obligations, medical bills, child-care expenses, and seasonal income variations. The corporation has established maximum income levels to be used by its grantees in determining client eligibility. These ceilings are 125 percent of the official government poverty threshold. The following maximum income levels are based on the poverty guidelines issued by the federal Office of Management and Budget:

Family Unit Size	Contiguous States	Alaska	Hawaii
1	$3,713	$ 4,650	$ 4,288
2	4,913	6,150	5,633
3	6,113	7,650	7,038
4	7,313	9,150	8,413
5	8,513	10,650	9,788
6	9,713	12,150	11,163
For more than 6, add per additional person	1,200	1,500	1,375

Most legal-services programs provide legal advice and representation in a wide variety of civil matters; some specialize in problems relating to a particular area of the law, such as consumer matters, problems of elderly persons, housing matters, administrative benefit problems or domestic-relations problems. A few legal-services programs have created special units to represent women who are being physically abused by their husbands and who seek relief from the court. If you need legal help but do not know where to go for assistance, contact the lawyer-referral service of your local bar association or the Public Affairs Office of the Legal Services Corporation.

Legal Services Corporation—
National Center on Women and Family Law
799 Broadway, Room 402
New York, New York 10003

Legal Services Corporation funds go to 355 legal-services programs in the United States that can provide legal services to domestic-violence victims who meet the low-income requirements. The corporation also funds the National Center on Women and Family Law, a new back-up center that provides support and technical assistance to attorneys, paralegals, clients, and client organizations. A priority of the center is to address the issue of violence against women in domestic relationships.

National Center on Child Abuse and Neglect
Office of Human and Human Services
Department of Health, Education, and Welfare
400 6th Street, S.W.
Washington, D.C. 20013
(202) 755-0587

The National Center on Child Abuse and Neglect was created by the Child Abuse Prevention and Treatment Act (P.L. 93-247), enacted 31 January 1974. The objectives of the center are to generate and disseminate knowledge and information and to facilitate their application in order to improve the capabilities of states and communities to prevent and treat child abuse and neglect.

The center accomplishes these objectives through a combination of grants and contracts that provide for 1) the conduct of research to develop new or improved service-delivery mechanisms; 2) the dissemination of information through a national clearinghouse; and 3) the award of grants to those states that satisfy eligibility requirements stipulated in the act.

All demonstration activity sponsored by the center is described in priority statements announced by the Administration for Children, Youth, and Families. Applications for grant funds received in response to such announcements are reviewed and competitively evaluated by an independent review panel composed of nongovernment professionals with expertise in relevant fields. To be put on the mailing list to receive grant applications, individuals may write the national center at P.O. Box 1182, Washington, D.C. 20013.

All contractual activity sponsored by the center is announced in the *Commerce Business Daily* and is competitively awarded based on proposals offerors submit in response to the government's request for proposal.

State grants are awarded based on eligibility statements that states submit annually to their respective regional offices.

National Center for Health Services Research
Health Resources Administration
Department of Health and Human Services
3700 East West Highway
Hyattsville, Maryland 20782
(301) 436-8936

Staff of the National Center for Health Services Research have conducted several discussions on the subject of battered spouses with potential investigators. To this time, they have focused upon the emergency department to which many battered women come for care. Possible health-services-research approaches include exploring the use of the emergency department as a case-finding site; identifying the relationship between battering and other conditions such as alcohol, drug abuse, and suicide; and examining the emergency medical management of battered women. The center would have authority, under Sections 305 and 1205 of the Public Health Service Act, to provide funds via grant and contract for research, research conferences, and demonstrations on the subject. The brochure, *The Program in Health Services Research*, provides additional information on the center's activities.

National Organization for Women (NOW)
425 13th Street, N.W.
Washington, D.C. 20004

Eleanor Cutri Smeal, president
(202) 347-2279
*Founded: 1966. Members: 120,000. Regional groups: 9. State groups: 50.
Local groups: 800.*

NOW is a group of men and women who support full equality for women in truly equal partnership with men. NOW acts to end prejudice and discrimination against women in government, industry, the professions, the churches, the political parties, the judiciary, the labor unions, education, science, medicine, law, religion, and every other field of importance in U.S. society. The group seeks passage of the Equal Rights Amendment, enforcement of federal legislation prohibiting discrimination on the basis of sex, a nationwide network of child-care centers and other social innovations to enable women to work while rearing a family, and reexamination of laws and mores governing marriage and divorce with an end to alimony. Its publications include *National NOW Times* (newsletter, monthly).

Office of Community Planning and Development
Department of Housing and Urban Development
451 7th Street, S.W.
Room 7212
Washington, D.C., 20410
(202) 755-6082

The Community Development Block Grant Program, under Title I of the Housing and Community Development Act of 1974, provides grants to units of local governments for a wide variety of community-development activities. Priorities for use of these funds are determined at the local level within the statutory objectives of the program. The following examples illustrate the types of projects that may be eligible under certain circumstances: acquisition, construction, or rehabilitation of publicly owned, multi- or single-purpose social-service centers; provision of social services such as counseling, legal aid, or health services administered by public or private agencies; and rehabilitation.

These types of activities, however, are eligible only under very restrictive conditions.

Office of Human Development
Department of Health, Education, and Welfare
6th Street S. W.
Washington, D.C. 30531
(202) 245-6462

The Administration on Public Services, under Title XX of the Social Security Act, may fund protective services for children and adults. There is no means test for receiving protective services. Funding is on a 75 percent federal and 25 percent matching basis. Protective services must be included in the state plan for the use of Title XX funds. (Note: Title XX funds can be used for emergency shelter for children only, not for adults.)

Currently, shelter can be provided to adults only when it is integral and subordinate to another social service. For example, states could have a service center for battered spouses in their service plan that provides a range of services but that could not fund an emergency shelter center for battered women.

The Administration on Public Services funds demonstration programs on residential treatment for multiproblem families with female heads. Battered spouses are identified as a component of the demonstration projects— that is, spouses with physical or sexual abuse—with a focus on the family.

As a component of their family-oriented services to abused and neglected children, the twenty demonstration treatment centers of the Administration on Children, Youth, and Families provide some services that either directly or indirectly assist abused spouses. For example, the Honolulu project has established an emergency shelter that is used exclusively to provide shelter to abused spouses and children. Additionally, the shelter staff provides other support services such as counseling and home finding so that the family might relocate back in the community and referral for financial assistance to the mother and family when needed.

The Chicago project coordinate community services such as legal aid to the abused spouse, couple counseling when appropriate, and emergency shelter (utilizing the Salvation Army) when needed.

The Philadelphia project provides psychiatric counseling to abused spouses and integrates its efforts with the Women-in-Transition Center, a local program designed especially for abused spouses.

The Yakima project is housed in a large residential structure that is open on a twenty-four-hour basis. It frequently provides emergency shelter to abused spouses and works with the families to reduce the incidence of such abuse.

In addition, although a number of projects do not have an in-house capability to provide emergency shelter, they arrange for and provide transportation to such facilities located elsewhere in the community.

Some examples of longer-range intervention services that are provided are legal assistance, psychological evaluations of adults, individual adult counseling, parent aid/lay therapy, couple/family counseling, group counseling/therapy, Parents Anonymous participation, education services, home making services, transportation support, residential shelters, short-term foster care, medical services, and day-care and babysitting services. Uniformly, all the demonstration treatment projects report that one of their most successful interventions with abusive and/or neglectful parents is in the area of improved socialization. Through various activities sponsored by the centers, parents are made to feel less isolated; they become involved in activities that foster interaction with other adults, often for the first time in their lives; and, they end up with a new and heightened sense of their own worth as individuals. This pattern is also borne out by the experience of individuals involved with Parents Anonymous.

Demonstration efforts are showing that the successful prevention, identification, and treatment of child abuse and neglect require that the services be provided to all members of the family unit.

Rape Crisis Center
P.O. Box 21005
Washington, D.C. 20009
Loretta J. Ross, director
(202) 333-7273
Founded: 1972. Members: 25.

Women at the Rape Crisis Center are united to provide counseling and information to victims of rape, community education materials and programs in regard to rape, and consulting services for other groups concerned with rape. The center provides self-defense-referral information for other professionals who deal with rape victims.

Technical Assistance Centers on Family Violence:

National Technical Assistance Center
202 East Huron, #101
Ann Arbor, Michigan 48104
Kathleen Modigliani, director
(313) 995-5460/5447

Region I includes Connecticut, Maine, Massachusetts, New Hampshire, Rhode Island, Vermont:
Domestic Violence Technical Assistance Project
Casa Myrna Vasquez, Inc.
P.O. Box 18019
Boston, Massachusetts 02118
Paulea Mooney, director
(617) 266-4305

Region II includes New Jersey, New York, Puerto Rico:
Volunteers against Violence Technical Assistance Project
American Friends Service Committee
New York Metropolitan Regional Office
15 Rutherford Place
New York, New York 10003
Yolanda Bako, director
(212) 777-4600

Region III includes Delaware, Maryland, Pennsylvania, Virginia, West Virginia, District of Columbia:

Pennsylvania Coalition against Domestic Violence
2405 North Front Street
Harrisburg, Pennsylvania 17110
Barbara Hart, director
(717) 233-6030, (800) 692-7445, (800) 932-4632

Region IV includes Alabama, Florida, Georgia, Kentucky, Mississippi, North Carolina, South Carolina, Tennessee:

University of Tennessee
Division of Continuing Education
426 Communication and University Extension Building
Knoxville, Tennessee 37916
Lucy Biggs
(615) 974-2327

Region V includes Illinois, Indiana, Missouri, Minnesota, Ohio, Wisconsin:

Domestic Violence Technical Assistance Project
Community Crisis Center, Inc.
600 Margaret Place
Elgin, Illinois 60120
Gretchan Vapnar, director
(312) 697-2380

Region VI includes Arkansas, Louisiana, New Mexico, Oklahoma, Texas:

Domestic Violence and Networking
Houston Area Women's Center
P.O. Box 20186, Room E 401
Houston, Texas 77025
Susan Eggert, director
(713) 792-4403

Region VII includes Iowa, Kansas, Missouri, Nebraska:

Rural Family Violence Center
Nebraska Task Force on Domestic Violence
2202 South 11th Street
Lincoln, Nebraska 68508
Joan Wilson, director
(402) 435-0027

Region VIII includes Colorado, Montana, North Dakota, South Dakota, Utah, Wyoming:

Domestic Violence Technical Assistance Center
Colorado Association for Aid to Battered Women

Colorado Women's College
Box 136
Montview and Quebec Streets
Denver, Colorado 80220
Lindsey Lawrence, director
(303) 355-7080

Region IX includes Arizona, California, Hawaii, Nevada, Guam:
Technical Assistance Center
Southern California Coalition on Battered Women
P.O. Box 5036
Santa Monica, California 90405
Kerry Lobel, director
(213) 396-7744

Region X includes Alaska, Idaho, Oregon, Washington:
State Networks Technical Assistance Project
Washington State Shelter Network
Technical Assistance Office
1063 South Capitol Way, Room 217
Olympia, Washington 98501
Carol Richards, director
(206) 753-4621

Women's Action Program (WAP)
Office of the Secretary
Department of Health, Education, and Welfare
438 F South Portal Building
200 Independence Avenue, S.W.
Washington, D.C. 20005
(202) 245-6604

The Women's Action Program (WAP), in the Office of the Assistant Secretary for Planning and Evaluation of HEW, is responsible for analyzing the effects of HEW programs and policies on women. Functioning in this capacity, it provides direct services to women.

In an effort to facilitate communication among interested persons, WAP brought together for the first time representatives of several offices engaged in discrete efforts related to wife abuse or family violence. Existing relevant HHS programs, the gaps in those programs, and the ways in which new federal legislation could most effectively assist providers in delivering services at the local level were discussed. While preparing recommendations for specific changes in HHS regulations, longer-range effort will focus on the

programmatic changes that may require legislation and/or budget alloca-
tions.

Women against Violence against Women
1727 North Spring Street
Los Angeles, California 90012
Joan Howarth, executive officer
(213) 223-8771
Founded: 1976. Staff: 1. Local groups: 25.

This group is an activist organization that is working to stop gratuitous use of
images of physical and sexual violence against women in mass media and the
real-world violence it promotes. It sponsors public education, consciousness
raising, and mass consumer action. Currently focusing on the recording
industry, the organization is pressing for an industrywide policy against the
use of violence against women in record advertising. It seeks to educate
people about sexist and violent exploitation in media and advertising by
maintaining a slide presentation that illustrates advertising violence against
women.

Women in Crisis
444 Park Avenue, South
New York, New York 10016
Jane Velez, conference administrator
(212) 686-1942
Founded: 1979. Staff: 3.

Women in Crisis is composed of national conference participants concerned
with the plight of women in crisis including victims of sexual discrimination
and poverty, battered wives, teenage prostitutes, rape and incest victims,
female offenders, female drug abusers and alcoholics, and other women
whose lives have been devastated by emotional starvation and neglect. The
group aims for an integrated approach in services to women involving the
areas of alcohol, mental health, drugs, and justice and for the initiation of a
network system of professionals in these areas.

Women in Transition
112 South 6th Street
7th Floor
Philadelphia, Pennsylvania 19102
Sarah Lynne McMahon, codirector
(215) 387-5556
Founded: 1971. Staff: 30.

This organization provides services to displaced homemakers including women experiencing marital distress, domestic violence, separation, divorce, and widowhood. It operates a telephone hotline for information and resource referrals and facilitates self-help support groups for abused women and for women in marital crisis. Women in Transition conducts special weekly workshops for Comprehensive Employment and Training Act (CETA) eligible displaced homemakers, and outreach programs and survival-skills workshops are available to low-income women and to professional organizations throughout the Philadelphia area.

Women's Bureau
Department of Labor
200 Constitution Avenue, N.W.
Washington, D.C. 20210
(202) 523-6611/6539

The Women's Bureau, which is primarily concerned with women's employment and which functions to promote programs and to advocate policies to improve working conditions and employment opportunities for women, does not have a special program for battered women. Solutions to the specific problem of violence and physical abuse are not within the purview of the Department of Labor.

However, most battered women, and particularly those who have left their husbands, do have pressing economic needs, and the Women's Bureau can assist by providing information and publications about legal rights, occupations, day care, employment, and training opportunities. In addition, in its function as a clearinghouse on women's issues, the bureau answers requests for information about current legislation that affects battered women, sources of funding for shelters and centers for abused women and their children, programs currently in operation, organizations that have an interest in and information about battered women, and bibliographies of books and articles on the subject.

Through CETA, which is administered by the Department of Labor, local prime sponsors have funded a number of projects to assist battered women. Under CETA Titles I, II, and IV, staff positions and projects have been funded to provide employment counseling, training, and related supportive services.

The Women's Bureau, through its ten regional offices, encourages the funding of such projects by prime sponsors and can provide examples of projects that have been funded.

Region I includes Connecticut, Maine, Massachusetts, New Hampshire, Rhode Island, Vermont:

Vivian L. Buckles, regional administrator
Patricia Kelly, management assistant
JFK Building, Room 1700-C
Boston, Massachusetts 02203
(617) 223-4036

Region II includes New Jersey, New York, Puerto Rico, Virgin Islands:
Mary E. Tobin, regional administrator
Florence Falk-Dickler, program development specialist
Mary Sanford, management assistant
1515 Broadway, Room 3575
New York, New York 10036
(212) 399-2935

Region III includes Delaware, District of Columbia, Maryland, Pennsylvania, Virginia, West Virginia:
Kathleen Riordan, regional administrator
Gateway Building, Room 15230
3535 Market Street
Philadelphia, Pennsylvania 19104
(215) 596-1183

Region IV includes Alabama, Florida, Georgia, Kentucky, Mississippi, North Carolina, South Carolina, Tennessee:
Vacant, regional administrator
Linda Guthrie, program development specialist
Dorris Muscadin, secretary
1371 Peachtree Street, N.E., Room 737
Atlanta, Georgia 30309
(404) 881-4461

Region V includes Illinois, Indiana, Michigan, Minnesota, Ohio, Wisconsin:
Vacant, regional administrator
Sandra Frank, acting regional administrator
Ethel Bouler, management assistant
230 South Dearborn Street, 8th Floor
Chicago, Illinios 60604
(312) 353-6985

Region VI includes Arkansas, Louisiana, New Mexico, Oklahoma, Texas:
Rhobia C. Taylor, regional administrator
555 Griffin Square Building, Room 505
Griffin and Young Streets
Dallas, Texas 75202
(215) 767-6985

Region VII includes Iowa, Kansas, Missouri, Nebraska:

Euphesenia W. Foster, regional administrator
Gwynn H. Gilliam, program development specialist
Diana Sue Nelson, management assistant
2511 Federal Building
911 Walnut Street
Kansas City, Missouri 64106
(816) 374-6108

Region VIII includes Colorado, Montana, North Dakota, South Dakota, Utah, Wyoming:

Lynn Brown, regional administrator
Janice Gerhardt, management assistant
1432 Federal Building
1961 Stout Street
Denver, Colorado 80202
(303) 837-4138

Region IX includes Arizona, California, Hawaii, Nevada:

Madeline Mixer, regional administrator
Elba Montes, program development specialist
Eleanor Cress, management assistant
Federal Building, Room 11411
450 Golden Gate Avenue
San Francisco, California 94102
(415) 556-2377

Region X includes Alaska, Idaho, Oregon, Washington:

Lazelle S. Johnson, regional administrator
Micki Sims, management assistant
Federal Office Building, Room 3032
909 First Avenue
Seattle, Washington 98174
(206) 442-1534

Women's Legal Defense Fund
1010 Vermont Avenue, N.W.
Washington, D.C. 20005
Judith Lichtman, executive director
(202) 638-1123
Founded: 1971. Members: 450. Staff: 1.

The Women's Legal Defense Fund is composed of attorneys, paralegals, administrators, and secretaries. Its purpose is to secure equal rights for women by providing volunteer legal representatives as well as sponsoring educational and informational activities on legal issues of special interest to women, including problems of battered wives. The organization conducts seminars on special legal topics and classes on women and the law and domestic-relations law. Its publications include a quarterly newsletter.

Women's Program Division
Office of the Assistant Secretary for Neighborhoods,
Voluntary Associations, and Consumer Protection
U.S. Department of Housing and Urban Development
451 7th Street, S.W.
Washington, D.C. 20410
(202) 755-6524

The Women's Policy and Programs Division plans, first, to determine whether any research-and-development projects or other centrally controlled programs include any facilities and/or services related to needs of battered spouses.

Second, the division has proposed letting a small contract for a study to ascertain where HUD-assisted shelters exist; to discover what typologies exist in terms of funding strategies, services, physical/organizational arrangements, and so forth; and to develop a how-to manual for use by other organizations.

Third, the division is convening planning sessions with representatives of key women's organizations, housing and community development agencies, and HUD officials to set programs and priorities for the office and to plan an action agenda for consideration.

Women's Rights Program Unit
Commission on Civil Rights
1121 Vermont Avenue, Room 410
Washington, D.C. 20425
(202) 254-8127

The U.S. Commission on Civil Rights is planning a national consultation on domestic violence. Previous subject areas included relevant research, legal aspects (the law and law enforcement), and support services (short and long term). Papers will be presented on each subject with a panel of experts to respond to each paper. Participants will be selected from those with expertise in the specific areas listed, and time will be designated for observers to comment. The proceedings of the consultation will be published and available for distribution by the commission.

In addition, the Connecticut and New Jersey State Advisory Committees of the commission are planning projects investigating domestic violence and the needs of battered women [Jacques Wilmors, regional director, Northeastern Regional Office, 26 Federal Plaza, Room 1639, New York, New York 10007, (212) 264-0400]. Further, the Rocky Mountain regional office has recently completed a study of and a film on domestic violence and services available to battered women in Denver [Shirley Hill Witt, regional director, 1405 Curtis, Room 1700, Denver, Colorado 80202, (303) 837-2211].

6 Programs for Men Who Batter

Alaska

Male Awareness Project
417 West 8th Street
Anchorage 99501
(907) 279-9581

This project is a nonprofit community organization that offers group counseling, therapy, and other assistance.

Arizona

Rainbow Retreat, Inc., Outpatient Program
4332 North 12th Street
Phoenix 85014
(602) 263-1113

The outpatient program operates as part of a battered women's shelter. Services include individual and marital counseling.

Victim Witness Advocate Program
111 West Congress
Suite 900
Tucson 85701
(602) 792-8021

Crisis intervention, mediation, referral, and follow-up services have been provided since 1976.

Arkansas

Family Services of North Little Rock
P.O. Box 500
North Little Rock 72115
(501) 758-1516 (Office)
(501) 375-1742 (Hot line)

As part of comprehensive counseling services to families, this agency provides individual, marital, and family counseling.

California

Alternatives to Violence, YWCA Womenshelter
3636 Atlantic Avenue
Long Beach 90807
(213) 426-1734

Project staff provide peer-group counseling for batterers. The project, which accepts court referrals or men who voluntarily seek counseling services, began in February 1979.

Batterers Anonymous
P.O. Box 29
Redlands 92373
(714) 885-6843

Batterers Anonymous, a mutual support group specifically for men who batter, began in February 1980.

Couple Counseling of the Neighborhood Facility
769 West 3rd Street
San Pedro 90731
(213) 547-0831

This YWCA shelter program, which began in 1977, provides individual and couple counseling.

Foothill Family Services—Family Life, Education Camp and Family Stress Center
118 South Oak Knoll
Pasadena 91106
(213) 795-6907

The center provides group counseling, informational workshops, and parent education.

Marin Abused Women's Services
1618 Mission Avenue
San Rafael 94901
(415) 924-6616

The project offers a ten-week counseling group for men who are involved in violent relationships. Counselors also conduct individual and marital counseling by referral. These services began in January 1980; a peer support group began in April 1980.

Positive Anger Control Program
2015 J Street
Suite 8
Sacramento 95814
(916) 448-2321

The program, which began in 1978, is a shelter outreach effort. The program offers telephone, individual, and couple and family counseling.

Riverside County Coalition for Alternatives to Domestic Violence
P.O. Box 910
Riverside 92502
(714) 684-1720 (Office)
(714) 683-0829 (twenty-four-hour crisis line)

Counseling, short-term support, and referrals by telephone have been available since January 1977.

Ken Ryan, Ph.D.
6128 Beaumont Avenue
La Jolla 92037
(714) 236-3381 (Office)
(714) 459-5562 (Office)

Since September 1977, Dr. Ryan has been providing individual counseling for men who batter.

Santa Barbara Family Violence Program
5689 Hollister Avenue
P.O. Box 1429
Galeta 93017
(805) 964-8857

This program provides individual, marital, and group counseling, as well as an anger-management course. Services started in 1978.

South County Alternatives
7751 Monterey Road
Gilroy 95020
(408) 842-3118

This project offers individual counseling for men and started in September 1978.

Stanislaus Women's Refuge Center (SWRC), Counseling Connection
430 12th Street
Suite D
Modesto 95354
(209) 578-1441

The Counseling Connection provides individual, group, and couple counseling for both women and men involved in domestic violence. Project staff also provide inservice training to agencies dealing with the batterer.

Youth and Family Services Bureau of the Hayward Police Department
300 West Winston Avenue
Hayward 94544
(415) 881-7048

The bureau provides crisis intervention and short-term marital counseling. Services began in 1973.

Women's Alliance (WOMA)
349 Willow Street
San Jose 95110
(408) 298-3505

WOMA operates a pilot project that offers a ten-week bilingual (English/ Spanish) counseling program.

Colorado

Abusing Men Exploring New Directions (AMEND)
144 West Colfax Avenue
Suite 302
Denver 80202
(303) 575-2621 (Office)
(303) 289-4441 (twenty-four-hour crisis line)

AMEND, a community-based program, has provided self-help group counseling since 1978.

Family Violence Counseling Service
830 Kipling Street
Suite 306
Lakewood 80215
(303) 234-1501
(303) 234-1525

Formerly counselors for a battered women's shelter, Egan and MacDonald provide individual counseling and offer two men's groups for batterers. The service began in March 1979.

Women's Assistance Services (WAS), Alternative to Family Violence
P.O. Box 385
Commerce City 80037
(303) 289-4441 (twenty-four-hour crisis line)

The program provides individual, couple, and group counseling to men on both a voluntary and court-referral basis.

Connecticut

Men and Stress Control of the Bridgeport Division of the YMCA
651 State Street
Bridgeport 06604
(203) 334-5551

Men and Stress Control is a group-counseling program for men who are physically abusive toward their wives or girlfriends or who feel they may lose control of their tempers in the future. It began in January 1980.

Salvation Army Family Service Bureau
855 Asylum Avenue
Hartford 06105
(203) 278-0240

In 1976, the Family Service Bureau began to provide individual and marital counseling.

Delaware

Family Violence Program of Child, Inc.
11th and Washington Streets
Wilmington 19801
(302) 655-3311

This private, nonprofit organization provides individual and short-term counseling services and began in 1979.

Peoples Place II
13 North Church Avenue

Milford 19963
(302) 422-8011

This agency provides individual counseling and offers a batterers' group that
started in September 1979.

District of Columbia

Hotline (Families and Children in Trouble)
36th Street, N.W.
Washington, D.C. 20007
965-1900 (Office)
628-FACT (twenty-four-hour crisis line)

This is a private, nonprofit community organization opened in 1976. Hot
line staff provide crisis counseling and referral.

Indiana

Family Violence Workshops of the Family Service Agency
225 North 4th Street
Lafayette 47901
(312) 423-5361

The project provides individual, couple, and group counseling. Services
began in September 1979.

**Men's Group for Temper Control, South Central Mental Health Founda-
tion**
640 South Rogers Street
Bloomington 47401
(812) 339-1691

The agency provides individual and marital counseling for battering men, as
well as a group for men with violent tempers. It began in January 1978.

Kentucky

Family Counseling Service
620 Euclid Avenue
Lexington 40502
(606) 266-0425

The services provided include individual, marital, group, and family counseling. These services have been provided since January 1980.

Lansdowne Mental Health Center
P.O. Box 790
Ashland 41101
(606) 324-1141

This program began in September 1979 and provides individual and couple counseling.

Maryland

Abused Persons Program Community Crisis Center
4910 Auburn Avenue
Bethesda 20014
(301) 654-1881 (twenty-four-hour crisis line)

Program services are limited to men referred by the state attorney's office or the court. The program's group for batterers began in April 1980. Plans are being made to include voluntary participants in the group.

Carrol County Battered Spouse Program
22 North Court Street
Westminster 21157
(301) 876-1233

The program, which began in 1977, is operated by Maryland Children's Aid Family Service Society. The program provides individual, marital, and family counseling.

House of Ruth
2437 Maryland Avenue
Baltimore 21218
(301) 889-0840 (Office)
(301) 889-7884 (twenty-four-hour crisis line)

Services began in April 1979 and include a twenty-four-hour crisis line and individual, group, and couple counseling. The project accepts court referrals.

Therapy for Abusive Behavior (TAB)
1211 Wall Street
Baltimore 21230

(301) 396-4340
or
271 Thelma Avenue
Glen Burnie 21060
(301) 761-7446

TAB provides group counseling for couples, group counseling for men who batter, and individual counseling.

Massachusetts

EMERGE
25 Huntington Avenue
Boston 02116
(617) 267-7690

EMERGE is a men's organization that focuses on men who batter. The project provides individual and group counseling.

Franklin/Hampshire Community Mental Health Center
P.O. Box 625
Northampton 01060
(413) 586-1257

The center offers a ten-week group educational program for batterers. The program, which accepts court referrals, began in January 1980.

Michigan

The Assailant Program
25 Sheldon Boulevard, S.E.
Grand Rapids 49503
(616) 451-2744

The Assailant Program is sponsored by the YWCA Community Center. The program started in 1979 and provides individual, couple, group, and family counseling.

Assailants Program
23 Strong Avenue
Muskegon 49441
(616) 726-4493

Services began in 1979 and include individual, group, and couple counseling.

Domestic Violence Project
202 East Huron
Suite 101
Ann Arbor 48104
(313) 995-5447
(313) 995-5444 (twenty-four-hour crisis line)

This private, nonprofit organization offers individual and couple counseling free of charge. Services for men began in 1979.

Shelter, Inc., Assailants Diversionary Program
P.O. Box 797
Alpena 49707
(517) 356-9650 (twenty-four-hour crisis line)

The diversionary program began in February 1979 and provides individual counseling on both a self-referred and court-referred basis.

Spouse Abuse Counseling
24331 Van Born Road
Taylor 48180
(313) 292-5690

Spouse Abuse Counseling is sponsored by Catholic Social Services. Since 1978, it has provided individual and marital counseling.

Minnesota

Domestic Abuse Project
2445 Park Avenue, South
Minneapolis 55404
(612) 870-8643

This project has as a major component group treatment for men who batter. The project also provides group counseling for women and therapy for children. The project formally began in January 1980.

Men and Women in Violent Relationships, Family and Children's Services
414 South 8th Street
Minneapolis 55404
(612) 340-7444

The family-service agency provides individual, group, and couple group counseling. Services began in 1977.

Men in Violent Relationships Project
P.O. Box 14299
University Station
Minneapolis 55414
(612) 729-8404 (Office)
(612) 874-1985 (Twenty-four-hour crisis line)

This nonprofit community organization has provided hot line counseling and referrals since 1978.

Violent Partner Program Family Service of Duluth
424 West Superior Street
Duluth 55802
(218) 722-7766

This family-service agency began to provide individual, marital, family, and couple counseling in 1977.

Missouri

Raven
P.O. Box 24159
St. Louis 63130
(314) 533-3372 (Monday–Friday, 7–10 P.M.)

Raven is a counseling and self-help organization for men. Its focus is on men who have been abusive to women. The staff provides crisis intervention and short- and long-term individual and group counseling. It began in October 1978.

Montana

Group for Battering Men, Family Court Services
Courthouse Annex
Great Falls 59501
(406) 761-6700

Individual, group, and marital counseling have been available since 1978.

Outpatient Services of the North Central Montana Community Mental Health Center
P.O. Box 3048
Great Falls 59403
(406) 761-2100

Outpatient services of the center include individual, marital, and group counseling that began in 1978.

Nebraska

Family Service Association of Lincoln
1133 H Street
Lincoln 68508
(402) 476-3327

The Family Service Association offers a counseling program for men and their families who are experiencing difficulties controlling their anger or aggressive behavior. Emphasis is placed on cognitive, interactional, and communication processes.

New Jersey

Alternatives to Domestic Violence of the Bergen County CAP
215 Union Street
Hackensack 07601
(201) 487-8484 (Twenty-four-hour crisis line)

The project offers individual, couple, group, and family counseling. It began in October 1978.

The Resolve Programs Plainfield Area Chapter of the American Red Cross
332 West Front Street
Plainfield 07060
(201) 756-0900

The project offers individual and family counseling.

Veterans Administration Hospital Violence Clinic
East Orange 07018
(201) 676-1000

Services are provided to veterans and include a psychiatric diagnosis, psychological evaluation, and a treatment program.

New Mexico

Esperanza
P.O. Box 5701
Santa Fe 87501
(505) 988-9731 (twenty-four-hour crisis line)

This project for battered families began in March 1978 to provide individual, couple, and group counseling. A group specifically for men who batter began in January 1980.

New York

Abused Women's Aid in Crisis (AWAIC)
G.P.O. 1699
New York 10116
(212) 686-3628 (Office)
(212) 686-1676 (Crisis line)

AWAIC's services include individual and group counseling for batterers. All men in the program participate voluntarily. Services began in January 1980.

Couple Communications, Inc.
574 Metropolitan Avenue
Brooklyn 11211
(212) 387-6902 (Twenty-four-hour crisis line)

The nonprofit organization, which began in December 1976, offers individual, group, and couple counseling.

Erie County Medical Center, Referral Outpatient
462 Grider Street
Buffalo 14215
(716) 898-3368

The outpatient department provides individual and marital therapy for men who batter. The psychiatry department of the center operates a twenty-four-hour walk-in mental-health-emergency center that provides crisis intervention and psychiatric evaluation.

The Humanistic Assemblage
141–155 85th Road
Jamaica 11435
(212) 297-1166

The assemblage is a private-practice organization that provides individual and group counseling.

Partners Anonymous, Inc.
159-34 Riverside Drive
New York 10032
(212) 586-6525

Partners Anonymous is a nonprofit organization dedicated to eliminating family violence. Services include individual and group psychotherapy and consultation.

Spouse Abuse Educational Workshop, Volunteer Counseling Service of Rockland County, Inc.
15 South Main Street
New City 10956
(914) 634-5729

The Spouse Abuse Educational Workshop is funded by an ACTION grant. The Volunteer Counseling Service, offering couple and family counseling, as well as educational workshops and other specialized programs, is a private nonprofit community organization.

Victims Information Bureau
496 Smithtown Bypass
Smithtown 11787
(516) 360-3730 (Office)
(516) 360-3606 (Twenty-four-hour crisis line)

This project is a community program that provides group, couple, and individual counseling and crisis intervention.

North Carolina

Focus
P.O. Box 1137
Greensboro 27402
(919) 272-0284

Focus offers individual advocacy for men and an eight-week-group-counseling program. The group-counseling program started in January 1980.

Resolve
108 Highland Avenue
Fayetteville 28305
(919) 323-4187

Resolve offers a six-week group-counseling program as well as individual counseling for men who batter.

Oregon

Men's Resource Center Counseling Service
3534 Southeast Main
Portland 97214
(502) 235-3433

The center is a private, nonprofit community organization that provides individual counseling.

Pennsylvania

Task Force on Men and Violence of the Pittsburgh Men's Collective
5512 Bartlett Street
Pittsburgh 15217
(412) 421-6405

The men's collective which began services in 1977, offers referral services, group counseling and rap and support groups, as well as consultation and education.

Tennessee

Alpha
5796 North Foxburrow Circle
Memphis 38118
(901) 362-0295

Alpha's program for men who batter requires that men attend individual counseling sessions, followed by group sessions. In the second phase of the program, group relationship counseling is offered to both the batterer and the victim.

Family Crisis Center
2535 Magnolia Avenue
Knoxville 37914
(615) 637-8000

The center began individual, group, and residential services in 1978.

Texas

Family Services Association of Lubbock
1220 Broadway
Suite 1405
Lubbock 79401
(806) 747-3488

Family Services provides individual, couple, and family counseling.

Houston Area Women's Center Council for Abused Women
Room E-435
University of Texas School of Public Health
6905 Bertner Street
Houston 77030
(713) 792-4664 (Crisis line, 9–9, Monday through Friday)

Services for men at the center began in March 1980 and include individual, marital, and group counseling.

Mental Hygiene Clinic, Veterans Administration Outpatient
1205 Texas Avenue
Lubbock 79401
(806) 762-7494

The clinic provides individual, group, marital, and family counseling on an outpatient basis to veterans. The clinic also offers relaxation and assertiveness training.

Washington

Domestic Assault Program, Psychology Service
American Lake Veterans Administration Medical Center
Tacoma 98493
(206) 582-8440, Ext. 383

The outpatient program is open only to veterans and their families. Services include individual and group counseling. Couple counseling is available only after violence has stopped.

Family Violence Project
11101 Northeast 8th Street
Bellevue 98004
(206) 477-3871

The project has provided individual, marital, and men's group counseling since 1978.

Hay and Nickle Associates
1704½ 4th Avenue
Olympia 98506
(206) 357-8293

The program provides individual, group, and couple therapy including specific programs for assaultive men. Referral sources include court and shelters for battered women.

Men's Counseling Program
405 Broadway
Tacoma 98402
(206) 383-2593

The YWCA Women's Support Shelter sponsors this program that offers men's and couples' groups. Services began in 1976, and the men's component began in 1978.

Northwest Treatment Associates
315 West Galer Street
Seattle 98119
(206) 283-8099

Northwest Treatment Associates operates as a private practice. Individual and couple therapy began in 1977.

Women's Association for Self-Help (WASH)
P.O. Box 2023
Bellevue 98004
(206) 454-WASH

Services for men began in January 1977 and include individual and couple counseling.

West Virginia

Northern Panhandle Mental Health Center
2121 Eoff Street
Wheeling 26003
(304) 233-6250 (Twenty-four-hour crisis line)

The center provides individual and group therapy, support groups, and consultation and education.

Wisconsin

Family Services, Alternatives to Aggression
214 North Hamilton
Madison 53703
(608) 251-7611

This agency began group services in 1978 and individual and couple counseling services in 1976.

Wyoming

Self-Help Center
1515 Burlington Street
Casper 82601
(307) 235-2814

The center initially provided services only to women. Services were expanded in June 1979 to include individual counseling for men who batter.

7 Services for Women

Alabama

Committee on Domestic Violence
2818 Dorchester Drive, S.E.
Decatur 35601

Domestic Abuse Shelter, Inc.
Box 4752
Montgomery 36101

Family Violence Project, Women's Center
2230 Highland Avenue
Birmingham 35205
(205) 322-1915

Penelope House, Inc.
P.O. Box 6871
Mobile 36606
(205) 471-1771 (Crisis)
(205) 471-1795 (Office)

Services: Legal aid (court costs only); counseling; referral; hot line (twenty-four hours); housing (maximum capacity fifteen to twenty, maximum three weeks, children permitted); child care.

Safe Place
316 Bayless Street
Florence 35630

Serve, Inc.
742 Ninth Avenue West
Birmingham 35204

Spouse Abuse Network
P.O. Box 4752
Montgomery 35401
(205) 556-3300

Women's Center
2230 Highland Avenue
Birmingham 35205
(205) 322-1915

Alaska

Aiding Women in Abuse and Rape Emergency
P.O. Box 809
Juneau 99802
(907) 586-6624

Services: Legal aid; counseling; referral; hot line (twenty-four hours); housing; child care; transportation.

Alaska Family Violence Project
338 Denali Street
Anchorage 99510

Arctic Women's Group
P.O. Box 69
Barrow 99723

AWAIC, Inc.
417 West Eighth Street
Anchorage 99501
(907) 274-4561

Services: Legal aid; counseling; referral; hot line (twenty-four hours); housing; child care; transportation.

Bering Sea Women's Coalition
P.O. Box 1596
Nome 99762
(907) 443-5259

Services: Legal aid; counseling; referral; child care; hot line (twenty-four hours); housing; transportation.

Iliuliuk Family and Health Services
Unalaska 99685

Services: Legal aid; counseling; referral; child care; hot line (twenty-four hours); housing; transportation.

Kenai Women's Resource Center
P.O. Box 2464
Seldotna 99669
(907) 262-9760

Services: Counseling; referral; transportation; housing (in safe homes).

Kodiak Women's Resource Center
Kodiak 99615

Services: Crisis counseling; referral; hot line; housing (in safe homes).

Kotzebue Women's Crisis Center
P.O. Box 595
Kotzebue 99752

Sitkans against Violence
P.O. Box 1091
Sitka 99835

Tundra Women's Coalition
P.O. Box 1034
Bethel 99559
(907) 543-3455

Services: Legal aid; counseling; referral; hot line (twenty-four hours); housing; child care; transportation.

Women in Crisis Counseling and Assistance, Inc.
331 Fifth Avenue
Fairbanks 99701
(907) 452-RAPE (Crisis)
(907) 452-2293 (Office)

Services: Community education; counseling (crisis, long term, peer support, family); emergency transportation; hot line (twenty-four hours); referral; legal aid; liaison (police, medical); victim advocacy; housing (maximum capacity five, maximum two weeks, children permitted).

Women in Safe Homes (WISH)
P.O. Box 6552
Ketchikan 99901
(907) 225-2730

Services: Counseling; referral; hot line; housing (in safe homes).

Arizona

Alice Paul Shelter for Women
P.O. Box 142
Sierra Vista 85635

Center against Sexual Assault
1131 East Missouri
Phoenix 85014
(609) 257-8095 (Crisis)
(609) 279 9824 (Office)

Services: Hot line (twenty-four hours); referral.

Citizen Participation and Support Project
7012 North 58th Drive
Glendale 85301
(602) 931-5593

Services: Counseling; referral; hot line (twenty-four hours); child care; housing purchased for client.

Copper Basin Behavioral Health Services, Inc.
P.O. Box 116
Hayden 85235

Family Violence Coalition
P.O. Box 57
Tucson 85701

Services: Counseling and referral; community education.

Flagstaff Women's Resource, Inc.
3 North Leroux
Suite 201
Flagstaff 86001
(602) 774-2727 (Crisis)
(602) 774-7353 (Office)
(602) 774-1008 (Office)

Services: Counseling; referral; housing (temporary, in safe homes); hot line (8 A.M.–5 P.M., Monday–Friday).

Friends-of-the-Family
6825 East Osborne Road
Scottsdale 85251
(602) 949-7256

Services: Legal aid; counseling; referral; hot line; child care; housing (maximum capacity twelve to fifteen, maximum thirty to forty-five days, children permitted, sliding-scale fee).

Information & Referral Inc./Help-on-Call Crisis Line
2302 East Speedway, #210
Tucson 85719
(602) 323-9373

Services: Counseling; referral; hot line (twenty-four hours).

New Directions for Young Women
246 South Scott
Tucson 85701
(602) 623-3677

Services: Counseling; referral; child care (1–3 P.M.); advocacy groups; GED for all girls twelve to eighteen years of age.

Pima County Attorney's Victim/Witness Advocacy Program
111 West Congress Street
Suite 900
Tucson 85701
(602) 792-6921

Services: Counseling and referral.

Rainbow Retreat, Inc.
4332 North 12th Street
Phoenix 85014
(602) 263-1113

Services: Child care; community education; counseling (crisis, long term, peer support, family, outpatient); hot line (twenty-four hours); referral; housing (maximum capacity twenty-three, maximum forty-five days, sliding-scale fee, children permitted).

Sojourner Center
P.O. Box 2649
Phoenix 85602
(602) 258-5344

Services: Counseling; referral; hot line; housing (maximum capacity twenty-five, maximum seven days, children permitted).

Southern Arizona Legal Aid, Inc.
Family Law Unit

155 East Alameda
Tucson 85701
(602) 623-9461

Services: Legal aid; referral.

Tucson Center for Women and Children
419 South Stone Avenue
Tucson 85701
(612) 792-1929 (Crisis)
(612) 792-1933 (Home)

Services: Counseling; referral; hot line (twenty-four hours); child care; housing (sliding-scale fee, maximum capacity ten women, maximum one to two weeks, children permitted); nutrition program.

Arkansas

Advocates for Battered Women
P.O. Box 1954
Little Rock 72203
(501) 376-3219

Services: Community education; counseling (crisis, long-term, peer support, group); emergency medical treatment; emergency transportation; hot line (twenty-four hours); referral; legal aid; liaison; victim advocacy; housing (maximum thirty days, children permitted).

Northwest Arkansas Project for Battered Women and Their Families
P.O. Box 1168
Fayetteville 72701
(501) 521-1394

Services: Referral; hot line (twenty-four hours); housing; counseling.

Women in Crisis
P.O. Box 5832
Pine Bluff 71611
(501) 534-7465 (Office)
Contact: Kaye Evans, Kaye Bounds, Leslie Woodmansee.

Services: Emergency housing (local motels); hot line (twenty-four hours); advocacy; referrals (employment, financial assistance); community education; advocacy and referrals for rape victims.

California

Alliance on Family Violence
(Mental Health Association in Kern County)
459 Haberfelde Building
1706 Chester Avenue
Bakersfield 93301
(805) 322-HELP (Crisis)
(805) 322-0365 (Office)

Services: Community education; counseling (crisis); hot line (twenty-four hours); referral; housing (maximum two weeks, children permitted).

Ammon Henecy House
632 North Brittania, East
Los Angeles 90033

Battered Women's Alternatives
P.O. Box 1095
Lafayette 94549

Battered Women's Center
Yolo County
203 F Street
Davis 95616

The Battered Women's Project
2187 Ulric Street
Suite D
San Diego 92111
(714) 565-7197 (Crisis)
(714) 565-7198 (Office)

Services: Legal aid; counseling; referral; hot line (twenty-four hours).

Battered Women's Services
P.O. Box 4007
San Diego 92104
(714) 234-3164 (Crisis)
Contact: Ashley Walker Hooper.

Services: Community education; counseling; (crisis, long term, peer support, family, child, couple); hot line (twenty-four hours, seven days); referral; legal aid; liaison (police, medical); victim advocacy; housing (maximum capacity twenty-five, maximum thirty to fourty-five days, no charge, children permitted).

Berkeley Community YWCA Women's Refuge
2134 Allston Way
Berkeley 94704

Berkeley Women's Refuge
2134 Allison Way
Berkeley 94704
(415) 849-2314 (Crisis)
(415) 845-9256 (Office)

Services: Counseling; referral; hot line (twenty-four hours); housing (maximum seven to ten days, maximum capacity twenty-three, children permitted).

Calaveras Women's Crisis Line
Box 426
Angels Camp 95222

Call/Battered Women's Alternatives
1035 Carol Line
Lafayette 94549
(415) 284-CARE (Crisis)
(415) 837-6939 (Office)

Services: Legal aid ($15 first consultation, sliding-scale fee); counseling; referral; hot line (twenty-four hours); child care (during support groups).

Casa De Amparo
4070 Mission Avenue
Oceanside 92068
(714) 757-1200

Services: Child care (twenty-four hours); community education; counseling (crisis, peer support, family); emergency transportation; hot line (twenty-four hours); referral; victim advocacy.

Casa De Esperanza
P.O. Box 56
Yuba City 95991
(916) 674-2040 (Crisis)
(916) 674-5400 (Office)

Services: Community education; counseling (crisis, peer support, batterer); emergency medical treatment; emergency transportation; hot line (twenty-four hours); referral; legal aid; liaison (police, medical); victim advocacy; housing (maximum capacity fifteen, maximum sixty days, sliding-scale fee, children permitted).

Catalyst
P.O. Box 4184
Chico 95926

Services: Referral.

Center for the Pacific-Asian Family, Inc.
2140 West Olympic Boulevard
Room 250
Los Angeles 90006
(213) 388-0446 (Crisis)
(213) 388-3944 (Office)

Services: Community education; counseling; hot line (twenty-four hours); referral; liaison (police, medical); victim advocacy; housing (maximum thirty days, children permitted).

Center for Women's Studies and Services Underground Railroad
for Battered Women
908 F Street
San Diego 92101
(714) 233-3088 (Crisis)
(714) 233-8984 (Office)

Services: Community education; counseling (crisis, long term, group); hot line (twenty-four hours); referral; housing (children permitted).

Central Valley Mental Health Option House
P.O. Box 861
Colton 92324

Chicana Service Action Center Shelter For Battered Women, E.L.A.
2244 Beverly Blvd.
Los Angeles 90057
(213) 384-0422 (Crisis)
(213) 384-0441 (Office)

Services: Community education; counseling; emergency transportation; hot line (twenty-four hours); referral; liaison (police, medical, court); victim advocacy; housing (maximum capacity eight to ten; maximum twenty-four hours/three weeks, children permitted, bilingual: English/Spanish).

Coalition for Alternatives to Domestic Violence
P.O. Box 910
Riverside 92502
(714) 686-HELP

Services: Legal aid (sliding-scale fee); counseling; referral; hot line (twenty-four hours); child care (unlimited); housing (maximum fourteen days, charge $1/woman, $0.50/child, sliding-scale fee).

Coalition to Eliminate Domestic Violence
P.O. Box 484
Grass Valley 95945

Coalition for the Prevention of Abuse of Women and Children/Domestic Violence Outreach Center
566 North Lugo
San Bernardino 92410
(714) 885-6819 (Office)
Contact people: Bea McNeary, Dee Miles

Services: Community Education; counseling (crisis and peer support); emergency transportation; hot line (twenty-four hours); referral; legal aid; liaison (police, medical); victim advocacy; housing.

Committee for Abused Women's Shelter
856 South Realto
Oxnard 93030
(805) 486-2728

Committee for Napa Emergency Women's Shelter
5 Villa Maria
Novalto 94947

Community Assistance/Assault and Rape Emergency
P.O. Box 764
Fort Bragg 95437

Concept 7 Group Homes
Box 4747

Anaheim 92803
Contact: Hugh Margesson.

Cumings, Jordan, and Morgan
96 Jessie Street
San Francisco 94105
(415) 495-4495

Services: Legal aid (charge involved).

Domestic Violence Unit Community Legal Services of Santa Clara County
210 South 1st Street
San Jose 95103
(408) 998-5200

Services: Legal aid; counseling; referral.

Emergency Shelter Program, Inc.
24518 Mission Boulevard
Hayward 94544
(415) 881-1244 (Crisis)
(415) 881-1246 (Office)

Services: Counseling; referral; hot line (twenty-four hours); housing (maximum ten days, maximum capacity 23, children permitted, bilingual shelter).

Emergency Shelter Project
235 West Tulare, #1
Visalia 93277

Family Emergency Shelter
1794 Tahoe
Salinas 93906

Family Violence Program, Community Action Commission
P.O. Box 1429
Goleta 93017
(805) 962-5245 (Crisis)
(805) 964-0509 (Office)

Services: Child care; community education; counseling (crisis, peer support, batterer's diversion); emergency medical treatment; emergency transportation; food and clothing; hot line (twenty-four hours); referral; legal aid; liaison (police, medical, court); victim advocacy; housing (maximum capacity fifteen, maximum thirty days, charge $1/women, $0.25/child).

Family Violence Program Community Action Commission
533 North H Street
Lompoc 93017
(805) 736-0965

Services: Child care; community education; counseling (crisis, peer support, batterer's diversion); emergency medical treatment; emergency transportation; food and clothing; hot line (twenty-four hours); referral; legal aid; liaison (police, medical, court); victim advocacy; housing (maximum capacity twelve, maximum thirty days, $1/day, $0.25/child).

Friends of Battered Women
Box 377
Merced 95340

Good Shepherd Shelter
2561 Venice Street
Los Angeles 90019

Harbor Area YWCA Refuge and Services for Victims of Domestic Violence
437 West 9th Street
San Pedro 90731
(213) 547-9343 (Crisis)
(213) 547-0831 (Office)

Services: Counseling; referral; hot line; housing (maximum fourteen days, maximum capacity ten, children permitted).

Haven Hills, Inc.
P.O. Box 66
Canoga Park 91305
(213) 887-6589 (Crisis)
(213) 340-2632 (Office)

Service: Legal aid; counseling (sliding-scale fee); referral; hotline (twenty-four hours); housing (maximum thirty days, maximum capacity fifteen, children permitted).

Haven House, Inc.
P.O. Box 2007

Pasadena 91107
(213) 681-2626

Services: Legal aid (sliding-scale fee); counseling; referral; hot line
(twenty-four hours); child care; housing (maximum thirty days, maximum
capacity thirty-five, children permitted).

House of Ruth, Inc.
P.O. Box 457
Claremont 91711
(714) 988-5559 (Crisis)
(714) 988-0308 (Office)

Services: Community education; Batterer's Anonymous group; hot line
(twenty-four hours); referral; shelter opening in summer 1981.

Humboldt Women for Shelter
P.O. Box 775
850 G Street
Suite H
Arcata 95521
(707) 822-5286 (Crisis)
(707) 822-7940 (Office)

Services: Community education; counseling (crisis, peer support); emergency transportation; hot line (9A.M.–9 P.M., Monday through Friday);
referral; liaison (police, medical); victim advocacy; housing (maximum
capacity three, maximum three days, children permitted).

Interface Community
3475 Old Conejo Road
Newbury Park 91320

Interval House
P.O. Box 3151
Seal Beach 90740

Jenesse Center, Inc.
P.O. Box 73837
Los Angeles 90003
(213) 582-4523 (Crisis)
Contact: Margaret Cambricee.

Services: Child care (7:30 A.M.–5:30 P.M.); community education; counseling (crisis, peer support, family, handicap shelter); emergency medical

treatment; emergency transportation; hot line (twenty-four hours); referral; liaison (police, medical); victim advocacy; housing (maximum capacity eighteen, maximum sixty days, $1/day, children permitted); job training and placement.

La Casa de las Madres
P.O. Box 15147
San Francisco 94115
(415) 626-9343 (Crisis)
(415) 626-7859 (Office)

Services: Legal aid; counseling; referral; child care; housing (maximum capacity thirty, children permitted).

Legal Aid Foundation of Long Beach
4790 East Pacific Coast Highway
Long Beach 90804
(213) 434-7421

Services: Legal aid; counseling; referral.

Lompoc Shelter
c/o Family Violence Program
P.O. Box 1429
Goleta 93101

Los Angeles Commission on Assaults against Women/Los Angeles Rape and Battery Hotline
5410 Wilshire Boulevard, #34
Los Angeles 90036
(213) 392-8381 (Crisis)
(213) 938-3662 (Office)
Contact: Judy Ravitz.

Services: Community education; crisis and family counseling; hot line (twenty-four hours); referral; legal aid; liaison (police, medical, and court); victim advocacy.

Marin Abused Women's Services
P.O. Box 2924
San Rafael 94901
(415) 924-6616 (Crisis)
(415) 457-4413 (Office)

Services: Legal aid; counseling; referral; hot line (twenty-four hours); child care (hours by arrangement); housing (maximum twenty-eight days, maximum capacity ten, children permitted).

Mariposa House
Box 2789
Santa Cruz 95062

Mariposa House Battered Women Shelter Project
P.O. Box 1123
Apto 95003
(408) 476-1489

Services: Legal aid; counseling; referral; hot line (twenty-four hours); child care; housing (maximum capacity fifteen, maximum four to six weeks, children permitted).

Mid-Peninsula Support Network
655 Castro Street
Suite 6
Mountain View 94041

Mother Lode's Crisis Center/Shelter
P.O. Box 3061
Sonora 95370

Mother's Emergency Stress Service
2515 J Street
Sacramento 95816
(916) 446-7811 (Crisis)
(916) 446-2791 (Home)

Services: Legal aid; counseling; referral; hot line (twenty-four hours); housing (maximum sixty days, maximum capacity fifteen, children permitted); pre-child-abuse and child-abuse counseling.

Mountain Sisters Collective
P.O. Box 426
Old Bank Mall
Angels Camp 95222
(209) 736-2723 (Crisis)
(209) 736-4801 (Office)

Services: Counseling; referral; community education.

Oakwood Wesley House
617 Broadway
Venice 90291

Option House
P.O. Box 861

Colton 92335
(714) 874-5570

Our House, Friends of Battered Women and Women's Shelter
P.O. Box 377
Merced 95340
(209) 383-7233 (Crisis)
(209) 383-7255 (Office)

Services: Community education; counseling (crisis, peer support, outside support group); emergency transportation; hot line (twenty-four hours); referral; liaison (police, medical, legal); victim advocacy; housing (maximum capacity fifteen, maximum six weeks, charge $1/woman, $0.25/child).

Our House Women's Shelter
Box 377
Merced 95340

Our Refuge For Battered Spouses
c/o 18781 Midland Way
Madera 93637

Pacific-Asian Rape Care-Line
c/o Council of Asian/Pacific Organizations
1543 West Olympic Boulevard
Room 323
Los Angeles 90015
(213) 388-0446

Services: Counseling; referral; hot line (8:30 A.M.–5 P.M., Monday through Friday); housing (planned); multilingual staff; prevention workshops.

Phoenix House YWCA
735 East Lexington
Glendale 92106

Placer Rape Crisis Line
701 High Street, #202
Auburn 95603

Porterville Mission Project Shelter
P.O. Box 2035
Porterville 93257

Project Sanctuary
P.O. Box 995
280 Oak Street
Ukiah 95482

Quest Center
2940 16th Street, #104
San Francisco 94103
(415) 861-2292
Contact: Rebecca Rodriguez

Services: Counseling; support groups; referrals (child care, legal aid, medical); preemployment counseling and testing; workshops; financial assistance.

Riverside Country Coalition/Alternatives to Domestic Violence
Box 910
Riverside 92502

Rosasharon
P.O. Box 4583
North Hollywood 91607
(213) 769-4237 (Crisis)
(213) 781-2722 (Crisis)
(213) 985-2006 (Office)

Services: Counseling; referral; hot line (twenty-four hours); child care; housing (maximum thirty to forty-five days, maximum thirty to forty, children permitted).

A Safe Place
P.O. Box 275
Oakland 94604
(415) 444-7233

Services: Legal aid; counseling; referral; hot line (twenty-four hours); child care; housing (maximum capacity thirty, maximum six weeks, children permitted, charge $1/adult, $0.50/child).

Salinas Family Emergency Center
6 West Gabilan #18
Salinas 93901

San Diego Women for Shelter
Box 81961
San Diego 92138

San Francisco Women's Center
63 Brady Street
San Francisco 94103
(415) 431-1180

Services: Legal aid; referral; housing.

San Joaquin Commisssion on the Status of Women, Task Force on Domestic Violence
215 West Stadium Drive
Stockton 95204
(209) 463-6957

Services: Community education; counseling (peer support); referral; liaison (police); victim advocacy.

San Mateo Women's Shelter
P.O. Box 652
San Mateo 94401
(415) 342-0850

Services: Legal aid; counseling; referral; hot line; child care; housing (maximum one month, children permitted).

Santa Barbara County Family Violence Program, Counseling/Diversion Component
c/o District Attorney's Office
118 Figueroa Street
Santa Barbara 93101
(805) 963-7100 (Office)
Contact: Roberta Foreman.

Services: Community education; counseling (crisis, long term); victim advocacy; housing referral; diversion counseling for offenders.

Santa Barbara Shelter
c/o Family Violence Program
P.O. Box 1429
Goleta 93101

Santa Monica Hospital Medical Center
1225 15th Street
Santa Monica 90404
(213) 451-1511

Services: Counseling; referral; medical care.

Save, Inc.
P.O. Box 2246
Fremont 94536

Shasta County Women's Refuge
Box 4211
Redding 96001

Shattered Women's Shelter
Box 520
Redondo Beach 90277

Sojourn
Ocean Park Community Center
245 Hill Street
Santa Monica 90405
(213) 399-9228

Services; Counseling; referral; hot line (twenty-four hours); child care; housing (maximum thirty days, maximum capacity four, children permitted).

Sojourn Shelter
925 Stonehill Lane
Los Angeles 90049

Solano Center for Battered Women
P.O. Box 2051
Fairfield 94533
(707) 429-HELP (Crisis)
(707) 425-9768 (Home)

Services; Counseling; referral; hot line (twenty-four hours); housing (maximum capacity six, children permitted).

South County Alternative
La Isla Pacifica
P.O Box 1326
Gilroy 95020
(408) 683-4118 (Crisis)
(408) 842-3118 (Office)

Services: Community education; counseling (crisis, long-term, peer support, family, batterers); emergency transportation; referral; liaison (police, medical); victim advocacy; housing; (maximum capacity fifteen, maximum one month, children permitted); all services in Spanish.

Southeast Emergency Quarters
4996 Holly Street
San Diego 92113

Stanislaus Women's Refuge Center
P.O. Box 2227
Modesto 95351

Su Casa Family Crisis and Support Center
12305 East 207 Street
Lakewood 90715
(213) 868-3800 (Crisis)
(213) 860-3921 (Office)
Contact: Petra Medelez.

Services: Counseling; hot line (twenty-four hours); referral; victim advocacy; housing (maximum capacity fifteen, maximum thirty days, children permitted).

Tri-Valley Haven for Women
P.O. Box 188
Livermore 94550
(415) 443-1955

Services: Counseling groups; referral; hot line (twenty-four hours); child care (limited); housing (maximum capacity ten, maximum thirty to sixty days, children permitted).

Tulare County Emergency Shelter Project
515 West School Street
Visalia, California 93277
(209) 732-5941 (Crisis)
(209) 732-0906 (Office)

Services: Counseling (crisis); emergency transportation; hot line (twenty-four hours); referral; liaison (police, medical); victim advocacy; housing (maximum capacity twenty, maximum thirty days, sliding-scale fee, children permitted).

Violence in the Family Project, Community Action Commission
735 State Street

Santa Barbara 93102
(805) 968-2556 (Crisis)
(805) 963-1526 (Office)

Services: Legal aid (sliding-scale fee); referral; hot line (twenty-four hours); housing (client advocate, small demonstration shelter).

Volunteers of America Brandon House, Emergency Shelter for Women and Children
1716 East San Antonio Street
San Jose 95116
(408) 258-3200 (Crisis)
(408) 258-3201 (Office)

Services: Child care (9 A.M. −5 P.M., Monday through Friday); community education; counseling (crisis, peer support, family, spiritual); emergency medical treatment; emergency transportation; hot line (twenty-four hours); referral; housing (maximum capacity forty, maximum thirty days, charge $10/day, children permitted).

Weave, Incorporated
P.O. Box 161356
Sacramento 95816

Weed
Station A
Box 111
Auburn 95603

The Women's Alliance (WOMA)
1509 East Santa Clara Street
San Jose 95116
(408) 251-6655

Services: Legal aid; counseling; referral; hot line; housing.

Woman Haven, Incorporated
P.O. Box 747
Hotville 92250

Womanspace Shelter for Battered Women
P.O. Box 106994
Sacramento 95816

(916) 446-7811 (Crisis)
(916) 446-2791 (Office)

Services: Legal aid; counseling; referral; hot line (twenty-four hours); child care; housing (maximum fifty-six days, maximum capacity fifteen, children permitted).

Women Against Domestic Violence
Box 196, Route 1
Carmel Highlands 93921

Women Against Emergency Services (WAVES)
P.O. Box 1121
Berkeley 94701
(415) 893-4357 (Crisis)
(415) 848-9130 (Office)
Contact: Valerie Herst.

Services: Hot line (twenty-four hours); counseling; referrals; legal advocacy; weekly support groups; community education.

Women and Child Crisis Shelter Incorporated
P.O. Box 1231
Whittier 90609

Women Encouraging Enterprise and Development (WEED)
Station A
P.O. Box 111
Auburn 95603
(916) 885-8406

Services: Legal aid; counseling; referral; hot line (twenty-four hours); housing (children permitted).

Women Escaping a Violent Environment
1606 H Street
Sacramento 95816
(916) 920-2952
(916) 448-2321
Contact: Marna Jones.

Services: Child services; community education; counseling; male positive anger control counseling; emergency transportation; hot line (twenty-four hours); referral, victim advocacy; housing.

Women's Center/San Joaquin Company Domestic Violence Project
930 Commerce
Stockton 95202

Women's Crisis Center
616 South Glendora
West Covina 91790

Women's Crisis Support
640 Capitola Road
Santa Cruz 95062
(408) 425-2058

Services: Counseling; referral; hot line (twenty-four hours)

Women's Litigation Unit, Neighborhood Legal Assistance
1095 Market Street
San Francisco 94103
(415) 626-3819

Services: Legal aid (residence and low-income requirement).

Womenspace, Unlimited
P.O. Box 13111
South Lake Tahoe 95702

Women's Resource Center, Incorporated
4070 Mission Avenue
Room 220
San Luis Rey 92068
(714) 757-3500

Services: Counseling; referral; hot line; housing (maximum capacity fifteen, maximum one day, children permitted).

Women's Shelter
P.O. Box 4222
Long Beach 90804
(213) 437-4663

Services: Counseling; referral; hot line; child care (for residents); housing (maximum twenty-eight days, maximum capacity twenty-one, children permitted).

Women's Shelter Program, San Luis Obispo Company
P.O. Box 125
San Luis Obispo 93406

Women's Transitional Living Center, Incorporated
P.O. Box 6103
Orange 92667
(714) 992-1931

Services: Counseling (donation requested); referral; child care; housing (charge $1/woman, $0.25/child, maximum thirty days, maximum capacity eighteen).

Women United Against Battering
P.O. Box 893
Placerville 95667
(916) 622-1235 (Crisis)
(916) 626-0338 (Office)

Services: Counseling; referral; hot line; child care; housing (maximum five days, children permitted).

YWCA
Fresno 93706

YWCA Marjorie Mason Center for Victims of Domestic Violence
1660 M Street
Fresno 93721
(209) 237-4701
Contact: Cindy Morrow, Norma Quintero.

Services: Child care; community education; counseling; (crisis, long term, peer support, family, and counseling to batterers); emergency transportation; hot line (twenty-four hours); referral; legal aid; liaison (police, medical, welfare); victim advocacy; housing (maximum capacity twenty-five, maximum three weeks, $1/day, children permitted).

YWCA Wings
P.O. Box 1464
West Covina 91793

YWCA Women Against Domestic Violence
P.O. Box 1362
Monterey 93940
(408) 649-0834

Services: Referral; hot line (10 A.M.–10 P.M.); housing (maximum fourteen days, maximum capacity thirty, children permitted, sliding-scale fee).

YWCA Women's Emergency Shelter
P.O. Box 3506
Santa Rosa 95402
(707) 546-1234 (Crisis)
(707) 546-1477 (Office)

Services: Legal aid; counseling; referral; hot line; child care.

YWCA Womenshelter
3636 Atlantic Avenue
Long Beach 90807

Youth and Family Services Bureau of the Hayward Police Department
300 West Winton
Hayward 94544
(415) 881-7049

Services: Counseling (crisis, family); hot line; referral; liaison (police).

Colorado

Abused and Battered Humans, Incorporated
1052 Barclay
Craig 81625
(303) 824-2923

Advocates for Victims of Assault
Alpine Mental Health
Box 565
Breckenridge 80424
(303) 453-2757

Alternative Horizons
333 13th Street
Durango 81301
(303) 247-5245

Alternatives
Box 385
Commerce City 80037
(303) 289-4441

Battered Women Project
205 North 4th Street
Grand Junction 81501
(303) 242-0190

Services: Counseling; referral; hot line (twenty-four hours); child care; housing (maximum fourteen days, children permitted).

Battered Women Project, Women's Resource Center
4th and Rood
Grand Junction 81501
(303) 243-0190

Services: Counseling; referral; hot line (twenty-four hours); housing (maximum fourteen days, maximum capacity four women, sliding-scale fee, children permitted).

Battered Women Services
12 North Meade
Colorado Springs 80907
(303) 633-4601 (Office)
(303) 471-HELP (Evenings and weekends)

Services: Counseling; referral; hot line (twenty-four hours); housing (in private homes, children permitted).

Boulder County Safehouse
P.O. Box 4157
Boulder 80306
(303) 449-8623

Boulder County Women's Resource Center
1406 Pine Street
Boulder 80302
(303) 447-9670

Services: Counseling; referral.

Brandun Guest House
1260 Pennsylvania
Denver 80203
(303) 832-7826

Services: Counseling; referral; hot line (twenty-four hours); child care; housing (maximum twenty-eight days, maximum fifty, children permitted).

Columbine Center
1331 Columbine
Denver 80206
(303) 399-0082 (Crisis)
(303) 399-4554 (Office)

Services: Legal aid (sliding-scale fee); counseling (sliding-scale fee); referral; hot line (twenty-four hours); child care; housing (maximum thirty days, maximum capacity twenty-five to thirty, children permitted).

Crossroads Shelter
P.O. Box 993
Fort Collins 80522
(303) 482-3502

Domestic Violence Prevention Center
P.O. Box 2662
Colorado Springs 80901
(303) 633-1462

Fremont County Task Force on Wife Abuse
Box 308
Canon City 81212
(303) 275-2318

Gateway
P.O. Box 914
Aurora 80040
(303) 343-1851

Longmont Coalition/Women in Crisis
P.O. Box 1458
Longmont 80501
(303) 772-0432

Park County Mental Health
P.O. Box 1694
Bailey 80421
(303) 838-7981 or 838-7653

Safe House
P.O. Box 18014
Denver 80218

(303) 388-4703 (Crisis)
(303) 388-4268 (Office)

Services: Legal aid; counseling; referral; hot line (10 A.M.–5 P.M.); child care; housing (maximum ninety days, capacity thirty, children permitted).

Tu Casa, Incorporated
1015 4th Street
Alamosa 81101
(303) 589-3671 (Mental health)
Contact: Cynthia Sandoval (589-4993).

Women in Crisis (WIC)
5250 Marshall Street
Arvada 80003
(303) 420-6752

Women in Crisis
P.O. Box 1955
Evergreen 80439
(303) 232-0996 (Crisis)
(303) 674-5504, 234-1494 (Home)

Services: Legal aid (sliding-scale fee); counseling; referral; hot line (twenty-four hours) child care; housing (maximum capacity forty, children permitted).

Women in Crisis
1426 Pierce Street
Lakewood 80214
(303) 232-0996 (Crisis)
(303) 234-1494 (Office)

Services: Legal aid, counseling, referral; hot line (twenty-four hours); housing (sliding-scale fee, maximum twenty-eight days, maximum capacity forty, children permitted).

Women's Assistance Services
P.O. Box 385
6571 Kearney
Commerce City 80037
(303) 289-4441

Services: Counseling; referral; advocacy; housing (maximum capacity twenty-six, children permitted, charge $1.75/person/day for food, $3.50/family/day for housing).

Women's Resource Center
1059 Rood Avenue
Grand Junction 81501
(303) 243-0190

Women's Resource Center
307 Main Street
Suite 7
Montrose 81401

YWCA Family Crisis Shelter
801 North Sante Fe
Pueblo 81003
(303) 545-8195

York Street Center
1632 York Street
Denver 80206
(303) 333-5626 (Crisis)
(303) 321-8191 (Sexual assault only)
(303) 388-0834 (Office)

Services: Legal aid; counseling; referral, hot line (twenty-four hours); child care (daytime only); housing (maximum fourteen days).

Connecticut

Battered Women's Program
551 Westcott Road
Danielson 06239

Battered Women's Project
P.O. Box 663
Meriden 06450
(203) 238-1501

Services: Information; referral; peer support; victim advocacy; housing.

Battered Women's Service
c/o YWCA
1862 East Main Street
Bridgeport 06610
(203) 334-6154

Services: Information; referral; peer support; victim advocacy; housing.

Battered Women's Services
256 Main Street
Danbury 06810

Battered Women's Task Force Stand, Incorporated
246 Main Street
Derby 06418
(203) 735-9553

Services: Counseling; referral.

Catholic Family Services
90 Franklin Square
New Britain 06051
(203) 225-3561

Services: Counseling (sliding-scale fee); referral.

Connecticut Task Force on Abused Women
148 Orange Street
New Haven 06510
(203) 562-1816

Services: Information on state services: referral.

Genesis House
P.O. Box 572
New London 06320
(203) 447-0366
Contact: Barbara Greenberg

Services: Child care (ten hours/week); community education; counseling (crisis, peer support, family, single parent); emergency medical treatment; emergency transportation; hot line (twenty-four hours); referral; legal aid; liaison (police, medical); victim advocacy; housing (maximum capacity twelve, maximum six weeks, children permitted).

Hartford Interval House
Hartford 06105
(203) 527-0550

Services: Information; referral; peer support; victim advocacy; housing.

Lower Naugatuck Valley Battered Women Project
P.O. Box 327

Ansonia 06497
(203) 736-0052

Services: Shelter, hot line (twenty-four hour); community overflow housing; community education support groups; legal advocacy; transportation; coalition member; brochure available.

Meriden-Wallingford Battered Women's Shelter
P.O. Box 663
Meriden 06450
(203) 238-1501

Services: Shelter; hot line (twenty-four hour); state housing; community education; support groups; legal advocacy; child care; transportation; coalition member; brochure available.

New Haven Legal Assistance Association
339 Temple Street
New Haven 06511
(203) 436-8230

Services: Legal aid; counseling; referral.

New Haven Project for Battered Women
P.O. Box 1329
New Haven 06505
(203) 789-8104

Services: Counseling; referral; hot line (9 A.M.–5 P.M.); child care; emergency housing.

Prudence Crandall Center for Women
P.O. Box 895
New Britain 06050
(203) 225-6357
(203) 229-6939

Services: Counseling; referral; child care; housing (maximum sixty days, maximum capacity ten women, children permitted).

Shelter Services for Abused Women
YWCA of Greater Bridgeport
1862 East Main
Bridgeport 06610

Sojourn House
Box 758
Middletown 06457

Task Force on Abused Women
Bridgeport 06610
(203) 334-6154

Services: Information; referral; peer support; victim advocacy; housing.

Task Force on Abused Women
Danielson 06239
(203) 774-2020

Services: Information; referral; peer support; victim advocacy; housing.

Women's Center of Southeastern Connecticut
P.O. Box 572
New London 06320
(203) 447-0366

Services: Child care (ten hours/week); community education; counseling (crisis, peer support, family, single parent); emergency medical treatment; emergency transportation; hot line (twenty-four hours); referral; legal aid; liaison (police, medical); victim advocacy; housing (maximum capacity twelve, maximum six weeks, children permitted).

Women's Crisis Service
c/o Leroy Downs Apartments
26 Monroe Street
South Norwalk 06854
(203) 852-1980

Services: Hot Line (twenty-four hours); state homes; community education; support groups; programs for batterers, legal advocacy; transportation; coalition members; brochure available.

Women's Emergency Shelter
Box 1503
Waterbury 06721

Yale/New Haven Hospital Rape and Sexual Assault Trauma Counseling Team
c/o Emergency Services
Yale/New Haven Hospital
789 Howear Avenue

New Haven 06510
(203) 436-1960

Services: Counseling, referral; medical treatment; emergency housing (in emergency room overnight).

Delaware

For information and referral concerning the state of Delaware's Family Violence Program, contact:
(302) 475-4111 (Newcastle County)
(302) 422-8058 (Kent and Sussex Counties)

Child, Inc.
11th and Washington Streets
Wilmington 19801
(302) 655-3311

Services: Counseling; referral.

Families in Transition Center
11–13 Church Avenue
Milford 19963
(302) 422-8058

Services: Community education; counseling (crisis, long term, peer support, family); emergency transportation; hot line (twenty-four hours); referral; legal aid; liaison (police, medical, courts); victim advocacy; housing (maximum thirty days; charge $1.50/day, children permitted).

New Beginnings, Arden House
2210 Swiss Line
Ardentown 19810
(302) 475-8424

Services: Legal aid; counseling; referral; child care; housing (maximum fourteen days, maximum capacity eight, children permitted).

People's Place
P.O. Box 301
Milford 19963

YWCA Family Violence Program
908 King Street

Ardentown 19810
(302) 475-4111

Services: Legal aid; counseling; referral; hot line.

District of Columbia

Citizen Complaint Center
Superior Court Building A
5th and F Street, N.W., F Street Entrance
Washington, D.C. 20001
(202) 724-5750

Services: Counseling; referral; information. Remedies obtainable through
the center are civil protection orders, prosecutors hearings, and occasionally, warrants. As of October 1979, center will institute a mediation service
using neighborhood and community volunteers. Complainant must know
the respondent's full name and mailing address. There are no income
guidelines for services. Hours are 8:30 A.M.–9:30 P.M., Monday through
Friday.

Fact Hotline (Families and Children in Trouble)
P.O. Box C
1690 36th Street, N.W.
Washington, D.C. 20007
(202) 628-FACT (Crisis)
(202) 965-1900 (Office)

Services: Community education; hot line (twenty-four hours); referral.

House of Imagene
214 P Street, N.W.
Washington, D.C. 20001
(202) 797-7460

Services: Counseling; referral; housing (maximum seven days, maximum
capacity twenty-five, children not permitted).

House of Ruth
459 Massachusetts Avenue, N.W.
Washington, D.C. 20001
(202) 347-9689

Services: Legal aid (emergency basis); counseling; referral; hot line (twenty-four hours); housing (maximum one night, maximum capacity thirty, children permitted).

House of Ruth
1215 New Jersey Avenue
Washington, D.C. 20001

My Sisters' Place
P.O. Box 3035
Washington, D.C. 20010
(202) 529-5991

Services: Counseling; referral; hot line (twenty-four hours); children's program; housing (maximum capacity fifteen, maximum six weeks, children permitted).

Women's Legal Defense Fund
1010 Vermont Avenue, N.W.
Suite 210
Washington, D.C. 20005
(202) 630-1123

Services: Legal counseling; referral.

Women's Right's Clinic of the Antioch School of Law
2633 16th Street, N.W.
Washington, D.C. 20009
(202) 265-9500

Services: Legal aid; victim advocacy.

Florida

ACT, INC.
Box 928
Fort Myers 33902

Brevard Family Aid
615 Citrus Court
Melvourne 32981

Citizen Dispute Settlement Center
1351 Northwest 12th Street

Miami 33125
(305) 547-7062

Services: Referral; mediation (domestic and neighbor).

Creative Services, Inc., Rape Crisis Center and Spouse Abuse Center
721 Northeast 3rd Street
Ocala 32670
(904) 622-8495

Services: Counseling; hot line (twenty-four hours); referral; victim advocacy; liaison (police, courts, mental health, social services); community education; housing (maximum capacity ten).

Dade County Victims Advocates/Safespace
1515 Northwest 7th Street
Room 112
Miami 33125
(305) 579-2915

Services: Community education; counseling (crisis, peer support, family, group); emergency transportation; hot line (twenty-four hours); referral; liaison (police, medical, courts); victim advocacy; housing (maximum capacity thirty, maximum six weeks, children permitted).

Domestic Assault Project
Pan American Building
307 North Dixie Highway
West Palm Beach 33402
(305) 588-1121 (Crisis)
(305) 837-2418 (Office)

Services: Counseling; referral; hot line (twenty-four hours).

Favor House
P.O. Box 17102
Pensacola 32522
(904) 438-4661

Services: Child care (8 A.M.–5 P.M.); community education; counseling (crisis, peer support); emergency medical treatment; emergency transportation; hot line (twenty-four hours); legal aid; referral; liaison (police, medical); housing (maximum capacity twenty, maximum thirty days, children up to age fourteen permitted).

Free Clinic
433 7th Avenue North
Saint Petersburg 33701

Hubbard House
1231 Hubbard Street
Jacksonville 32206
(904) 354-3114

Services: Legal aid; counseling; referral; hot line (twenty-four hours); child care; housing (charge $1/day, maximum capacity twenty-five, children permitted).

Pensacola YWCA
1417 North 12th Avenue
Pensacola 32504
(904) 438-2171

Services: Referral.

Rape Prevention Center
3800 South Tamiami Terrace
Sarasota 33579

Refuge House of Leon County, Inc.
P.O. Box 12304
Tallahassee 32308
(904) 878-6089

Safe Place and Rape Crisis Center of Sarasota
P.O. Box 1675
Sarasota 33578
(813) 365-1976 (Crisis)
(813) 365-0208 (Office)

Services: Community education; counseling (crisis, long term, peer support, family); emergency medical treatment; emergency transportation; hot line (twenty-four hours); referral; legal aid; liaison (police, medical); victim advocacy; housing (maximum capacity six, maximum two weeks, children permitted).

Safespace: Battered Women's Shelter
P.O. Box 186

Miami 33137
(305) 358-4357 (Crisis)
(305) 579-2915 (Office)

Services: Community education; counseling (crisis support, family); hot line (twenty-four hours); referral; legal aid; liaison (police, medical, social-service agencies); victim advocacy; housing (maximum capacity thirty, maximum four to six weeks, children permitted).

Safe Space of Indian River County
P.O. Box 427
Vero Beach 32960
(305) 562-5713

Saint Petersburg Free Clinic Shelter
433 7th Avenue, North
Saint Petersburg 33701
(813) 821-1200

Sexual and Physical Abuse Resource Center
P.O. Box 12367
University Station
Gainesville 32603
(904) 377-TALK (Crisis)
(904) 377-RAPE (Office)

Services: Community education; counseling (crisis, long term, peer support); emergency transportation; hot line (twenty-four hours); referral; liaison (police, medical, jobs, housing); housing (maximum capacity fifteen, maximum three weeks, children permitted).

Spouse Abuse, Inc.
c/o We Care, Inc.
112 Pasadena Plain
Orlando 32803
(305) 628-1227 (twenty-four hours)
(305) 425-2624 (8 A.M. to midnight)

Services: Legal aid; counseling; referral; hot line (twenty-four hours); child care (referrals); housing (maximum twenty-one days).

Spouse Abuse of Polk County, Inc.
P.O. Box 797
Lakeland 33802
(813) 687-4461

Spouse Abuse Shelter
721 Northeast 3rd Street
Ocala 32670

The Spring, Inc.
P.O. Box 11087
Tampa 33610
(813) 835-4471 (Crisis)
(813) 835-9481 (Office)

Services: Legal aid; counseling; referral; hot line (twenty-four hours) child care (when available); housing (maximum three weeks, children permitted).

Victim Advocate Program
Fort Lauderdale Police Department
1300 West Broward Boulevard
Fort Lauderdale 33312
(305) 761-2143

Services: Counseling; referral; hot line (twenty-four hours).

Volunteer Abused Shelter
2105 Fogarty Street
Key West 33040

Women in Distress of Broward County, Inc.
P.O. Box 676
Fort Lauderdale 33302
(305) 761-1133

YWCA Domestic Assault Shelter
901 South Olive Avenue
West Palm Beach 33401
(305) 833-2439

Services: Legal aid; counseling; referral; hot line (twenty-four hours); child care; housing (maximum capacity ten to thirteen).

YWCA of Jacksonville
325 East Duval Street
Jacksonville 32202
(904) 354-6681

Services: Counseling; referral; job training and placement; housing (charge

$30/week, maximum sixty days, maximum capacity eighty-six, children permitted).

Georgia

Athens Council on Domestic Violence
c/o YWCA
560 Research Road
Athens 30605
(404) 543-2221 (Crisis)
(404) 542-7614 (Office)
Contact: Diane Glendron.

Services: Community education; crisis counseling; hot line (evenings and weekends); referral; victim advocacy.

Council on Battered Women, Inc.
P.O. Box 54737
Atlanta 30308
(404) 873-1766

Services: Community education; counseling (crisis, peer support); hot line (twenty-four hours); referral; victim advocacy; housing (maximum capacity thirty, maximum two weeks, charge $3/day, children permitted).

Domestic Crisis Intervention Unit of Child Service and Family Counseling Center
1105 West Peachtree Street, N.E.
Atlanta 30357
(404) 658-6666 (Crisis)
(404) 873-6916 (Office)
(404) 658-6074 (Office)

Services: Community education; counseling (crisis, long term, family); referral; liaison (police).

Family Crisis Shelter
Box 612
Hilo 96720

Hospitality House for Women
216 South Broad Street
Rome 30161
(912) 235-4673

Services: Legal aid; counseling; referral; child care; housing (maximum capacity ten, maximum five days, children permitted).

Rescue Mission
971 Washington Avenue
Macon 31201

Safe Shelter
P.O. Box 22487
Savannah 31328

Salvation Army Shelter
399 Meigs Street
Athens 30601

Women in Distress
Route 1
Box 151G
Naylor 32541

YWCA Crisis Center
48 Henderson Street
Marietta 30064
(404) 973-8890

Services: Referral; housing (maximum five days, maximum capacity three, children permitted, sliding-scale fee).

Hawaii

"The Family Crisis Shelter, Inc." *Pu'uhonua*
2020 Kinoole Street
Hilo 96720
(808) 959-8400 (Crisis)
(808) 959-9252 (Office)

Services: Community education; counseling (crisis, peer support, family); emergency transportation; hot line (twenty-four hours); referral; liaison (police, medical); housing (maximum capacity twenty-six, maximum forty-five days, children permitted).

Shelter
R.R. 1

Box 295
Kapaa 96746

Shelter for Abused Spouses and Children
c/o Kokua Kalihi Valley
1888 Owawa Street
Honolulu 96819
(808) 841-0822 (Crisis)
(808) 841-3275 (Office)

Services: Community education; referral; housing (maximum capacity five families, maximum five days, children permitted).

Women's Counseling Clinic and Resource Center
1314 South King Street
Suite 754
Honolulu 96814
(808) 536-9976

Services: Legal aid (referral); counseling; referral; hot line (twenty-four hours); child care (limited); housing.

Idaho

Battered Women's Group
P.O. Box 2301
Salmon 83467

Battered Women's Help Center
P.O. Box 1061
Blackfoot 83226
(208) 785-4181

Services: Emergency housing; counseling; crisis intervention; referral.

Couer d'Alene Women's Center
421½ Sherman Avenue
Coeur d'Alene 83814
(208) 664-9303

Services: Emergency housing; counseling; crisis intervention; referrals; information.

Crisis Line Emergency Services, Inc.
Weisgerber Building
Room 302

Clarkston 83501
(208) 746-9658 (Business)
(208) 746-9655 (Twenty-four-hours crisis)
Contact: Glenda Johnson.

Services: Safe homes; counseling; support group.

Emergency Housing Services, Inc.
P.O. Box 286
815 North 7th Street
Boise 83701
(208) 343-7541

Services: Referral; housing (maximum fourteen days, maximum capacity eighteen, children permitted).

The Woman's Advocates
454 North Garfield
Pocatello 83201
(208) 232-HELP (Crisis)
(208) 232-9169 (Answering service)

Services: Counseling; referral; hot line; child care; housing (maximum three days, maximum capacity one, children permitted).

Women against Violence
P.O. Box 323
Idaho Falls 83401
(208) 524-5040 (Crisis)
(208) 529-4200 (Office)
Contacts: Jean Gullixson.

Services: Community education; counseling; emergency transportation; hot line (twenty-four hours); referral; victim advocacy; housing (two days free, $5.50/day longer, children permitted).

Illinois

Against Domestic Violence
203 East Hickory Street
Streator 61364

Services: Shelter may be arranged.

Call for Help, Women's Crisis Shelter
P.O. Box 284

Bellerville 62222
(618) 397-0963 (Crisis)
(618) 235-0892 (Office)

Services: Community education; counseling (crisis, peer support, individual/group); emergency transportation; informational programming; hot line (twenty-four hours); referral; legal aid; housing (maximum capacity eighteen, maximum three weeks, children permitted).

Chicago Abused Women Coalition Shelter Task Force
53 West Jackson Street, #516
Chicago 60604

Community Crisis Center
600 Margaret Place
Elgin 60120
(312) 697-1093

Services: Legal aid; counseling; referral; hot line (twenty-four hours); child care; housing (maximum twenty-one days, maximum capacity ten, children permitted).

Cook County Legal Assistance Foundation, Inc.
19 South LaSalle
Suite 1419
Chicago 60603
(312) 263-2267

Services: Legal assistance; legal counseling; referral.

Countering Domestic Violence
P.O. Box 3572
Bloomington 61701

Services: Shelter may be arranged.

Crisis Center/South Suburbia
P.O. Box 10
Palos Park 60464

Services: Shelter may be arranged.

Des Plaines Valley Community Center, Family Crisis Center
6125 South Archer Road
Summit 60501
(312) 485-5254 (Crisis)
(312) 458-6920 (Office)

Services: Community education; counseling (crisis, long term, peer support, family, group); hot line (twenty-four hours); referral; legal aid; housing (maximum capacity twelve, maximum three weeks, children permitted).

Emergency Department of the Illinois Masonic Medical Center
836 Wellington
Chicago 60657
(312) 525-2300

Services: Counseling; referral.

Family Counseling Agency in Will County, Battered Women's Program
168 North Ottawa Street
Suite 304
Joliet 60431
(815) 722-3344 (Crisis)
(815) 727-4584 (Office)

Services: Community education; counseling (crisis, long term, peer support, family); hot line (twenty-four hours); referral; legal aid; liaison (police); victim advocacy; housing (maximum capacity three families, children permitted).

Family Shelter Service Hanson House Shelter
415 Melrose
Box 646
Glen Ellyn 60137

Gospel League
955 West Grand Avenue
Chicago 60622
(312) 243-2480

Services: Legal aid; referral; hot line; child care; housing (maximum capacity forty, children permitted).

Lake County Crisis Center
P.O. Box 1067
Waukegan 60085

Mujeres Latinas en Accion
1823 West 17th Street
Chicago 60608

Mutual Ground
P.O. Box 843

Aurora 60507
(312) 898-4490 (Crisis)
(312) 859-8350 (Office)

Services: Community education; counseling (crisis, peer support); emergency transportation; hot line (twenty-four hours); referral; victim advocacy; housing (maximum capacity sixteen to eighteen, donations accepted, children permitted).

Oasis Women's Center
111 Market Street
Alton 62002

Rape and Sexual Abuse Care Center
P.O. Box 154
Southern Illinois University
Edwardsville 62026
(618) 692-2197

Services: Legal aid; counseling; referral; hot line (twenty-four hours).

Rock Island County Council on Alcoholism (New Hope League)
R.R. 2
P.O. Box 288
East Moline 61244
(309) 797-4220 (Crisis)
(309) 792-0292 (Office)

Services: Counseling; referral; hot line (twenty-four hours); child care; housing (maximum capacity eighteen, children permitted).

Salvation Army Emergency Lodge
800 West Lawrence Avenue
Chicago 60640
(312) 275-9383

Services: Legal aid; counseling; referral; housing (maximum capacity 125, children permitted).

Salvation Army Project Shelter
Unified Command Headquarters
875 North Dearborn Street
Chicago 60610

Sojourn Women's Center, Incorporated
915 North 7th Street

Springfield 62702
(217) 544-2484 (Crisis)
(217) 525-0313 (Office)

Services: Counseling; hot line (twenty-four hours); housing (maximum capacity eight, children permitted).

Southwest Women Working Together
3201 West 63rd Street
Chicago 60629

Tri-County Women Strength
301 Northeast Jefferson
Peoria 61602
(309) 674-4443

Services: Peer counseling; referral; hot line (twenty-four hours); child care (twenty-four hours); housing (maximum capacity fourteen, maximum three weeks, children permitted).

Uptown Center Hull House
4520 North Beacon Street
Chicago 60640

WAVE Program (Working against Violent Environments)
630 North Church Street
Rockford 61103
(815) 962-6102

Services: Community education; counseling (crisis, peer support, family, relationship, batterer); emergency transportation; hot line (twenty-four hours); referral; liaison (police, medical); victim advocacy; housing (maximum capacity fourteen, maximum four weeks, children permitted).

A Woman's Place
505 West Green
Urbana 61801
(217) 384-4390

Services: Counseling (peer); referral; hot line (twenty-four hours); housing (sliding-scale fee, maximum twenty-one days, children permitted).

Women's Alternative Shelter
Box 553
Danville 61832

Women's Center
408 West Freeman
Carbondale 62901
(618) 457-0346

Services: Legal aid; counseling; referral; hot line (twenty-four hours); housing.

Women's Crisis Service
1101 Main Street
Peoria 61606
(309) 674-4443
(309) 676-0200

Services: Counseling; referral; hot line; housing (maximum twenty-one days, maximum capacity six, children permitted).

Women's Services Department/Loop YWCA
37 South Wabash
3rd Floor
Chicago 60603
(312) 372-6600

Services: Legal advice; consultation; referral.

YWCA
436 North Main Street
Decatur 62521

YW CARES
South Suburban YWCA
300 Plaza
Park Forest 60466

Indiana

Alternatives, Incorporated
P.O. Box 1302
Anderson 46015

A Better Way, Incorporated
P.O. Box 734
Muncie 47305
(317) 289-0404

Services: Referral; peer support; legal/legislative advocacy; housing (maximum five days, children permitted); emergency transportation; hot line (twenty-four hours); community education; speaker's bureau; newsletter.

Caring Place
568 East Second Street
Hobart 46342

Commission on Status of Women
475 Broadway
Suite 509
Gary 46402

Council on Spouse Abuse
Virgo County Line
P.O. Box 392
Terre Haute 47807

Family Crisis Shelter
512 West Wabash Avenue
Crawfordsville 47933

Friends of Battered Women
P.O. Box 1161
Richmond 47374
(317) 966-5158 (Crisis)
(317) 935-3920 (Office)

Services: Child care; community education; counseling (crisis, peer support, family); emergency transportation; hot line (twenty-four hours); referral; legal aid; liaison (police, medical); victim advocacy; housing (maximum capacity four, maximum three days, children permitted).

Kokomo YWCA Shelter Program
Sycamore Street
Kokomo 46901

Marion County Victim Advocate Program, Incorporated
4602 Thornleigh Drive
Indianapolis 46226
(317) 545-1116

Services: Community education; counseling (crisis, long term, peer support); emergency transportation; hot line (twenty-four hours); referral; liaison (police, medical); victim advocacy.

Salvation Army Family Service, Domestic Violence Program
234 East Michigan
Indianapolis 46204
(315) 637-5551
Contact: Drindee McCauley.

Services: Child care (9–12 A.M.); counseling (crisis, long term, peer support, family); hot line (twenty-four hours); referral; mental-health liaison; housing (maximum capacity thirty, time limit by case, children permitted). Funding: Title XX.

Women's Alternatives Shelter House
P.O. Box 1302
Anderson 46011

Women's Center
P.O. Box 103
Columbus 47201

Women's Shelter Advisory Committee of the YWCA
802 North LaFayette Boulevard
South Bend 46601
(219) 232-3344 (Crisis)
(219) 233-9491 (Women's Center)

Services: Legal aid; counseling; referral; hot line.

Woman's Shelter of the YWCA
118 Vine Street
Evansville 47708

YWCA
P.O. Box 1121
Hammond 46325

YWCA Shelter for Women Victims of Violence
P.O. Box 5338
Fort Wayne 46805
(219) 424-2554 (Crisis)
(219) 424-2621 (Office)

Services: Counseling; referral; hot line (twenty-four hours); child care; housing (maximum capacity thirty, children permitted).

YWCA Women's Shelter
P.O. Box 695
South Bend 46624

Iowa

Adult Family Life Crisis Center
P.O. Box 446
Ottumwa 52501
(515) 683-3122 (Crises)
(800) 452-1019 (Crisis for other counties served)

Services: Emergency housing (maximum thirty days); transportation; referral; counseling; hot line (twenty-four hours).
Area served: Monroe, Jefferson, Wapello, Van Buren, Mahaska, Appanoose, Lucas, Keokuj, Daris, and Wayne Counties.

Aid and Alternatives
Victims of Spouse Abuse
P.O. Box 733
Iowa City 52244

Battered Women Project of the Council on Sexual Assault and Domestic Violence Incorporated
722 Nebraska
Sioux City 51101
(712) 252-1861 (Crisis)
(800) 352-4929 (Crisis for other counties served)

Services: Emergency housing (maximum three days); advocacy; crisis intervention; support groups; referral; hot line (twenty-four hours).
Area served: Woodbury, Monana, Ida, Plymouth, and Cherokee Counties.

Battered Women's Project of the YWCA
722 Nebraska Street
Sioux City 51101
(712) 255-7432 (Twenty-four hour crisis line)
Contact: Mary Ann Garrigan.

Services: Temporary emergency shelter; hot line; counseling; support groups; abuser group, Batterer's Anonymous; referrals; advocacy.
Area served: Sioux City and surrounding area.

Buena Vista County Task Force on Domestic Violence and Sexual Assault
800 Oneida
Storm Lake 50588
(712) 732-6295 (Twenty-four hour crisis line)
Contact: Mary Ann McGowan.

Services: Temporary emergency housing (maximum three days); hot line, support group, teen rap group, Batterers Anonymous for men; advocacy; counseling and referrals.
Area served: Buena Vista and Cherokee Counties.

Citizens for the Prevention of Abuse
315 West Pierce
Council Bluffs 51501
(712) 328-3086

Services: Emergency housing; referral; support groups; counseling.

Domestic Violence Program
315 West Pierce
Council Bluffs 51501
(712) 322-8747 (Twenty-four-hour crisis line)
Contact: Peggy Hammes.

Services: Temporary housing; counseling; hot line; referrals to services.
Area served: Eight counties in southwest Iowa.

Domestic Violence Program of Council Bluffs (Satellite Program)
315 West Pierce
Council Bluffs 51501
(800) 432-0242 (Twenty-four-hour crisis line)
(712) 328-0266

Services: Hot line; temporary emergency housing (twenty-four hour limit); counseling; referrals.
Area served: Shelby County.

Domestic Violence Project
P.O. Box 733
Iowa City 52244
(319) 351-1043 (Twenty-four-hour crisis line)
(319) 351-1042 (Office)
Contact: Susan Dickinson.

Services: Temporary shelter (limit fourteen days, capacity twelve to fifteen); hot line; advocacy; transportation to services, referrals, support groups.
Area served: Iowa City and Johnson County.

Domestic Violence Project, The Door Opener

215 North Federal Avenue
Mason City 50401
(515) 567-3740 (Crisis)
(515) 424-9071 (Office)

Services: Legal aid (through referral only); counseling; child care; housing (maximum five days, children permitted); hot line (twenty-four hours); referral.

The Door Opener

215 North Federal Avenue
Mason City 50401
(505) 424-9071 (Crisis line)
Contact: Shirley Sandage.

Services: Temporary emergency housing (limit one week maximum); advocacy; support group; counseling; referrals.

Family and Children's Service

115 West Sixth Street
Davenport 52803
(319) 323-1852 (Office and crisis line)
Contact: Berlinda Tyler-Jamison.

Services: Counseling, referrals.
Area served: Davenport and Quad City area.

Family Violence Center

Iowa Children's and Family Services
1101 Walnut Street
Des Moines
(515) 288-1981 (Office)
(515) 243-6147 (Twenty-four hour crisis line)
Contact: Glory Gray.

Services: Emergency housing six weeks maximum, capacity twelve to sixteen families); counseling for women and children; support groups; hot line; referrals; advocacy.

Family Violence Center Incorporated of North Central Iowa
P.O. Box 379
Fort Dodge 50501
(515) 955-5456 (Twenty-four hour crisis line)
Contact: Marj Ramthun.

Services: Limited temporary shelter; counseling, advocacy; hot line; referrals.
Area served: Webster County.

Gateway YWCA Women's Resource Center
317 Seventh Avenue, South
Clinton 52732
(319) 242-2118 (Twenty-four hour crisis line)
Contact: Maggie Charnoska.

Services: Temporary emergency housing (thirty days maximum), capacity ten; hot line; counseling; support groups; referrals to all services; advocacy.
Area Served: Clinton County and surrounding Gateway area including northwestern Illinois.

Helping Services for Northeast Iowa
Services for Abused Women
Box 372
Decorah 52101
(319) 382-2989 (Twenty-four-hour crisis line).

Services: Temporary emergency housing; hot line, counseling; advocacy; referrals.
Area served: Alamakee, Clayton, Howard, Fayette, and Winneshiek Counties.

Human Services Planning and Coordinating
Eldrige City Hall
Eldrige 52748
(309) 285-4841

Services: Child care; community education; counseling (crisis, peer support, family); emergency transportation; referral; liaison (police, medical).

Integrated Crisis Service
301½ Main Street
Cedar Falls 50613
(319) 277-4735 (Twenty-four hour crisis line)

Contact: Sue Sweet.

Services: Temporary emergency housing; hot line; counseling; referrals.
Area Served: Black Hawk County.

Iowa Coalition against Domestic Violence
318 Fifth Street, S.E.
Cedar Rapids 52401
(319) 363-2093
Martha Garner, chairperson

Iowa Commission on the Status of Women
507 10th Street
Des Moines 50319

Services: Referral.

Legal Services Corporation
315 East 5th Street
Des Moines 50309
(515) 243-2151

Services: Legal aid.

Muscatine County Rape/Assault Care Services
Medical Arts Building
Muscatine 52761
(319) 263-8080 (Twenty-four-hour crisis line)
Contact: Kathy Groth.

Services: Temporary emergency housing (maximum three days); hot line;
counseling; referrals to services and low-rent housing; advocacy.
Area served: Muscatine and surrounding townships.

Project Dove
Matura Action Corporation
129 North Pine Street
Creston 50801
(515) 782-8433 (Twenty-four hour crisis line)
(515) 782-8431 (Office)
Contact: Joyce Schreck.

Services: Temporary housing; hot line; support groups; advocacy; referrals.
Area served: Clarke and Union Counties.

Rape and Battered Women Program of the Gateway YWCA Women's Resource Center
317 7th Avenue, South
Clinton 52732
(319) 243-3611 (Crisis)
(319) 242-2118 (Office)

Services: Counseling; referral; hot line (twenty-four hours); child care; housing (maximum capacity eight, children permitted); support groups; victim advocacy; community education.

Reverend Angus McDonald
Ministerial Alliance
425 Morgan Street
Keokuk 52632
(319) 524-6841 (Home)
(319) 524-1090 (Church Office)

Services: Counseling and referrals.
Area Covered: Keokuk.

Services for Abused Women, Helping Services for Northeastern Iowa
P.O. Box 372
Decorah 52101
(319) 382-2989 Crisis)
(319) 382-2980 (Office)

Services: Legal aid; counseling; referral; hot line (twenty-four hours); support groups; child care (flexible hours); housing (maximum capacity one family, maximum three days); emergency transportation; community education.

Spouse Abuse Victims Advocacy Programs, Crisis Center
112½ East Washington Street
Iowa City 52240
(319) 351-0140 (Crisis)
(319) 351-2726 (Office)

Services: Counseling; advocacy; crisis intervention; transportation; emergency housing; shelter to be open soon.

Story County Sexual Assault Care Center and Battered Women's Project
P.O. Box 1150
Welch Avenue Station
Ames 50010

(515) 295-4976 (Twenty-four-hour crisis line)
Contact person: Lois Hamilton

Services: Counseling; referrals; hot line; temporary emergency housing; advocacy.
Area served: Story County.

YWCA
409 North 4th Street
Burlington 52601
(319) 752-4531

Services: Housing (emergency); referral; information.

YWCA
35 North Booth Street
Dubuque 52001
(319) 588-4016 (Crisis)
(319) 556-3371 (Office)

Services: Emergency housing; counseling; referral.

YWCA Women's Emergency Shelter
318 5th Street, S.E.
Cedar Rapids 52401
(319) 363-2093 (Shelter)
(319) 365-1458 (YWCA)

Services: In process of developing legal-help system for those women not eligible for legal aid; counseling; referral; support groups; hot line (twenty-four hours); child care (hours negotiated); housing (maximum capacity thirteen to fifteen, maximum two weeks, children permitted).

Kansas

Battered Women Task Force
P.O. Box 1883
Topeka 66601
(913) 295-8499 (Crisis)
(913) 233-1750 (Office)

Services: Community education; counseling (crisis, peer support, short term, parent support group); emergency transportation; hot line (twenty-four hours); referral; liaison (police, medical-emergency room); victim advocacy; housing (maximum capacity fifteen, maximum one month, charge $2.50/day, children permitted).

Battered Women's Task Force
P.O. Box 160
Emporia 66801

Battered Women's Task Force
644 Quindaro
Kansas City 64101
(816) 931-1653 (twenty-four hour crisis line)
(913) 321-1566
(913) 321-1569
(913) 321-0951
Contact: Pat O'Brien.

Services: Temporary shelter (thirty-day limit); hot line; counseling; support group; referrals; advocacy.
Area served: Wyandotte County.

Coalition against Spouse Abuse of Reno County
P.O. Box 537
Hutchinson 67501
(316) 663-2522 (Twenty-four-hour crisis line)
Contact: Paula Berglund.

Services: Temporary emergency housing; hot line; counseling; support group; referrals; advocacy.
Area served: Reno County.

Dickinson County Crisis Hotline
Box 442
Abilene 67410
(913) 263-1120 (Sunday–Thursday, 1 P.M.–Midnight; Friday and Saturday, 1 P.M.–7 A.M.).
Contact: Larry Dursham.

Services: Temporary emergency housing (one day); hot line; counseling; referrals.
Area served: Dickinson County.

Domestic Violence Association of Central Kansas
651 East Prescott
Salina 67401
(913) 822-4433 (Twenty-four hour crisis line)

(913) 827-5862 (Office)
Contact: Cindy Entriken.

Services: Temporary housing; hot line, counseling; support groups; referrals; advocacy.
Area served: North central Kansas.

Domestic Violence Task Force
P.O. Box 272
Concordia 66901
(913) 243-1094 (Twenty-four hour crisis line)
(913) 243-1234 (Hospital phone)
Contact: Sr. Marilyn Wall.

Services: Counseling; referrals.
Area served: Coud County.

Garden City Task Force on Domestic Violence
c/o Kansas Rural Legal Services
118½ Grant Street
Garden City 67846
(316) 275-0238 (8 A.M. to 5 P.M.)
Contact: Cynthia Hale.

Service: Referrals.

Johnson County Task Force for Battered Persons
c/o Johnson County District Attorney's Office
Box 728
Olathe 66061
(913) 782-5000 (Office)
(913) 931-1653 (Twenty-four hours crisis line)

Services: hot line; counseling; advocacy; support group; referrals.
Area served: Johnson County.

Kansas Association of Domestic Violence Programs
Wichita Women's Crisis Center
P.O. Box 1579
Wichita 67201
(316) 263-6520
Contact: Jeri Swinton.

Margaret W. Jordan
2515 West 91st Street

Leawood 66206
(913) 649-7691

Services: Legal aid; counseling; referral.

Pawnee Mental Health Center
320 Sunset Street
Mànhattan 66502

Services: Counseling (sliding-scale fee); referral.

Regional Crisis Center for Victims of Family Abuse or Rape
P.O. Box 164
Manhattan 66502
(913) 539-2785

Services: Child care (twenty-four hours); community education; counseling (crisis, peer support); emergency medical treatment; emergency transportation; hot line (twenty-four hours); referral; legal aid; liaison (police, medical) victim advocacy; housing (in private homes, maximum three days, children permitted).

Safehouse
Box 313
Pittsburg 66762
(316) 231-8251 (Weekdays)
(316) 231-1700 (Weekend)
Contact: Liz Ann Saia.

Services: Temporary housing (three days); support group; referrals; advocacy.
Area served: Southeast Kansas.

SOS, Incorporated
Services for Rape Victims and Battered Women
Box 1191
Emporia 66801
(316) 342-6116 (Monday through Friday, 8–5)
(316) 343-2626 (After-hours phone)
Contact: Jan Jones.

Services: Temporary emergency housing (72 hours); hot line; counseling; information on pregnancy and venereal disease; referrals; advocacy.
Area served: Lyon County and surrounding seven counties.

Wichita Women's Crisis Center
1158 North Waco
Wichita 67203
(316) 263-9806 (Crisis)
(316) 263-6520 (Office)
Services: Legal counseling; referral; hot line (twenty-four hours); housing (maximum twenty-one days, maximum capacity fifteen, children permitted).
Area served: Wichita and surrounding area.

Women's Safe House
Box 313
Pittsburg 66762

Women's Transitional Care Services
P.O. Box 633
Lawrence 66044
(316) 864-3506
(316) 841-2345

Services: Legal aid; counseling; referral; hot line (twenty-four hours); housing (maximum twenty-one days, children permitted).

Wyandot Mental Health Center
Eaton at 36th Avenue
Kansas City 66103
(913) 831-9500

Services: Counseling (fee); referral; hot line (twenty-four hours).

Kentucky

Adaire County Shelter House
Columbia 42728

Battered Women's Unit of Legal Aid
317 South 5th Street
Louisville 40202
(502) 637-5301

Services: Legal aid; referral.

Brass, Incorporated
P.O. Box 1945
Bowling Green 42101

Cumberland Valley Women's Shelter
P.O. Box 70
Barbourville 40906

Gateway, Buffalo Trace Shelter
Box 532
Morehead 40351

Green River Comprehensive Care Center
P.O. Box 950
Owensboro 42301
(800) 482-7972 (Crisis)
(502) 683-0227 (Office)

Services: Counseling (sliding-scale fee); referral; hot line (twenty-four hours); housing.

Mission House
1305 West Market Street
Louisville 40203
(502) 584-4024

Services: Referral; housing (maximum five days, maximum capacity eight, children permitted).

Northeast Kentucky Legal Services
P.O. Box 679
320 East Main Street
Morehead 40351
(606) 784-8921

Services: Legal aid; referral.

Social Work Service
U.S. Army Hospital
Fort Campbell, 42223
(502) 798-2103 (Crisis)
(502) 798-4187 (Office)

Services: Counseling; referral; hot line (twenty-four hours, through emergency room); housing (maximum capacity four, seven days, children permitted); limited funds for transportation.

Women's Crisis Center
321 York Street
Newport 41071

YWCA Spouse Abuse Center
604 South 3rd Street
Louisville 40202
(502) 585-2331

Services: Child care (9 A.M.–5 P.M., Monday through Friday); community education; counseling (crisis, long term, peer support, family); hot line (twenty-four hours); referral; legal aid; liaison (police, medical, social services); victim advocacy; housing (maximum capacity thirty-four, maximum thirty days, sliding-scale fee, children permitted).

YWCA Spouse Abuse Project Shelter for Battered Women
1060 Cross Keys Road
Lexington 40504
(606) 255-9808

Services: Community education; counseling (crisis, long-term, peer support, family, child); hot line (twenty-four hours); referral; liaison (police); housing (maximum capacity fifteen, maximum two weeks, sliding-scale fee, children permitted).

Louisiana

Battered Women's Program
P.O. Box 2133
Baton Rouge 70821
(504) 389-3001

Services: Community education; counseling (crisis, peer support); emergency transportation; emergency money ($5–$35 as available);hot line (8:30 A.M.–4:30 P.M.); referral (includes Volunteers of America that will shelter women and young children for seven days, location of a shelter out of city or state, and provision of gasoline or bus ticket money is also provided); liaison (police, medical, food stamps, legal).

Calcasieu Women's Shelter
P.O. Box 276
Lake Charles 70601
(318) 436-4552

Services: Legal aid (must qualify for low-income guidelines, referral);

counseling; referral; hot line (twenty-four hours); child care (twenty-four hours); housing (emergency, maximum capacity eighteen, children permitted).

Crescent House, an Associated Catholic Charities Program
2929 South Carrollton Avenue
New Orleans 70118
(504) 821-5390

Services: Community education; counseling (crisis, peer support, family, couples); emergency transportation; referral; liaison (police, medical); victim advocacy; housing (maximum capacity twenty-one, children permitted).

Salvation Army Women's Care Center (for Abused Women)
P.O. Box 3504
Lafayette 70502
(318) 235-2407

Services: Child care (twenty-four hours); community education; counseling (crisis, long-term, peer support, family); emergency medical treatment; emergency transportation; hot line (twenty-four hours) referral; legal aid; liaison (police, medical) housing (maximum capacity seventeen, children permitted).

Women's Resource Center of the YWCA
710 Travis Street
Shreveport 71101
(318) 222-0556 (Crisis)
(318) 222-2116 (Office)

Services: Legal aid; counseling; referral; hot line (twenty-four hours); child care (during counseling); housing (maximum capacity forty-four, children permitted).

YWCA Battered Women's Program
3433 Tulane Avenue
New Orleans 70119
(504) 486-0377

Services: Counseling; referral; hot line (twenty-four hours).

Maine

Abused Women's Advocacy Project
P.O. Box 713
Auburn 04210

Services: Counseling; referral; housing (maximum fourteen days, maximum capacity six, children permitted).

Caring Unlimited
P.O. Box 955
Biddeford 04005
(207) 282-4435

Services: Legal aid; counseling; referral; hot line (twenty-four hours); housing (maximum capacity twelve, children permitted).

Caring Unlimited
P.O. Box 384
Kennebunk 04090
(207) 985-6272

Services: Hot line (twenty-four hours); office (9 A.M.–5 P.M., Monday through Friday); shelter (twenty-four hours, capacity of nine includes children, fifteen days); overflow housing; community education, programs for batterers; legal advocacy; transportation; coalition members; brochure available.

Family Crisis Shelter, Inc.
Box 4255
Station A
Portland 04101

Family Support Center
4 Epworth Street
Presque Isle 04769

Family Violence Assistance Project
Box 304
Augusta 04330

Spruce Run
44 Central Street
Bangor 04401
(207) 947-0496 (Business hours)
(207) 947-6143 (Evenings and weekends)

Services: Legal referral; counseling; referral; hot line; counseling (child).

Waldo Women's Shelter
Union Street
Searsport 04774
Contact: Patty Plourde

The Washington County Domestic Violence Project
P.O. Box 493
Machias 04652
(207) 255-4785

Services: Hot line (twenty-four hours); office (8 A.M.–5 P.M., Monday through Friday); state homes; community education; support groups; legal advocacy; transportation; coalition members.

Woman Care/Aegis Association
10 West Main Street
Dover-Foxcroft 04426

Maryland

Abused Persons Program
4910 Auburn Avenue
Bethesda 20014

Assisi
P.O. Box 203
Upper Marlboro 20870
(301) 529-0611 (Crisis)
(301) 568-6385 (Office)

Services: Counseling; hot line (twenty-four hours); child care (flexible hours); housing (maximum capacity nine, maximum thirty days, children permitted); court advocacy; transportation; support groups.

Battered Partners Program
Carroll County Department of Social Services
95 Carroll Street
Westminster 21157
(301) 848-5060

Services: Counseling (sliding-scale fee); referral; child care (fee); housing (fee, maximum fourteen days, children permitted, Carroll County resident only).

Casa, Inc.
101 Summit Avenue
Hagerstown 21740
(301) 739-6000 (Crisis)
(301) 797-4161 (Office)

Services: Legal aid; counseling; referral; employment aid; housing (children permitted).

Center for Individual and Family Studies
31 Allegheny Avenue
Towson 21204
(301) 321-6068

Services: Community education; counseling (crisis, long term, peer support, family); referral (legal aid); liaison (police; Sexual Assault Center, Baltimore City).

Citizens Against Spousal Assault (CASA)
P.O. Box 915
Columbia 21044
(301) 997-2272

Services: Legal aid; counseling; referral; hot line (twenty-four hours); child care; housing (maximum capacity seven, maximum one week, children permitted).

Citizens Assisting and Sheltering the Abused (CASA of Cecil County)
North East 21901
(301) 287-5780

Services: Counseling (weekly mutual support group); hot line (twenty-four hours).

Community Crisis Center, Abused Persons Program
4910 Auburn Avenue
Bethesda 20014
(301) 656-9161 (Crisis)
(301) 656-9526 (Office)

Services: Legal aid; counseling (crisis intervention, self-help groups); referral; hot line (twenty-four hours); housing (maximum three weeks, children permitted).

Family Abuse Program
c/o General Delivery
La Plata 20646
(301) 645-0001 (Crisis)
(301) 934-3556 (Office)

Services: Counseling; referral; hot line (twenty-four hours); child care; housing (maximum three days, children permitted).

Family Service Society
22 North Court Street
Westminster 21157

Frederick County Battered Spouse Program
118 North Market Street
Frederick 21701
(301) 662-2873 (Crisis)
(301) 662-6151 (Office)
(301) 663-6161 (City police)

Services: Community education; counseling (crisis, long term, peer support); emergency transportation; hot line (Monday through Thursday, 8 P.M.–Midnight; Friday through Sunday, 4 P.M.–Midnight); referral; legal aid; liaison (police, medical); victim advocacy; housing (in motels, maximum two days, children permitted).

Garrett County Mental Health and Addictions Services
Medical Building
4th Street
Oakland 21550
(301) 334-8111

Services: Counseling (sliding-scale fee); referral; housing (available through House of Hope, 4th Street, Oakland 21550, maximum capacity two families).

Good Neighbors Unlimited
208 Duke of Gloucester Street
Annapolis 21401

Services: Legal aid; counseling; referral; child care; housing (maximum ten days, maximum capacity twelve, children permitted, must be referred through police department).

House of Ruth
2402 North Calvert Street
Baltimore 21218
(301) 899-7884

Services: Counseling (sliding-scale fee); referral; housing (maximum capacity fifteen, children permitted).

Maryland's Children's Aid and Family Society
22 North Court Street

Westminster 21157
(301) 848-3111 (Crisis)
(301) 876-1233 (Office)

Services: Counseling; referral; housing (children permitted).

Sexual Assault and Domestic Violence Center, Baltimore City
Medical Arts Building
Suite 112
9101 Franklin Square Drive
Rosedale 21237
(301) 391-2345 (Crisis)
(301) 391-2396 (Office)

Services: Community education; counseling (crisis, peer support, family); emergency medical treatment; emergency transportation; hot line (twenty-four hours); referral; liaison (police, medical); victim advocacy.

Sexual Assault/Spouse Abuse Resource Center
34 North Philadelphia Boulevard
Room 311
Aberdeen 21001
(301) 272-7050

Services: Legal aid; counseling; referral; hot line.

Violence Clinic/Department of Psychiatry
University of Maryland Hospital
645 West Redwood Street
Baltimore 21201
(301) 528-6475

Services: Counseling (psychiatric evaluation); referral (fee).

Woman's Place
150 Maryland Avenue
Rockville 20850
(301) 279-8346

Services: Legal aid; counseling; referral.

Woman's Refuge
Seton Plaza,
Suite 201
952 Seton Drive

Cumberland 21502
(301) 777-1509

Services: Counseling; referral; housing (maximum six days, children permitted).

YWCA Women's Center
167 Duke of Gloucester Street
Annapolis 21401
(301) 268-4393

Services: Counseling; referral; child care; housing (maximum ten days, maximum capacity six).

Massachusetts

Abby Kelley Foster House, Incorporated
23 Crown Street
Worcester 01609
(617) 756-5486 (Crisis)
(617) 753-1957 (Office)

Service: Hot line; referral; liaison (police, Department of Mental Health); housing (maximum capacity twelve, maximum three to five days, children permitted).

Adult/Adolescent Counseling in Development, Services Against Family Violence
170 Pleasant Street
Malden 02148
(617) 324-2221 (Crisis)
(617) 324-2218 (Office)

Services: Child care; community education; counseling (crisis, long term, peer support, family); emergency transportation; hot line (twenty-four hours); referral; legal aid; victim advocacy.

Alternative House
Box 2096
Highland Station
Lowell 01851

Battered Women's Task Force
Women's Services Center

33 Pearl Street
Pittsfield 01201
(617) 443-0089 (Hot line)
(617) 443-2425 (Administration)

Services: Twenty-four hour hot line; safe homes; community education; support groups; legal advocacy; transportation; brochure available.

Boston College Legal Assistance Bureau
21 Lexington Street
Waltham 02154
(617) 893-4793

Services: Legal aid ($1 fee); referral.

Cambridge-Somerville Legal Services
24 Thorndike Street
East Cambridge 02141
(617) 492-5520

Services: Legal aid; referral.

Cape Shelter, Incorporated
54 Main Street
Hyannis 02601

Casa Myrna Vazquez
c/o Pat Quintana
P.O. Box 18019
Boston 02118
(617) 262-9381

Services: Counseling; hot line (twenty-four hours); referral; legal aid; housing (maximum capacity twenty-five, maximum six weeks, children permitted); Spanish speaking.

Central Massachusetts Legal Services, Incorporated
455 Main Street
Fitchburg 01420
(617) 345-1946

Services: Referral; legal aid.

Central Massachusetts Legal Services, Incorporated
339 Main Street

Worcester 01608
(617) 752-3718

Services: Referral; legal aid.

Daybreak, Incorporated
93 Grand Street
Worcester 01610
(617) 791-6562 (Crisis)
(617) 755-5371 (Office)

Services: Legal aid; counseling (sliding-scale fee); referral; hot line (twenty-four hours); child care (hours vary); housing (maximum capacity fifteen to seventeen, maximum six weeks, children permitted).

Domestic Violence Program
Countryside Drive
Milford 01757
(617) 478-0820 (Days)
(617) 478-2412 (Evenings and weekends)
(617) 478-0820 (Administration)

Services: Twenty-four hour hot line; community education; support groups; legal advocacy; child care; transportation.

DOVE
P.O. Box 287
Quincy 02269
(617) 471-1234 (Hot line)
(617) 471-5087 (Administration)

Services: Twenty-four hour hot line; shelter; community education; support groups; legal advocacy; child care; brochure available.

Elizabeth Stone House
108 Brookside Avenue
Jamaica Plain 02130
(617) 522-3417

Services: Counseling; housing (maximum 180 days, maximum capacity six).

Gardner Women's Center
175 Connors Street
Gardner 01462
(617) 632-5150

Services: Legal aid; referral; counseling; hot line (9 A.M.–4 P.M.).

Greater Lowell YWCA
29 Hawks Street
Lowell 01852
(617) 454-5405

Services: Child care (7:30 A.M. –5:30 P.M.); community education; counseling; housing (maximum capacity twenty-three, maximum one year,
charge $30/week).

Hampden County Women's Center
764 Alden Street
Springfield 01109
(413) 783-4004 (Hot line)
(413) 783-3020 (Administration)

Services: Shelter; twenty-four hour hot line; community education; support groups; legal advocacy; child care; transportation; coalition members;
brochure available.

Harbor Area Task Force on Battered Women
c/o Children's Community Corner
185 Shurleff Street
Chelsea 02150
(617) 884-0739 (Hot line)
(617) 884-HELP (After hours)

Services: Twenty-four hour hot line; community education; support
groups; legal advocacy; coalition members; brochure available.

Help for Abused Women
9 Crombie Street
Salem 01970
(617) 744-6841 (Hot line)
(617) 744-8552 (Administration)

Services: Shelter; twenty-four hour hot line; community education; support groups; programs for batterers; legal advocacy; child care; coalition
members; brochure available.

Hegira, Incorporated
71 Broad Street
Westfield 01085
(413) 568-0966 (Hot line)

Services: Shelter; twenty-four hour hot line; safe homes; overflow housing;
community education; support groups; legal advocacy; child care; transportation; coalition members; brochure available.

Hotline to End Rape and Abuse (HERA)
P.O. Box 126
Springfield 01108
(413) 733-2561 (Hot line)
(413) 783-0325 (Administration)

Services: Shelter; twenty-four hour hot line; community education; program for batterers; transportation; coalition members.

Independence House
c/o Community Action Committee
583 Main Street
Hyannis 02601
(617) 771-1080 (Hot line)
(617) 771-1727 (Administration)

Services: Shelter; twenty-four hour hot line; community education; support groups; legal advocacy; child care; transportation; brochure available.

Lynn District Court Clinic
580 Essex Street
Lynn 01907
(617) 598-5200

Services: Legal aid; counseling; referral; hot line (9 A.M.–4 P.M.).

Massachusetts Task Force on Battered Women
P.O. Box 911
75 Day Street
Fitchburg 01420

Necessities/Necesidades
P.O. Box 745
Northhampton 01060
(413) 586-5066 (Hot line)
(413) 586-1125 (Administration)

Services: Twenty-four hour hot line; safe homes; support groups; legal advocacy; child care; transportation; coalition members; brochure available.

New Bedford Women's Center
Battered Women's Project
252 County Street
New Bedford 02740
(617) 992-4222 (Hot line)
(617) 996-3345 (Administration)

Services: Shelter; twenty-four-hour hot line; community education; support groups; legal advocacy; child care; transportation; coalition members; brochure available.

New England Learning Center for Women in Transition
310 Main Street
Greenfield 01301
(413) 672-0125

Services: Legal aid; counseling; referral; child care (9 A.M.–4 P.M., Monday through Friday); housing (maximum thirty days, maximum capacity ten, children permitted); support groups; transportation; victim advocacy; crisis intervention.

New Hope, Incorporated
P.O. Box 48
Attleboro 02703
(617) 695-2113 (Hotline)
(617) 222-2113 (Administration)

Services: Shelter; twenty-four hour hot line; overflow housing; community education; support groups; legal advocacy; child care; transportation; brochure available.

Program Hope
54 Main Street
Hyannis 02601
(617) 771-3486

Services: Community education; counseling (crisis, long term), peer support, family, alcoholism); emergency transportation; hot line; referral; legal aid; victim advocacy; housing (maximum two nights, contributions, children permitted).

Renewal House
Franklin Square Ministry
1575 Tremont Street
Boston 02120
(617) 566-6881

Services: Twenty-four hour hot line; community education; legal advocacy.

Respond
1 Summer Street
Somerville 02143
(617) 623-5900

Services: Legal aid; counseling; referral; child care; housing (maximum capacity four, children permitted).

Services against Family Violence
166 Pleasant Street
Malden 02148
(617) 324-2221 (Hot line)
(617) 324-2221 or 2218 (Administration)

Services: Community education; support groups; legal advocacy; child care; transportation; brochure available.

Social Service Department of Saint Luke's Hospital
101 Page Street
New Bedford 02740
(617) 997-1515

Services: Counseling; referral.

South Shore Women's Center
14 Main Street
Plymouth 02360
(617) 746-2664

Services: Community education; counseling (crisis, long term, peer support, family); hot line (twenty-four hours); referral; legal aid; liaison (police, medical); victim advocacy; housing (maximum six weeks, children permitted).

Suffolk County District Attorney's Office
503 Washington Street
Dorchester 02124
(617) 287-1195

Services: Legal aid; counseling; referral.

Transition House, Women's Center
P.O. Box 530
Harvard Square Station
Cambridge 02138
(617) 661-7203 (Crisis)
(617) 354-2676 (Office)

Services: Counseling; hot line; referral; legal aid; housing (maximum twenty-eight days, charge $1.50/day, children permitted).

Womanshelter/Companeras
P.O. Box 6099
Holyoke 01040
(413) 536-1628 (Hot line)
(413) 536-1629 (Administration)

Services: Shelter; twenty-four hour hot line; community education; support groups; legal advocacy; child care; transportation; coalition members; brochure available.

Womanspace, Feminist Therapy Collective, Incorporated
636 Beacon Street
Boston 02215
(617) 267-7992

Services: Counseling (fee negotiable); referral.

Women Helping Women
P.O. Box 1552
Brockton 02401
(617) 584-2477 (Hot line)
(617) 583-0234 (Administration)

Services: Shelter; twenty-four hour hot line; overflow housing; support groups; legal advocacy; child care; transportation; coalition members.

Women's Law Collective
678 Massachusetts Avenue
P.O. Box 125
Cambridge 02139
(617) 492-5110

Services: Legal aid (sliding-scale fee); referral.

Women's Protective Services
c/o YWCA
231 Bacon Street
Natick 01760
(617) 872-6161 (Hot line)
(617) 235-5613 (Administration)

Services: Twenty-four hour hot line; safe homes; community education; support groups; legal advocacy; transportation; brochure available.

Women's Resource Center
38 Lawrence Street
Lawrence 01840
(617) 685-2480 (Hot line)
(617) 685-2480 (Administration)

Services: Shelter; twenty-four hour hot line; safe homes; community education; support groups; legal advocacy; coalition members; brochure available.

Women's Services Center of Berkshire County
33 Pearl Street
Pittsfield 01201
(413) 443-0089 (Crisis)
(413) 442-9458 (Office)

Services: Counseling (sliding-scale fee); referral; hot line (twenty-four hours); child care; emergency housing (children permitted).

YWCA Women against Violence
Natick 01760
(617) 872-6161 (Crisis)
(617) 369-6112 (Crisis)
(617) 653-4464 (Office)

Services: Legal aid; counseling; referral; hot line (twenty-four hours); child care; housing (fee for food).

Michigan

Assault Crisis Center
4009 Washtenaw Avenue
Ann Arbor 48104

Assault Crisis Center
Box 48
Hart 49420

Assault Crisis Center
561 North Hewitt Street
Ypsilanti 48197
(313) 668-8888 (Crisis)
(313) 434-9881 (Office)

Services: Counseling; referral; hot line (twenty-four hours); housing (maximum three days, children permitted).

AWARE
2904 Francis Street
Jackson 49203

Bay County Women's Center/Rape and Crisis
P.O. Box 646
Bay City 49707

Bright House
Council against Domestic Assault
P.O. Box 14149
Lansing 48901

Call Someone Concerned, Incorporated
155 North Main Street
Adrian 49221

Center for Women in Transition
834 Grant Street
Grand Rapids 49417

Chippewa County Down with Violence Program, Incorporated
P.O. Box 636
Sault Ste. Marie 49783

Council against Domestic Assault
P.O. Box 14149
Lansing 48901
(517) 372-5572

Council on Domestic Violence
P.O. Box 2289
Midland 48640

Dares, Incorporated
2920 Lapeer Street
Port Huron 48060

Domestic Assault Program of the YWCA
211 South Rose Street
Kalamazoo 49007

Domestic Harmony
63½ North Howell Street
Suite 3
Hillsdale 49242

Domestic Violence Program
Iron River City Hall
Iron River 49935

Domestic Violence Program/Threshold
723 Woodward Heights
Hazel Park 48030

Domestic Violence Project, Incorporated
202 East Huron
Suite 101
Ann Arbor 48104
(313) 995-5444 (Crisis)
(313) 995-5447 (Office)
(313) 995-5460 (Office)

Services: Community education; counseling (crisis, peer support, family
batterer); emergency transportation; hot line (twenty-four hours); referral;
victim advocacy; housing (maximum capacity thirty, maximum thirty days,
children permitted).

**Domestic Violence Shelter Program of Family and Children Service
of
Calhoun County**
182 West Van Buren Street
Battle Creek 49017

Domestic Violence/Victim Assistance Project
1917 Washtenaw Avenue
Ann Arbor 48104
(313) 995-5444 (Crisis)
(313) 995-5460 (Office)

Services: Referral; hot line (twenty-four hours).

Domestic Violence/Victim Assistance Shelter Program
108 East Washington Street
Ionia 48846

Every Woman's Center
310 East 3rd Street
Flint 48503
(313) 238-7671

Services: Counseling (sliding-scale fee); referral.

Every Woman's Place, Incorporated
Rape/Spouse Assault Crisis Center
23 Strong Avenue
Muskegon 49441

First Step
West Wayne County Project/Domestic Assault
8381 Farmington Street
Westland 48185

Heartline
8201 Sylvester Street
Detroit 48214

HERS
410 West Upton Avenue
Reed City 49677

LaBelle Shelter
1599 LaBelle Street
Detroit 48227

Outer Drive Hospital Social Work Services Department
26400 Outer Drive
Lincoln Park 48146
(313) 386-2000, Ext. 346

Services: Community education; crisis counseling; emergency medical
treatment; referral.

Perfect Place
1110 Howard Street
Saginaw 48601

Perfect Place, Women's Crisis Shelter
1765 East Genesee
Saginaw 48601
(517) 754-8361

Services: Community education; counseling (crisis, peer support); emergency medical treatment; emergency transportation; hot line (twenty-four
hours); referral; legal aid; liaison (police, medical); victim advocacy housing (maximum capacity ten, sliding-scale fee).

Project Shelter, Women's Center
Marquette 49855
(616) 227-2219

Services: Legal aid; counseling; referral; housing (maximum three days, maximum capacity ten, children permitted).

Rape/Spouse Assault Crisis Center
29 Strong Avenue
Muskegon 49441
(616) 722-3333 (Crisis)
(616) 726-4493 (Office)

Services: Legal aid; counseling; referral; hot line (twenty-four hours); child care (8 A.M.–6 P.M.); housing (children permitted).

Region 4 Assault Crisis Center
P.O. Box 48
Hart 49420

SAFE House
32 North Washington Street
Ypsilanti 48197

Salvation Army
1331 Trumbell Street
Detroit 48216

Shelter Home for Abused Women
302 Iroquis
Laurium 49913

Shelter Home for Abused Women, Incorporated
P.O. Box 27
Calumet 49913
(906) 337-5623
Contact: Fran Hella, Priscilla Malnar, Linga Gregorich.

Services: Chid care; community education; counseling; referral for assailants; emergency medical treatment; emergency transportation; legal aid; liaison (police, medical); victim advocacy; housing (maximum capacity ten, children permitted).

Shelter, Incorporated
136 East Washington

P.O. Box 797
Alpena 49707
(517) 356-9650

Services: Community education; counseling (crisis, peer support); emergency medical treatment; emergency transportation; hot line; referral; legal aid; liaison (police, medical); housing (maximum capacity ten, maximum twenty-one days, children permitted).

Sisters for Human Equality (SHE)
1320 South Washington Street
Lansing 48910
(517) 374-0818 (Crisis)
(517) 484-1905 (Office)

Services: Legal aid; referral.

Spouse Abuse Center
108 East Washington Street
Ionia 48846
(616) 527-1360
Contact: Ms. June Parsons.

Spouse Abuse Shelter Project, Incorporated
P.O. Box 517
Marquette 49855

Spouse Abuse Shelter Project of the Women's Resource Center
North Central Michigan College
Petosky 49770

Turning Point
P.O. Box 308
New Baltimore 48047

Underground Railroad, Incorporated
P.O. Box 565
Saginaw 48606
(517) 755-0411

Services: Counseling (crisis); emergency medical treatment; hot line (twenty-four hours); referral; liaison (police, medical); housing (maximum capacity twenty-five, maximum thirty days, sliding-scale fee, children permitted).

Washtenaw County Legal Aid Society
212 East Huron
Ann Arbor 48104
(313) 665-6181

Services: Legal aid; referral.

Western Wayne County Project on Domestic Assault
First Step
32715 Dorsey
Westland 48185
(313) 595-1111
Contact: Deborah Benjamin.

WIT
1114 Washington Street
10th Floor
Radisson Cadillac
Detroit 48226

Women in Transition
834 Grant Street
Grand Haven 49417
(616) 842-7970
(616) 842-6310

Services: Counseling; referral; community education.

Women in Transition
1114 Washington Boulevard
Suite 1018
Detroit 48226

Women in Transition
218½Washington Street
Grand Haven 49417
(616) 842-7970
(616) 842-6310

Services: Counseling; referral; community education.

Women's Aid Service, Incorporated, Domestic Violence Project
113 East Palmer Street
Mount Pleasant 48858

Women's Crisis Center
211 South Rose Street
Kalamazoo 49006
(616) 343-9496

Services: Legal aid; counseling; referral; hot line (twenty-four hours); child care (daytime); housing (maximum twenty-one days, maximum capacity ten families).

Women's Justice Center
651 East Jefferson
Detroit 48226
(313) 961-7073

Services: Legal referral; counseling.

Women's Resource Center
918 West Front Street
Traverse City 49684

Women's Survival Center
70 Whittemore
Pontiac 48058
(313) 335-1520 (Crisis)
(313) 335-2685 (Office)

Services: Counseling; referral; hot line (9 A.M.–5 P.M.).

Women's Survival Center of Oakland County
171 West Pike Street
Pontiac 48053

YWCA Domestic Crisis Center
25 Sheldon S.E.
Grand Rapids 49503

YWCA Domestic Violence Shelter
269 West Huron Street
Pontiac 48053

YWCA Metro-Detroit Interim House
2230 Witherell Street
Detroit 48201

YWCA of Pontiac/North Oakland Domestic Crisis Shelter
269 West Huron Street
Pontiac 48053
(313) 332-HELP (Crisis)
(313) 334-0973 (Office)

Services: Counseling; referral; hot line (twenty-four hours); child care; housing (maximum twenty-one days, maximum capacity eleven, children permitted).

YWCA Safe House Domestic Violence Shelter
310 East 3rd Street
Flint 48502
(313) 238-8761

Services: Hot line (twenty-four hours); child care (9 A.M.–5 P.M.); community education; counseling (crisis, peer support); emergency medical treatment; referral; legal advocacy; liaison (police, medical); housing (maximum capacity twenty, maximum five weeks, sliding-scale fee, children permitted).

YWCA Spouse Abuse Shelter of Berrial County
508 Pleasant Street
Saint Joseph 49085

Minnesota

Alexandra House
P.O. Box 131
Anoka 54404

Alexandra House
P.O. Box 32142
Fridley 55432

Anoka County Task Force for Battered Women, Incorporated
P.O. Box 131
Anoka 55303
(612) 780-1376

Services: Legal aid; counseling; referral; hot line; housing (emergency, as available).

Battered Women's Task Force
P.O. Box 934

Winona 55987
(507) 452-4440

Services: Community education; counseling (crisis); emergency transportation; referral; legal aid; liaison (police, medical, courts); victim advocacy; housing (in safe homes, as available, maximum seven days, children permitted).

B. Robert Lewis House
4750 Cedar
Eagan 55122
(612) 452-7488

Chrysalis Center for Women
2104 Stevens Avenue, South
Minneapolis 55404
(612) 871-2603 (Crisis)
(612) 871-0118 (Office)

Services: Legal aid; counseling; referral; hot line (9 A.M.–8 P.M., Monday through Friday).

Committee against Domestic Violence
Box 466
Mankato 56001

Community Action Council, Incorporated
13760 Nicollet Avenue, South
Burnsville 55337
(616) 894-2424 (Crisis)
(616) 894-4212 (Office)

Services: Counseling; referral; hot line; child care; housing (maximum thirty days, children permitted).

Community Planning Organization
333 Sibley, #503
St. Paul 55101
(612) 291-8323

Services: Information; referral.

Fairbault Area Victim Support Program
P.O. Box 354
Fairbault 55021
(507) 334-2555 (Crisis)
Contact: Donna Miller.

Services: Community education; emergency transportation; hot line (twenty- four hours); referral; liaison (police, courts, welfare); victim advocacy.

Family Resource Center
Route 1
Box 1-C
Shafer 55074
(612) 257-2400
Contact: Maggie Sivigny.

Services: Community education; counseling (crisis, long term, family); referral; victim advocacy.
Funding: CETA; WEP; state DPW; possible county and some fees for service.

Harriet Tubman Shelter
30001 Oakland
Minneapolis 55414
(612) 827-2841

Services: Legal aid; counseling; referral; hot line (twenty-four hours); child care (8 A.M.–5 P.M.); housing (maximum capacity thirty, children permitted).

Home Free
3401 East Medicine Lake Boulevard
Plymouth 55441

Hopkins Project
P.O. Box 272
Hopkins 55343
(612) 933-7422

Lewis House
4750 Cedar Avenue
Eagan 55122

Listening Ear Crisis Center
111 17th Avenue, East
Alexandria 56308

Martha Rogers Ripley Alliance for Battered Women, Incorporated
P.O. Box 96

Thief River Falls 56701
(218) 281-4224

Services: Child care; community education; counseling (crisis, peer support); emergency transportation; hot line (twenty-four hours); referral; legal aid; liaison (police, medical); victim advocacy; housing (maximum capacity twelve, children permitted).

Mid-Minnesota Women's Center, Incorporated
P.O. Box 602
Brainerd 56401
(218) 828-1216

Services: Counseling; referral; hot line (twenty-four hours); housing (maximum capacity sixteen, children permitted).

Northeastern Coalition for Battered Women, Incorporated
2 East 5th Street
Duluth 55805
(218) 722-0222

Services: Counseling; referral; hot line (twenty-four hours); child care; housing (maximum capacity twelve, children permitted).

Northfield Victim Support Program
P.O. Box 171
Northfield 55057
(507) 645-5555 (Crisis)
Contact: Kathy Keasline.

Services: Community education; emergency transportation; hot line (twenty- four hours); referrals; liaison (police, courts, welfare); victim advocacy.
Funding: United Way

Northwoods Coalition for Battered Women
P.O. Box 563
Bemidji 56601
(218) 751-0211

Region IV Council on Domestic Violence
P.O. Box 815
Fergus Falls 56537
(218) 939-4491

Ripley Alliance for Battered Women
P.O. Box 96
Thief River Falls 56701

St. Joseph's House
2101 Portland Avenue
Minneapolis 55404
(612) 874-8867

Service: Legal aid; referral; hot line (twenty-four hours); housing (maximum capacity fifteen, children permitted, maximum thirty days).

Shelter House
1125 Southeast 6th Street
Willmar 56201
(612) 235-4613

Sojourner House
P.O. Box 272
Hopkins 55343

South Suburban Family Service
633 South Concord
South St. Paul 55075
(612) 451-1434

Services: Counseling (fee); referral.

Southwest Women's Shelter
111 East Main Street
Marshall 56258
(507) 532-2350 (Crisis)
(507) 532-4604 (Office)

Services: Legal aid; counseling; referral; hot line (twenty-four hours); child care (twenty-four hours); housing (flexible time limit, children permitted).

Stevens County Battered Women's Committee
Box 111
Morris 56267
(612) 589-1481
Contact: Ms. Janet Senjemor.

Victim's Crisis Center/Freeborn Mowe Mental Health Center
908 Northwest 1 Drive

Austin 55912
(507) 437-6680

Services: Legal aid; counseling; referral; hot line; child care; housing (children permitted).

Walk-in Counseling Center
2421 Chicago Avenue
Minneapolis 55404
(612) 870-0565

Services: Counseling; referral.

Woman House
P.O. Box 195
St. Cloud 56301
(612) 252-1603

Woman's Advocates
584 Grand Avenue
St. Paul 55103
(612) 227-8284

Services: Legal aid; counseling; referral; hot line (twenty-four hours); housing.

Women's Coalition
P.O. Box 3205
Duluth 55803
(218) 728-3679

Women's Resource Center/Battered Women's Task Force
205 Exchange Building
Winona 55987
(507) 452-4440
Contact: Jan Gaspard.

Services: Community education; counseling (crisis); emergency transportation; referral; legal aid; liaison (police, medical, courts); victim advocacy; housing; (in safe homes, as available, maximum seven days, children permitted).
Funding: State Task Force on Battered Women

Women's Shelter
P.O. Box 61

Rochester 55901
(507) 285-1010

Services: Legal aid; counseling; referral; hot line (twenty-four hours); child care (limited hours); housing.

Mississippi

Aid to Battered Women, Incorporated, Project Safe
P.O. Box 334
c/o Information Place
Tupelo 38801
(601) 842-5222

Services: Counseling; referral; hot line; housing (maximum capacity ten, children permitted).

Catholic Charities
P.O. Box 2248
Jackson 39209

Coalition against Spouse Abuse
P.O. Box 9227
Southern Station
(601) 544-4357 (Crisis)
(601) 266-7200 (Office)

Services: Counseling; referral; hot line (twenty-four hours); housing (maximum capacity five, children permitted).

Gulf Coast Women's Center
P.O. Box 333
Biloxi 39533

Gulf Coast Women's Center, Incorporated
Box 444
Biloxi 39531
(601) 435-1968 (Crisis)
Contact: Rosmary DeCamp.

Services: Counseling (crisis, peer support, rape/sexual abuse); emergency medical treatment; emergency transportation; hot line (twenty-four hours); referral; legal aid; liaison (police, medical); victim advocacy; housing (maximum capacity fifty, maximum eight weeks, children permitted).
Funding: Community.

Harbor House
Route 2
Box 164
Tupelo 38801

Person's Service, Incorporated
115 Front Street
Hattiesburg 39401

Project Safe
P.O. Box 1014
New Albany 38652

Project Save Battered Women
Box 334
Tupelo 38801

Salvation Army
P.O. Box 784
Pasagoula 39567

Missouri

Abuse, Assault Crisis Center
P.O. Box 1827
Columbia 65205
(314) 443-3322 (Twenty-four hour crisis line)
(315) 449-7721 (Office, noon–4 P.M.)
Contact: Ann Fullman.

Services: Hot line; temporary housing; referrals; services to rape victims.
Area served: Columbia and central Missouri.

Battered and Abused Women's Program
624 South Clay
Springfield 65803
(417) 855-1728 (Twenty-four hour crisis line)
Contact: Susie David.

Services: Counseling; hot line; temporary housing; support group; referrals.
Area served: Springfield and thirty-mile surrounding area.

Bridgeway Counseling Services, Incorporated
125 North Fifth Street

St. Charles 63301
Contact: Janet Silverstein Woodburn.

Services: Counseling; referral; hot line (twenty-four hours); housing (maximum capacity eight).

Child Center of Our Lady of Grace
7900 Natural Bridge
St. Louis 63121
(314) 383-0200

Services: Counseling (fee); child care.

Crisis Intervention, Incorporated
P.O. Box 585
Joplin 64801
(417) 623-8310

Services: Referral; hot line (twenty-four hours).

Family Self-Help Center
P.O. Box 1185
Joplin 64801
(417) 782-1772 (Twenty-four hour crisis line)

Services: Hot line, temporary housing (capacity thirty); support group; children's group; men's group; advocacy; referrals; job services.
Area served: Four-state area: southwest Missouri, northeast Oklahoma, northwest Arkansas, southeast Kansas.

Hope House
1635 North Summit
Springfield 65803
(417) 864-8452
Contact: Sr. Mary William Goeckner.

Services: Temporary shelter (capacity eight); mental-health center; referrals.

Howell County Volunteers
People's Park
West Plains 65775
(417) 256-5759 (Crisis line)
Contact: Pat Jones

Services: Counseling; referrals; temporary shelter (maximum seven to ten); hot line.
Area served: Howell County and three surrounding counties.

Legal Services of Eastern Missouri, Incorporated
607 North Grand Avenue
St. Louis 63103
(314) 533-3000

Services: Legal advice; counseling; referral.

Linda Cobb, Social Service Department, Malcolm Bliss Mental Health Center
1420 Grattan Street
St. Louis 63110

Services: Counseling; workshops for community organizations.

McCambridge Center for Women
1108 Walnut Street
Columbia 65201
(314) 449-3953
Contact: Vicki Lewis.

Services: Counseling; transportation; medical treatment; referrals.
Area served: Columbia and surounding area.

Missouri Coalition against Domestic Violence
706 Fairview Avenue
Columbia 65205
(314) 443-2005
Contact: Diane Huneke.

Missouri Ozarks Economic Opportunity Corporation Outreach Program
P.O. Box 69
Richland 65556
(314) 765-3263
Contact: Kenita Johnson.

Services: Counseling; referrals.
Area served: Camden, Crawford, Gaconade, Leclede, Maries, Miller, Phelps, Pulaski Counties.

News, Neighborhood House
811 Benton Boulevard
Kansas City 64124
(816) 931-1653 (Twenty-four hour crisis line)
Contact: Rev. Sharon Garfield.

Services: Hot line; temporary housing (six weeks, capacity fifteen to eighteen); support group; counseling; advocacy; referrals.

Raphael House
3740 Grandel Square
St. Louis 63108
(314) 533-1219 (Crisis line, 7:30 A.M.–10 P.M.)
Contact: Sr. Melinda Reed.

Services: Temporary housing (three-day renewable contract, capacity eighteen to twenty); support group; counseling; referrals; advocacy. Area served: Greater St. Louis.

Redevelopment Opportunities for Women
1408 Kings Highway
St. Louis 63113
(314) 454-1100

Services: For single-female head-of-household and battered, abused women; career and life planning; assertiveness training; job-search skills; counseling; referrals.

Rose Brooks Center
Box 27067
Kansas City 64110
(816) 931-1653 (Twenty-four hour crisis line)
(816) 931-3189 (Office)
Contact: Linda May.

Services: Counseling; hot line; temporary housing (six weeks); support groups; referrals.

Saint George's Home for Women
1600 East 58th Street
Kansas City 64110
(816) 444-4750

Services: Counseling; housing (maximum ninety days, maximum capacity sixteen, children permitted).

Saint Louis Abused Women's Support Project, Incorporated
P.O. Box 24193
St. Louis 63130
(314) 535-8424 (Twenty-four hour crisis line)
(314) 535-8811 (Office)
Contact: Brenda Mamon.

Services: Counseling; temporary shelter for sixty days or more; hot line; referrals; abuser program (RAVEN).
Area Served: St. Louis.

Sojourner Truth Center for Women
Box 164
Caruthersville 63830
(314) 333-1652 (Crisis line, 8 A.M.–5 P.M.)
Contact: Debbie Bowling, Joy Higgins.

Services: Counseling; hot line; referrals; rape crisis.
Area served: Boothill section of southeast Missouri, Pemiscot, Dunkline,
New Madrid, and Mississippi Counties.

Survival, Adult Abuse Program
P.O. Box 344
Warrensburg 64093
(816) 429-2847
Contact: Barbara Heath.

Services: Referrals; advocacy; counseling; limited transportation.

Webster County Support Group
204 Pine Ridge
Marshfield 65706
Contact: Jean Stafford.

Women's Center
P.O. Box 51
St. Charles 63301
(314) 946-6854 (Twenty-four hour crisis line)
Contact: Janet Woodburn.

Services: Temporary housing (capacity eight); support group; counseling;
child-care specialist; hot line; referrals to all services.
Area served: Six-county area of St. Charles, Lincoln, Warren, St. Louis,
Jefferson, and Franklin.

Women's Center and Safe House
737 Themis
Cape Cirardeau 63701
(314) 334-7795 (Twenty-four hour crisis line)
Contact: Susan Frane.

Services: Counseling; hot line; temporary housing (thirty days, capacity
fifteen); referrals; support group.
Area served: Eighteen counties in southeast Missouri.

Women's Counseling Center
6808 Washington Street

St. Louis 63130
(314) 725-9158

Services: Counseling (sliding-scale fee); referral.

Women's Self Help Center
27 North Newstead Avenue
St. Louis 63108
(314) 531-2003 (Twenty-four hour crisis line)
(314) 531-2005 (Office, 9–5)
Contact: Louise Bauschard.

Services: Support group; advocacy; referrals; hot line.
Area served: Greater St. Louis.

YWCA Women's Growth Center
Jules and 8th Street
St. Joseph 64501
(816) 641-2100 (Twenty-four hour crisis line)
(816) 232-4481 (Office)
Contact: Joyce McVey, Mary Jean Falkner, executive director.

Services: Temporary housing; counseling; hot line; referrals; support group.
Area served: St. Joseph area.

Montana

Battered Spouse Center
Yellowstone County
907 Wyoming
Billings 59101
(406) 259-8100

Big Horn County Crisis Line
809 North Custer Street
Hardin 59034
(406) 665-1405

Billings Rape Task Force
1245 North 29th Street
Room 218
Billings 59101
(406) 259-6506

Services: Counseling; referral; hot line (twenty-four hours).

Bozeman Area Battered Women's Network
137 West Main Street
Bozeman 59715
(406) 586-0263

Bozeman Help Center
323 South Wall Street
Bozeman 59715
(406)586-3333

Services: Counseling; referral; hot line.

Community Resources
1937 Florida Avenue
Butte 59701
(406) 792-2616

Services: Legal aid (donation); counseling; referral; child care; housing (maximum capacity eight, children permitted).

Eastern Montana Spouse Abuse Program
306 North Kendrick
Glendive 59330
(406) 365-3364

Glendive Task Force against Spouse Abuse
Hagenston Building
Glendive 59330
(406) 365-2412 (Crisis)
(406) 365-3364 (Office)

Services: Counseling; referral; hot line; housing.

Great Falls Mercy Home
P.O. Box 6183
Great Falls 59406

Services: Counseling; referral; hot line (twenty-four hours); housing (maximum capacity thirteen, children permitted).

Helena Women's Center
146 East 6th Street
Helena 59601
(406) 443-5353

Kalispell Rape Crisis Line
Box 1385

Kalispell 59901
(406) 755-5067

Mercy Home, Incorporated
Box 6183
Great Falls 59408
(406) 483-6511

Women's Place
210 North Higgins
Room 218
Missoula 59801
(406) 543-7606

Women's Resource Center
University of Montana
Missoula 59812
(409) 243-4153

Services: Referral.

Women's Resource Center of Dillon
213 West Glendale Street
Dillon 59725
(406) 683-5630

YWCA Battered Women's Shelter
1130 West Broadway Avenue
Missoula 59801
(406) 543-8277

Nebraska

Alcoholism Help Line	**(800) 652-9300**
Food Hot Line	**(800) 742-7743**
Hot Line for Handicapped	**(800) 742-7594**
Legal Aid	**(800) 742-7555**
Poison Control	**(800) 642-9999**

National Runaway (Chicago)   **(800) 621-4000**

Operation Peace of Mind   **(800) 231-6946**

Alliance Task Force on Domestic Violence
Box 446
Alliance 69301
(308) 635-3171 (Twenty-four hour crisis line)
Contact: Margo Young.

Services: Counseling; hot line; temporary shelter; referrals; transportation.
Area served: Box Butte County.

ASK, Incorporated
601 Sioux Lane
Route 2, Box 337
North Platte 69101
(308) 662-2908 (Twenty-four hour crisis line)
Contact: Sonja Ulrich.

Services: Transportation.
Area served: Lincoln County.

Cheyenne County Task Force of Domestic Violence
P.O. Box 608
Sidney 69161
(308) 254-4510
Contact: Willi Walker.

Services: Temporary emergency shelter; referrals.

Clay County Domestic Violence Task Force
Box 173
Clay Center 68933
(402) 762-3805 (Crisis)
Contact: Joyce Dane.

Services: Counseling; hot line; temporary shelter; referral; transportation.

Community Social Services
303 West 4th Street
Hastings 68901
(402) 463-2112

Services: Counseling; referral.

Coordinated Intervention System for Domestic Abuse, Incorporated
Box 73
Crete 68333
(402) 826-4422 (Hot line)
(402) 826-2332 (Office)
Contact: Anne Nation.

Services: Counseling; hot line; temporary housing; referrals; transportation.
Area served: Butler, Fillmore, Gage, Jefferson, Polk, Saline, Saunders, Seward, Thayer, and York Counties.

Custer County Domestic Violence Task Force, Incorporated
Box 183
Broken Bow 68822
(308) 872-5988 (Twenty-four hour crisis line)
Contact: Cathy Fiorelli.

Services: Counseling; hot line; temporary housing; referrals; transportation.
Area served: Custer and surrounding counties.

DAWN Incorporated, Family Rescue Shelter
309 North Main Street
Gordon 69343
(308) 282-2492
Contact: Susan Phillips.

Services: Counseling; hot line (twenty-four hours); shelter house; referrals; transportation.
Area served: Sheridan County.

Dawson County Parent-Child Center
Box 722
610 North Washington Street
Lexington 68850
(308) 324-4856 (Twenty-four hour crisis line)
Contact: Amy Richardson.

Services: Counseling; hot line; temporary housing; referral; transportation.
Area served: Dawson and Gosper Counties.

Domestic Abuse Program of Sarpy County
1912 Hancock Street

Bellevue 68005
(402) 291-6065 (Twenty-four hour crisis line)
Contact: Rita Abdouch.

Services; Hot line; temporary housing (seventy-two hours); advocacy; counseling; referrals; transportation.
Are⸱ ₃erved: Sarpy County and surrounding area of metropolitan Omaha.

Domestic Violence Task Force
1102 Prospect Avenue
Norfolk 68701

Dundy County Domestic Violence Task Force
Box 68
Benkelman 69021
(308) 423-2384 (Twenty-four hour crisis line)
Contact: Wanda Mindt.

Services: Temporary housing (three days); advocacy; counseling; referrals, transportation.
Area served: Dundy County.

Family Rescue Shelter
309 North Main Street
Gordon 69343
(308) 282-2494 (Office)

Family Service Association
Rape/Spouse Abuse Crisis Center
1133 H Street
Lincoln 68508
(402) 476-3327 (Office)
(402) 465-7273 (Twenty-four hour crisis line)
Contact: Jo Ann Dunn.

Services: Crisis line; shelter available at Friendship Home; counseling; referrals; transportation; abuser counseling (Bill Dick).
Area served: Lincoln and Lancaster Counties.

Friendship Home
P.O. Box 95125
Lincoln 68509
(402) 475-7273 (Twenty-four hour crisis line)
(402) 474-4709 (Office, twenty-four hours)
Contact: Sister Janet Wolf.

Services: Temporary housing (limit two weeks, capacity fourteen); referrals.

Grand Island Task Force on Domestic Violence and Sexual Assault, Incorporated
P.O. Box 1008
Grand Island 68801
(308) 381-0555 (Hot line)
(308) 384-4390 (Office)
Contact: Pam Fegley.

Services: Counseling; hot line (twenty-four hours); temporary housing; referrals; transportation.
Area served: Grand Island area.

Hastings Task Force on Domestic Violence
Community Health Center
P.O. Box 50
Hastings 68901
(402) 462-6800 (Hot line)

Services: Temporary emergency shelter; transportation; crisis line (twenty-four hours); counseling; referrals.

Haven House Family Services
416 Main Street
Wayne 68787
(402) 375-1633 (Hot line)
Contact: Hallie Sherry.

Services: Hot line; temporary shelter (seventy-two hours); advocacy; counseling; referrals; transportation.
Area served: Wayne County.

Immanuel Medical Center
6901 North 72nd Street
Omaha 68122
(402) 572-2225 (Crisis)
(402) 572-2259 (Office)

Services: Counseling; referral; hot line (twenty-four hours).

Kearney Task Force on Domestic Violence and Sexual Assault
2402 Avenue G
Kearney 68847

(308) 234-2491 (Hot line)
Contact: Mary Anna Vargas.

Services: Temporary emergency shelter; referrals; twenty-four hour hot line; transportation.
Area served: Buffalo County.

Lutheran Family and Social Service Domestic Violence Program
2204 14th Street Columbus 68601
(402) 564-1616 (Hot line)
Contact: Jamie Snyder.

Services: Counseling; twenty-four hour hot line; temporary housing; referrals; transportation.
Area served: Platte, Boone, Madison, Colfax, and Nance Counties.

McCook Task Force on Domestic Violence
504 West E
McCook 69001
(308) 345-5534 (Hot line)
Contact: Roxanne Bernard.

Services: Hot line (twenty-four hours); temporary housing (three days); advocacy; referrals; counseling; transportation.
Area served: Redwillow County.

Mayor's Commission on Women
1819 Farnam Street, #501
Omaha 68102
(402) 444-5032

Services: Legal advocacy; crisis intervention; referral.

Nebraska Task Force on Domestic Violence
930 Manchester Drive
Lincoln 68528
Contact: Shirley J. Kuhle, president.

Norfolk Task Force on Domestic Violence
Box 1231
Norfolk 68701
(402) 379-3798 (Crisis)
Contact: Sharyn Nore.

Services: Hot line; temporary housing (children permitted) counseling;

referrals; transportation.
Area served: Norfolk and five surrounding counties.

Operation Bridge, Incorporated
3929 Harney Street
Suite 124
Omaha 68131
(402) 346-7102

Services: Counseling.

Papillion Multi-Service Center
122 East 3rd Street
Papillion 68046
(492) 339-2544 (Crisis)
Contact: Marge Gunn.

Services: Temporary emergency shelter; transportation; referrals to services; counseling.
Area served: Sarpy County.

People's City Mission
124 South 9th Street
Lincoln 68508
(402) 467-2596 (Office, 9–5)
Contact: Pastor Jerry Dunn.

Services: Temporary housing; referrals.
Area served: City of Lincoln.

Rape/Spouse Abuse Crisis Center, Family Service Association
1133 H Street
Lincoln 68508
(402) 475-7273 (Crisis)
(402) 432-3327 (Office)

Services: Counseling; referral; hot line (twenty-four hours).

Salvation Army
511 North 20th Street
Omaha 68102
(402) 346-5155

Services: Referral; housing (maximum fourteen days, maximum capacity thirty, children permitted).

Scottsbluff County Domestic Violence Task Force (DOVES)
P.O. Box 434
Scottsbluff 69361
(308) 436-HELP (Hotline)
Contact: Debbie Stanko.

Services: Hot line (twenty-four hours); temporary housing (seventy-two hours); advocacy; self-help groups; counseling; referrals; transportation. Area served: Scottsbluff, Morill, Banner, and Sioux Counties.

Seward County Task Force on Domestic Violence
1301 North 1st Street
Seward 68434
(402) 643-2640

Services: Community education; emergency medical treatment; emergency transportation; referral; legal aid; liaison (police); victim advocacy; housing (children permitted).

The Shelter
Box 4346
Omaha
(402) 558-5700

Services: Twenty-four hour crisis line; temporary shelter (capacity twenty); referrals to all services and Women against Violence.
Area served: Greater Omaha metropolitan area.

The Shelter, A Center for Victims of Family Violence
P.O. Box 14510
Omaha 68124
(402) 496-3300

Services: Legal aid; counseling; referral; hot line (twenty-four hours); child care (during groups); housing (maximum capacity fifteen, maximum ten weeks, charge $4/adult $2/child/day, children permitted).

Shiloh Youth Revival Center
1045 North 34th Street
Omaha 68131
(402) 553-3947

Services: Counseling; hot line; housing (maximum three days, maximum capacity ten, children not permitted).

Siena House
804 North 19th Street
Omaha 68102
(402) 341-1821 (Crisis)
Contact: Joni Geer.

Services: Twenty-four hour hot line; temporary housing (limit fourteen days, capacity sixteen people); referrals to services.
Area served: Douglas and Sarpy Counties.

Women Against Violence
3929 Harney Street
Room 100
Omaha 68131
(402) 342-2748 (Crisis)
(402) 345-7273 (Office)

Services: Twenty-four hour crisis line; counseling; refer to shelter; referrals to all services; abuser program in conjunction with the shelter.
Area Served: Omaha and vicinity.

Nevada

Advocates for Abused Women
Box 2529
Carson City 89701

Committee to Aid Abused Women (CAAW)
235 Pyramid Way
Sparks 89431
(702) 323-6111 (Crisis, nights and weekends)
(702) 358-4150 (Office, weekdays)

Services: Community education; counseling (crisis, long term, family, rape); emergency transportation; hot line (twenty-four hours); referral; legal aid; liaison (police, medical, social services); victim advocacy; housing (maximum capacity twelve to fifteen, maximum four weeks, children permitted).

Las Vegas Family Abuse Center
3135 Industrial
Las Vegas 89109

Temporary Assistance for Women, Incorporated, Women's Crisis Shelter
P.O. Box 43264
Las Vegas 89109
(702) 382-4428 (Crisis)
(702) 382-2509 (Office)

Services: Counseling; referral; hot line (twenty-four hours); housing (sliding-scale fee), maximum capacity twelve to sixteen, maximum eight weeks, children permitted).

New Hampshire

Concord Task Force on Battered Women
20 South Main Street
Concord 03301
(800) 852-3311 (Crisis)
(603) 228-0571 (Office)

Services: Community education; counseling (crisis); emergency transportation; hot line (twenty-four hours); referral; victim advocacy; housing (in safe homes, maximum three to four days, children permitted).

Family Violence Program of the Upper Valley
P.O. Box 221
Lebanon 03766
(603) 448-4400 (Hot line)
(603) 448-4872 (Administration)

Services: Shelter; twenty-four hour hot line; safe homes; community education; support groups; legal advocacy; brochure available.

Lakes Region Family Services
Beacon Street East
Belkin Mill
Laconia 03246
(603) 524-5834 (Administration, 9 A.M. – 5 P.M., Monday through Friday).

Rape and Assault Committee for Nashua Area, Incorporated
P.O. Box 217
Nashua 03054
(603) 883-3044 (Hot line)
(603) 889-5762 (Administration)

Services: Shelter; twenty-four hour hot line; community education; support groups; legal advocacy; transportation; brochure available.

A Safe Place, Seacoast Task Force on Family Violence
P.O. Box 674
Portsmouth 03901
(800) 852-3311 (Crisis)
(603) 436-7924 (Office)

Services: Community education; counseling (crisis, peer support); emergency transportation; hot line (twenty-four hours); referral; legal aid; liaison (police, medical, welfare); victim advocacy; housing (maximum capacity twelve, maximum four weeks, charge $5/family, $2.50/single woman, children permitted).

Stafford County Information and Referral
Administration and Justice Building
County Farm Road
Dover 03820
(800) 582-7183 (Hot line)
(603) 742-8078 (Administration)

Services: Community education; support groups; programs for batterers.

Task Force on Family Violence
57 Green Street
Berlin 03570
(603) 752-2599 (Hot line)
(603) 752-4222 (Administration)

Services: Twenty-four hour hot line; safe homes; community education; legal advocacy; transportation; coalition members.

Women's Crisis Service
23 Center Street
Keene 03431
(603) 352-3782 (Administration)

Services: Safe homes; community education; support groups; programs for batterers; legal advocacy; child care; transportation; coalition members.

Women's Crisis Service
72 Concord Street
Manchester 03101
(603) 688-2299 (Crisis)
(603) 625-5785 (Office)

Services: Child care (9 A.M.–1 P.M.); community education; hot line (twenty-four hours); referral; liaison (police, medical, courts); victim advocacy.

Women's Supportive Services
94 Sullivan Street
Claremont 03743
(603) 543-0155

Services: Shelter; twenty-four hour hot line; safe homes; community education; legal advocacy; coalition members; brochure available.

New Jersey

ACWC, Abuse Center
Northfield 08225
(609) 646-6767

Services: Counseling; referral; hot line (twenty-four hours); child care (9 A.M.–5 P.M. and selected other hours); housing (maximum capacity eighteen, maximum thirty days, children permitted, charge $7.60/person/ day for nonwelfare).

Alternatives for Women Now/R-CCWC
517 Penn Street
Camden 08102
(609) 964-8034 (Crisis)
(609) 365-0672 (Office)

Services: Child care (9 A.M.–5 P.M.); counseling (crisis, educational/ career); referral; legal aid; victim advocacy; housing (maximum capacity twenty, maximum thirty days, children permitted).

Atlantic County Women's Center
P.O. Box 84B
R.D. 3
West Hickory Street
May's Landing 08330
(609) 653-8411

Services: Counseling; referral; hot line (twenty-four hours); housing (maximum thirty days, maximum capacity twenty, children permitted).

Atlantic County Women's Hotline
2 South Oakland Avenue

Ventnor 08406
(609) 822-2178

Services: Emergency transportation; hot line (twenty-four hours); referral; liaison (police, medical); victim advocacy.

Battered Person Resource Center
R.D. 2
P.O. Box 246
Sussex 07461
(201) 875-7561

Services: Shelter; counseling.

Battered Women's Project
Elizabeth 07201
(201) 355-4357

Services: Community education; counseling (crisis, long term, peer support); hot line; referral; legal aid; victim advocacy; housing (maximum thirty days, charge $5/day/person, children permitted).

Bergen County Community Action Program
215 Union Street
Hackensack 07601
(201) 487-8484 (Crisis)
(201) 487-8446 (Home)

Services: Counseling; referral; hot line (twenty-four hours); child care; housing (maximum twenty-eight days, maximum capacity twelve, children permitted, currently using motels and private residences).

Camden Regional Legal Services
11 West Union Street
Burlington 08016
(609) 386-6660

Services: Legal aid; referral.

Community Action Program
215 Union Street
Hackensack 07601

Family Violence Project
Essex 07021
(201) 484-4446

Services: Counseling; hot line (twenty-four hours); housing (children permitted).

Hudson County Battered Women's Project of the YWCA
111 Storms Avenue
Jersey City 07306
(201) 333-5700

Services: Legal aid; counseling; referral; hot line (twenty-four hours); child care (twenty-four hours); housing (maximum capacity twenty-eight, maximum thirty days, children permitted).

Jersey Battered Women's Service, Inc.
P.O. Box 7
Greystone Park 07950
(201) 267-4763 (Crisis)
(201) 455-1910 (Office)

Services: Counseling (peer support); hot line (twenty-four hours); referral; victim advocacy; housing (maximum capacity thirty, maximum one month, sliding-scale fee, children permitted).

OWLA
c/o Our Lady of Help Church
17 North Clinton Avenue
East Orange 07019
(201) 762-5208

Services: Counseling; hot line (twenty-four hours).

Providence House, Willingboro Shelter
P.O. Box 424
Burlington 08016
(609) 387-3151

Services: Community education; counseling (crisis, peer support, short term); emergency transportation; court accompaniment; hot line (twenty-four hours); referral; housing (maximum capacity twenty-five, charge $7.50/person/day, children permitted).

Resource Center for Women and Their Families
22 North Bridge Street
Somerville 08876
(201) 685-1122 (Crisis)
(201) 685-1126 (Office)

Services: Community education; counseling (crisis, peer support); emergency transportation; hot line (twenty-four hours, Monday through Friday); referral; liaison; housing (received grant money to guarantee space in a shelter outside our county).

SAFE (Shelter Abused Females)
1400 Morgan Avenue
Cinnaminson 08077
(609) 829-6771

Services: referral.

Shelter for Abused Women
Salem Road
Willingboro 08046

Shelter our Sisters
133 Cedar Avenue
Hackensack 07601
(201) 342-1185

Services: Legal advice; counseling; referral; hot line (twenty-four hours); child care; housing (maximum ninety days, children permitted).

Shelter Our Sisters, Inc.
2357 Lemoine Avenue
Fort Lee 07024
(201) 944-9600

Services: Child care; community education; counseling (crisis, long term, peer support); emergency medical treatment, emergency transportation; hot line (twenty-four hours); referral; legal aid; liaison (police, medical); victim advocacy; housing (children permitted).

Volunteers of America
318 Cooper Street
Camden 08102
(609) 964-5100

Services: Housing; hot line (twenty-four hours).

Western Center (Savvy)
P.O. Box 95 Cassville
Jackson 08527

(201) 240-6100 (Crisis)
(201) 928-0014 (Office)

Services: Counseling.

Womanspace, Inc., Mercer County Women's Center
P.O. Box 7182
Trenton 08628
(609) 394-9000

Services: Child care; community education; counseling (crisis); emergency medical treatment; emergency transportation; hot line (twenty-four hours); referral; legal aid; liaison (police, medical, welfare); victim advocacy; housing (maximum capacity twenty-four, maximum six weeks, children permitted).

Women Helping Women, Abused Women's Services
New Jersey Job Corps
Building 852
Plainfield Avenue
Edison 08817
(201) 968-0905 (Crisis)
(201) 968-6563 (Office)

Services: Child care (twenty-four hours); counseling (crisis, peer support); emergency transportation; hot line; referral; legal aid; liaison (police, medical, counseling); victim advocacy; housing (maximum capacity four to six families, maximum six weeks, children permitted).

Women's Crisis Center
56 College Avenue
New Brunswick 08903
(201) 828-RAPE (Crisis)
(201) 932-7599 (Office)

Services: Community education; counseling (crisis); emergency transportation; hot line; referral; liaison (police, medical); victim advocacy.

Women's Crisis Service
P.O. Box 217
Annandale 08801
(201) 782-4357

Services: Counseling; peer support; hot line (twenty-four hours); referrals; victim advocacy; housing.

Women's Crisis Services
26 Main Street
Flemington 08822
(201) 782-HELP (Crisis)
(201) 788-4044 (Office)

Services: Community education; counseling (crisis, peer support); hot line (twenty-four hours); referral; liaison (police, medical, hospital emergency room); victim advocacy; housing (in safe homes, maximum one to two nights).

Women's Haven
185 Carroll Street
Paterson 07505
(201) 881-1450 (Crisis)
(201) 881-0033 (Office)

Services: Community education; counseling (crisis, long term peer support, family, men's group); emergency medical treatment; emergency transportation; hot line (twenty-four hours); referral; legal aid; liaison (police, medical, welfare); victim advocacy; housing (maximum capacity fifteen, sliding-scale fee, children permitted).

Women's Referral Central
(800) 322-8092

Services: Keeps an update list of New Jersey shelters and family-violence resources. A service of Together, Inc., and the New Jersey State Division on Women.

Women's Resource and Survival Center
57 West Front Street
Keyport 07735
(201) 264-4111

Services: Legal aid; counseling; referral; hot line (twenty-four hours); child care; housing (maximum three days).

YWCA Battered Women
111 Storms Street
Jersey City 07306

New Mexico

Battered Families Project
211 South Main

Portales 88130
(505) 356-4779 (Crisis)
(505) 356-8320 (Office)

Services: Counseling; referral; hot line (twenty-four hours); child care (as needed); housing (maximum capacity six families, children permitted).

Battered Women's Project
P.O. Box 5701
Santa Fe 87501
(505) 988-9731

Services: Counseling; referral; hot line (twenty-four hours); housing (maximum capacity seventeen, children permitted).

Information and Referral Resource Center
808 Spruce Street
Las Cruces 88001
(505) 524-3594

Services: Referral (8:30 A.M.–5 P.M., Monday through Friday).

Option
Box 2213
Hobbs 86240

San Juan Mental Health Service Center Against Sexual Assault
805 Maniapal Drive
Room 109
Farmington 87401
(505) 327-9825

Services: Counseling; referral; hot line; housing.

Shelter for Victims of Domestic Violence
8915 Central, N.E.
Albuquerque 87112
(505) 247-4219 (Crisis)
(505) 299-7845 (Office)

Services: Counseling; referral; hot line (twenty-four hours); housing (maximum capacity twenty, maximum two weeks, children permitted, $2/day, sliding scale).

Women's Community Association, Inc.
P.O. Box 6472
Albuquerque, New Mexico 87197

(505) 247-4219 (Crisis)
(505) 299-7845 (Office)

Services: Counseling; referral; hot line (twenty-four hours); housing (maximum capacity twenty, maximum two weeks, children permitted, charge $2/day, sliding-scale fee).

New York

Abused Spouse Assistance Services
29 Sterling Avenue
White Plains 10606
(914) 949-6741 (Crisis)
(914) 949-1741 (Office)

Services: Legal aid; counseling; referral; hot line.

Abused Women
Box 285
Nurses Residence
Nassau County Medical Center
East Meadow 11534

Abused Women Hotline, YWCA of the Tonawandas
49 Tremont Street
North Tonawanda 14120
(716) 692-5580

Abused Women's Aid in Crisis, Inc.
P.O. Box 1699
New York 10001
(212) 686-1676 (Crisis)
(212) 686-3628 (Office)

Services: Referral; counseling; hot line.

Advocates Against Family Violence, YWCA
1000 Cornelia Street
Utica 13502
(315) 797-7740 (Crisis)
(315) 736-0883 (Office)

Services: Peer counseling; referral; hot line (twenty-four hours); child care (9 A.M.–11 A.M.); YWCA housing fund for motel (Maximum three days).

Aid to Battered Women, YWCA
18 Bancroft Road
Poughkeepsie 12601
(914) 454-6160 (Crisis)
(914) 454-6770 (Office)
Contact: Trudy Grundon.

Services: Counseling (crisis, peer support); emergency transportation; emergency shelter in safe homes (one to three nights); hot line (twenty-four hours); referral; liaison (police, medical); victim advocacy.

Aid to Women Victims of Violence, YWCA
14 Clayton Avenue
Cortland 13045
(607) 756-6363

Services: Victim advocacy; referral hot line; housing (maximum three days, children permitted, in private homes).

Alternatives for Battered Women
380 Andrews Street
Rochester 14604

Battered Women Shelter
250 Church Street
13th Floor
New York 10013

Battered Women's Law Project
2 Cannon Street
Poughkeepsie 12601
(914) 473-4818

Services: Legal aid; referral; community education.

Brooklyn Legal Services Corporation
152 Court Street
Brooklyn 11201
(212) 855-8029

Services: Legal aid; referral.

Cayuga County Action Program
60 Clark Street
Auburn 13021

(315) 252-2024 (Crisis)
(315) 253-4057 (Crisis)
(315) 255-1703 (Office)

Services: Legal aid; counseling; referral; hot line; child care (emergency only); housing (in safe homes; maximum one to five days).

Chemung County Task Force for Victims of Domestic Violence
Chemung County Department of Social Services
203–209 William Street
Elmira 14901

Services: Legal aid; counseling; referral; hot line.

Children and Youth Development Services
262 9th Street
Brooklyn 11215
(212) 788-4800

Services: Counseling; referral; hot line (9 A.M.–5 P.M., Monday through Friday).

Coalition against Human Abuse in Columbia-Greene Counties
10 Orchard Drive
Kinderhook 12106
(518) 758-9420

Services: Legal aid; counseling; referral.

Coalition for Abused Women
P.O. Box 94
East Meadow 11554
(516) 542-2594 (Crisis)
(516) 542-2846 (Office)

Services: Legal aid; counseling; referral; hot line (twenty-four hours); community education.

Community Action Organization of Erie County, Incorporated
70 Harvard Place
Buffalo 14209
(716) 881-5150

Services: Legal aid; counseling; referral; hot line (9 A.M.–5 P.M.).

C.W. Post Women's Center
Greenvale 11548
(516) 299-2461

Services: Community education; counseling (crisis, peer support, short term); referral; victim advocacy.

Domestic Violence Program
23 West Main Street
Middletown 10940
(914) 343-3750

Services: Legal aid; counseling; referral; hot line.

Domestic Violence Prosecution Program
Westchester County District Attorney's Office
111 Grove Street
White Plains 10601
(914) 682-2127
(914) 682-2944

Services: Legal counseling; referral; investigation and prosecution.

Eastern Women's Center
14 East 60th Street
New York 10022
(212) 832-0099 (Crisis)
(212) 832-0033 (Office)

Services: Counseling; referral; hot line (twenty-four hours).

Erie County Coalition for Victims of Domestic Violence, Haven House
P.O. Box 45
Niagara Square Station
Buffalo 14201

Services: Counseling; referral; hot line; child care; housing (maximum capacity thirty-eight, children permitted).

Family Abuse Project, Manhattan Family Court
60 Lafayette
New York 10013
(212) 766-9588 (Office)
(212) 766-9587 (Office)

Services: Legal aid, counseling; referral.

Family and Women's Advocates
44 Washington Avenue
Schenectady 12305
(518) 572-5473

Services: Advocacy; decisional counseling; referral.

Family Counseling Service of the Finger Lakes, Incorporated
91 Genesee Street
Geneva 14456
(315) 789-2613

Services: Counseling; referral (sliding-scale fee for all services).

Family of Woodstock, Incorporated
16 Rock City Road
Woodstock 12498
(914) 338-2370

Services: Counseling; legal aid; referral; hot line (twenty-four hours); child care; housing (children permitted).

Family Service Center
26 Grove Street
Kingston 12401
(914) 331-1488

Services: Counseling; referral (sliding-scale fee).

Family Service Department of the Salvation Army
749 South Warren Street
Syracuse 13032
(315) 475-1688

Services: Counseling; referral; hot line (twenty-four hours); child care (day-care available); housing (maximum capacity eight, short term, children permitted).

Farnham Youth Development Center
145 East Bridge Street
Oswego 13126
(315) 342-4472

Services: Counseling; referral; hot line (twenty-four hours); housing (maximum two, maximum forty-eight hours, children permitted).

Franklin County Community Mental Health Services
Main Office
16 Elm Street
Malone 12953
(518) 483-3261

Services: Counseling; referral (sliding-scale fee).

Greene County Department of Social Services
465 Main Street
Catskill 12414
(518) 943-3300 (Crisis, on call)
(518) 943-3200 (Office)

Services: Counseling; referral; child care; housing (emergency only, children permitted).

Greene County Mental Health Center
P.O. Box P
Montain Avenue
Cairo 12413
(518) 943-6666 (Crisis)
(518) 622-9163 (Office)

Services: Counseling; referral; hot line (twenty-four hours).

Haven House
Erie County Domestic Violence
Box 45
Niagara Square Station
Buffalo 14201

Henry Street Settlement Program for Victims of Domestic Violence
265 Henry Street
New York 10002
(212) 766-9300

Services: Legal aid; counseling; referral; child care (planned); housing (maximum capacity eighteen families, maximum three months, children permitted).

Hotline for Battered Women
Box 573
Dunkirk 14048
(716) 366-1220
Contact: Jean Fragokis.

Services: Community education; counseling; emergency transportation; hot line (twenty-four hours); referral; liaison (police, medical, social services); victim advocacy; housing (safe homes, maximum three days, children permitted).

Hudson Guild Family Life Center
441 West 26th Street

New York 10001
(212) 760-9844

Services: Counseling; referral.

Jane Addams Center for Battered Women, Incorporated
P.O. Box 848
New York 10004
(212) 732-2627

Services: Advocacy; counseling; referral; hot line (9 A.M.–5 P.M., Monday through Friday); liaison medical.

The Jefferson County Women's Center, Incorporated
50–52 Public Square
Watertown 13601
(315) 782-1855

Services: Legal aid; counseling; referral; hot line; child care (when needed); housing (maximum capacity twelve, children permitted).

Karen Delrow
116 Benedict Avenue
Syracuse 13210
(315) 478-4910

Services: Legal advice; referral.

Legal Aid of Oneida County, Incorporated
53 West Street
Ilion 13357
(315) 895-7789

Services: Legal aid; referral.

Legal Aid Society Domestic Violence Legal Unit
40 Steuben Street
Albany 12207
(518) 462-6765

Services: Legal aid; referral.

Litigation Coalition for Battered Women
759 10th Avenue
New York 10019
(212) 581-2810

Services: Legal aid.

Long Island Women's Coalition, Incorporated
P.O. Box 183
Islip Terrace 11752
(516) 589-1658
(516) 581-5179
(516) 757-7797

Services: Legal aid; counseling; referral; hot line; housing (temporary, in private homes, maximum capacity six women with children).

Lutheran Community Services, Incorporated
33 Worth Street
New York 10013
(212) 431-7470

Services: Child care (twenty-four hours); community education; counseling (crisis, long term, peer support, family, phobic); referral.

Mental Health Association
Niagara County—SAFE Families
88 East Avenue
Lockport 14094

Mercy House
12 St. Joseph Terrace
Albany 12210
(518) 434-3531

Services: Counseling; referral; housing (maximum capacity nine, limit according to temporary need, children not permitted).

Mid-Hudson Legal Services, Incorporated
50 Market Street
Poughkeepsie 12486
(914) 452-7911

Services: Legal aid; referral.

New York City Human Resources Administration Battered Women's Shelter Program
250 Church Street
New York 10013
(212) 581-4911 (Crisis)
(212) 581-4912 (Office)

Services: Child care; counseling (crisis); hot line (twenty-four hours); referral; legal aid; liaison (medical, day care); housing (maximum capacity sixty families, children permitted).

Niagara County Legal Aid Society, Incorporated
257 Portage Road
P.O. Box 844
Niagara Falls 14302

Services; Legal aid; counseling; referral.

North County Legal Services, Incorporated
Box 61
Upper Jay 12987

Services: Legal aid.

Oswego County Council on Battered Women, Catholic Charities of Oswego
26 West Bridge Street
Oswego 13126
(315) 342-1600 (Crisis, will accept collect calls)
(315) 343-2824 (Office)
(315) 343-9540 (Office)

Services: Child care (hours vary); community education; counseling (crisis, peer support); referral (legal aid, court systems, long term, counseling); victim advocacy; emergency transportation (to hospital ER); hot line (twenty-four hours); housing (in safe homes, maximum capacity as available, children permitted).

Outreach
41 Sussex
Port Jervis 10940
(212) 856-5800

Services: Counseling; referral.

Outreach Women's Defense
665 Greene Avenue
Brooklyn 11221
(212) 452-9835 (Crisis)
(212) 237-7070 (Office)
(212) 237-7071 (Office)

Services: Legal aid; counseling; referral; hot line (twenty-four hours); child care (9 A.M.–4 P.M.); housing (maximum capacity one hundred, maximum one month, children permitted).

Park Slope Safe Homes Project
P.O. Box 429
Van Brun Station

Brooklyn 11215
(212) 449-2151 (Crisis)

Services: Legal aid; advocacy; counseling; referral; hot line (9 A.M.–
9 P.M.); housing (maximum three days).
Funding: Combination city, state, private funding supplemented by community funding.

Park Slope Safe Homes Project, Children and Youth Development Services
262 9th Street
Brooklyn 11215
(212) 449-2151 (Crisis)
(212) 788-4800 (Office)

Services: Legal aid; advocacy; counseling; referral; hot line (9 A.M.–9
P.M.), child care (9 A.M.–9 P.M.); housing (maximum three days, children
permitted).

Prison Families Anonymous, Incorporated
91 North Franklin Street
Room 304
Hempstead 11550
(516) 538-6065

Project Green Hope, Services for Women, Incorporated
448 East 119th Street
New York 10035
(212) 369-5100

Services: Counseling; referral; housing (maximum six months, children not
permitted); parenting education program.

Project Reach, Incorporated
18 South Lackawanna Street
Wayland 14572
(716) 728-5010

Services: Legal aid; referral; housing (maximum three days).

Rape Crisis Center
66 Chenango Street
Binghamton 13901
(607) 722-4256

Services: Counseling; referral; hot line (twenty-four hours).

Rape Crisis Service of Schenectady, Incorporated, YWCA
44 Washington Avenue

Schenectady 12305
(518) 346-2266

Services: Legal aid; psychological and medical information; counseling; referral; hot line (twenty-four hours).

Rockland Family Center
P.O. Box 517
Nyack 10960

Services: Legal aid; counseling; referral; hot line; housing (sliding-scale fee, maximum capacity fourteen, maximum six weeks).

St. Luke's Hospital Battered Women Program
114th Street and Amsterdam Avenue
New York 10025
(212) 870-6080

Services: Counseling (crisis, referral); emergency medical treatment; emergency transportation; staff education; referral; liaison (police, medical, Jane Addams Center, Community Agency).

Salvation Army
414 Lake Street
P.O. Box 459
Elmira 14902
(607) 732-0314

Simple Gifts
80 Richmond Avenue
Buffalo 14222
(716) 884-5330

Services: Legal advocacy; counseling; referral; hot line (twenty-four hours); child care; housing (maximum capacity ten, maximum two months, children permitted).

SOS Shelter, Incorporated
P.O. Box 393
Endicott 13760

Services: Counseling; referral; child care; housing (maximum capacity thirteen, maximum two weeks, children permitted).

Staten Island Women's Crisis Center
159 Richmond Avenue

Staten Island 10302
(212) 727-1509

Services: Community education; counseling (crisis, peer support); emergency transportation; hot line (8 A.M.–8 P.M.); referral; legal aid; liaison (police, medical); victim advocacy; housing referral.

Steuben County Spouse Abuse Task Force
c/o Steuben County, DSS
Box 631
Bath 14810
(607) 776-7611

Task Force for Battered Women
112 The Commons
Ithaca 14850

Tompkins County Task Force for Battered Women
112 The Commons
Ithaca 14850
(607) 272-1616 (Crisis)
(607) 277-3203 (Office)

Services: Legal aid; counseling; referral; hot line (twenty-four hours); housing (in private homes, maximum three days, children permitted).

Tri-Lakes Shelter
P.O. Box 102
Saranac Lake 12983

Vera House, Incorporated
P.O. Box 62
Syracuse 13207
(315) 422-2271

Services: Counseling; referral; hot line (twenty-four hours); housing (maximum capacity ten, maximum three months).

Victims Information Bureau of Suffolk, Incorporated
501 Route 111
Hauppauge 11787
(516) 360-3606 (Crisis)
(516) 360-3730 (Office)

Services: Legal aid; counseling; referral; hot line (twenty-four hours); child care; housing (maximum thirty days, maximum capacity twenty, children permitted).

Victims of Domestic Violence, Department of Social Services
207 William Street
Elmira 14901
(607) 737-2996

Services: Counseling; referral; child care; housing (maximum capacity eight, children permitted).
Funding: Department of Social Services.

Victim/Witness Assistance Project
50 Court Street
Brooklyn 11201
(212) 834-7444 (Crisis)
(212) 834-7450 (Office)

Services: Counseling; referral; hot line; in-court assistance.

Volunteer Counseling Service of Rockland County, Incorporated, Spouse Abuse Educational Workshop
151 South Main Street
New City 10956
(914) 634-5729/9527

Services: Community education; counseling (crisis, long term, peer support, family, education workshop, marital); referral; liaison (police, mental-health service); victim advocacy.

Women Incorporated
P.O. Box 44
Plattsburgh 12901
(518) 563-6904

Services: Counseling; referral; hot line; housing (maximum one night with children, four nights without).

Women's Center of Yonkers
2 Monroe House Square
Yonkers 10701
(914) 969-5800

Services: Legal aid; counseling; referral (child care, housing).

Women's Resource Center of the Jamestown Girls Club
532 East 2nd Street

Jamestown 14701
(716) 484-1820

Services: Counseling; legal information; referral; hot line (9 A.M.–
5 P.M.); housing (maximum seven days, maximum capacity five families,
children permitted).

Women's Shelter
P.O. Box 474
Canton 13617
(315) 386-4130

Services: Child care (as needed); community education; counseling (crisis,
peer support, family); emergency transportation; hot line (twenty-four
hours); referral; liaison (police, mental health); victim advocacy; housing
(maximum capacity ten, maximum six weeks, charge $2/day, children per-
mitted).

Women's Shelter and Personal Assistance Project
3 Chapel Street
Canton 13617
(315) 386-4130

Services: Counseling; referral; hot line (twenty-four hours); child care (as
needed); housing (maximum capacity seven, maximum six weeks, children
permitted).

Women's Survival Space
P.O. Box 279
Bay Ridge Station
Brooklyn 11220
(212) 439-7281 (Crisis)
(212) 439-4612 (Office)

Services: Legal aid; counseling; referral; hot line (9 A.M.–5 P.M.); child
care; housing (charge $5/day, sliding-scale fee, maximum forty-two days,
maximum capacity forty, children permitted).

Yonkers Court Assistance Program for Abused Spouses
45 South Broadway
6th Floor
Yonkers 10701
(914) 963-7450, Ext. 423

Services: Legal aid; counseling; referral.

Yonkers Women's Task Force
32 Pallisades Avenue

Yonkers 10701
(914) 968-4347

Services: Legal aid; counseling; referral; hot line (twenty-four hours); child care (twenty-four hours); housing (charge $3/day, maximum capacity ten, children permitted).

Yonkers Women's Task Force, Incorporated (The Shelter)
P.O. Box 395
Main Post Office
Yonkers 10702
(914) 968-4345 (Crisis)
(914) 968-4347 (Office)

Services: Legal aid; counseling; referral; hot line (twenty-four hours); housing (maximum capacity eight, maximum three weeks, children permitted).

YWCA of Binghamton
Hawley and Exchange Streets
Binghamton 13901
(607) 772-0340

Services: Counseling; referral; child care (mornings only); housing (maximum three days, maximum capacity three, children permitted).

YWCA
401 North Main Street
Jamestown 14701
(716) 485-1137

Services: Child care (sliding-scale fee, 6:30 A.M.–5:30 P.M.); housing (maximum capacity twenty, children permitted).

YWCA Aid to Women Victims
14 Claton Street
Cortland 13045

YWCA For Family Violence
1000 Cornelia Street
Utica 13502

YWCA of the Tonawandas
49 Tremont Street
Tonawanda 14120

(716) 692-5643 (Crisis)
(716) 692-5580 (Office)

Services: Counseling; referral (legal); hot line (twenty-four hours); child care; housing (maximum one day, maximum capacity two, children permitted).

YWCA Services to Families in Violence
44 Washington Avenue
Schenectady 12308

Services: Legal aid; counseling; referral; hot line (twenty-four hours); child care (twenty-four hours); housing (maximum capacity fourteen, maximum twenty-eight days, children permitted).

North Carolina

Battered Women's Crisis Line at Hasslehouse
1022 Urban Avenue
Durham 27701
(919) 688-4353

Services: Legal aid; counseling; referral; hot line (twenty-four hours); housing.

Battered Women's Project
312 Umstead Street
Durham 27707

Battered Women's Service
1201 Glade Street
Winston Salem 27101

Beacon House
Route 3
Box 107
Newport 29570

Care (Citizens Aware and Responding to Emergencies) Center
108 Highland Avenue
Fayetteville 28301
(919) 323-4187

Services: Legal aid; counseling; referral; hot line; housing (maximum two weeks, children permitted).

Carteret County Council on the Status of Women
Beacon House
Route 3
P.O. Box 107
Newport 29570
(919) 726-7039

Services: Emergency shelter; counseling; transportation; advocacy; referral; community education.

Christ Clinic for Women
(919) 353-2115

Services: Counseling; medical services; referral.

Council on Status of Women
Box 344
Vanceboro 28586

Craven County Council on the Status of Women
(919) 247-0867

Services: Housing (emergency); food; counseling; referral.

Domestic Violence Program
406 South Chestnut Street
Henderson 27536
(919) 492-3000

Services: Community education; counseling (crisis, long term, peer support); emergency transportation; hot line (twenty-four hours); referral; liaison (police); victim advocacy; housing (maximum capacity ten adults, children permitted).

Faith Teaching Center
Murphy 28906
(704) 837-7840

Services: Emergency shelter.

Family Crisis Center
301 South Brevard Street
Charlotte 28202
(704) 332-9034 (Days)
(704) 332-0982 (Nights and weekends)

Services: Housing (emergency); counseling; child care; referral; community education.

Family Crisis Council
211 North Church Street
Salisbury 28144

Greensboro Legal Aid Foundation
917 Southeastern Building
Greensboro 27401
(919) 272-0148

Services: Legal aid (no charge for financially eligible clients); referral.

Halifax County Mental Health Center
P.O. Box 757
Roanoke Rapids 27870
(919) 537-2909 (Crisis)
(919) 537-6174 (Office)

Services: Counseling (fee); referral; hot line (twenty-four hours).

Hasslehouse
1022 Urban Avenue
Durham 27701

Helpmate
Asheville Buncombe Community Relations Council
331 College Street
Asheville 28801
(704) 252-8102 (Crisis)
(704) 252-4713 (Office)

Services: Community education; counseling (crisis, long term, peer support); hot line (5 P.M.–8:30 A.M.); referral (housing); liaison (police, medical); victim advocacy.

High Point Women's Shelter
P.O. Box 826
High Point 27261
(919) 889-6636

Services: Emergency shelter; counseling; transportation; child care; referral.

Oasis, Watauga Mental Health Clinic
Watauga County Department of Social Services
King Street
Boone 28607
(704) 264-HELP

Services: Housing (emergency); counseling; transportation; referral; community education.

Orange-Durham YWCA Coalition for Battered Women
809 Proctor Street
Durham 27707
(919) 929-7177 (Crisis)
(919) 688-9353 (Crisis)
(919) 688-4396 (Office)

Services: Legal aid; counseling; referral; hot line (twenty-four hours); housing (temporary motels and boarding homes); victim advocacy.

Randolph County Women's Aid, Incorporated
603 Worth Street
Asheboro 27203
(919) 629-9132

Services: Counseling; transportation; housing (emergency); child care; victim advocacy; referral; community education.

Rape and Abuse Prevention Group of Statesville/Iredell County, Incorporated
Statesville 28677
(704) 872-3403

Services: Counseling; referral; community education.

Rape, Child and Family Crisis Council of Salisbury-Rowan
211 North Church Street
Salisbury 28144
(704) 636-9222

Services: Counseling; referral (fee); hot line (twenty-four hours); housing (as available, fee); community education.

Reach
P.O. Box 1828
Sylva 28779
(704) 568-5647

Services: Emergency shelter; counseling; advocacy, referral.

Real Crisis Intervention, Incorporated
1117 Evans Street

Greenville 27834
(919) 758-HELP

Services: Emergency shelter; counseling; referral; community education.

Shelter
Box 220312
Charlotte 28222

Shelter Home of Caldwell County, Incorporated
907 Harper Avenue, Southwest
Lenior 28645
(704) 758-0888

Services: Community education; counseling (crisis, peer support); emergency transportation; hot line (twenty-four hours); referral; job counseling; victim advocacy; housing (maximum capacity twenty-five, maximum two weeks, in-county $1.50/day/person, out-of-county women $5/day, one child $3, two children $4, three to five children $5).

Support through Sharing
Box 822
Roanoke Rapids 27870

Supporting Ourselves through Sharing
P.O. Box 822
Roanoke Rapids 27870
(919) 537-2909

Services: Emergency shelter; counseling; child care; advocacy.

Switchboard, Battered Women's Project
312 Umstead Street
Durham 27701
(704) 688-1140

Services: Legal aid; counseling; referral; hot line (twenty-four hours); housing.

Task Force against Domestic Violence
(919) 343-4959

Services: Emergency shelter; counseling; child care; referral; community education.

Task Force against Domestic Violence
P.O. Box 595
Wilmington 28402
(800) 672-2930
(919) 762-1900

Services: Emergency shelter; counseling; child care; referral; community education.

Task Force Battered Women
300 South Garden Street
Henderson 27536

Task Force/Family Violence
Box 595
Wilmington 28402

Task Force on Battered Women
Council on the Status of Women
526 North Wilmington Street
Raleigh 27604

Vance County Task Force on Battered Women
(919) 492-5000

Services: Emergency shelter; counseling; advocacy; referral.

Victims Assistance Program
825 East 4th Street
Charlotte 28202
(704) 334-5656

Services: Counseling (crisis); referral; liaison (police); victim advocacy; housing referral.

Wake County Women's Aid: Services for Abused Women, Incorporated
718 Hillsborough Street
Raleigh 27603
(919) 832-4769

Services: Community education; counseling (crisis, long term, peer support); emergency transportation; hot line (twenty-four hours); referral; liaison (police, medical, social service, counseling, housing); victim advocacy (court); housing (in motels, maximum one to two nights, children permitted).

Wake County Women's Aid Services for Abused Women, YWCA
1012 Oberlin Road
Raleigh 27605
(919) 828-3205

Women's Aid Services for Abused Women
P.O. Box 1137
Greensboro 27402
(919) 275-0896 (Crisis)
(919) 379-5256 (Office)

Services: Legal aid; counseling; referral; hot line (twenty-four hours); child care (various hours); housing (emergency, in safe homes, maximum capacity as available, children permitted).

Women's Shelter
P.O. Box 826
High Point 27260

YWCA Battered Women
809 Proctor Street
Durham 27707

North Dakota

Abused Women's Resource Closet
Box 167
Bismarck 58502
(701) 222-8370

Abused Women's Resource Closet
219 North 7th Street
Bismarck 58501
(800) 472-2911 (Crisis)
(701) 258-2240 (Office)

Services: Support group; referral; hot line (twenty-four hours); housing (in safe homes, children permitted).

Abused Women's Services
P.O. Box 471
Washburn 58577
(701) 462-8643

Family Crisis Shelter
Box 1893
Williston 58801
(701) 572-8126

Fargo-Moorhead YWCA
411 Broadway
Fargo 58102
(701) 232-2546

Services: Counseling; referral; housing (temporary, maximum capacity fourteen, children permitted, charge $7/night, $35/week, $125/month plus tax).

Fort Berthoud Reservation
Box 923
New Town 58763
(701) 472-2911 (Hot line)

Legal Assistance of North Dakota
420 North 4th Street, #324
Bismarck 58501
(701) 258-4270

Services: Legal aid (just filing fees in certain cases).

Lutheran Social Service
1407 24th Avenue, South
Grand Forks 58021

McLean County Outreach Abused Women's Services
P.O. Box 506
Washburn 58577
(701) 462-8643

Northwest Human Resources Center/Family Crisis Shelter
P.O. Box 1568
Williston 58801

Office of State Networking Coordinator
710½ East Broadway
Bismarck 58502
(701) 258-6914

Rape and Abuse Crisis Center
P.O. Box 1655

Fargo 58107
(701) 293-7273

SAFE
P.O. Box 1934
Jamestown 58401
(701) 251-2300

Safe Alternatives for Abused Families
Box 657
Devils Lake 58310
(701) 662-8123 or 662-4311
(701) 472-2911 (Hot line)

Safe House
Box 327
Belcourt 58316
(701) 477-5661

Women Abuse, Children's Village, Family Service
1721 South University Drive
Fargo 58102
(800) 472-2911 (Crisis)
(701) 235-6433 (Office)

Services: Counseling; referral; hot line (7 P.M.–1 A.M.); housing.

Women's Action and Resource Center
Beulah 58523
(701) 873-2274

Women's Action Program, Incorporated (Services for Battered Women)
P.O. Box 881
400 22nd Avenue, N.W.
Minot 58701
(701) 857-2000 (Crisis)
(701) 852-1251 (Office)

Services: Counseling; referral; hot line (5 P.M.–9 A.M., weekends, holidays); child care (limited hours); housing (emergency, maximum 1 to 3 days, children permitted).

Women's Alliance
Box 1081
Dickinson 58601
(701) 225-4506

Ohio

Action for Battered Women in Ohio
P.O. Box 15673
Columbus 43215

Akron Task Force on Battered Women
146 South High School Street
Akron 44305

Services: Legal aid; counseling; referral; hot line (10 A.M.–6 P.M., Monday through Friday); child care (for weekly support group only); housing (as available, maximum capacity three women, children permitted).

Alice Paul House, YWCA Battered Women's Shelter
9th and Walnut Streets
Cincinnati 45202
(512) 961-0680

Services: Legal aid; counseling; referral; hot line; housing (maximum capacity seventeen, maximum thirty days, children permitted).

Battered Persons Crisis Center
25 West Rayen Street
Youngstown 45503

Battered Women Project of Youth Services, Incorporated
401 Broadway Building
Lorain 44052
(216) 245-4821 (Weekdays)
(206) 245-3131 (Nights and weekends)

Services: Community education; counseling (crisis, long term, peer support, family); emergency medical treatment; emergency transportation; hot line (twenty-four hours); referral; legal aid; liaison (police, medical, social service); victim advocacy; housing (maximum three weeks, children permitted).

Butler County Woman's Crisis Shelter
5021 Fairfield Circle
Fairfield 45014
(513) 874-3690

Services: Legal aid; counseling (sliding-scale fee); referral; hot line (twenty-four hours); housing (sliding-scale fee, maximum capacity twelve, maximum three to five days, children not permitted).

Canton Battered Service Corporation
1341 Market Avenue, North
Canton 44714

Choices for Victims of Domestic Violence
P.O. Box 8323
Columbus 43201
(614) 294-3381 (Crisis)
(614) 294-7876 (Office)

Services: School and preschool (9 A.M.–11:30 A.M., 1 P.M.–3:30 P.M.); community education; counseling (crisis, long term, peer support); hot line (twenty-four hours); referral; legal information liaison (police, medical); victim advocacy; housing (maximum capacity thirty-two, charge $2.50/day for woman with one child, $3/day for any number of children).

Concerned Citizens against Violence against Women, Incorporated, Turning Point Shelter
P.O. Box 822
Marion 43302
(614) 382-8988 (Crisis)
(614) 382-9192 (Office)

Services: Child care; community education; counseling (crisis, long term, referral, peer support); emergency medical treatment; emergency transportation; hot line (twenty-four hours); referral; legal aid; liaison (police, medical); victim advocacy; housing (maximum capacity eighteen, maximum ninety days, $2 charge, children permitted).

Crossroad Crisis Center
P.O. Box 643
Lina 45804

Every Women's House
245 North Buckeye Street
Wooster 44691

Family Crisis Network
965 South Echo Street
Celina 45822
(419) 586-1133 (Crisis)
(419) 586-4054 (Office)

Services: Child care (for women going to court); community education; counseling (family, alcoholism, mental health); emergency medical treatment; emergency transportation; hot line (twenty-four hours); referral; legal aid; housing (short stay, children permitted).

Family Service Association
122 West Church Street
Newark 43055
(614) 345-HELP (Crisis)
(614) 345-4498 (Office)

Services: Counseling; referral; hot line; housing (maximum three nights, sliding-scale fee).

Family Services of Greater Toledo
Suite 414
1 Stranahan Square
Toledo 43604
(419) 244-5511

Services: Counseling (crisis, long term, family, marital).

Furnace Street Mission
P.O. Box 444
Akron 44309
(216) 923-0174

Services: Counseling; referal; hot line (twenty-four hours); housing (maximum seven days, children permitted).

Genesis House Program for Battered Women
401 Broadway
Lorain 44052

Greene County Crisis Center
53 North Collier Street
Xenia 45385
(513) 376-2993 (Crisis)
(513) 376-9471 (Office)

Services: Counseling (sliding-scale fee); referral; hot line (twenty-four hours); housing (maximum two nights, children permitted).

Heidi House
P.O. Box 8053
Columbus 43201
(614) 294-2720

Services: Legal aid; counseling; referral; child care; housing (maximum capacity four, $1.50/day, maximum six months, children permitted).

Homesafe, Inc.
P.O. Box 702
Ashtabula 44004

Lake County Committee on Sexual Assault and Domestic Violence, Inc./ Forbes House
P.O. Box 702
Plainsville 44077
(216) 354-6838 (Crisis)
(216) 953-0600 (Office)

Services: Counseling; hot line (twenty-four hours); victim advocacy; support groups; housing (Forbes House, children permitted).

My Sister's Place
P.O. Box 1158
Athens 45701
(614) 593-3402

Services: Counseling; referral; hot line (twenty-four hours); child care; housing (maximum capacity twelve, maximum one month, children permitted).

Newark Battered Women Services
122 West Church Street
Newark 43055

Night Prosecutor's Program
City Hall Annex
67 North Front Street
Columbus 43215
(614) 222-7483

Services: Counseling; referral; hot line (8 A.M.–midnight); mediation.

Northwestern Ohio Crisis Line
P.O. Box 13
Defiance 43512

Phoenix House
P.O. Box 823
Columbus 43201

Pike County Battered Women's Task Force
418 West Emitt Avenue
Waverly 45690

Services: Referral; housing.

Project Woman
712½ North Fountain Avenue
Springfield 45504

Project Women
22 East Grand
Springfield 45506
(513) 325-3707

Services: Counseling; referral; hot line (twenty-four hours); housing (maximum seven days, place women in other facilities).

Rescue-Crisis Center
One Stranahan Square, #141
Toledo 43604

Richland County Task Force on Domestic Violence
P.O. Box 1524
Mansfield 44901
(419) 526-4450

Services: Legal aid; counseling; referral; hot line; child care; housing (maximum capacity sixteen, maximum two weeks, children permitted).

Task Force/Battered Women
P.O. Box 9074
Akron 44305

Templum
P.O. Box 5466
Cleveland 44101

Toledo YWCA Battered Women Services
1018 Jefferson
Toledo 43624

Transitions, Inc.
P.O. Box 326
Zanesville 43701

Services: Counseling; job placement; child care; legal aid; temporary residential services.

Turning Point
P.O. Box 822
Marion 43302

Van Wert Crisis Center Line
P.O. Box 266
Van Wert 45801

Witness/Victim Service Center of Cuyahoga County
Justice Center
1215 West 3rd Street
Cleveland 44113
(216) 623-7345

Services: Legal information; counseling; referral; child care (8:30 A.M.–4:30 P.M.).

Woman Together, Inc.
P.O. Box 6331
Cleveland 44104
(216) 961-4422 (Crisis)
(216) 631-3556 (Office)

Services: Legal aid; counseling; referral; hot line (twenty-four hours); child care (9 A.M.–4 P.M., 6 P.M.–8 P.M.); housing (maximum capacity eight women, twenty children).

Women's Crisis Shelter
5021 Fairfield
Fairfield 45014

Women Shelter
Box 545
Ravenna 44266

Women Shelter, Inc.
1206 North Mantua
Kent 44240

YWCA, Alice Paul House
9th and Walnut
Cincinnati 45202

YWCA Battered Women Project
141 West Third Street
Dayton 45402

YWCA Battered Women's Shelter
1018 Jefferson Street
Toledo 43624

YWCA of Clermont County
55 South 4th Street
Batoria 45103
(216) 732-0450

Services: Counseling; referral.

YWCA Protective Shelter
Battered Women and Their Children
244 Dayton Avenue
Hamilton 45011

Oklahoma

Legal Services of Eastern Oklahoma, Inc.
23 West 4th Street
Tulsa 74103
(918) 584-3211

Services: Legal aid; referral.

New Directions Shelter for Battered Women
P.O. Box 1684
Lawton 73502
(405) 355-7575

Services: Hot line (twenty-four hours); advocacy; emergency shelter; community education.

Stillwater Domestic Violence Service
619 West 12th
Stillwater 74074
(405) 624-3020
Contact: Sherry Maxwell.

Services: Hot line (twenty-four hours); community education; advocacy; referrals for abusers.

Tulsa Force for Battered Women, Inc.
524 South Boulder
Room 206
Tulsa 74103
(918) 622-2345 (Crisis)
(918) 585-8917 (Office)

Services: Counseling; referral; hot line (twenty-four hours); child care (limited).

Women's Resource Center/Norman, Oklahoma Task Force for Battered Women
P.O. Box 474
Peters and Gray
Norman 73070
(405) 364-9424

Services: Counseling; referral; hot line; housing (maximum three days, children permitted).

YWCA Option House Shelter
525 South Quincy
Erid 73701
(405) 234-7644

Services: Hot line (twenty-four hours); community education; emergency housing; permanent housing assistance; referrals for abusers.

YWCA Passageway, A Women's Crisis Center
135 Northwest 19th
Oklahoma City 73103
(405) 528-5508 (Crisis)
(405) 528-5540 (Office)

Services: Counseling; referral; hot line (twenty-four hours); housing (maximum three days, children permitted); community education; advocacy; liaison (police).

YWCA Women's Resource Center
3626 North Western Avenue
Oklahoma City 73118
(405) 528-5540

Services: Counseling; referral; hot line (daytime hours only); housing (maximum three days, children permitted).

Oregon

Beware
P.O. Box 494
Hillsboro 97123
(503) 640-1171 (Crisis)
(503) 640-5352 (Office)

Services: Community education; counseling (crisis, peer support, group therapy); hot line (twenty-four hours); referral; legal aid; liaison (police, medical); victim advocacy; housing (maximum two to three weeks, charge $3/day, children permitted).

Bradley/Angle House
P.O. Box 40132
Portland 97240
(503) 281-2442 (Crisis)
(503) 281-8275 (Office)
(503) 249-8117 (Child program)

Services: Legal aid; counseling; referral; hot line (twenty-four hours); child care; housing (maximum capacity fifteen, children permitted).

Central Oregon Battering and Rape Alliance/Women's Crisis Service, Cobra/WCS
P.O. Box 1086
Bend 97701
(503) 389-7021
(503) 382-4961
Contact: Connie Hyatt.

Services: Community education; counseling; emergency transportation; hot line (twenty-four hours); referral; legal aid; liaison (police, medical, district attorney); victim advocacy; housing (children permitted).

Coos County Women's Crisis Service, Inc.
P.O. Box 772
Coos Bay 97420
(503) 267-2020

Services: Community education; counseling; emergency transportation; hot line (twenty-four hours); referral; liaison (medical, other agencies); victim advocacy; housing (maximum capacity three families, maximum three days, charge negotiable, children permitted).

Domestic Violence Intervention Center
19600 South Molalla Avenue
Oregon City 97045
(503) 657-8400, Ext. 404
Contact: Kathleen Normile, Paul Moon.

Services: Community education; counseling; limited emergency transportation; hot line (8 A.M.–4 P.M.); referral; liaison; victim advocacy.

Domestic Violence Resource Center Shelter
Box 494
Hillsboro 97123

Family Shelter
369 Highway 99, North
Eugene 97402
(503) 689-7156

Services: Legal aid; counseling (including support group); referral; housing (maximum capacity eight, maximum two to four weeks, children permitted); $5–$10/week requested for services.

Jackson County Task Force on Household Violence
P.O. Box 369
Ashland 97520
(503) 779-HELP

Services: Child care (hours vary); community education; counseling (crisis, peer support, child); emergency medical treatment; emergency transportation; hot line (twenty-four hours); referral; legal aid; liaison (police, medical, Social Services Agency); victim advocacy; housing (maximum capacity sixteen, maximum three weeks, A.F.S. room/board, children permitted).

Lincoln Shelter and Services, Incorporated
P.O. Box 426
Lincoln City 97367
(503) 994-5959

Services: Counseling; hot line (twenty-four hours); referral; housing (maximum three weeks, children permitted).

Parents Anonymous of Oregon
3214 S.E. Holgate
Room 311

Portland 97202
(503) 238-8818 (Crisis)
(503) 238-8819 (Office)

Services: Counseling (self-help group); hot line (twenty-four hours); referral; self-help program for child-abusing parents.

Rape Relief Hotline
522 S.W. 5th
6th Floor
Portland 97202
(503) 235-5333 (Crisis)
(503) 224-7125 (Office)

Services: Counseling; referral; hot line (twenty-four hours).

Raphael House
P.O. Box 10797
Portland 97210
(503) 223-4544

Services: Legal aid; counseling (support group); referral; housing (maximum capacity ten, maximum eight days, children permitted).

Refuge House
920 S.E. Cass
Roseburg 97470
(503) 673-0240

Services: Counseling; referral; housing (maximum capacity four families including men, maximum two weeks, $5/day fee for four family members).

Union County Task Force on Domestic Violence
1007 4th Street
La Grande 97850
(503) 963-8156 (Crisis)
(503) 963-3188 (Office)

Services: Child care; community education; counseling (including batterer); emergency medical treatment; emergency transportation; hot line (twenty-four hours); referral; legal aid; liaison (police, medical); victim advocacy; housing (in safe homes).

Volunteers of America
2000 S.E. 7th
Portland 97208
(503) 232-6562

Services: Counseling; referral; hot line (twenty-four hours); housing (maximum capacity fifty-four, maximum thirty days, $5/day/person, children permitted).

Womanspace
P.O. Box 21167
Eugene 97402
(503) 485-6513

Services: Legal aid; counseling (support group); referral; hot line (twenty-four hours); housing (maximum capacity eighteen, maximum two to three weeks, children permitted, sliding-scale fees $2–5 or welfare per diem grant for services).

Womanspace
P.O. Box 3030
Eugene 97403
(503) 485-6513

Services: Counseling; referral; hot line; housing (sliding-scale, children permitted).

Women's Crisis Service
P.O. Box 851
Salem 97308
(503) 399-7722 (Crisis)
(503) 378-1572 (Office)

Services: Child care (hours vary); community education; counseling (crisis, long term, peer support, parent training); emergency transportation; hot line (twenty-four hours); referral; liaison (police, medical); victim advocacy; housing (maximum capacity eighteen, $14/day, children permitted).

Women's Crisis Support Team
c/o Bethany Presbyterian Church
748 N.W. 5th Street
Grants Pass 97526
(503) 479-HELP (Crisis, ask for Women's Crisis Team)
(503) 479-9349 (Office)

Services: Community education; counseling (crisis); emergency transportation; hot line (twenty-four hours); referral; liaison (police, medical; victim advocacy.

Women's Place Resource Center
1915 N.E. Everett

Portland 97232
(503) 234-7044

Services: Community education; counseling (peer support); referral.

Women's Resource Center of Lincoln for Battered Women
908 S.W. Hurbert
Newport 97365
(503) 265-2491 (Crisis)
(503) 265-7551 (Office)

Services: Counseling; referral; hot line (twenty-four hours); housing ($1/
night, maximum capacity ten, children permitted).

Pennsylvania

Access-York, Incorporated
c/o Mrs. Jane Tucker
R.D. 2
P.O. Box A-402
Dallastown 17313
(717) 845-3656 (Crisis)
(717) 845-6624 (Office)

Services: Counseling (crisis, long term, family, emergency); hot line (twenty-
four hours); referral.

A Woman's Place
108 Main Street
Sellersville 18960
(215) 257-0188

Services: Counseling; referral; hot line (twenty-four hours); housing (maximum capacity six, maximum fourteen days, $2.50/day, children permitted).

A Women's Place, Incorporated
P.O. Box 946
Doylestown 18901
(215) 348-9780 (Crisis)
(215) 752-8035 (Crisis)
(215) 343-9241 (Office)

Services: Community education; counseling (crisis, peer support); emergency transportation; hot line (twenty-four hours); referral; legal aid;
liaison (police, medical); victim advocacy; housing (maximum capacity
fourteen, maximum thirty days, $2.50/night, children permitted).

Berks County Women in Crisis
P.O. Box 803
Reading 19603
(215) 372-9540 (Crisis)
(215) 373-2053 (Office)

Services: Community education; counseling (crisis, peer support); emergency transportation; hot line (twenty-four hours); referral; legal aid; liaison (police, medical, welfare); victim advocacy; housing.

Berks Women in Crisis
c/o Jacque Melton
1045 Moss Street
Reading 19604
(215) 372-7273

Services: Legal aid; counseling; referral; hot line.

Central Pennsylvania Legal Services
524 Washington Street
Reading 19604
(215) 376-8656

Services: Legal advice; counseling; referral.

Centre County Women's Resource Center and Rape/Abuse Crisis Line
108 W. Beaver Avenue
State College 16801
(814) 234-5050 (Crisis)
(814) 234-5222 (Office)

Services: Counseling; referral; hot line (twenty-four hours); housing (in private homes, maximum two to three days, children permitted).

Clearfield/Jefferson Community Mental Health Center
102 Hospital Avenue
DuBois 15801
(800) 262-0707 (Crisis)
(814) 371-1100 (Office)

Services: Community education; counseling (crisis, long term, family, child); hot line (twenty-four hours); referral; liaison (police); victim advocacy.

Clinton County Women's Center
132½ E. Main Street
P.O. Box 504

Lock Haven 17745
(717) 748-9509
(717) 748-9500

Services: Community education; counseling (crisis, peer support); emergency transportation; referral; liaison (medical, area agencies).

Domestic Abuse Program of Erie County, Incorporated
335 W. 8th Street
Erie 16502
(814) 453-5656 (Crisis)
(814) 453-7102 (Office)

Domestic Violence Program at the Women's Resource Center, Incorporated
312-15A Bank Towers Building
Scranton 18503
(717) 346-4671

Services: Community education; counseling (crisis, long term); hot line (twenty-four hours); referral; liaison (police, medical, legal); victim advocacy.

Domestic Violence Service Center
P.O. Box 1662
Wilkes Barre 18703
(717) 823-7312 (Crisis)
(717) 823-5834 (Office)

Services: Legal aid; counseling; referral; hot line; housing (maximum capacity seventeen, children permitted); community education.

Elk City Crisis Line
c/o Ruth Arick, Patti Smith
316 W. Theresia Road
Saint Mary's 15857
(814) 834-1227

Services: Counseling; referral; hot line (twenty-four hours); housing (maximum capacity ten, maximum two to three days, children permitted).

Fayette County Family Abuse Council
64 S. Beeson Boulevard
Uniontown 15401
(412) 785-7532 (Crisis)
(412) 438-1470 (Office)

Services: Legal aid; counseling; referral; hot line (day and evenings); child care (limited, days); housing (in private homes).

Horizon House
Union City 16438
(814) 438-2675

Services: Counseling (crisis, long term, peer support, family); legal aid; liaison (police); housing (maximum capacity eight, maximum thirty days, $2/day, children permitted).

Hospitality House
240 E. 10th Street
Erie 16503
(814) 454-8161

Services: Counseling; hot line (twenty-four hours); referral; housing (maximum five days, children permitted).

Hotline for Abused Women/Kensington and Lutheran Settlement House/Women's Program
1340 Frankford Avenue
Philadelphia 19125
(215) 739-9999 (Crisis)
(215) 426-8610 (Office)

Services: Community education; counseling (crisis, long term, peer support); hot line (weekday hours); referral; liaison (bilingual services); victim advocacy.

Lancaster Shelter for Abused Women
P.O. Box 359
Lancaster 17604
(717) 299-1249 (Crisis)
(717) 299-9677 (Office)

Services: Child care (hours vary); community education; counseling (crisis, long term, peer support, family); hot line (twenty-four hours); referral; legal aid; liaison (police, medical); victim advocacy; housing (maximum capacity twenty-five, maximum thirty-three days, children permitted, no charge).

Marital Abuse Project
P.O. Box 174
Media 19063

Marital Abuse Project of Delaware County, Incorporated
P.O. Box 294
Wallingford 19086
(215) 565-4590 (Crisis)
(215) 565-6272 (Office)

Services: Counseling; referral; hot line.

The Open Door of Indiana, Pennsylvania
1008 Philadelphia Street
Indiana 15701
(412) 465-2605

Services: Community education; counseling (crisis, long term, family); hot line (twenty-four hours); referral; liaison (police, medical, agencies); victim advocacy.

Pennsylvania Coalition against Domestic Violence
2405 N. Front Street
Harrisburg 17110
(717) 233-6030

Services: Legal aid; counseling; referral; hot line.

Southern Alleghenys Legal Aid, Incorporated
P.O. Box 202
Bedford 15522
(814) 623-6189

Services: Referral; legal aid.

Susquehanna Valley Women in Transition, Incorporated
P.O. Box 502
Sunbury 17801
(717) 379-9625

Services: Legal aid; counseling; referral; hot line.

Turning Point of Lehigh Valley
522½ Cedar Street
Allentown 18102
(215) 437-3369 (Crisis)
(215) 776-1341 (Office)

Services: Community education; counseling (peer support); hot line (twenty-four hours); referral; liaison (police, medical); victim advocacy.

Turning Point of Lehigh Valley
P.O. Box 5162
Bethlehem 18015
(215) 437-3369

Services: Counseling; referral to limited housing (six to ten beds, maximum three nights).

Volunteers against Abuse Center
Calvin United Presbyterian Church
Grandview Avenue
Zelienople 16063
(412) 452-5710

Services: Legal aid; counseling; referral; hot line (six hours, Monday through Friday).

Wise Options for Women, YWCA
815 W. 4th Street
Williamsport 17701
(717) 322-4714

Services: Counseling; referral; hot line (twenty-four hours); child care (daytime); housing; (maximum capacity eight, maximum thirty days, children permitted).

Woman's Aid Center, Incorporated
67 N. Church Street
Hazelton 18201
(717) 455-9971 (Crisis)
(717) 455-9972 (Office)

Services: Community education; counseling (crisis, long term, hot line (5 P.M.–midnight); referral; legal aid; liaison (police, medical).

Woman's Place
P.O. Box 946
Doylestown 18901

Womanplace
631 Share Avenue
McKeesport 15132
(412) 678-4616

Services: Community education; counseling; hot line (twenty-four hours); referral.

Womanspace East
3274 Parkview Street
Pittsburgh 15213

Women against Abuse
P.O. Box 12233
Philadelphia 19144
(215) 386-7777 (Crisis)
(215) 386-1280 (Office)
(215) 386-5773 (Office)

Services: Child care; counseling; hot line (twenty-four hours); referral;
legal aid; housing (maximum capacity thirty, maximum thirty days, sliding-
scale fee, children permitted).

Women in Crisis
4th and Market Streets
Harrisburg 17101
(717) 238-1068

Services: Legal aid; counseling; referral; hot line (twenty-four hours); child
care (daytime hours only); housing $2/night, maximum thirty days, maxi-
mum capacity seven, children permitted).

Women in Crisis
R.D. 1
P.O. Box 314A
Hummelstown 17036
(717) 534-1101 (Crisis)
(717) 535-1103 (Office)

Services: Community education; counseling (crisis, group); emergency
transportation; hot line (twenty-four hours); referral; liaison (police, medical, agencies); victim advocacy; housing (maximum capacity ten families,
maximum thirty days, sliding-scale fee, children permitted).

Women in Crisis/YWCA
8th and Washington Streets
Reading 19604
(717) 372-7273

Services: Legal aid; counseling; hot line (twenty-four hours).

Women in Need
P.O. Box 25

Chambersburg 17201
(717) 264-4444 (Crisis)
(717) 264-3056 (Office)

Services: Counseling; referral; hot line (twenty-four hours); housing (maximum two days, children permitted).

Women in Transition
4025 Chestnut Street
Suite 303
Philadelphia 19104
(215) 382-7016 (Crisis)
(215) 382-7019 (Office)

Services: Legal aid; counseling (sliding-scale fee); referral; hot line (10 A.M.–noon, 2 P.M.–4 P.M.).

Women Services of Westmoreland County
223 North Maple Street
Greensburg 15601

Womencenter
76 C. Jefferson Avenue
Sharon 16146
(412) 528-2110

Services: Community education; counseling (crisis, peer support, short term); hot line (twenty-four hours); referral; liaison (police, medical, social service); victim advocacy.

Womencenter Domestic Violence Service Center
P.O. Box 621
Wilkes Barre 18703
(717) 829-7868

Services: Legal aid; counseling; referral; hot line.

Women's Alternative Center
Station Road
Wawa 19063
(215) 459-9177

Services: Child care (8:30 A.M.–4:30 P.M.); counseling (long term, peer support, family); housing (maximum capacity eight to ten mothers, fifteen children, maximum three to six months, sliding-scale fee); residential program for female-headed families.

Women's Center
1305 Third Avenue
Beaver Falls 15101

Women's Center and Shelter of Greater Pittsburgh
616 North Highland Avenue
Pittsburgh 15206
(412) 661-6066

Services: Counseling; referral; hot line (twenty-four hours); child care; housing (maximum capacity nineteen, maximum six days, $2/night, children permitted).

Women's Center and Shelter of Greater Pittsburgh, North Hills
Zoar Home Annex
Mount Royal Boulevard
Allison Park 15101
(215) 487-4700

Services: Counseling (crisis); emergency transportation; hot line (10 A.M.–4 P.M.); referral; legal aid; liaison (police).

Women's Center Family Support System
P.O. Box 221
Bloomsburg 17815
(717) 784-6631

Services: Community education; counseling (crisis, peer support); hot line (twenty-four hours); referral; liaison (police); housing (maximum three days, charge $3, children permitted).

Women's Center of Beaver County
175 West Washington Street
Rochester 15074
(412) 775-0131

Services: Counseling; referral; hot line (twenty-four hours); child care (9 A.M.–noon); housing (maximum capacity twenty, maximum seven days, $2 donation required, children permitted).

Women's Center of Montgomery County, Domestic Violence Committee
1030 York Road
Abington 19001
(215) 885-5020

Services: Community education; counseling (crisis, peer support); emergency transportation; hot line (twenty-four hours) referral; liaison (police, medical); victim advocacy.

Women's Center, Williamsport, Inc.
P.O. Box 1292
151 West 4th Street
Williamsport 17701
(717) 323-4529

Services: Counseling; referral; hot line (twenty-four hours).

Women's Help Center/YWCA
526 Somerset Street
Johnstown 15901

Women's Place
108 Main Street
Sullersville 18960

Women's Resource Center of Chester County/YWCA
123 North Church Street
West Chester 19380
(215) 431-1430

Services: Referral; hot line (twenty-four hours); counseling; child care (daytime); housing (maximum fourteen days, children permitted).

Women's Resource Network
4025 Chestnut Street
Philadelphia 19104
(215) 387-0420

Services: Legal aid; counseling; referral.

Women's Services, Greenhouse
P.O. Box 637
Meadville 16335
(814) 333-9766

Services: Referral; hot line (twenty-four hours); housing (maximum capacity ten, maximum seven days, charge $4/adult, $2/child, children permitted).

Women's Services of Westmoreland County
Bank and Trust Building
Greensburg 15601
(412) 836-1122 (Crisis)
(412) 837-9540 (Office)

Services: Counseling; referral; hot line (twenty-four hours).

YWCA
Lancaster Shelter
Box 359
Lancaster 17604

YWCA Women's Center
123 North Church Street
West Chester 19380

YWCA Women's Help Center
526 Somerset Street
Johnstown 15901
(814) 536-5361

Services: Legal aid; counseling; referral; hot line (9 A.M. – 9 P.M., Monday through Friday).

Rhode Island

Elizabeth Buffum Chase House, Inc.
P.O. Box 9018
Conimicut Station
Warwick 02889
(401) 738-1700

Services: Hot line (9 A.M. – 5 P.M., Monday through Friday); safe homes; community education; support groups; legal advocacy; coalition members; brochure available.

Newport County Women's Resource Center
P.O. Box 151
Broadway Station
Newport 02840
(401) 847-2533 (Crisis)
(401) 846-5263 (Office)

Services: Hot line (twenty-four hours); shelter (capacity nine, maximum three days); overflow housing; community education; support groups; legal advocacy; transportation; brochure available.

Rhode Island Legal Services, Inc.
77 Durance Street
Providence 02903
(401) 274-3140

Services: Legal aid; referral.

Sojourner House
P.O. Box 5667
Weybosset Hill Station
Providence 02903
(401) 751-1262 (Crisis)
(401) 521-4921 (Office)

Services: Hot line (twenty-four hours); shelter (maximum capacity five women and their children, maximum five weeks); community education; legal advocacy; child care; transportation; coalition members; brochure available.

Woman's Resource Center of Wood River
P.O. Box 358
Wyoming 02898
(401) 539-2569 (Crisis)
(401) 539-2028 (Office)

Services: Hot line (9 A.M.–9 P.M. Monday and Wednesday; 9 A.M.–5 P.M., Tuesday, Thursday, and Friday); shelter (maximum capacity three women, six children, maximum four to six weeks); safe homes; overflow housing; community education; support groups; legal advocacy; coalition members; brochure available.

Women's Center, Inc.
45 East Transit Street
Providence 02906
(401) 861-2760

Services: Hot line (twenty-four hours); shelter (maximum capacity fourteen women, ten children, maximum four to six weeks); community education; support groups; legal advocacy; child care; coalition members; brochure available.

San Juan Islands

Friday Harbor
Evelyn: 378-2847
Susan G.: 378-2474 (Home), 378-4994 (Work)
Susan R.: 378-4916 (Work)

Lopez
Josie: 486-2586
Rosie: 486-2496
Jeannie: 486-2671
Leona: 486-2868

Orcas
Fran: 376-2643
Lois: 376-4675
Ruth: 376-4347

South Carolina

My Sister's House
Charleston 29404

Providence Home, Women's Shelter
3425 North Main Street
Columbia 29203
(803) 779-4706
(803) 252-5264
Contact: Sr. Kathy Riley, Sr. Helen Cullen.

Services: Community education; counseling; emergency transportation; referral; liaison (police, medical); housing (maximum capacity sixteen).

Sister Care, YWCA
1505 Blanding Street
Columbia 29201

Women in Crisis/Family Counseling Service
P.O. Box 10306
Greenville 29603
(803) 271-0220 (Crisis)
(803) 232-2434 (Office)

Services: community education; counseling (crisis, peer support, long term, family, marriage); hot line (twenty-four hours); referral; legal aid;

housing (maximum capacity fourteen, maximum fourteen days, children permitted).

Women's Advocacy Center
P.O. Box 501
Charleston 29402
(803) 881-0099 (Crisis)
(803) 884-2070 (Office)
Contact: Sally Gartzke.

Services: Community education; counseling (crisis, long term, family, husband/male); emergency transportation; hot line (twenty-four hours); referral; legal aid; liaison (police, medical, magistrate); victim advocacy.

South Dakota

Anpo-Techa (New Dawn)
c/o Judy Brown
Eagle Butte 57625
(605) 964-6602

Brookings Women's Center
802 11th Avenue
Brookings 57006
(605) 692-4359 (Crisis)
(605) 688-4518 (Office)

Services: Counseling; referral; housing ($4/per day, children permitted).

Citizens against Rape and Domestic Violence
Sioux Falls Citizens against Rape and Domestic Violence
P.O. Box 297
Sioux Falls 57101
(605) 688-4518

Crisis Intervention Team
301 South 5th Street
Hot Springs 57747
(605) 745-6070

Domestic Violence Prevention Center
White Buffalo Calf Women's Society, Incorporated
P.O. Box 227
Mission 57555
(605) 747-2283 or 747-2284

Domestic Violence Task Force
Lake County Women's Caucus
P.O. Box 236
Madison 57042
(605) 246-6551

People Helping People, Incorporated
P.O. Box 96
Wagner 57380
(605) 384-5911

Sacred Shawl Women's Society, Incorporated
P.O. Box 273
Pine Ridge 57770
(605) 867-5138

South Central Community Act Program
P.O. Box 6
Lake Andes 57356
(605) 487-7634

Services: Legal aid; counseling; referral; hot line (twenty-four hours);
housing (maximum capacity fourteen, children permitted).

South Dakota Coalition against Domestic Violence
Box 500
Eagle Butte 57625
(609) 964-2175

Women and Violence, Incorporated
P.O. Box 3042
Rapid City 57709
(605) 341-4808 (Crisis)

Women in Crisis Coalition, Incorporated
P.O. Box 110
Northern Black Hills Area
Deadwood 57732
(605) 642-7844

Women in Crisis Task Force/Women's Crisis Task Force
c/o Missouri Shores Women's Resource Center
P.O. Box 101
Pierre 57501
(605) 224-6224

Women's Place
c/o YWCA
P.O. Box 647
Aberdeen 57401
(605) 225-7159 (8 A.M.–5 P.M.)
(605) 225-1010 or 225-1014 (After hours)
Contact: Sandra Peterson.

Services: Child care (8 A.M.–5 P.M.); community education; counseling; hot line (twenty-four hours); referral; liaison (police, medical, legal, social services, housing assistance); housing (maximum capacity fourteen, maximum four weeks, $5/day if possible, children permitted).

Women's Resource Center
P.O. Box 781
Watertown 57201
(605) 886-4300

Yankton Task Force Contact Center
P.O. Box 675
Yankton 57078
(605) 665-4725

YWCA Women's Place
P.O. Box 647
Aberdeen 57401
(605) 225-1010 or 225-7159 (Crisis line)

Tennessee

Child and Family Services
114 Dameron Street
Knoxville 37919

Child and Family Services, Family Crisis Center
2535 Magnolia Avenue
Knoxville 37914
(615) 637-8000 (Crisis)
(615) 524-7483 (Office)

Services: Community education; counseling (crisis, long term, peer support, group, individual); emergency transportation; hot line (twenty-four hours); referral; liaison (police, medical); victim advocacy; housing (maximum capacity ten, maximum two weeks, no charge, children permitted).

Knoxville Women's Center
406 Church Avenue
Knoxville 37902
(615) 546-1873

Services: Community education; referral.

Legal Services of Middle Tennessee
111 South 2nd Street
Clarksville 37040
(615) 552-6656

Services: Legal aid.

Lexington-Henderson County Counseling Center
107 East Church Street
Lexington 38351
(901) 968-3322 (Crisis)
(901) 968-8197 (Office)

Services: Counseling (crisis, long term, peer support, group, family); hot line (6 P.M.–10 P.M.); referral; victim advocacy.

Nashville Consortium on Domestic Violence
c/o Council of Community Services
250 Venture Circle
Nashville 37228

Services: Community education.

Oasis House
1013 17th Avenue, South
Nashville 37212
(615) 327-4455

Services: Counseling (crisis, long term, peer support, family, groups); hot line (twenty-four hours); referral; legal aid; liaison; victim advocacy; housing for children (maximum capacity nine, maximum thirty days, no charge, only children permitted).

Salvation Army Emergency Family Shelter
200 Monroe Street
Memphis 38103
(901) 526-1066

Services: Counseling (crisis); emergency transportation; referral; victim advocacy; housing (maximum capacity forty-five, no charge, children permitted).

Services for Women in Crisis, Incorporated
P.O. Box 3240
Nashville 37219
(615) 254-1168

Services: Job training; victim advocacy.

Tennessee Commission on the Status of Women
100 Andrew Jackson Building
Nashville 37219
(800) 342-1189 (Office)
(616) 741-1013 (Office)

Services: Referral.

"The Shelter" Victims of Domestic Violence, Incorporated
P.O. Box 3388
Bristol 37620
(703) 466-2312
(615) 968-9612
Contact: Pam Eisenbise.

Services: Community education; counseling; hot line (twenty-four hours); referral; emergency medical treatment; emergency transportation; legal aid; liaison (police, medical); housing (maximum capacity twelve, maximum two weeks, $1.50/adult $0.50/child).

Victim Advocacy/District Attorney's Staff
107 Cumberland Avenue
Ashland City 37015
(615) 292-9623 (Crisis)
(615) 292-4404 (Office)

Services: Legal aid; counseling; referral; hot line.

Wife Abuse Crisis Service
4995 Patterson
Memphis 38111
(901) 458-1661 (Crisis)
(901) 324-4969 (Office)

Services: Counseling; referral; hot line (9 A.M.–5 P.M.); limited child care.

YWCA Domestic Violence Program
1608 Woodmont Boulevard
Nashville 37215
(615) 385-3952

Services: Community education; counseling (crisis, peer support); training for direct service personnel; community organizing; referral; victim advocacy.

Texas

Anderson County Shelter
1504 West Reagan
Palestine 75801

Services: Counseling; referral; housing (maximum capacity five women, limit three months, children permitted).

Center for Battered Women
P.O. Box 5631
Austin 78763
(512) 472-HURT (Crisis)
(512) 472-4879 (Office)

Services: Legal aid; counseling; referral; hot line (twenty-four hours); child care; housing (maximum twenty-eight days, maximum capacity fourteen, children permitted).

Domestic Violence Intervention Alliance, The Family Place
P.O. Box 19803
Dallas 75219
(214) 521-4290 (Crisis)
(215) 386-5055 (Office)

Services: Child care (8 A.M.–4 P.M.); community education; counseling (peer support); emergency transportation; hot line (twenty-four hours); referral; liaison (police); victim advocacy; housing (maximum capacity ten women, maximum three weeks, no charge, children permitted).

Family Abuse Center
P.O. Box 1812
Waco 76703

Family Place
P.O. Box 4216
Dallas 75203

Family Shelter and Referal Service, Institute of Cognitive Development, Incorporated
P.O. Box 5018
San Angelo 76902
(915) 655-5774 (Crisis)
(915) 944-4484 (Office)
Contact: Verneta Graham.

Services: Community education; counseling; emergency transportation; hot line (twenty-four hours); referral; liaison (police, medical, legal, long-term counseling); housing (maximum capacity fifteen women, sliding-scale fee, children permitted).

Family Violence Center, Incorporated
P.O. Box 5914
Beaumont 77706
(713) 832-7575

Services: Peer-support counseling; emergency medical transportation; hot line (twenty-four hours); referral; victim advocacy temporary shelter (maximum capacity eight, maximum fourteen days, $7 charge if affordable, children permitted).

First Step, Incorporated
P.O. Box 773
Wichita Falls 76307
(817) 723-0821 (Crisis)
(817) 767-4933 (Office)
Contact: Holly Harris.

Services: Community education (manuals available); counseling (crisis, peer, family); emergency transportation; hot line (twenty-four hours); liaison (police, medical); victim advocacy; housing (maximum capacity eight to ten, maximum two weeks, children permitted, no charge).

Hays County Women's Center
P.O. Box 234
San Marcos 78666
(512) 396-HELP (Crisis)
(512) 396-3403 (Office)
Contact: Jan Wells or Gloria Salazar.

Services: Community education; counseling (crisis, peer support, family, work with abusers); emergency medical treatment; emergency transportation; hot line (twenty-four hours); referral; legal aid; liaison (police, medical, judicial); victim advocacy; housing (maximum capacity four women, ten to fourteen children, maximum thirty days); shelter.

Houston Area Women's Center, Incorporated
P.O. Box 20186
Room E401
Houston 77025
(713) 527-0718 (Crisis)
(713) 792-4411 (Office)

Services: Counseling; referral; hot line; child care; housing (maximum capacity eleven, children permitted).

***Mujeres Unidas*/Women Together**
P.O. Box 566
Alamo 78516
(512) 781-3399 (Crisis)
(512) 781-8781 (Office)
Contact: Sandy Hall.

Services: Community education; job training; housing assistance; thrift shop; counseling (crisis, long term, peer, family); emergency medical treatment; emergency transportation; hot line (twenty-four hours); legal aid; liaison (police, medical, social-service agencies); victim advocacy; housing (maximum capacity five families, maximum three weeks, children permitted, no charge).

***Mujeres Unidas*/Women Together**
1615 West Kuhn Street
Edinburg 78539
(512) 383-4950 (Crisis)
(512) 383-4959 (Office)

Services: Referral; hot line (9 A.M.–9 P.M., Monday through Friday); housing (through referral, maximum three days, children permitted).

Noah Project, Incorporated
P.O. Box 875

Abilene 79601
(915) 676-7107
Contact: Dianne Mehoffey.

Services: Community education; counseling; emergency medical treatment; referral; legal aid; liaison (police, medical); victim advocacy; housing (maximum capacity fifteen, maximum thirty days, children permitted).

Transitional Living Center, Incorporated
P.O. Box 13265
El Paso 79912
(915) 859-4156 (Crisis)
(915) 859-4148 (Office)

Services: Legal aid; counseling; referral; hot line (twenty-four hours); child care (twenty-four hours); housing (maximum capacity thirty-six, maximum thirty days, children permitted).

Tree House
613 South 9th Street
Temple 76501
(817) 778-1499

Services: Community education; counseling; hot line (twenty-four hours); referral; police liaison; victim advocacy; housing (maximum capacity twenty, maximum six months, sliding-scale fee, children not permitted).

Trims
c/o Mary Beth Holley
1300 Moursand
Texas Medical Center
Houston 77030
(713) 797-1976

Services: Counseling; referral.

Women's Center
Box 20186
Room E401
Houston 77025

Women's Haven, Incorporated
P.O. Box 12180
Fort Worth 76116
(214) 336-3355 (Crisis)
(214) 336-1711 (Office)

Services: Legal aid; counseling; referral; hot line (twenty-four hours); child care; housing (maximum capacity twenty, children permitted); job assistance.

Women's Help, Incorporated
P.O. Box 11449
Dallas 75223
(214) 827-5260 (Crisis)
(214) 827-5261 (Office)

Services: Counseling; referral; hot line (twenty-four hours).

Women's Services Project
P.O. Box 1322
Denton 76201
(817) 387-4357 (Crisis)
(817) 387-1612 (Office)

Services: Legal aid (charge for service); counseling; referral; hot line (twenty-four hours); child care (ten hours per week); housing (maximum capacity eight, maximum thirty days, children permitted).

Women's Shelter, Incorporated
P.O. Box 3368
Corpus Christi 78404
(713) 881-8888

Services: Counseling; referral; hot line (twenty-four hours); child care; housing (maximum capacity sixteen, children permitted).

Women's Shelter of Bexar County, Incorporated
P.O. Box 10-393
San Antonio 78210
(512) 532-7648

Services: Legal aid (sliding-scale fee, court costs); counseling; referral; housing (maximum capacity fifty, maximum one month, children permitted).

Women's Shelter of East Texas, Incorporated
P.O. Box 569
Nacogdoches 75961
(713) 569-8850

Services: Child care; community education; counseling (crisis, peer support); hot line (twenty-four hours); referral; victim advocacy.

YWCA Women's Resource and Crisis Center
621 Moody
Galveston 77550
(713) 763-5606 (Crisis)
(713) 763-8505 (Office)

Services: Legal aid; counseling; referral; hot line (twenty-four hours); housing (sliding-scale fee, maximum capacity fifty, maximum twenty-one days, children permitted).

Utah

Eastern Utah Families in Crisis Project
Office of Community Operations
90 North 1st Street, East
Price 84581
(801) 637-6850

Eastern Utah Families in Crisis Project
Energy Building
Room 2
Moab 84532
(801) 259-5331 (Crisis)
(801) 259-6128 (Office)

Services: Community education; counseling; referral; legal aid; liaison (police); victim advocacy; housing (maximum capacity two families; maximum two weeks, children permitted).

Eastern Utah Families in Crisis Project
1052 West Market Drive
Vernal 84078
(801) 789-2511 (Crisis)
(801) 789-4888 (Crisis)
(801) 789-5850 (Office)

Services: Child care; community education; counseling; emergency transportation; referral; legal aid; liaison (police, court); victim advocacy; housing (maximum capacity three families, maximum thirty days, children permitted).

Rape Crisis Center, Incorporated
776 West 200, North
Salt Lake City 84116

(801) 532-RAPE (Crisis)
(801) 532-7286 (Office)

Services: Legal aid; counseling; referral; hot line (twenty-four hours).

Women in Jeopardy Program, YWCA
322 East 3rd Street
Salt Lake City 84111
(801) 355-2804

Women's Crisis Center, YWCA
505 27th Street
Ogden 84403
(801) 392-7273 (Crisis)
(801) 394-9456 (Office)

Services: Counseling; referral; community education; hot line (twenty-four hours); housing (children permitted).

YWCA Women in Jeopardy Program
322 East 3rd Street
Salt Lake City 84111

YWCA Women's Crisis Center
505 27th Street
Ogden 84403

Vermont

Alma Canter Domestic Violence Project
30 Union Street
P.O. Box 46
Windsor 05089
(802) 674-5273 (Hot line)
(802) 674-6785 (Administration)

Services: Shelter; twenty-four hour hot line; safe homes; overflow housing; support groups; programs for batterers; legal advocacy; child care; transportation; coalition member; brochure available.

Central Vermont Shelter Project
28 Pearl Street
Montpelier 05602
(802) 229-9495

Services: Shelter.

Katie Did . . . , Incorporated
53 Frost Street
Brattleboro 05301
(802) 257-1990 (Administration)

Services: Community education; support groups, legal advocacy; coalition members; brochure available.

Lamoille Family Center
P.O. Box 274
Morrisville 05661
(802) 888-5817 (Administration)

Services: Safe homes; support groups; child care; transportation; brochure available.

Rutland County Battered Women Network
P.O. Box 327
Rutland 05701
(802) 775-1000 (Hot line)
(802) 772-3232 or 6788 (Administration)

Services: Shelter; twenty-four hour hot line; safe homes; community education; support groups; programs for batterers; legal advocacy; transportation; coalition members.

Support for Change, Incorporated
44 Saxtons River Road
Bellow Falls 05101
(802) 463-3244 (Administration)

Services: Safe homes; community education; support groups; legal advocacy; transportation; coalition members; brochures available.

Umbrella of Saint Johnsbury, Incorporated
79 Railroad Street
Saint Johnsbury 05819
(802) 748-8645

Services: Referral; hot line; (daytime only); child care (emergency); housing (maximum fourteen days, maximum capacity twelve, children permitted).

Vermont Legal Aid, Incorporated
3 Summer Street
Springfield 05156
(802) 885-5181

Services: Legal aid; referral.

Women's Crisis Center
14 Green Street
Brattleboro 05301
(801) 254-6954

Services: Legal advice; counseling; referral; hot line (twenty-four hours); child care; housing ($10/week, maximum sixty days, maximum capacity four, children permitted).

Women's House of Transition, Incorporated
P.O. Box 194
Winooski 05404
(802) 863-9117

Services: Counseling (crisis, peer support); emergency transportation; hot line (twenty-four hours); referral; liaison; victim advocacy; housing (maximum capacity fifteen, maximum two months, rent charge, children permitted).

Virginia

Action in Community through Service
South Main Street
Dunfries 22026

Alexandria Battered Women's Support Project
P.O. Box 178
Alexandria 22313
(703) 768-1400 (Answering service)
(703) 750-6631 (Office)

Services: Community education; counseling (crisis, peer support); emergency transportation; hot line (twenty-four hours); referral; legal aid; liaison (police, all relevant city services); victim advocacy; housing (in motels, maximum two to three days, children permitted).

Battered Women's Support Project
Box 178
Alexandria 22313

Cease (Community Effort for Abused Spouses)
8119 Holland Road
Alexandria 22306
(703) 360-6910

Services: Legal aid; counseling (fee); referral; hot line (twenty-four hours); child care; housing (motel, maximum several days, children permitted).

Community Service to Abuse Victims
325 West 29th Street
Norfolk 22507

Connections Social Services
2800 North Pershing Drive
Arlington 22201
(703) 528-3200

Services: Legal aid; counseling; referral; hot line (twenty-four hours).

Fairfax County Victim Network
8119 Holland Road
Alexandria 22306

Fairfax County Women's Shelter
P.O. Box 1174
Vienna 22180
(703) 527-4077 (Crisis)
(703) 827-0090 (Office)

Services: Counseling; referral; hot line (twenty-four hours); child care (twenty-four hours); housing (maximum fourteen days, maximum capacity eight, children permitted).

First Step: Response to Domestic Violence
P.O. Box 69B
Keezletown 22832
(703) 434-2538 (Crisis)

Mahala
P.O. Box 2416
Roanoke 24010
(703) 342-4076

Services: Six apartment units for low rental; week-to-week leasing; children permitted; legal aid; counseling; referral; hot line; child care; housing.

Monticello Area Community Action Agency, SHE Project (Shelter for Help in Emergency)
201 5th Street, N.W.

Charlottesville 22901
(804) 295-3174

Services: Child care (nine when mother is with the children); community education; counseling (crisis, peer support); emergency medical treatment; emergency transportation; referral; legal aid; liaison (police, medical); victim advocacy; housing (maximum capacity fifteen, maximum six weeks, charge, children permitted).

Rappahannock Council on Domestic Violence, The Haven
P.O. Box 1785
College Station
Fredericksburg 22401
(703) 371-1212 (Crisis)
(703) 898-0299 (Office)

Services: Community education; counseling (crisis, peer support); emergency transportation; hot line (twenty-four hours) referral; liaison (police, court, counselor); victim advocacy; housing (maximum capacity ten, maximum thirty days, charge sliding-scale $0.50 to $5, children permitted).

Shelter for Help in Emergency
P.O. Box 3013
University Station
Charlottesville 22903
(804) 924-5564 (Crisis)
(804) 295-3174 (Office)
Contact: Ann Wood, Peggy Whipple.

Services: Community education; counseling (crisis, peer support); hot line; referral; liaison (police, medical, social services); housing (maximum capacity fifteen, maximum six weeks, sliding-scale fee, children permitted).

Virginia Peninsula Counseling for Battered Women
P.O. Box 561
Hampton 23669

Woman to Woman
420 East Market Street
Harrisonburg 22801
(703) 434-1231 (Crisis)
(703) 434-1766 (Office)

Services: Counseling; referral; hot line (noon–midnight).

Women's Resource Center of the New River Valley, Incorporated
P.O. Box 278
Christiansburg 24073
(703) 951-3434 (Crisis)
(703) 382-6751 (Office)
(800) 542-5988 (Crisis, toll free)

Services: Community education; counseling (crisis); hot line (twenty-four hours); referral; legal aid; liaison (police, counseling, legal aid); housing (maximum capacity fifteen, maximum four weeks, no charge, children permitted).

Women's Victim Advocacy Program/YWCA
6 North 5th Street
Richmond 23219
Contact: Shelia Crowley.

Services: Public education; training; individual and group counseling; hot line (twenty-four hours); emergency transportation; housing; child care; referral; victim advocacy.

YWCA/Crisis Shelter
600 Monroe Street
Lynchburg 24504
(804) 528-1041 or 847-7751 (Crisis)

Services: Child care (7 A.M.–6 P.M.); community education; counseling (crisis, peer support); emergency medical treatment; emergency transportation; referral; legal aid; liaison (police, medical); housing (maximum capacity nineteen, maximum thirty days, children permitted).

YWCA Women's Victim Advocacy Program
6 North 5th Street
Richmond 23215

Washington

Abused Women's Network
4747 12th Avenue, N.E.
Seattle 98105
(206) 523-2187

Services: Legal aid (referrals and victim advocacy); counseling (individual and group); referral.

ALIVE (Alternatives to Living in Violence)
611 Highland
Bremerton 98310
(206) 479-1980

Services: Counseling; referral; housing.

Alternative to Violence/Women's Center
Cub B-27
Pullman 99164
(509) 335-6830 (Office)
(509) 332-1505 (Crisis)
Contact: Anne DePuydt.

Services: Hot line (twenty-four hours); safe homes for women and children; counseling for women; counseling for children; counseling for batterers; support group for women; employment/job training/career counseling.

Alternatives to Violence Program
605 South Infirmary Road
Colville 99114
(509) 684-6139 (Crisis)
Contact: Gael Treesiwin, Anne Williams.

Services: Hot line (twenty-four hours); safe homes for women and children; counseling for women; support group for women.

Anger Control Group
Tacoma 98401
(206) 531-6314
Contact: Gary Benton.

Anger Control Groups
Seattle
(206) 789-4513
Contact: Stuart Dautoff.
(206) 363-0910
Contact: Julee Rosanoff.

ARISE (Action Resulting in Safe Environment)
P.O. Box 2126
Longview 98632
(206) 425-2620 (Crisis)

Services: Crisis line (twenty-four hours); women and children; counseling for children; counseling for women; counseling for batterers; support group for women.

Battered Women's Program
829 West Broadway
Spokane 99201
(509) 327-9534 (Office)
(509) 838-4428 (Crisis)
Contact: Valerie Norisada, director; Lynn Ackley, head counselor;
Victoria Davis, counselor.

Services: Crisis line (twenty-four hours); shelter for women and children;
support group for women.

Battered Women's Project
City Attorney's Office
Municipal Building
10th Floor
Seattle 98104
(206) 625-2119 (Crisis)
(206) 625-2002 (Office)

Services: Community education; counseling (crisis, peer support); referral;
liaison (police, courts); victim advocacy.

Catherine Booth House, Salvation Army
925 North Pike Street
Seattle 98122
(206) 281-4646 or 332-7959
Contact: Victor Doughty.

Services: Twenty-four hour crisis line; women and children; counseling for
women; counseling for children.

Claham County Safe House Program
c/o Vicki Roth
Department of Social and Health Services
P.O. Box 2148
Port Angeles 98362
(206) 452-8958

Services: Counseling; referral; hot line (twenty-four hours); housing
(twenty houses, maximum forty-eight hours, children permitted).

Community Abuse and Assault Center
366 Chase Street
P.O. Box 158A
Route 5
Walla Walla 99362

(509) 529-3377
Contact: Beryle Bias.

Services: Community education; counseling (crisis); emergency medical treatment; emergency transportation; hot line (twenty-four hours); referral; liaison (police, medical referral); victim advocacy.

Community Service Officers Section of the Seattle Police
1810 East Yesler
Seattle 98122
(206) 625-4661

Services: Counseling; referral.

Dawn
P.O. Box 5174
Kent 98031
(206) 854-7867 or 854-STOP
Contact: Sharon Atkins.

Services: Twenty-four hour crisis line; safe home; women and children; counseling for women; advocacy.

Dawson House
15 North Naches Avenue
Yakima 98901
(509) 248-7796

Services: Legal aid; counseling; referral; hot line (twenty-four hours); child care (daytime only); housing (maximum fourteen days, maximum capacity nine, children permitted).

Domestic Violence Program
P.O. Box 743
Port Townsend 98368
(206) 385-4748 (Crisis)
(206) 385-5291 (Office)

Services: Community education; counseling; emergency transportation; hot line (twenty-four hours); referral; liaison (police, medical); victim advocacy; housing.

Domestic Violence/Rape Relief Services
Family Service and Counseling Center
103 West 5th Street
Ellensburg 98926

(509) 925-4168 (Crisis)
(509) 925-9861 (Office)
Contact: Ann Glover.

Services: Community education; counseling; hot line (twenty-four hours);
referral; emergency transportation and medical treatment; liaison (police,
medical); victim advocacy; housing (in motels).

Eastside Domestic Violence Program
Eastgate,
King County 98004
643-0932
Contact: Lee or Mary
641-2418
Contact: Christy.

Services: No crisis line; women's and men's support groups.

Emergency Support Program
P.O. Box 2126
Longview 98632
(206) 425-2620 (Crisis)
(206) 425-1176 (Office)

Services: Community education; counseling; hot line (twenty-four hours);
emergency transportation; referral; legal aid; liaison (police, medical); victim advocacy; housing (fourteen beds, maximum thirty days, $3/day, chil-
dren permitted).

Evergreen Human Services
3604 East G Street
Tacoma 98404
(206) 474-2294
Contact: Linda Avreayl.

Services: Counseling, safe homes.

Evergreen Legal Services
1712½ Howitt Street
Everett 98201
(206) 258-2681

Services: Legal aid; counseling; referral.

Evergreen Legal Services
109 Prefontaine Plaza, South

Seattle 98104
(206) 464-5911

Services: Legal advocacy.

Family Crisis Program
c/o YMCA
15 North Naches Avenue
Yakima 98902
(509) 575-4200
Contact: Flora Johnson.

Services: Twenty-four hour crisis line; women and children; counseling for women; counseling for children; counseling for batterers; support for women.

Family Service and Counseling
103 5th Avenue
Ellensburg 98925
(509) 925-4168 (Crisis)
(509) 925-9861 (Business)
Contact: Arlene Bennett.

Services: Twenty-four hour crisis line; counseling for women; counseling for children; counseling for batterers.

Family Support Center
Box 2058
Omak 98841
422-3221 (Office)
Contact: Evelyn Rallios.

Services: Safe homes; women and children; counseling for women; support group for women; employment/job training; career counseling.

Family Violence Project, Family and Child Service of Metropolitan Seattle
107 Cherry Street
500 Lowman Building
Seattle 98104
(206) 447-3871 (Crisis)
(206) 447-3883 (Office)

Services: Community education; counseling (crisis, long-term, peer support, family, abused women's groups, men's groups); referral; housing (maximum open, sliding-scale fee, children permitted).

Forks Abuse Program
P.O. Box 1644
Forks 98331
(206) 374-2273
Contact: Pat Mansfield.

Services: Community education; counseling (crisis, violence, peer support); arrange for emergency medical treatment; emergency transportation; hot line (twenty-four hours); referral; legal aid; victim advocacy; housing (children permitted).

Group Health Cooperative of Puget Sound Domestic Abuse Program
1600 East John Street
Seattle 98112
(206) 326-7050

Services: Counseling (crisis, long term, peer support, family, spouse); referral; victim advocacy.

Harbor Shelter Service
P.O. Box 1825
Aberdeen 98520
(206) 533-5100
Contact: Lee Terry.

Services: Safe homes.

Harborview Medical Center
Emergency Trauma Center/Sexual Assault Program
325 9th Avenue
Seattle 98164
(206) 223-3074 (Crisis)
(206) 223-3086 (Social Work Department)

Services: Counseling; emergency medical treatment; emergency transportation; hot line (twenty-four hours); referral; liaison (medical, police); victim advocacy.

Inc Spot Counseling Center
P.O. Box 171
17516 Bothell Way, N.E.
Bothell 98011
(206) 485-6541

Services: Counseling (initial $20 fee, free thereafter); referral; hot line.

Kitsap County YWCA/Family Violence Project
611 Highland
Bremerton 98310
(206) 479-0599 (Crisis)
(206) 479-5116 (Office)
Contact: Tim Gerstann, Pam Greenway.

Klickitat County Council on Domestic Violence
P.O. Box 233
Goldendale 98620
(509) 773-4022 (Crisis, Goldendale)
(509) 493-1101 (Crisis, White Salmon)

Services: Child care during counseling; counseling (crisis, long term, peer support, religious); emergency transportation and medical treatment; hot line (twenty-four hours); referral; legal aid; liaison (police, medical, social services); victim advocacy; housing (seventy-two hours in safe homes).

New Beginnings
217 9th Avenue, North
Seattle 98109
(206) 622-8194

Services: Counseling; referral; housing (sliding-scale fee, maximum thirty days, maximum capacity ten, children permitted).

New Beginnings for Battered Women
P.O. Box 261
North Gate Station
Seattle 98125
(206) 522-9475

Services: Counseling (crisis, group); hot line (twenty-four hours); referral; victim advocacy; housing (maximum capacity eighteen, maximum two weeks, sliding-scale fee, children permitted).

Nuestro Lugar (Our Place)
P.O. Box 506
Moses Lake 98837
(509) 765-1717 (Crisis)
Contact: Alice Rendon.

Services: Safe homes; twenty-four hour crisis line; women and children; counseling for women; support group for women.

Odgen Hall for Women/Gospel Mission
2825 West Dean Avenue
Spokane 99201
327-7737 (Crisis)
Contact: Betty Jolly.

Services: Twenty-four hour crisis line; shelter; women; counseling for women; counseling for children; counseling for batterers.

Pacific County Family Abuse Alternatives
P.O. Box 950
South Bend 98586
(206) 875-6655
Contact: Pat Simpson-Stanton.

Services: Counseling for women; safe homes.

People Assistance Team
P.O. Box 1995
Vancouver 98663
(206) 696-8226 (Crisis)
(206) 696-8292 (Office)

Services: Counseling; referral.

Safe Homes
105½ East 1st Street
Suite 31
P.O. Box 592
Port Angeles 98362
(206) 452-7002 (Crisis)

Services: Twenty-four hours crisis line; women and children; counseling for women; counseling for children; support group for women.

Services for Victims of Domestic Violence
P.O. Box 1644
Forks 98331
(206) 374-2273 (Crisis)
(206) 374-6193 (Office)
Contact: Kay Sullivan, Pat Mansfield.

Services: Twenty-four hour crisis line; safe homes; women and children; counseling for women; counseling for batterers; support group for women.

Skagit Rape Relief/Battered Women's Program
P.O. Box 301
Mount Vernon 98273
(206) 336-2162 (Crisis)
(206) 336-9591 (Office)
Contact: Vi Fifield.

Services: Safe home; women and children; counseling for women; support group for women; employment/job training/career counseling.

Sojourner Truth House
P.O. Box 975
Cehalis 98532
(206) 748-6601 (Crisis)
(206) 748-6306 (Office)

Services: Child care (emergency); community education; counseling (crisis, peer support, family); emergency transportation; hot line (twenty-four hours); referral; legal aid; liaison (police, medical, welfare); victim advocacy; housing (maximum capacity fifteen, maximum thirty days, charge, children permitted).

Stop Abuse
2731 10th Street
Everett 98201
(206) 252-2873 (Crisis)
(206) 258-3543 (Office)

Services: Women and children; counseling for women; counseling for batterers.

Survival Center of Snohomish County
5205 South 2nd Street
Everett 98203
(206) 25A-BUSE (Crisis)
(206) 268-3543 (Home)

Services: Counseling; referral; hot line (twenty-four hours); child care; housing (children permitted).

Tacoma's Support Shelter
405 Broadway
Tacoma 98402
(206) 383-2593 (Crisis)
Contact: Gracie Brooks.

Services: Twenty-four hour crisis line; women and children; counseling for women; counseling for children; support group for women; information and referral.

Vancouver Women's Resource Center
602 West Evergreen Boulevard
Vancouver 98663
(206) 695-6386

Services: Counseling; referral.

Vancouver Women's Resource Center/Rape Relief/Victim Advocacy
1115 Esther Street
Vancouver 98660
(206) 695-6386 (Crisis)
(206) 695-0790 (Office)

Services: Community education; counseling (crisis, peer support, telephone support); hot line (9 A.M.–5 P.M., Monday through Friday); referral; legal referral; liaison (police, medical, prosecution); victim advocacy.

Washington State Shelter Network
1063 South Capital, #27
Olympia 98501
(800) 562-6025 (Crisis, can be called only within Washington)
(206) 753-4621 (Office)

Services: Crisis counseling; referral; hot line (twenty-four hours); linking victims with programs throughout the United States.

Washington State Women's Council
15th and Columbia Streets
Olympia 98504
(206) 753-2870

Services: Information and educational services.

Whatcom County Crisis Services Domestic Violence Program
124 East Holly
Bellingham 98225
(206) 734-7271 (Crisis)
(206) 671-5755 (Office)

Services: Legal aid; counseling referral; hot line (twenty-four hours); housing (service has affiliation with shelter programs; maximum capacity seven, children permitted).

Woman's Survival Center
9261 First Street
Snohomish 98290

Womencare Shelter
P.O. Box 4094
Bellingham 98227
(206) 734-3438 (Crisis)
Contact: Jamie Moore

Services: Twenty-four hour crisis line; women and children; counseling for women.

Women's Association of Self Help
11100 Northeast 2nd Street
Bellevue 98008
(206) 454-9274

Services: Counseling; referral.

A Women's Place
1440 Kimball Street
Richland 99352
(509) 946-0329

Services: Legal aid; referral; counseling; hot line (twenty-four hours); housing (maximum twenty-one days, children permitted).

Women's Resource Center/YWCA
829 West Broadway
Spokane 99201
(509) 838-4428 (Crisis, evenings and weekends)
(509) 327-1508 (Office)

Services: Counseling; referral; hot line.

Women's Shelter and Support Services Program
220 East Union
Olympia 98502
(206) 352-0593

Services: Counseling; referral.

YWCA Battered Women's Program
15 North Naches Avenue

Yakima 98901
(509) 248-7796
Contact: Pat Tucker.

Services: Child care; community education; counseling (crisis, peer support, family, couples); emergency transportation; hot line (twenty-four hours); referral; liaison (police, medical); victim advocacy; housing (maximum capacity sixteen, maximum two weeks, charge $3/day, children permitted).

YWCA Emergency House
1012 West 12th Street
Vancouver 98660
(206) 695-0501

Services: Counseling; referral; hot line; housing (sliding-scale fee, maximum twenty-one days, maximum capacity thirteen, children permitted).

YWCA Emergency Housing Program for Women in Crisis
1118 5th Avenue
Seattle 98101
(206) 447-4882

Services: Community education; counseling (crisis, peer support, feminist therapy referral, support groups for abused women); hot line (twenty-four hours); referral; legal referral; liaison (police, medical,welfare); victim advocacy; housing (maximum capacity fourteen, maximum one week, charge, children not permitted).

YWCA Family Crisis Program
15 North Naches Avenue
Yakima 98901
(509) 248-7796

YWCA Pasada
1026 North Forest
Bellingham 98225
(206) 734-4820

Services: Counseling; referral.

YWCA Women's Shelter Program
220 East Union
Olympia 98501

(206) 352-2211 (Crisis)
(206) 352-0593 (Office)

Services: Child care; community education; counseling (crisis, peer support, battered women's group); referrals to batterer's counseling; emergency transportation; hot line (twenty-four hours); referral; legal aid; liaison (police, medical, legal); victim advocacy; housing (maximum two weeks, charge, children permitted).

YWCA Women's Support Shelter
405 Broadway
Tacoma 98402
(206) 383-2593 (Crisis)
(206) 272-4181 (Office)

West Virginia

Battered Women's Resource Center
Box 145
Hamlin 25523

Branches, Incorporated
P.O. Box 448
Huntington 25766

Braxton Victim Advocate Center
307 Main Street
Sutton 26601

Charleston Domestic Violence Center, Incorporated
Suite 305
Morris Square
1212 Lewis Street
Charleston 25301

Council on Abused Persons
P.O. Box 1423
Beckley 25801
(304) 252-7817 (Crisis)
(304) 253-9672 (Office)

Services: Community education; counseling (crisis, long term); emergency transportation; hot line (twenty-four hours); referral; legal aid; liaison (police, medical, community agencies); victim advocacy; housing (maximum capacity four, maximum three weeks, children permitted, not in shelter but arrangements are made with Department of Welfare).

Domestic Violence Center
31 Hillcrest Street
Charleston 25303
(304) 345-0848 (Crisis)
(304) 346-9471 Ext. 283 (Office)

Services: Legal aid; counseling; referral.

Family Refuge Center
105 Church Street
Lewisburg 24901

Potomac Highlands Mental Health Guild/Domestic Violence Program
P.O. Box 1179
Petersburg 26847
(304) 257-1155

Services: Community education; counseling (crisis, long term, peer support, family, alcohol and drug abuse); emergency transportation; referral; liaison (police, medical, legal services); victim advocacy; housing (maximum capacity one family; maximum two weeks, children permitted).

Rape and Domestic Violence Information Center (RDVIC)
P.O. Box 4228
Morgantown 26505
(304) 599-6800 (Crisis)
(304) 599-6801 (Office)

Services: Community education; counseling (crisis, long term support, family, family incest program); emergency medical treatment; emergency transportation; hot line (twenty-four hours); referral; legal aid; liaison (police, criminal-justice system); victim advocacy; housing (maximum capacity fifteen, maximum three weeks, children permitted).

Rape Information Service
221 Willey Street
Morgantown 26505
(304) 292-1212 (Crisis)
(304) 292-5015 (Office)

Services: Counseling; referral; hot line; child care; housing (maximum fourteen days, children permitted); transportation; victim advocacy.

Shenandoah Women's Center
P.O. Box 1083
410 West Roce Street
Martinsburg 25401
(304) 263-8292 (Crisis)
(304) 263-8522 (Office)

Services: Community education; counseling (crisis, peer support, family); emergency transportation; hot line (9 A.M.–9 P.M. weekdays, 5 A.M.–9 P.M. weekends); referral; liaison (police); victim advocacy; housing (maximum thirty days, no charge, children permitted).

Upshur County Home Crisis Aid
34 West Florida Street
Buckhannon 26201

West Virginia Legal Services Plan
222 North College Street
Martinsburg 25401
(304) 263-8871

Services: Legal aid; referral.

West Virginia Women's Commission
WB-9, Capitol Complex
Charleston 25305
(304) 348-8816

Services: Referral.

Women's Aid in Crisis
Box 2062
Elkins 25523

Women's Resource Center
Box 1476
Beckley 25801

YWCA of Wheeling
1100 Chapline Street
Wheeling 26003

Wisconsin

Abused Persons Economic and Resource Shelter
Box 474
Wisconsin Dells 53965

Abused Women's Project
Lake View Drive
Wausau 54401
(715) 842-1636

Services: Counseling; referral; hot line (twenty-four hours).

Association for Abused Women
P.O. Box 398
Manitowoc 54220
(414) 684-5770

Services: Counseling; referral; hot line.

Domestic Abuse and Sex Assault Victims Service
P.O. Box 172
Wausau 54401

Domestic Violence Center
1203 North 18th Street
Manitowoc 54220

Domestic Violence of Door County
Box F
Sturgeon Bay 54235

FACTS
P.O. Box 112
Superior 54880

Family Crisis Center
Portage County
1503 Water Street
Stevens Point 54481

Family Resource Center and Association for Prevention of Family Violence
718 Wisconsin Avenue
Lake Geneva 53147

Family Service
North Hamilton Street
Madison 53703
(414) 251-7611

Services: Counseling (fee); referral.

Friends of Battered Women of Washington County Shelter
P.O. Box 61
West Bend 53096

Hotline
P.O. Box 221
Green Bay 54301
(414) 437-9008 (Crisis)
(414) 468-3479 (Office)

Services: Legal aid; counseling; referral; hot line (twenty-four hours).

Lakeshore Association for Abused Women
P.O. Box 398
Manitowoc 54220
(414) 684-5770

Services: Counseling; referral; hot line.

Morningpoint for Victims of Domestic Abuse, Inc.
Woodworth 54011
(715) 273-4438

Services: Counseling; referral; volunteer housing (maximum three days).

National Organization for Women, North Central Wisconsin Chapter
P.O. Box 793
Wausau 54401
(715) 842-7636

Services: Counseling; referral; hot line; child care; housing.

New Horizons, YWCA Women's Center
P.O. Box 2031
La Crosse 54601

Passages Shelter
Viola 54664

Personal Development Counseling, Inc.
P.O. Box 395
Marshfield 54449

Rape and Domestic Violence Center Shelter
P.O. Box 333
Marinette 54143

Refuge House
P.O. Box 482
Eau Claire 54701
(715) 834-9578

Services: Counseling; referral; hot line (twenty-four hours); child care (twenty-four hours); housing (maximum capacity fifteen, children permitted).

Saint Nicholas Hospital
Social Services Department
Sheboygan 53081

Sheboygan County Advocates for Battered Women
427 Bell Avenue
Sheboygan 53081
(414) 457-7924 (Crisis)
(414) 452-2213 (Office)

Services: Counseling; referral; hot line (twenty-four hours); housing (temporary in hotels and motels).

Sojourner Truth House
P.O. Box 008110
Milwaukee 53208
(414) 933-2722

Services: Counseling; referral; hot line (twenty-four hours); housing (maximum capacity eighteen, children permitted).

Southwestern Wisconsin Community Action Program Project on Battered Women
403 Warner Hall
Platteville 53818
Contact: Jan Myers-Eisner.

Services: Child care (arranged hours); community education; counseling; emergency transportation; referral; hot line (8 A.M.–5 P.M., Monday through Friday); liaison (medical, police, social services); victim advocacy; housing (children permitted).

Tapers, Inc.
Box 474
Wisconsin Dells 53965

Task Force on Abused Women, Mental Health Association in Portage County
945 A Main Street
Stevens Point 54481
(715) 344-5759

Services: Counseling; referral; housing (maximum two days, maximum capacity three, children permitted).

Time-Out
Domestic/Violence Abuse Shelter
502 Lake Avenue East
Ladysmith 54849

Tri-County Counseling
Domestic Violence, Inc.
Box 496
Eagle River 54501

Tri-County on Domestic Violence, Inc.
P.O. Box 446
Eagle River 54521
(715) 362-5619 (Collect, or dial 0 and ask for Enterprise 6292)
(715) 479-6960 (Office)
Contact: Marcy Wheiting.

Services: Child care; community education; counseling; emergency transportation; hot line (twenty-four hours); referral; victim advocacy; housing (three days, children permitted).

Turning Point for Victims of Domestic Abuse, Inc.
Ellsworth 54011
(715) 273-4438

Services: Counseling; referral; volunteer housing (maximum three days).

Victim Assistance Support Project
419 North Grand Avenue
Waukesha 53186

Waukesha County Battered Women's Task Force
1303 Fleetfoot Drive
Waukesha 53186
(414) 547-3388 (Crisis)
(414) 691-3200 (Office)

Services: Counseling; referral; hot line; housing (private).

Womencenter, Inc.
P.O. Box 2352
Appleton 54913

Services: Peer Counseling; referral; hot line (twenty-four hours); housing (in private homes, children permitted).

Women's Coalition, Inc./Sojourner Truth
2211 East Kenwood Boulevard
Milwaukee 53211
(414) 964-6117

Services: Community education; referral.

Women's Horizons, Inc.
1630 56th Street
Kenosha 53140
(414) 652-1846

Services: Legal referral; counseling; hot line (twenty-four hours); child care; housing.

Women's Resource Center
Main Street
Stevens Point 54481
(715) 346-4851

Services: Referral; hot line (9 A.M.–9 P.M.).

Women's Resource Center of Racine, Inc.
P.O. Box 1764
Racine 53401
(414) 633-3233
Contact: Marialyce Gottschalk.

Services: Counseling; referral; hot line (twenty-four hours); victim advocacy; housing (maximum capacity nine, thirty days, children permitted).

Women's Resource Center of the YWCA
740 College Avenue
Racine 53403
(414) 633-3233

Services: Counseling; referral; hot line (twenty-four hours); housing (maximum fourteen days, children permitted).

Women's Service Center Domestic Violence Project
102 North Monroe
Green Bay 54301
(414) 432-4244

Services: Counseling (sliding-scale fee); referral; hot line (twenty-four hours); child care; housing (maximum thirty days, maximum capacity sixteen, children permitted).

YWCA Women's Resource Center
740 College Avenue
Racine 53403

Wyoming

Carbon County Human Services Project
P.O. Box 713
Rawlins 82301
(307) 328-0400

Fremont Counseling
P.O. Box 618
Lander 82520
(307) 332-2231

Gillette Refuge
900 West 6th
Gillette 82716
(307) 682-4762

Grandma's Safe House
Box 1621
Cheyenne 82001
(307) 632-2072

Parents Anonymous
c/o Community Resource Center, Inc.
P.O. Box 713
Rawlins 82301
(307) 328-0400

Rape Crisis Center
222 East 17th

Cheyenne 82001
(307) 635-5212

Safe House
P.O. Box 1621
Cheyenne 82001
(307) 632-2072

SAFE Services
2154 North 16th
Laramie 82070
(307) 766-6258

Safe Task Force
36 10th Street
Evanston 82930
(307) 789-9039

Self Help Center
1515 Burlington Street
Casper 82601
(307) 235-2814

Sheridan Women's Center
P.O. Box 5002
Sheridan 82801
(307) 672-9358

Sweetwater County Task Force on Sexual Assault
450 South Main
Rock Springs 82901
(307) 382-4381

Sweetwater Shelter House
P.O. Box 601
Rock Springs 82901
(307) 382-6925 (Crisis)
(307) 362-7923 (Office)
Contact: Diane Brice (Crisis line), Lisa Smith (Shelter).

Services: Child care; counseling (individual, crisis, peer support); hot line
(twenty-four hours); referral; legal aid; liaison (police, medical); victim
advocacy; housing (maximum capacity five women, nine children, no time
limit).

Task Force on Violence against Women
P.O. Box 2323
Jackson 83001
(307) 733-6817

Turning Point
Box 64
Kemmerer 83101
(307) 877-9209

Women's Self Help Center, Inc.
1515 Burlington
Casper 82601
(307) 235-2814

Services: Community education; counseling; hot line (twenty-four hours); referral; liaison (police, medical, family); referrals to temporary housing (two weeks).

YWCA
P.O. Box 601
Rock Springs 82901
(307) 362-9718 or 362-6370

8 Films and Videotapes on Spouse Abuse

Center for Women Policy Studies

Audio

Feminist Radio Network. *Ain't It a Shame: Battered Women.* Washington, DC: PRN, 1981.

Battered women, feminist activists, and attorneys describe the experiences of battered women—their economic dependence, isolation, and fear—and the indifference of some service providers. They draw parallels between woman abuse and the sexism and violence of our culture and describe the real alternatives offered by shelters and women's support groups.

Additional Information: Audio reels (7½ ips, 3¾ ips) and audio cassettes, 29 minutes. Purchase 7½ ips $12.50, 3¾ ips $10, cassettes, $10.

Ordering Information: Feminist Radio Network, P.O. Box 5537, Washington, DC 20016. Telephone: (202) 244-2331.

Films and Videotapes

Byrd, Jeff, and Cook, Jacqueline (Producers). *She's Mine, Ain't She.* Rochester, New York: WXXI Television (PBS), 1980.

This documentary relates the experiences of five former battered women. They come from various backgrounds, a fact which serves to break down stereotypes about who battered women are. The film portrays battered women who have found a way out and who share their terrorizing experiences with others. Their poignant stories reflect a daily struggle to cope with

Prepared under grant number 79-TA-AX-0024 of the Law Enforcement Assistance Administration, U.S. Department of Justice, and under grant number 90-CW-2189 (01) of the Office of Domestic Violence, U.S. Department of Health and Human Services.

The Law Enforcement Assistance Administration and the Office on Domestic Violence reserves the right to reproduce, publish, translate, or otherwise use and to authorize others to publish and use all or any part of the copyrighted material contained in this publication.

Films and Videotapes on Spouse Abuse, copyright © 1980 by the Center for Women Policy Studies, is reprinted by permission of the Center for Women Policy Studies, 2000 P Street N.W., Suite 508, Washington, D.C.

a life-threatening home environment common to many women in our society.

Additional Information: Color, 55 minutes. Available in ¾-inch video cassette, ½-inch reel to reel; other formats available upon request. Purchase $200. Rental $75.

Ordering Information: Video Spectrum, attention distribution Coordinator, 288 Warren Street, Brooklyn, N.Y. 11201. Telephone: (212) 233-5851.

Campbell, Peg (Producer). *A Common Assault.* Vancouver, British Columbia: United Way of the Lower Mainland, 1981.

This slide tape presents actors protraying a husband and wife involved in wife battering who take steps to resolve the problem. The intervention professionals play themselves in their work. Part I, Crisis intervention (15 minutes), shows Canadian police accompanied by a crisis intervention specialist arriving at the home after a battering incident and provides immediate crisis counseling. In Part II, Transition (11 minutes), the battered woman goes to Transition House Shelter for support and safety. In Part III, Court (9 minutes), the couple appears in the family court system, which seeks to provide the legal intervention that will stop the battering. Although the show is Canadian based, the description of the entire intervention process would be of interest to American audiences. The slide tape is engrossing and award winning for its most innovative use of the medium.

Additional Information: Slide tape and ¾-inch cassette color videotape. Three parts, 35 minutes total length. Available in English, Cantonese, French, Greek, Italian, Portuguese, Punjabi and Vietnamese. Purchase $200. Rental $30 ($17.50 to women's shelters per showing.)

Ordering Information: IDERA, 2524 Cypress Street, Vancouver, B.C., Canada V6J, 3N2. Telephone: (604) 738-8815.

Campbell, Peg (Producer). *A Rule of Thumb.* Vancouver, British Columbia: United Way of the Lower Mainland, 1977 (Videotape).

This tape opens with the common-law practice in the early United States that allowed a husband "the right to whip his wife, provided he used a switch no bigger than his thumb." The theme is that society still gives approval to "a rule of thumb" of men's physical domination over women. The commentary by Jillian Ridington, then a staff member of Vancouver Transition House, is supported by the personal story of a battered wife. Their comments are interspersed with examples from "love" comics, soap operas, magazine articles, and advertisements that show the media influence in perpetuating attitudes that "it's all right" for women to be beaten.

Additional Information: 25 minutes; ½-inch video tape; free rental.
Ordering Information: Flora MacLeod, Coordinator, Task Force on Family Violence, Social Planning and Research, United Way of Greater Vancouver, 1625 West 8th Avenue, Vancouver, B.C., Canada V6J 1T9. Telephone: (604) 731-7781, local 258.

Campbell, Peg (Producer). *A Sign of Affection.* Vancouver, British Columbia: United Way of Greater Vancouver, 1977 (Videotape).

This videotape is a survey of attitudes and opinions on wife battering, ranging from women who have been battered to the people who are supposed to be there to help: social workers, police, a doctor, a priest, and the Minister of Human Resources. Interviews were conducted in Burns Lake and Vancouver, Canada. The relationship of alcohol to wife battering is examined with case workers saying that alcohol is involved in 85 percent of their cases. But the general consensus is that it is a catalyst to the violence, not a cause: "Alcohol cannot trigger a problem that wasn't there to begin with."
Additional Information: 25 minutes; ½-inch videotape; free rental.
Ordering Information: Flora MacLeod, Coordinator, Task Force on Family Violence, Social Planning and Research, United Way of Greater Vancouver, 1625 West 8th Avenue, Vancouver, B.C., Canada V6J 1T9. Telephone: (604) 731-7781, local 258.

Choy, Christine (Director). *To Love, Honor and Obey.* New York, New York: Third World Newsreel, 1981.

This is one of the best and most current films describing the experiences and concerns of battered women. Unlike other films on the subject, which rely solely on the use of actors, *To Love, Honor and Obey* is a documentary in the truest sense. The film shows what actually happens when a battered woman goes to an emergency room or when she must be escorted by the police to her home to get her belongings before she goes to a shelter. It places battering in a total cultural perspective considering how our illusions about marriage, sex roles, and childrearing form and perpetuate a framework for battering. Interviews with battered women, shelter workers, counselors, men who batter, and children who have come from battering situations are included. A woman who killed her husband after violent battering is interviewed. This film is in the best of documentary traditions. It is particularly recommended for public education for urban audiences, but would be good for any audience.

Additional Information: 16 mm. color film, 55 minutes. Purchase $650. Rental $85 plus shipping.

Ordering Information: Third World Newsreel, 160 Fifth Avenue, Suite
                       911, New York, N.Y. 10010. Telephone: (212)
                       243-2310.

Cine Design, Inc. (Producer). *A Women, A Spaniel, A Walnut Tree.* Washington, D.C.: U.S. Commission on Civil Rights, 1977 (Film).

The title of this short investigation of wife beating comes from the old English proverb, "A woman, a spaniel, a walnut tree. The more you beat them, the better they be." In the film, a victim describes her beatings and helps to dispel some common myths about the problem. Although the film only touches on solutions, it does address one of the questions most commonly asked of abused women: "Why did you stay?" This film was done in conjunction with a report issued by the U.S. Commission on Civil Rights, "The Silent Victims: Denver's Battered Women," which may also be obtained by writing to the address above.

Additional Information: 13 minutes; free rental.
Ordering Information: Barbara Brooks, Public Information Office. U.S.
                       Commission on Civil Rights, 1121 Vermont Avenue, N.W., Washington, DC 20425. (Orders must
                       be placed in writing.)

Cochran, Peter (Producer). *Violence in the Family.* Pleasantview, New York: Human Relations Media, 1978 (Filmstrip and audio cassettes).

The filmstrip series, *Violence in the Family*, gives four overview perspectives on domestic violence. Part I, Dynamics of Family Violence, runs 10 minutes and provides an introduction to the subject of family violence. It presents the traditional idealized vision of the American home and family life and contrasts that picture with statistics on child, wife, and adolescent abuse. Part II, Child Abuse and Neglect, runs 12 minutes. It describes common misconceptions about child abusers, discusses the cyclical nature of abuse, and briefly shows a family history of abuse. Part III, Battered Wives, runs 12 minutes and gives reported and estimated figures on abuse and a brief history of wife beating. It suggests a process for seeking help and tells where wives can go if they are being beaten. Part IV, Adolescent Abuse, runs 10 minutes and discusses ways that children entering adolescence may experience family stress which can result in an abusive atmosphere. It also discusses runaways and runaway services.

Additional Information: 4 filmstrips with audio cassettes, $135.
Ordering Information: Human Relations Media, 175 Tompkins Avenue,
                       Pleasantview, NY 10570.

Consortia (Producer). *Officer Survival: An Approach to Conflict Management.* Hagerstown, Maryland: Harper & Row Media, Inc., 1976 (Film).

This series is designed to encourage and support expansion of family crisis police intervention programs and is geared to police training. Films I and II deal with officer/citizen safety in conflict situations. Film III explores techniques for calming a hostile individual without using physical force. Film IV looks at communications skills needed for effective interviewing, while Films V and VI deal with mediation and referral. The films are not practical for roll call training.

Additional Information: Six part series: 16 mm, 22 minutes for each part; rental $60 per week per part; purchase $380 per part, $2,124.60 complete set.
Ordering Information: Harper & Row Media, Inc., Order Fulfillment/ Customer Service, 2350 Virginia Avenue, Hagerstown, MD 21740. Telephone: (301) 733-2700, ext. 64.

Crawford, Clare (Producer). *Wife Beating.* National Broadcasting Company. 1976 (Film).

This investigative report was produced for NBC's "Weekend." In it, Crawford lets the abused women tell their stories. The film highlights the lack of judicial protection for victims of family violence and concludes that there will be no aid from the criminal justice system as it now exists. A visit to women's Advocates, a shelter in Minneapolis, shows one possible solution to the problem, although the staff of the refuge quickly point out that shelters constitute only one approach to an overwhelming problem.

Additional Information: 25 minutes; rental $35/day; purchase $375.
Ordering Information: Films Inc., 733 Greenbay Road, Wilmette, IL 60091. Telephone: (800) 323-4222.

Domestic Violence Project (Producer). *How To Help Battered Women.* Michigan State University, East Lansing:Domestic Violence Project, 1977 (Slides).

The show is divided into three 30-minute segments. The first describes the treatment of domestic violence cases by the criminal justice system: the response of the police, prosecutor, and court to both victim and abuser. The second segment presents a summary of services available to battered women; they include medical, psychological, financial, and employment resources. The final component focuses on the problem of establishing a shelter/emergency housing facility, and points out groups that have developed model programs of service to victims. The slides are available in a carousel (90) slides with a tape and script. Instructions for self-teaching are included.

Additional Information: 90 minutes; slide presentation; free rental; *available only in Michigan.*

Ordering Information: Agriculture and Natural Resources Education Institute (ANDREI), 410 Agriculture Hall, Cooperative Extension Service, Michigan State University, East Lansing, MI 48824. Telephone: (517) 355-6580.

Donahue, Phil (Host). *Battered Women* (Show #09230). Cincinnati, Ohio: The Phil Donahue show. May 1980.

This show features an interview with Beverly Webster, director of Women Together, a shelter for battered women and their children in Cleveland, Ohio. Ms. Webster discusses the plight of battered women and the services that a shelter offers to end the violence.

Additional Information: Color videotape, 47 minutes. Purchase $300.

Ordering Information: Multi-media Program Productions, Attention Mike Brown, 14 West 9th Street, Cincinnati, Ohio 45202. Telephone: (513) 352-5044.

Donahue, Phil (Host). *Battered Women—Abusive Men* (Show #05290). Cincinnati, Ohio: The Phil Donahue Show. May 1980.

This show focuses on the usefulness of counseling programs for spouses who want to stop their abusive behavior. The show features interviews with two batterers who have completed counseling, their wives, and a therapist from AMEND, a counseling service for men who batter in Denver, Colo. The former batterers discuss the social, psychological, and emotional factors that led them to beat their wives and the improvement counseling has brought to their relationships.

Additional Information: Color videotape, 47 minutes. Purchase $300.

Ordering Information: Available from Multi-Media Program Productions, Attention: Mike Brown, 14 West 9th Street, Cincinnati, Ohio 45202. Telephone: (513) 352-5044.

Eggplant Media Productions (Producer). *Coming Out of Violence.* Connecticut: Eggplant Media Productions, 1978 (Videocassette).

Coming Out of Violence is a videotape of the 1977 Public Hearings in

Hartford, Conn. It includes testimony and interviews with battered women and persons working in social service agencies, shelters, courts, police departments, hospitals, and support groups. Battered women testify about the psychological and physical manifestations of battering and relate their experiences with various social service and legal agencies. Lisa Leghorn, an organizer of Transition House in Cambridge, Mass., describes myths and facts about wife abuse. Each segment of the tape closes with findings and recommendations made by the U.S. Commission on Civil Rights.

Additional Information: ¾-inch videocassette; 56 minutes; rental $50, purchase $200.

Ordering Information: Eggplant Media Productions, P.O. Box 14001, Hartford, CT 06114. Telephone: (203) 233-8756.

George, W. (Producer). *Battered Wives: Women.* New York, New York: WNED Television (Sponsoring Agency, The Ford Foundation), 1976 (Videocassette).

This videotaped recording of an episode in the television series, "Woman," conducted by Sandra Elkin, presents a panel discussion about wife abuse. The panel defines "battered wives" as women who have been subjected to either physical or emotional abuse from their husbands. Panelists discuss the scope of the problem and the kinds of women who become battered wives. They recommend the development of more crisis centers and battered women's shelters throughout the United States and stress the need for greater resources and programs for women who seek alternatives to returning to their husbands upon leaving shelters.

Additional Information: Videocassette; 29 minutes; color; rental $68; purchase $175.

Ordering Information: Public Television Library, 475 L'Enfant Plaza, S.W., Washington, DC 20024.

Graham, Nancy (Producer). *Triage: In Need of Special Attention.* Berkeley, CA: ODN Productions, 1981.

Directed by Christina Crawley (who made *Battered Women: Violence Behind Closed Doors*) and narrated by Loretta Swit of the television series, MASH, this film is designed to teach nurses, doctors, and medical social workers how to identify a battered woman when she presents herself for hospital treatment. The goal is to inspire hospitals to develop a protocol for treating battered women and to improve hospital intervention. The word "triage" refers to the triage nurse in the emergency room. Loretta Swit notes that emergency rooms should not be like MASH units, but unfortunately some are. The film is drama, rather than documentary, and is accompanied by a training manual and film guide.

Additional Information: 16 mm color, 16 minutes. Contact ODN for information on purchase/rental.
Ordering Information: ODN Productions, 1454 Sixth Street, Berkeley, CA
94710. Telephone: (415) 527-9120.

Howard, Glen (Producer). *Battered Spouses.* Kentucky: National Crime
Prevention Institute, University of Louisville, 1978 (Film).

This film offers a panoramic view of the problem of spouse abuse as it affects
victims, abusers, police, justice system officials, shelters, and other service
agencies. It is designed to encourage the development of crisis aid programs.
The major focus is on the diversity of programs available to help the victim
legally and emotionally. Participants in the film point to police crisis intervention teams, victim assistance programs in prosecutors' offices, private
doctors' watchful screening of female patients for possible cases of wife
battery, and federal support of service programs as measures that can
prevent domestic violence.

Additional Information: 16 mm; 23 minutes; color; rental $50/week; pur-
chase $380.
Ordering Information: Harper & Row Media, Inc., Order Fulfillment/
Customer Service, 2350 Virginia Avenue, Hagers-
town, MD 21740. Telephone: (301) 733-2700, ext.
64.

Jaffee, Henry (Producer). *Battered Wives.* Henry Jaffee Enterprises Inc.,
1978.

Karen Grassle (of "Little House on the Prairie") and Cynthia Lovelace
Sears wrote the screenplay for this film originally shown on TV in late 1978.
The well-publicized drama constituted commercial television's sensitive
coverage of domestic violence. Through the stories of four women who are
beaten by their husbands, the film presents the general characteristics of
wife abuse cases and some of the alternative solutions available to persons in
that situation. At the same time, the film addresses some of the public's most
common misconceptions about the problem.

Additional Information: 16 mm, 45 minutes; color, rental $50/three days;
purchase $495. Also available as a 70 mm, 98 min-
utes, motion picture; rental $75/three days, $850/
five years.
Ordering Information: Learning Corporation of America, Customer Relations Department, 1350 Avenue of the Americas,
New York, NY 10009. Telephone: (212) 397-9361.

Landon, Barbara, and Reilly, Susan (Producers). *The Fear Inside.* Roanoke, Virginia: WBRA-Television (PBS), 1980.

This film, geared to a rural audience, depicts what a day in a shelter is like. It describes the services that are available and the alternatives open to a battered woman who is in a shelter. The tape explores the pros and cons of returning to the husband, moving in with family or relatives and leaving to start a new life.

Additional Information: 30 minutes. Black and white ½-inch reel to reel and color ¾-inch videocassette. Written material included. Send blank tape, no fee for reproduction.

Ordering Information: Virginia Tech University, Department of Communications Studies, Attention: Dr. Susan Reilly, Blacksburg, VA 24060. Telephone: (703) 961-7136.

Media Loft, Inc. (Producer). *Battered Women: A Hidden Crime.* St. Paul, Minnesota: Minnesota Department of Corrections, 1978 (Slides).

The first part of the program is aimed at general audiences, based on real people and real injuries, and dramatizes the facts of domestic violence. It explores why women remain in the situation, the impact of violence on children, and how shelters operate. The second part of the program, aimed at the professional, presents a general overview of the social services and criminal justice response to battered women. The presentation considers possible responses by officials that will provide the battered woman with the economic assistance, physical safety, and emotional support she needs to leave a violent home.

Additional Information: 10 minutes; slide and tape presentation; $60.

Ordering Information: Minnesota Department of Corrections, Battered Women's Programs, Victim Services Division. Suite 430, Metro Square Building, Seventh and Roberts Streets, St. Paul, MN 55101. Telephone: (612) 296-6133.

Mitchell, J. Gary (Producer). *Battered Women: Violence Behind Closed Doors.* J. Gary Mitchell Film Company, 1977. (Film)

In this film, battered women describe their feelings of helplessness, shame about being a failure as a wife, and fear of being alone. The strongest impact, however, comes not from the women interviewed but from the statements of the batterers who insist, even though they have seriously injured their wives, that they have a right to discipline "My woman." The film explores a number of options for women in battering situations and discusses methods for police intervention and family crisis counseling.

Additional Information: 24 minutes; rental $60/week; purchase $395.

Ordering Information: MTI Teleprograms, 4825 N. Scott Street, Schiller Park, IL 60176, Telephone: (800) 323-1900.

Mitchell, J. Gary, and McDonald, John (Producers). *Burnout.* Schiller Park, Illinois: MTI Teleprograms, Inc.

Although this film does not specifically address family violence, it considers a problem experienced by service providers—"burnout." The symptoms of "burnout" include feelings of frustration, uselessness, exhaustion, and irritability about one's job. Organizational results include absenteeism, low morale, high job turnover, and inadequate delivery of services. This film describes the signs of "burnout" and suggests ways of working with it. A workshop manual and leader's guide accompany the film for a workshop on burnout.

Additional Information: 16 mm film or ¾ inch cassette, 28 minutes. Purchase for film $460, for video $415. Rental for one week, $70 (applicable towards purchase price).
Ordering Information: MTI Teleprograms, 4825 N. Scott St., Suite 23, Schiller Park, IL 60176. Telephone: (800) 323-5343. (Alaska, Illinois or Hawaii call collect (312) 671-0141) Audrey Smith.

Moses, Harry (Producer). *The New Police: Family Crisis Intervention.* Harry Moses Productions, Inc., 1974. (Film)

This documentary film deals mainly with the training of police officers in the generalist-specialist method of responding to domestic disturbances. The film was shot during the experimental phase of Oakland police departments' work in family crisis intervention. It will be of value mainly to police departments interested in training a limited number of officers as family crisis specialists.

Additional Information: 16 mm; 14 minutes; rental $50/week; purchase $295.
Ordering Information: Motorola Teleprograms, Inc., 4825 N. Scott Street, Suite 23, Schiller Park, IL 60176. Telephone: (800) 323-1900.

Rather, Dan (Narrator). *A Place to Go.* New York, New York: Sixty Minutes 1981.

The opening of this segment from the CBS newsprogram *Sixty Minutes* provides information on battered women and the problem of battering among all races and classes. It highlights the Center for Battered Women in Austin, Tex., and one man's successful effort with the local Homebuilder's Association to raise several hundred thousand dollars for a new shelter. It shows, in an upbeat way, how one person's interest in fundraising made a difference, and provides a role model for entrepreneurs in other communities to become involved in finding a solution to the very serious problem of battering. The narrator speculates that this may be the very first building designed as a shelter specifically to meet the need of battered women.

Additional Information: Also 16 mm film or ¾-inch color videotape, 15 minutes. Purchase $295 plus shipping costs. One week rental $60.

Ordering Information: MTI Teleprograms, Inc., #70 Commercial Ave., Northbrook, IL 60062. Telephone: (800) 323-5343.

Shadburne, Susan (Director, Co-producer). *A Family Affair.* Portland, Oregon: Will Vinton Productions, 1981.

Commissioned by the Association of Family Conciliation Courts and funded by the Law Enforcement Assistance Administration, this film is geared primarily to judges but could also be used for a general audience. The film is a documentary drama that depicts, through the experience of one violent couple, the legal remedies available for domestic abuse and the role that judges, law enforcement officials, and attorneys can play in preventing subsequent abuse. The film begins by showing the dynamics of one violent incident and then follows the battered woman through her efforts to stop the abuse by calling the police, filing a petition for a protection order, and filing criminal charges. The film is the best available audiovisual summary of American court response to spouse abuse.

Additional Information: 16 mm. color film, 28 minutes.

Ordering Information: For information about availability, contact the Center for Women Policy Studies.

Sheriff's Department (Producer). *415: Domestic Disturbance.* California: Sheriff's Department of Santa Barbara. (Film)

415 traces police reaction to a domestic disturbance involving a husband and wife. The film covers what happens from dispatch of the call and police arrival through resolution, referral, and police departure. Its effective safety message is aimed exclusively at domestic disturbance situations. It is good for use in teaching police refresher courses or in roll call training where officers have had previous in-depth instruction in family crisis intervention skills.

Additional Information: Send a blank 30 minute, ½-inch videotape to Sgt. Jim Thomas, Training Division, Santa Barbara Sheriff's Department, 4434 Calle Real, Santa Barbara, CA 93110.

Shortell-McSweeney, Jacqueline; Zimmerman, Debra; and Maguire, Genny (Directors). *Why Women Stay*. New York, New York: Women Make Movies, Inc. 1980. (Videocassette)

This video documentary considers the reasons why women stay in battering situations. Using animation, video rewrite and interviews, the film considers the stories of two women trapped within the historical and social context of the oppression of women. It analyzes the attitudes of helping professionals towards battered women, and makes the case that there is a critical need for shelters because of the help and peer support they provide battered women. *Why Women Stay* is a good film for putting the problems of battered women in a larger social context.

Additional Information: Black and white ¾-inch videocassette, and reel-to-reel, 30 minutes. Purchase $200. Rental $30 plus $6 shipping fee. Previews are available for purchase consideration only for a fee of $10, which is deductible from sale price if bought within 30 days.

Ordering Information: Women Make Movies, Inc., 257 West 19th St., New York, N.Y. 10011. Telephone: (212) 929-6477.

Third World Newsreel (Producer). *Violence in America: Women, Family and Society*. New York, New York: Third World Newsreel (Christine Choy, Director), 1980. (Film).

This realistic documentary explores the cultural, psychological, and social factors that contribute to violence against women in the home and in society at large. The film looks at the self-described experience of the battered woman and considers the shelter experience and other aspects of attempts to get help.

Additional Information: 40 minutes, color; price not known.
Ordering Information: Third World Newsreel, 160 Fifth Avenue, Suite 911, New York, NY 10010. Telephone: (212) 243-2310.

Tiseo, Mary, and Greenwald, Carol (Producers). *We Will Not Be Beaten*. Boston, Massachusetts: Transition House Films, 1979. (Film)

This film documents the work of Transition House, a refuge for battered women and their children in Cambridge, Massachusetts. The film depicts the active discussions of women recounting their violent experiences and efforts to escape a battering relationship. The film conveys the urgent plight of battered women and explores the social and economic barriers that make it difficult to end the violence.

Additional Information: Black and white, 38 minutes. Available in 16 mm. film. Purchase $395; rental $40; sliding scale fee for community groups.

Ordering Information: Transition House Films, Attention: Carol Greenwald, 120 Boylston Street, Room 708, Boston, MA 02116. Telephone: (617) 426-1912.

Wachter, Oralee. *Time Out Series: Deck the Halls, Up the Creek, Shifting Gears.* New York, New York and Berkeley, California: ODN Productions, 1981. (Films)

These three films are about three different phases in the battering experience focusing on the man who batters. They may be used singly or together and come with a curriculum guide.

Deck the Halls (18 min.) focuses on the battering experiences in a uppermiddle class family. Al has a financially successful career in sales but is unable to control his anger and discuss his feelings. The aftermath of a Christmas party degenerates into violence against his wife and the alienation of his teenaged son. A very powerful example of the battering incident.

Up the Creek (14 min.) focuses on the experiences of a working-class man, Tommy, after a battering has occurred and his wife has left him for the shelter. He tries to find her and cannot. His wife files a complaint of assault and battery against him with the District Attorney's office. A good example of the denial in a man who batters, although the D.A.'s involvement is not fully presented.

Shifting Gears (12 min.) explores the change experienced by a man who batters, Buddy, after he has been involved in a counseling program for men who batter. When his best friend P.K. beats his wife and then explodes in front of Buddy, Buddy offers him the possibility of changing his behavior. The focus on change and the interrelationship of both men make this a particularly powerful film.

Additional Information: For purchase information, contact ODN.

Ordering Information: ODN Productions, Inc. Attn: Nancy Graham, 1454 Sixth St., Berkeley, CA 94710 (415) 527-9120; or Attn: Oralee Wachter, 74 Varick St., Suite 304, New York, NY 10013. Telephone: (212) 431-8923.

WIIC-Television. *Wife Abuse.* Pittsburgh, Pennsylvania: WIIC-Television, 1977. (Videocassette)

In a 5-part series done for a local Pittsburgh news show, Donna Tabor reports on the issues while victims tell their stories. Simulated scenes of abuse and police intervention are used.

Additional Information: ¾ inch videocassette; 29 minutes; free rental; pur-
  chase $50.
Ordering Information: Donna Tabor, WIIC-TV, 341 Rising Main Avenue,
  Pittsburgh, PA 15214.

Woman's Eye Productions (Producer). *Battered Wives: A Legacy of Violence.* Falls Church, Virginia: Woman's Eye Productions, 1978. (Film)

A therapist, a shelter director, a police officer, attorneys, and scholars
present facts about spouse abuse. Through its educational format, the film
explores the roots of wife abuse in history, religion, culture, and the law. It
focuses on the particular problems that women face because of existing laws,
such as those of the Commonwealth of Virginia, where a woman jeopardizes
her support rights if she leaves the home. Finally, it examines the solutions
available to victims, with special emphasis on those chosen by the three
battered women whose moving testimony lends a sobering quality to the
film.

Additional Information: 16 mm; 28½ minutes; color; rental $35; purchase
  $375.
Ordering Information: Woman's Eye Productions, 7909 Sycamore Drive,
  Falls Church, VA 22042. Telephone: (703) 698-1691.

Woroner, Murray (Producer). *Officer Down: Code Three.* 1975. (Film)

Though not aimed exclusively at domestic disturbance situations, this police
officer survival training film is an excellent aid in teaching the safety component of such situations. The message is powerful enough to reach veteran
officers as well as recruit classes and provokes discussion. This film recreates
actual case histories of police incidents and emphasizes the importance of
constant vigilance on the part of the officers, lists in general terms the
improper practices that make officers most vulnerable to death or serious
injury, and dramatizes each of those practices in graphic detail.

Additional Information: 26 minutes; rental $60/week, purchase $395.
Ordering Information: Motorola Teleprograms, Inc., 4824 N. Scott Street,
  Schiller Park, IL 60176. Telephone: (800) 323-1900.

Appendix A
Alphabetical Listing of Shelters, Projects, and Agencies

Abby Kelley Foster House, Incorporated, Worcester, Massachusetts
Abuse, Assault Crisis Center, Columbia, Missouri
Abused and Battered Humans, Incorporated, Craig, Colorado
Abused Persons Economic and Resource Shelter, Wisconsin Dells, Wisconsin
Abused Persons Program, Bethesda, Maryland
Abused Spouse Assistance Services, White Plains, New York
Abused Women, East Meadow, New York
Abused Women Hotline, YWCA of the Tonawandas, North Tonawanda, New York
Abused Women's Advocacy Project, Auburn, Maine
Abused Women's Aid in Crisis, Incorporated, New York, New York
Abused Women's Network, Seattle, Washington
Abused Women's Project, Wausau, Wisconsin
Abused Women's Resource Closet, Bismarck, North Dakota
Abused Women's Services, Washburn, North Dakota
Access-York, Incorporated, Dallastown, Pennsylvania
Act, Incorporated, Fort Myers, Florida
Action for Battered Women in Ohio, Columbus, Ohio
Action in Community through Service, Dunfries, Virginia
ACWC Abuse Center, Northfield, New Jersey
Adaire County Shelter House, Columbia, Kentucky
Adult/Adolescent Counseling in Development, Malden, Massachusetts
Adult Family Life Crisis Center, Ottuma, Iowa
Advocates against Family Violence, YWCA
Advocates for Abused Women, Carson City, Nevada
Advocates for Battered Women, Little Rock, Arkansas
Advocates for Victims of Assault, Breckenridge, Colorado
Against Domestic Violence, Streator, Illinois
Aid and Alternatives, Iowa City, Iowa
Aiding Women in Abuse and Rape Emergency, Juneau, Alaska
Aid to Battered Women, Incorporated, Project Safe, Tupelo, Mississippi
Aid to Battered Women, YWCA, Poughkeepsie, New York
Aid to Women Victims of Violence, YWCA, Cortland, New York
Akron Task Force on Battered Women, Akron, Ohio

Alaska Family Violence Project, Anchorage, Alaska
Alexandra House, Anoka, Minnesota
Alexandra House, Fridley, Minnesota
Alexandria Battered Women's Support Project, Alexandria, Virginia
Alice Paul House, YWCA Battered Women's Shelter, Cincinnati, Ohio
Alice Paul Shelter for Women, Sierra Vista, Arizona
Alive (Alternatives to Living in Violence), Bremerton, Washington
Alliance on Family Violence, Bakersfield, California
Alliance Task Force on Domestic Violence, Alliance, Nebraska
Alma Canter Domestic Violence Project, Windsor, Vermont
Alternative Horizons, Durango, Colorado
Alternative House, Lowell, Massachusetts
Alternative to Violence/Women's Center, Pullman, Washington
Alternatives, Commerce City, Colorado
Alternatives for Battered Women, Rochester, New York
Alternatives for Women Now/R-CCWC, Camden, New Jersey
Alternatives, Incorporated; Anderson, Indiana
Alternatives to Violence Program, Colville, Washington
Ammon Henecy House, Los Angeles, California
Anderson County Shelter, Palestine, Texas
Anger Control Groups, Seattle, Washington
Anger Control Groups, Tacoma, Washington
Anoka County Task Force for Battered Women, Incorporated, Anoka,
    Minnesota
Anpo-Techa (New Dawn), Eagle Butte, South Dakota
Arctic Women's Group, Barrow Alaska
ARISE, Longview, Washington
Ask, Incorporated, North Platte, Nebraska
Assault Crisis Center, Ann Arbor Michigan
Assault Crisis Center, Hart, Michigan
Assault Crisis Center, Ypsilanti, Michigan
Assisi, Upper Marlboro, Maryland
Association for Abused Women, Manitowoc, Wisconsin
Athens Council on Domestic Violence, Athens, Georgia
Atlantic County Women's Center, May's Landing, New Jersey
Atlantic County Women's Hotline, Ventnor, New Jersey
AWAIC, Incorporated, Anchorage, Alaska
Aware, Jackson, Michigan

B. Robert Lewis House, Eagan, Minnesota
Battered and Abused Women's Program, Springfield, Missouri
Battered Families Project, Portales, New Mexico
Battered Partners Program, Westminster, Maryland
Battered Person Resource Center, Sussex, New Jersey

Battered Persons Crisis Center, Youngstown, Ohio
Battered Spouse Center, Billings, Montana
Battered Women Project, Sioux City, Iowa
Battered Women Project of Youth Services, Incorporated, Lorain, Ohio
Battered Women's Alternatives, Lafayette, California
Battered Women's Center, Davis, California
Battered Women's Crisis Line at Hasslehouse, Durham, North Carolina
Battered Women's Group, Salmon, Idaho
Battered Women's Help Center, Blackfoot, Idaho
Battered Women's Shelter, New York, New York
Battered Women's Law Project, Poughkeepsie, New York
Battered Women's Program, Baton Rouge, Louisiana
Battered Women's Program, Danielson, Connecticut
Battered Women's Project, Durham, North Carolina
Battered Women's Project, Elizabeth, New Jersey
Battered Women's Project, Grand Junction, Colorado
Battered Women's Project, Meriden, Connecticut
Battered Women's Project, San Diego, California
Battered Women's Project, Santa Fe, New Mexico
Battered Women's Project, Seattle, Washington
Battered Women's Project, Sioux City, Iowa
Battered Women's Project, Spokane, Washington
Battered Women's Project, Women's Resource Center, Grand Junction,
    Colorado
Battered Women's Resource Center, Hamlin, West Virginia
Battered Women's Service, Bridgeport, Connecticut
Battered Women's Services, Colorado Springs, Colorado
Battered Women's Services, Danbury, Connecticut
Battered Women's Services, San Diego, California
Battered Women's Services, Winston Salem, North Carolina
Battered Women's Support Project, Alexandria, Virginia
Battered Women's Task Force, Emporia, Kansas
Battered Women's Task Force, Kansas City, Kansas
Battered Women's Task Force, Pittsfield, Massachusetts
Battered Women's Task Force, Topeka, Kansas
Battered Women's Task Force, Winona, Minnesota
Battered Women's Task Force Stand, Incorporated, Derby, Connecticut
Battered Women's Unit of Legal Aid, Louisville, Kentucky
Bay County Women's Center/Rape and Crisis, Bay City, Michigan
Beacon House, Newport, North Carolina
Bergen County Community Action Program, Hackensack, New Jersey
Bering Sea Women's Coalition, Nome, Alaska
Berkeley Community YWCA Women's Refuge, Berkeley, California
Berkeley Women's Refuge, Berkeley, California

Berks County Women in Crisis, Reading, Pennsylvania
Berks Women in Crisis, Reading, Pennsylvania
Better Way, A, Incorporated, Muncie, Indiana
Beware, Hillsboro, Oregon
Big Horn County Crisis Line, Hardin, Montana
Billings Rape Task Force, Billings, Montana
Boston College Legal Assistance Bureau, Waltham, Massachusetts
Boulder County Safehouse, Boulder, Colorado
Boulder County Women's Resource Center, Boulder, Colorado
Bozeman Area Battered Women's Network, Bozeman, Montana
Bozeman Help Center, Bozeman, Montana
Bradley/Angle House, Portland, Oregon
Branches, Incorporated, Huntington, West Virginia
Brandun Guest House, Denver, Colorado
Brass, Incorporated, Bowling Green, Kentucky
Braxton Victim Advocate Center, Sutton, West Virginia
Brevard Family Aid, Melbourne, Florida
Bridgeway Counseling Services, Incorporated, Saint Charles, Missouri
Bright House, Lansing, Michigan
Brookings Women's Center, Brookings, South Dakota
Brooklyn Legal Services Corporation, Brooklyn, New York
Buena Vista County Task Force on Domestic Violence, Storm Lake, Iowa
Butler County Woman's Crisis Shelter, Fairfield, Ohio

C.W. Post Women's Center, Greenvale, New York
Calaveras Women's Crises Line, Angels Camp, California
Calcasieu Women's Shelter, Lake Charles, Louisiana
Call/Battered Women's Alternatives, Lafayette, California
Call for Help: Women's Crisis Shelter, Belleville, Illinois
Call Someone Concerned, Incorporated, Adrian, Michigan
Cambridge-Somerville Legal Services, East Cambridge, Massachusetts
Camden Regional Legal Services, Burlington, New Jersey
Canton Battered Service Corporation, Canton, Ohio
Cape Shelter, Incorporated, Hyannis, Massachusetts
Carbon County Human Services Project, Rawlins, Wyoming
Care (Citizens Aware and Responding to Emergencies) Fayetteville, North
    Carolina
Caring Place, Hobart, Indiana
Caring Unlimited, Biddeford, Maine
Caring Unlimited, Kennebunk, Maine
Carteret County Council on the Status of Women, Newport, North Carolina
Casa, Columbia, Maryland
Casa de Amparo, Oceanside, California

Casa de Esperanza, Yuba City, California
Casa, Incorporated, Hagerstown, Maryland
Casa Myrna Vazquez, Boston, Massachusetts
Catalyst, Chico, California
Catherine Booth House, Seattle, Washington
Catholic Charities, Jackson, Mississippi
Catholic Family Services, New Britain, Connecticut
Cayuga County Action Program, Auburn, New York
CEASE (Community Effort for Abused Spouses), Alexandria, Virginia
Center against Sexual Assault, Phoenix, Arizona
Center for Battered Women, Austin, Texas
Center for Individual and Family Studies, Towson, Maryland
Center for the Pacific-Asian Family, Incorporated, Los Angeles, California
Center for Women in Transition, Grand Rapids, Michigan
Center for Women's Studies and Services, Underground Railroad for
    Battered Women, San Diego, California
Central Massachusetts Legal Services, Incorporated, Fitchburg, Massachu-
    setts
Central Massachusetts Legal Services, Incorporated, Worcester, Massachu-
    setts
Central Oregon Battering and Rape Alliance/Women's Crisis Service
    (COBRA/WCS), Bend, Oregon
Central Pennsylvania Legal Services, Reading, Pennsylvania
Central Valley Mental Health Option House, Colton, California
Central Vermont Shelter Project, Montpelier, Vermont
Centre County Women's Resource Center, Rape/Abuse Crisis Line, State
    College, Pennsylvania
Charleston Domestic Violence Center, Incorporated, Charleston, West
    Virginia
Chemung County Task Force for Victims of Domestic Violence, Elmira,
    New York
Cheyenne County Task Force of Domestic Violence, Sidney, Nebraska
Chicago Abused Women Coalition Shelter Task Force, Chicago, Illinois
Chicana Service Action Center, Los Angeles, California
Child and Family Services, Knoxville, Tennessee
Child and Family Services, Family Crisis Center, Knoxville, Tennessee
Child Center of Our Lady of Grace, Saint Louis, Missouri
Child, Incorporated, Wilmington, Delaware
Children and Youth Development Services, Brooklyn, New York
Chippewa County Down with Violence Program, Incorporated, Sault
    Ste. Marie, Michigan
Choices for Victims of Domestic Violence, Columbus, Ohio
Chrysalis Center for Women, Minneapolis, Minnesota

Citizen Complaint Center, Washington, D.C.
Citizen Dispute Settlement Center, Miami, Florida
Citizen Participation and Support Project, Glendale, Arizona
Citizens against Rape and Domestic Violence, Sioux Falls, South Dakota
Citizens against Spousal Assault (CASA), Columbia, Maryland
Citizens Assisting and Sheltering the Abused (CASA), North East, Maryland
Citizens for the Prevention of Abuse, Council Bluffs, Iowa
Claham County Safe House Program, Port Angeles, Washington
Clay County Domestic Violence Task Force, Clay Center, Nebraska
Clearfield/Jefferson Community Mental Health Center, DuBois, Pennsylvania
Clinton County Women's Center, Lock Haven, Pennsylvania
Coalition against Human Abuse in Columbia-Greene Counties, Kinderhook, New York
Coalition against Spouse Abuse, Hattiesburg, Mississippi
Coalition against Spouse Abuse of Reno County, Hutchinson, Kansas
Coalition for Abused Women, East Meadow, New York
Coalition for Alternatives to Domestic Violence, Riverside, California
Coalition for the Prevention of Abuse of Women and Children Domestic Violence Outreach Center, San Bernardino, California
Coalition to Eliminate Domestic Violence, Grass Valley, California
Columbine Center, Denver, Colorado
Commission on Status of Women, Gary, Indiana
Committee against Domestic Violence, Mankato, Minnesota
Committee for Abused Women's Shelter, Oxnard, California
Committee for Napa Emergency Women's Shelter, Novalto, California
Committee on Domestic Violence, Decatur, Alabama
Committee to Aid Abused Women (CAAW), Sparks, Nevada
Community Abuse and Assault Center, Walla Walla, Washington
Community Action Council, Incorporated, Burnsville, Minnesota
Community Action Organization of Erie County, Incorporated, Buffalo, New York
Community Action Program, Hackensack, New Jersey
Community Assistance/Assault and Rape Emergency, Fort Bragg, California
Community Crisis Center, Elgin, Illinois
Community Crisis Center Abused Persons Program, Bethesda, Maryland
Community Planning Organization, Saint Paul, Minnesota
Community Resources, Butte, Montana
Community Service Officers Section, Seattle Police, Seattle, Washington
Community Service to Abuse Victims, Norfolk, Virginia
Community Social Services, Hasting, Nebraska

Concept 7 Group Homes, Anaheim, California
Concerned Citizens against Violence against Women, Incorporated, Turning Point Shelter, Marion, Ohio
Concord Task Force on Battered Women, Concord, New Hampshire
Connecticut Task Force on Abused Women, New Haven, Connecticut
Connections Social Services, Arlington, Virginia
Cook County Legal Assistance Foundation, Incorporated, Chicago, Illinois
Cooper Basin Behavioral Health Services, Incorporated, Hayden, Arizona
Coordinated Intervention System for Domestic Abuse, Incorporated, Crete, Nebraska
Coos County Women's Crisis Service, Incorporated, Coos Bay, Oregon
Couer d'Alene Women's Center, Couer d'Alene, Idaho
Council on Abused Persons, Beckley, West Virginia
Council on Battered Women, Incorporated, Atlanta, Georgia
Council on Domestic Violence, Midland, Michigan
Council on Spouse Abuse, Terre Haute, Indiana
Council on Status of Women, Vanceboro, North Carolina
Countering Domestic Violence, Bloomington, Illinois
Creative Services, Incorporated, Rape Crisis Center and Spouse Abuse Shelter, Ocala, Florida
Crescent House, An Associated Catholic Charities Program, New Orleans, Louisiana
Crisis Center/South Suburbia, Palos Park, Illinois
Crisis Intervention, Incorporated, Joplin, Missouri
Crisis Intervention Team, Hot Springs, South Dakota
Crisis Line Emergency Services, Incorporated, Clarkston, Idaho
Crossroad Crisis Center, Lima, Ohio
Crossroads Shelter, Fort Collins, Colorado
Cumberland Valley Women's Shelter, Barbourville, Kentucky
Cumings, Jordan, and Morgan, San Francisco, California
Custer County Domestic Violence Task Force, Incorporated, Broken Bow, Nebraska

Dade County Victims Advocates/Safespace, Miami, Florida
Dane County Advocates for Battered Women, Madison, Wisconsin
Dares, Incorporated, Port Huron, Michigan
Dawn, Kent, Washington
DAWN, Incorporated, Gordon, Nebraska
Dawson County Parent-Child Center, Lexington, Nebraska
Dawson House, Yakima, Washington
Daybreak, Incorporated, Worcester, Massachusetts
Desplaines Valley Community Center, Family Crisis Center, Summit, Illinois

Dickinson County Crisis Hotline, Abilene, Kansas
Domestic Abuse and Sex Assault Victims Service, Wausau, Wisconsin
Domestic Abuse Program of Erie County, Incorporated, Erie, Pennsylvania
Domestic Abuse Program of Sarpy County, Bellevue, Nebraska
Domestic Abuse Shelter, Montgomery, Alabama
Domestic Assault Program, YWCA, Kalamazoo, Michigan
Domestic Assault Project, West Palm Beach, Florida
Domestic Crisis Intervention Unit of Child Service and Family Counseling Center, Atlanta, Georgia
Domestic Harmony, Hillsdale, Michigan
Domestic Violence Association of Central Kansas, Salina, Kansas
Domestic Violence Center, Charleston, West Virginia
Domestic Violence Center, Manitowoc, Wisconsin
Domestic Violence Intervention Alliance, The Family Place, Dallas, Texas
Domestic Violence Intervention Center, Oregon City, Oregon
Domestic Violence of Door County, Sturgeon Bay, Wisconsin
Domestic Violence Prevention Center, Colorado Springs, Colorado
Domestic Violence Prevention Center, Mission, South Dakota
Domestic Violence Program, Council Bluffs, Iowa
Domestic Violence Program, Henderson, North Carolina
Domestic Violence Program, Iron River, Michigan
Domestic Violence Program, Middletown, New York
Domestic Violence Program, Milford, Massachusetts
Domestic Violence Program, Port Townsend, Washington
Domestic Violence Program at the Women's Resource Center, Incorporated, Scranton, Pennsylvania
Domestic Violence Program of Council Bluffs, Council Bluffs, Iowa
Domestic Violence Program/Threshold, Hazel Park, Michigan
Domestic Violence Project, Iowa City, Iowa
Domestic Violence Project, Incorporated, Ann Arbor, Michigan
Domestic Violence Project, The Door Opener, Mason City, Iowa
Domestic Violence Prosecution Program, White Plains, New York
Domestic Violence/Rape Relief Services, Ellensburg, Washington
Domestic Violence Resource Center Shelter, Hillsboro, Oregon
Domestic Violence Service Center, Wilkes Barre, Pennsylvania
Domestic Violence Shelter Program of Family and Children Service of Calhoun County, Battle Creek, Michigan
Domestic Violence Task Force, Concordia, Kansas
Domestic Violence Task Force, Madison, South Dakota
Domestic Violence Task Force, Norfolk, Nebraska

Domestic Violence Unit, Community Legal Services of Santa Clara County, San Jose, California
Domestic Violence/Victim Assistance Project, Ann Arbor, Michigan
Domestic Violence Victim Assistance Shelter Program, Ionia, Michigan
Door Opener, Mason City, Iowa
DOVE, Quincy, Massachusetts
Dundy County Domestic Violence Task Force, Benkelman, Nebraska

Eastern Montana Spouse Abuse Program, Glendive, Montana
Eastern Utah Families in Crisis Project, Moab, Utah
Eastern Utah Families in Crisis Project, Price, Utah
Eastern Utah Families in Crisis Project, Vernal, Utah
Eastern Women's Center, New York, New York
Eastside Domestic Violence Program, East King County
Elizabeth Buffum Chace House, Incorporated, Warwick, Rhode Island
Elizabeth Stone House, Jamaica Plain, Massachusetts
Elk City Crisis Line, Saint Mary's, Pennsylvania
Emergency Department/Illinois Masonic Medical Center, Chicago, Illinois
Emergency Housing Services, Incorporated, Boise, Idaho
Emergency Shelter Program, Incorporated, Hayward, California
Emergency Shelter Project, Visalia, California
Emergency Support Program, Longview, Washington
Erie County Coalition for Victims of Domestic Violence, Haven House, Buffalo, New York
Evergreen Hamon Services, Tacoma, Washington
Evergreen Legal Services, Everett, Washington
Evergreen Legal Services, Seattle, Washington
Every Woman's Center, Flint, Michigan
Every Woman's Place, Incorporated, Muskegon, Michigan
Every Woman's House, Wooster, Ohio

Fact Hotline (Families and Children in Trouble), Washington, D.C.
Facts, Superior, Wisconsin
Fairbault Area Victim Support Program, Fairbault, Minnesota
Fairfax County Victim Network, Alexandria, Virginia
Fairfax County Women's Shelter, Vienna, Virginia
Faith Teaching Center, Murphy, North Carolina
Families in Transition Center, Milford, Delaware
Family Abuse Center, Waco, Texas
Family Abuse Program, La Plata, Maryland
Family Abuse Project, Manhattan Family Court, New York, New York

Family and Children's Service, Davenport, Iowa
Family and Women's Advocates, Schenectady, New York
Family Counseling Agency in Will County, Joliet, Illinois
Family Counseling Service of the Finger Lakes, Incorporated, Geneva,
    New York
Family Crisis Center, Charlotte, North Carolina
Family Crisis Center, Stevens Point, Wisconsin
Family Crisis Council, Salisbury, North Carolina
Family Crisis Network, Celina, Ohio
Family Crisis Program, c/o YMCA, Yakima, Washington
Family Crisis Shelter, Crawfordsville, Indiana
Family Crisis Shelter, Hilo, Georgia
Family Crisis Shelter, Williston, North Dakota
Family Crisis Shelter, Incorporated, Portland, Maine
Family Crisis Shelter, Incorporated (Pu'Uhonua), Hilo, Hawaii
Family Emergency Shelter, Salinas, California
Family of Woodstock, Incorporated, Woodstock, New York
Family Place, Dallas, Texas
Family Refuge Center, Lewisburg, West Virginia
Family Rescue Shelter, Gordon, Nebraska
Family Resource Center, Shafer, Minnesota
Family Resource Center and Association for Prevention of Family Vio-
    lence, Lake Geneva, Wisconsin
Family Service and Counseling, Ellensburg, Washington
Family Service Association, Newark, Ohio
Family Shelter and Referral Service, Institute of Cognitive Development,
    Incorporated, San Angelo, Texas
Family Support Center, Omak, Washington
Family Violence Assistance Project, Augusta, Maine
Family Violence Center, Des Moines, Iowa
Family Violence Center, Incorporated, Beaumont, Texas
Family Violence Center, Incorporated, Fort Dodge, Iowa
Family Violence Coalition, Tucson, Arizona
Family Violence Program, Goleta, California
Family Violence Program, Lompoc, California
Family Violence Program of the Upper Valley, Lebanon, New Hampshire
Family Violence Project, Family and Child Service of Metropolitan Seattle,
    Seattle, Washington
Family Violence Project of the Women's Center, Birmingham, Alabama
Family Self-Help Center, Joplin, Missouri
Family Service, Madison, Wisconsin
Family Service Association, Lincoln, Nebraska
Family Service Center, Kingston, New York

Family Service Department, Salvation Army, Syracuse, New York
Family Service Society, Westminster, Maryland
Family Services of Greater Toledo, Toledo, Ohio
Family Shelter, Eugene, Oregon
Family Shelter Service/Hanson House, Glen Ellyn, Illinois
Family Support Center, Presque Isle, Maine
Family Violence Project, Essex, New Jersey
Fargo-Moorhead YWCA, Fargo, North Dakota
Farnham Youth Development Center, Oswego, New York
Favor House, Pensacola, Florida
Fayette County Family Abuse Council, Uniontown, Pennsylvania
First Step, Incorporated, Wichita Falls, Texas
First Step: Response to Domestic Violence, Keezletown, Virginia
First Step, West Wayne County Project, Westland, Michigan
Flagstaff Women's Resource, Incorporated, Flagstaff, Arizona
Forks Abuse Program, Forks, Washington
Fort Berthoud Reservation, New Town, North Dakota
Franklin County Community Mental Health Services, Malone, New York
Frederick County Battered Spouse Program, Frederick, Maryland
Free Clinic, Saint Petersburg, Florida
Fremont Counseling, Lander, Wyoming
Fremont County Task Force on Wife Abuse, Canon City, Colorado
Friendship Home, Lincoln, Nebraska
Friends of Battered Women, Merced, California
Friends of Battered Women, Richmond, Indiana
Friends of Battered Women of Washington County, West Bend, Wisconsin
Friends-of-the-Family, Scottsdale, Arizona
Furnace Street Mission, Akron, Ohio

Garden City Task Force on Domestic Violence, Garden City, Kansas
Gardner Women's Center, Gardner, Massachusetts
Garrett County Mental Health and Addictions Services, Oakland, Maryland
Gateway, Aurora, Colorado
Gateway-Buffalo Trace Shelter, Morehead, Kentucky
Gateway YWCA Women's Resource Center, Clinton, Iowa
Genesis House, New London, Connecticut
Genesis House Program for Battered Women, Lorain, Ohio
Gillette Refuge, Gillette, Wyoming
Glendive Task Force Against Spouse Abuse, Glendive, Montana
Good Neighbors Unlimited, Annapolis, Maryland
Good Shepherd Shelter, Los Angeles, California
Gospel League, Chicago, Illinois

Grand Island Task Force on Domestic Violence and Sexual Assault, Incorporated, Grand Island, Nebraska
Grandma's Safe House, Cheyenne, Wyoming
Greater Lowell YWCA, Lowell, Massachusetts
Great Falls Mercy Home, Great Falls, Montana
Greene County Crisis Center, Xenia, Ohio
Greene County Department of Social Services, Catskill, New York
Greene County Mental Health Center, Cairo, New York
Green River Comprehensive Care Center, Owensboro, Kentucky
Greensboro Legal Aid Foundation, Greensboro, North Carolina
Group Health Cooperative of Puget Sound Domestic Abuse Program, Seattle, Washington
Gulf Coast Women's Center, Biloxi, Mississippi
Gulf Coast Women's Center, Incorporated, Biloxi, Mississippi

Halifax County Mental Health Center, Roanoke Rapids, North Carolina
Hampden County Women's Center, Springfield, Massachusetts
Harbor Area Task Force On Battered Women, Chelsea, Massachusetts
Harbor Area YWCA Refuge and Services for Victims of Domestic Violence, San Pedro, California
Harbor House, Tupelo, Mississippi
Harbor Shelter Service, Aberdeen, Washington
Harborview Medical Center, Seattle, Washington
Harriet Tubman Shelter, Minneapolis, Minnesota
Harriet Tubman Women's Shelter, Minneapolis, Minnesota
Hartford Interval House, Hartford, Connecticut
Hasslehouse, Durham, North Carolina
Hastings Task Force on Domestic Violence, Hastings, Nebraska
Haven Hills, Incorporated, Canoga Park, California
Haven House, Buffalo, New York
Haven House Family Services, Wayne, Nebraska
Haven House, Incorporated, Pasadena, California
HAWC, Salem, Massachusetts
Hays County Women's Center, San Marcos, Texas
Heartling, Detroit, Michigan
Hegira, Incorporated, Westfield, Massachusetts
Heidi House, Columbus, Ohio
Helena Women's Center, Helena, Montana
Help for Abused Women, Salem, Massachusetts
Helping Services for Northeast Iowa, Decorah, Iowa
Helpmate, Asheville, North Carolina
Henry Street Settlement Program for Victims of Domestic Violence, New York, New York

Hera (Hotline to End Rape and Abuse), Springfield, Massachusetts
HERS, Reed City, Michigan
High Point Women's Shelter, High Point, North Carolina
Home Free, Plymouth, Minnesota
Homesafe, Incorporated, Ashtabula, Ohio
Hope House, Springfield, Missouri
Hopkins Project, Hopkins, Minnesota
Horizon House, Union City, Pennsylvania
Hospitality House, Erie, Pennsylvania
Hospitality House for Women, Rome, Georgia
Hotline, Green Bay, Wisconsin
Hotline for Abused Women/Kensington, Kensington, Pennsylvania
Hotline for Abused Women/Kensington and Lutheran Settlement House/
   Women's Program, Philadelphia, Pennsylvania
Hotline for Battered Women, Dunkirk, New York
House of Imagene, Washinton, D.C.
House of Ruth, Baltimore, Maryland
House of Ruth, Washington, D.C.
House of Ruth, Incorporated, Claremont, California
Houston Area Women's Center, Incorporated, Houston, Texas
Howell County Volunteers, West Plains, Missouri
Hubbard House, Jacksonville, Florida
Hudson County Battered Women's Project of the YWCA, Jersey City,
   New Jersey
Hudson Guild Family Life Center, New York, New York
Human Services Planning and Coordinating, Eldridge, Iowa
Humboldt Women for Shelter, Arcata, California

Iliuliuk Family and Health Services, Unalaska, Alaska
Immanuel Medical Center, Omaha, Nebraska
Inc Spot Counseling Center, Youth Services, Bothell, Washington
Independence House, c/o Community Action Committee, Hyannis, Massa-
   chusetts
Information and Referral Inc./Help-on-Call Crisis Line, Tucson, Arizona
Information and Referral Resource Center, Las Cruces, New Mexico
Integrated Crisis Service, Cedar Falls, Iowa
Integrative Crisis Services, Cedar Falls, Iowa
Interface Community, Newbury Park, California
Interval House, Seal Beach, California
Iowa Coalition against Domestic Violence, Cedar Rapids, Iowa
Iowa Commission on the Status of Women, Des Moines, Iowa

Jackson County Task Force on Household Violence, Ashland, Oregon

Jane Addams Center for Battered Women, Inc., New York, New York
Jefferson County Women's Center, Inc., Watertown, New York
Jenesse Center, Inc., Los Angeles, California
Jersey Battered Women's Service, Inc., Greystone Park, New Jersey
Johnson County Task Force for Battered Persons, c/o Johnson County
    District Attorney's Office, Olathe, Kansas

Kalispell Rape Crisis Line, Kalispell, Montana
Kansas Association of Domestic Violence Programs, Wichita, Kansas
Karen Delrow, Syracuse, New York
Katie Did . . . , Inc., Brattleboro, Vermont
Kearney Task Force on Domestic Violence and Sexual Assault, Kearney,
    Nebraska
Kenai Women's Resource Center, Seldotna, Alaska
Kitsap County YWCA/Family Violence Project, Bremerton, Washington
Klickitat County Council on Domestic Violence, Goldendale, Washington
Knoxville Women's Center, Knoxville, Tennessee
Kodiak Women's Resource Center, Kodiak, Alaska
Kokomo YWCA Shelter Program, Kokomo, Indiana
Kotzebue Women's Crisis Center, Kotzebue, Alaska

Labelle Shelter, Detroit, Michigan
La Casa de las Madres, San Francisco, California
Lake County Committee on Sexual Assault and Domestic Violence, Inc./
    Forbes House, Painesville, Ohio
Lake County Crisis Center, Waukegan, Illinois
Lakeshore Association for Abused Women, Manitowoc, Wisconsin
Lakes Region Family Services, Laconia, New Hampshire
Lamoille Family Center, Morrisville, Vermont
Lancaster Shelter for Abused Women, Lancaster, Pennsylvania
Las Vegas Family Abuse Center, Las Vegas, Nevada
Legal Aid Foundation of Long Beach, Long Beach, California
Legal Aid of Oneida County, Inc., Ilion, New York
Legal Aid Society Domestic Violence Legal Unit, Albany, New York
Legal Assistance of North Dakota, Bismarck, North Dakota
Legal Services Corporation, Des Moines, Iowa
Legal Services of Eastern Missouri, Inc., St. Louis, Missouri
Legal Services of Eastern Oklahoma, Inc., Tulsa, Oklahoma
Legal Services of Middle Tennessee, Clarksville, Tennessee
Lewis House, Eagan, Minnesota
Lexington-Henderson County Counseling Center, Lexington, Tennessee
Lincoln Shelter and Services, Inc., Lincoln City, Oregon
Linda Cobb, Social Service Department, Malcolm Bliss Mental Health
    Center, St. Louis, Missouri

Listening Ear Crisis Center, Alexandra, Minnesota
Litigation Coalition for Battered Women, New York, New York
Lompoc Shelter, Goleta, California
Long Island Women's Coalition, Inc., Islip Terrace, New York
Longmont Coalition/Women in Crisis, Longmont, Colorado
Los Angeles Commission on Assaults Against Women/Los Angeles Rape
    and Battery Hotline, Los Angeles, California
Lower Naugatuck Valley Battered Women Project, Ansonia, Connecticut
Lutheran Community Services, Inc., New York, New York
Lutheran Family and Social Service Domestic Violence Program, Columbus,
    Nebraska
Lutheran Social Service, Grand Forks, North Dakota
Lynn District Court Clinic, Lynn, Massachusetts

Mahala, Roanoke, Virginia
Margaret W. Jordan, Leakwood, Kansas
Marin Abused Women's Services, San Rafael, California
Marion County Victim Advocate Program, Inc., Indianapolis, Indiana
Mariposa House, Santa Cruz, California
Mariposa House Battered Women Shelter Project, Aptos, California
Marital Abuse Project, Media, Pennsylvania
Marital Abuse Project of Delaware County, Inc., Wallingford, Pennsyl-
    vania
Martha Rogers Ripley Alliance for Battered Women, Inc., Thief River
    Falls, Minnesota
Maryland Children's Aid and Family Society, Westminster, Maryland
Mayor's Commission on Women, Omaha, Nebraska
McCambridge Center for Women, Columbia, Missouri
McCook Task Force on Domestic Violence, McCook, Nebraska
McLean County Outreach Abused Women's Service, Washburn, North
    Dakota
Mental Health Association, Lockport, New York
Mercy Home, Inc., Great Falls, Montana
Mercy House, Albany, New York
Meriden-Wallingford Battered Women's Shelter, Meriden, Connecticut
Mid-Hudson Legal Services, Incorporated, Poughkeepsie, New York
Mid-Minnesota Women's Center, Inc., Brainerd, Minnesota
Mid-Peninsula Support Network, Mountain View, California
Mission House, Louisville, Kentucky
Missouri Coalition Against Domestic Violence, Columbia, Missouri
Missouri Ozarks Economic Opportunity Corp., Richland, Missouri
Montachusetts Task Force on Battered Women, Fitchburg, Massachusetts
Monticello Area Community Action Agency SHE Project (Shelter for Help
    in Emergency), Charlottesville, Virginia

Morningpoint for Victims of Domestic Abuse, Inc., Woodsworth, Wisconsin
Mother Lode's Crisis Center/Shelter, Sonora, California
Mother's Emergency Stress Shelter and Service, Sacramento, California
Mountain Sisters Collective, Angels Camp, California
Mujeres Latinas en Accion, Chicago, Illinois
Mujeres Unidas/Women Together, Alamo, Texas
Mujeres Unidas/Women Together, Edinburg, Texas
Muscatine County Rape/Assault Care Services, Muscatine, Iowa
Mutual Ground, Aurora, Illinois
My Sister's House, Charleston, South Carolina
My Sister's Place, Athens, Ohio
My Sister's Place, Washington, D.C.

Nashville Consortium on Domestic Violence, Nashville, Tennessee
National Organization for Women, North Central Chapter, Wausau, Wisconsin
Nebraska Task Force on Domestic Violence, Lincoln, Nebraska
Necessities/Necesidades, Northhampton, Massachusetts
Neward Battered Women Services, Neward, Ohio
New Bedford Women's Center, New Bedford, Massachusetts
New Beginnings, Seattle, Washington
New Beginnings Arden House, Ardentown, Delaware
New Beginnings for Battered Women, Seattle, Washington
New Directions for Young Women, Tucson, Arizona
New Directions Shelter for Battered Women, Lawton, Oklahoma
New England Learning Center for Women in Transition, Greenfield, Massachusetts
New Haven Legal Assistance Association, New Haven, Connecticut
New Haven Project for Battered Women, New Haven, Connecticut
New Hope, Incorporated, Attleboro, Massachusetts
New Horizons, YWCA Women's Center, La Crosse, Wisconsin
Newport County Women's Resource Center, Newport, Rhode Island
News, Neighborhood House, Kansas City, Missouri
New York City Human Resources Administration Battered Women's Shelter Program, New York, New York
Niagara County Legal Aid Society, Incorporated, Niagara Falls, New York
Night Prosecutor's Program, Columbus, Ohio
Noah Project, Incorporated, Abilene, Texas
Norfolk Task Force on Domestic Violence, Norfolk, Nebraska
North County Legal Services, Incorporated, Upper Jay, New York
Northeastern Coalition for Battered Women, Incorporated, Duluth, Minnesota

Northeast Kentucky Legal Services, Morehead, Kentucky
Northfield Victim Support Program, Northfield, Minnesota
Northwest Arkansas Project for Battered Women and Their Families, Fay-
    etteville, Arkansas
Northwestern Ohio Crisis Line, Defiance, Ohio
Northwest Human Resources Center/Family Crisis Shelter, Williston, North
    Dakota
Northwoods Coalition for Battered Women, Bemidji, Minnesota
Nuestro Lugar (Our Place), Moses Lake, Washington

Oakwood Wesley House, Venice, California
Oasis House, Nashville, Tennessee
Oasis, Watauga Mental Health Clinic, Boone, North Carolina
Oasis Women's Center, Alton, Illinois
Office of State Networking Coordinator, Bismarck, North Dakota
Ogden Hall for Women/Gospel Mission, Spokane, Washington
Open Door of Indiana, Pennsylvania, Indiana, Pennsylvania
Operation Bridge, Incorporated, Omaha, Nebraska
Option, Hobbs, New Mexico
Option House, Colton, California
Orange-Durham YWCA Coalition for Battered Women, Durham, North
    Carolina
Oswego County Council On Battered Women, Catholic Charities of Oswe-
    go, Oswego, New York
Our House, Friends of Battered Women, Merced, California
Our House Women's Shelter, Merced, California
Our Refuge for Battered Spouses, Madera, California
Outer Drive Hospital Social Work Services Department, Lincoln Park,
    Michigan
Outreach, Port Jervis, New York
Outreach Women's Defense, Brooklyn, New York
OWLA, Our Lady of Help Church, East Orange, New Jersey

Pacific-Asian Rape Care Line, Los Angeles, California
Pacific County Family Abuse Alternatives, South Bend, Washington
Papillion Multi-Service Center, Papillion, Nebraska
Parents Anonymous, Rawlins, Wyoming
Parents Anonymous of Oregon, Portland, Oregon
Park County Mental Health, Bailey, Colorado
Park Slope Safe Homes Project, Children and Youth Development Services,
    Brooklyn, New York
Passages, Viola, Wisconsin
Pawnee Mental Health Center, Manhattan, Kansas

Penelope House, Incorporated, Mobile, Alabama
Pennsylvania Coalition against Domestic Violence, Harrisburg, Pennsylvania
Pensacola YWCA, Pensacola, Florida
People Assistance Team, Vancouver, Washington
People Helping People, Incorporated, Wagner, South Dakota
People's City Mission, Lincoln, Nebraska
People's Place, Milford, Delaware
Perfect Place, Saginaw, Michigan
Perfect Place, Women's Crisis Shelter, Saginaw, Michigan
Personal Development Counseling, Incorporated, Marshfield, Wisconsin
Persons Service, Incorporated, Hattiesburg, Mississippi
Phoenix House, Columbus, Ohio
Phoenix House, YWCA, Glendale, California
Pike County Battered Women's Task Force, Waverly, Ohio
Pima County Attorney's Victim/Witness Advocacy Program, Tucson, Arizona
Placer Rape Crisis Line, Auburn, California
Porterville Mission Project Shelter, Porterville, California
Potomac Highlands Mental Health Guild/Domestic Violence Program, Petersburg, West Virginia
Prison Families Anonymous, Incorporated, Hempstead, New York
Program Hope, Hyannis, Massachusetts
Project Dove, Crosston, Iowa
Project Green Hope, Services for Women, Incorporated, New York, New York
Project Reach, Incorporated, Wayland, New York
Project Safe, New Albany, Mississippi
Project Sanctuary, Ukiah, California
Project Save Battered Women, Tupelo, Mississippi
Project Shelter, Women's Center/NMU, Marquette, Michigan
Project Women, Springfield, Ohio
Providence Home Women's Shelter, Columbia, South Carolina
Providence House, Willingboro Shelter, Burlington, New Jersey
Prudence Crandall Center for Women, New Britain, Connecticut

Quest Center, San Francisco, California

Rainbow Retreat, Incorporated, Phoenix, Arizona
Randolph County Women's Aid, Incorporated, Asheboro, North Carolina
Rape and Abuse Crisis Center, Fargo, North Dakota
Rape and Abuse Prevention Group of Statesville/Iredell County, Incorporated, Statesville, North Carolina

Rape and Assault Committee for Nashua Area, Incorporated, Nashua, New Hampshire

Rape and Battered Women Program of the Gateway YWCA Women's Resource Center, Clinton, Iowa

Rape and Domestic Violence, Marinette, Wisconsin

Rape and Domestic Violence Information Center (RDVIC), Morgantown, West Virginia

Rape and Sexual Abuse Care Center, Edwardsville, Illinois

Rape, Child and Family Crisis Council of Salisbury, Salisbury, North Carolina

Rape Crisis Center, Binghamton, New York

Rape Crisis Center, Cheyenne, Wyoming

Rape Crisis Center, Incorporated, Salt Lake City, Utah

Rape Crisis Service of Schenectady, Incorporated, YWCA, Schenectady, New York

Rape Information Services, Incorporated, Morgantown, West Virginia

Rape Prevention Center, Sarasota, Florida

Rape Relief Hotline, Portland, Oregon

Rape/Spouse Abuse Crisis Center of the Family Service Association, Lincoln, Nebraska

Rape/Spouse Assault Crisis Center, Muskegon, Michigan

Raphael House, Portland, Oregon

Raphael House, Saint Louis, Missouri

Rappahannock Council on Domestic Violence, The Haven, Fredericksburg, Virginia

Reach, Sylva, North Carolina

Real Crisis Intervention, Incorporated, Greenville, North Carolina

Redevelopment Opportunities For Women, Saint Louis, Missouri

Refuge House, Eau Clare, Wisconsin

Refuge House, Roseburg, Oregon

Refuge House of Leon County, Incorporated, Tallahassee, Florida

Region 4 Assault Crisis Center, Hart, Michigan

Region 4 Council on Domestic Violence, Fergus Falls, Minnesota

Regional Crisis Center for Victims of Family Abuse or Rape, Manhattan, Kansas

Renewal House, Boston, Massachusetts

Rescue-Crisis Center, Toledo, Ohio

Rescue Mission, Macon, Georgia

Resource Center for Women and Their Families, Somerville, New Jersey

Respond, Somerville, Massachusetts

Rev. Angus McDonald, Keokuk, Iowa

Rhode Island Legal Services, Incorporated, Providence, Rhode Island

Richland County Task Force on Domestic Violence, Mansfield, Ohio

Ripley Alliance for Battered Women, Thief River Falls, Minnesota
Riverside County Coalition/Alternatives to Domestic Violence, Riverside, California
Rock Island County Council on Alcoholism (New Hope League) East Moline, Illinois
Rockland Family Shelter, Nyack, New York
Rosasharon, North Hollywood, California
Rose Brooks Center, Kansas City, Missouri
Rutland County Battered Women Network, Rutland, Vermont

Sacred Shawl Women's Society, Incorporated, Pine Ridge, South Dakota
SAFE (Services for Abused Families and Emergency Shelter), Jamestown, North Dakota
SAFE (Shelter Abused Females), Cinnaminson, New Jersey
Safe Alternatives for Abused Families, Devils Lake, North Dakota
Safe Homes, Port Angeles, Washington
Safe House, Belcourt, North Dakota
Safe House, Cheyenne, Wyoming
Safe House, Denver, Colorado
Safehouse, Pittsburg, Kansas
Safe House, Ypsilanti, Michigan
Safe Place, Florence, Alabama
Safe Place, Oakland, California
Safe Place and Rape Crisis Center of Sarasota, Sarasota, Florida
Safe Place, Seacoast Task Force on Family Violence, Portsmouth, New Hampshire
SAFE Services, Laramie, Wyoming
Safe Shelter, Savannah, Georgia
Safespace, Battered Women's Shelter, Miami, Florida
Safe Space of Indian River County, Vero Beach, Florida
Safe Task Force, Evanston, Wyoming
Saint George's Home for Women, Kansas City, Missouri
Saint Joseph's House, Minneapolis, Minnesota
Saint Louis Abused Women's Support Project, Incorporated, Saint Louis, Missouri
Saint Luke's Hospital Battered Women Program, New York, New York
Saint Nicholas Hospital, Sheboygan, Wisconsin
Saint Petersburg Free Clinic Shelter, Saint Petersburg, Florida
Salinas Family Emergency Center, Salinas, California
Salvation Army, Detroit, Michigan
Salvation Army, Elmira, New York
Salvation Army, Omaha, Nebraska
Salvation Army, Rasagoula, Mississippi

Salvation Army Emergency Family Shelter, Memphis, Tennessee
Salvation Army Emergency Lodge, Chicago, Illinois
Salvation Army Family Service, Indianapolis, Indiana
Salvation Army Project, Chicago, Illinois
Salvation Army Shelter, Athens, Georgia
San Diego Women for Shelter, San Diego, California
San Francisco Women's Center, San Francisco, California
San Joaquin Commission on the Status of Women, Stockton, California
San Juan Mental Health Service Center Against Sexual Assault, Farming-
    ton, New Mexico
San Mateo Women's Center, San Mateo, California
Santa Barbara County Family Violence Program, Santa Barbara, California
Santa Barbara Shelter, Goleta, California
Santa Monica Hospital Medical Center, Santa Monica, California
Save, Incorporation, Fremont, California
Scottsbluff County Domestic Violence Task Force, DOVES, Scottsbluff,
    Nebraska
Self Help Center, Casper, Wyoming
Serve, Incorporated, Birmingham, Alabama
Services against Family Violence, Malden, Massachusetts
Services for Abused Women, Helping Services for Northeastern Iowa,
    Decorah, Iowa
Services for Victims of Domestic Violence, Forks, Washington
Services for Women in Crisis, Incorporated, Nashville, Tennessee
Seward County Task Force on Domestic Violence, Seward, Nebraska
Sexual and Physical Abuse Resource Center, Gainesville, Florida
Sexual Assault and Domestic Violence Center of Baltimore City, Rosedale,
    Maryland
Sexual Assault/Spouse Abuse Resource Center, Aberdeen, Maryland
Shasta County Women's Refuge, Redding, California
Shattered Women's Shelter, Redondo Beach, California
Sheboygan County Advocates for Battered Women, Sheboygan, Wisconsin
Shelter, Charlotte, North Carolina
Shelter, Kapaa, Hawaii
Shelter, Omaha, Nebraska
Shelter, A Center for Victims of Family Violence, Omaha, Nebraska
Shelter for Abused Women, Willingboro, New Jersey
Shelter for Abused Spouses and Children, Honolulu, Hawaii
Shelter for Help in Emergency, Charlottesville, Virginia
Shelter for Victims of Domestic Violence, Albuquerque, New Mexico
Shelter Home for Abused Women, Incorporated, Calumet, Michigan
Shelter Home for Abused Women, Laurium, Michigan
Shelter Home of Caldwell County, Incorporated, Lenior, North Carolina

Shelter House, Willmar, Minnesota
Shelter, Incorporated, Alpena, Michigan
Shelter Our Sisters, Incorporated, Fort Lee, New Jersey
Shelter Our Sisters, Hackensack, New Jersey
Shelter Services for Abused Women, Bridgeport, Connecticut
Shelter, Victims of Domestic Violence, Incorporated, Bristol, Tennessee
Shenandoah Women's Center, Martinsburg, West Virginia
Sheridan Women's Center, Sheridan, Wyoming
Shiloh Youth Revival Center, Omaha, Nebraska
Siena House, Omaha, Nebraska
Simple Gifts, Buffalo, New York
Sister Care, YWCA, Columbia, South Carolina
Sisters for Human Equality (SHE), Lansing, Michigan
Sitkans against Violence, Sitka, Alaska
Skagit Rape Relief/Battered, Mount Vernon, Washington
Social Service Department of Saint Luke's Hospital, New Bedford, Massachusetts
Social Work Service, Fort Campbell, Kentucky
Sojourn, Santa Monica, California
Sojourn House, Middletown, Connecticut
Sojourn Shelter, Los Angeles, California
Sojourner Center, Phoenix, Arizona
Sojourner House, Hopkins, Minnesota
Sojourner House, Providence, Rhode Island
Sojourner Truth Center for Women, Caruthersville, Missouri
Sojourner Truth House, Cehalis, Washington
Sojourner Truth House, Milwaukee, Wisconsin
Sojourner Women's Center, Incorporated, Springfield, Illinois
Solano Center for Battered Women, Fairfield, California
SOS, Incorporated, Emporia, Kansas
SOS Shelter, Incorporated, Endicott, New York
South Central Community Act Program, Lake Andes, South Dakota
South County Alternative, Gilroy, California
South Dakota Coalition against Domestic Violence, Eagle Butte, South Dakota
Southeast Emergency Quarters, San Diego, California
Southern Alleghenys Legal Aid, Incorporated, Bedford, Pennsylvania
Southern Arizona Legal Aid, Incorporated, Tucson, Arizona
South Shore Women's Center, Plymouth, Massachusetts
South Suburban Family Service, South Saint Paul, Minnesota
Southwestern Wisconsin Community Action Program Project on Battered Women, Platteville, Wisconsin
Southwest Women Working Together, Chicago, Illinois

Southwest Women's Shelter, Marshall, Minnesota
Spouse Abuse Center, Ionia, Michigan
Spouse Abuse, Incorporated, Orlando, Florida
Spouse Abuse Network, Montgomery, Alabama
Spouse Abuse of Polk County, Incorporated, Lakeland, Florida
Spouse Abuse Shelter, Ocala, Florida
Spouse Abuse Shelter Project, Petoskey, Michigan
Spouse Abuse Shelter Project, Incorporated, Marquette, Michigan
Spouse Abuse Victims Advocacy Programs, Crisis Center, Iowa City, Iowa
Spring, Incorporated, Tampa, Florida
Spruce Run, Bangor, Maine
Stafford County Information and Referral, Dover, New Hampshire
Stanislaus Women's Refuge Center, Modesto, California
Staten Island Women's Crisis Center, Staten Island, New York
Steuben County Spouse Abuse Task Force, Bath, New York
Stevens County Battered Women's Committee, Morris, Minnesota
Stillwater Domestic Violence Service, Stillwater, Oklahoma
Stop Abuse, Everett, Washington
Story County Sexual Assault Care Center and Battered Women's Project,
    Ames, Iowa
Su Casa Family Crisis and Support Center, Lakewood, California
Suffolk County District Attorney's Office, Dorchester, Massachusetts
Support For Change, Incorporated, Bellow Falls, Vermont
Supporting Ourselves Through Sharing, Roanoke Rapids, North Carolina
Support Through Sharing, Roanoke Rapids, North Carolina
Survival, Adult Abuse Program, Warrensburg, Missouri
Survival Center of Snohomish County, Everett, Washington
Susquehanna Valley Women in Transition, Incorporated, Sunbury, Penn-
    sylvania
Sweetwater County Task Force on Sexual Assault, Rock Springs, Wyoming
Sweetwater Shelter House, Rock Springs, New York
Switchboard, Battered Women's Project, Durham, North Carolina

Tacoma's Support Shelter, Tacoma, Washington
Tapers, Incorporated, Wisconsin Dells, Wisconsin
Task Force Against Domestic Violence, Wilmington, North Carolina
Task Force and Spouse Abuse, Glendive, Montana
Task Force/Battered Women, Akron, Ohio
Task Force Battered Women, Henderson, North Carolina
Task Force/Domestic Violence, Mansfield, Ohio
Task Force for Battered Women, Ithaca, New York
Task Force on Abused Women, Bridgeport, Connecticut
Task Force on Abused Women, Danielson, Connecticut

Task Force on Abused Women, Mental Health Association in Portage County, Stevens Point, Wisconsin
Task Force on Battered Women, Raleigh, North Carolina
Task Force on Family Violence, Berlin, New Hampshire
Task Force on Family Violence, Wilmington, North Carolina
Task Force on Violence against Women, Jackson, Wyoming
Templum, Cleveland, Ohio
Temporary Assistance for Women, Incorporated, Las Vegas, Nevada
Tennessee Commission on the Status of Women, Nashville, Tennessee
Time-Out, Ladysmith, Wisconsin
Toledo YWCA Battered Women Services, Toledo, Ohio
Tompkins County Task Force for Battered Women, Ithaca, New York
Transitional Living Center, Incorporated, El Paso, Texas
Transition House, Women's Center, Cambridge, Massachusetts
Transitions, Incorporated, Zanesville, Ohio
Tree House, Temple, Texas
Tri County Council on Domestic Violence, Incorporated, Eagle River, Wisconsin
Tri County Counseling, Eagle River, Wisconsin
Tri County Women Strength, Peoria, Illinois
Tri Lakes Shelter, Saranac Lake, New York
Trims, Houston, Texas
Tri Valley Haven for Women, Livermore, California
Tu Casa, Incorporated, Alamosa, Colorado
Tucson Center for Women and Children, Tucson, Arizona
Tulare County Emergency Shelter Project, Visalia, California
Tulsa Task Force for Battered Women, Incorporated, Tulsa, Oklahoma
Tundra Women's Coalition, Bethel, Arkansas
Turning Point, Kemmerer, Wyoming
Turning Point, Marion, Ohio
Turning Point, New Baltimore, Michigan
Turning Point for Victims of Domestic Abuse, Incorporated, Ellsworth, Wisconsin
Turning Point of Lehigh Valley, Allentown, Pennsylvania
Turning Point of Lehigh Valley, Bethlehem, Pennsylvania

Umbrella of Saint Johnsbury, Incorporated, Saint Johnsbury, Vermont
Underground Railroad, Incorporated, Saginaw, Michigan
Union County Task Force on Domestic Violence, La Grande, Oregon
Upshur County Home Crisis Aid, Buckhannon, West Virginia
Upton Center Hull House, Chicago, Illinios

Vance County Task Force on Battered Women,
Vancouver Women's Resource Center, Vancouver, Washington

Vancouver Women's Resource Center/Rape Relief/Victim Advocacy, Van-
   couver, Washington
Van Wert Crisis Center Line, Van Wert, Ohio
Vera House, Incorporated, Syracuse, New York
Vermont Legal Aid, Incorporated, Springfield, Vermont
Victim Advocacy/District Attorney's Staff, Ashland City, Tennessee
Victim Advocate Program, Fort Lauderdale, Florida
Victim Assistance Support Project, Waukesha, Wisconsin
Victims Assistance Program, Charlotte, North Carolina
Victim's Crisis Center/Freeborn Mowe Mental Health Center, Austin, Tex-
   as
Victims Information Bureau of Suffolk, Incorporated, Hauppauge, New
   York
Victims of Domestic Violence, Elmira, New York
Victim/Witness Assistance Project, Brooklyn, New York
Violence Clinic/Department of Psychiatry, Baltimore, Maryland
Violence in the Family Project of the Community Action Commission,
   Santa Barbara, California
Virginia Peninsula Counseling for Battered Women, Hampton, Virginia
Volunteer Abused Shelter, Key West, Florida
Volunteer Counseling Service of Rockland County, Incorporated, Spouse
   Abuse Educational Workshop, New City, New York
Volunteers against Abuse Center, Zelienople, Pennsylvania
Volunteers of America, Camden, New Jersey
Volunteers of America, Portland, Oregon
Volunteers of America, Brandon House, San Jose, California

Wake County Women's Aid, Services for Abused Women, Incorporated,
   Raleigh, North Carolina
Waldo Women's Shelter, Searsport, Maine
Walk-in Counseling Center, Minneapolis, Minnesota
Washington County Domestic Violence Project, Machias, Maine
Washington State Shelter Network, Olympia, Washington
Washington State Women's Council, Olympia, Washington
Washtenaw County Legal Aid Society, Ann Arbor, Michigan
Waukesna County Battered Women's Task Force, Waukesna, Wisconsin
WAVE Program (Working against Violent Environments), Rockford, Illi-
   nois
Weave, Incorporated, Sacramento, California
Webster County Support Group, Marshfield, Missouri
WEED, Auburn, California
Western Center (Savvy), Jackson, New Jersey
Western Community Development Center, Jackson, New Jersey
Western Wayne County Project on Domestic Assault, Westland, Michigan

West Virginia Legal Services Plan, Martinsburg, West Virginia
West Virginia Women's Commission, Charleston, West Virginia
Whatcom County Crisis Services Domestic Violence Program, Bellingham, Washington
WIC (Women in Crisis), Arvada, Colorado
Wichita Women's Crisis Center, Wichita, Kansas
Wife Abuse Crisis Service, Memphis, Tennessee
Wise Options for Women, YWCA, Williamsport, Pennsylvania
WIT, Detroit, Michigan
Witness/Victim Service Center of Cuyahoga County, Cleveland, Ohio
WOMA (The Women's Alliance), San Jose, California
Woman Care/Aegis Association, Dover-Foxcroft, Maine
Woman Haven, Incorporated, Hotville, California
Woman House, Saint Cloud, Minnesota
Womanplace, McKeesport, Pennsylvania
Woman's Advocates, Pocatello, Idaho
Woman's Advocates, Saint Paul, Minnesota
Woman's Aid Center, Incorporated, Hazleton, Pennsylvania
Womanshelter/Companeras, Holyoke, Massachusetts
Womanspace, Eugene, Oregon
Womanspace East, Pittsburgh, Pennsylvania
Womanspace, Feminist Therapy Collective, Incorporated, Boston, Massachusetts
Womanspace, Incorporated, Mercer County Women's Center, Trenton, New Jersey
Womanspace Shelter for Battered Women, Sacramento, California
Woman's Place, Doylestown, Pennsylvania
Woman's Place, Rockville, Maryland
Woman's Place, Sellersville, Pennsylvania
Woman's Place, Urbana, Illinois
Woman's Place, Incorporated, Doylestown, Pennsylvania
Woman's Place, Incorporated, Greeley, Colorado
Woman's Survival Center, Snohomish, Washington
Woman to Woman, Harrisonburg, Virginia
Woman Together, Incorporated, Cleveland, Ohio
Woman Abuse, Children's Village, Family Service, Fargo, North Dakota
Woman against Abuse, Philadelphia, Pennsylvania
Women against Domestic Violence, Carmel Highlands, California
Women against Emergency Services (WAVES), Berkeley, California
Women against Violence, Idaho Falls, Idaho
Women against Violence, Omaha, Nebraska
Women and Child Crisis Shelter Incorporated, Whittier, California
Women and Violence, Incorporated, Rapid City, South Dakota

Womencare Shelter, Bellingham, Washington
Womencenter, Sharon, Pennsylvania
Womencenter Domestic Violence Service Center, Wilkes Barre, Pennsylvania
Womencenter, Incorporated, Appleton, Wisconsin
Women Encouraging Enterprise and Development (WEED), Auburn, California
Women Escaping a Violent Environment, Sacramento, California
Women Helping Women, Brockton, Massachusetts
Women Helping Women, Abused Women's Services, Edison, New Jersey
Women Incorporated, Plattsburgh, New York
Women in Crisis, Evergreen, Colorado
Women in Crisis, Harrisburg, Pennsylvania
Women in Crisis, Hummelstown, Pennsylvania
Women in Crisis, Lakewood, Colorado
Women in Crisis, Pine Bluff, Arkansas
Women in Crisis Coalition, Deadwood, South Dakota
Women in Crisis, Counseling and Assistance, Incorporated, Fairbanks, Alaska
Women in Crisis/Family Counseling Service, Greenville, South Carolina
Women in Crisis Task Force, Pierre, South Dakota
Women in Crisis/YWCA, Reading, Pennsylvania
Women in Distress, Naylor, Georgia
Women in Distress of Broward County, Incorporated, Fort Lauderdale, Florida
Women in Jeopardy Program, Salt Lake City, Utah
Women in Need, Chambersburg, Pennsylvania
Women in Safe Homes (WISH), Ketchikan, Alaska
Women in Transition, Detroit, Michigan
Women in Transition, Grand Haven, Michigan
Women in Transition, Philadelphia, Pennsylvania
Women Services of Westmoreland County, Greensburg, Pennsylvania
Women Shelter, Ravenna, Ohio
Women Shelter, Incorporated, Kent, Ohio
Women United against Battering, Placerville, California
Women's Action and Resource Center, Beulah, North Dakota
Women's Action Program, Incorporated (Services for Battered Women), Minot, North Dakota
Women's Advocacy Center, Charleston, South Carolina
Women's Aid in Crisis, Elkins, West Virginia
Women's Aid Service, Incorporated, Mount Pleasant, Michigan
Women's Aid, Services for Abused Women, Greensboro, North Carolina
Women's Alliance, Dickinson, North Dakota

Women's Alternative Center, Wawa, Pennsylvania
Women's Alternative Shelter, Danville, Illinois
Women's Alternatives Shelter House, Anderson, Indiana
Women's Assistance Services, Commerce City, Colorado
Women's Association of Self-Help, Bellevue, Washington
Women's Care Center (for Abused Women), Lafayette, Louisiana
Women's Center, Beaver Falls, Pennsylvania
Women's Center, Birmingham, Alabama
Women's Center, Carbondale, Illinois
Women's Center, Columbus, Indiana
Women's Center, Houston, Texas
Women's Center, Saint Charles, Missouri
Women's Center and Safe House, Cape Girardeau, Missouri
Women's Center and Shelter of Greater Pittsburgh, North Hills, Allison
    Park, Pennsylvania
Women's Center and Shelter of Greater Pittsburgh, Pittsburgh, Pennsyl-
    vania
Women's Center, Family Support System, Bloomsburg, Pennsylvania
Women's Center, Incorporated, Providence, Rhode Island
Women's Center of Beaver County, Rochester, Pennsylvania
Women's Center of Montgomery County Domestic Violence Committee,
    Abington, Pennsylvania
Women's Center of Southeast Connecticut, New London, Connecticut
Women's Center of Yonkers, Yonkers, New York
Women's Center/San Joaquin Company Domestic Violence Project, Stock-
    ton, California
Women's Center, Williamsport, Incorporated, Williamsport, Pennsylvania
Women's Coalition, Duluth, Minnesota
Women's Coalition, Incorporated/Sojourner Truth, Milwaukee, Wisconsin
Women's Community Association, Incorporated, Albuquerque, New Mex-
    ico
Women's Counseling Center, Saint Louis, Missouri
Women's Counseling Clinic and Resource Center, Honolulu, Hawaii
Women's Crisis Center, Brattleboro, Vermont
Women's Crisis Center, Kalamazoo, Michigan
Women's Crisis Center, New Brunswick, New Jersey
Women's Crisis Center, Newport, Kentucky
Women's Crisis Center, West Covina, California
Women's Crisis Center, Wichita, Kansas
Women's Crisis Center, YWCA, Ogden, Utah
Women's Crisis Service, Annandale, New Jersey
Women's Crisis Services, Flemington, New Jersey
Women's Crisis Services, Keene, New Hampshire
Women's Crisis Services, Manchester, New Hampshire
Women's Crisis Services, Peoria, Illinois

Women's Crisis Services, Salem Oregon
Women's Crisis Services, South Norwalk, Connecticut
Women's Crisis Shelter, Fairfield, Ohio
Women's Crisis Support, Santa Cruz, California
Women's Crisis Support Team, Grants Pass, Oregon
Women's Crisis Task Force, Pierre, South Dakota
Women's Emergency Shelter, Waterbury, Connecticut
Women's Haven, Paterson, New Jersey
Women's Haven, Incorporated, Fort Worth, Texas ·
Women's Help Center/YWCA, Johnstown, Pennsylvania
Women's Help, Incorporated, Dallas, Texas
Women's Horizons, Incorporated, Kenosha, Wisconsin
Women's House of Transition, Incorporated, Winooski, Vermont
Women's Justice Center, Detroit, Michigan
Women's Law Collective, Cambridge, Massachusetts
Women's Legal Defense Fund, Washington, D.C.
Women's Litigation Unit, Neighborhood Legal Assistance, San Francisco,
    California
Womenspace, Unlimited, South Lake, Tahoe, California
Women's Place, Aberdeen, South Dakota
Women's Place, Missoula, Montana
Women's Place, Richland, Washington
Women's Place, Sullersville, Pennsylvania
Women's Place Resource Center, Portland, Oregon
Women's Protective Services, Natick, Massachusetts
Women's Referral Central, New Jersey
Women's Refuge, Cumberland, Maryland
Women's Resource and Survival Center, Keyport, New Jersey
Women's Resource Center, Beckley, West Virginia
Women's Resource Center, Grand Junction, Colorado
Women's Resource Center, Lawrence, Massachusetts
Women's Resource Center, Missoula, Montana
Women's Resource Center, Montrose, Colorado
Women's Resource Center, San Luis Rey, California
Women's Resource Center, Stevens Point, Wisconsin
Women's Resource Center, Traverse City, Michigan
Women's Resource Center, Watertown, South Dakota
Women's Resource Center, Winona, Minnesota
Women's Resource Center/Norman, Oklahoma Task Force for Battered
    Women, Norman, Oklahoma
Women's Resource Center of Chester County, YWCA, West Chester,
    Pennsylvania
Women's Resource Center of Dillon, Dillon, Montana
Women's Resource Center of the Jamestown Girls Club, Jamestown, New
    York

Women's Resource Center of Lincoln for Battered Women, Newport, Oregon
Women's Resource Center of the New River Valley, Incorporated, Christiansburg, Virginia
Women's Resource Center of the YWCA, Racine, Wisconsin
Women's Resource Center of the YWCA, Shreveport, Louisiana
Women's Resource Center of Wood River, Wyoming, Rhode Island
Women's Resource Center/YWCA, Spokane, Washington
Women's Resource Network, Philadelphia, Pennsylvania
Women's Rights Clinic of the Antioch School of Law, Washington, D.C.
Women's Safe House, Pittsburg, Kansas
Women's Self Help Center, Saint Louis, Missouri
Women's Self Help Center, Incorporated, Casper, Wyoming
Women's Service Center Domestic Violence Project, Green Bay, Wisconsin
Women's Services Center of Berkshire County, Pittsfield, Massachusetts
Women's Services Department/Loop YWCA, Chicago, Illinois
Women's Services, Greenhouse, Meadville, Pennsylvania
Women's Services of Westmoreland County, Greensburg, Pennsylvania
Women's Services Project, Denton, Taxas
Women's Shelter, Canton, New York
Women's Shelter, High Point, North Carolina
Women's Shelter, Long Beach, California
Women's Shelter, Rochester, Minnesota
Women's Shelter, San Antonio, Texas
Women's Shelter Advisory Committee of YWCA, South Bend, Indiana
Women's Shelter and Personal Assistance Project, Canton, New York
Women's Shelter and Support Services Program, Olympia, Washington
Women's Shelter, Incorporated, Corpus Christi, Texas
Women's Shelter of Bexar County, Incorporated, San Antonio, Texas
Women's Shelter of East Texas, Incorporated, Nacogdoches, Texas
Women's Shelter of the YWCA, Evansville, Indiana
Women's Shelter Program/San Luis Obispo Company, San Luis Obispo, California
Women's Supportive Services, Claremont, New Hampshire
Women's Survival Center, Pontiac, Michigan
Women's Survival Center Oakland County, Pontiac, Michigan
Women's Survival Space, Brooklyn, New York
Women's Transitional Care Services, Lawrence, Kansas
Women's Transitional Living Center, Incorporated, Orange, California
Women's Victim Advocacy Program/YWCA, Richmond, Virginia
Wyandot Mental Health Center, Kansas City, Kansas

Yale/New Haven Hospital Rape and Sexual Assault Trauma Counseling Team, New Haven, Connecticut
Yankton Task Force, Yankton, South Dakota
Yonkers Court Assistance Program for Abused Spouses, Yonkers, New York
Yonkers Women's Task Force, Yonkers, New York
Yonkers Women's Task Force, Incorporated, Yonkers, New York
York Street Center, Denver, Colorado
YWCA, Burlington, Iowa
YWCA, Decatur, Illinois
YWCA, Fresno, California
YWCA, Hammond, Indiana
YWCA, Jamestown, New York
YWCA, Lancaster, Pennsylvania
YWCA, Rock Springs, Wyoming
YWCA, Advocates for Family Violence, Utica, New York
YWCA, Aid To Women Victims, Cortland, New York
YWCA, Alice Paul House, Cincinnati, Ohio
YWCA, Battered Women, Dubuque, Iowa
YWCA, Battered Women, Durham, North Carolina
YWCA, Battered Women, Jersey City, New Jersey
YWCA, Battered Women Project, Dayton, Ohio
YWCA, Battered Women's Program, New Orleans, Louisiana
YWCA, Battered Women's Program, Yakima, Washington
YWCA, Battered Women's Shelter, Missoula, Montana
YWCA, Battered Women's Shelter, Toledo, Ohio
YWCA, Crisis Center, Marietta, Georgia
YWCA, Crisis Shelter, Lynchburg, Virginia
YWCA, Domestic Assault Shelter, West Plam Beach, Florida
YWCA, Domestic Crisis Center, Grand Rapids, Michigan
YWCA, Domestic Violence Program, Nashville, Tennessee
YWCA, Domestic Violence Services, Flint, Michigan
YWCA, Domestic Violence Shelter, Pontiac, Michigan
YWCA, Emergency House, Vancouver, Washington
YWCA, Emergency Housing Program for Women, Seattle, Washington
YWCA, Family Crisis Program, Yakima, Washington
YWCA, Family Crisis Shelter, Pueblo, Colorado
YWCA, Family Violence Program, Ardentown, Delaware
YWCA, Marjorie Mason Center for Victims of Domestic Violence, Fresno, California
YWCA, Metro-Detroit Interim House, Detroit, Michigan
YWCA, of Binghamton, Binghamton, New York

YWCA, of Clermont County, Batoria, Ohio
YWCA, of Jacksonville, Jacksonville, Florida
YWCA, of Pontiac/North Oakland Domestic Crisis Shelter, Pontiac, Michigan
YWCA, of the Tonawandas, Tonawanda, New York
YWCA, of Wheeling, Wheeling, West Virginia
YWCA, Option House Shelter, Enid, Oklahoma
YWCA, Pasada, Bellingham, Washington
YWCA, Passageway, A Women's Crisis Center, Oklahoma City, Oklahoma
YWCA, Program for Women in Jeopardy and Their Children, Salt Lake City, Utah
YWCA, Protective Shelter, Hamilton, Ohio
YW CARES, Park Forest, Illinois
YWCA, Safe House Domestic Violence Shelter, Flint, Michigan
YWCA, Services to Families in Violence, Schenectady, New York
YWCA, Shelter for Women Victims of Violence, Fort Wayne, Indiana
YWCA, Spouse Abuse Center, Louisville, Kentucky
YWCA, Spouse Abuse Project Shelter for Battered Women, Lexington, Kentucky
YWCA, Spouse Abuse Shelter of Berrian County, Saint Joseph, Michigan
YWCA, Wings, West Covina, California
YWCA, Women against Domestic Violence, Monterey, California
YWCA, Women against Violence, Natick, Massachusetts
YWCA, Women's Center, Annapolis, Maryland
YWCA, Women's Center, West Chester, Pennsylvania
YWCA, Women's Emergency Shelter, Cedar Rapids, Iowa
YWCA, Women's Emergency Shelter, Santa Rosa, California
YWCA, Women's Growth Center, Saint Joseph, Missouri
YWCA, Women's Help Center, Johnstown, Pennsylvania
YWCA, Women's Place, Aberdeen, South Dakota
YWCA, Women's Resource and Crisis Center, Galveston, Texas
YWCA, Women's Resource Center, Oklahoma City, Oklahoma
YWCA, Women's Resource Center, Racine, Wisconsin
YWCA, Womenshelter, Long Beach, California
YWCA, Women's Shelter, South Bend, Indiana
YWCA, Women's Shelter Program, Olympia, Washington
YWCA, Women's Support Shelter, Tacoma, Washington
YWCA, Women's Victim Advocacy, Richmond, Virginia
Youth and Family Services Bureau, Hayward Police Department, Hayward, California

Appendix B
U.S. Cities with One or
More Services

Aberdeen, Maryland
Aberdeen, South Dakota
Aberdeen, Washington
Abilene, Kansas
Abilene, Texas
Abington, Pennsylvania
Adrian, Michigan
Akron, Ohio
Alamo, Texas
Alamosa, Colorado
Albany, New York
Albuquerque, New Mexico
Alexandria, Minnesota
Alexandria, Virginia
Allentown, Pennsylvania
Alliance, Nebraska
Allison Park, Pennsylvania
Alpena, Michigan
Alton, Illinois
Ames, Iowa
Anaheim, California
Anchorage, Alaska
Anderson, Indiana
Angels Camp, California
Annandale, New Jersey
Annapolis, Maryland
Ann Arbor, Michigan
Anoka, Minnesota
Ansonia, Connecticut
Appleton, Wisconsin
Aptos, California
Arcata, California
Ardentown, Delaware
Arlington, Virginia
Arvada, Colorado
Asheboro, North Carolina
Ashland, Oregon
Ashland City, Tennessee
Ashtabula, Ohio
Athens, Georgia
Atlanta, Georgia
Attleboro, Massachusetts
Auburn, California
Auburn, Maine

Auburn, New York
Augusta, Maine
Aurora, Colorado
Austin, Minnesota
Austin, Texas

Bailey, Colorado
Bakersfield, California
Baltimore, Maryland
Bangor, Maine
Barbourville, Kentucky
Barrow, Alaska
Bath, New York
Baton Rouge, Louisiana
Batoria, Ohio
Battle Creek, Michigan
Bay City, Michigan
Beaumont, Texas
Beaver Falls, Pennsylvania
Beckley, West Virginia
Bedford, Pennsylvania
Belcourt, North Dakota
Belleville, Illinois
Bellevue, Nebraska
Bellevue, Washington
Bellingham, Washington
Bellow Falls, Vermont
Bemidji, Minnesota
Bend, Oregon
Benkelman, Nebraska
Berkeley, California
Berlin, New Hampshire
Bethel, Arkansas
Bethesda, Maryland
Bethlehem, Pennsylvania
Beulah, North Dakota
Biddeford, Maine
Billings, Montana
Biloxi, Mississippi
Binghamton, New York
Birmingham, Alabama
Bismarck, North Dakota
Blackfoot, Idaho
Bloomington, Idaho

Derby, Connecticut
Des Moines, Iowa
Detroit, Michigan
Devils Lake, North Dakota
Dickinson, North Dakota
Dillon, Montana
Dover, New Hampshire
Dorchester, Massachusetts
Dover-Foxcroft, Maine
Doylestown, Pennsylvania
DuBois, Pennsylvania
Dubuque, Iowa
Duluth, Minnesota
Dunfries, Virginia
Dunkirk, New York
Durango, Colorado
Durham, North Carolina

Eagan, Minnesota
Eagle Butte, South Dakota
Eagle River, Wisconsin
East Cambridge, Massachusetts
East Meadow, New York
East Moline, Illinois
East Orange, New Jersey
Eau Claire, Wisconsin
Edinburg, Texas
Edison, New Jersey
Edwardsville, Illinois
Eldridge, Iowa
Elgin, Illinois
Elizabeth, New Jersey
Elkins, West Virginia
Ellensburg, Washington
Ellsworth, Wisconsin
Elmira, New York
Elmira, New York
El Paso, Texas
Emporia, Kansas
Endicott, New York
Enid, Oklahoma
Erie, Pennsylvania
Essex, New Jersey
Eugene, Oregon
Evanston, Wyoming
Evansville, Indiana
Everett, Washington
Evergreen, Colorado

Fairbanks, Alaska
Fairbault, Minnesota

Fairfield, California
Fairfield, Ohio
Fargo, North Dakota
Farmington, New Mexico
Fayetteville, Arizona
Fayetteville, North Carolina
Fergus Falls, Minnesota
Fitchburg, Massachusetts
Flagstaff, Arizona
Flemington, New Jersey
Flint, Michigan
Florence, Alabama
Forks, Washington
Fort Bragg, California
Fort Campbell, Kentucky
Fort Collins, Colorado
Fort Dodge, Iowa
Fort Lauderdale, Florida
Fort Lee, New Jersey
Fort Myers, Florida
Fort Wayne, Indiana
Fort Worth, Texas
Frederick, Maryland
Fredericksburg, Virginia
Fremont, California
Fresno, California
Fridley, Minnesota

Gainesville, Florida
Galveston, Texas
Garden City, Kansas
Gardner, Massachusetts
Gary, Indiana
Geneva, New York
Gillette, Wyoming
Gilroy, California
Glendale, Arizona
Glendale, California
Glendive, Montana
Glen Ellyn, Illinois
Goldendale, Washington
Goleta, California
Gordon, Nebraska
Grand Forks, North Dakota
Grand Haven, Michigan
Grand Island, Nebraska
Grand Junction, Colorado
Grand Rapids, Michigan
Grants Pass, Oregon
Grass Valley, California
Great Falls, Montana

Greeley, Colorado
Green Bay, Wisconsin
Greenfield, Massachusetts
Greensboro, North Carolina
Greensburg, Pennsylvania
Greenvale, New York
Greenville, North Carolina
Greenville, South Carolina
Greystone Park, New Jersey

Hackensack, New Jersey
Hagerstown, Maryland
Hamilton, Ohio
Hamlin, West Virginia
Hammond, Indiana
Hampton, Virginia
Hardin, Montana
Harrisburg, Pennsylvania
Harrisonburg, Virginia
Hart, Michigan
Hartford, Connecticut
Hastings, Nebraska
Hattiesburg, Mississippi
Hauppauge, New York
Hayden, Arizona
Hayward, California
Hazel Park, Michigan
Hazleton, Pennsylvania
Helena, Montana
Hempstead, New York
Henderson, North Carolina
High Point, North Carolina
Hillsboro, Oregon
Hillsdale, Michigan
Hilo, Georgia
Hilo, Hawaii
Hobart, Indiana
Hobbs, New Mexico
Holyoke, Massachusetts
Honolulu, Hawaii
Hoplins, Minnesota
Hot Springs, South Dakota
Hotville, California
Houston, Texas
Hummelstown, Pennsylvania
Huntington, West Virginia
Hutchinson, Kansas
Hyannis, Massachusetts

Idaho Falls, Idaho
Ilion, New York

Indiana, Pennsylvania
Indianapolis, Indiana
Ionia, Michigan
Iowa City, Iowa
Iron River, Michigan
Islip Terrace, New York
Ithaca, New York

Jackson, Michigan
Jackson, Mississippi
Jackson, New Jersey
Jackson, Wyoming
Jacksonville, Florida
Jamaica Plain, Massachusetts
Jamestown, New York
Jamestown, North Dakota
Jersey City, New Jersey
Johnstown, Pennsylvania
Joliet, Illinois
Joplin, Missouri
Juneau, Alaska

Kalamazoo, Michigan
Kalispell, Montana
Kansas City, Kansas
Kapaa, Hawaii
Kearney, Nebraska
Keene, New Hampshire
Keezletown, Virginia
Kemmerer, Wyoming
Kennebunk, Maine
Kensington, Pennsylvania
Kenosha, Wisconsin
Kent, Ohio
Kent, Washington
Keokuk, Iowa
Ketchikan, Alaska
Keyport, New Jersey
Key West, Florida
Kinderhook, New York
Kingston, New York
Knoxville, Tennessee
Kodiak, Alaska
Kokomo, Indiana
Kotzebue, Alaska

Laconia, New Hampshire
La Crosse, Wisconsin
Ladysmith, Wisconsin
Lafayette, California
Lafayette, Louisiana

La Grande, Oregon
Lake Andes, South Dakota
Lake Charles, Louisiana
Lake Geneva, Wisconsin
Lakeland, Florida
Lakewood, California
Lakewood, Colorado
Lancaster, Pennsylvania
Lander, Wyoming
Lansing, Michigan
La Plata, Maryland
Laramie, Wyoming
Las Cruces, New Mexico
Las Vegas, Nevada
Laurium, Michigan
Lawrence, Kansas
Lawrence, Massachusetts
Lawton, Oklahoma
Leawood, Kansas
Lebanon, New Hampshire
Lenior, North Carolina
Lewisburg, West Virginia
Lexington, Kentucky
Lexington, Nebraska
Lexington, Tennessee
Lincoln, Nebraska
Lincoln City, Oregon
Lincoln Park, Michigan
Little Rock, Arkansas
Livermore, California
Lock Haven, Pennsylvania
Lockport, New York
Lompoc, California
Long Beach, California
Longmont, Colorado
Longview, Washington
Lorain, Ohio
Los Angeles, California
Louisville, Kentucky
Lowell, Massachusetts
Lynchburg, Virginia
Lynn, Massachusetts

Machias, Maine
Macon, Georgia
Madera, California
Madison, South Dakota
Madison, Wisconsin
Malden, Massachusetts
Malone, New York
Manchester, New Hampshire

Manhattan, Kansas
Manitowoc, Wisconsin
Mankato, Minnesota
Mansfield, Ohio
Marietta, Georgia
Marinette, Wisconsin
Marion, Ohio
Marquette, Michigan
Marshall, Minnesota
Marshfield, Missouri
Marshfield, Wisconsin
Martinsburg, West Virginia
Mason City, Iowa
May's Landing, New Jersey
McCook, Nebraska
McKeesport, Pennsylvania
Meadville, Pennsylvania
Media, Pennsylvania
Melvourne, Florida
Memphis, Tennessee
Merced, California
Meriden, Connecticut
Miami, Florida
Middletown, Connecticut
Middletown, New York
Midland, Michigan
Milford, Delaware
Milwaukee, Wisconsin
Minneapolis, Minnesota
Minot, North Dakota
Mission, South Dakota
Missoula, Montana
Moab, Utah
Mobile, Alabama
Modesto, California
Monterey, California
Montgomery, Alabama
Montpelier, Vermont
Montrose, Colorado
Morehead, Kentucky
Morgantown, West Virginia
Morris, Minnesota
Morrisville, Vermont
Moses Lake, Washington
Mount Pleasant, Michigan
Mount Vernon, Washington
Mountain View, California
Muncie, Indiana
Murphy, North Carolina
Muscatine, Iowa
Muskegon, Michigan

Nacogdoches, Texas
Nashville, Tennessee
Nashua, New Hampshire
Natick, Massachusetts
Naylor, Georgia
New Albany, Mississippi
Newark, Ohio
New Baltimore, Michigan
New Bedford, Massachusetts
New Britain, Connecticut
New Brunswick, New Jersey
Newbury Park, California
New Haven, Connecticut
New London, Connecticut
New Orleans, Louisiana
Newport, Kentucky
Newport, North Carolina
Newport, Oregon
Newport, Rhode Island
New York, New York
New Town, North Dakota
Niagara Falls, New York
Nome, Alaska
Norfolk, Nebraska
Norfolk, Virginia
Norman, Oklahoma
Northhampton, Massachusetts
North East, Maryland
Northfield, Minnesota
Northfield, New Jersey
North Hollywood, California
North Platte, Nebraska
North Tonawanda, New York
Novalto, California
Nyack, New York

Oakland, California
Oakland, Maryland
Ocala, Florida
Oceanside, California
Ogden, Utah
Oklahoma City, Oklahoma
Olathe, Kansas
Olympia, Washington
Omaha, Nebraska
Omak, Washington
Orange, California
Oregon City, Oregon
Orlando, Florida
Oswego, New York
Ottuma, Iowa

Owensboro, Kentucky
Oxnard, California

Painesville, Ohio
Palestine, Texas
Palos Park, Illinois
Papillion, Nebraska
Park Forest, Illinois
Pasadena, California
Pasagoula, Mississippi
Paterson, New Jersey
Pensacola, Florida
Peoria, Illinois
Petersburg, West Virginia
Petroskey, Michigan
Philadelphia, Pennsylvania
Phoenix, Arizona
Pierre, South Dakota
Pine Bluff, Arkansas
Pine Ridge, South Dakota
Pittsburg, Kansas
Pittsburgh, Pennsylvania
Pittsfield, Massachusetts
Placerville, California
Platteville, Wisconsin
Plattsburgh, New York
Plymouth, Massachusetts
Plymouth, Minnesota
Pocatello, Idaho
Pontiac, Michigan
Port Angeles, Washington
Port Huron, Michigan
Port Jervis, New York
Port Townsend, Washington
Portales, New Mexico
Porterville, California
Portland, Maine
Portland, Oregon
Portsmouth, New Hampshire
Poughkeepsie, New York
Price, Utah
Presque Isle, Maine
Providence, Rhode Island
Pueblo, Colorado
Pullman, Washington

Quincy, Massachusetts

Racine, Wisconsin
Raleigh, North Carolina
Rapid City, South Dakota

Ravenna, Ohio
Rawlins, Wyoming
Reading, Pennsylvania
Redding, California
Redondo Beach, California
Reed City, Michigan
Richland, Missouri
Richland, Washington
Richmond, Indiana
Richmond, Virginia
Riverside, California
Roanoke, Virginia
Roanoke Rapids, North Carolina
Rochester, Minnesota
Rochester, New York
Rochester, Pennsylvania
Rockford, Illinois
Rock Spring, New York
Rock Springs, Wyoming
Rockville, Maryland
Rome, Georgia
Roseburg, Oregon
Rosedale, Maryland
Rutland, Vermont

Sacramento, California
Saginaw, Michigan
Saint Charles, Missouri
Saint Cloud, Minnesota
Saint Johnsbury, Vermont
Saint Joseph, Michigan
Saint Joseph, Missouri
Saint Louis, Missouri
Saint Mary's, Pennsylvania
Saint Paul, Minnesota
Saint Petersburg, Florida
Salem, Massachusetts
Salem, Oregon
Salina, Kansas
Salinas, California
Salisbury, North Carolina
Salmon, Idaho
Salt Lake City, Utah
San Angelo, Texas
San Antonio, Texas
San Bernardino, California
San Diego, California
San Francisco, California
San Jose, California
San Luis Obispo, California
San Luis Rey, California

San Marcos, Texas
San Mateo, California
San Petro, California
San Rafael, California
Santa Barbara, California
Santa Cruz, California
Santa Fe, New Mexico
Santa Monica, California
Santa Rosa, California
Saranac Lake, New York
Sarasota, Florida
Sault Ste. Marie, Michigan
Savannah, Georgia
Schenectady, New York
Scottsbluff, Nebraska
Scottsdale, Arizona
Scranton, Pennsylvania
Seal Beach, California
Searsport, Maine
Seattle, Washington
Seldotna, Arkansas
Sellersville, Pennsylvania
Seward, Nebraska
Shafer, Minnesota
Sharon, Pennsylvania
Sheboygan, Wisconsin
Sheridan, Wyoming
Shreveport, Louisiana
Sidney, Nebraska
Sierra Vista, Arizona
Sioux City, Iowa
Sioux Falls, South Dakota
Sitka, Alaska
Snohomish, Washington
Somerville, New Jersey
Somerville, Massachusetts
Sonora, California
South Bend, Washington
South Bend, Indiana
South Lake Tahoe, California
South Norwalk, Connecticut
South Saint Paul, Minnesota
Sparks, Nevada
Spokane, Washington
Springfield, Illinois
Springfield, Massachusetts
Springfield, Missouri
Springfield, Ohio
Springfield, Vermont
State College, Pennsylvania
Staten Island, New York

Statesville, North Carolina
Stevens Point, Wisconsin
Stillwater, Oklahoma
Stockton, California
Storm Lake, Iowa
Streator, Illinois
Sturgeon Bay, Wisconsin
Sullersville, Pennsylvania
Summit, Illinois
Sumbury, Pennsylvania
Superior, Wisconsin
Sussex, New Jersey
Sutton, West Virginia
Sylva, North Carolina
Syracuse, New York

Tacoma, Washington
Tallahassee, Florida
Tampa, Florida
Temple, Texas
Terre Haute, Indiana
Thief River Falls, Minnesota
Toledo, Ohio
Tonawanda, New York
Topeka, Kansas
Towson, Maryland
Traverse City, Michigan
Trenton, New Jersey
Tucson, Arizona
Tulsa, Oklahoma
Tupelo, Mississippi

Ukiah, California
Unalaska, Alaska
Union City, Pennsylvania
Uniontown, Pennsylvania
Upper Jay, New York
Upper Marlboro, Maryland
Urbana, Illinois
Utica, New York

Vanceboro, North Carolina
Vancouver, Washington
Van Wert, Ohio
Venice, California
Ventnor, New Jersey
Vernal, Utah
Vero Beach, Florida
Vienna, Virginia
Viola, Wisconsin
Visalia, California

Waco, Texas
Wagner, South Dakota
Walla Walla, Washington
Wallingford, Pennsylvania
Waltham, Massachusetts
Warrensburg, Missouri
Warwick, Rhode Island
Washburn, North Dakota
Washington, District of Columbia
Waterbury, Connecticut
Watertown, New York
Watertown, South Dakota
Waukegan, Illinois
Waukesna, Wisconsin
Wausau, Wisconsin
Waverly, Ohio
Wawa, Pennsylvania
Wayne, Nebraska
Wayland, New York
West Bend, Wisconsin
West Chester, Pennsylvania
West Covina, California
West Palm Beach, Florida
West Plains, Missouri
Westfield, Massachusetts
Westland, Michigan
Westminster, Maryland
Wheeling, West Virginia
White Plains, New York
Whittier, California
Wichita, Kansas
Wichita Falls, Texas
Wilkes Barre, Pennsylvania
Williamsport, Pennsylvania
Willingboro, New Jersey
Williston, North Dakota
Willmar, Minnesota
Wilmington, Delaware
Wilmington, North Carolina
Windsor, Vermont
Winona, Minnesota
Winooski, Vermont
Winston Salem, North Carolina
Wisconsin Dells, Wisconsin
Woodstock, New York
Woodworth, Wisconsin
Wooster,Ohio
Worcester, Massachusetts
Wyoming, Rhode Island

Xenia, Ohio

Yakima, Washington
Yankton, South Dakota
Yonkers, New York
Youngstown, Ohio
Ypsilanti, Michigan
Yuba City, California

Zanesville, Ohio
Zelienople, Pennsylvania

The following guide is intended to assist the reader in locating the various articles by subject.

A = Abuse: women, wife, assault, battering, beating, sexual, psychological, violence.

B = Agencies: centers, havens, programs, resources, cases, manuals, methods, reports, research, and so on.

C = Crisis: analysis, prevention, intervention, treatment.

D = Harrassment.

E = Incest.

F = Law.

G = Rape.

H = Victimology: victims, aggression, victimization, violence.

Bibliography

Abarbanel, G. "Helping Victims of Rape." *Social Work* 21 (November 1976):478–482.   G

> It is observed that, despite the frequency of the crime, victims of rape frequently prefer to remain silent and fail to take advantage of the services their communities may offer. An effective rape-treatment program designed to overcome such reluctance is described. Components of the program reflect its psychosocial focus and include information dissemination, medical care, supportive services, staff training, coordination with education services, coordination with other agencies, and program evaluation.

Abbott, D., and J.M. Calonico. "Black Man, White Woman: The Maintenance of a Myth: Rape and the Press in New Orleans." In *Crime and Delinquency: Dimensions of Deviance*, edited by M. Riedel and T.P. Thornberry, P. 211. New York: Praeger, 1974.   G

> The chapter examines news media and public attitudes toward interracial rape.

Abel, G.G. "Assessment of Sexual Deviation in the Male." In *Behavioral Assessment: A Practical Handbook*, edited by M. Hersen and A.S. Bellack. New York: Pergamon, 1976.   G
———. "The Behavior Assessment of Rapists." Paper presented at Brown University and Butler Hospital, Providence, Rhode Island, 21 October 1976.   G
———. "Treatment of Sexual Aggressives." *Criminal Justice and Behavior* 5 (1978):291–293.   G

> The psychological treatment needs of rapists and child molesters are discussed. In an attempt to bring together individuals involved with the assessment and treatment of sexual aggressiveness, a national conference was held in April 1977 in Memphis, Tennessee. Participants concluded that consistent components in the various treatment programs for sexual aggressiveness include methods of decreasing sexual arousal to thoughts of rape and sexual aggressiveness; development of appropriate heterosexual arousal; the teaching of various social skills; instruction in sexual knowledge; and treatment of sexual dysfunction or marital problems. Any one rapist or child molester may need treatment in any one or all five areas of treatment, but assessment must be made on an individual basis.

The *Annotated Bibliography on Spouse Abuse*, copyright 1980 by the Center for Women Policy Studies, has been incorporated into this bibliography by permission of the Center for Women Policy Studies, 2000 P Street N.W., Suite 508, Washington, D.C. 20036.

Abel, G.G., and E.B. Blanchard. "The Role of Fantasy in the Treatment of Sexual Deviation." *Archives of General Psychiatry*, 1974, p. 467.   G
———. "Biofeedback Treatment of a Rape-Related Psychophysiological Cardiovascular Disorder." *Psychosomatic Medicine*, 1975, p. 85.   G
Abel, G.G.; E.B. Blanchard; D.H. Barlow; and D. Guild. "The Components of Rapists' Sexual Arousal." *Archives of General Psychiatry* 34 (August 1977):895–903.   G

Audio descriptions of rape and nonrape sexual scenes varying in aggressive behavior and victim's age: 14–51-year-old rapists and 20–30-year-old nonrapists.

Abel, G.G.; E.B. Blanchard; D.H. Barlow; and M. Mavissakalian. "Identifying Specific Erotic Cues in Sexual Deviation by Audio-Taped Descriptions." *Journal of Applied Behavior Analysis* 8:247–260.   G
Abel, G.G.; E.B. Blanchard; and J.V. Becker. "An Integrated Treatment Program for Rapists." In *Clinical Aspects of the Rapist*, edited by R. Rads. New York: Grune and Stratton.   G
———. "Psychological Treatment for Rapists." In *Sexual Assault*, edited by S. Brodsky and M. Walker. Lexington, Mass.: Lexington Books, D.C. Heath and Company, 1976.   G
Abrahams, S. *Law in Family Conflict*. New York: Law-Arts, 1970.   F
———. "Abused Wives Not an Uncommon Problem." *East Liberty Gazette* 16 (April 1976).   A
Abramson, P.R. "Familial Variables Related to the Expression of Violent Aggression in Preschool Age Children." *Journal of Genetic Psychology* 122 (June 1973):345–346.   H
Achiron, M. "Sexual Harassment on the Job." *Mademoiselle* 85 (October 1979):116–118.   D
Acquaintance Rape Prevention. Schiller Park, Illinois: Produced by MTI Teleprograms, 1978. Incorporated. Distributed by Association Films, Incorporated, Arlington, Virginia.   G

Presents four films to raise the consciousness of teenage and young-adult audiences in an effort to reduce acquaintance rape. Demonstrates that (1) acquaintance rape can result from ineffective communications; (2) behavior associated with traditional sex roles increases the probability of such rape; (3) peer pressure and labeling contribute to such rape; and (4) assertiveness can help to prevent it. The four films, *The Party Game*, *The Date*, *Just One of the Boys*, and *End of the Road* are accompanied by a program guide and display concept poster, four teacher film guides, and thirty student fact sheets.

Adams, C. "Wife Beating as a Crime and Its Relation to Taxation."

Philadelphia: Philadelphia Social Science Association, 1886, pp. 3 and 17.   A

Adams, J. "Women, Success and Men: From Women on Top." *Glamour* 77 October 1979:60.   D

Adams, M.S. "Incest: Genetic Considerations." *American Journal of Diseases of Children* 132 (1978):124.   E

> Genetic considerations bearing on management of incest cases are suggested. It is noted that progeny of incest unions have an inbreeding intensity four times that of first-cousin marriage.

Adams, P.L. "Language Patterns of Opponents to a Child Protection Program." *Child Psychiatry & Human Development* 11 (Spring 1981):135–157.   E

> Discusses the high incidence of incest and presents vocabulary used by health-care and legal professionals as well as community members to deny or obsure the occurrence of father-daughter incest. It is suggested that this lexicon can assist the clinician in promoting child protection and in checking actual efforts to condone incest.

Adleman, C. "Teaching Police Officers Techniques of Crisis Intervention with Victims of Rape." *Victimology: An International Journal* 2 (1977): 51.   G

> A training program in crisis intervention for police officrs from the sex-crime-analysis unit is described and evaluated. Police were taught how to apply crisis theory to their work with rape victims.

Adorno, T.W.; E. Frenkel-Brunswik; D.J. Levinson; and R.N. Sanford. *The Authoritarian Personality*. New York: Harper & Row, 1950. A

Adrian, M. "Montana: A Study of Spouse Battering." Montana Board of Crime Control, Helena, Montana, 1978.   A

> The environment of domestic violence, specifically spouse battering, in Montana was studied in relation to victims, assailants, children, patterns of violence, legal remedies, and law enforcement.

"After Rape: A Reliable Record." *Emergency Medicine* 7 (1975):252. G

Agolian, C., and G. Agolian. "Interracial Forcible Rape in a North American City: An Analysis of 63 Cases." *Victimology: A Reader*, 1974. G

"Ain't It a Shame-Battered Women." Washington, D.C.: Feminist Radio Network, 1978.   A

Various women on this radio program discuss the problems of battered women in the United States. They point out that this abuse occurs in all classes, poor and rich, black and white, and in urban and rural locations.

Aitken. "Rape Prosecutions." *Women Law Journal* 60 (1974):192.   G
Akesson, H.O. "Historic and Contemporary Views on Incest in Sweden." *Nordisk Psykiatrisk Tidsskrift* 33 (1979):176–181.   E

Changes in the Swedish attitudes toward incest and the early and present legislation are reviewed. In preceding centuries incest was looked upon as an act of sin committed by two people. Society claimed severe sentences; the death penalty was prescribed for both partners, irrespective of age. During the nineteenth century the death penalty was abolished and replaced by long-term prison sentences. Legislation today is characterized by concern about the sexual abuse of the child or minor, a crime punished by law. Incest committed voluntarily by adults will soon cease to be considered a criminal act.

Akers, R.L. *Deviant Behavior: A Social Learning Approach*. Belmont, Calif.: Wadsworth Publishing, 1977.   E
Alan Guttmacher Institute. *Abortion 1974–1975: Need and Services in the United States, Each State and Metropolitan Area*. New York, 1976. E
Alberti, R., and M. Emmons. *Your Perfect Right*. San Luis Obispo, Calif.: Impact, 1974.   L,C
Albi, F.J. "Prosecutor-Based Investigation: An Alternative Model for the Specialized Handling of Rape Cases." *Journal of Political Science* 5 (June 1977):129–137.   C,G
Albin, R.S. "Psychological Studies of Rape." *Signs* 3 (Winter 1977):423–435.   G

Reviews the treatment of rape within the mental-health professions from the Freudian to the feminist perspectives. The psychoanalytic school is seen as responsible for the notion of rape as a victim-precipitated phenomenon.

Aldous, J. "Occupational Characteristics and Males' Role Performance in the Family." *Journal of Marriage and the Family* 31 (November 1969): 707–712.   A
Alexander, C.S. "Blaming the Victim: A Study of the Assignment of Responsibility to Victims of Violence." *Abstracts International* 41 (1980):731–738.   H

The extent to which rape victims are viewed as blameworthy was examined by using a self-administered questionnaire administered to 368 police and 312 nurses. Initial analysis of the data revealed no statistically significant differences in the levels of blame assigned to rape victims as compared with beating victims. The total amount of blame attributed to victims of either crime was quite small relative to that accorded to their assailants.

―――. "The Responsible Victim: Nurses' Perceptions of Victims of Rape." *Journal of Health and Social Behavior* 21 (1980):22–33.   G

The attitude of nurses toward the victim's responsibility for rape was investigated. A sample of 312 nurses was questioned about vignettes involving rape or nonsexual assault. The psychological characteristics of the nurse, the type of crime, and the victim's dress, marital status, extent of injury, and relationship to the assailant were among the variables tested. Psychological attributes of the nurse were found to be the strongest predictors of victim blaming. Those who assigned blame to the victim were most likely to blame victims described as divorced, scantily dressed, casually acquainted with the assailant, and uninjured as a result of the crime. The victims least often blamed were described as married, conservatively dressed, not acquainted with the assailant, and seriously injured.

Alexander, S. *Alexander's State-By-State Guide to Women's Legal Rights*. Los Angeles: Wollstonecraft, 1975.   F

Alexander, "Simple Question of Rape." *Newsweek*, 28 October, 1974. G

Alive. "Haven for Spouses of Alcoholics." Pamphlet published by Alcoholics Anonymous. February 1976.   B

"The All-American Crime." *Human Behavior*, April 1974, p. 43.   G

Allard, A. *The Human Imperative*. New York: Columbia University Press, 1972.   G

"Alleged Rape: An Invitational Symposium." *Journal of Reproductive Medicine*, 1974, p. 133.   G

Allen, C.L. "Testimony by Clara L. Allen on July 10, 1979, Concerning H.R. 2977." Domestic Violence Prevention and Services pp. 71–83, 1979.   F,H

The New Jersey State Division on Women expresses its support for the Domestic Violence Prevention and Services Act (H.R. 2977) and recognizes the need for increased intergovernmental cooperation regarding service centers.

Allen, C.M., and M.A. Straus. "Resources, Power, and Husband-Wife Violence." Paper read at the 1975 annual meeting of the National Council on Family Relations.   H

Allen, G. "A Reply to Roy Schenk." *Humanist* 39 (1979):50–51.   G

Roy Schenk's analysis of the causes of rape are questioned. In an article Dr. Schenk proposes that rape is a violent response by some men to the nonphysical violence committed by all women against all men. This violence consists of sexual deprivation, teasing, and moral superiority. Schenk argues that women are as much a victim as men and that both society and the educational system reinforce double standards of sexuality. He suggests that when men commit rape they are attacking society as well as an individual woman and argues that society must reorder its priorities before rape can be eliminated.

Allen, P. *Free Space*. Washington, N.J.: Times Change Press, 1970.   *G*

Allison, T.S., and S.L. Allison. "Time-out from Reinforcement: Effect on Sibling Aggression." *Psychological Record* 21 (Winter 1971):81–86. *A*

Allport, G.W. *The Nature of Prejudice*. Reading, Mass.: Addison-Wesley, 1954.   *A*

Almond, G., and H.D. Lasswell. "Aggressive Behavior by Clients toward Public Relief Administrators: A Configurative Analysis." *American Political Science Review* 28 (1934):643–655.   *C*

Alper, B.S. "Affluence as Victim." *Victimology: An International Journal* 2 (1977):51.   *H*

In a paper presented at the Second International Symposium on Victimology, held in Boston, September 1976, the problem of increasing economic crimes, the theft of property, is discussed. The increase in television sets has led to an increase in television thefts, likewise with automobiles and all the products of affluence. Measures that may be taken to reduce the toll taken by house breakers are suggested. Police, manufacturers, insurance companies, and the general public have a part to play in programs for the prevention of such thefts, it is reported. Restitution and arbitration procedures are recommended to speed the disposition of such cases.

Alpert, J. "Mother Right: A New Feminist Theory." *Off Our Backs*, July/August 1973, p. 30.   *A,C*

Alpert, M., and S. Schechter. "Sensitizing Workers to the Needs of Victims: Common Worker and Victim Responses." *Victimology* 4 (1979):385–389.   *C,D*

Within the context of a crisis-intervention training program, worker and victim responses to rape and abuse are discussed. By sensitizing the worker to her own needs and those of the victim inservice training, it was hoped to create a greater sense of empathy, lessen punitive responses and distancing, and ameliorate worker burnout. Sensitizing exercises are used to enable workers to understand their own vulnerabilities and reactions to victimization, making it more difficult for them to label and blame the victim. Other exercises are included.

Alstrom, C.H. "A Study of Incest with Special Regard to the Swedish Penal Code." *Acta Psychiatrica Scandinavica* 56 (November 1977):357–372.   *E*

Presents a historical review of incest penalties in Sweden, with particular emphasis on the special incest section of the current Swedish penal code. It is argued that there is no logical justification for retaining the incest paragraph in the code.

The American Family: What Is its Future? Current Research on Marriage, Families and Divorce. New York: Atcom Publishing, 1979. *A,H,C,E*

Eighteen articles on the future of the U.S. family, taken from the newsletter "Marriage and Divorce Today," cover the issues of changes in public policy necessary to keep the family a viable unit; the changing nature of the family; the families-in-transition program; a family-impact seminar that assessed the impact of public policies on families; the number of children who live with separated or divorced families; the role of the church in helping families in crisis; a study to determine who would be good parents; a program to help save teenage marriages; the way childbirth strengthens the husband-wife relationship; family encounter groups; incest; family violence; the implications of role reversal in abused/neglected families; situational stress as a source of child abuse; family conflict and children's self-concepts; the impact on children of conjugal crime; solutions to present problems by confronting parental relationships; and birth parents who relinquished babies for adoption revisted.

American Jurisprudence. *Husband and Wife to Indictments and Informations.* Rochester, N.Y.: Lawyers Cooperative Publishing Company; and San Francisco: Bancroft-Whitney Company, 1968.   *C,F*

"American Psychiatric Association Issues Rape Treatment Guidelines." *Psychiatric News*, 7 May 1976, p. 11.   *F,G*

American Public Health Association. *Health and Work in America: A Chart Book.* Washington, D.C., 1975.   *A,D*

American Public Health Association. *Women in Health Careers.* Washington, D.C., 1975.   *D*

American Society of Anesthesiologists. "Occupational Disease among Operating Room Personnel: A National Study." *Anesthesiology* 41 (1974).   *D*

Amidar Corporation. *Community Work in Israeli Housing Estates.* Tel Aviv, 1964.   *A*

Amidon, H.T., and T.A. Wagner. "Successful Investigation and Prosecution of the Crime of Rape: A Descriptive Model." *Journal of Police Science and Administration* 6 (June 1978):141–156.   *G*

Amir, M. "Patterns in Forcible Rape: With Special Reference to Philadelphia, Pennsylvania, 1958 and 1960." *Dissertation Abstracts International* 66 (4-A) (1960):1126–1127.   *G*

———. *Report of the Commission on Violent Behavior in Government Social Welfare Offices.* Jerusalem: Szold Institute, 1967.   *B*

———. *Patterns of Forcible Rape.* Chicago, Ill.: University of Chicago Press, 1971.   *G*

———. "The role of the Victim in Sex Offenses." *Sexual Behaviors: Social, Clinical, and Legal Aspects.* Boston: Little, Brown, 1972.   *H*

Discusses research data concerning the demographic characteristics of female victims of sex offenses. Victim-offender relationships and victim precipitation of offenses are considered. A classification of victims is proposed based on behavior during the offense.

Amir, M., and D. Amir. "Rape Crisis Centers: An arena for Ideological Conflicts." *Victimology* 4 (1979):247–257.   *C*

Ideological and service features of a sample of rape crisis centers were investigated as part of a larger study of rape crisis centers as a social phenomenon. The main ideological features of the centers are described and analyzed in light of their social and community backgrounds. The special processes that led to different organizational characteristics and service delivery among various centers are also described. A common ideology was found that explains rape because of the nature of man's world, the values that guide people and institutions toward women, and the biases that mark the institutional arrangements that have been created to deal with rape victims. The need for centers to appear as nonactivist services-delivery organizations while working toward changing the services and agencies that deal directly with rape victims is noted.

Analysis on Police Department Costs Relative to 'Victimless Crime' report by Walter Quinn, budget analyst, for San Francisco Board of Supervisors. 23 October, 1974.   *H*

Andelin, H. *Fascinating Womanhood.* New York: Bantam, 1975. *A,D,H*

Anderiesz, G.J. *Violation.* London: Satellite Books, 1978.   *A,G*

Andersen, I. "Wife Battering in the Netherlands: Needs and Incidence." Paper presented at the International Sociological Association Seminar on Sex Roles, Deviance, and Agents of Social Control in Dublin, Ireland, 1977.   *A*

Anderson, A. "Prostitution and Social Justice." *Social Service Review*, June 1974.   *G*

Anderson, D., and R.W. Ten-Bensel. "Counseling the Family in which Incest Has Occurred." *Medical Aspects of Human Sexuality* 13 (1979): 143–144.   *E*

Guidelines are presented for the counseling of families in which incest has occurred. It is maintained that physicians are in a key position to identify and aid victims of incest. Adolescent pregnancy, behavioral problems, somatic complaints, and depression are identified as possible indicators of incest.

Anderson, G.A., and S. Lythcott. *Information on Domestic Violence in Wisconsin, Extent and Services Available*. Rockville, Md.: NCJRS Microfiche Program, 1978.   A

> Tabular data derived by questionnaire is presented on the extent of domestic violence and services available to abused spouses in Wisconsin.

Anderson, G.M. "Wives, Mothers, and Victims." *America* 137 (30 July 1977):46–50.   A,H

Anderson, M.L., and C. Renzetti. "Rape Crisis Counseling and the Culture of Individualism." *Contemporary Crisis* 4 (1980):323–339.   G,H

> Theoretical explanations of rape are examined, and the manner in which the theories are reflected in the beliefs of practicing female rape crisis counselors is discussed. It is contended that in the absence of a theoretical framework that analyzes the political and economic causes of rape, population explanations mask understanding of rape as the rules of women's position in society. This assumption is supported by analysis of rape counselors' beliefs about feminism and the individualistic theories of rape they tend to hold. These beliefs emphasize rape as psychological or learned problem. Individualism and personal growth is emphasized as the proper step toward eliminating rape.

Anderson, M.L., and G. Shafer. "The Character-Disordered Family: A Community Treatment Model for Family Sexual Abuse." *American Journal of Orthopsychiatry* 49 (July 1979):436–445.   B,E

> Presents a collaborative approach to treating sexually abusive character-disordered individuals. This model, unlike traditional voluntary treatment models, assumes that effective intervention requires authoritative control and careful coordination of all professional activity. Phases of treatment are outlined, and a case history is presented.

And Now You May Hit the Bride." Produced by WIIC, Channel 11, Pittsburgh, Pennsylvania, aired 9 and 19 October 1976.   A

Andrea, J. "New Rights for Rape Victims." *Majority Report*, no. 4, 8 February 1975.   F,G

Anon, H., and W. Anon. "Sexual Assaults on Children." *British Medical Journal* 2 (1961):1628.   E

Ansbacher, H.L. "Love and Violence in the view of Adler." *Humanitas* 2 (1966):109–127.   H

Anson, A. "That Championship Season." *New Times*, 20 September 1974, p. 46.   A,H

"Anti-Rape Technique: An Interview with Susan Brownmiller." *Harper's Bazaar*, March 1976, p. 119.   C

Anttila, I. "Who Are the Victims of Crimes?" *Victimology: An International Journal* 2 (1977):52.   H

In a paper presented at the Second International Symposium on Victimology, held in Boston, September 1976, the identity of the victim of crime is dicussed. Victimless crimes and cases where the victim has only been endangered but not injured are the foci of the discussion. In both cases there are indirect consequences to which researchers should attend. It is recommended that further research be directed toward what interests are harmed, as an extension of the notion of a victim, to clarify what actual or supposed interests such victimless acts are directed against.

Appell; Bashin; and Smith. "The First Half-Hour." *Journal of Practical Nursing*, 1975, p. 16.   A

Appleton, W. "Battered Women Syndrome." *Annals of Emergency Medicine* 9 (February 1980):84–91.   A,C

Six hundred and twenty adult women volunteers and 30 acutely battered adult women were studied during a ten-week period to establish criteria for diagnosis, define therapy, and conceptualize a theoretical model of the battered-women syndrome.

Arcel, L.T.; B. Bonnesen; A. Jacobsen; J. Jensen; L. Karpatchof; V. Larsen; N. Ostenfeld; and K. Lewis. "Rape Is a Serious Issue—But Serious for Whom?" *Bulletin of the British Psychological Society* 32 (August 1979):317–320.   B

A rape advisory center run by the Joan Sisters, an interdisciplinary group of twenty-two women in Denmark, is described. The aims of the center are to provide information and to offer psychological, legal, and social support to victims of rape and similar offenses. Following a discussion of Danish rape laws and attitudes toward rape and the victim of rape, psychological reactions to rape are considered. The counseling procedure used by the center is designed to help the victim deal with the traumatic experience of the rape itself and with the consequences of the rape.

Archer, D., and R. Gartner. "Violent Acts and Violent Times: A Comparative Approach to Postwar Homicide Rates." *American Sociological Review* 41 (December 1976):937–963.   A,H

Ardrey, R. *The Territorial Imperative*. New York: Atheneum, 1966.
                                                                                        A,C,D,H

Arendt, H. *On Violence*. London: Allen Lane, Penguin Press, 1970.   H

"Arguing about Death for Rape." *Time*, 11 April 1977, p. 80.   F

Aries, P. *Centuries of Childhood: A Social History of Family Life*. New York: Random House, 1965.   E

Arkus, M. "Ban on Wife Selling." *San Francisco Chronicle*, 28 March 1975.   A

Armentroug, J.A., and A.L. Hauer. "MMPI of Rapists of Adults, Rapists of Children, and Non-Rapist Sex Offenders." *Journal of Clinical Psychology* 34 (April 1978):330–332.   E

Compared MMPI group mean profiles of thirteen rapists of adults, twenty-one rapists of children, and seventeen nonrapist sex offenders.

Armstrong, L. *Kiss Daddy Goodnight: A Speak-Out on Incest.* New York: Hawthorn Press, 1978.   E

Interviews with 183 victims of father-daughter incest are presented. It is suggested that incest is repellent and criminal. Girls whose fathers abuse them are encouraged to fight their way out of this form of paternal tyranny. It is hoped that by this discussion of father-daughter incest, victims will gather courage, see that their plight is not unique, and be able to do something about it.

Arnold, J.E.; A.G. Levine; and G.R. Patterson. "Changes in Sibling Behavior Following Family Intervention." *Journal of Consulting and Clinical Psychology* 43 (October 1975):683–688.   E
Arnold, M. "Making the Criminal Pay Back His Victim." *National Observer* 16 (1977):1.   H
Aromaa, K. "Alcohol Consumption and Victimization to Violence: Correlations in a National Sample." Research Report Summaries, *1977.* Helsinki: Research Institute of Legal Policy, *1978.*   H

A report on new survey results on alcohol consumption and victimization to violence obtained from the interview material of the 1973 National Gallup Survey, "Violence Gallup," is summarized. An overview and explanations of the alcohol-consumption measure and victimization measure are presented. The descriptions of victimization incidents of the recent survey seem to indicate that the alcohol variable only infrequently measures the number of risk-increasing states of drunkenness.

———. "Three Victim Surveys, 1970–1976: Gallup Surveys on Victimization to Violence." Research Report Summaries, *1977.* Helsinki: Research Institute of Legal Policy, *1978.*   H

Results and analyses of three National Gallup Surveys on victimization to violence, conducted in 1970, 1973, and 1976, are summarized. The surveys, which had small samples, indicate that the victimization density of the average population as a whole first increased a small amount, mainly among young men in white-collar occupations who live in cities and towns. From 1973 to 1976, the increase was somewhat larger, and whereas the increase in the first period was limited mainly to young urban men, most of the increase in the second period was found in the rural population. The increase of the victimization rate in the rural population is not limited to any single subcategory of people. Differences between victim surveys and police statistics are discussed, and statistical considerations in interpretating the data are outlined.

Aronson, E., and H.M. Carlsmith. "Experimentation in Social Psychology." In *The Handbook of Social Psychology*, edited by G. Lindzey and E. Aronson. Reading, Mass.: Addison-Wesley, 1954, pp. 1–80.   *H*
———. "Performance Expectancy as a Determinant of Actual Performance." *Journal of Abnormal and Social Psychology* 65 (1962): 178–182.   *H*
Ashley, J. *Report of House of Commons Debate*. Hansard, pp. 218–227. 17 July 1973.   *F*
Ashworth, C.D., and S.S. Feldman. "Perceptions of the Effectiveness of the Criminal Justice System: The Female Victim's Perspectives." *Criminal Justice and Behavior* 5 (September 1978):227–240.   *F,H*

> Twenty-six female rape victims, 26 female assault victims, and 51 matched nonvictimized controls completed a questionnaire at several time periods during a one-year interval. The questionnaires assessed the participants' perceptions of the effectiveness of the police, judiciary, and penal system in handling several types of crimes. Findings indicate that rape victims' perceptions of the effectiveness of the criminal-justice system decline with time, that the system was seen as least effective in handling rape cases, and that assault victims, when compared to the other study participants, perceived the criminal-justice system as less effective in dealing with the crime of assault.

"Assault under the Influence." *Human Behavior*, January 1975, p. 73. *A*
Athens, L.H. "A Symbolic Interactionist's Approach to Violent Criminal Acts." *Dissertation Abstracts International* 37 (1-A) (July 1976):627–628.   *H*

> Symbolic interactionist's approach to understanding the problem of violent criminal acts.

Atkinson, D. "The Academic Situation." In *Student Power*, edited by J. Nagel. London: Merlin Press, 1969.   *D*
Atkinson, J.W. "Motivational Determinants of Risk-Taking Behavior." *Psychological Review* 64 (1957):359–372.   *H*
Attacking the Last Taboo." *Time*, 14 April 1980, p. 72.   *E*
Aubert, V. "Law as a Way of Resolving Conflicts: The Case of a Small Industrialized Society." In *Law in Culture and Society*, edited by L. Nader. Chicago: Aldine, 1969.   *F*

Auerbach, J.S. "Perceptions of Police and Psychiatric Mandates in Family Disputes." *Dissertation Abstracts International* 39 (3):1465-B, 1978.
C,F

A model was developed and tested for its ability to explain several phenomena, including agency selection by potential clients, stigma attached to former clients of particular agencies, and the difficulty of getting both agency and the public to accept new roles for social-service organizations.

Aumer, S.M. *Battered Women: An Effective Response*. St. Paul: Minnesota Department of Corrections/Programs and Services for Battered Women, 1979.
A

This Minnesota study addresses the problem of battered women, reviews their common psychology and that of their abusers, and looks to community, legal, medical, and judicial responses.

Austin, G.B.; M.M. Maher; and C.J. Lomonaco. "Women in Dentistry and Medicine: Additudinal Survey of Educational Experience." *Journal of Dental Education* 40 (1976):11–13.
D

Australian Institute on Criminology. National Conference on Rape Law Reform. Australia, 1980.
F,G

Axelberd, M.M. "The Effects of Family Crisis Intervention Training on Police Behavior and Level of Anxiety in Response to a Domestic Dispute." *Dissertation Abstracts International*, p. 112, 1977.
C

The effectiveness of training fifty police officers to function as crisis interveners in domestic disputes was assessed on the basis of a forty-hour block of instruction on family-crisis intervention. Differences between the scores on the behavioral scale for measuring police effectiveness in a domestic dispute were found to be significant for all but the safety item between the members of the treatment group and two comparison groups. It was found that no significant differences existed between members of the treatment and comparison groups on level of anxiety. It is concluded that police officers can be trained effectively as paraprofessional mental-health agents to intervene in domestic disputes.

Axelberd, M. and J. Valle. "Development of the Behavioral Scale for Measuring Police Effectiveness in Domestic Disputes." *Crisis Intervention* 9 (1978):69–80.
C

Developed and tested the ten-item behavioral scale for measuring police effectiveness in domestic disputes. The scale was designed for use with police officers or other law-enforcement personnel whose effectiveness was measured by defining specific officer behaviors that have been identified to be most beneficial when dealing with this type of disturbance. These behaviors include appropriate safety procedures, defusing techniques, assessment skills, mediation skills, and referral strategies. This test was used to evaluate a crisis-intervention training program and allowed instructors and officers to become aware of problem areas.

Ayh, A. "The Pattern of Rape in Singapore." *Singapore Medical Journal*, 1974, p. 49.   G

Bach, G.R. "Hate and Aggression." *Voices: The Art and Science of Psychotherapy*, 1965, p. 1.   C

————. "Episodic Dyscontrol: A Study of 130 Violent Patients." *American Journal of Psychiatry* 127 (May 1971):1473–1478.   C

The authors report a two-year study of 130 patients with a chief complaint of explosive violent behavior. When pertinent and possible, neurological and psychological tests, EEGs, pneumoencephalograms, and other tests were made. The authors noted that the patients' lives mirrored their backgrounds: Family histories revealed a high incidence of violence and alcoholism. The patients reported that they had frequently sought help in the past for control of violent impulses but usually in vain. The authors believe that severe psychopathology should not exclude neurological examination and management, nor should positive neurological findings exclude psychiatric management. A plea is made to view these patients as having a multidetermined problem.

Bach, G.R., and H. Goldberg. *Creative Aggression*. New York: Doubleday and Company, 1972.   A,G,H

Bach, G.R., and P. Wyden. *The Intimate Enemy*. New York: Morrow, 1969.   D,E,G,H

Bacon, G.M. "Parents Anonymous." *Victimology* 2(1977): 331–337.   H

Bacon, M.K.; H. Barry; and I.L. Child. "A Cross-Cultural Study of Correlates of Crime." *Journal of Abnormal and Social Psychology* 66 (1963): 291.   A,H

Bagley, C. "Incest Behavior and Incest Taboo." *Social Problems* 16 (1969): 505–519.   E

Critically examines some recent theories of the incest taboo and certain theoretical positions in the light of information on 425 published cases of incest behavior. Five distinct types of incest emerge: (1) functional, (2) accidental or disorganized, (3) pathological, (4) object fixation, and (5) psychopathic. The functional type is discussed at some length since it appears to show that the taboo on incest is not universal. The implications of the findings for the understanding and treatment of incest behavior are discussed.

Bahr, S.J. "Effects on Power and Division of Labor in the Family." In *The Employed Mother in America*, edited by L.W. Hoffman and F.I. Nye. Chicago: Rand McNally, 1974.   C

Bahr, S.J.; C.E. Bowerman; and V. Gecas. "Adolescent Perceptions of Conjugal Power." *Social Forces* 52 (March 1974):357–367.   E

Bailey, B. "Child Abuse: Causes, Effect and Prevention." *Victimology* 2 (1977):337–342.   E

Bailey, C.F. "Incest—Practical Investigative Guide." *Police Chief* 46 (1979):36–38.   E

Bailey, R. "The Family and Social Management of Intolerable Dilemmas." In *Contemporary Social Problems*, edited by R. Bailey and J. Young. C

Bakan, D. *Slaughter of the Innocents*. San Francisco: Jossey-Bass, 1971.   E,H

Baker, A.L., and C. Peterson. "Self-Blame by Rape Victims as a Function of the Rape's Consequences: An Attributional Analysis." *Crisis Intervention* 8 (1977):92–104.   G

Used attribution theory to predict individual differences in self-blame by rape victims as a function of the severity of the rape's consequences. Data from thirty-four female rape victims aged at least fourteen years indicated that self-blame was inversely proportional to severity. It is concluded that rape victims take into account the rape's consequences in determining whether the rape was more representative of victimization or of their own characteristics.

Baker, A.; Telfer; Richardson; and Clark. "Chromosome Errors in Men with Antisocial Behavior: Comparison of Selected Men with Klinefelter's Syndrome and XYZ Chromosome Pattern," *Journal of the American Medical Association* 214 (1970):869.   H

Ball, P. "The Effect of Group Assertiveness Training on Selected Measures of Self-Concept for College Women." Ph.D. dissertation, University of Tennessee, 1976.   C

Ball, P.G., and E. Wyman. "Battered Wives and Powerlessness: What Can Counselors Do." *Victimology: An International Journal* 2(1978):545–552.   A

Techniques for feminist counseling of battered wives are presented. Assertiveness training and a dialectical approach to eliminating learned helplessness are discussed in light of their applicability to aiding battered wives. It is asserted that the feminist approach is particularly relevant to battered wives, especially since psychologists have done little in the past to train counselors and therapists in the specific counseling needs of battered women.

Ball, R.A. "The Victimological Cycle." *Victimology* 1 (1976):379–395. H

Using the distinction between micro- and macroprocesses, the concept of the victimological cycle is treated in terms of processes of mutal victimization at the level of interaction among individuals and at the level of relationships between different societies or segments of society. The victimological cycle is regarded as a form of dysfunctional dialectics that can occur at various levels of system complexity. Transactional analysis is used as an example of microprocess analysis, and the theory of subcultures is used as an example of macroprocess analysis. The focus is on basic process forms rather than on types of victims. The fundamental victimological processes are categorized as regression and resignation.

Ball, R.A., and J.J. Simoni. "The Institutionalization of Victimization: The Case of the Mexican Medicine Huckster." *Victimology: An International Journal* 2 (1977):52–53.   H

In a paper presented at the Second International Symposium on Victimology, held in Boston, September 1976, the case of the Mexican medicine huckster is presented for a focus upon cross-cultural patterns of victimization. One hundred victims of medicine hucksters were studied and were found to show great faith in the huckster even after repeated victimization.

Ballard, R.G. "The Interrelatedness of Alcoholism and Marital Conflict." *American Journal of Orthopsychiatry* 1959, p. 29.   C

Balliett, B. "Selling the Pain of Women." *Casa, The Newsletter for the Center against Sexual Assault* 4 (1977).   A,H

Baluss, M.E. "Integrated Services for Victims of Crime: A County-Based Approach," pp. 21–22. Prepared for the National Associations for Counties Research Foundation. 27 September 1974.   B,H

Bancroft, S. *Programs Providing Services to Battered Women*. Rockville, Md.: NCJRS Microfiche Programs, 1978.   B

The location, program components, and funding sources of groups providing services to battered women are listed.

Bandura, A. "Influence of Model's Reinforcement Contingencies on the Acquisition of Imitated Responses." *Journal of Personality and Social Psychology* 1 (1965):589–595.   B

———. *Aggression—A Social Learning Analysis*. Englewood Cliffs, N.J.: Prentice-Hall, 1973.   C

Bandura, A.; D. Ross; and S.A. Ross. "Transmission of Aggression through Imitation of Aggressive Models." *Journal of Abnormal and Social Psychology* 63 (1961):757–782.   C

———. "Imitation of Film-Mediated Aggressive Models." *Journal of Abnormal and Social Psychology* 66:(1963):3–11.   C

———. "Vicarious Reinforcement and Imitative Learning." *Journal of Abnormal and Social Psychology* 67 (1963):601–607.   C,F

Bannon, J.D. "Law Enforcement Problems with Intra-Family Violence." Paper presented at the Annual Meeting of the American Bar Association in Montreal, Canada, 1975.   F

Barabee, H.E. "Reduction of Deviant Arousal–Satiation Treatment for Sexual Aggressors." *Criminal Justice and Behavior* 5 (1978):294–304. *B*

Barbaree, H.E.; W.L. Marshall; and R.D. Lanthier. "Deviant Sexual Arousal in Rapists." *Behavior Research and Therapy* 17 (1979):205–222.   *G*

Measured increases in penile circumference of ten incarcerated rapists and ten graduate students during verbal descriptions of mutually consenting sex, rape, and violent nonsexual assault. Mutually consenting sex evoked sexual arousal in both groups. Rape evoked comparable arousal in rapists but significantly less arousal in nonrapists.

Barber. "Judge and Jury Attitudes to Rape." *Australian and New Zealand Journal of Criminology* 7 (1974):157.   *F,G*

———. "Rape as a Capital Offense in Nineteenth Century Queensland." *Australian Journal of Politics and History* 21 (1975):31.   *G*

Bard, M. "Extending Psychology's Impact through Existing Community Institutions." *American Psychologist* 24 (1969):610–612.   *B,C*

———. "Family Intervention Police Teams as a Community Mental Health Resource." *Journal of Criminal Law, Criminology and Police Science* 60 (1969):247–250.   *B,C*

———. "Alternatives to Traditional Law Enforcement." *Police*, November/December 1970, pp. 20–23.   *F*

———. "The Study and Modification of Intra-Familial Violence." In *The Control of Aggression and Violence: Cognitive and Psychological.* New York: Academic Press, 1971, p. 154.   *A,C*

———. "Police Family Crisis Intervention and Conflict Management: An Action Research Analysis." Report No. PB-230-973. Springfield, Va.: National Technical Information Service, 1972.   *B,C*

———. "The Rape Victim: Challenge to the Helping Systems." *Victimology* 1 (1976):263–271.   *B,G*

Common findings of recent research on the rape victim are analyzed for their program and policy implications. Roles for the helping systems are discussed, and strategies for change are outlined in order for such systems to serve victims of sexual assault effectively.

———. *Police and Family Violence—Policy and Practice.* Rockville, Md.: NCJRS Microfiche Programs, 1978.   *A,B,C*

An overview of police policy and practice in the management of domestic violence is presented with special emphasis on the problem of wife battering and trends in family-crisis intervention.

Bard, M., and B. Berkowitz. "Family Disturbance as a Police Function."

Law Enforcement Science and Technology II, Chicago: IIT Research Institute, 1969.   *A, C*

Bard, M., and K. Ellison. "Crisis Intervention and Investigation of Forcible Rape." *Police Chief*, May 1974, p. 68.   *G*

Bard, M., and D. Sangrey. *The Crime Victim's Book*. New York: Basic Books, 1979.   *H*

A book addressing the emotional needs of the victim is presented. The sources of people's expectations about victimization are described. The stages a victim of crime moves through and the appropriate support such a person should receive at each stage are examined. Information about how to get help including resources for emotional support, medical care, legal assistance, and crime-victim compensation is provided. It is noted that the victim's feelings of guilt and shame, a sense of being stigmatized by the victimization, are often strengthened by the insensitivity of others.

Bard, M., and R. Shellow. *Issues in Law Enforcement: Essays and Case Studies*. Reston, Va.: Reston Publishing Company, 1976.   *F*

Presents a series of ten detailed articles on police function and dynamics. Four essays focus on the role and duties of the police, professionalism in policing, the development of professional skills, and problems confronting police organizations. The six case studies examine the operation of a family-crisis unit, investigations of forcible rape, the anatomy of a siege, neighborhood police teams, and a pilot police district project for improving relations between the police and inner-city residents.

Bard, M., and J. Zacker. "Design for Conflict Resolution." *Police*, November/December 1970.   *B, C*

———. "The Prevention of Family Violence: Dilemmas of Community Intervention." *Journal of Marriage and the Family* 33 (November 1971): 677–682.   *C*

———. "Assaultiveness and Alcohol Use in Family Disputes: Police Perceptions." *Criminology: An Interdisciplinary Journal* 12 (November 1974):281–292.   *A, H*

Notes that systematic naturalistic observation often contradicts experimental laboratory findings and idiosyncratic personal perceptions. In the present study, family disputes managed by police officers trained in interpersonal conflict management yielded uniform observational data on 962 families visited 1,388 times during a 22-month period. The view shared by police and by social scientists that family disputes are likely to involve assaultiveness and that such behavior is typically caused by alcohol use was not supported by these data. Instead, the findings suggest that assaults do not usually precede arrival of police, that disputes are not usually influenced by alcohol use, and that assaults are less common when alcohol has been used.

————. "How Police Handle Explosive Squabbles." *Psychology Today* 113 (November 1976):71–74.   *B,C*

Bard, P., and M. Johnson. *At the Risk of Being a Wife.* Grand Rapids, Mich.: Zondervan, 1973.   *A,H*

Barden, C., and J. Barden. "The Battered Wife Syndrome." *Viva Magazine,* May 1976, pp. 79–81, 108–110.   *A,H*

Discusses which men might have tendencies toward wife beating as well as what should incite husbands to violence. The need for protective shelters and counseling is recognized. In 1974 a study conducted in Norwalk, Connecticut, revealed that police received roughly four to five charges of wife abuse each night. Law-enforcement officials estimate that there are about ten unreported cases of wife beatings for every call they receive asking help. The Norwalk study also indicates that police across the country probably receive about one-half million calls each year to aid battered wives. Alcohol does not play a big role in family violence according to the psychologists who directed the Harlem and Norwalk studies. In the Harlem study, police found that in only 21 percent of the assault cases had the husband even had a drink and in only 6 percent was he intoxicated. In Norwalk, police judged alcohol as a factor in family violence in about the same low percentage of cases.

Barden, J.C. "Wife Beaters: Few of Them Ever Appear before a Court of Law." *The New York Times,* 21 October 1974, Sect. 2, p. 38.   *A*

Figures reported as 17,277 family-violence cases, of which the wife was plaintiff in 82 percent.

Bardwick, J., and E. Douvan. "Ambivalence: The Socialization of Women." In *Woman in Sexist Society,* edited by V. Gornick and B. Moran. New York: Basic Books, 1971.   *A*

Baril, C., and I.B.S. Couchman. "Legal Rights." *Society* 13 (July 1976):15–17.   *F*

Barkas, J.L. *Victims.* New York: Charles Scribner's Sons, 1978.   *H*

Victims is a compilation of firsthand accounts by people who have been brutally victimized. Motivated by the killing of her brother by would-be robbers, Barkas has written the book to allow the victims to tell their stories of the crimes that either were perpetrated directly against them or affected them because of their close association with a victim. Many of the victims in Barkas's case studies are battered or murdered women, and a common theme in each chapter is the victimization of women at the hands of husbands, lovers, strangers, and institutions geared to protect citizens.

For programs that train volunteers to work in victim-oriented services, the book can serve as an orientation because it provides an invaluable perspective on the feelings and fears of victims. For professions working with victims, *Victims* can increase understanding of the issues and clarify the areas where further advocacy is needed. Barkas weaves into every chapter an issue that she does not resolve but rather leaves for the reader to ponder. It is a question that has been debated for centuries in philosophy books and that is resurfacing in modern debate: Has the criminal-justice system gone too far in protecting offenders' rights, thereby failing to protect victims' rights or to deter violent criminal acts?

Barkas, J.L. "What about the Victims." *Journal of Current Social Issues* 16 (1979):27–29.   H

The plight of victims of crime is discussed. Whereas crime victims undergo intense trauma, help is usually provided by volunteers rather than highly trained professionals. Many victims of crime are stigmatized by their peers for their unfortunate fate. It is suggested that crime victims need a national self-help support network. Such a network would provide a necessary psychological outlet for victims of crime.

Barker. "She Felt Like a Defendant." *Washington Post*, 2 December 1972, sec. E, p. 1, col. 5.   A
Barlow, D.H. "Crime Victims and the Sentencing Process." *Victimology: An International Journal* 2 (1977):53.   H

In a paper presented at the Second International Symposium on Victimology, held in Boston, September 1976, the role of the victim in the sentencing process is explored. Criminal-justice roles available to crime victims under anglo-American doctrines of criminal procedure are examined. A review of factors thought to impinge upon the success or failure of the victim as judicial consultant is presented, and from this, generalizations regarding variations in the adoption and impact of this role are enumerated. The recognition of a formal victim role in sentencing is proposed, with implications for substantive and procedural law discussed in light of the proposal.

Barlow, D.H.; G.G. Abel; E.B. Blanchard; A. Bristow; and L. Young. "A Heterosocial Skills Checklist for Males." *Behavior Therapy* 1:229–239.
                                                                      C,G
Barnes, D.L. "Rape: A Bibliography, 1965–1975." P.O. Box 322, Troy, New York: Whitston, 1977.   G
Barnes, G.B.; R.S. Chabon; and L.J. Hertzbert. "Team Treatment for Abusive Families." *Social Casework* 55 (December 1974).   A,H
Barnett, N.J., and H.S. Field. "Sex Differences in University Students' Attitudes toward Rape." *Journal of College Student Personnel* 18 (March 1977):93–96.   G

Rape is being recognized by university administrators as a major problem on campuses. A questionnaire was administered to 200 male and 200 female undergraduates to investigate the nature of sex differences among college students' attitudes toward rape. Men were quite different from women in their attitudes and tended to support many of the myths regarding rape. Of the women, 40 percent felt that rape is a male exercise in power over women, while only 18 percent of the men agreed with this idea. Men were significantly more likely than women to attribute a desire for sex as being most rapists' basic motivation for rape. Male students were concerned with protecting men from a false charge of rape. Forty percent of the men, compared with 18 percent of the women, felt that a women's degree of resistance should be the major factor in determining if a rape has occurred. Responses also indicated the insensitivity of male students to the physiological and psychological trauma of rape for women. Almost one-third of the men believed that it would do some women some good to be raped. Results point up the need for rape education programs involving men as well as women.

―――. "Character of the Defendant and Length of Sentence in Rape and Burglary Crimes." *Journal of Social Psychology* 104 (1978):271–277.
F,G

The possibility that the effects of defendant character or attractiveness on juror decision making by Americans may be juror specific or crime specific was tested. Defendant character, sex, race, and nature of the crime (rape and burglary) were systematically varied in written cases that were distributed to 120 randomly selected men and women. Character of the defendant had a signficant effect in a case involving rape but played only a minor role in juror sentencing in a burglary case. The results confirm earlier findings that suggest that defendant attractiveness influences juridic judgment in person-oriented crimes to a greater degree than in property-oriented crimes.

Baroff, M. University of California, Los Angeles, School of Public Health.
A,B,D,E,H

Mental-health and social-policy programs include aging, alcohol abuse, criminal justice, marital dysfunction, drug abuse, juvenile delinquency, neurosis, psychosis, schizophrenia, sexual variance, sociocultural problems, suicide, unemployment, welfare, child behavior problems, smoking, rape, population problems (including contraception and abortion), weight problems, and child abuse.

Bar-on-bat-ami; D. Chalfie; S. Graff; K. Jensen; S. McKinley; E. McCrate; and C. Sparks. "A Rape Prevention Program in an Urban Area: Community Action Strategies to Stop Rape." *Journal of Women in Culture and Society* 5 (1980):S238–241.
B,G

A three-year research/demonstration project recently completed by Women against Rape of Columbus, Ohio, a feminist rape-prevention program based on community-action strategies, is described. The demonstration component of the project included four component programs: (1) a series of women's rape-prevention workshops that included discussions on the politics of rape and feminist prevention strategies, confrontation training, and self-defense; (2) a whistle alert program; (3) a shelter house; and (4) a women's rape-prevention network. The project's primary goal was to change women's attitudes about their status as potential rape victims and to increase community awareness of and responsiveness to rape and to programs designed to reduce women's vulnerability to victimization.

Barr, J. *Within a Dark Wood*. New York: Doubleday, 1979.   *A,E,G*

Barr, N.A., and Carrier, J.W. "The Economic Case for State Assistance to Battered Wives." *Policy and Politics* 6 (1978):333–350.   *A,B*

Barrett, C. "Implications of Women's Liberation and the Future of Psychotherapy." *Psychotherapy Theory Research and Practice* 11 (1974):11–15.   *B,C*

Barrett, C.E. "Gonorrhea and the Pediatrician." *American Journal of Diseases of Children* 125 (February 1973):233–238.   *E,H*

Barry, S. "Spousal Rape—The Uncommon Law." *American Bar Association Journal* 66 (1980):1088–1091.   *A,F,G*

Barsegiants, K. "Voprosu issledovanii spermy i sliuny v odnom i tom zhe piatne [Examination of sperm and saliva in a single stain]. *Sudebno-Meditsinskaia Ekspertiza* (Russian) 14 (October/December 1971):30. *G*

Bart, P.B. "Sexism and Social Science: From the Gilded Cage to the Iron Cage, or the Perils of Pauline." *Journal of Marriage and the Family* 33 (November 1971):734–745.   *H*

———. "Rape Doesn't End with a Kiss." *Viva*, June 1975, pp. 39–42 and 100–102.   *G*

———. "Victimization and its Discontents." *Continuing Medical Education: Syllabus and Proceedings in Summary Form*. Washington, D.C.: American Psychiatric Association, 1978.   *H*

A summary of a paper read at the 131st Annual Meeting of the American Psychiatric Association, held in Atlanta, May 1978, is presented. Theories of aggression against women—notably, those in the mental-health literature as well as in sociology—are discussed as a form of aggression against women. These theories have lead to further victimization of women by holding them responsible for the crimes that are committed against them (rape, incest, battering, molesting). Although a comparative study of victims and avoiders could lead to blaming the victim, such interpretations can be averted by locating the source of the problem within the social structure rather than within the personality structure. It is concluded that such theories serve a social-control function.

———. "Rape as a Paradigm of Sexism in Society—Victimization and its Discontents." *Women's Studies International Quarterly* 2(1979):347– 357.   G

The endemic nature of violence against women found during the course of a study of women who were attacked and avoided being raped and rape victims is described. The various forms of violence against women are reviewed (rape by a known rapist, rape by a stranger, woman abuse, and incest). Definitional issues, social class, individual responses, and institutional responses to rape and its victim are discussed as manifestations of sexism. Topics discussed include the double standard in rape, the ideology of the rapist as mentally ill, the ideology of the imperative nature of male sexuality, and responses of the police, hospital, courts, and mental-health professionals to rape.

———. "Research on Rape." *Psychology Today* 12 (1979).   G
Baruch, D.W. *New Ways in Discipline*. New York: McGraw-Hill, 1949, p. 35.   B,C
Bass, D., and J. Rice. "Agency Responses to Wife Abuse." *Social Casework* 60 (1979):338–342.   A,B

The responses of social-service agencies to the problems faced by abused wives was examined. Twenty-one interviews were conducted with counselors and caseworkers who did family counseling over a two-month period in nine separate social-service agencies in a county of a northeastern state. Findings indicated that only nine of the professional service workers in social-service agencies gave accurate descriptions of community services that exist specifically to deal with the abused wife. It is concluded that large gaps in communication exist between social-service agencies due to the tendency of agency personnel to classify problem areas by fitting them into their agency's service repertoire and the tendency of family counselors to view wife abuse within the context of interaction between family members.

Bassett, S. *Battered Rich*. Port Washington, N.Y.: Ashley Books, 1980. A

This book explores the world of rich, battered women through personal interviews.

Bassuk. "Organizing a Rape Crisis Program in a General Hospital." *Journal of American Medical Women Association* 1975, p. 486.   B
Bateman, P. *Fear into Anger—A Manual of Self-Defense for Women*. Chicago: Nelson-Hall, 1978.   B

Self-defense strategies and techniques are described and illustrated in a manual directed to women.

Battelle Memorial Institute, Columbus, Ohio, Law and Justice Study Center. "Forcible Rape." Washington, D.C.: National Institute of Law Enforcement and Criminal Justice, U.S. Department of Justice, Law Enforcement Assistance Administration, National Institute of Law Enforcement and Criminal Justice, 1977.   *G*

"Battered but Unbeaten." Washington Star, 19 March 1976, p. 19.   *A*

"Battered Wife Syndrome." *Washington Post*, 13 September 1975, pp. A6–B1.   *A*

"Battered Wives." Capitol Women. Lansing: Michigan House of Representatives, December 1975.   *A*

"Battered Wives: Chiswick Woman's Aid." *Newsweek*, 9 July 1973. *A,B*

"Battered Wives: Help for the Victim Next Door." *Ms.* 5 (August 1976): 95–98.   *A,B*

> A collection of several short articles dealing with different aspects of wife abuse. Contained is a general overview, a case history, a legal overview, a review of *Scream Quietly* by E. Prizzey, and discussion of Great Britain's experience. It also contains a description of Rainbow Retreat, a refuge in Phoenix, Arizona; a state-by-state listing of sources; a short bibliography; and a list of upcoming conventions dealing with the topic.

"Battered Wives: Now They're Fighting Back." *U.S. News & World Report*, 20 September 1976.   *A,C*

"Battered Wives: Where to Get Help." *Ms.*, August 1976.   *A,B*

"Battered Women." *Trial* 13 (November 1977):20.   *A*

"Battered Woman: Family Violence in America." *Behavioral Medicine*, 6 (1979):38–41.   *A,C,H*

> Facts about wife beating in the United States and the role of the family physician are examined. The Women against Abuse shelter in Philadelphia has to turn away women because of limited space, and many have to return to violent homes because they have no money, family, or friends to help them. Wife battering has occurred across all socioeconomic lines, and the typical batterer has a problem with self-confidence and uses physical violence to counteract feelings of frustration, impotence, and powerlessness. Women should be told that battering happens to million of other women, that it is against the law, and that the beatings are not her fault.

Battered Women and Social Work. New York: Wiley & Sons, 1978.   *H*

> The attitudes and ideology generally held by English social-services personnel are shown to undermine practical help for battered wives, and suggestions for change are offered.

Battered Women—A National Concern. Rockville, Md.: NCJRS, 1980.
                                                                     A,C

This paper, a problem statement from the National Clearing House on Domestic Violence, discusses wife abuse, stating that it has become a major social problem.

Battered Women in Hartford, Connecticut. Rockville, Md.: NCJRS, 1979.
A,B

This study of battered women in the Hartford, Connecticut, area focuses on their treatment by the criminal-justice system and social-service agencies.

Battered Women—Issues of Public Policy. Washington, D.C.: U.S. Commission on Civil Rights, 1978. *A*

Proceedings of a consultation on battered women sponsored by the U.S. Commission on Civil Rights are presented. Participants included experts in law, law enforcement, psychology, sociology, and support services for women.

Battered Women—Part I. Rockville, Md.: NCJRS Microfiche Program, 1978. *A*

A New York State study of battered spouses attempts to find how many battered women (and men) there are, where they are, and how their needs are being met by the social-service delivery system.

Battered Women—Part II. Rockville, Md.: NCJRS Microfiche Program, 1978. *A,B*

Profiles of the services offered to battered women are presented, county by county, in the state of New York.

Battered Women, Refuges, and Womens' Aid—A Report—England. London: National Women's Aid Federation. *A,B*

The booklet provides information on operating a shelter and providing supportive services for battered wives based on the experiences of women's aid groups in the United Kingdom.

Battered Women: The Hidden Problem. Saint Paul, Minn.: Community Planning Organization, 1976. *A,C*

Battered Women Need Refuges. A Report. London: National Women's Aid Federation. *A,B*

Bauer. "Triebverbrechen Jugendlicher und Minderjahriger Delinquenten. *Praxis Der Kinder-Psychologie Und Kinderpsychiatrie* 19 (1970):234.*A*

———. "Der Serien-Notzuchter Bernhard N. Bericht uber einen Morder,

der als 'Freiganger' aus dem Gefangnis kam." *Archiv Fur Kriminologie* 147 (March/April 1971):65.   A

Bauermeister, M. "Rapists, Victims and Society." *International Journal of Offender Therapy and Comparative Criminology* 21 (1977):238–248.
                                                                    G,H

Notes that rape is predatory behavior most typical in group settings of male violence where it often serves the purpose of acquiring power and prestige within the peer group.

Beardslee, C. "Shelter—Viable Alternative." *Domestic Violence* (1978): 355–363.   B

The development of a shelter program for battered wives and their children in St. Paul, Minnesota, is described by a staff member of women's advocates to the Senate Subcommittee on Child and Human Development.

Beck, M.J. "Pathological Narcissism and the Psychology of the Married Victim." *Family Therapy* 6 (1979):155–159.   H

Pathological narcissism is examined as an aspect of the psychology of the victimized spouse in two case reports. In both cases, the women were victimized by their spouses.

Becker, J.R. "Men and the Victimization of Women." In *Victimization of Women*, edited by J.R. Chapman and M. Gates. Beverly Hills, Calif.: Sage Publications, 1978.   C,D,H

Differential effects of aggression on men and women, rape as a prototype of victimization, and possible forms of treatment for rapists are discussed. A psychological classification of rapists is presented.

Becker, J.V. "Sexual Assault of Children and Adolescents." *Contemporary Psychology* 24 (1979):49–50.   E,G

Becker, J.V., and G.G. Abel. "The Treatment of Victims of Sexual Assault." *Quarterly Journal of Corrections* 1 (Spring 1977):38–42. G,H

Discusses the definition and prevalence of rape. Several misconceptions about rape are presented, as follows: that only young, attractive women are raped; that the rapist preselects the victim; and that there is a typical rape victim. Rape is reviewed as a crisis in coping, describing the psychological, medical, and legal needs of the rape victim.

Becker, J.V. et. al. "Evaluating Social Skills of Sexual Aggressives." *Criminal Justice and Behavior* 5 (December 1978):357–368.   G,H

Reviews current means of assessing social skills and applying skills-training treatments to sexual aggressives when needed. A major finding is that treatment in one skills area does not generalize into other skills areas—that is, specific skills deficits must be resolved by treatment to improve that very deficit since generalization from other skills areas is minimal.

Becker, J.V.; G.G. Abel; and L.J. Skinner. "The Impact of a Sexual Assault on the Victim's Sexual Life." *Victimology* 4 (1979):229–235.
G,H

The role of sexual satisfaction in the motivation of rapists is explored via analysis of published studies, and the impact of a sexual assault on the victim's sexual life is explored.

Bedard, V.S. "Wife Beating." *Glamour* 76 (August 1978):85–86.
Bedrosian, R.C., and S.A. Kagel. "A Woman under the Influence: An Example of Multiple Victimization within a Family." *American Journal of Family Therapy* 7 (1979):51–58.
A,G

Rather than portraying the persecution of a single individual by other members of the family, this film's drama demonstrates that the complex interactions within the extended family victimizes all the participants.

Beghard, P. *Sex Offenders: An Analysis of Types*. New York: Harper & Row, 1965.
D,E,G
Beit, H.B. "Motivation for Murder: The Case of G." *Corrective Psychiatry and Journal of Social Therapy* 17 (1971):25–30.
A

The study was based on psychotherapy done with a convicted murderer in a prison psychiatric clinic.

Bell, J.N. "New Hope for the Battered Wife." *Good Housekeeping* 183 (August 1976):94.
B
Bell, J.N. "Rescuing the Battered Wife." *Human Behavior*, June 1977, pp. 16–23.
A,C
Bell, M. "Issues of Violence in Family Casework." *Social Casework* 58 (January 1977):3–12.
A,H
Bell, R.R. "Sexual Exchange of Marriage Partners." Paper presented with Lillian Silvan at the Society for the Scientific Study of Social Problems Meeting, Washington, D.C., 1 September 1970. See also *Philadelphia Magazine*, pp. 76–160, September 1969.
A
———. *Social Deviance*. Homewood, Ill.: Dorsey Press, 1971.
A,H
Bellak, L. *The Porcupine Dilemma*. New York: Citadel Press, 1970. A,H
Bellak, L., and M. Antell. "An Intercultural Study of Aggressive Behavior

on Children's Playgrounds." *American Journal of Orthopsychiatry* 44 (1974):503–511. *E,H*

Belson, R. "You Have to Know Who Is Who." *Journal of Family Counseling* 2 (Spring 1974):55–59. *C,H*

Ben-David, J. "The Kibbutz and the Moshav." In *Agricultural Planning and Village Community in Israel.* Paris: UNESCO, 1964. *C*

Bender, L. "Children and Adolescents Who Have Killed." *American Journal of Psychiatry* 116 (1959):510–513. *E,G,H*

Bender, L., and A. Blau. "The Reaction of Children to Sexual Relations with Adults." *American Journal of Orthopsychiatry* 8 (1937):500–518. *E,G*

Bender, L., and F.J. Curran. "Children and Adolescents Who Kill." *Criminal Psychopathology* 3 (1940):297–322. *C,E,H*

Bender, M. "Changing Rules of Office Romances." *Esquire* 91 (1979):46–47. *D*

Benhorin. "Is Rape a Sex Crime?" *Nation*, 16 August 1975. *G,H*

Benjamin, H., and R. Masters. *Prostitution and Morality.* New York: Julien Press, 1964. *H*

Bennett, J.R. "A Model for Evaluation: Design for a Rape Counseling Program." *Child Welfare* 56 (June 1977):395–400. *B,G*

Describes an evaluation design for a rape and counseling service, emphasizing that similar procedures can be used in other social-services programs. The three-part program described includes assistance to the victim, community education about rape, and education of police, medical personnel, and other professionals who work with rape victims.

Bennett, M.H. "Father-Daughter Incest: A Psychological Study of the Mother from an Attachment Theory Perspective." *Dissertation Abstracts International* 41 (6):2381-B, 1980. *E*

Childhood background of attachment disruption, presence of a separation disorder, ways of expressing anger, and levels of self-esteem were examined with mothers from incestuous families and control mothers with a daughter between the ages of eleven and seventeen years.

Benshoff, D.L. "A Comparison of Types of College Students and Their Attitudes toward the Phenomenon of Rape." *Dissertation Abstracts International* 38 (9-B):4533, March 1978. *G*

Compares masculinity, femininity, androgyny, aggressiveness, feminism stand, and attitudes toward rape of tested college students.

Bensing, R.C., and O. Schroeder. *Homicide in an Urban Community.* Springfield, Ill.: CC Thomas, 1960. *A,H*

Benward, J., and J. Densen-Gerber. "Incest as a Causative Factor in Antisocial Behavior: An Exploratory Study." *Contemporary Drug Problems* 4 (Fall 1975):323–340.　　　　　　　　　　　　　E

Investigated the prevalence of incest among a sample of 188 female drug addicts in residence in Odyssey House Centers serving twenty-six states. Female interviewers conducted standardized interviews. Samples were white, black, Hispanic, Indian, Protestant, Catholic, Jewish, Mormon from lower socioeconomic class, unmarried, and 13–42 years old when interviewed.

Berelson, B., and G.A. Steiner. *Human Behavior: An Inventory of Scientific Findings.* New York: Harcourt, Brace & World, 1964.　　　H

Berger, E.H. *The Betrayed Wife.* Chicago: Nelson-Hall, 1971.　　　A

Berkowitz, L. "The Expression and Reduction of Hostility." *Psychological Bulletin* 55 (1958):257–283.　　　　　　　　　　　　H

———. Aggression: A Social Psychological Analysis. New York: McGraw-Hill, 1962.　　　　　　　　　　　　　　　　　　　　　H

———. "Aggressive Cue on Aggressive Behavior and Hostility Catharsis." *Psychological Review* 71(1964):104–122.　　　　　　　　H

———. *Roots of Aggression: A Re-examination of the Frustration-Aggression Hypothesis.* New York: Atherton, Jr., 1969.　　　　　H

———. "Experimental Investigations of Hostility Catharsis." *Journal of Consulting and Clinical Psychology* 35 (1970):1–7.　　　　　H

———. "The Case for Bottling up Rage." *Psychology Today*, July 1973, pp. 24–31.　　　　　　　　　　　　　　　　　　　　　　　H

Berliner, L. "Child Sexual Abuse: What Happens Next." *Victimology: An International Journal* 2 (1977):327–331.　　　　　　　　　E

The outcome of cases of sexually abused children is considered. It is noted that the sexually abused child is not only a victim of sexual exploitation but also of societal attitudes that tend to disbelieve or blame the child. Suggestions to rectify this situation include providing acute medical care and crisis counseling.

Bermant, G.; H.C. Kelman; and D.P. Warwick. *The Ethics of Social Intervention.* Washington, D.C.: Series in Clinical and Community Psychology, 1978.　　　　　　　　　　　　　　　　　　　B

Ethical concerns of social scientists and policymakers implementing social-intervention programs are investigated by considering behavior modification, encounter groups, organizational development, community-controlled educational reform, intervention in community disputes, income-maintenance experiments, federally funded housing programs, and family planning programs.

Bernard, J. *The Future of Marriage*. New York: Bantam, 1973.   *A,C*
———. "Moving Mountains: Appalachia Women Organize." *Ms.*, Sept-
   ember 1975, p. 21.   *A,B*
———. "The Paradox of the Happy Marriage." In *Woman in Sexist Society:
   Studies in Power and Powerlessness*, Edited by V. Gornick and B.K.
   Moran, pp. 145–162. New York: Mentor, 1972.   *A*
———. *Women, Wives, Mothers: Values and Options*. Chicago: Aldine,
   1975.   *A,H*
Berns, W. "Terms of Endearment: Sexual Harassment." *Harpers* 261
   (October 1980):14–16.   *D*
Bernstein, B.F. "The Social Worker as an Expert Witness." *Social Case-
   work* 58 (1977):412–417.   *B*

   The role that social workers could play in judicial procedures in cases
   involving family disputes, child-custody suits, and parent-child interactions
   is discussed. It is argued that social workers, by training, experience, and
   education, gain an insight into the social welfare of family life.

Bernstein, G.A. "Physician Management of Incest Situations." *Human
   Sexuality* 13 (1979):67, 71, 75, 79, 83, 87.   *E*

   Case examples of incest situations involving father and daughter and
   their management by family physicians are presented. It is contended
   that physicians should understand the dynamics of incestuous families in
   order to be effective. Victims seldom report the situation for fear of dis-
   rupting the family unit or fear of retaliation, and they often present
   with a variety of other symptoms such as depression and somatic complaints.

Bernstein, P. "Sexual Harassment on the Job." *Harper's Bazaar* 109 (Au-
   gust 1976):12.   *D*
Bernstein and Rommel. "Rape: Exploding the Myths." *Today's Health*,
   October 1975, p. 36.   *G*
Berry, B. "NOW's National Task Force on Marriage, Divorce, and Family
   Relations." *Newsletter*, 25 May 1973, pp. 3–4.   *B*
Berry. G.W. "Incest: Some Clinical Variations on a Classical Theme."
   Journal of the American Academy of Psychoanalysis 3 (April 1975):
   151–161.   *E*

   Presents seven clinical cases to illustrate four incest variations: (1) incest
   and homosexuality, (2) brother-sister incest, (3) incest as a transmissible
   phenomenon, and (4) incest envy. The findings question whether incest is
   as uncommon as classical psychoanalytic theory implies. A real act of incest
   is considered as much a psychic reality as a fantasied one.

Berry, P. "The Rape of Demeter/Persephone and Neurosis." *Spring*, 1975, pp. 186–198.   G

Analyzes the myth of Demeter and her experience of the rape of her daughter, Persephone. Demeter's neurosis occurs because of Persephone's rape, and this connection in the archetype is seen as relevant to therapy.

Besharov, J.D. "Building a Community Response to Child Abuse and Maltreatment." *Children Today* 4 (1975):2.   B

Bessmer, S. "The Laws of Rape." Ann Arbor, Michigan, University, *Dissertation Abstracts International*, 1976.   F,G

A sociocultural analysis of rape laws and adjudicatory practices concerning rape of chaste and unchaste women is presented. An analysis of rape laws in all jurisdictions indicates that such laws reflect societal norms concerning coercion as in forcible rape, the protection of children from premature sexual contact, and the protection of the institution of monogamous marriage.

Best, C.L., and D.G. Kilpatrick. "Psychological Profiles of Rape Crisis Counselors." *Psychological Reports*, 40 (June 1977):1127–1134.   B

To describe the psychological characteristics of volunteer rape-crisis counselors, a battery of psychological tests was administered to twenty female counselors and fourteen pediatric nurses matched for age and education.

Bethschneider, J.L. "A Study of Father-Daughter Incest in the Harris County Child Welfare Unit." Sam Houston State University, Huntsville, Texas, Institute of Contemporary Corrections and the Behavioral Sciences, 1973.   E

Betries. "Rape: An Act of Possession." *Sweet Fire*, Early Summer 1972, p. 12.   G

Bettelheim, B. "Children Should Learn about Violence." *Saturday Evening Post*, 12 March 1967, p. 100.   E,H

Bettner, J. "How to Tame the Office Wolf—Without Getting Bitten." *Business Week* 107 (1 October 1979).   D

Beyer, M. "Runaway Youths: Families in Conflict." Mimeographed. Paper presented at the Eastern Psychological Association Meeting, 3–4 May 1973, Washington, D.C.   C

Biaggi, G.R. *Battered Women—A Legal Handbook for New Jersey Women*. Trenton: New Jersey State Law Enforcement Planning Agency, 1979.   A,F

The booklet describes where to go and what to do if husbands or male friends are physically abusive, emphasizing an understanding of the legal system and use of the courts in New Jersey.

Biane, H.T., and H. Barry. "Sex of Siblings of Male Alcoholics." *Archives of General Psychiatry* 32 (November 1975):1403–1405.   E

Bickman, L. "Bystander Intervention in a Crime." Paper presented at the International Advanced Study Institute on Victimology and the Needs of Contemporary Society, Bellagio, Italy, 1–12 July 1975.   B

Bieber, I. *Homosexuality: A Psychoanalytic Study.* New York: Basic Books, 1962.   H,C

Bienen, H. *Violence and Social Change.* Chicago: University of Chicago Press, 1968.   H

Bienen, L. "Rape II." *Women Rights Law Reporter* 3 (1977):90–137.G,F

Bierer, J. "Generation of Homosexuals: An Unusual Case of Anorexia Nervosa." International Journal of Social Psychology 26 (Autumn 1980):153–157.   H

Bigger, S.F. "Family Laws of Leviticua 18 in Their Setting." *Journal of Bible Literature* 98 (June 1979):187–203.   F

Biggs, J.M. *The Concept of Matrimonial Cruelty.* Atlantic Highlands, N.J.: Athlone Press Humanities, 1962.   A

Biles, D., and J. Braithwaite. "Crime Victims and the Police." *Australian Psychologist* 14 (1979):345–355.   H

> A survey conducted by the Australian bureau of statistics investigated the reasons why crime victims do not report their victimization to the police. The most common reason for nonreporting was that the victims considered that the offense was too trivial, but a large number of victims expressed the view that the police could not do anything about it.

Bill M. "How I Stopped Beating My Wife." *Ms.* 5 (August 1976):53.   A

> Case history of a wife beater, describes one man's experience. Gives personal background and motivations operating in this instance. Bill M. came from a family in which his mother was abused. He had always felt a strong need to express manhood as imposed through peer groups, married, and became heavily in debt. Claims that drinking contributed to his violent responses.

Biller, H., and D. Meredith. *Father Power.* New York: David McKay Company, 1974.   A,E

Billings, "How To Tell if You're Being Raped and What to Do about It." *Redbook,* 1974, p. 70.   B,G

Binford, S. "Apes and Original Sin." *Human Behavior* 1 (1972):64–71.G,H

Birnbaum, R. "The Battered Wife—The Legal System Attempts to Help."
University of Cincinnati Law Review 48 (1979):419–434.   *A,B,F*

The legal barriers erected by the common law and state legislatures that
deny abused women legal redress are described, and the legal system's
recent attempts to provide remedies for the battered woman are explored.

Bischof, N. "The Biological Foundations of the Incest Taboo." *Social
Science Information* 11 (December 1972):7–36.   *E*

Discusses the background and significance of the incest taboo. Topics
covered include anthropological significance, cross-cultural universals and
differences, biological and sociological advantages and conditions, incest-
preventing mechanisms in mammals, biological import of incest avoidance,
and incest barriers in man.

Bittner, E. "Police Discretion in Emergency Apprehension of Mentally Ill
    Persons." *Social Problems* 14 (1967):278.   *C*
Black, D.J., and A.J. Reiss. "Studies in Crime and Law Enforcement
    in Major Metropolitan Areas." Patterns of Behavior in Police and
    Citizen Transaction. Washington, D.C.: U.S. Government Printing
    Office, 1967.   *B,C*
Black, K.D., and C.B. Broderick. "Systems Theory versus Reality." Paper
    presented at the 1972 meeting of the National Council on Family Rela-
    tions, University of Southern California, Los Angeles.   *C*
Blackstone, Sir W. *Commentaries on the Laws of England.* London:
    Houghton Mifflin, 1768.   *F*
Blanchard, W. "The Group Process in Gang Rape." *Journal of Social
    Psychology* 49:259–266.   *G*
———. "An Experimental Case Study of the Biofeedback Treatment of a
    Rape-Induced Psychophysiological Cardiovascular Disorder." *Behav-
    ior Therapy* 7 (1976):113.   *G*
Blesofsky, S. "Victim Restitution: The MAPS Model." *Victimology: An
    International Journal* 2 (1977):54–55.   *H*

In a paper presented at the Second International Symposium on Victimology, held in Boston, September 1976, a mutual agreement programming
(MAPS) -type victim-restitution program is described. The program involves the victim in the preliminary contract hearing as one of the decision
makers along with the inmate, representatives of the institution, and a
parole board member. The contract that emerges is designed to identify
clearly the responsibilities of all parties involved and what an inmate can do
to earn a guaranteed parole release date. The institution provides programs
that address the inmate's needs and allow him to make restitution from

funds earned while in prison. The concept is presented as a due-process-type parole release—that is, the inmate has it in his power to succeed or fail.

Blitman, G. "Inez Garcia on Trail." *Ms.*, May 1975, p. 49.   *A*

Block, R. "Victim and Offender in Violent Crime." *Victimology: An International Journal* 2 (1977):55.   *H*

In a paper presented at the Second International Symposium on Victimology, held in Boston, September 1976, data based upon police records of homicide, robbery, and aggravated assault in Chicago are used to examine the relationship between victim-offender interaction and outcome in robbery and aggravated assault.

Blood, R., and D.M. Wolfe. *Husbands and Wives: The Dynamics of Married Living*. Glencoe, Ill.: Free Press, 1960.   *A,C*

Bloom, M. "Conciliation Court—Crisis Intervention in Domestic Violence." *Crime Prevention Review* 6 (October 1978):19–27.   *C*

The initiation of a domestic-violence program in 1977 by the San Diego County Conciliation Court in California to provide protestion and counseling to victims of domestic violence in the family is examined.

Bluglass, R. "Incest." *British Journal of Hospital Medicine* 22 (1979):152, 154–157.   *E*

The history, demography, and current legal status of incest is discussed. It is believed that incest is far more common than appears from police records. Sibling relationships are probably the most frequent form of incest although father-daughter incest is the most commonly reported type. Incest offenders exhibit a higher intelligence than other sex offenders. Psychopathological traits tend to include maladjustment at work, alcoholism, and violence. Wives of incestuous fathers tend to promote incest between their own children and the father. The younger daughters involved are often the victims of sexual assault by violent, drunken, or psychopathic fathers. It is suggested that since incest is a family offense it might be best dealt with in a family court.

Blumberg, M.L. "Psychopathology of the Abusing Parent." *American Journal of Psychotherapy* 28 (1974):21–29.   *A*

Blumberg, and Bohmer. "The Rape Victim and Due Process." *Case and Comment*, 1975, p. 3.   *F,G*

Blumenthal, M. *Justifying Violence: The Attitudes of American Men*. Ann Arbor: Institute for Social Research, University of Michigan, 1972.*H*

Blumfeld, A.I. "The Adolescent Rape Offender: A Psychological Profile." *Dissertation Abstracts International* 40 (1979):2353-B.   *G*

The intellectual and personality characteristics of the adolescent rape offender were examined to provide a baseline of data describing the psychological profile of such subjects.

Bode, J. *Fighting Back*. New York: Macmillan, 1978.   G
———. *Rape*. New York: Watts, 1979.   G
Boekelheide, P.D. "Incest and the Family Physician." *Journal of Family
    Practice* 6 (1978):87–90.   E

    Reviews incest from epidemiologic, familial, and individual points of view.
    The incest taboo has characterized almost every culture and society
    throughout the ages. Respect for the incest barrier is a cultural demand
    made by society and is not a physiological or biological imperative.

———. "Sexual Adjustment in College Women Who Experience Incestu-
    ous Relationships." *Journal of the American College Health Association*
    26 (1978):327–330.   E

    The effect of incestuous relationships on the sexual adjustment of college
    women is discussed in several case studies of actual incest and incestuous
    fantasies. For most of the cases it was found that the women suffered
    traumas from the experience, leading to promiscuity and an inability to
    form lasting heterosexual relationships.

Boese. "Kinder sind anders." *Kriminalistik* 16 (1962):471.   H
Bohanan, P. *African Homicide and Suicide*. New York: Atheneum, 1960. H
Bohmer. "Judicial Attitudes toward Rape Victims." *Judicature* 57 (1974):
    303.
Boissevain, J.F. "Patronage in Sicily." *Man* n.s. 1 (1966):18–33.   E,G
Boisvert, M.J. "The Battered Child Syndrome." *Social Casework* 53
    (October 1972):475–480.   E
Bolin, D.C. "The Pima County Victim/Witness Program: Analyzing Its
    Success." *Evaluation and Change* Special Issue (1980):120–126. B

    The Pima County Victim/Witness Program in Tucson, Arizona, which
    began as a project to reduce crime and which responded to a variety of
    client and community needs through innovative services delivery, is des-
    cribed.

———. "Police-Victim Interactions: Observations from the Police Foun-
    dation." *Evaluation and Change* Special Issue (1980):110–115.   C

    Research conducted or stimulated by the police foundation that concerns
    police functions, the manner in which the police and public interact, and the

ways in which police and the courts respond to the victims of crime is considered.

Bolton, F.G. "Domestic Violence Continuum—A Pressing Need for Legal Intervention." *Women Lawyers Journal* 66 (Winter 1980):11–17. *C,H*

This article examines domestic violence in the context of its etiology and effects and focuses on the necessity and role of legal intervention.

Bond, S.B. "Self-Defense against Rape: The Joanne Little Case." *Black Scholar*, March 1975, p. 29.   *G*
———. "Affective and Sexual Reactions to Guided Imagery of Rape: Implications for Counseling." *Dissertation Abstracts International* 40 (10):5369-A, 1980.   *G*

Affective and sexual reactions were examined in 104 female students presented with guided imagery scenarios of a sex fantasy of rape and realistic imagery of rape with unambiguous rapist responsibility or with ambiguous rapist/victim responsibility.

Borafia, A.W. "Compensation to Victims of Crime." *Victimology: An International Journal* 2 (1977):55.   *H*

The revival of the African custom of having the offender compensate his victim is strongly advocated. The ineffectiveness of prisons, forms of social controls, and current provisions in Tanzanian law are seen as unique factors that make compensation desirable.

Borgida, E. "Evidentiary Reform of Rape Laws: A Psycholegal Approach." In *New Directions in Psycholegal Research*, edited by P. Lipsitt. New York: Van Nostrand Reinhold, 1980.   *F,G*

The impact of the common-law rules of evidence in rape cases versus two types of revised evidentiary rules on the decisions of simulated juries are examined. The peculiar legal status of rape and the issue of admissibility of third-party prior-sexual-history evidence are considered.

Borgida, E., and P. White. "Social Perception of Rape Victims: The Impact of Legal Reform." *Law and Human Behavior* 2 (1978):339–351. *G*

The extent to which the types of legal reform affect social perception of the victim, as well as the conviction rate, in a videotaped consent defense rape trial was examined.

Borkenhagen. "You Asked for It." *Imprint*, December 1975, p. 22. *A,D,G*

Borsa, N. "Battered Women." *Western Canadian Women's News*, 15
September 1975.   A

The battered woman, not only wives but also a large portion of women
involved in common-law relationships, is still an unknown fact in today's
statistics. Her age ranges from twenty to sixty years and she comes from
almost every economical background, but little more is known about her.
Psychosis, alcohol, and drugs are major contributors to the problem of
battered wives.

Boschan, S. *Europaisches Familienrecht Handbuch*. Berlin: P. Vahlen,
1965.   A

Boskey, J.B. *Spousal Abuse in the United States—The Attorney's Role*.
Scarborough, Ont.: Butterworth, 1978.   A

The range of criminal and civil remedies available to a battered spouse in
the U.S. and the difficulties that occur with the enforcement of each are
surveyed. The attorney's role in securing remedies is reviewed.

Boston Women's Health Book Collective. *Our Bodies, Ourselves: A Book
by and for Women*. New York: Simon & Schuster, 1973. See especially
"Rape and Self-Defense."   B

Written by women for women, to communicate the excitement about the
power of shared information, to assert that, in an age of professionals,
women are the best experts on themselves and their feelings.

Boudouris, J. "Homicide and the Family." *Journal of Marriage and the
Family* 33 (1971):667–676.   C

In an analysis of 6,839 homicides occurring in the city of Detroit from
1927–1968, a classification of homicides based on social interaction was
made. It is proposed that homicides involving family members represent
problems in family interaction and maladjustment, and that the proper
training of persons in family counseling and crisis intervention may help to
reduce the homicide rate.

Boulding, E. "Women and Social Violence." *International Social Science
Journal* 30 (1978):801–815.   H

Women are discussed as victims of the institutional structures of society and
as aggressors under specified conditions of structural and behavioral violence.

Bowden, P. "The Psychology of Violence." *Nursing Mirror and Midwives
Journal* 146 (1978):13–16.   H

Violence, defined as the exertion of force so as to inflict injury or damage to a person or property, should be distinguished from aggression, which is an attacking process by which dominance is gained. Lorenz believes that it is instinctual behaviors that seek release, while the adherents of the other group maintain that violence always requires a stimulus. Violence within the family and rape are discussed to illustrate specific forces at work in violent behavior.

————. "Rape." *British Journal of Hospital Medicine* 20 (1978):205–290. G

The history and prevalence of rape, personality characteristics of rapists, and the after effects of rape on the victim are discussed.

Bower, R.K. *Solving Problems in Marriage*. Grand Rapids, Mich.: Berd-mans, 1972.   A
Bow Group. *Battered Wives—A Report from the Bow Group*. London: WCIV.   A
Bowker, L.H. "The Criminal Victimization of Women." *Victimology* 4 (1979):371–384.   A,G,H

Criminal victimization of women in the United States in the categories of property crime, murder, assault, and rape is examined.

Box, S. *Deviance, Reality and Society*. London: Holt, 1971.   H
Boyatzis, R.E. "The Effect of Alcohol Consumption on the Aggressive Behavior of Men." *Quarterly Journal of Studies of Alcohol* 35 (1974): 959–972.   H
Boycott, R. "Battered Women Find Refuge." *Spare Rib* 14 August 1973, p. 3.   A,B
Brabec. "Rape: The Ultimate Violence." Prime Time, September 1974, p. 36.   G
Bracki, M.A., and G. Connor. "Survey of Police Attitudes Toward Rape in Du Page County, Illinois." *Crisis Intervention* 6 (1975):28–42.   C,G

Compared civilian and police attitudes toward rape using a survey questionnaire with items on perception of the victim, perception of the perpetrator, and general conceptions about the crime itself. Results indicate no significant differences between police and civilian attitudes toward rapist and the victim.

Brady, K. *Father's Days*. New York: Playboy Press, 1979.   A,E
Brain, J.L. "Sex, Incest, and Death: Initiation Rites Reconsidered." *Current Anthropology* 18 (June 1977):191–208.   E

Uses concepts derived from social and physical anthropology and from psychoanalysis to show why initiation and/or puberty rites occur in so many societies and why they take the shape they do. The rites are seen as part of a general human concern with categorization and the attribution of power/danger to what is not classifiable.

Brain, P. "Report on National Conference on Crime and Violence in Modern Society." *Aggressive Behavior* 2 (1976):233–235.   *A,H*

Briefly describes the papers at a conference on crime and violence held in London in 1976. Topics included anthropological perspectives of violence, how moral judgments influence perceptions of violence, the relationship between food impurities and violence, social coherence and new towns, violent sex crimes, corporal punishment in education, battered wives, and concepts of social control.

Bralove, M. "A Cold Shoulder: Career Women Decry Sexual Harassment by Bosses and Clients." *Wall Street Journal* 15 January 1976.   *D*

Branch. "Putting the Sex Back into Rape." *Washington Monthly*, March 1976, p. 56.   *G*

Brandwein, R.A.; C.A. Brown; and E.M. Fox. "Women and Children Last: The Social Situation of Divorced Mothers and their Families." *Journal of Marriage and the Family* (August 1977):498–514.   *H*

Brant, R.S.T., and V.B. Tisza. "The Sexually Misused Child." *American Journal of Orthopsychiatry* 47 (1977):80–90.   *E*

Braucht, G.N.; F. Loya; and K.J. Jamieson. "Victims of Violent Death: A Critical Review." *Psychological Bulletin* 87 (1980):309–333.   *H*

The present state of knowledge regarding victims of suicide, accidental death, and homicide is assessed, and the formal characteristics of the empirical research models that have yielded this body of knowledge are analyzed. It is shown that knowledge of these victims and their circumstances is fragmented because few investigators have studied more than one mode of violent death and because few studies have examined data from both the individual and environmental levels of analysis.

Breckenridge, S.P. *Marriage and the Civil Rights of Women*. Finch, 1931.*F*

Breen; Greenwald; and Gregori. "The Molested Young Female. Evaluation and Therapy of Alleged Rape." *Pediatrics Clinics of North America* 19 (1972):717.   *B,C,E*

Breiter, T. "Battered Women." *Essence* 10 (June 1979):74–75.   *A*

Brenner, R.H. *Children and Youth in America: A Documentary History*. Cambridge: Harvard University Press, 1970.   *E,G,H*

Breuer, J., and S. Freud. "Studies on Hysteria." In *Standard Edition*, Vol. 2, edited by J. Strachey. London: Hogarth (First German Edition 1865), 1955.   *H*

Brewster, P.G. *The Incest Theme in Folksong*. Helsinki: Suomalainen Tiedaekatemia, 1972.   *E*

Briddell, D.W.; D.C. Rimm; G.R. Caddy; G. Krawitz; D. Sholis; and R.J. Wunderlin. "Effects of Alcohol and Cognitive Set on Sexual Arousal to Deviant Stimuli." *Journal of Abnormal Psychology* 87 (1978):418–430.

G

Independent and interactive effects of the cognitive and pharmacological factors associated with alcohol consumption on sexual arousal to highly deviant stimuli was investigated with male social drinkers. Forty-eight undergraduate male social drinkers were randomly assigned to one of two expectancy set conditions in which they were led to believe the beverage administered contained alcohol or no alcohol.

Briffault, R., and B. Malinowsky. *Marriage—Past and Present.* Boston: P. Sargent, 1971.   A,C

"Britain: Battered Wives." *Newsweek*, 9 July 1973, p. 39.   A

Report on Chiswick Women's Aid Refuge. Center has received more requests than any other similar agency in its first year and a half of operation. They have also won laborite M.P. Jack Ashley's support for national reform in the community.

Brockett, L.P. *Woman: Her Rights, Wrongs, Privileges, and Responsibilities.* Plainview, N.Y.: Books for Libraries, 1869.   F

Broderick, C.B. "Beyond the Five Conceptual Frameworks: A Decade of Development in Family Theory." *Journal of Marriage and the Family* 33 (February 1971):139–159.   H

Brodsky, S. "Prevention of Rape: Deterrence by the Potential Victim." In *Sexual Assault*, edited by H. Walker and S. Brodsky. Lexington, Mass.: Lexington Books, D.C.Heath and Company, 1976.   B,G

———. "Sexual Assault: Perspectives on Prevention and Assailant." In *Sexual Assault*, edited by M. Walker and S. Brodsky. Lexington, Mass.: Lexington Books, D.C. Heath and Company, 1976.   B,G

Treatment programs for sexual aggressives operate from a set of assumptions called blame models, each of which hypothesizes why sexual assault occurs. Four models are reviewed.

Brodyaga, L.; M. Gates; S. Singer; M. Tucker; and R. White. *Rape and Its Victims: A Report for Citizens, Health Facilities, and Criminal Justice Agencies.* Washington, D.C.: U.S. Government Printing Office, 1975.

B,G

Bromberg, W., and E. Coyle. "Rape, A Compulsion to Destroy." *Medical Insight* 22 (1974):21–25.   G

Bronfenbrenner, U. "The Changing American Child: A Speculative Analysis." *Journal of Social Issues* 17 (January 1961):6–18. Also repre-

sented in Rose Coser, ed. *Life Cycle and Achievement in America*. New
York: Harper & Row, Harper Torchbooks, 1969.   E
———. *Two Worlds of Childhood: U.S. and U.S.S.R.* New York: Russell
Sage Foundation, 1970.   E
Brothers, J. "A Quiz on Crime." *San Francisco Sunday Examiner and
Chronicle, Sunday Scene*, 22 June 1975, p. 6.   H
Brown, C. *Manchild in the Promised Land*. New York: New American
Library, 1965. Reprinted as "The Family and the Subculture of Vio-
lence." In *Violence in the Family*, edited by S.K. Steinmetz and M.A.
Straus. New York: Dodd, Mead, 1974.   H
Brown, S. "Clinical Illustrations of the Sexual Misuse of Girls." *Child
Welfare* 58 (1979):435–442.   B,E

Clinical examples are given of the sexual misuse of young girls, emphasizing
that such abuse is usually incestuous and often results in profound psychological impairment that is sometimes transmitted to the next generation.
The problem is a family phenomenon and involves sexual stimulation by a
father figure.

Brown, V.B. "Community Rape Prevention Program." Final Report.
Washington, D.C.: National Institute of Mental Health, Grant R18-
MH-29308, 1979.   B,G

A rape-consultation and rape-education project, which was a collaborative
effort between the Didi Hirsch Community Mental Health Center and the
Los Angeles Commission on assaults against women, and which was concerned with the prevention of rape and with the aftermath of rape, is
discussed.

Browne, S.F. *In Sickness and in Health—Analysis of a Battered Women
Population*. Denver, Colo.: Denver Anti-Crime Council, 1980.   A

Seventy-three women in a Denver, Colorado, safe house for battered
women completed a self-administered questionnaire in a study that explored some leading theoretical assumptions about battered women.

Browning, D.H., and B. Boatman. "Incest: Children at Risk." *American
Journal of Psychiatry* 134 (January 1977):69–72.   E

A review of fourteen cases of incest revealed that the typical family constellation was that of a chronically depressed mother, an alcoholic and violent
father or stepfather, and an eldest daughter who was forced to assume
many of her mother's responsibilities, with ensuing role confusion. Discussion also focuses on the higher incidence of incest with defective children or
those born out of wedlock.

Brownmiller, S. *Against Our Will*. New York: Simon & Schuster, 1975. *G*

> Against historical background and factual evidence, the author traces the use and meaning of rape in war, from biblical times through the world wars to Bangladesh and Vietnam. In addition, she examines every aspect of rape through the ages—legal, interracial, rape in prison, molestation of children, and so forth.

———. "Heroic Rapist." *Mademoiselle*, September 1975, p. 128.   *G*
———. "Real Spoils of War." *Ms.*, December 1975, p. 82.   *G*
———. "Anti-Rape Technique; Interview." *Harper's Bazaar* 109 (March 1976):119.   *B,G*
Bruce. "The Rape of Sheila Robinson." *Imprint*, December 1975, p. 32. *G*
Bruckman, J.C. "Project Rape Response: Evaluation, Conclusions, and Recommendations." *Dissertation Abstracts International* 38 (6-B):2936–2937E, December 1977.   *B,G*
Brunold. *Beobachtungen und Katamnestische Feststellungen nach im Kindesalter Erlittenen Sexualtraumen*. Praxis (Switzerland) 1962, p. 965.
Bryan, M. *Battered Spouses—Resource Manual*. New York: Harper & Row, 1978.   *A,B*

> The nature and scope of spouse abuse, the roles of social-service and law-enforcement agencies in dealing with spouse abuse and information about programs to assist abused spouses and their children are presented.

Bryant, C.D., and J.G. Wells. *Deviancy and the Family*. Philadelphia: F.A. Davis, 1973.   *A,E*
Bryant, G., and P. Cirel. *A Community Response to Rape*. Washington, D.C.: Department of Justice, Law Enforcement Assistance Administration, National Institute of Law Enforcement and Criminal Justice, Office of Technology Transfer.   *B,G*
Bryant, H.D. "Physical Abuse of Children: An Agency Study." *Child Welfare* 42 (1963):125–130.   *B,E*
Buckley, W.F., Jr. "Sex and Judicial Progress." *National Review* 30 (3 March 1978):299.   *F*
Bulcroft, R.A., and M.A. Straus. "Validity of Husband, Wife, and Child Reports of Conjugal Violence and Power." Mimeographed. Durham: University of New Hampshire, 1975.   *A*
Bullough, V., and B. Bullough. *The Subordinate Sex: A History of Attitudes towards Women*. Chicago: University of Illinois Press, 1974.   *A*
Bulter, S. *Conspiracy of Silence: The Trauma of Incest*. San Francisco: New Guide Publications, 1978.   *E*

> Questions some of society's most basic attitudes about sex, the sanctity of the nuclear family unit, male/female role expectations, and the rights of

children over their own minds and bodies. By opening up a dialogue, the author hopes to create a supportive atmosphere in which incest victims can acknowledge their painful experiences and begin to heal.

Buren, A.V. "Dear Abby." *San Francisco Chronicle*, 11 April 1975.   *A*

Burgess, A.W.; A.N. Groth; L.L. Holmstrom; S.M. Sgroi. *Sexual Assault of Children and Adolescents*. Lexington, Mass.: Lexington Books, D.C. Heath and Company, 1978.   *E*

Issues involved in the sexual assault of children and adolescents are examined. Characteristics of offenders and victims are delineated, and guidelines are offered for the provision of treatment and services for victims.

Burgess, A.W., and L.L. Holmstrom. "The Rape Victim in the Emergency Ward." *American Journal of Nursing* 73 (October 1973):1740–1745. *B*

Describes the care and treatment administered to rape victims by a twenty-four-hour crisis-intervention service. Reactions of rape victims and traumas associated with their assault are discussed.

———. "Accountability and Rights of Rape Victims." *American Journal of Orthopsychiatry* 44 (1974):182.   *F,G*

———. "Crisis and Counseling Requests of Rape Victims." *Nursing Research* 23 (May 1974):196–202.   *C,G*

A study of 109 17–73-year-old women and 37 children who were victims of sexual assault revealed a positive response by the victims to psychological intervention during the crisis period. Victims were interviewed at a hospital immediately following the assault and were followed up with telephone calls from the two investigator-counselors.

———. "Rape Trauma Syndrome." *American Journal of Psychiatry* 131 (September 1974):981–986.   *B,G*

Interviewed and followed 146 patients admitted during a one-year period to the emergency ward of a city hospital with a presenting complaint of having been raped. Based upon an analysis of the 92 adult women rape victims in the sample, existence of a rape trauma syndrome is documented, and its symptomatology as well as that of two variations—compounded reaction and silent reaction—is delineated.

———. "Rape Victim Counseling: The Legal Process." *Journal of National American Women Deans, Administrators and Counselors* 38 (1974): 24.   *B,F,G*

———. *Rape: Victims of Crisis*. Bowie, Md.: Robert J. Brady, 1974. *C,G*

———. "Sexual Assault: Signs and Symptoms." *Journal of Emergency Nursing*, March/April 1975, p. 10.   *B,G*

————. "Sexual Trauma of Children and Adolescents." *Nursing Clinics of North America* 10 (1975):551.   E
————. "Coping Behavior of the Rape Victim." *American Journal of Psychiatry* 133 (April 1976):413–418.   B,G

Data from ninety-two women having rape trauma show that most of them used verbal, physical, or cognitive strategies when threatened, although thirty-four were physically or psychologically paralyzed. The actual rape prompted coping behaviors in all but one victim.

————. "Child Sexual Assault by a Family Member: Decisions Following Disclosure." *Victimology: An International Journal* 2 (1977):236–250.
                                                                    E

Forty-four cases of child sexual assault by a family member were analyzed to determine the key decision points and issues faced by the victim and family. In eight cases, decisions were made for the family by the hospital for court-ordered foster placement. Decisions made by the family included handling the situation as a family matter, mental-health intervention, and/or legal intervention. A major issue facing families is whether to place their loyalty in the child or in the offender.

————. "Study by Recovering from Rape." *Human Behavior* 7 (November 1978):59–60.   B,G
————. "Adaptive Strategies and Recovery from Rape." *American Journal of Psychiatry* 136 (1979):1278–1282.   B,G

A follow-up study of eighty-one victims was conducted to analyze the effect of adaptive or maladaptive response to rape on recovery over a four-to-six-year period. It was found that victims recovering fastest used more-adaptive strategies, including positive self-assessment; defense mechanisms of explanation, minimization, suppression, and dramatization; and increased action.

————. "Rape: Disclosure to Parental Family Members." *Women and Health* 4 (1979):255–268.   B,G

As part of a longitudinal study, a follow-up was conducted of rape victims four to six years following initial contact. The study analyzes whether victims told parental family members of the rape at the time of the rape and their reasons for telling or not telling.

————. "Rape: Sexual Disruption and Recovery." *American Journal of Orthopsychiatry* 49 (1979):648–657.   B,G

In a longitudinal study of eighty-one adult rape victims reinterviewed four to six years later, effects of the rape on subsequent sexual functioning were analyzed.

Burgess, A.W., and A.T. Laszlo. "Courtroom Use of Hospital Records in Sexual Assault Cases." *American Journal of Nursing* 77 (4 January 1977):64–68.   *B,F*

Burke, R.J., and T. Weir. "Patterns in Husbands' and Wives' Coping Behaviors." *Psychological Reports* 44 (1979):951–956.   *A,B*

To examine patterns in husbands' and wives' coping behaviors, eighty-five husband-wife pairs indicated separately how likely they were to use each of thirty-eight coping responses.

Burnham, D. "The Life of the Afro-American Woman in Slavery." *International Journal of Women's Studies* 1 (1978):363–377.   *H*

The life of the Afro-American woman in slavery is reconstructed from slave narratives, recorded interviews with ex-slaves, and reports of observers. The reports deal with the work of slaves in the field, household, and factory with the living conditions provided for the slaves.

Burnham, J.T. "Incest Avoidance and Social Evolution." *Mankind* 10 (December 1975):93–98.   *E*

Burns, S. "On Being an Abused Wife . . . and Living in Fear." *Mademoiselle* 85 (December 1979):56.   *A*

Burr; Hill; Nye and Reiss. *Contemporary Theories about the Family*. New York: Free Press, 1977.   *H*

Burt, M.R. "Attitudes Supportive of Rape in American Culture." Final Report of Minnesota Center for Social Research. Minneapolis: University of Minnesota, 1978. NIMH Grant R01-MH-I9023.   *G*

One hundred social-service workers, 598 Minnesota adults (eighteen years old and over), and thirty-six rapists were interviewed to determine the distribution of rape-relevant attitudes in these populations. The effects of the respondents' age, sex, class, and education on rape-relevant attitudes were determined.

———. "Cultural Myths and Supports for Rape." *Journal of Personality and Social Psychology* 38 (1980):217–230.   *B,G*

The rape is described; hypotheses are derived from social-psychological and feminist theory that acceptance of rape myths can be predicted from attitudes such as sex-role stereotyping, adversarial sexual beliefs, and sexual conservatism; and acceptance of interpersonal violence is tested.

Burton, G., and H.M. Kaplan. "Group Counseling in Conflicted Marriages Where Alcoholism Is Present: Clients' Evaluation of Effectiveness." *Journal of Marriage and the Family* (February 1968):74–79.   *C*

Burton, J.W. "Women and Men in Marriage: Some Atuot Texts." *Anthropos* 75 (1980):710–720.   *A*

Marriage in Atuot society, a pastoral society in Africa, is described and the causes for its dissolution examined.

Burton, R.V. "Folk Theory and the Incest Taboo." *Ethos* 1 (1973):504–516.   *C,E*

Busch, R.D., and J. Gundlach. "Excess Access and Incest: A New Look at the Demographic Explanation of the Incest Taboo." *American Anthropologist* 79 (December 1977):912–914.   *E*

Bush, J.P. "Sex Offenses." *Australian Family Physician* 7 (1978):1433–1441.   *E,G*

Buss, A.H. *The Psychology of Aggression.* New York: Wiley & Sons, 1961.   *H*

———. "Physical Aggression in Relation to Different Frustrations." *Journal of Abnormal and Social Psychology* 67 (1963):1–7.   *H*

Butler, S. *Conspiracy of Silence: The Trauma of Incest.* San Francisco: New Guide, 1978.   *E*

Incestuous assault as one of the major sources of psychological trauma for children and adolescents is examined. It is felt that professionals who provide services to children should become more sensitive to the possibility of incestuous assault when they have evidence of child abuse.

Butts, B. *Rape and Infidelity.* New York: Vantage Press, 1979.   *G*

Buzawa, E.S. "Legislative Responses to the Problem of Domestic Violence in Michigan." *Wayne Law Review* 25 (March 1979):859–881.   *F*

Michigan legislation dealing with spouse abuse is described and analyzed, and suggestions for future domestic-violence legislation are offered.

Cain, A.A., and M. Kravitz. "Victim/Witness Assistance—A Selected Bibliography." Rockville, Md.: NCJRS Microfiche Program, 1978.   *B*

Documents on victim/witness services, compensation, and restitution are cited in a two-part annotated bibliography compiled from the collection of the NCJRS.

Calhoun L. G.; J.W. Selby; A. Cann; and G.T. Keller. "The Effects of Victim Physical Attractiveness and Sex of Respondent on Social Reactions to Victims of Rape." *British Journal of Social & Clinical Psychology* 17 (June 1978):191–192.   *G*

Results of a study with forty-five female and twenty-eight male college students are in agreement with other data showing sex differences in social reactions to victims of rape. Men were more likely than women to perceive the victim as playing a role in her own assault.

Calhoun, L.G.; J.W. Selby; G.T. Long; and S. Laney. "Reactions to the Rape Victim as a Function of Victim Age." *Journal of Community Psychology* 8 (1980):172–175.   G

The effects of the age of a victim on social reactions to a rape incident were investigated to test the hypothesis that victims of extreme age range would be perceived as playing less of a causal role in their attack than victims in the middle-age range.

Calhoun, L.G.; J.W. Selby; and L.J. Warring. "Social Perception of the Victim's Causal Role in Rape: An Exploratory Examination of Four Factors." *Human Relations* 29 (June 1976):517–526.   G

Sex of respondent, victim's history of rape, number of rapes in the area, and victim acquaintance with the rapist were investigated by having samples respond to a standardized videotape of an interview with a presumed victim.

California Department of Justice. *Handbook on Domestic Violence.* Los Angeles: California Office of the Attorney General Crime Prevention Unit, 1979.   A,B,G

The information provided is intended to assist victims, families, law-enforcement officers, and other people who aid victims to learn the legal protections and emergency and long-range victim services provided in California.

California. Senate. Subcommittee on Nutrition and Human Needs. *Hearings on Marital Violence and Family Violence.* 21 July 1975.   C
California Unemployment Insurance Appeals Board. Decision of the Referee, Case #SJ-5963. Sacramento, 1975a.   B,C
California Unemployment Insurance Appeals Board. Benefit Decision, Case #75-5225. Sacramento, 1975b.   B,C
Calvert, R. "Criminal and Civil Liability in Husband-Wife Assaults." In *Violence in the Family*, edited by S.K. Steinmetz and M.A. Straus. New York: Dodd, Mead, 1974.   B,F

References may be found in ancient law to the right of the husband to use physical punishment on his wife. It is assumed that the long series of laws that have gradually given more and more equal rights to women were the means by which the rights of the husbands to use physical force on their wives were called to a halt. This article makes it clear that the change did not occur in this way. If there has been a reduction in wife beating, it has come about through gradual increases in the socioeconomic level and education of the population rather than by legislation. The decisions reached by judges and juries have tended to reflect these changes in social practice.

———. "Is Rape What Women Really Want." *Mademoiselle*, March 1974,
p. 134.   G

Campbell, P.B. "Are We Encouraging Rape?" *Crisis Intervention* 6 (1975):
20–27.   G

Presents evidence that society encourages rape through perpetration of
stereotypic sex roles, discrimination toward the rape victim, and the development of aggression in men and passivity in women.

Cann, A.; L.G. Calhoun; J.W. Selby. "Attributing Responsibility to the
Victim of Rape: Influence of Information Regarding Past Sexual Experience." *Human Relations* 32 (January 1979):57–67.   G

Information regarding a rape victim's past sexual behaviors was presented
to 128 college students in specially constructed newspaper stories describing testimony at the trial. Findings are discussed in reference to attribution-
theory predictions and recent interest in laws regarding rape.

"Capital Punishment for Rape Constitutes Cruel and Unusual Punishment
When No Life Is Taken or Endangered." *Minnesota Law Review* 56
(1971):95.   B,F,G

Caplan, N., and S.D. Nelson. "Who's to Blame?" *Psychology Today* 99
(November 1974):104.   G

Capraro. "Sexual Assault of Female Children." *Annals of New York Academy of Science* 142 (1967):817.   E

Capuzzi, D., and A. Hensley. "Rape—Relationships and Recovery." *Personnel and Guidance Journal* 58 (1979):133–138.   B,C,G

A group-counseling model for use at the end of crisis-oriented rape-counseling programs is described. The model gives factual information and
process following rape and aids in the expression of interpersonal feelings
that result from the attack.

Carbary. "Treating Terrified Rape Victims." *Journal of Practical Nursing*,
February 1974, p. 20.   B,G

Carder, J.H. "Families in Trouble." Paper presented at the Twenty-fourth
International Institute on the Prevention and Treatment of Alcoholism,
1978.   A,B

The family structure, socioeconomic status, and abuse factors are reported
for battered women, using data obtained from interviews with abused
women who called a crisis center over a three-month period.

Carlson, B.E. "Battered Women and Their Assailants." *Social Work*, 22
(November 1977):455–465.   A

Data on incidence of assault are presented, and sources of family violence, its relationship to alcoholism, and problems involved in leaving the assailants are also discussed. In addition to improving men's and women's ability to support themselves and their families, the author recommends that efforts be made to eliminate the beliefs that men's status must be higher than women's, that men who are not dominant are not masculine and not adequate, and that physical power and coercion are valid means of solving disputes.

Carns, D. "Talking about Sex: Notes on First Coitus and the Double Sexual Standard." *Journal of Marriage and Family* 35 (1973):677–688.   B
Carper, J.M. "Emergencies in Adolescents: Runaways and Father-Daughter Incest." *Pediatric Clinics of North America* 26 (1979):883–894. E
Carr, B.F. *Five Years of Rape and Murder.* New York: Dutton, 1979. *B,G*
——. *Woman Abuse Bibliography.* Monticello, Ill.: Vance Bibliographies, 1979.   *A,B*

This bibliography lists references on abuse of women in order to aid efforts at identification, intervention, and prevention of the woman-abuse phenomenon.

Carrow, D. *Rape: Guidelines for a Community Response.* Washington, D.C.: U.S. Government Printing Office, 1980.   B,G
Carver, C.A. "Psychological Androgyny and Its Relationship to Jurors' Decisions in Sexual Assault Cases." *Dissertation Abstracts International* 39(9-B):4645–4646P, March 1979.   B

Psychological androgyny of jurors, decisions regarding victim and defendant responsibility, and punishment in sexual-assault cases.

Center for Law and Health Sciences. Boston: Boston University.   B

Research includes legal and ethical implication of health-care delivery, health insurance, human experimentation, rights of adolescents in mental-health treatment, rape, patient rights, child development, environmental health, health-care delivery, and the dying.

Centre of Criminology. Toronto: University of Toronto.   B

Research in all aspects of criminology including mentally disordered offenders, violence in society, rape, public attitudes to crime, and legal education in schools.

"Certification of Rape under the Colorado Abortion Statute." *University of Colorado Law Review* 42 (1970):121.   F,G

Chafetz, J.S. *Masculine/Feminine or Human?* Itasca, Ill.: F.E. Peacock, 1974.   *A*

Chaneles. "Child Victims of Sexual Offenses." *Federal Probation*, 31 (June 1967):52.   *E*

Chapman, J.R. "Economics of Women's Victimization." In *Victimization of Women*, edited by Chapman and M. Gates. Beverly Hills, Calif.: Sage Publications, 1978.   *A,D,E,H*

The economic factors contributing to and the costs of wife beating, child sexual abuse, rape, prostitution, pornography, and harassment and biased medical care are assessed. Costs faced by victims are discussed.

Chapman, J.R., and M. Gates. *Women into Wives: The Legal and Economic Impact of Marriage*. Beverly Hills, Calif.: Sage Publications, 1977.   *H*
————. *The Victimization of Women*. Beverly Hills, Calif.: Sage Yearbooks in Women's Policy Studies, 1978.   *H*

The different aspects of abuse, sexual and otherwise, of women and children are examined. Chapters cover the following topics: the role of men in the victimization of women, rape, sexual abuse of children, battered women, treatment alternatives for battered women, victimization of prostitutes, sexual harassment, the side-effects of sex bias, the economics of women's victimization, and the inevitability of victimization.

Chappell, D. "Forcible Rape and Criminal Justice System." In *Sexual Assault*, edited by M. Walker and S. Brodsky. Lexington, Mass.: Lexington Books, D.C. Heath and Company, 1976.   *F,G*

Chappell, D. "Forcible Rape and the Criminal Justice System—Surveying Present Practices and Projecting Future Trends." *Crime and Delinquency* 22 (1976):125.   *F,G*

Chappell, D. "Victim Selection and Apprehension from the Rapist's Perspective: A Preliminary Investigation." *Victimology: An International Journal* 2 (1977):55–56.   *G*

The study indicated that stranger against stranger, rape was frequently a planned event, with the offender selecting locations for victim contact that minimized the chances of his apprehension and maximized the vulnerability of the woman.

Chappell, D. "Rape in Marriage—The South Australian Experience." In *Violence in the Family—A Collection of Conference Papers*, 1980.   *A*

New south Australian legislation with regard to marital rape and the reasons for its lack of impact are discussed.

Chappell, D., and F. Fogary. *Forcible Rape*. Washington, D.C.: Depart-
ment of Justice, Law Enforcement Assistance Administration, National
Institute of Law Enforcement and Criminal Justice, 1978.   G
Chappell, D.; G. Geis; and F. Forgarty. "Forcible Rape: Bibliography."
Journal of Criminal Law and Criminology 64 (June 1974):248–263.
                                                                  B,G

> Demonstrates a large change of emphasis between pre-1969 and post-1969
> materials. Earlier cases deal mainly with aspects of protecting an accused
> rapist from vindictive charges, while the more recent literature stresses the
> protection of the rape victim.

Chappell, D.; R. Geis; and G. Geis. "Forcible Rape: A Comparative Study
of Offenses Known to the Police in Boston and Los Angeles." In *Studies
in the Sociology of Sex*, edited by J.M. Henslin. New York: Columbia
University Press, 1971.   B,G
Chappell, D.; R. Geis; and G. Geis. "Forcible Rape: The Crime, the
Victim, and the Offender. New York: Columbia University Press,
1977.   C,G

> A collection of behavioral-science studies of rape is presented. Among the
> topics discussed are rape and the law, a statistical analysis of rape, rape and
> race, the rights of the accused, judicial attitudes toward victims, compara-
> tive incidence of rape in various major cities, the psychology of rapists,
> traumatization of the victim, hitchhiking and rape, crisis intervention for
> the rape victim, and the Philadelphia Rape Victim Project.

Chappell, D., and J. Monahan, eds. *Violence and Criminal Justice*. Lex-
ington, Mass.: Lexington Books, D.C. Heath and Company, 1975. H
Charney, I.W. "Love and Hate, Honor and Dishonor, Obey and Disobey."
In *Cooperative, Nonviolent Tension: The Need for a Revised Marriage
Contract and a Revised Offer of Help by the Marriage Counselor*. Pre-
sented to the Family Workshop, Family Service of Chester County,
Pennsylvania, 27 September 1967.   A,B
———. *Marital Love and Hate*. New York: Macmillan, 1973.   A
Chase. "Rape and Police Professionalism." *Carolina Law* 24 (1974):67.
                                                                  B,C,G
Chesler, P. *Women and Madness*. New York: Avon, 1973.   A,D,G,H
Chesler, P., and E. Goodman. *Women, Money and Power*. New York:
William Morrow and Company, 1976.   D
Chester, R. "Health and Marriage Breakdown." *British Journal of Preven-
tive and Social Medicine* 25 (November 1971):231–235.   A,H
Chester, R., and J. Streather. "Cruelty in English Divorce: Some Empiri-
cal Findings." *Journal of Marriage and the Family*, 1972, 706–712.
                                                                  A,H

Child. "Ohio's New Rape Law: Does It Protect Complainant at the Expense of the Rights of the Accused?" *Akron Law Review* 9 (1975):337. *F*

Childhood Sexual Abuse. Schiller Park, Ill.: Motorola Teleprograms, Incorporated, 1977.   *E*

> Presents in-depth cases of four victims of childhood sexual abuse. The women describe their abuse experience during a weekend reality therapy group in an attempt to relive and begin to cope with their feelings about the mistreatment. 16mm film, color.

"Children of Incest." *Newsweek*, 9 October 1972, p. 58.   *E*

Children's Bureau. U.S. Department of Health, Education and Welfare. *Bibliography on the Battered Child.* Washington, D.C., 1969.   *B,E*

Chimbos, P.D. *Marital Violence—A Study of Interspouse Homicide.* Washington, D.C.: Law Enforcement Assistance Administration Library, 1978.   *A,H*

> Interviews with thirty-four men and women who had killed their legal or common-law spouses are the basis of an analysis of the social conditions and marital conflict that lead to lethal violence in Canada.

Chiswick Women's Aid. *Nemesis*, nos. 1 et seq. (1974b).   *B*

Chiswick Women's Aid. *Women's Aid and the Problem of Battered Women.* 1974a.   *B*

Chiswick Women's Aid and Inter-Action. *A Strategy for Chiswick Women's Aid*, 1973.   *B*

Chriss, N.C. "Can a Black Be Acquitted? Indictment of R. Holloway." *Nation* 211 (28 December 1970):690–691.   *G*

Christensen, H.T. *Handbook of Marriage and the Family*. Chicago: Rand McNally, 1964.   *B*

Christensen, K. "Sexual Harassment—the Quiet Job Threat." *Chicago Daily News*, 20 August, pp. 33, 38.   *D*

Cicourel, A.V. *Method and Measurement in Sociology*. New York: Free Press Studies in Argentine Fertility, 1967; also Wiley & Sons, 1967. *H*

Citizens Advice Bureau. "Experience of the Problem of Battered Women." Memorandum for the DHSS. London W.C.1.: National Citizen's Advice Bureau Council.   *A*

City of Oakland Police Services. "Techniques of Dispute Intervention." Training Bulletin III-J, 19 June 1975.   *B,C*

Clark, G.L. *Domestic Relations, Cases and Text*. New York: Bobbs-Merrill Company, 1954.   *B,F*

Clark, H.H. *The Law of Domestic Relations in the United States*. Saint Paul, Minn.: West Publishing Company, 1963.   *B,F*

Clark, L.M. "Group Rape in Vancouver and Toronto." *Canada's Mental Health* 28 (1980):9–12. G

The approach to rape research and to the rape offender is criticized for having failed to take into account group rape occurrences. A comparison of rape statistics in Toronto and Vancouver indicates that in both cities single-offender cases were classified as found at twice the rate of multiple-offender cases.

Clark, T.P. "Counseling Victims of Rape." *American Journal of Nursing* 76 (December 1976):1964. C,G

Clarke, H.I. *Social Legislation*, 2d ed. New York: Appleton-Century-Crofts, 1957. F

Claster, D., and D.S. David. "The Resisting Victim: Extending the Concept of Victim Responsibility." *Victimology: An International Journal* 2 (1977):56–57. H

The concept of resistance is examined within the theoretical framework of victimology. It is argued that the range of victim responsibility should extend from victim as precipitator to victim as register, with the innocent victim in the middle.

Cleaver, E. "White Woman, Black Man: The Allegory of the Black Eunuchs." In *Soul on Ice*, edited by E. Cleaver. New York: Dell, 1968. B

Climent, C.E., and F.R. Ervin. "Historical Data in the Evaluation of Violent Subjects." *Archives of General Psychiatry* 27 (1972):621–624. B

Clinard, M. *Sociology of Deviant Behavior*. New York: Rinehart, 1959. B

———. Summary of Comparative Crime Victimization Surveys: Some Problems and Results." *Victimology: An International Journal* 2 (1977): 57. B

Problems encountered in cross-cultural crime victimization surveys are discussed. On the basis of surveys conducted in several countries, differences are found to exist in perceptions of behavior considered to be a crime.

"Closing Chiswick's Open Door." *Economist* (Great Britain) 266 (28 January 1978):25. B

Coates, C.J., and D.J. Leong. *Conflict and Communication for Women and Men in Battering Relationships*. Washington, D.C.: U.S. Department of Justice, Law Enforcement Assistance Administration, 1980. H

A sample of forty-four women and nineteen men who have been involved in family violence was interviewed to determine characteristics of battered women and abusive patterns of violence, positive aspects of the relationship, and communication styles.

Cobb, K., and N. Schauer. "Legislative Note: Michigan's Criminal Sexual Assault Law." *Journal of Law Reforms* 81 (1974):221.   F

"Code R, for Rape." *Newsweek*, 13 November 1972, p. 75.   B, G

Cohen. "Sexual Molestations in Hospitals: The Role of the Physician and Other Suggestions of Management." *Clinic Pediatrics* 3(1964):689. C, G

Cohen, A.K. Delinquent Boys: The Culture of the Gang. Glencoe, Ill.: Free Press, 1955.   H

Cohen, D. "To Avoid Rape, Be Ready to Struggle at Home." *Psychology Today* 12 (1978):124–125.   G

Cohen, J.A. "Theories of Narcissism and Trauma." *American Journal of Psychotherapy* 35 (January 1981):93–100.   E

Presents a theoretical point of view that emphasizes the effects of psychic trauma on the organization of memory, drives, and affects. Using illustrative material from a case of father-daughter incest, the usefulness of this point of view for understanding pathogenesis and the process of psychotherapeutic change is demonstrated.

Cohen, L., and C. Backhouse. "Putting Rape in Its Legal Place." (Reform of Canadian Law) *Macleans* 93 (30 June 1980):6.   F, G

Cohen, M.; R. Garofalo; and R. Boucher. "Family Interaction Patterns, Drug Treatment, and Change in Social Aggression." *Archives of General Psychiatry* 19 (July 1968):50–56.   H

———. "The Psychology of Rapists." *Seminars in Psychiatry* 3 (August 1971):307–327.   G

Discusses the laws, punishments, treatment, and typology of rapists. Three clinical classifications of rape are proposed in which the aim of the rape is the differentiating factor: (1) aggressive, (2) sexual, and (3) sex-aggression diffusion.

Cohen, S. "Funding Family Violence Programs—Sources and Potential Sources for Federal Monies." *Prosecutor* 15 (November/December 1979):128–132.   B

A descriptive listing of federal funding sources for shelters and other support services to victims of domestic violence is submitted as an aid to establishing assistance services in the family-violence field.

Cohen, Y. "The Disappearance of the Incest Taboo." *Human Nature* 1 (1978):72–73.   E

The reduction in incest taboos in contemporary industrial societies is discussed. Because the sources of the taboo lie in patterns of trade, prohibitions become less encompassing as society becomes more complex.

Cohn. "Succumbing to Rape?" In *Rape Victimology*, edited by L. Schultz. 1975.   *G*

Cohn, E.S.; L.H. Kidder; and J. Harvey. "Crime Prevention vs. Victimization Prevention: The Psychology of Two Different Reactions." *Victimology* 3 (1978):285–296.   *H*

The results of two studies of reactions to crime are presented. In the first, eighty-one residents of a white working-class neighborhood in Philadelphia were interviewed. Those who belonged to the community organization reported less fear of crime and more control over crime than those who did not belong. In the second study, thirty-seven women enrolled in a personal defense course reported feeling more active, brave, in control, independent, and so on and were less worried about being home alone or out after dark after the course.

Colburn, K. "Hedonism, Incest and the Problem of Difference." *Theory and Society* 2 (1975):351–374.   *E*

Coleman, D.H. *Alcohol Abuse and Family Violence*. Rockville, Md.: National Institute of Mental Health, 1979.   *H*

This overview of alcohol-abuse studies and family violence found that true alcoholics rather than those disinhibited by alcohol are in effect anesthetized and unlikely to commit violent acts.

Coleman, K.H.; M.L. Weinman; and P. Hsi-Bartholomew. "Factors Affecting Conjugal Violence." *Journal of Psychology* 105 (July 1980): 197–202.   *H*

Presents information on thirty couples involved in marital violence within a sample of sixty couples who were seeking psychiatric assistance for marital conflict.

Coles, F.S. "Social Scorn and the Rape Victim." *Human Behavior* 7 (May 1978):70.   *G*

Coles, R. *Uprooted Children*. New York: Harper & Row, 1970.   *E*

Colianni, E. "How They Caught the Oakland-Shadyside Rapist." Pittsburgh, 19 July 1974, p. 36.   *B,G*

———. "Battered Wives: A New Issue Comes out of the Closet." *Pittsburgh Forum* 4 (11 October 1974):1 and 11.   *A*

Illustrates a local case history and experience with local office and police officials.

"Comment: Employment Discrimination-Sexual Harassment and Title VII." *New York University Law Review* 51 (April 1976):148–167. *D*

A Community Fights Rape. Schiller Park, Ill.: MTI, 1979. 16 mm sound film, 12 mins.   *B,G*

Spotlights San Jose, California, a community whose awareness of and statistics for legal action against rape are far higher than the national norm.

Connell, H.M. "Incest—A Family Problem." *Medical Journal of Australia (Glebe)* 2 (1978):362.   *B,E*

The subject of incest is examined in a discussion that views it as only one fact of gross family pathology. The family in which incest occurs usually is large and living in poor socioeconomic and overcrowded conditions.

Conran, M.B. "Incestuous Failure: Studies of Transference Phenomena with Young Psychotic Patients and Their Mothers." *International Journal of Psycho-Analysis* 57 (1976):477–481.   *E*

Reports observations of twenty disorganized psychotic boys in a hospital ward. A strategy of treatment is described that involved the patient-nurse relationship and work with the parents. It is suggested that a significant factor in the development of schizophrenia is a failure of the early mother-son incestuous relationship.

———. "Schizophrenia as Incestuous Failure Issues." *Mental Health* 56 (1978):55–64.   *E*

Constantine, J., and L. Constantine. "Jealousy—The Marriage Killer." *Penthouse Forum*, March 1974, 59–60.   *H*

The Constitutionality of the Death Penalty for Non-Aggravated Rape. (*Ralph* v. *Warden*), 1972 Washington *University Law Quarterly*, 1972. *F*

Cook, M.J. "Battered Wives and the Law." *Law Society Gazette* 73 (1976): 123.   *A,F*

Cooke, G. "The Behavioral Treatment of the Rapist." *Prison Journal* 58 (1978):47–52.   *B,G*

Coon, L.F. "Felony Assaults in Family Court." *Criminal Law Bulletin*, May 1965.   *F*

Cooper, H.A. "The Terrorist and the Victim." *Victimology* 1 (Summer 1976):229–239.   *H*

Suggests that terror and terrorism are extraordinarily difficult concepts to handle in normative terms. Terror is certainly an element in the commission of many easily identifiable crimes of universal recognition and condemnation.

Cooper, J.K. "Decriminalization of Incest—New Legal Clinical Responses." In *Family Violence: An International and Interdisciplinary Study*, edited by J.M. Eekelaar and S. Katz. Toronto: Butterworths, 1978, pp. 518–528.   *E*

Cooper, K.D. "Incest in Today's Society: An Orientation for Graduate Students in the Helping Professions." *Dissertation Abstracts International* 40 (11-A), May 1980:5730.   *B,E*

Development of functional incest curriculum, awareness of and attitudes toward incest, and graduate students in helping professions.

Coote, A. "Police, the Law, and Battered Wives." *Manchester Guardian*, 23 May 1974, p. 11.   *A,C,F*

———. "Hellbent on Destroying the Domestic Violence Act." *New Statesman* 95 (16 June 1978):814.   *H*

Coote, A., and T. Gill. *Women's Rights, A Practical Guide*. New York: Penguin, 1974.   *B,F*

Copeland et al. *Sexual Abuse of Children*. San Francisco: Queen's Beach Found, September 1976.   *E*

"Coping with Crime." *Christianity Today* 19 (6 June 1975):30–31.   *B*

Corea, G. "Northern Ireland: The Violence Isn't All in the Street." *Ms.* 8 (July 1979):94.   *B*

Corfman, E. "Family Violence and Child Abuse." Rockville, Md.: NCJRS Microfiche Program, 1979.   *B,H*

Three papers on family violence and child abuse focus on physical violence in families, child-abuse research, and treatment approaches for abused children and their families.

Corin, J. *Mating, Marriage and the Status of Women*. New York: AMS Press, 1976.   *A,D*

Cormier, B.M. "Psychodynamics of Homicide Committed in a Marital Relationship." *Corrective Psychiatry and Journal of Society Therapy* 8 (1962):187–194.   *A*

Described are some aspects of the psychopathology of men who have killed a woman with whom they are bound either in a true marriage or in an equivalent relationship. In the eight cases investigated, the murder was neither a product of mental illness nor motivated by material gain or similar consideration. It was committed as a result of a deep-seated conflict between the individuals involved.

Cormier, B.M., and P. Boulanger. "Life Cycle and Episodic Recidivism." *Canadian Psychiatric Association Journal* 18 (August 1973):283–288. *B*

Presents a study of episodic recidivism and recurrent psychopathological states in two incestuous families to illustrate the psychosexual and psycho-social aspects of deviant behavior in the nuclear group of society.

Cormier, B.M. and S. Sickert. "Forensic Psychiatry: The Problem of the Dangerous Sexual Offender." *Canadian Psychiatric Association Journal* 14 (1969):329–335.   G
Coser, L.A. *The Functions of Social Conflict*. Glencoe, Ill.: Free Press, 1956.   B
———. "Some Social Functions of Violence." *Annals of the American Academy of Political and Social Sciences* 364 (1966):8–18.   H
———. *Continuities in the Study of Social Conflict*. New York: Free Press, 1967.   B
Cottell, L. "Rape: The Ultimate Invasion of Privacy." *FBI Law Enforcement Bulletin*, May 1974, pp. 2–4.   G
Council for Exceptional Children. "Child Abuse: A Selective Bibliography." Exceptional Child Bibliography Series, #601. Reston, Va., 1975.
                                                                                 B,E
"Council Gives a House." *Nemesis*, April 1974.   B
Court, J. "Attack on Women." *Australian Nursing Journal* 4 (September 1975):1.   A,G
———. "Violence in the Home." *Social Work Today* 9 (1978):1.   B

Violence in the home, a pattern that is difficult to change since the couple becomes locked in a negative interactive process reflecting the hierarchy of power in the family, is reviewed. Children are physically powerless, and the weaker marital partner often employs the same techniques the child uses to survive.

Courtois, C.A. "Characteristics of a Volunteer Sample of Adult Women Who Experienced Incest in Childhood or Adolescence." *Dissertation Abstracts International* 40(6):3194-A, 1979.   B

Characteristics of a volunteer sample of thirty adult women who experienced incest in childhood or adolescence were investigated via structured interviews.

———. "The Incest Experience and Its Aftermath." *Victimology* 4 (1979): 337–347.   E

The incest experience and its long-and short-term psychological sequelae were explored in a voluntary sample of thirty-one women who had incest experiences in childhood or adolescence. Compared to three previous studies, the women in this sample differed in that the majority of their incestuous encounters were cross-generational, involved different types of sexual activity, and were begun at an older age.

————. "Victims of Rape and Incest." *Counseling Psychologist* 8 (1979): 38–40.   E

> Discusses the counseling of victims of rape or incest. Research indicates that the incidence of these crimes is increasing. At the same time, attitudes toward victims are changing. Counselors may become involved with rape or incest victims during the crisis stage immediately following the assault or during the reorganization period that follows, during which the victim recovers from the experience. Treatment is predicated on the personal situation and characteristics of the individual client. General principles are recommended as guidelines for the knowledge base, skills, and attitudes required by counseling victims of rape or incest.

Craft, M. "The Natural History of Psychopathic Disorder." *British Journal of Psychiatry* 115 (1969):39–44.   B
Craven, C. "Rape Victim Strikes Back." *Ebony* 33 (September 1978):154–156.   B,G
Craven, C., and B. Beals, "Crime: Work of Rape Victim." *People* 9 (27 February 1978):97–98.   G,H
Crick, B. *Crime, Rape and Gin.* Buffalo, N.Y.: Prometheus Books, 1974. G
"Crime and the Family—Some Aspects of the Report of the Royal Commission on Human Relationships, Australia." Institute of Criminology, Sydney University Law School, Sydney, Australia, 1979.   A,H

> Papers on child abuse, sexual offenses, family violence, and community justice are presented at a seminar in Australia devoted to issues raised by the report of the royal commission on human relationships.

"The Crime of Incest against the Minor Child and the States Statute on Response." Journal of Family Law. 17(1):93–115, 1978–79.   E,F
"Crimes of Violence." Staff Report to the National Commission on the Causes and Prevention of Violence. Washington, D.C.: U.S. Government Printing Office, 1969, p. 360.   B,H
Cromwell, P.E. "Women and Mental Health." Washington, D.C.: Department of Health, Education, and Welfare, 1974.   G

> A bibliography of materials on women and mental health, including topics such as abortion, aging, alcoholism and drug abuse, contraception, divorce, lesbianism, marriage, menstruation and menopause, prostitution, rape, single motherhood, and the women's liberation movement.

Crowley, C.J.; J. Jordan; L. Iperen; and P. Vennard. "Physically Abused Women and Their Families—The Need for Community Services: Program Development Guide." Trenton: New Jersey Department of Human Services, 1978.   A,B

This preliminary guide to community program development for abused women and their children discusses the scope of the wife-abuse problem, current program-development activity, and recommendations for program development.

Crum. "Counseling Rape Victims." *Journal of Pastoral Care* 28 (1974):112.
                                                                                                                    B,G

An emergency-room chaplain presents a case verbatim of counseling a rape victim. Counseling focused first on the patient's need for help in managing the psychological, social, and legal issues raised by the family and the police and then on her need for recall of the trauma and private reflection on it.

Cryer, L.G. "Group Therapy: An Alternative Treatment Approach for Rape Victims." *Journal of Sex and Marital Therapy* 6 (Spring 1980): 40–46.   *B,G*

Describes a pilot project in which nine rape victims were treated in group therapy. Objective measures of psychological disturbance before and after nineteen weeks of treatment revealed that the victims experienced substantially reduced anxiety, fear, and hostility levels.

————. "Life Change Measurement: An Outcome Evaluation Study of a Public Health Nursing Program to Assist Rape Victims." *Dissertation Abstracts International* 40(11-B):5389, May 1980.   *B,G*

Evaluation of public-health nursing program to assist rape victims.

Cuddeback, G.L. "An Evaluation of the Victim/Witness Advocate Program for Victims and Witnesses of Criminal Acts." *Dissertation Abstracts International.*   *B*

The effectiveness of a victim/witness advocate program implemented in Danville, Illinois, was assessed using survey data obtained from police officers, local prosecutors, and social-agency personnel.

Cummings, E.; I. Cumming; and L. Edell. "Policeman as Philosopher, Guide and Friend." *Social Problems* 12 (1964):276.   *B,C*
Cummings, E. *Systems of Social Regulation.* New York: Atherton Press, 1968.   *B*
Curley, E.M. *Philos and Public Affairs* 5 (Summer 1976):325–60.   *B*
Curtis. "Present and Future Measures of Victimization in Forcible Rape." *Sexual Assault,* 1976, p. 66.   *B,G,H*
Curtis. "Rape, Race, and Culture: Some Speculations in Search of Theory." *Sexual Assault,* 1976, p. 61.   *G*

Curtis. "Victim Precipitation and Violent Crime." *Social Problems* 21 (1974):594.   H

Curtis, D. "The Divorce Furies." *San Francisco Sunday Examiner and Chronicle, Sunday Punch Section,* 6 July 1975.   A,H

Curtis, G.C. "Violence Breeds Violence—Perhaps?" *American Journal of Psychiatry* 120 (1963):386–387.   H

Curtis, L. "For Women Only." *Denver Post,* December 1974.   A,F,G

Curtis, L.A. "Criminal Violence: Inquiries into National Patterns and Behavior." *Dissertation Abstracts International* 33(12-A), (June 1973) 7052.   B,H

National patterns of criminal homicide, aggravated assault, forcible rape, and robbery.

———. "Victim Precipitation and Violent Crime." *Social Problems* 21 (April 1974):594–605.   H

Defines victim precipitation and estimates its incidence in a U.S. national sample of police reports on serious violent crime. Provocation appears not uncommon in criminal homicide and aggravated assault, less frequent but still empirically noteworthy in robbery, and perhaps least frequent in forcible rape.

———. "On a Conservative Mentality and the Dangers of Victimology." *Victimology: An International Journal* 2 (1977):58.   H

In a paper presented at the Second International Symposium on Victimology, held in Boston, September 1976, the risk to the study of victimology from the current conservative mentality in the United States, and the reactions against the antipoverty and anticrime programs, are analyzed.

Dada, H. "A Study of Selected Socio-Economic Variables Associated with Criminal Victimization in Rural Ohio." *Dissertation Abstracts International* 40(1):476-A, 1979.   B,H

Selected demographic and socioeconomic variables associated with criminal victimization in rural Ohio were investigated via analysis of questionnaire responses of 899 heads of households.

Dadrian, V. "An Attempt at Defining Victimology." In E. Viano, *Victims and Society,* edited by E. Viano, pp. 40–42. Washington, D.C. Visage Press, 1976.   H

Dahl, T.S. "Violence of Privacy" (review article). *Acta Sociologica* 18 (1975):269–273.   H

———. "Domestic Violence—Crimes against Women." *Crime and Crime Control in Scandinavia,* 1976–1980, p. 26.   A,G,H

Feminists in Scandinavian countries, particularly Norway, have had some success in convincing officials and the public of the need for legislation enforcing equality of the sexes in both public and private life and of need for crisis centers to aid abused women.

Daniels, R. "Battered Women—The Role of Women's Aid Refuges." *Social Work Today* 9 (1977):10–13.   *A,B*

The program for battered women and their children operated by the national women's aid federation in Great Britain is described. The federation is an affiliation of over 100 groups, some of which offer as many as five refuges for battered women.

Danto, B.K. "Violent Sex and Suicide." *Mental Health and Society* 5 (1978): 1–13.   *G,H*

Violence, sexual deviations, psychosexual behavior, and sexual sadism are discussed. Reviews early literature on the relationships between sexual problems, especially violent sexual ones, and suicide. The relationship between guilt feelings and suicide is viewed from the standpoint of current observations about sexually violent behavior and suicide. It is postulated that sexual perversions constitute a defensive means of coping with internal stress. Suicide is viewed as serving the same aim. Specific violent sexual behaviors such as sexual asphyxia and rape are discussed in terms of suicide.

Daugherty, M.K. "The Crime of Incest against the Minor Child and the States' Statutory Responses." *Journal of Family Law* 17 (1979):93–115.
                                                                          E

Sexual abuse of children within the family is examined, and an analysis of the crime itself is followed by an exploration of the state laws dealing with the crime. The need to distinguish incest from other sexual abuse of the child is urged.

Davenport, J., III, and J.A. Davenport. "Role Playing Helps Rape Victims Prepare for Next Ordeal." *Innovations* 5 (1978):35.   *B,G*

An effort to prepare rape victims for their own encounters with police, lawyers, and others is described. At the rape-crisis center of the Weems Regional Community Mental Health Center in Meridian, Mississippi, rape-crisis workers used role playing to help rape victims deal with the complexities of their predicament.

———. "Role-Playing in a Rape Crisis Center." *Health and Social Work* 5 (1980):65–68.   *B,G*

The ways in which role playing can be used successfully with the rape victim are described. It is suggested that the social worker and the client should be prepared for this type of intervention.

Davenport, W.H. "The Cultural Pattern of Close Consanguinea Matings and Marriages in Old Hawaii." *Social Class and Social Behavior*, 1979.
                                                                           E

The cultural pattern of close Consanguinea matings and marriages in old Hawaii is described and analyzed. The Hawaiian pattern, under certain conditions, permitted—even urged—siblings and other close Consanguinea to mate in what repeatedly has been analyzed as an exception to the universal incest prohibition of sexual relations, mating, and marriage between siblings.

Davidson, T. *Conjugal Crime*. New York: Hawthorne Books.   *A,G,H*
Davies, R.K. "Incest: Some Neuropsychiatric Findings." *International Journal of Psychiatry in Medicine* 9 (1979):117–121.   E

The medical records of twenty-two subjects who were the children or younger members of an incestuous relationship were examined. A higher than expected incidence of abnormal neuropsychiatric findings was found.

Davis, Kerr; Atkin; Holt; and Meek. "The Decision Processes of 6- and 12-Person Mock Juries Assigned Unanimous and Two-Thirds Majority Rules." *Journal of Personality and Social Psychology* 32 (1975):1. *F*
Davis. "Medical Care for the Sexually Assaulted." *Journal of Florida Medical Association* 61 (1974):558.   *B*
Davis, A. "JoAnne Little: The Dialectics of Rape." *Ms.* 3 (June 1975):74–77.   *G*
Davis, A.Y. "Racism and Contemporary Literature on Rape" (review article). *Freedomways* 16 (1976):25–33.   *B,G*
———. "Rape, Racism, and the Capitalist Setting." *Black Scholar* 9 (1978): 24–30.   *G*

It is argued that the incentives for rape are social in nature, being caused by the capitalist system. The infrequent occurrence of rape in socialist countries is cited to show that the roots of the urge to rape lie in social relations of capitalism.

Davis, E.G. *The First Sex*. New York: Putman, 1971.   *C,G,F*
Davis, K. "The Sociology of Prostitution." *American Sociological Review* 2 (1937):744–755.   *A*
Davis, L.J. "Rape and Older Women." In *Rape and Sexual Assault: Management and Intervention*. Germantown, Md.: Aspen Systems, 1980. *G*

The prevalence and problem of victimization of older women and ways to reduce their vulnerability to sexual crime are considered. Special vulnerabilities of older women, types of crimes against older women, characteristics of rapes against older women, and the aftermath of victimization for raped older women are addressed.

Davis, S.K., and P.W. Davis. "Meaning and Process in Erotic Offensiveness: A Study of Some Victims of Exhibitionism." *Victimology: An International Journal* 2 (1977):58–59.   H

In a paper presented at the Second International Symposium on Victimology, held in Boston, September 1976, reactions to the exhibitionist were investigated. Interviews with twenty-four women who had encountered an exhibitionist were conducted to examine the retrospective social meanings associated with the experience.

Davoren, E. "Testimony of Elizabeth Davoren on March 8, 1978." *Domestic Violence*, 270–278, 1978.   A,G

Testimony by a representative of the National Association of Social Workers is presented dealing with domestic violence. The testimony is before the Senate Committee on Child and Human Development.

Day, L.E. "Technical Assistance Project—Domestic Violence." Chicago: Illinois Law Enforcement Commission, 1978.   B

This report on a recent study concerning how law-enforcement agencies handle domestic violence concludes that a low response rate, conflicting answers to some questions, and a low rate of record keeping point to a need for further research.

Deal, R. *Women in Crisis—Help on the Way*. Pittsburgh, Pa.: Know, Incorporated, 1978.   B

Assistance to women who are beaten by their husbands or male friends is needed to provide them with temporary shelter, emotional support, help in finding jobs and housing, and help in obtaining welfare and legal aid.

DeBeauvoir, S. *The Second Sex*. New York: Vintage Books, 1974.   G
DeCourcy, P., and J. DeCourcy. *The Silent Tragedy*. New York: Alfred Publishing, 1973.   E
DeCrow, K. *Sexist Justice*. New York: Random House, 1974.   F
"Defending Yourself against Rape: Excerpts from Our Bodies, Ourselves." *Ladies Home Journal* 90 (July 1973):62.   G
DeFleur, M.L.; W.V. D'Antonio; and L.B. DeFleur. *Sociology: Man in Society*. Glenview, Ill.: Scott, Foresman and Company, 1970.   H

DeFrancis, V., ed. *Protecting the Battered Child*. Denver: American Humane Association, 1962.   E

———. "Protecting the Child Victims of Sex Crimes Committed by Adults." Final report. Denver: *American Humane Association, Children's Division*, 1969.   E

DeGramont, N.R. "Couple-Speak: Rape, True and False." *Vogue* 157 (June 1971):108–109.   G

Del Drago. "The Pride of Inez Garcia." *Ms.*, May 1975, p. 54.   A,G

Delfiner, R. "Battered Wives: The Quiet Crime." *New York Post*, 23 August 1975, p. 21.   A

Delgado, J.N. *Physical Control of the Mind*. New York: Harpers, 1969.G

Delin, B. *The Sex Offender*. Boston: Beacon, 1978.   E

Delsordo, J.D. "Protective Casework for Abused Children." *Children* 10 (November/December 1963):213–218.   E

DeMause, L. *The History of Childhood*. New York: Psychohistory Press, 1974.   E

Deming, R.R. "Advocating the Concept of the Victim-Offender Relationship." *Victimology: An International Journal* 2 (1977):59.   H

The importance of the concept of the victim-offender relationship in any theoretical construct is discussed. The concept of the victim-offender relationship should be examined prior to, at the time of, and after the offense.

Demott, B. "The Pro-Incest Lobby." *Psychology Today* 13 (1980): 11–12, 15–16.   E,F

Recent signs of impatience with the incest taboo and doubts that the taboo ought to retain its force are discussed. A wide range of cultural forces and assumptions involved in this movement are outlined.

Densen, G.J., and S.F. Hutchinson. "Incest and Drug Related Child Abuse: Systematic Neglect by the Medical and Legal Professions." *Contemporary Drug Problems* 6 (1977):135–172.   E

Department of Health and Social Security. "Non-Accidental Injury to Children." Circular LASS 13. Washington, D.C., 1974.   E

Deutsch, H. "The Significance of Masochism in the Mental Life of Women." *International Journal of Psychoanalysis* 11 (1930):48–60.
                                                                D,H

Deutsch, M., and R.M. Krauss. "The Effect of Threat upon Interpersonal Bargaining." *Journal of Abnormal and Social Psychology* 61 (1960): 181–189.   D

"Developing a Pertinent Rape Prevention Program." *Law and Ordinances* 24 (1976):64.   B,G

DeVos, G.A. "Affective Dissonance and Primary Socialization: Implica-

tions for a Theory of Incest Avoidance." *Ethos* 3 (Summer 1975):165–
182.   *B,E*

Contends that, in developing a psychocultural theory, based on the concept
of affective dissonance, both psychological and social structural forces must
be considered to determine why a society inhibits or periodically allows the
appearance of unsanctioned incest behavior.

Dewsbury, A.R. "Battered Wives—Family Violence Seen in General Practice." *Royal Society of Health Journal* 95 (1975):290–294.   *A*
Dicks, H.V. "Conflict in the Family." *New Society* 2 (November 1963):11–
12.   *C,H*
Dietz, C.A., and J.L. Craft. "Family Dynamics of Incest: A New Perspective." *Social Casework* 61 (1980):602–609.   *C,E*

Perceptions of protective workers regarding the relationship between incest and other forms of sexual abuse of children and the role of the mother
in such situations were investigated.

Dimsdale, J.E. *Survivors, Victims, and Perpetrators: Essays on the Nazi
Holocaust.* Washington, D.C.: Hemisphere Publishing Corporation,
1980.   *A,D,E,G,H*

Essays by psychologists, psychiatrists, historians, and sociologists are presented of the psychological impact of the Nazi holocaust.

Dinitz, S.R., and A.C. Clarke. *Deviance: Studies in the Process of Stigmati-
zation and Societal Reaction.* New York: Oxford University Press,
1969.   *C*
Disney, D.C. "I Was a Battered Wife." *Ladies Home Journal* 96 (April
1979):18.   *A*
District of Columbia City Council. Public Safety Committee Task Force on
Rape. Report. Washington, D.C., 9 July 1973.   *B,G*
Divasto, P.; A. Kaufman; R. Jackson; L. Ballen. "Caring for Rape Victims:
Its Impact on Providers." *Journal of Community Health* 5 (1980):204–
208.   *B,G*

The effects of working with and providing counseling services for rape
victims were studied. All of the students reported heightened awareness of
their own vulnerability.

Dobash, R.E., and R.P. Dobash. *Battered Wives: The Case against Patriarchy.* New York: Free Press.   *A*
Dobash, R.E. "The Relationship between Violence Directed at Women
and Violence Directed at Children within the Family Setting." Appen-

dix 38 in the Second Report of the House of Commons Select Committee on Violence in the Family. London: Her Majesty's Stationery Office, 1976.   *C,H*

———. "Negotiation of Daily Life and the Provocation of Violence—A Patriarchial Concept in Support of the Wife Beater." Paper presented at the Ninth World Congress of Sociology, Uppsala, Sweden, August 1978.   *A*

This paper defines and explores implications of the provocation-of-violence concept used by husbands and social-science researchers to explain, and sometimes to defend, wife beating.

Dobash, R.E., and R.P. Dobash. "Violence between Men and Women within the Family Setting." Presented at the Seventh World Congress of Sociology, Toronto, August 1974.   *C,H*

———. "The Importance of Historical and Contemporary contexts in Understanding Marital Violence." Paper presented at the Annual Meeting of the American Sociological Association, New York, 1976.   *C*

———. "Love, Honour and Obey: Institutional Ideologies and the Struggle for Battered Women." Paper presented at the Annual Meeting of the Society for the Study of Social Problems, New York, 1976.   *H*

———. "The Role of the Sociologist in the Struggle of Women against Repression." Paper presented at the Annual Meeting of the American Sociological Association, New York, 1976.   *H*

———. "Wife-Beating—Still a Common Form of Violence." *Social Work Today* 9 (1977):14–17.   *A,H*

Police domestic-relations and violent-offenses statistics for Edinburgh and Glasgow (Scotland) during 1974 are reviewed, and factors relating to wife beating are discussed.

———. "With Friends Like These Who Needs Enemies—Institutional Supports for the Patriarchy and Violence against Women." Paper presented at the Ninth World Congress of Sociology, Uppsala, Sweden, August 1978.   *A*

This paper discusses problems encountered by battered women in getting help from social agencies, doctors, courts, and police, and the effects of common social attitudes about wife beating.

———. "Wives: The Appropriate Victims of Marital Violence." *Victimology: An International Journal* 2 (1978):426–442.   *A*

The historical, legal, religious, and cultural underpinnings of marital violence against women are explored. Evidence is presented from diverse sources to document the prevalence of violence directed at wives in contemporary societies.

————. *Violence against Wives: A Case against the Patriarchy*. New York: Free Press, 1979.   A

Patriarchal domination through force is explored in history, biography, institutional processes, and culture.

Dobash, R.E.; R.P. Dobash; C. Cavanaugh; and M. Wilson. "Wife Beatings: The Victims Speak." *Victimology: An International Journal* 2 (1978):608–622.   A

Excerpts from 3 out of 109 interviews with battered women that give accounts of violent episodes are presented. The incidents recounted are the first violent incidents in a marriage and the two worst incidents.

Dobell, E.R. "Self Defense: Ideas of F. Storaska." *Seventeen* 36 (April 1977):194–195.   A,G

Dodson. "People vs. Rincon-Pineda: Rape Trials Depart the Seventeenth Century—Farewell to Lord Hale." *Tulsa Law Journal* 279 (1975):11.
                                                                            F,G

Dollard, J., et al. *Frustration and Aggression*. New Haven, Conn. Yale University Press, 1939.   C,H

Dominian, J. "Marital Pathology: A Review." *Postgraduate Medical Journal* 48 (September 1972):517–525.   B

This paper considers a selected number of medical and psychological factors related to the etiology and complications of marital pathology. The difficulty of description and definition of marital pathology is recognized.

Dominick, J.R. "The Influence of Social Class, the Family and Exposure to Television Violence on the Socialization of Aggression." *Dissertation Abstracts International* 31(12-A), (June 1971):664.   H

Donadio. "Seven Who Were Raped." *Nursing Outlook* 245 (1974):22. G

Donath, D. *L'evolution de la femme Israelite à fes*. Aix-en-Provence: Faculte de Lettres, 1962.   A

Donovan, R.J. *The Assassins*. New York: Harper & Row, 1955.   G,H

Dormanen, S. "Helping the Victim in a Sample City." *Evaluation and Change* (Special Issue) (1980):16–17.   B

Services offered to victims by public and private agencies in Minneapolis and Hennepin County, Minnesota, are described.

Double Jeopardy. Schiller Park, Ill.: MTI Teleprograms, Incorporated, 1977. 16 mm film, sound, color, 40 min.   *B*

Sensitizes helping professionals to the problems of the child victim during judicial proceeding using case histories.

Dowie, M., and T. Johnston. "A Case of Corporate Malpractice." *Mother Jones* 1 (1976):37.   *F*

Downing, N.E. "An Evaluation of the Effectiveness of a Training Program for Paraprofessional Rape Crisis Hotline Volunteers." *Dissertation Abstracts International* 41(5):1890-B, 1980.   *B*

The effectiveness of a sixteen-hour training program designed for paraprofessional rape-crisis hot-line volunteers is evaluated.

Drapkin, I. "On Human Indifference: Violence, Suffering, Human Rights and the Prison Inmate." *Victimology: An International Journal* 2 (1977):59.   *H*

The extent to which we live in an era of violence, a reign of terror, that affects all levels and members of the human community is discussed.

Drapkin, I., and E. Viano, eds. *Victimology: A New Focus*. Lexington, Mass.: D.C. Heath and Company, 1973.   *H*

Dreifus, C. *Woman's Fate*. New York: Bantam, 1973.   *C*

———. "It Can Happen to Any Woman." *Redbook* 152 (March 1979):35.
                                                                          C,G

Driver, E.D. "Interaction and Criminal Homicide in India." *Social Forces* 40:153–138.   *C*

Article discusses homicide statistics in India. Reports show that 45 percent of all homicides are perpetrated by spouses, parents, and lovers. Attacks usually occurred as a result of the violation of important social norms. This pattern is quite similar to those of Western countries that have been studied.

Drucker, D. "The Common Law Does Not Support a Marital Exception for Forcible Rape." *Women's Rights Law Reporter* 5 (1979):181–200. *G*

Dukes, R.L., and C.L. Mattley. "Predicting Rape Victim Reportage." *Sociology and Social Research* 62 (1977):63–84.   *G*

The findings support a model that suggests that for crimes in which victim fear is a characteristic, if police are perceived as providing a haven for an extremely frightened victim, she is likely to report the crime to them.

Durbin, K. "Wife Beating." *Ladies Home Journal*, June 1974.   *A*

————. "Intelligent Woman's Guide to Sex: D. Martin's Battered Wives."
Mademoiselle, December 1976.   *B*

Durkheim, E. *The Rules of Sociological Method*. Chicago: Free Press,
1938 (French original, 1895).   *B*

————. *Suicide: A Study in Sociology*. London: Routledge & Kegan Paul,
1952 (French original, 1897).   *B*

Dussich, J.P. "The Victim Ombudsman Revisited." *Victimology: An International Journal* 2 (1977):59–60.   *H*

> The implementation of the victim-ombudsman concept is advocated. The
> position could serve as a governmental commission monitoring all victim-
> related activities within a given jurisdiction and insuring that the best
> interests of the victims are protected. The ombudsman could also serve as a
> lobbyist for victims' rights and as a referral service for victims to other
> helping agencies.

Dutton, D.G. "Social Psychological Research and Relevant Speculation on
the Issue of Domestic Violence." In *Female Offender*, 1980.   *B*

> Key research findings on domestic violence are reviewed, and based on the
> findings, program recommendations are offered.

Dweck, C.S., and N.D. Reppucci. "Learned Helplessness and Reinforcement Responsibility in Children." *Journal of Personality and Social
Psychology* 25 (1973):109–116.   *B*

Dweck, C.S.; W. Davidson; and S. Nelson. "Sex Differences in Learned
Helplessness; (II) The Contingencies of Evaluative Feedback in the
Classroom." Paper presented at the meeting of Society for Research in
Child Development, Denver, 1975.   *B*

Dworkin, A. *Woman Hating*. New York: E.P. Dutton, 1974.   *A,H*

Easson, W.E. "De-Glamorize the Rapist." *Journal of Clinical Psychiatry* 39
(1978):180.   *G*

> Factors that promote and encourage the continuing increase in the inci-
> dence of rape in the United States are discussed, and the need to deglamor-
> ize the rapist is emphasized.

Eastman, W. "First Intercourse: Some Statistics on Who, Where, When,
And Why." *Sexual Behavior* 2:22–27.   *G*

Eaton, A.P., and E. Vastbinder. "The Sexually Molested Child: A Plan of
Management." *Clinical Pediatrics* 8 (August 1969):438–441.   *E*

Eaton, J.W. *Culture and Mental Disorders*. Glencoe, Ill.: Free Press, 1955.
   B

Edelhortz, H., and G. Geis. *Public Compensation to Victims of Crime*. New
    York: Praeger, 1974.   H
"Edinburgh Women's Aid." *Newsletter*, 26 February 1975, p. 6.   B
Edmiston, S. "The Wife Beaters." *Woman's Day*, March 1976, pp. 61,
    110–111.   A

    This article reviews the current research in the area of conjugal violence. In
    particular, estimates of the incidence of wife beating and alcoholism are
    discussed. The psychodynamics of violence are also discussed.

————. "If You Loved Me, You Wouldn't Hurt Me." *Redbook* 153 (May
    1979):99–100.   A
Edmunds, M. "Rape Education and Awareness—A Model for Training
    Health Care." *Journal of the American College Health Association* 27
    (1978):40.   G

    At the fifty-sixth Annual Meeting of the American College Health Associa-
    tion held in New Orleans, March 1978, the rape education and awareness
    program at the Indiana University Student Health Service was described.

Edwards, J.N. *Sex and Society*. Chicago: Markham Publishing Company,
    1972.   E,G

    A group of articles covers the following topics: unmarried heterosexual
    relations, homosexuality, prostitution, sex among the postmarried, incest,
    marital sex, and extramarital sex, with an overview by the editor.

Eekelaar, J.M., and S.N. Katz. *Family Violence: An International and
    Interdisciplinary Study*. Toronto: Butterworths, 1978.   B,F

    A series of essays on family violence written by law professors, law-
    enforcement authorities, psychiatrists, and behavioral-science profession-
    als is presented.

Egner, D. "Dish of Legal Sauce: Judge Serves up Surprise." *San Jose
    Mercury*, 5 November 1975, p. 67, Sec. 4C.   F
Ehrenreich, B. And D. English. *Witches, Midwives and Nurses: A History
    of Women Healers*. Old Westbury, N.Y.: Feminist Press.   B
Ehrlich, F.M. "Rape." *New England Journal of Medicine* 298 (1978):167. G

    In a letter to the editor, the semantic interaction between terms *sexual
    dysfunction* and *rape* is addressed. It is maintained that rape itself is a sexual
    dysfunction and that potency or impotence during the act of rape is immate-
    rial to the abnormality of the act itself.

Eibl-Eibesfeldt, I. *Love and Hate: The Natural History of Behavior Patterns*. New York: Library of Human Behavior, 1971.   *A,G*

Eidson, R. "The Constitutionality of Statutory Rape Laws." *UCLA Law Review* 27 (1980):757–815.   *F*

The history and rationale behind statutory-rape laws are examined, and the constitutionality of these laws is measured against the standards of review currently applied in the equal protection context.

Eisenberg, A.D. "Abolishing Cautionary Instructions in Sex Offense Cases: *People* v. *Rincon-Pineda*." *Criminal Law Bulletin* 58 (1976):12.   *G*

———. "Overview of Legal Remedies for Battered Women—Part 1." *Trial* 15 (August 1979):28–31.   *A,F*

Orders of protection, issued under the New York Family Court Act of 1962, are easily and immediately enforceable remedies to the problem of spouse abuse.

Eisenburg, A.D. "The Self-Defense Plea and Battered Women." *Trial* 14 (1978):34–36, 41–42, 68.   *A,F*

The use of the self-defense plea in representing women who have been beaten by their husbands or lovers and who have retaliated with murder is discussed. The failure of the legal system to delineate clearly and provide strong penalties for criminal behavior within the household is described.

———. "Overview of Legal Remedies for Battered Women—Part 2." *Trial* 15 (October 1979):42–45, 60, 69.   *A,F*

Civil remedies for battered women are reviewed with particular focus on restitution, rehabilitation, and victim compensation.

Eisenburg, S.E., and P.L. Micklow. "The Assaulted Wife: 'Catch 22' Revisited." Ann Arbor: University of Michigan Law School. Revised version in *Women's Rights Law Reporter*, June 1976.   *A*

This article reports a study of twenty wife-assault cases in Michigan and focuses particularly on the historical, psychological, cultural, legal, and social forces involved. Although the authors discuss Michigan law in their overview of the legal issues concerning wife assault, the scope of their study is as broad as the problem itself.

Eist, H.I., and A.U. Mandel. "Family Treatment of Ongoing Incest Behavior." *Family Process* 7 (1968):216–232.   *B,C,E*

Describes a three-year period of conjoint therapy for a family of eight with six children. The family began in therapy originally to help the eldest son who had been referred for psychiatric help. However, conjoint exploration revealed a chaotic, tumultuous tangle of relationships among family members and led eventually to divulsion of incestuous behavior among several family members.

Elbow, M. "Theoretical Considerations of Violent Marriages." *Social Casework* 58 (November 1977):515–526.   H

Eldridge, J.E.G. *Max Weber: The Interpretation of Social Reality*, especially Part One, "Sociological Analysis and Research Methodology" London: Michael Joseph, 1970.   B

Elliot, E., and W. Susco. "Legal Briefs: Questions and Answers." *Working Women* 4 (May 1979):10.   F

Ellis, D. "The Marks of Abel: Factors Influencing the Selection of Victims of Interpersonal Violence." Research proposal, York University, Downsview, Ontario (date unknown).   H

Ellis, E.M. "An Assessment of Long-Term Reaction to Rape." *Journal of Abnormal Psychology* 90 (June 1981):263–266.   G

Examined reactions to rape by interviewing twenty-seven female rape victims at least one year after the assault and assessing their current functioning through such measures as the Beck depression inventory and profile of mood states. Victims were significantly more depressed and reported less pleasure in daily activities than twenty-six matched nonvictim controls.

Ellis, H. "The Love Rights of Women." In *Masculine/Feminine*, edited by B. Roszuk and T. Roszoch, pp. 61–67. New York: Harper & Row, 1969.   A

Ellison, K.W. "The 'Just World' in the 'Real World': Attributions about Crime as a Function of Group Membership, Victim Precipitation and Injury." *Dissertation Abstracts International* 37 (8-B):4215, February 1977.   H

Elmer, E. *Children in Jeopardy: A Study of Abused Minors and Their Families*. Pittsburgh, Pa.: University of Pittsburgh, 1967.   E

Elston, E.; J. Fuller; and M. Murch. "Battered Wives: The Problems of Violence in Undefined Divorce Cases." Unpublished paper. Department of Social Work, University of Bristol, 1976.   A

Elwell, M.E. "Sexually Assaulted Children and Their Families." *Social Casework* 60 (1979):227–235.   E

Recent research studies on sexually assaulted children and their families are reviewed to determine what is known currently about the phenomenon. Topics discussed include statistics, definitions, emotional effects, relationship of offender/victim, characteristics of female victims, nature of attack, coercion versus participation, and categories of victimization.

Elwin, V. *Maria Murder and Suicide*, 2d ed. Bombay: Oxford University Press, 1951.   *H*

Ember, M. "On the Origin and Extension of the Incest Taboo." *Behavior Science Research* 10 (1975):249–281.   *E*

Presents new evidence and a model that are consistent with the theory that the prohibition of familial mating became universal and may have originated because of the problem of inbreeding. The new evidence is concerned with why the incest taboo is extended to first cousins; of all the available theories, only the inbreeding theory can explain the cross-cultural variation in cousin marriages.

Emde, R.N.; C. Boyd; and G.A. Mayo. "Family Treatment of Folie à Deux." *Psychiatric Quarterly* 42 (1968):698–711.   *E*

Perhaps the syndrome of Folie à Deux is a result of a disturbed family that tries desperately to stay together; resulting pathological relationships solve something for the family, and the family has a need to maintain them.

Emerson, R.D. *Violence against Wives*. New York: Free Press, MacMillan, 1979.   *A,H*

Emerson, R.M. "Power-Dependence Relations." *American Sociological Review* 27 (1962):31–41.   *H*

Engein, R. "Behavior Modification Techniques Applied to a Family Unit: A Case Study." *Journal of Child Psychiatry and Allied Disciplines* 9 (1968):245–252.   *H*

Engels, F. *The Origin of Family, Private Property and the State*. Moscow: Progress, 1948, p. 42.   *B*

Ennis, P.H. "Crime, Victims, and the Police." *Transaction* (June 1967): 36–44.   *H*

Enos, and Beyer. "Standard Rape Investigation Form." *Virginia Medical Monthly* 101 (1974):43.   *C,F,G*

Enos; Beyer; and Mann. "The Medical Examination of Cases of Rape." *Journal of Foreign Science* 17 (1972):50.   *G*

Erikson, E. *Gandhi's Truth*. New York: W.W. Norton and Company, 1969.   *H*

Estabrook, B.; R. Fessenden; M. Dumas; and T.C. McBride. "Rape on Campus: Community Education and Services for Victims." *Journal of the American College Health Association* 27 (1978):72–74.   *G*

A comprehensive community-education and victim-services program implemented at the University of Massachusetts at Amherst is described.

Etzioni, A. "Violence." In *Contemporary Social Problems*, 3rd ed., edited by R.K. Merton and R.A. Nisbet, chap. 14. New York: Harcourt Brace Jovanovich, 1971. **H**

Evan, W.M. *Organizational Experiments: Laboratory and Field Research.* New York: Harper & Row, 1971. **B**

Evans, H.I. "Psychotherapy for the Rape Victim: Some Treatment Models." *Hospital and Community Psychiatry* 29 (May 1978):309–312. **G**

> Notes that a victim of rape immediately feels an acute disruption of her life-style and coping skills and a great stress on her ego. In order to achieve long-term integration, she must resolve a lack of trust of men, paranoia about her physical safety, guilt, and a grief reaction.

Evans, H.I., and N.B. Sperekas. "Community Assistance for Rape Victims." *Journal of Community Psychology* 4 (October 1976):378–381. **G**

> Describes a program designed to use trained volunteer companions in crisis intervention with rape victims in a public hospital emergency room. A six-week, female-volunteer training course.

Evans, J.L., and G.J. Leger. "Canadian Victimization Surveys: A Discussion Paper." *Canadian Journal of Criminology* 21 (1979):166–183. **G,H**

> A program of methodological research designed to produce victimization data in a cost-efficient manner is described, and the uses to which this data may be put are discussed.

Evans, L.H. *Our Marriage—Duel or Duet?* Old Tappan, N.J.: Revell. **A**

Evans, P. "Patterns of Violence." *New Behavior*, 5 June 1975. **H**

Evans-Pritchard, E.E. *Witchcraft, Oracles and Magic among the Azande.* Oxford: Clarendon Press, 1937. **B**

———. *The Nuer: A Description of the Modes of Livelihood and Political Institutions of a Nilotic People.* Oxford: Clarendon Press, 1940. **B**

———. *Kinship and Marriage among the Nuer.* Oxford: Clarendon Press, 1951. **E**

"Even Experts Lack a Formula for Helping Battered Wives." *Reading Times*, 18 September 1975. **A**

Everly, K. "Premarital Pregnancy—The Quality of Life." *Impact: Journal of National Family Sex Education Week* 1 (1978):22–23. **C,G**

Evrard, F. "Rape: The Medical, Social, and Legal Implications." *American Journal of Obstetrics and Gynecology* 197 (1971):111. **G**

———. "The Sex Offender." In Successful Parole 88, Springfield, 1971. **G**

Ewing, C.P. *Crisis Intervention as Psychotherapy.* New York: Oxford University Press, 1978. **E,H**

An overview of current theory, clinical practice, and evaluation of crisis intervention is presented. Crisis intervention is characterized as a widely applicable form of psychotherapy, and various principles and practices that at present are gathered under that label are questioned.

"Exposed . . . Wife Beating Is Fought." *Reading Times*, 17 September 1975.   A

Eyman, J.S. *How to Convict a Rapist*. New York: Stein & Day, 1980. *F,G*

Faier, J. "Sexual Harassment on the Job." *Harpers Bazaar* 112 (August 1979):90–91.   D

Fairstein. "DICTA: Rape Law Revisions Increase Indictments." *Virginia Law Weekly* 28 (1975):21.   G

Fairweather, G.W. *Methods for Experimental Social Innovation*. New York: Wiley & Sons, 1967.   B

Family Consultant Service with the London Police Force. "Discussion, Evaluation, and Proposed Structure for Continuation of the Program." London, Ontario, September 1975.   B

Family Crisis Center Feasibility Study. Prepared with the aid of the National Council on Alcoholism and submitted to Santa Clara County Alcoholism Advisory Board, 1 July 1975, p. 3.   B,C

Family Violence Program Background Paper. Domestic Violence Prevention and Services, pp. 480–490, 1978.   B

Background information and supplementary explanations are provided for those who wish to apply for grants for LEAA's family-violence program.

Family Violence—The Battering Syndrome. Pleasantville, N.Y.: Audio Visual Narrative Arts, Incorporated, 1978.   A,B,C

The underlying causes of family stress as the trigger for the rising incidence of family violence are examined in this audio cassette and filmstrip series for teachers and educators.

Fanon, F. *The Wretched of the Earth*. New York: Penguin, 1967.   A,H

Faraone, and Modica. "Considerazioni in tema di deflorazione" [Consideration on the subject of defloration]. *Archivio di Medicina Legale, Sociale e Criminologica* 7 (1971):101.   G

Farberow, N.L., and E.S. Shneidman *The Cry for Help*. New York: McGraw-Hill, 1961.   A,C

Farrington, D.P., and D.J. West. "A Comparison between Early Delinquents and Young Aggressives." *British Journal of Criminology* 2 (October 1971):341–358.   C,H

Fasteau, M.F. *The Male Machine*. New York: McGraw-Hill, 1975.   G

Fattah, E.A. "The Use of the Victim as an Agent of Self-Legitimization: Toward a Dynamic Explanation of Criminal Behavior." *Victimology* 1 (Spring 1976):29–53.   H

Most theories of criminal and deviant behavior, whether attempting to define causation or association, offer only static explanations. However, since criminal behavior is dynamic, the author contends that it can be explained only through a dynamic approach, in which the delinquent, the act, and the victim are inseparable elements of a total situation that conditions the dialectic of the antisocial conduct.

————. "Perceptions of Violence, Concern about Crime, Fear of Victimization, and Attitudes to the Death Penalty." *Canadian Journal of Criminology* 21 (1979):22–38.   H

The relationship between violent-crime rates and public attitudes toward the death penalty was examined in Canadian and U.S. samples, along with the influence of fear of victimization and concern about crime on such attitudes.

————. "Some Recent Theoretical Developments in Victimology." *Victimology* 4 (1979):198–213.   H

The current status of victimology is analyzed and recent trends and developments in theoretical and applied victimology are reviewed.

Faulk, M. "Men Who Assault Their Wives." *Medicine, Science, and the Law* 14 (July 1974):180–183.   A

There is virtually no literature on the psychiatric disturbance of men who assault their wives. This paper is an account of twenty-three men seen during the period of remand in custody awaiting trial on charges of seriously assaulting their wives or cohabitees. All the men were interviewed, and information available in the prison records and depositions was incorporated where available. A questionnaire on each subject was then completed by the interviewer.

Faulkner, R. "On Respect and Retribution: Toward an Ethnography of Violence." *Sociological Symposium* 9 (Spring 1973):17–35.   H
Federal Bureau of Investigation Law Enforcement Bulletin, January 1963, p. 27.   F
Federal Bureau of Investigation. *Unified Crime Reports*. Washington, D.C.: U.S. Government Printing Office, 1973.   F
————. *Unified Crime Reports*. Washington, D.C.: U.S. Government Printing Office, 1976.   F

Field, H.S. "Attitudes toward Rape: A Comparative Analysis of Police,
Rapists, Crisis Counselors, and Citizens." *Journal of Personality and
Social Psychology* 36 (February 1978):156–179.   G

This study was designed to examine the dimensionality of rape attitudes;
explore the relationships between perceptions of rape and background
characteristics of rapists, police, female rape-crisis counselors, and citizens;
and determine how these groups might differ with regard to rape attitudes.

———. "Juror Background Characteristics and Attitudes toward Rape."
Law and Human Behavior 2 (1978):73–93.   G

Empirical data on the link between juror characteristics and juror decisions
in rape trials are presented. Using data from 896 citizens serving as mock
jurors, it was found that juror's backgrounds and attitudinal variables are
associated with their decisions.

———. "Rape Trials and Jurors' Decisions: A Psycholegal Analysis of the
Effects of Victim, Defendant, and Case Characteristics." *Law and
Human Behavior* 3 (1979):261–284.   G

Data collected for 896 citizens as mock jurors for a rape case indicate that
the factors of defendant and victim race, victim physical attractiveness and
sexual experience, strength of evidence, and type of rape had significant
effects.

Field, H.S., and N.J. Barnett. "Forcible Rape: An Updated Bibliography." *Journal of Criminal Law and Criminology* 68 (March 1977):146–
156.   G
Fein, L.J. *Politics in Israel.* Boston: Little, Brown, 1967.   A,F,G
Feldman, S.S.; P.E. Gordon; and J.R. Meagher. "The Impact of Rape on
Sexual Satisfaction." *Journal of Abnormal Psychology* 88 (1979):101–
105.   G

Adult rape victims were asked to rate, retrospectively, their satisfaction
with twenty-three sex-related activities prior to and after the rape.

Feldman, S.S., and K. Lidner. "Perceptions of Victims and Defendants in
Criminal Assault Cases." *Criminal Justice and Behavior* 3 (June 1976):
135–150.   A,F,G

Conducted an experiment with 300 undergraduates, equally divided by sex,
to ascertain how male and female samples perceive the victim and the
defendant involved in criminal assault. Characteristics of the victim, type of
crime committed, and sex of the sample were systematically varied.

Feldman, S.S., and G.C. Palmer. "Rape as Viewed by Judges, Prosecutors, and Police Officers." *Criminal Justice and Behavior* 7 (1980):19–40. G

> Beliefs about rape held by judges, prosecutors, and police officers were compared with beliefs held by social-service personnel.

Felice, M. "Follow-Up Counseling of Adolescent Rape Victim." *Medical Aspects of Human Sexuality* 14 (1980):67–68.   G

> Follow-up counseling of adolescent rape victims is discussed. It is important that the physician investigate the adolescent's feelings about the assault, encourage her to ventilate her fears and frustrations, and help her to mobilize her strengths to deal with the crisis.

Fenichel, O. *The Psychoanalytic Theory of Neurosis.* New York: Norton, 1945.   B

Ferracuti, F. *Incest between Father and Daughter.* Boston: Little, Brown, 1972.   E

Ferracuti, and Newman. "Acts of Violence from the Point of View of the Criminologist." *Quad. Criminology Clin.*, January/March 1975.   H

Ferreira, A. "Family Myth and Homeostasis." *Archives of General Psychiatry* 9 (1963):457–463. (As reprinted in *The Family*, edited by N.W. Bell and E.F. Vogel. New York: Free Press.)   H

Ferrin, D. *Battered Spouses.* Hagerstown, Md.: Harper & Row, 1978. A

> This film explores the psychological, social, and legal aspects of spouse abuse and discusses intervention techniques, agencies, and projects to aid victims. Recommendations for future services are made.

Feshbach, S. "The Catharsis Hypothesis and Some Consequences of Interaction with Aggressive and Neutral Play Objects." *Journal of Personality* 24 (1956):449–462.   H

———. "The Stimulating versus Carthartic Effects of a Vicarious Aggressive Activity." *Journal of Abnormal Psychology* 63 (1961):381–385. H

———. "Aggression." In *Carmichael's Manual of Child Psychology*, 3rd. ed., edited by P.H. Mussen. New York: Wiley & Sons, 1970.   H

Feshbach, S., and N. Feshbach. "The Young Aggressors." *Psychology Today*, April 1973, pp. 90–96.   H

Feuer, L.S. *The Conflict of Generations: The Character and Significance of Student Movements.* New York: Basic Books, 1969.   H

Field, M.H., and H.F. Field. "Marital Violence and the Criminal Process: Neither Justice nor Peace." *Social Service Review* 47 (1973):221–240. A

Fields, M. "Representing Battered Wives, or What to do Until the Police Arrive." Family Law Reporter 3(22), April 1977.   A,F

This article reviews the legal obstacles a battered woman can expect to encounter. Fields bases her discussion on her experience in dealing with battered women at the Brooklyn Legal Services Corporation.

―――. "Does this Vow Include Wife Beating?" *Human Rights* 7 (Summer 1978):40–45.   *A*

Wife beating is viewed as a significant civil-rights problem, the unresponsiveness of the legal system to the problem is addressed, and services to aid battered wives are described.

Fields, M.D. "Wife Beating: The Hidden Offense." *New York Law Journal* 175 (29 April 1976).   *A*

This article gives a summary of the current state of affairs regarding spouse abuse, giving statistics and citing sources from New York; Ann Arbor and Detroit, Michigan; and Seattle, Washington. It also discusses efforts being made in the United Kingdom to deal with the crime.

―――. "Wife Beating: Facts and Figures." *Victimology* 2 (1977–1978): 643–647.   *A*

Discusses the extent of wife beating, its economic implications, and the social costs involved. The author calls for a stronger social response to end the cycle of violence, with better protection for the victims of family violence as a starting point.

―――. "Wife Beating—Government Intervention Policies and Practices." Rockville, Md.: NCJRS Microfiche Program, 1978.   *A*

Typical responses of police, prosecutors, and judges to cases of wife beating are discussed along with spouse murder, statutes related to wife beating, and judicial interpretation of such statutes.

―――. "Battered Wife—How the Lawyer and Psychologist Can Work Together." *Family Advocate* 2 (Fall 1979):20–22.   *A*

Battered wives are caught in a trap of unresponsive criminal-justice practitioners and the generally unsympathetic attitudes of a male-dominated society in their fight for physical and emotional survival.

Fields, M.D., and R.M. Kirchner. "Summary of English and Scottish Shelters." Unpublished paper, 1976.   *B*
―――. "Battered Women Are Still in Need: A Reply to Steinmetz." *Victimology* 3 (1978):216–222.   *A*

A critique of Steinmetz' article "The Battered Husband Syndrome" is presented. It is suggested that Steinmetz' paper is filled with baseless conjecture that gives substance to a latent backlash against the movement to aid battered wives.

Finch, S.M. "Adult Seduction of the Child: Effects on the Child." *Medical Aspects of Human Sexuality* 7 (March 1973):170–187.   E
Findley. "Cultural Context of Rape." *Women Law Journal* 60 (1974):99. G
Finer. *Report of the Committee on One Parent Families.* 1974.   B
Finkelhor, D. "Psychological, Cultural and Family Factors in Incest and Family Sexual Abuse." *Journal of Marriage and Family Counseling* 4 (1978):41–49.   E

A review of clinical and sociological research on incest and family sexual abuse is presented with attention to psychological, cultural, and family etiological factors.

———. *Sexually Victimized Children.* New York: Free Press, 1979.   E

Sexual victimization and incest were explored among 796 students at six British colleges and universities by a questionnaire and interviews concerning family composition, social and demographic background, and parental-role adequacy.

Finnelly, A. "Rape Investigation." *Police Law Quarterly* 8 (1978):20–24. G

Police investigation problems in dealing with rape victims are discussed with particular reference to how the public often views the victim as a participant in the crime. The importance of establishing a rapport with the victim and gently eliciting the most critical information is emphasized.

Fiora, G.N. "Battered Wives Who Kill: Double Standard Out of Court, Single Standard In." *Law and Human Behavior* 2 (1978):133–165. A

The law regarding murder, manslaughter, and self-defense is examined as it relates to the battered-wife defendant. The legal distinctions between the three legal categories are described, along with the reasonable-man standard as it applies to the elements of manslaughter.

Firth, R. "Suicide and Risk-Taking in Tikopia Society." *Psychiatry* 24 (1961):1–17.   H
———. "Authority and Public Opinion in Tikopia." In *Essays on Social Organization and Values.* London: Athlone Press, 1967.   B
Fischer, J.L.; R. Ward; and M. Ward. "Ponapean Conceptions of Incest." *Journal of the Polynesian Society* 85 (1976):199–208.   E

Fisher, and Rivlin "Psychological Needs of Rapists." *British Journal of Criminology* 11 (1971):182.   G

Fisher, G. *The Abusers.* Milford, Mich.: Mott Media, no date.   *A, G*

Fisher, T., and M.P. Winston. "The Grim Plight of Destitute Mothers Who Need Free Rooms on a Stormy Night." *Los Angeles Times*, 12 March 1973, p. 7.   B

Fisher, W.S. "Predictability of Victim Injury in Incidents of Rape." *Dissertation Abstracts International* 40(5), (1979):2912-A.   *G,H*

Data from 814 cases of rape and attempted rape were employed to form a multivariate model predictive of physical injury to the rape victim. A multiple-regression equation accounting for 29 percent of the variance in victim injury was obtained.

Fishman, G. "Police, Law and Victimization: Differential Patterns and Attitudes." *Victimology: An International Journal* 2 (1977):60–61. *F,H*

In a paper presented at the Second International Symposium on Victimology, held in Boston, September 1976, differential victimization patterns in various residential areas and among different socioeconomic groups are discussed.

Fithian, P.V. *Journal and Letters of Philip Vickers Fithian.* Princeton, N.J.: Princeton University Press, 1945.   B

Fammang. "Interviewing Child Victims of Sex Offenders." *Rape Victimology*, 1975.   E

Flax, M.L. "Couples Therapy in Battering Relationships." Paper presented at Colorado Women's College Conference on Battered Women, Denver, 1977.   *A, C*

Flax, M.L., and L.E. Walker. "Conjoint Marital Therapy with Battered Wives and Their Spouses." (Forthcoming.)   *A, C*

Flax, M.L.; L.E. Walker; and K.J. Schreiber. "The Battered Women Syndrome." Symposium presented at the American Psychological Association Convention, Washington, D.C., 3 September 1976.   A

Fleming, J.B. "Wife Abuse." Unpublished paper. Philadelphia, 1975, p. 3.
                                                                                           A

———. *Stopping Wife Abuse: A Guide to the Emotional, Psychological, and Legal Implications for the Abused Woman and Those Helping Her.* Garden City: Anchor Press/Doubleday, 1979.   A

This is a comprehensive how-to book that addresses the myriad of personal and institutional problems associated with wife abuse. Fleming is both theoretical and practical in her approach and both critical and hopeful in her assessment of the problem itself and of attempts to alleviate it.

Fleming, J.D. "Shop Talk about Shop Sex." *Working Women* 4 (July 1979): 31. *B,D*

Fletcher, R. *The Family and Marriage in Britain, 1973.* *A,C*

"Flipside of the Japanese Miracle." *Alternative Press Digest* 3 (1975):66.*A*

"Florida's Sexual Battery Statute: Significant Reform but Bias against the Victim Still Prevails." *University of Florida Law Review* 30 (1978):419–445. *F*

The new sexual-battery statute approved by the Florida state legislature in 1974 is discussed. The new code acknowledges forcible violations other than sexual intercourse, has specific provisions for varying degrees of sexual battery, and is sex neutral.

Fluehr, L.C. *An Analysis of Homicide in the Afro-Arab Sudan.* 1972. *H*

Flynn, J.P. "Recent Findings Related to Wife Abuse." *Social Casework* 58 (January 1977):13–20. *A*

Summarizes findings from a study of thirty-three victims of wife abuse. Sexist attitudes are held to support wife beating, resulting in blaming victims rather than offering effective help.

Flynn, J.; P. Anderson; B. Coleman; M. Finn; C. Moeller; H. Nodel; R. Novara; C. Turner; and H. Weiss. *Spouse Assault: Its Dimensions and Characteristics in Kalamazoo County, Michigan.* Kalamazoo: Western Michigan University School of Social Work, 1975. *A*

FOCUS (Fellowship of Christian Union Leadership) on Change in Seattle. "Shelter for Abused Women." Majority report. Seattle, 25 January 1975. *B*

Fojtik, K.M. *Handbook for Victims of Domestic Violence.* Ann Arbor, Mich.: Washingnaw County NOW, no date. *B*

———. *How to Develop a Wife Assault Task Force and Project.* Washtenaw Avenue, Ann Arbor, Michigan 48104. *B*

———. "NOW Domestic Violence Project." *Victimology: An International Journal* 2 (1978):653–657. *B,H*

The activities of the NOW domestic-violence project are described. The project has established a twenty-four-hour crisis line and provides emergency housing, transportation, advocacy with social-service agencies, legal and medical information and referrals, and peer counseling for battered women.

Follingstad, D.R. "A Reconceptualization of Issues in the Treatment of Abused Women: A Case Study." *Psychotherapy: Theory, Research and Practice* 17 (1980):294–303. *A*

The personality profile of abused women is examined, and a case study is presented to illustrate a behavior-therapy/congnitive-restructuring approach to working with such clients. It is contended that the profile of these women needs to be reconceptualized as a result of living in an abusive situation, rather than the antecedent that provokes abuse from the spouse.

Fonseka, S. "A Study of Wife-Beating in the Camberwell Area." *British Journal of Clinical Practice* 28 (December 1974):400–402.   *A*

Two groups of cases of wife beating seen in King's College Hospital, Camberwell, were studied in order to analyze the incidence, associated factors, and patterns of injury, especially from a radiological viewpoint.

Fontana, V.J. *The Maltreated Child*. Springfield, Ill.: Charles C Thomas, 1964.   *E*
———. *Somewhere a Child Is Crying: The Battered Child*. New York: Macmillan, 1973.   *E*
Foote, C. *Cases and Materials on Family Law*, 2d ed. Boston: Little, Brown, 1976.   *F*
———. "Getting Tough about Rape: Self-Defense Work of M. Thomas." *Human Behavior* 7 (December 1978):24–26.   *G*
Footlick. "Rape Alert." *Newsweek*, 21 November 1975, p. 70.   *G*
Footlick, Clift & Camper. "Right to Privacy: Overturning a Georgia Statute Forbidding Publication of a Rape Victim's Name." *Newsweek*, 17 March 1975, p. 66.   *F,G*
Footlick, J.K., and E. Sciolino. "Wives Who Batter Back." *Newsweek*, 30 January 1978, p. 54.   *B*
"For Victims of Rape: Many New Types of Help." *U.S. News & World Report* 79 (8 December 1975):44.   *A,G*
Forcible Rape. New York: Columbia University Press, 1977.   *G*
Ford, C.S., and F.A. Beach. *Patterns of Sexual Behavior*. New York: Harper & Row, 1951.   *E,G*
Ford, R.E., and L. Keitner. "The Circular Population: The Victims and Offenders of Violent Offenses." *Victimology: An International Journal* 2 (1977):61.   *H*

In a paper presented at the Second International Symposium on Victimology, held in Boston, September 1976, research to test the hypothesis that victims of violent crimes are themselves as likely as the offenders to be active participants in the criminal milieu is reported.

Ford, R.P.; S. Kearns; and M.F. Nichols. "Pat Ford-Roegner Panel on Battered Wives." *Bulletin of the American Academy of Psychiatry and the Law* 5 (1977):402–407.   *A*

A panel discussion by three women who work with battered women in the Atlanta, Georgia, area is presented.

Foreman, B.D. "Cognitive Modification of Obsessive Thinking in a Rape Victim: A Preliminary Study." *Psychological Reports* 47 (1980):819–822.   G

The use of cognitive restructuring in the treatment of multiple behavior problems, including obsessive thinking, of a twenty-two-year-old female rape victim is reported.

Foreman, B.D. "Psychotherapy with Rape Victims." *Psychotherapy: Theory, Research and Practice* 17 (1980):304–311.   G

Literature on psychological response and treatment of rape victims is reviewed.

Forer, L.G. *Protection from and Prevention of Physical Abuse—The Need for New Legal Procedures.* Flushing, N.Y.: Spectrum Publications, 1978.   F

Ways of improving legal protection for those who by age, mental condition, institutionalization, or legal status are particularily vulnerable to physical abuse are suggested.

Forrest, L.M. "Rape Victim Characteristics and Crime Circumstances: Their Relationship to the Victim's Perception of the Treatment Received from Criminal Justice Personnel." *Dissertation Abstracts International* 40(7):4245-A, 1980.   G

The relationship of victim characteristics and crime circumstances to victim perceptions of treatment by criminal-justice personnel was examined in questionnaire data of 146 female victims of forcible rape.

Forrest, T. "The Family Dynamics of Maternal Violence." *Journal of the American Academy of Psychoanalysis* 2 (1974):215–230.   C,H

Fortune, M.M., and D. Hormann. *Family Violence—A Workshop Manual for Rural Communities.* Washington, D.C.: U.S. Department of Justice Law Enforcement Assistance Administration, 1980.   C

This manual was designed to be used as a resource tool by individuals and groups working on family violence in rural areas.

Forward, S., and C. Buck. "Family Crime Nobody Talks about: Excerpt from *Betrayal of Innocence: Incest and Its Devastation.*" *Ladies Home Journal* 95 (November 1978):116.   E

———. *Betrayal of Innocence: Incest and Its Devastation.* New York: Penguin, 1979.   E

The psychological implications of incest and the causes, consequences, and treatment are explored.

———. *Betrayal of Innocence.* New York: Penguin Books, 1981.   E

Fosburgh, L. "Berkeley Rapist." *The New York Times*, 15 May 1978, pp. 28–32.   G

Foucault, M. *Madness and Civilization: A History of Insanity in the Age of Reason.* Social Science Paperback, 1967.   C

Four Translation New Testament. New York: Iversen Associates, 1966.
                                          C,H

Fox and Scherl. "Crisis Intervention with Victims of Rape." *Rape Victimology*, 1975.   C,H

Fox, G.L. "Another Look at the Comparative Resources Model: Assessing the Balance of Power in Turkish Marriages." *Journal of Marriage and the Family* 35 (1973):718–729.   B

Fox, J.A., and P.E. Tracy. "The Randomized Response Approach: Applicability to Criminal Justice Research and Evaluation." *Evaluation Review* 4 (1980):601–622.   B

Developments in the use of the randomized-response approach in criminal-justice research and evaluation are examined, with emphasis on efforts to refine this method of reducing evasive-answer bias in surveys of sensitive information.

Fox, R. *The Red Lamp of Incest.* New York: Dutton, 1980.   E

Francis, C. "Singer Forges a New Life After the Trauma of Rape Ended Her Career. *People*, 26 January 1981, p. 78.   G

Frances, V., and A. Frances. "The Incest Taboo and Family Structure." *Family Process* 15 (June 1976):235–244.   E

The evolutionary advantage of outbreeding has influenced the family structure and the mating, attachment, and dominance behaviors of all animals.

Francke, L.B. "Battered Women." *Newsweek*, 2 February 1976.   A

Frank and Frank. "Medical Aspects of Rape." *Mademoiselle*, February, 1976.   G

Frank, E. "Psychological Response to Rape: An Analysis of Response Patterns." *Dissertation Abstracts International* 41(1):351-B, 1980.   G

Initial response to sexual assault of fifty adolescent and adult women were investigated using self-report inventories, a structured interview, and behavioral role-playing assessments, and their responses were compared to responses of a group of twenty-two demographically comparable, nonvictimized women.

Frank, E., and S.M. Turner. "Depressive Symptoms in Rape Victims." *Journal of Affective Disorders* 1 (1979):269–277. G

Thirty-four recent rape victims were assessed for depressive symptomatology using a well-validated self-report instrument in combination with formal psychiatric evaluation.

Frank, E.; S.M. Turner; and B.D. Stewart. "Initial Response to Rape: The Impact of Factors within the Rape Situation." *Journal of Behavioral Assessment* 2 (1980):39–53. G

The relationship between specific aspects of the rape situation and immediate postrape measures of depression, fear, anxiety, and social and interpersonal functioning was investigated in fifty recent victims of sexual assault. The data did not reveal any significant relationships between rape-situation variables and the nature or severity of the victim's psychological response.

Franklin, H.B. *The Victim as Criminal and Artist*. New York: Oxford University Press, 1978. H

The thesis that exploitation, violence, racism, and especially classicism of the United States from colonial times has produced a mass of victims who have produced poetry, novels, and biography that are among the most significant in U.S. literary history is expounded.

Frappat, B. "Battered Women: A Social Plague." *Le Monde*, November. A

Frazier, W.H., and B. Moynihan. "The Emergency Service Based Rape Counseling Team." *Connecticut Medicine* 42 (1978):91–94. G

The structure, functions, and treatment protocols of an emergency-service-based rape-counseling team are presented. Most rape victims present initially to an emergency service for evaluation and treatment, and a planned approach to intervention is essential.

Frederick, C.J. "Effects of Natural vs. Human-Induced Violence upon Victims." *Evaluation and Change* Special Issue (1980):71–75. H

Some of the major characteristics of the experience of natural violence and the experience of human-induced violence such as crimes and acts of terrorism are compared and contrasted in terms of the associated phases, psychological disturbances, and social processes.

Frederick, R.E. "Domestic Violence—A Guide for Police Response." Harrisburg, Pa.: Pennsylvania Coalition against Domestic Violence, 1979.   *H*

This manual is intended to increase police awareness of the history and scope of domestic violence and to provide them with tools for more-effective and skillful confrontations with the problem.

Freeman, A.M., III. "Planning Community Treatment for Sex Offenders." *Community Mental Health Journal* 14 (1978):147–152.   *B*

Treatment needs of sex offenders served by community programs are discussed. In California and in Great Britain, plans are being made to move the treatment setting for many sex offenders from large state hospitals to community sites.

Freeman, J. "The Building of the Gilded Cage." In *Radical Feminism*, edited by A. Koedt, E. Levine, and A. Rapone, pp. 127–150. New York: Quadrangle, 1973.   *B*
Freeman, M.D. "Phenomenon of Marital Violence and the Legal and Social Response in England." Scarborough, Ont.: Butterworth, 1978.   *H*

Four explanations of the etiology of wife battering are put forth, the status of women in English law generally and their status under the criminal law are examined, and the role of the courts is reviewed.

————. *Violence in the Home*. Westmead, England: Saxon House, Tear-field Limited, 1979.   *H*

Focusing on violence in the home, its consequences for the family, and legal responses to the problem, this volume examines both wife and child abuse and briefly considers other forms of domestic violence.

Freeman, N.R. "Victim Advocate." Rockville, Md.: NCJRS Microfiche Program, 1978.   *H*

The nature and extent of spouse abuse, specifically wife beating, are outlined along with the responsibilities of prosecutors in spouse-assault cases.

Freerksen, G.N., and D.M. Tuke. "Young Persons in the Legal Literature: An Annotated Bibliography." *Law in American Society* 4 (September 1975):33–38.   E
Freiberg, P., and M.W. Bridwell. "An Intervention Model for Rape and Unwanted Pregnancy." *Counseling Psychologist* 6 (1976):50–53.   G

The analytic grief process, consisting of the interrelated stages of denial, depression, anger, and resolution, is presented as a framework for understanding and helping a woman who is confronted with feelings arising from unwanted pregnancy or rape.

Freilich. "Rape: Hospitals Can Do More Than Treat the Victim." *Hospital Medical Staff,* September 1975, p. 1.   G
French, J.R., and B. Raven. "The Bases of Social Power." In *Studies in Social Power*, edited by D. Cartwright, pp. 150–165. Ann Arbor: Research Center for Group Dynamics, Institute for Social Research, University of Michigan, 1959.   B
Freud, S. "Repression." In *Collected Papers,* edited by E. Jones. London: Hogarth, 1924.   C
———. "On the History of the Psychoanalytic Movement." In *Collected Papers*, edited by E. Jones, pp. 284–389. London: Hogarth, 1924. C
———. *Civilization and its Discontents*. London: Hogarth, 1930.   C,H
———. *Group Psychology and the Analysis of the Ego*. London: Hogarth, 1948.   C
———. *Complete Introductory Lectures on Psychoanalysis*, translated and edited by J. Strachey. New York: Norton, 1966.   C
———. "Anatomy Is Destiny." In *Masculine/Feminine*, edited by B. Roszak and T. Roszak, pp. 19–29. New York: Harper & Row, 1969. C
Freund, K. "Diagnosis and Treatment of Forensically Significant Anomalous Erotic Preferences." *Canadian Journal of Criminology and Corrections* 18 (July 1976):181–189.   C

Three abnormal erotic preferences are discussed: sadism, pedophilia (child molesting), and courtship disorders.

Friedan, B. *The Feminine Mystique*. New York: Dell Books, 1974. *A,H*
Friedman, A.S. *Therapy with Families of Sexually Acting-Out Girls*. New York: Springer Publishing Company, 1971.   C

Deals with family therapy in one area—namely, that of families with daughters who have problems related to sexual behavior, such as vagrancy, promiscuity, incest, homosexuality, and so on. Case examples are given with detailed reports of progress from the therapy and the problems that arise. It also approximates a guide to practice by reporting on the learning process of the beginning family therapist and on the role of his supervisor.

Friedman, D.M. "Information Gathering for a Victim Service Program." *Victimology: An International Journal* 2 (1977):61–62.   *B,H*

In a paper presented at the Second International Symposium on Victimology, held in Boston, September 1976, an information-gathering system for a victim service-delivery program serving a diverse population of victims is described. Policy issues regarding the collection of data from a victim-service program and advantages of the techniques employed are covered.

Friedman, K.O. "Image of Battered Women." *American Journal of Public Health* 67 (August 1977):722–823.   *A*
———. *Battered—A Survival Manual for Battered Women*. Baltimore: Maryland Committee for Women, 1978.   *A*

This manual for battered women advised victims and potential victims of spouse abuse about criminal and civil responses to abuse and lists crisis shelters for battered women in Maryland.

Fromm, E. *The Anatomy of Human Destructiveness*. New York: Holt, Rinehart, and Winston, 1973.   *A*
Fromson, T.L. "Case for Legal Remedies for Abused Women." *New York University Review of Law and Social Change* 6 (Spring 1977):135–174.   *A,F*

The abuse of women is viewed as a social and political problem, and the ability of the legal system to protect victims, deter perpetrators, and reduce the incidence of abuse is examined.

Frosch, W.A. "Geographic Reinforcement of the Incest Taboo: Three Case Vignettes." *American Journal of Psychiatry* 138 (May 1981): 679–680.   *E*

Reports the cases of three patients—a forty-three-year-old merchant seaman, a thirty-eight-year-old traveling salesman, and a thirty-two-year-old female secretary—in whom the impulse to wander provided a geographical reinforcement of the incest taboo and resembled the situation that K. Abraham termed neurotic exogamy.

Frost, J.W. *The Quaker Family in Colonial America*. New York: Saint Martin's Press, 1973.   *B,H*
Fuchs, V.R. *Who Shall Live: Health, Economics and Social Choice*. New York: Basic Books, 1974.   *H*

Fulero, S.M., and C. Delara. "Rape Victims and Attributed Responsibility: A Defensive Attribution Approach." *Victimology* 1 (Winter 1976): 551–563.   G

C. Jones and E. Aronson found that a divorcee rape victim was attributed less responsibility than married or virgin rape victims, a finding that is explained in terms of M. Lerner's just-world theory.

Fuller, R.C., and R.R. Myers. "The Natural History of a Social Problem." *American Sociological Review*, 1941, p. 320.   H

Fullerton, G.P. "Marital Conflict: Hostility in Intimacy." *Survival in Marriage*. New York: Holt, Rinehart, and Winston, 1972.   A

Futterman, S. "Personality Trends in Wives of Alcoholics." *Journal of Psychiatric Social Work*, October 1959, pp. 37–41.   C

This article focuses on the wife of the alcoholic who sought help in her family situation because of the husband's alcoholism. The bulk of the material is derived from clients in social agencies and the remainder about evenly from patients seen in a mental-hygiene clinic and in private practice.

Gabor, A. "I Am Joe's Punching Bag." *Homemaker's Magazine* 11 (May 1976):137–148.   A

Discusses the etiology and dynamics of the battered-wife syndrome. Drinking plays a major role in domestic violence.

Gage, R.W. "Program for Rape Victims Applauded." *Journal of the American College Health Association* 27 (1978):67.   B,G

Rape social issues are briefly discussed in an editorial and the rape program described by Estabrook. It is proposed as a model for other community programs for rape victims. Rape is an especially detestable form of assault and is a blatant expression of the widespread exploitation of women.

Gager, N., and C. Schurr. *Sexual Assault: Confronting Rape in America*. New York: Grosset & Dunlap, 1976.   G

Gagnon, J. "Female Child Victims of Sex Offenses." *Social Problems* 13 (1965):176–192.   E

Gagnon, J.H. and W. Simon. *Sexual Conduct*. Chicago: Aldine, 1973. G
———. *Sexual Encounters between Adults and Children*. Siecus Study Guide, 1970.   E

A discussion of the nature of adult-child sexual encounters, the identity of sex offenders, the consequences for the child involved, and the important role that parents play in mitigating the possible effects of such incidents.

Galaway, B.R., and W. Marsella. "Study of the Perceived Fairness of Restitution as a Sanction for Juvenile Offenders." *Victimology: An International Journal* 2 (1977):62.   *C,E*

In a paper presented at the Second International Symposium on Victimology, held in Boston, September 1976, an exploratory study to determine the extent to which restitution, imposed as a probation condition on juvenile property offenders, is perceived as a fair requirement is described.

Gallen, R.T. *Wive's Legal Rights*. New York: Dell, 1967.   *F*

Gallup, G. "Guns Found in 44% of Homes." *San Francisco Chronicle*, 7 July 1975.   *H*

Galton. "Police Processing of Rape Complaints: A Case Study." *American Journal of Criminology* 4 (1975–1976):15.   *F,G*

Galtung, J. *Theory and Methods of Social Research*. London: George Allen & Unwin, 1973.   *B*

Galy, L. "Family Violence: A Psychiatric Perspective." *Journal of the Irish Medical Association* 68 (1975):450–453.   *B*

Gammon, M.A. *Violence in Canada*. Ontario: Methuen Publications, 1978.   *B*

Violence in Canada is presented from different perspectives in a book of essays covering rape, child abuse, domestic violence, violence and the media, and origins of violence.

Gaquin, D.A. "Spouse Abuse: Data from the National Crime Survey." *Victimology: An International Journal* 2 (1978):632–643.   *A*

The phenomenon of spouse abuse is examined, using the national crime survey as the data base. Though the data are not as accurate as it would be with a larger survey and are amenable to biases, some conclusions were reached about the nature and frequency of spouse abuse.

Garcia, L.T., and W. Griffitt. "Authoritarianism—Situation Interactions in the Determination of Punitiveness: Engaging Authoritarian Ideology." *Journal of Research in Personality* 12 (December 1978):469–478.   *B*

An analysis of previously reported authoritarianism-situation interactions in the determination of punitiveness suggested that the extent to which target-person characteristics or behaviors engage the important ideology content dimensions of the authoritarianism syndrome is a potent mediator of authoritarianism-punitiveness relationships.

Garfinkel, H. *Studies in Ethnomethodology*. Englewood Cliffs, N.J.: Jersey: Prentice-Hall, 1967.   *B*

Garofalo, J. "Social Stratification and Criminal Victimization." *Dissertation Abstracts International*, Ann Arbor, Michigan, University, 1978. *H*

A conceptualization of social stratification based on differential ability to control the environment was developed and applied to criminal-victimization surveys of eight large U.S. cities. Indicators of social-power dimensions were derived and applied to the analysis of personal theft and household burglary victimizations.

———. "Victimization and the Fear of Crime." *Journal of Research in Crime and Delinquency* 16 (1979):80–97.   *H*

The determinants of the fear of crime are examined with special attention to how the risk and experience of criminal victimization affect that fear. Using data from victimization and attitude surveys in eight U.S. cities, a model of the determinants of the fear of crime was developed and evaluated in a preliminary fashion.

Garofalo, J., and J. Laub. "The Fear of Crime: Broadening our Perspective." *Victimology* 3 (1978):242–253.   *H*

Evidence in fear of crime research is reviewed, and it is discovered that what are taken as expressions of the fear of crime are not simply reflections of anxiety about being the victim of specific criminal acts or of actual experiences with victimization.

Garrett, C.A., and M.S. Ireland. "A Therapeutic Art Session with Rape Victim." *American Journal of Art Therapy* 18 (1980):103–106.   *B,G*

A group art therapy procedure implemented with victims of sexual assault is described. The purpose is to provide, as alternative to individual psychotherapy, an additional therapeutic experience for individuals in psychotherapy, and a follow-up group support to rape victims in order to promote integration of the traumatic event into the person's ongoing life.

Garrett, T.B., and R. Wright. "Wives of Rapists and Incest Offenders." *Journal of Sex Research* 11 (May 1975):149–157.   *A,E,G*

Interviewed eighteen wives of forcible rapists and incest offenders who had been committed to hospitals and prisons. The wives were better educated than their husbands. They gained satisfaction from the hospitalization of their husbands because it put them in the role of martyrs.

Gates, M. *Victims of Rape and Wife Abuse: Women in Courts*. Williamsburg, Va.: National Center for State Courts, 1978.   *A,F,G*

Attitudes toward victims of rape and wife beating are discussed as they affect law and the criminal-justice system. Consequences for the victims are discussed, and reforms in progress are mentioned.

Gayford, J.J. "Battered Wives." *Medicine, Science, and the Law* 15 (1975): 237–245.   A

A battered wife is defined as a woman who has received deliberate, severe, and repeated demonstrable physical injury from her marital partner. Some of the details of a survey of 100 battered wives are presented, including the types of injuries seen, age, and nationality, backgrounds to the cases, type of relationship, influence on the children, and psychological symptoms.

——. "Battered Wives." *Royal Society of Health Journal* 95 (1975):288–289.   A
——. "Research on Battered Wives." *Royal Society of Health Journal* 95 (1975):288–290.   A,B
——. "Wife Battering: A Preliminary Survey of 100 Cases." *British Medical Journal*, 1975, pp. 194–197.   A,B,F

One hundred battered wives were interviewed. All had bruising, often together with other injuries such as lacerations and fractures.

——. "Plight of the Battered Wife." *International Journal of Environmental Studies* 10 (1977):283–286.   A
——. "Aetiology of Repeated Serious Physical Assaults by Husbands on Wives." *Medicine, Science, and the Law* 19 (January 1979):19–24. A,B

Following a review of significant studies of wife battering, methodology and results are reported from a study of etiological factors in 100 battered wives.

——. "Battered Wives." *British Journal of Hospital Medicine* 22 (1979): 496, 498, 500–503.   A

The terminology, epidemiology, etiology, classifications, and treatment of wife abuse are discussed, and dynamics of violence in marriage are described.

Geddes, D. "Run Joey Run." Big Tree Records, 1975.   C
Geis, G. "Group Sexual Assaults." *Medical Aspects of Human Sexuality* 5 (May 1971):100–113.   G

Discusses group rape in terms of well-established principles of collective behavior. It is noted that rape is the most underreported major criminal offense in the United States and that group rape is the most understudied.

―――. *The Case of Rape: Legal Restrictions on Media Coverage of Deviance in England and America.* Beverly Hills, Calif.: Sage, 1978.
B,F,G

Legal restrictions on the press in the United Kingdom and the United States are contrasted by considering press liberty and personal privacy in rape cases.

Geis, G., and D. Chappell. "Forcible Rape by Multiple Offenders." *Abstract on Criminology and Penology* 11 (1971):431.   G
Geis, G., and R. Geis. "Rape Reform: An Appreciative Critical Review." *Bulletin of the American Academy of Psychiatry and Law* 6 (1978):301– 312.   *B,F,G*

Major developments in rape reform are examined from the perspective of the feminist campaign for public and scientific acceptance of the view that rape is the quintessential expression of male exploitation of women.

―――. "Rape in Stockholm: Is Permissiveness Relevant?" *Criminology* 17 (1979):311–322.   *B,G*

The relationship between Swedish sexual behavior and the rate of rape in Stockholm was examined. The rate of rape in Stockholm was found to be equivalent to comparably sized U.S. jurisdictions.

Geis, G.; T.L. Huston; and R. Wright. "Crime Victims as Seen by Interviewing Bystanders." *Victimology: An International Journal* 2 (1977): 63.   H

Research findings regarding the manner in which onlookers who intervene in criminal episodes view the victim of the crime are reported.

Geiser, R.L. *Hidden Victims: The Sexual Abuse of Children.* Boston: Beacon Press, 1979.   E

The sexual misuse of female and male children is explored by examining incest, pornography, obscenity, prostitution, and deviant sexual environments.

Geller, J.A., and J.C. Walsh. "A Treatment Model for the Abused Spouse." *Victimology* 2 (1977–1978):627–632.   *A,B*

Describes a treatment model developed at a social-service center providing crisis intervention, counseling, and advocacy for victims of spouse abuse, rape, and assault and their families.

Gelles, R.J. *The Violent Home*. Beverly Hills, Calif.: Sage Publications, 1972.   *A,H*

Gelles presents a study of eighty people and their experiences with conjugal violence. The information for his work was collected through unstructured, informal interviews.

————. *The Violent Home—A Study of Physical Aggression between Husbands and Wives*. Beverly Hills, Calif.: Sage Publications, 1972.   *H*

Gelles's research was undertaken in order to narrow existing gaps in the systematic knowledge concerning the extent and nature of violence between husbands and wives.

————. "Child Abuse as Psychopathology: A Sociological Critique and Reformulation." *American Journal of Orthopsychiatry* 43 (July 1973): 611–621.   *E*
————. "An Exploratory Study of Intra-Family Violence." Ph.D. dissertation, University of New Hampshire, Durham, 1973.   *C,H*
————. *Conjugal Violence: A Study of Physical Aggression between Husband and Wife*. Beverly Hills, Calif.: Sage Publications, 1974.   *A,H*
————. "Toward an Integrated Theory of Family Violence." Paper presented at the 1974 Conference of the National Council on Family Relations. Available from the University of New Hampshire, Sociology Department, Durham.   *B,H*
————. "Violence and Pregnancy: A Note on the Extent of the Problem and Needed Services." *Family Coordinator* 24 (January 1975):81–86.
                                                                                                 A,H
————. "The Social Construction of Child Abuse." *American Journal of Orthopsychiatry* 44 (April 1975):363–371.   *E*
————. "On the Association of Sex and Violence in the Fantasy Production of College Students." *Suicide* 5 (Summer 1975):78–85.   *B*
————. "Battered Wives Find It Hard To Get Help: Study." *Psychology Today* 11 (June 1977):36.   *A,B*
————. "Power, Sex, and Violence: The Case of Marital Rape." *Family Coordinator* 26 (October 1977):339–347.   *G,H*

The available evidence on marital violence indicates that a number of women are pressured into having sexual relations with their husbands through intimidation or physical force. This paper examines the issue of marital rape by discussing some of the controversies involved in such a phenomenon.

————. "Methods for Studying Sensitive Family Topics." *American Journal of Orthopsychiatry* 48 (1978):408–424.   *B*

Problems associated with carrying out research on sensitive topics in the family are discussed, and solutions that can be and have been implemented in the course of research on child abuse, wife abuse, family violence, and sexual behavior are presented.

————. "Profile of Violence toward Children in the U.S." Paper presented at the Annenberg School of Communications Conference on Child Abuse: Cultural Roots and Policy Options, Philadelphia, 20 November 1978. *B*

This national study of violence toward children in the United States examines factors related to the use of violence by parents and the extent of child abuse.

————. *Violence in the American Family*. New York: Wiley & Sons, 1978. *C,H*

The extent of family violence in the United States, contributing causes, and public response are discussed.

————. *Family Violence*. Beverly Hills, Calif.: Sage Publications, 1979. *H*

This is a compilation of eleven essays that are products of three federally funded and related research projects. The essays are arranged under subtopics as follows: violence toward children, marital violence, studying family violence, and the impact of family violence.

————. "Physical Violence in Families." In *Family Violence and Child Abuse*, edited by E. Corfman. Rockville, Md.: U.S. Department of Health, 1979. *C,H*

Results from the first survey of family violence in the United States are discussed, and their implications are analyzed.

————. "Violence in the Family: A Review of Research in the Seventies." *Journal of Marriage and the Family* 42 (1980):873–885. *C,H*

Research in the 1970s on family violence is reviewed. The issue of family violence became increasingly visible as a social and family issue in the decade of the 1970s.

Gelles, R.J., and M.A. Straus. "Family Experience and Public Support of the Death Penalty." *American Journal of Orthopsychiatry* 45 (July 1975):596–613. *C,H*

————. "Determinants of Violence in the Family: Toward a Theory Inte-

gration." In *Contemporary Theories about the Family*, edited by W.R. Burr, R. Hill, F.I. Nye, and I.L. Reiss, New York: Free Press, 1977.
                                                                                                    B,H
Gelles, R.J.; D.J. Pittman; and W. Handy. "Patterns in Criminal Aggravated Assault." *Journal of Criminal Law, Criminology and Police Science* 55 (1964):463.   *H*
Genet, J. *Miracle of the Rose.* New York: Grove Press, 1966.   *A,B,H*
Gentry, C.E. "Incestuous Abuse of Children: The Need for an Objective View." *Child Welfare* 57 (June 1978):355–364.   *E*

Discusses the need for more data on incestuous abuse of children and examines the victim's, the abuser's, and the family's response to the incestuous behavior.

Gentzler, R. *The Abused—Advocacy Programs for Abused Women.* Lancaster, Pa.: Pennsylvania Coalition against Domestic Violence, 1977. *A*

This manual covers all the important stages of planning a shelter and provides a sound foundation on which to build a successful program.

Gephard, P., et al. *Sex Offenders: An Analysis of Types.* New York: Harper & Row, 1965.   *C,E*
Geracimos, A., ed. "How I Stopped Beating My Wife." *Ms.*, August 1976.
                                                                                                        A
Gergen, K.J. *The Psychology of Behavior Exchange.* Reading, Mass.: Addison-Wesley, 1969.   *B*
———. "Methodology in the Study of Policy Formation." In *The Study of Policy Formation*, edited by R.A. Bauer and K.J. Gergen. New York: Free Press, 1971.   *B*
Gerth, H., and C.W. Mills. *Character and Social Structure: The Psychology of Social Institutions.* New York: Harcourt, Brace & World, 1953. *B*
Gesell, A. *The Guidance of Mental Growth in Infant and Child.* New York: Macmillan, 1930.   *B*
"Getting into Violence." *San Francisco Chronicle*, 23 April 1975.   *H*
Getzels, J.W., and P.W. Jackson. *Creativity and Intelligence.* New York: Wiley & Sons, 1962.   *B*
Giancinti, T., and C. Tjaden. "The Crime of Rape in Denver, 1973." A report of the Denver Anti-Crime Council.   *B,G*
Giarretto, H. "The Treatment of Father-Daughter Incest: A Psycho-Social Approach." *Children Today*, July/August 1976.   *E*

Studies the previous and subsequent convictions of 200 men charged with rape in 1961, together with circumstances of the criminal offense.

———. "Humanistic Treatment of Father-Daughter Incest." *Child Abuse and Neglect* 1 (1977):411–426. *B,E*
———. "Integral Psychology in the Treatment of Father-Daughter Incest." *Dissertation Abstracts International* 41(6):2319-B, 1980. *B,F*

The development and activities of the child sexual-abuse treatment program are reviewed. It is noted that typical community reactions, particularly law enforcement, tend to aggravate the family's troubled state when father-daughter incest is suspected or confirmed.

Gibbens, T.C. "Violence in the Family." *Medico-Legal Journal* 43:76–88. *H*
Gibbens, T.C., and J. Prince. *Child Victims of Sex Offences*. London, 1963. *E,H*
Gibbens, T.C.; K.L. Soothill; and C.K. Way. "Sibling and Parent-Child Incest Offenders." *British Journal of Criminology* 18 (1978):40–52. *E*

Results from a study of all incest cases, some involving minors, in 1951 and 1961 are reported. About half of incest cases known to the police reached court.

Gibbons, D.C. "Violence in American Society: The Challenge of Corrections." *American Journal of Correction* 31 (March/April 1969):6–11. *H*
Gibson, E. "Homicide in England and Wales 1967–1971." Home Office Research Study no. 31. London: Her Majesty's Stationery Office, 1975. *C,H*
Gibson, E., and S. Klein. *Murder, 1957–1968*. London: Her Majesty's Stationery Office, 1969. *C,H*
Gibson, L.; R. Linden; and S. Johnson. "A Situational Theory of Rape." *Canadian Journal of Criminology* 22 (1980):51–65. *B,G*

A situational theory of rape is described and contrasted with psychological or psychiatric theories of rape, and the theory is evaluated using data obtained from a western Canadian city.

Gil, D.G. *Violence against Children*. Cambridge: Harvard University Press, 1970. *E,H*
———. "A Conceptual Model of Child Abuse and Its Implications for Social Policy." In "Violence against Children," *Journal of Marriage and the Family* 33 (1971):644–648. *B,E*
———. "A Sociocultural Perspective on Physical Child Abuse." *Child Welfare* 50 (July 1971):389–395. *E*
———. "Violence against Children." *Journal of Marriage and the Family* 33 (1971):637–648. *B,E*

———. "Unraveling Child Abuse." *American Journal of Orthopsychiatry* 45 (1975):346–356.   *B,E*

Gil, D.G., and J.H. Noble. "Public Knowledge, Attitudes and Opinions about Physical Child Abuse in the United States." *Child Welfare* 48 (1969):395–401.   *E*

Gilder, G.F. *Visible Man.* New York: Basic Books, 1978.   *H*

Giles, S. "The Admissibility of a Rape-Complainant's Previous Sexual Conduct: The Need for Legislative Reform." *New England Law Review* 11 (1976):497.   *G*

———. "Stability and Change in Patterns of Wife Beating: A Systems Theory Approach." *Dissertation Abstracts International* 41(6):2781-A, 1980.   *A*

A longitudinal study, using a systems-theory approach was conducted to examine patterns of stability and change in wife beating.

Gill. "Victims of Sexual Assault." *Imprint*, December 1975.   *A,E*

Gill, J.S. "Psycho-Sociological Attitudes of the Male toward Rape, Using the Rape Attitudes Scale." *Dissertation Abstracts International* 39(10): 5103-B, (1979).   *G*

Psychosociological attitudes of thirty college students and thirty county jail inmates toward rape were measured, and the interaction of age, education, ethenicity, religious commitment, and sex by force upon rape attitudes was studied.

Gill, T., and A. Coote. *Battered Women: How to Use the Law.* London: Women's Rights Publications, Cobden Trust, January 1975.   *A,F*

This booklet explains how the law best can be used to help women who are assaulted by the men with whom they live, whether they are married or not.

Gillen, J.L. *The Wisconsin Prisoner: Studies in Crimogenisis.* Madison: University of Wisconsin Press, 1946.   *H*

Gillespie, D.L. "Who Has the Power? The Marital Struggle." *Journal of Marriage and the Family* 33 (August):445–458.   *F*

Gillis, P. "Sexual Harassment—No Longer a Dirty Joke." *Parents Magazine* 55 (August 1980):24.   *D*

Gillman, I.S. "An Object-Relations Approach to the Phenomenon and Treatment of Battered Women." *Psychiatry* 43 (1980):346–358. *A,B,C*

Problems experienced by battered women are addressed from the standpoint of object relations and psychoanalytic theory.

Gilula, M.F., and G. Daniels. "Violence and Man's Struggle to Adapt."
    Science, 164 (1969):396–405.   *C,H*
Gingold, J. "Most American Violence Happens in the Home." *Ms.*, pp.
    51–54, 94–98.   *H*
———. "One of These Days—POW—Right in the Kisser: The Truth about
    Battered Wives." *Ms.*, August 1976.   *A*
Gipson, N. *Battered Women—Rights and Options*. Urbana, Ill.: Woman's
    Fund, Incorporated, 1978.   *A,F*

    This booklet examines male-female relational patterns that are abusive
    toward women and suggests steps women can take to remedy the situation.

Gittelson. "Avoiding Rape: Whose Advice Should You Take?" McCalls,
    May 1976, p. 66.   *B,G*
Gittelson, N.L.; S.E. Eacott; and B.M. Mehta. "Victims of Indecent Expo-
    sure." *British Journal of Psychiatry* 132 (1978):61–66.   *H*

    One hundred female nurses at a psychiatric hospital were interviewed in an
    attempt to assess the overall frequency of having been the victim of inde-
    cent exposure and to describe it as experienced by the victim.

Glair, S. "Making the Legal System Work for Battered Women." *Battered
    Women*, 1979, pp. 101–118.   *A,F*

    Civil and criminal laws can be better enforced and supplemented by more-
    explicit laws to help make the legal system more responsive to the needs of
    battered women.

Glasgow, J.M. "The Marital Rape Exemption: Legal Sanction of Spouse
    Abuse." *Journal of Family Law* 18 (1980):565–586.   *F,G*

    The legal sanction of spouse abuse, the marital-rape exemption, is exam-
    ined from its historical origin to the current efforts to reform the law.

Glasgow Women's Aid (Interval House). *Report for the Year*. Glasgow,
    1974–1975.   *B*
Glasser, P.H., and N. Lois. *Families in Crisis*. New York: Harper & Row,
    1970.   *C*
Glastonbury, B; M. Burdett; and R. Austin. "Community Perceptions and
    the Personal Social Services." *Policy and Politics* 1 (1973):3.   *B*
Glatzle, M. "Terror in Franz Siegel Park (attempted rape of policewoman
    decoy; excerpt from *Muggable Mary*, edited by E. Fiore)." *Readers
    Digest* 116 (April 1980):23–24.   *G*

Glauberman, L.A. "Training the Police in Crisis Intervention Techniques."
    Dissertation Abstracts International 38(5-B), 2428, November 1977. C
Gless, "Nebraska's Corroboration Rule." *Nebraska Law Review* 54 (1975):
    93.   F
Gligor, A.M. "Incest and Sexual Delinquency: A Comparative Analysis of
    Two Forms of Sexual Behavior in Minor Females." *Dissertation Ab-
    stracts International* 67, 27(10-B), 3671.   E
Gluckman, M. *Custom and Conflict in Africa*. Oxford: Basil Blackwell,
    1955.   H
———. "Ethnographic Data in British Social Anthropology." *Sociological
    Review* 9 (1961):5–17.   B,H
———. "Tribalism, Ruralism, and Urbanism in South and Central Afri-
    ca." In *Profiles of Change: The Impact of Colonialism on Africa*.
    Cambridge: Cambridge University Press, 1970.   H
Glueck, E., and S. Glueck. *Physique and Delinquency*. New York: Har-
    per & Row, 1956.   H
Goffman, E. *Encounters: Two Studies in the Sociology of Interaction*. In-
    dianapolis: Bobbs-Merrill, 1961.   B
———. *Behavior in Public Places: Notes on the Social Organization of
    Gatherings*. New York: Free Press, 1963.   B
Gold, A.R.; P.G. Landerman; and K.W. Bullock. "Reactions to Victims of
    Crime: Sympathy, Defensive Attribution, and the Just World." *Social
    Behavior and Personality* 5 (1977):295–304.   H

    Explored in two experiments observers' perceptions of the responsibility of
    a victim of her involvement in a premeditated crime.

Gold, M. "Suicide, Homicide and the Socialization of Aggression." *Ameri-
    can Journal of Sociology* 63 (1958):651–661.   H
Gold, S., and M. Wyatt. "The Rape System: Old Roles and New Times."
    Catholic University Law Review 27 (1978):695–729.   F,G
Goldberg, P. "Are Women Prejudiced against Women?" *Trans-Action*,
    1968, 28–30.   C
Golde, M. "Federal Programs Provide Housing Assistance for Battered
    Women." *Journal of Housing* 37 (August 1980):443–447.   A,B
Golden. "The Ugly Crime of Rape." *Essence*, June 1975, p. 36.   G
Goldman, V.S. "Research Relating to Children." *Bulletin* 25. Washington,
    D.C.: Clearinghouse for Research in Child Life, EDRS, January/May
    1970.   B
———. "Research Relating to Children." Bulletin 26. Washington, D.C.:
    Clearinghouse for Research in Child Life, EDRS, January/May 1970. B
Goldner. "Rape as a Heinous but Understudied Offense." *Journal of Crimi-
    nology* 63 (1972):402.   G

Goldstein, J.H. *Aggression and Crimes of Violence*. New York: Oxford University Press, 1975.   H
———. "Social and Psychological Aspects of Child Abuse: A Bibliography." *Catalog of Selected Documents in Psychology* 5 (1976).   B
Goldstein, Kant; Judd; Rice; and Green. "Experience with Pornography: Rapists, Pedophiles, Homosexuals, Transsexuals, and Controls." Archives of Sexual Behavior 1 (1971):1.   G
Goldstein, J., and J. Katz. *Family and the Law*. New York: Free Press.
                                                                                           F
Goldstein, M.J. "Exposure to Erotic Stimuli and Sexual Deviance." *Journal of Social Issues* 29:197–219.   G

Interviewed samples of convicted male rapists, pedophiles, homosexuals, transsexuals, heavy pornography users, and a community control group to assess experience with erotic material in photographs, films, and books during adolescence and adulthood.

Gonzalez, C.F. "Victimologia." *Policia Ciientifica* 3 (1965):19–23.   H
Goode, E., and R. Troiden. *Sexual Deviance and Sexual Deviants*. New York: William Morrow & Company, 1974.   G,H

A collection of articles that discusses the social side of sex: pornography, prostitution, male homosexuality, lesbianism, rape, and kinky sex.

Goode, W.J. *Violence among Intimates. Crimes of Violence*. Washington, D.C.: U.S. Government Printing Office, 1969.   H
———. "Force and Violence in the Family." *Journal of Marriage and the Family* 33 (November 1971):624–636.   A,G,H
———. "Force and Violence in the Family." In Violence in the Family, edited by pp. 25–44. New York: Dodd, Mead, 1974.   A,G,H
Goode, W.J.; Hopkins; and H.M. McClure. *A Propositional Inventory in the Field of the Family*. Indianapolis: Bobbs-Merrill, 1971.   B
Goode, W.M. "Family Disorganization." *Contemporary Social Problems*, 1966.   H
Goodman, E. "Victim of Rape—What Progress." *Australian Journal of Social Issues* 14 (1979):21–27.   G
Goodman, E.J. "Abused by Her Husband—and the Law." *The New York Times*, 7 October 1975, Op-Ed page.   A,F,G
Goodwin, J., and P. Divasto. "Mother-Daughter Incest." *Child Abuse and Neglect* 3 (1979):953–957.   E

A case report of mother-daughter incest is described, and similarities and contrasts between homosexual and heterosexual incest are discussed.

Goodwin, J., and J.M. Fried. "Rape." *New England Journal of Medicine* 298 (1978):167.   G

In a letter to the editor, the importance of physical examinations in caring for suspected rape victims is discussed with reference to the unreliability of physical examinations as a means of establishing the veracity of rape claims in children.

Goodwin, J.; D. Sahd; and R.T. Rada. "Incest Hoax: False Accusations, False Denials." *Bulletin of the American Academy of Psychiatry and Law* 6 (1978):269–276.   E

Clinical aspects of false accusations or false denials of incest are discussed using case examples.

Goodwin, J.; M. Simms; and R. Bergman. "Hysterical Seizures: A Sequel to Incest." *American Journal of Orthopsychiatry* 49 (October 1979): 698–703.   E

Describes six cases in which hysterical seizures developed after incest and disappeared after psychotherapeutic exploration of the incestuous experience.

Goody, J. *Kinship*. New York: Penguin Books, 1972.   E

This collection of readings illuminates many aspects of a diversified field of study and includes material by writers such as Malinowski and Radcliffe-Brown. Discusses incest and sex, the developmental cycle, joking relationships, marriage transactions, plural marriage, divorce, kin terms, and ritual kinship.

Goppinger, H. "The Victim as Seen by the Offender." *Victimology: An International Journal* 2 (1977):63.   H

In a paper presented at the Second International Symposium on Victimology, held in Boston, September 1976, the results of the statistical evaluation of the relevant data of the Tubingen Life Imprisonment Project and of the Tubingen Young Offender Comparative Investigation are presented. Offenders' social dependencies, personality, and the type and behavior of the victim were examined to determine the offender's view of his victim.

Gordon, L. "Incest as Revenge against the Preoedipal Mother." *Psychoanalytic Review* 42 (1955) 284–292.   E

Gordon, M.T., and S. Riger. "The Fear of Rape Project." *Victimology* 3 (1978):346–347.   B,G

The fear-of-rape project at the center for urban affairs, Northwestern University, which is assessing the impact of the fear of rape and other crimes on the lives of women living in San Francisco, Chicago, and Philadelphia, is described. In the first stage of the project, several large secondary data sets were analyzed to determine baseline levels of fear of crime in various cities and the ways in which people's behavior was affected by that fear.

————. "Fear and Avoidance: A Link between Attitudes and Behavior." *Victimology* 4 (1979):395–402.   H

The relationship between perceived risk of victimization and preventive/avoidance behaviors was examined using 1973 data from a police survey of 1,161 persons. Factor analysis of twelve risk-assessment items yielded three factors: street risk, home risk, and property risk.

Gordon, M.T.; S. Riger; R.K. Lebailly; and L. Heath. "Crime, Women, and the Quality of Urban Life." *Signs: Journal of Women in Culture and Society* 5 (1980):S144–S160.   C,G

The relationship between fear and risk of rape victimization and the consequences of fear of crime for both men and women were examined in in-depth interview data for 299 women and 68 men in Chicago, San Francisco, and Philadelphia. Findings strongly support previous research: Urban fear of crime was pervasive, but women reported significantly more fear than men both in terms of perceived neighborhood safety and of worry about physical safety in day-to-day activities.

Gornick, V., and B.K. Moran, eds. *Woman in Sexist Society*. New York: Mentor, 1972.   A,F,G
Gottesman, D.M. "The Psychological Effects of Crisis." *Dissertation Abstracts International* 41(4-B):1504, October, 1980.   C

Life crisis, anxiety level versus depression versus self-esteem versus locus of control, operable cancer versus minor operable patients versus rape victims versus normals.

Gottesman, S. "Police Attitudes toward Rape before and after a Training Program." *Journal of Psychiatric Nursing and Mental Health Services* 15 (1977):14–18.   B,G
Gouge, W. *Of Domesticall Duties, Eight Treaties*, 3rd ed. London: George Miller, 1634.   B
Gove, W.B. "The Relationship between Sex Roles, Marital Status, and Mental Illness." *Social Forces* 51 (September 1972):34–44.   B,H
Gove, W., and J. Tudor. "Adult Sex Roles and Mental Illness." *American Journal of Sociology* 78 (1973):812–835.   E,G

Graff, T.T. "Personality Characteristics of Battered Women." *Dissertation Abstracts International* 40(7):3395-B, 1980.   *A*

The personality characteristics of women involved in physical marital violence were investigated. Several instruments were administered to abused women, nonabused women, and standard women.

Graham, H.D., and T.R. Gurr. *Violence in America: Historical and Comparative Perspectives.* New York: Bantam Books, 1969.   *A,E,F,G,H*
Grambs, M. "Refuge for Battered Wives: Casa de Las Madres." *Intellect* 106 (March 1978):353.   *A,B*
Gray, D. "Turning-Out: A Study of Teen-Age Prostitution." *Urban Life and Culture*, January 1973, pp. 401–425.   *B*
Gray, E. "Courting Regression on Rape (Supreme Court Decisions in Canada) *Macleans* 93 (28 July 1980):44–45.   *G*
Grayson, B. "A Comparison of Criminal Perceptions of Potential Victims of Assault and a Movement Analysis Based on Labanalysis." *Dissertation Abstracts International* 40(1):476-A, 1979.   *H*

Criminals' perceptions of the nonverbal communication of potential victims of assault were investigated, and the utility of movement analysis based on Labanalysis dance-notation system in describing these nonverbal communications was assessed.

Great Britain. Home Office. *Criminal Statistics on England and Wales.* London: Her Majesty's Stationery Office, 1969.   *B*
Great Britain. *Parliamentary Papers.* "Reports to the Secretary of State for the Home Department on the State of the Law Relating to Brutal Assaults," 1875.   *A*
Green, A.H. "Psychopathology of Abused Children." *Journal of the American Academy of Child Psychiatry* 17 (1978):92–103.   *B,C*

The major types of psychopathology and behavioral deviance observed in physically abused children during their participation in clinical research and treatment programs are described.

Green, A.W. "The Middle Class Male Child and Neurosis." *American Sociological Review* 11 (February 1946):31–41.   *B,E*
Green, C.P., and S.J. Lowe. *Teenage Pregnancy: A Major Problem for Minors.* New York: Alan Guttmacher Institute, 1976.   *E*
Green, K. "The Echo of Marital Conflict." *Family Process* 2 (1963).   *A*
Green, M.R. *Violence and the Family.* Boulder, Colo.: Westview Press, 1980.   *H*

A sociological perspective on the causes of family violence, the effect of television viewing on aggressive behavior in preschool children, ethno-psychiatric dimensions in family violence, and functions of the police in family violence are discussed in this book.

Green, R., and R. Pigg. "Acquisition of an Aggressive Response and its Generalization to Verbal Behavior." *Journal of Personality and Social Psychology* 19:165–170. H

Greenberg. "Letter: Serological Tests For Syphilis in Rape Cases." *Journal of the American Medical Association* 227 (1974):1381. G,H

Greenwald, H. *The Elegant Prostitute.* New York: Ballantine, 1970. C

Greer. "Seduction Is a Four Letter Word." In Rape Victimology. L. Schultz, ed., 1975. G,H

Greve, J. *London's Homeless.* London: G. Bell and Sons, 1964. B,C

Griffen, S. "Rape: The All American Crime." *Ramparts*, September 1971, pp. 26–35. G

Griffin. "A Self Defense Program for Women." *FBI Law Enforcement Bulletin* 9 (1974):43. B

Griffin, B.S. "Rape: Risk, Confrontation and Normalization." *Dissertation Abstracts International* 39(5):3160-A, 1978. G

The processes of rape victimization were defined, the relationships between risk, confrontation, and normalization variables were tested, and those factors that significantly affect the victimization process were identified.

Griffin. S. *Rape: The Power of Consciousness.* New York: Harper & Row, 1979. G

Grimshaw, A.D. "Interpreting Collective Violence: An Argument for the Importance of Social Structure." *Annals* 391 (September 1970):9–20. H

Grimstad, K., and S. Rennie, eds. *The New Woman's Survival.* New York: Alfred A. Knopf, 1975. B

Grohmann, S.W. "Dane County Advocates for Battered Women Emergency Shelter Facility—Monitor Report." Madison: Wisconsin Council on Criminal Justice, April 1979. B

An emergency shelter for battered women in Dane County, Madison, Wisconsin, is evaluated at the end of its first year of operations.

Groner, E. "Delivery of Clinical Social Work Services in the Emergency Room: A Description of an Existing Program." *Social Work in Health Care* 4 (1978):19–29. B

A program of social-work delivery in an emergency room is described. The application of crisis-intervention theory as practiced by the emergency-room social worker and the utilization of a system of clinical evaluation, community referral, and advocacy are delineated. Problem categories and protocols in social-work treatments of patients and families in cases of death, rape, child abuse, and suicide attempt are discussed.

Gropper, A., and J. Currie. "A Study of Battered Women." School of Social Work Library, University of British Columbia, March, 1976. *A*

This research project specifically addresses itself to the following question: What are the factors within the transition process that lead to success for women who have used Ishtar Transition House and who have been physically abused?

Gross, M. "One Woman's War against Rape." *Good Housekeeping* 184 (April 1977):84.   *G*
———. "Incestuous Rape: A Cause for Hysterical Seizures in Four Adolescent Girls." *American Journal of Orthopsychiatry* 49 (1979):705–708.   *E,G*

Four cases of hysterical seizures in adolescent girls that occurred as a result of forced incestuous relationships with fathers are presented.

Gross, R.J.; H. Doerr; D. Cladirola; G.M. Guzinska; and H. Ripley. "Borderline Syndrome and Incest in Chronic Pain Patients." Psychiatry in Medicine 10 (1980):1.   *E*
Groth, A.N. "The Older Rape Victim and Her Assailant." *Journal of Geriatric Psychiatry* 11 (1978):203–215.   *G*

Specific data relating to the rape of elderly women is presented. The elderly are not immune from rape, and the biopsychosocial impact of rape may be aggravated by the diminished physical, social, and economic resources that accompany aging.

———. *Men Who Rape: The Psychology of the Offender.* New York: Plenum Publishing, 1979.   *G*

Explores the motivation of the rapist, revealing the psychological and emotional pressures that make him react with sexual violence.

———. *Psychological Characteristics of the Rapist: The Psychology of the Offender.* New York: Plenum, 1979.   *G*

The psychological characteristics of the rapist are examined in support of the view that rape is a clinical syndrome worthy of inclusion in the major classifications of psychiatric disorders.

————. "Sexual Trauma in the Life Histories of Rapists and Child Molesters." *Victimology* 4 (1979):10–16.   E,G

Sexual trauma in the life histories of 348 rapists and child molesters was investigated to examine factors that lead to the formation of the sexual-assault symptom.

Groth, A.N., and J.J. Birnbaum. "Adult Sexual Orientation and Attraction to Underage Persons." *Archives of Sexual Behavior* 7 (1978):175–181.
                                                                             E
Groth, A.N., and A.W. Burgess. "Rape: A Sexual Deviation." *American Journal of Orthopsychiatry* 47 (July 1977):400–406.   G
————. "Sexual Dysfunction during Rape." *New England Journal of Medicine* 297 (October 1977):764–766.   E,G

Results of a study with 170 men convicted of sexual assault and 92 adult women and 37 children who reported having been victims of sexual assault suggest that negative results of physical and laboratory examination of the victim do not rule out sexual assault and penetration.

————. "Impotent Rape." *Human Behavior* 7 (June 1978):54.   G
————. "Rape." *New England Journal of Medicine* 298 (1978):167–168.
                                                                             G

In a letter to the editor, the authors of an article on sexual dysfunction during rape respond to several letters commenting on that article and comment on the relation between sexual dysfunction and forced sexual behavior.

————. "Rape: A Pseudosexual Act." *International Journal of Women's Studies* 1 (March/April 1978):207–210.   G

It is concluded that laws requiring the presence of sperm to confirm an act of rape fail to recognize rape as a pseudosexual act motivated more by feelings of hostility and power than of sexual desire.

————. "Male Rape: Offenders and Victims." *American Journal of Psychiatry* 137 (1980):806–810.   G

Descriptive characteristics of male rape, dynamics of the offender, and impact of the rape on the victim were investigated and compared with comparable reports for female victims of rape.

Groth, A.N.; Burgess; and L. Holmstron. "Rape: Power, Anger, and Sexuality." *American Journal of Psychiatry* 134 (November 1977):1239–1243.   G

Accounts from both offenders and victims of what occurs during a rape suggest that issues of power, anger, and sexuality are important in understanding the rapist's behavior.

Gundlach, R.H. "Birth Order among Lesbians: New Light on an Only Child." *Psychological Report* 40 (February 1977):250.   *E*
———. "Sexual Molestation and Rape Reported by Homosexual and Heterosexual Women." *Journal of Homosexuality* 2 (Summer 1977): 367–384.   *E, G*

Questionnaire returns from 225 homosexual and 233 heterosexual adult women revealed 115 cases of rape or attempted rape.

Gunn, J.C. *Violence*. London: David and Charles, 1973.   *H*
———. *Psychopathological Effects of Violence*. London: Edward Arnold Limited, 1978.   *H*

The psychological factors leading to violence factors that affect interactions between victim and attacker and the psychological aftereffects of violence are reviewed. The aftereffects are often underestimated.

Guss, G.H. "The Woman's Role in the Victim-Offender Relationship in Forcible Rape." *Dissertation Abstracts International* 36 (11):5761, May, 1976.   *G, H*
Gutheil, T.G., and N.C. Avery. "Multiple Overt Incest as Family Defense against Loss." *Family Process* 16 (March 1977):105–116.   *E*

Presents a case report of father-daughter incest to illustrate the way in which overt incest can function as a multidetermined familial defense against separation and loss.

Haber, S. *Society's Recognition and Control of Violence*. San Francisco: Jossey-Bass, 1978.   *H*

Factors influencing society's recognition of an act as violent, interpretation of a violent act as either appropriate or inappropriate, and control of inappropriate violence are explored.

Haden-Guest, A. "Melonie Haller's Lost Weekend." *New Yorker* 13 (12 May 1980):44–47.   *G*
Haffner, S. *Frauenhauser. Gewalt in der Ehe und was Frauen dagegen tun*. Berlin: Wagenbach, 1976.   *B*
———. "Wife Abuse in West Germany." *Victimology: An International Journal* 2 (1978):472–476.   *A*

The development of the battered-women movement and the founding of
one of the first refuges in West Berlin is described. A directory of West
Germany's refuges and initiative groups is provided.

————. "A Refuge for Battered Women: A Conversation with Erin Pizzy."
Victimology 4 (1979):100–112.   B

An interview with Erin Pizzy, the founder of Chiswick Women's Aid
Program, is presented. This refuge for battered women began in 1971 as a
community center for mothers and children who were alone and isolated
and is largely financed by government funds.

Hageman, M.J., and C. Hastings. "Patterns in Forcible Rape in Wichita,
Kansas: A Case of the Open System Theory." *Journal of Police Science
Administration* 6 (September 1978):318–323.   G
Haines. "The Character of the Rape Victim." *Chitty's Law Journal* 23
(1975):57.   G
Haley, J. "The Family of the Schizophrenic: A Model System." *Nerve and
Mental Disorder* 129 (October 1959):357–374.   B
Hall, B.J. *Incest: Breaking the Tabu.* Vancouver: Pulp Press, 1975.   E
Hall, R.L. "Empathetic Behavior in a Simulated Rape Interview by Police
Applicants." *Dissertation Abstracts International* 40 (5):2365-B, 1979.
                                                                      G

The roles of similarities of race and sex were measured on the degree
of empathetic behavior present in a simulated rape interview.

Halleck, S.L. "The Physician's Role in Management of Victims of Sex
Offenders." *Journal of the American Medical Association* 180 (Febru-
ary 1970):273–278.   G
Haller, J.S. "Abuses in Gynecological Surgery: An Historical Appraisal."
In *Women and Their Health: Research Implications for a New Era,*
edited by U.S. Department of Health, Education, and Welfare. Rock-
ville, Md.   C
Halpern, S. *Rape: Helping the Victim.* Dradell, N.J.: Economics, 1978.G

Guidelines for the care and treatment of the rape victim are presented.
Among the topics discussed are common misconceptions about rape, the
managment of child victims, investigation of the patient, long-term patient
needs, the role of the police, and the role of family and friends.

Hamilton, J.W. "Multiple Group Rape: Psychosocial Considerations."
Journal of Nervous and Mental Disease 167 (February 1979):128–130.
                                                                      G

Psychiatric examinations of several participants in repeated episodes of rape demonstrated that sexual assault combined with stealing represents symbolically an attack on the bad mother, such hostile acting out enabling the individual to defend against strong but ambivalent wishes to be nurtured.

Hamilton, M. "Don't You Come Home Mort Gordon." *American Home*, 79 (March 1976):100.   *A*

Hamlin, D.E.; D.B. Hurwitz; and G. Spieker. "Perspectives." *Alcohol Health and Research World* 4 (Fall 1979):17–22.   *H*

This interview presents recommendations of counselors on how to deal with domestic violence in view of such problems as resistance to societal regulations, the need to understand better the relationship between alcoholism and domestic violence, and fragmentation of services.

Hammel, E.A., et al. "Demographic Consequences of Incest Tabus: A Microsimulation Analysis." *Science* 7 September 1979, pp. 972–977. *E*

Hammer, J. "Community Action, Women's Aid and the Women's Liberation Movement." In *Women in the Community*, edited by M. Mayo. *B*

Hammer, J. "Violence and the Social Control of Women." Paper presented at the Annual Meeting of the British Societological Association in Sheffield, England, 1977.   *B,H*

Handleman, D. "The Dynamics of Developing Relationships: Social Workers and Clients." Unpublished, 1970.   *B*

Hanks, S.E., and C.P. Rosenbaum. "Battered Women: A Study of Women Who Live with Violent Alcohol-Abusing Men." *American Journal of Orthopsychology* 47 (April 1977):291–306.   *A*

Hannon, R.T. "Effects of a Rape Victim's Past History on Outcomes of Juror Deliberations." *Dissertation Abstracts International* 40 (3-B): 1423, 1979.   *G*

Hanss. "Another Look at the Case of Rape Victim." *Journal of Arizona Medicine* 32 (1975):634.   *G*

Harakas, M. "Wife Beating: Catch 22 Trauma." *Fort Lauderdale Sun-Sentinel*, a series of three articles, August 1975.   *A*

Harbert, T.L.; D. Marlow; M. Hersen; and J. Austin. "Measurement and Modification of Incestuous Behavior: A Case Study." *Psychological Reports* 34 (February 1974):79–86.   *E*

Describes treatment of a fifty-two-year-old man complaining of repeated incestuous behavior with his daughter from the time she was twelve years old until she was seventeen, when treatment was initiated.

Hardgrove, G. "An Interagency Service Network to meet needs of Rape Victims." *Social Casework* 57 (April 1976):245–253.   *G*

Describes a coordinated interagency network in California for rape-crisis intervention that offers support information for victims and hot line services manned by trained volunteers.

"Hard Look at Domestic Violence." *Royal Canadian Mounted Police Gazette* 40(8) (Fall 1978):8–12.   H

While abuse and neglect are leading causes of death in children, crimes committed within the home are nearly unpunishable. Society needs to face the fact that the family relationship is no excuse for assault or murder.

Hare, D. "The Victim Is Guilty." *Federation Procedures* 35 (1974):2223–2225.   H

Harper, F.V. *Problems of the Family*, rev. ed. New York: Bobbs-Merrill, 1962.   C,H

Harpole. "Rape, Seduction, and Love—Ethics in Public and Private Communications." *Speech Teacher* 24 (1975):303.   G

Harrington, J.A. "Violence: A Clinical Viewpoint." *British Medical Journal* 1 (1972):228–231.   H

Harris. "Towards a Consent Standard in the Law of Rape." *University of Chicago Law Review* 43 (1976):613.   F,G

Harris, J. "Networks Claim They've Been Toned Down but . . . " *National Enquirer*, 19 August 1975, p. 14.   H

Harris, L.H. "Middle Class High School Dropouts: Incidence of Physical Abuse, Incest, Sexual Assault, Loss, Symptomatic Behaviors, and Emotional Disturbance." *Dissertation Abstracts International* 41(5): 2058-A, 1980.   E

The possible relationship between dropout-prone behaviors and general psychosocial maladjustment was examined with a group of sixty-seven dropout-prone high school youths and sixty-eight controls.

Harris, L., and associates. Poll Conducted for the National Commission on the Causes and Prevention of Violence, 1968.   H

Harris, S.P. "Three Psychological Determinants of a Woman's Response to a Sexual Assault." *Dissertation Abstracts International*, Michigan University, Ann Arbor, Michigan: 1977.   G

The possible relationship between three psychological components of a woman's personality and her resistance or submission to a sexual assault were investigated.

Harrison, B. "Toward a Just Social Order." *Journal of Current Social Issues* 15 (1978):63–70.   E,G

The connections between human sexuality, sexual ethics, and social justice are examined. The relationship between the personal liberties of consenting adults and the needs of public order is discussed in relation to sex codes concerning child molestation, rape, pornography, and prostitution.

Harrison, P. "Compulsory Psychiatry." *New Society* 16 (May 1974):377–380.   C

Hart, A.W. "Thomas Promised that He Would." *The New York Times*, 10 June 1975.   A

Hartik, L.M. *Identification of Personality Characteristics and Self-Concept Factors of Battered Wives*. Palo Alto, Calif.: R & E Research Associates, Inc., 1982.   A

This book is an important contribution to the subject. With a national awareness of family abuse now in the spotlight, it is the intention to provide libraries, educators, students, counselors, and the general population with educational information, somewhat hard hitting but real accounts and solutions to the national disgrace.

Hartman. "Rape." *Illinois Medical Journal* 145 (1974):518.   G

Hartmann, H. "Capitalism, Patriarchy, and Job Segregation by Sex." In *Women and the Workplace*, edited by M. Blaxall and B. Reagan. Chicago: University of Chicago Press, 1976.   H

Hartogs, R. "Discipline in the Early Life of Sex-Delinquent and Sex Criminals." *Nervous Child* 9 (March 1951):167–173.   E,H

Hartwig, S. "Rape Victims: Reasons, Responses, and Reforms." *Intellect* 103 (1975):507.   G

Harvey, A. "April and the Homeless." *New Society* 21 (March 1974):707–708.   B

Haskell, M. *From Reverence to Rape: The Treatment of Women in the Movies*. New York: Holt, Rinehart & Winston, 1974.   C,G

Havemann, P.L. *Professional Education and the Violent Family*. Toronto: Butterworth, 1978.   D

The current status of training of professionals to deal with both marital violence and child abuse is surveyed. The problems of curriculum evaluation are examined, and possible components for curricula are presented.

Haven House Project. Proposal Submitted to County of Los Angeles Department of Urban Affairs, 15E–17E, 12 March 1975.   B

Havens, L.L. "Youth, Violence, and the Nature of Family Life." *Psychiatric Annals* 2 (February 1972):18–29.   H

Havernick, W. *Schlage als Strafe*. Hamburg: 1964.

Hawkes, W. "Crime and Punishment in an Anglo-Saxon Cemetery." *Antiquity* 49 (1975):118.   B

Hayman. "Roundtable: Rape and Its Consequences." *Medical Aspects of Human Sexuality* 6 (February 1972):12.   G

Hayman. "Letter: Serological Tests for Syphilis in Rape Crisis." *Journal of American Medical Association* 228 (1974):1227.   G

Hayman. "Sexual Assaults on Women and Girls." *Annals of Internal Medicine* 72 (1970):277.   E,G

Hayman, and Lanza. "Sexual Assault on Women and Girls." *American Journal of Obstetrics and Gynecology* 109 (1971):480.   E,G

———. "Victimology of Sexual Assault." *Medical Aspects of Human Sexuality* 5 (October 1971):112.   G,H

Hayman; Lanza; and Fuentes. "Sexual Assault on Women and Girls in the District of Columbia." *Southern Medical Journal* 62 (1969):1227. E,G

Hayman; Lanza; Fuentes; and Algor. "Rape in the District of Columbia." *American Journal of Obstetrics and Gynecology* 113 (1972):93.   G

Hayman; Lewis; Steward; and Grant. "A Public Health Program for Sexually Assaulted Females." In *Human Sexuality and Social Work*, edited by H. Gochros and L. Schultz. New York, 1972.   B,G

Haywood, C.H. "Emergency, Crisis and Stress Services for Rape Victims." *Crisis Intervention* 6 (1975):43–48.   C,G

Discusses services for rape victims in terms of the individual characteristics and needs of the victim as well as the nature of the crime.

"Healthy Rise in Rape." *Newsweek*, 31 July 1972, p. 72.   G

Heath, L. "A Multi-Methodological Examination of the Effects of Perceptions of Control on Women's Attitudes toward and Behaviors Concerning Rape." *Dissertation Abstracts International* 41 (6):2386-B, 1980. G

The effects of perceptions of the ability to control rape on women's fear, worry, and concern about rape as well as on their self-protective behaviors regarding rape were examined in two studies.

Heath, R.G. "Electrical Self-Stimulation of the Brain in Man." *American Journal of Psychiatry* 120 (1963):571–577.   B

Hebrew University. Institute of Criminology. *Proceedings of the Seminar on Violence in Israel*. Jerusalem, 1967 (Hebrew text, English summary).   H

Hecker, E.A. *A Short History of Women's Rights: From the Days of Augustus to the Present Time. With Special Reference to England and the United States*, 2d ed. Westport, Conn.: Greenwood Press, 1972. 124–127   A,C,E,G

Examines the legal status of women from the foundations of Roman law. On pages 124 through 127 are specific references to "the right of a husband to correct and chastise the wife." The evolution of law with regard to physical punishment and to what extent and for what misdemeanors it was accepted is examined. From dated readings it is found that abuse was not confined to a specific social rank. It asserts that wife beating is still "a flagrantly common offense" in England.

Heer, D.M. "The Measurement and Bases of Family Power: An Overview." *Marriage and Family Living* 25 (1963):133–139.   B,H

Hegeler, I., and S. Hegeler. *The XYZ of Love: Frank Answers to Every Important Question about Sex in Today's World.* New York: Crown, 1970.   B,E,G

"Heilbron Draws a Veil." *Economist*, 13 December 1975. (Great Britain).
          B

Heilbrun, A.B., Jr. "Presumed Motive in the Male and Female Perception of Rape." *Criminal Justice and Behavior* 7 (1980):257–274.   G

Sexual differences in rape stereotypes and the subjective impressions of rape generated by information and misinformation about the act were investigated.

Heilbrun, A.B., Jr., and J.M. Cross. "An Analysis of Rape Patterns in White and Black Rapists." *Journal of Social Psychology* 108 (1979):83–87.   B,G

To identify patterns of rape, a number of characteristics of rapists in the state of Georgia, their victims, and the acts of rape themselves were correlated and submitted to independent factor analyses for black and white rapists. Results show that factor 1 for black rapists loaded positively with age, negatively with education, and negatively with the use of psychological threat. Factor 1 for white rapists included a plus loading for age and a minus loading for education.

Heimel. "I Should Have Known: It's August." *Majority Report*, 22 August 1974, p. 1.   G

Heins, M., and S. Horn. Brief on behalf of claimant appellant in the matter of the claim of Carmita Wood for unemployment insurance benefits. Ithaca, N.Y., 1975.   F

Heins, M. et al. "Productivity of Women Physicians." *Journal of the American Medical Association* 236 (1976):1961–1964.   D

Heintzelman, C.A. "Differential Utilization of Selected Community Resources by Abused Women." *Dissertation Abstracts International* 41 (2):806-A, 1980.   A

The influences of pregnancy, abuse patterns in wife's family, length of marriage, husband's criminal-assault record, and wife's socioeconomic status on the wife's decision to contact a shelter or nonshelter agency for abused women were examined.

Heinz. "Time for a Change in this Nation's Rape Laws." 120 *Congressional Record* E2709, May 2, 1974.   F

Heiskanen, I., and V. Stohe. "Contextual Analysis and Theory Construction in Cross-Cultural Family Research." *Journal of Comparative Family Studies* 3 (Spring 1972):33–50.   B

Helfer, R.E., and C.H. Kempe. *The Battered Child*. Chicago: University of Chicago Press, 1968.   E

Helfer, R.M., M.D. "The Etiology of Child Abuse." *Pediatrics* LI 4 (April 1973):777–779.   E

Helmholtz, R.H. *Marriage Litigation in Medieval England*. Cambridge: Cambridge University Press, 1974.   A,F

"Help for Families Coping with Incest," *Practice Digest* 1 (September 1978):19–22.   E

"Help for the Rape Victim." Report of the Pennsylvania Commission for Women. Harrisburg, 1975.   A,G

Henderson, D.J. "Incest: A Synthesis of Data." *Canadian Psychiatric Association Journal* 17 (August 1972):299–313.   E

Hendin, H. "Suicide: A Psychoanalytic Point of View." In *The Cry for Help*, edited by H.L. Farberow and S. Shneidman. New York: McGraw-Hill, 1961.   C,H

Hendricks, J. "Transactional Analysis and the Police: Family Disputes." *Journal of Police Science and Administration* 5 (December 1977):416–420.   C,F

Examines the application of transactional analysis to police contacts with family disputes. The basic transactional-analysis concepts of parent, adult, child, and psychological games are discussed and illustrated.

Hendrix, M.J., and G.E. Lagodnam. "Battered Wife." *American Journal of Nursing* 78 (1978):650–653.   A

Henig, J., and M.G. Maxfield. "Reducing Fear of Crime: Strategies for Intervention." *Victimology* 3 (1978):297–313.   H

The gap between existing theoretical and empirical literature dealing with the fear of crime and the policy needs of urban decision makers are examined. Factors related to fear and crime include misperceptions of the threat of crime, urban social disintegration, and physical characteristics of the environment.

Henn, F.A.; Herjanic; and R.H. Vanderpearl. "Forensic Psychiatry: Pro-

files of Two Types of Sex Offenders." *American Journal of Psychiatry*
133 (June 1976):694–696.   B

Examined records of 239 individuals charged with sexual offenses and
referred by the courts to a forensic service. Defendants charged with rape
were typically under thirty with histories of antisocial behavior that included other types of violence.

Henry, R.A. "Urban Disturbances and Black Community Victimization."
Victimology: An International Journal 2 (1977):63–64.   H

In a paper presented at the Second International Symposium on Victimology, held in Boston, September 1976, the patterns and conditions involved in direct victimization of the black community during periods of
massive urban disturbances are explored. Direct victimization and analytical neglect are taken as the hallmark of the minority situation.

Hepburn, J.R. "Violence in Interpersonal Relationships." *Sociological
Quarterly* 14 (1973):419–429.   H
Hepperle, W.L., and L. Crites. *Women in the Courts*. Virginia: National
Center for State Courts, 1978.   D

Ten contributing authors assess the wide range of women's participation in
the judicial system.

Heppner, M.J. "Counseling the Battered Wife: Myths, Facts, and Decisions." *Personnel and Guidance Journal* 56 (1978):522–525.   A,C,G

Counseling for the battered wife is discussed with particular emphasis on
myths that contribute to the current inadequacy of service and the psychological patterns of battered wives that must be understood if effective
counseling is to be provided.

Heppner, P.P., and M.J. Heppner. "Rape: Counseling the Traumatized
Victim." *Personnel and Guidance Journal* 56 (1977):77–80.   C,G
Herman, E. "Battered Women: Why Some Can't Escape the Abuse."
Chicago Tribune 26 August 1976, Tempo section.   A

Begins with a case example, and reports that estimates show that thousands
of women are battered in the Chicago area each year. Cites studies showing
25 percent of abuse occurs in white-collar professional homes.

Herman, J., and L. Hirschman. "Father-Daughter Incest." *Signs* 2 (Summer 1977):735–756.   E

Explores the extent and possible causes of father-daughter incest and
common professional attitudes toward this problem. The outstanding fea-

tures of the incestuous constellation are analyzed on the basis of a clinical study of fifteen victims.

————. "Families at Risk for Father-Daughter Incest." *American Journal of Psychiatry* 138 (July 1981):967–970.   E

Compared forty women who had incestuous relationships with their fathers during childhood with twenty women whose fathers had been seductive but not overtly incestuous. More of the women who had experienced overt incest reported that their fathers had been violent and that their mothers had been chronically ill, disabled, or battered.

Herman and Sedlacek, "Female University Student and Staff Perceptions of Rape." *Journal of National Association of Women Deans, Administrators, and Counselors* 38 (1974):20.   G

Herner and Company. *Child Abuse and Family Violence.* Washington, D.C.: National Center for Child Abuse and Neglect, 1978.   E,H

Herold, E.S.; D. Mantle; and O. Zemitis. "A Study of Sexual Offenses against Females." *Adolescence* 14 (Spring 1979):65–72.   A,E,G

Data from 103 females in two university classes reveal that 84 percent had been the victim of a sexual offense. The offenses included obscene telephone calls (61 percent), sexual molestation (44 percent), exhibitionism (27 percent), being followed (24 percent), attempted rape (16 percent), and rape (1 percent).

Herrmann, K.J., Jr. "Getting Action from Social Agencies." *Trooper* 3 (July/August 1978):55–57.   B

The work of social agencies is discussed, and cooperation between the police and these agencies is urged. Reasons for the seemingly poor response by social agencies to police referrals are presented.

Hespel, J. "Emotional Frustration in Juvenile Delinquents Seen through the P.N." *Revue de Psychologie Appliquee* 1–8 (1968):147–158.   A

Hess, A.G. "Rape: A Psychosocial Study." *Dissertation Abstracts International*, Ann Arbor, Michigan University 1977.   G

Personality characteristics of two groups of rapists who were identified as mentally disordered sex offenders were studied.

Hess, J. "French Mothers to Get Equal Say in Raising Children." *The New York Times*, 17 April 1970.   C

Hibey. "The Trial of a Rape Case: An Advocate's Analysis of Corroboration, Consent, and Character." *Rape Victimology* 1975.   B,F

Hicks. "On Rape." *Parade Magazine* 12 February 1976, p. 10.   G

Hicks, D.J. "Imitation and Retention of Film-Mediated Aggressive Peer

and Adult Models." *Journal of Personality and Social Psychology* 2
(1965):97–100.   *B*

Hicks & Platt. "Medical Treatment for the Victim: The Development of a
Rape Treatment Center." In *Sexual Assault*, edited by M. Walker and
S. Brodsky. 1976.   *B,H*

Higgins, J.G. *Social Services for Abused Wives*. New York: Family Service
Association of America, 1978.   *A,B*

An inventory of social service available to battered wives in the United
States and Canada is given.

"High Court Backs Naming of Rape Victims in News." *Editor and Publisher*
8 March 1975, p. 11.   *F,G*

Hilberman, E. "Rape: The Ultimate Violation of the Self." *American
Journal of Psychiatry* 133 (1976):436.   *G*

———. *The Rape Victim*. New York: Basic Books, 1976.   *G*

Dr. Hilberman points out that the profound impact of rape stress is best
understood in the context of rape as a crime against the whole person and
not just the body.

———. "Rape: A Crisis in Silence." *Psychiatric Opinion* 14 (September/
October 1977):32–35.   *G*

Discusses some of the myths surrounding rape and the results of these
myths on the reporting of rape. It is suggested that in order to treat rape
victims adequately, clinicians should inform themselves about hospital
policy, criminal-justice procedures, rape statutes, and community attitudes
about and services for rape victims.

———. "Overview: The Wife-Beater's Wife Reconsidered." *American
Journal of Psychiatry* 137 (November 1980):1336–1347.   *G*

This article describes both the family and societal contexts in which the
physical abuse of wives can be understood, suggests alternative theoretical
constructs to traditional theories of masochism as explanation of why
women remain in violent marital relationships, and discusses treatment
issues and the clinician's role.

Hilberman, E., and K. Munson. "Sixty Battered Women." *Victimology:
An International Journal* 2 (1978):460–470.   *A*

The psychological impact of marital violence on sixty women referred to a
rural health clinic for psychiatric evaluation was examined. It was observed
that physical abuse played a causative role in paralyzing anxiety, low
self-image, and chronic tranquilizer use in the wife.

Hill, C.E.; M.F. Tanney; M.M. Leonard; and J.A. Reiss. "Counselor Reactions to Female Clients: Type of Problem, Age of Client, and Sex of Counselor." *Journal of Counseling Psychology* 24 (January 1977): 60–65.   B

Eighty-eight male and female graduate students in counseling, staff of a university counseling center, and faculty in counseling and clinical psychology viewed videotaped vignettes of two thirty-five-year-old women and two twenty-year-old women who portrayed problems about feared rape, existential anxiety, choice of a college major in social work, or choice of a college major in engineering.

Hill, R. *Families under Stress*. New York: Harper and Brothers, 1949. *C,H*
———. "General Features of Families under Stress." In *Crisis Intervention*, edited by H.J. Parad. 1965.   *B,C,H*
———. *Family Development in Three Generations: A Longitudinal Study of Changing Family Patterns of Planning and Achievement*. Cambridge, Mass.: Schenkman, 1970.   B
———. "Modern Systems Theory and the Family: A Confrontation." *Social Science Information* 10 (October 1970):7–26.   B
Hill, R., and R. Konig. *Families East and West*. Paris: Mouton, 1970. B
Hill, W.F. *Learning: A Survey of Psychological Interpretations*, rev. ed. Scranton, Pa.: Chandler Publishing, 1971.   B
Hinde, R.A. "The Nature and Control of Aggressive Behaviour," *International Social Science Journal* 23 (1971):48–52.   H
Hindelang, M.J. "Race and Involvement in Common Law Personal Crimes." *American Sociological Review* 43 (1978):93–109.   F

Data from a national victimization survey were compared with official arrest statistics to examine possible relationships between race and involvement in rape, robbery, and assault; to assess the relative accuracy of these two types of data and self-report data; and to determine whether overrepresentation of black offenders is a function of disproportionate black-criminal involvement or criminal-justice-system selection biases.

———. "Sex Differences in Criminal Activity." *Social Problems* 27 (1979): 143–156.   B

National victimization survey data for 1972 were examined to investigate the extent to which they accord with *Uniform Crime Report* data regarding the offender's sex. The results for common-law crime, both personal and property crime, parallel arrest data showing male involvement in these crimes to be much greater than female involvement.

Hindman, M.H. "Family Violence: An Overview." *Alcohol, Health and Research World* 4 (1979):2–11.   H

The association between alcohol use and family violence is discussed. The underreporting of child and spouse abuse is cited, and it is estimated that 1.7 million spouses and 1 million children are assaulted or abused each year.

Hinkel, D.B. "Intrafamily Litigation—Husband and Wife." *Insurance Law Journal*, 1970.   F
Hinton, J.W.; M.T. Oneill; and S. Webster. "Psychophysiological Assessment of Sex Offenders in a Security Hospital." *Archives of Sexual Behavior* 9 (June 1980):205–216.   B

Studied the sexual orientation and responsiveness of male sexual offenders in a maximum security hospital who had been referred to the psychology department for sexual assessment.

Hiroto, D.S. "Locus of Control and Learned Helplessness." *Journal of Experimental Psychology* 102 (1974):187–193.   B
Hirsch. B.D. *Divorce: What a Woman Needs to Know*. New York: Bantam, 1973.   B
Hirsch, M.F. *Women and Violence*. New York: Litton Educational Publishing Company, 1981.   H

This volume probes the manifestations of abuse of women from anthropological, sociological, and psychological viewpoints. Biological and behavioral differences in men and women are discussed, and the minority status of women throughout history is explored.

Hirschel D. "Providing Rape Victims with Assistance at Court: The Erie County Volunteer Supportive Advocate Court Assistance Program." *Victimology* 3 (1978):149–154.   B,F,H

Services offered by the Erie County Volunteer Supportive Advocate Court Assistance Program are described. Initiated by the department of antirape and sexual assault, the program is now operated by crisis services under the supervision of the citizens advisory committee on rape and sexual assault.

Hirschman, L.N. "Incest and Seduction: A Comparison of Two Client Groups." *Dissertation Abstracts International* 40 (9):4485-B, 1980. *E,G*

Family dynamics, client dynamics, and problems of therapeutic treatment were investigated among adult women in therapy who had experienced incestuous and seductive sexual relations with their fathers. The incest and seduction client groups were found to differ with regard to mother's social adjustment, realistic portrayals of parents, and maternal role of daughters.

Hobsbawm, E.J. *Primitive Rebels: Studies in Archaic Forms of Social Movement in the 19th and 20th Centuries.* Manchester: Manchester University Press, 1959.   B

Hoene, R.E. "Annotated Bibliography on Delinquent Girls and Related Research." *Catalog of Selected Documents in Psychology* 8 (May 1978): 40–41.   B

Female delinquency, incest, and lesbianism are covered.

Hofeller, K.H. *Social, Psychological, and Situational Factors in Wife Abuse.* Palo Alto, Calif.: R & E Research Associates, 1982.   A

Provides a thorough discussion of domestic violence and contains information of interest to sociologists, psychologists, social workers, and researchers. The book presents an extensive analysis of both quantitative and qualitative data and includes the social, legal, economic, and religious factors that were associated with the presence of wife abuse in the past and continue to contribute to its incidence today; a review of the literature in this field and an integration of the results of this work with previous research; personality characteristics and family backgrounds of violent men and battered women; detailed case histories that illustrate the dynamics of wife abuse and interaction patterns among violent couples; and comparison of violent and nonviolent marriages on selected variables.

Hoff, L.A., and T. Williams. "Counseling the Rape Victim and Her Family." *Crisis Intervention* 6 (1975):2–13.   C,G

Discusses crisis intervention as a basis for counseling the rape victim and her family.

Hoffman, L.W. "Effects of Employment of Mothers on Parental Power Relations and the Division of Household Tasks." *Marriage and Family Living* 22 (February 1960):27–35.   C

Hoffman, M.L. "Power Assertion by the Parent and Its Impact on the Child." *Child Development* 31 (1960):129–143.   C

———. "Parent Discipline and the Child's Consideration for Others." *Child Development* 34 (1963):573–588.   C

Hofstadter, R., and M. Wallace. *American Violence: A Documentary History.* New York: Alfred A. Knopf, 1970.   H

———. "The Hatfields and the McCoys." In R. Hofstadter and M. Wallace, *American Violence: A Documentary History.* New York: Alfred A. Knopf, 1970.   H

Hoggard, M.J. "An Initial Response to Rape Prevention and Control."
   Health and Social Work 3 (1978):173–181.   *B,C,G*

> An exploratory project initiated in a small rural county of South Carolina to
> find an appropriate method of prevention and control of rape is described.
> It is suggested that the efforts of the task force have been successful in
> increasing awareness of the problem and improving community services.

Holland, J.L. "A Theory of Vocational Choice." *Journal of Counseling
   Psychology* 6 (1959):35–45.   *B*
———. "Explorations of a Theory of Vocational Choice and Achieve-
   ment." *Psychological Reports* 12 (1963):547–594.   *B*
———. "Explorations of a Theory of Vocational Choice: Part II, Self-
   Descriptions and Vocational Preference." *Vocational Guidance Quar-
   terly*, Autumn 1963 pp. 17–23.   *B*
———. "Explorations of a Theory of Vocational Choice: Vocational Images and Choice." *Vocational Guidance Quarterly*, Summer 1963, pp.
   232–237.   *B*
Hollender, M.H. "Prostitution, the Body and Human Relatedness." *International Journal of Psychoanalysis* 42 (1961):404–413.   *C*
Holley, K.C. *Sexual Misuse of Children: Tools for Understanding*. Tacoma, Wash.: Pierce County Rape Relief, Allenmore Medical Center,
   1979.   *E*

> This manual is designed to help parents and teachers educate children and
> youth about sexual misuse. Information and statistics regarding sexual
> misuse are presented along with approaches for teaching children.

Hollingshead, A., and F. Redlich. *Social Class and Mental Illness*. New
   York: Wiley & Sons, 1958.   *B*
Holmes, D.J. *Psychotherapy*. Boston: Little, Brown, 1972.   *B,C*
Holmes, K.A. "Reflections by Gaslight: Prostitution in Another Age."
   Issues in Criminology 83 (Winter 1972).   *H*
———. "Rape-As-Crisis: An Empirical Assessment." *Dissertation Ab-
   stracts International* 40 (3):1685-A, 1979.   *C,G*

> The experience of rape was examined in terms of selected crisis concepts
> using data from semistructured interviews from an accidental sampling of
> sixty-one rape victims contacted through two rape-service organizations.
> Methodological limitations are examined, and implications of findings to
> service delivery and education are discussed.

Holmes, K.A., and J.E. Williams. "Problems and Pitfalls of Rape Victim
   Research: An Analysis of Selected Methodological, Ethical and Prag-
   matic Concerns." *Victimology* 4 (1979):17–28.   *B,G*

Methodological issues and problems encountered in research with rape victims are described with emphasis on analysis of moral and ethical concerns.

Holmstrom. "Rape, the Victim, and the Criminal Justice System." *International Journal of Criminology* 3 (1975):101.   *F,G*

Holmstrom, L.L., and A.W. Burgess. "Assessing Truama in the Rape Victim." *American Journal of Nursing* 75 (1975):1288.   *C,G*

———. "Rape: The Victim Goes on Trial." In 3 *Victimology: A Net Focus* edited by I. Drapkin and E. Viano. 1975.   *G,H*

———. "Rape Reconsidered: The Victim's View." Paper delivered at the American Sociological Association Annual Meeting in San Francisco, 29 August 1975.   *G*

———. "Delays in the Criminal Justice System: The Impact on the Rape Victim." *Victimology: An International Journal* 2 (1977):64.   *F*

The attrition process that occurred in a sample of rape cases in the criminal-justice system over three years is examined. The percentage of cases that do not result in a conviction and the various steps at which prosecution is dropped and the reasons therefore are discussed.

———. *The Victim of Rape: Institutional Reactions.* New York: Wiley & Sons, 1978.   *G*

The reactions of the rape victim to the institutions and the institutionalized responses that she must face are examined. The institutional norms that apply are discussed, and the emotionally brutalizing effects of dealing with the criminal-justice system are examined.

———. "Rape: The Husband's and Boyfriend's Initial Reactions." *Family Coordinator* 28 (1979):321–330.   *G*

The reaction of husbands and boyfriends to the rape of a wife or girlfriend was investigated using data from interviews with sixteen couples. Findings indicate that the man's reaction to the rape has two main components: (1) is his own response (his perceptions of who is the victim, wanting to go after the assailant, and if-only feelings) (2) involves his interaction with the raped woman, then the issues are whether the couple can discuss the rape, how they deal with the woman's new phobias, and the resumption of sexual relations.

———. "Rapists-Talk: Linguistic Strategies to Control the Victim." *Deviant Behavior* 1 (1979):101.   *G*

———. "Sexual Behavior of Assailants during Reported Rapes." *Archives of Sexual Behavior* 9 (1980):427–439.   *G*

Reports on the forced sexual, excretory, and sadistic acts that occur during rape. Analyzing the social meanings attached to forced sex makes a contribution to knowledge about the use of sex to express nonsexual issues.

Home Office. *Report on the Work of the Probation and After-Care Service, 1969–1971*. Cmnd 5158 1972.   B
———. *Criminal Statistics, England and Wales, 1972*. Cmnd. 5402. 1973. B
———. *Criminal Statistics, England and Wales, 1973*. Cmnd. 5677. 1974. B
"Home Strife Number One Cause of Murders in Atlanta." 6 February 1973.
                                                                                   H
"Home Strife Number One Cause of Murders in Atlanta." *Boston Globe*, 6 February 1973.   H
Hook, S. "Violence." In *Encyclopedia of the Social Sciences* 15:1930–1935, New York: Macmillan.   H
Hooper, A. "Eating Blood: Tahitian Concepts of Incest." *Journal of the Polynesian Society* 85 (1976):227–242.   E
Hoover, C.F."Conflict between the Parents of Schizophrenics." *Dissertation Abstracts International* 34 (3-A): September, 1973.   C
Hoplins, K. "Brother-Sister Marriage in Roman Egypt." *Comparative Studies in Society and History* 22 (1980):303–354.   E
Horgan, P.T. "Legal Protection for the Victim of Marital Violence." *Irish Jurist* 12 (Winter 1978):233–253.   F,H

The article compares the 1976 provisions enacted by the legislatures in the Republic of Ireland and England that afford varying degrees of protection to victims of marital violence.

Horney, K. "The Problem of Feminine Masochism." In *Feminine Psychology*. New York: W.W. Norton, 1967.   B
———. *The Neurotic Personality of Our Time*. New York: W.W. Norton, 1973.   H
Horoshak. "Learn to Fight Rape—Without Hangups." *Registered Nurse* 39 (July 1976): 52.   G
Hosken, F.P. "Female Circumcision in Africa." *Victimology: An International Journal* 2 (1978):487–498.   A

The practice and consequences of female genital mutilation in Africa are examined. The potential effects of these procedures are listed as extreme pain, frigidity, risk of infection, damage to adjacent and internal organs, and death. The belief, myths, and values supporting such customs are outlined.

"Hospital-Based Family Services Help SIDS Families, Battered Wives; Safe Homes for Battered Wives." *Hospitals* 53 (1979):32.   A,B

Hostetler, J.A. *Amish Society*. Baltimore: Johns Hopkins University Press, 1968.   B

Hotchkiss, S. "The Realities of Rape." *Human Behavior* 7 (1978):18–23. G

Rape in the United States is reviewed in relation to government spending to investigate and prevent rape.

House of Commons. "Report from the Select Committee on Violence in Marriage Together with the Proceedings of the Committee." London: Her Majesty's Stationery Office, 1975.   B

Howard. "Racial Discrimination in Sentencing." *Judicature* 59 (1975):121.
                                                                    L

Howard, J. "*Against Our Will* by S. Brownmiller." *Mademoiselle* 82 (January 1976):6.   G

Howard, P.F. *Wife Beating: A Selected Annotated Bibliography*. San Diego: 1978.   B

"How Do You Handle Sex on the Job?" Questionnaire. *Redbook* 146 (January 1976):74–75.   D

Howell, L.M. "Clinical and Research Impressions Regarding Murder and Sexually Perverse Crimes." *Psychotherapy and Psychosomatics* 21 (1973):156–159.   B

Background and summarizing observations and data collections made by the author while in a clinical center concerning the background, motives, personality dynamics, and treatment of rapists, murderers, and pedophiles.

"How to Protect Yourself from Rape." *Good Housekeeping*, September 1975, p. 157.   G

"How to Start a Rape Crisis Center." Washington, D.C.: Rape Crisis Center, August 1972.   B,G

"How You Can Help the Rape Victim." *Nursing*, October 1974, p. 11. B,G

Hricko, A., and M., Brunt. *Working for Your Life: A Women's Guide to Job Health Hazards*. Berkeley, Calif.: Labor Occupational Health Program, Center for Labor Research and Education, Institute of Industrial Relations, University of California, 1976.   B,D

Hudson, R.P.; J. Humphrey; and H. Kupferer. "Regional Variations in the Characteristics of Victims of Violence." *Victimology: An International Journal* 2 (1977):64–65.   H

Variations in the characteristics of victims of violence in the four regions of North Carolina—mountains, peidmont, coastal plains, and tidewater—are examined. Implications are drawn for prevention and intervention.

Huggins, M.D., and M.A. Straus. "Violence and the Social Structure as

Reflected in Children's Books from 1850–1970." Mimeographed. Durham: University of New Hampshire, 1974. *H*

Hughes, M.M. *The Sexual Barrier: Legal, Medical, Economic, and Social Aspects of Sex Discrimination*. Washington, D.C.: Hughes Press.*B,F*

A compendium of sources on women's rights and issues.

Humphrey, J.A., and S. Palmer. "A Comparison of Homicide and Suicide Victims in North Carolina during 1972–1973." *Victimology: An International Journal* 2 (1977):65. *H*

Hunt, A. et. al. *Families and Their Needs*. 1973. *C*

Hunt, V.R. *Occupational Health Problems of Pregnant Women*. University Park: Pennsylvania State University, 1975. *D*

Huntsman, J., and A. Hooper. "The Desecration of Tokelau Kinship." *Journal of the Polynesian Society* 85 (1976):257–274. *B,E*

Hursch, C.J. *The Trouble with Rape*. Chicago: Nelson Hall, 1977. *G*

This book is a psychologist's report of federally funded research project begun in Denver, 1973, for the purpose of studying victims, resisters, and perpetrators.

Huston, M. "Abused Women: Who's at Fault?" *Milwaukee Journal*, 27 January 1976. *A*

Huston, T.L.; G. Geis; R. Wright; and T. Garrett. "Good Samaritans as Crime Victims." *Victimology* 1 (1976):284–294. *C,H*

Good samaritans and other bystanders play a critical role in determining the course and outcome of criminal events. Issues concerning the value of encouraging samaritans in regard to crime are also examined.

Iglitzin, L.B. *Violent Conflict in American Society*. San Francisco: Changler, 1972. *H*

Ihinger, M. "The Referee Role and Norms of Equity: A Contribution toward a Theory of Sibling Conflict." *Journal of Marriage and the Family* 37 (August 1975):515–524. *E*

Ilfeld, F.W. "Overview of the Causes and Prevention of Violence." *Archives of General Psychiatry* 20 (June 1969):675–689. *C*

This paper reviews the causes of violence and the various ways in which violence might be prevented or reduced.

"I Married My Sister: Case of D. Goddu and V. Pittorino." *Newsweek* 2 July 1979, p. 36. *C*

"Incest and Family Disorder." *British Medical Journal* 13 May 1972, pp. 364–365. *E*

"Incest and Vulnerable Children: Study by R.K. Davies." *Science News*, 13 October 1979, pp. 244–245. E

"Incest: Out of Hiding." *Science News*, 5 April 1980, pp. 218–220. Discussion: 117–243, April 19, 1980. E

Incest: The Victim Nobody Believes. 16 mm, sound, color, 23 min. Schiller Park, Ill.: MTI Teleprograms, Incorporated, 1978. E

Discusses the issue of incest and sexual abuse of children to heighten public awareness and helping-services professionals who must deal with this problem.

Incest: The Victim Nobody Believes. 23 min. Schiller Park, Ill.: MTI Teleprograms Incorporated, 1976. E

The first film to openly discuss the issue of sexual abuse/misuse.

Inciardi, J.A. "The Pickpocket and His Victim." *Victimology* 1 (Fall 1976): 446–453. H

"Incidents of Battered Wives Said Under-reported." *Psychiatric News* 13 (19 May 1978):25–29. A

Comments of two psychiatrists are reported regarding the underreporting and lack of social-service response to wife battering and the dynamics of violence in the marital relationship.

"I Never Set Out to Rape Anybody." *Ms.*, December 1972, p. 22. G

Ingraham vs. Wright." *U.S. Law Week* 45 (1977):4364. F

Ipema, D.K. "Rape: The Process of Recovery." *Nursing Research* 28 (1979):272–275. G

The rape victim's perspective and her current situation were examined, utilizing tape-recorded interviews with eleven victims on the victims' reports of rape, rape sequelae, and disruptions of her social system.

Ireland, M.J. "Reform Rape Legislation: A New Standard of Sexual Responsibility." *University of Colorado Law Review* 49 (1978):185–204. F,G

Reforms in rape legislation that emphasize a new standard of sexual responsibility are discussed. The goal of these regulation reforms are to create sex-neutral crime laws that would provide neither special sex-based benefits nor sex-based disadvantages to any class of witness or defendants.

Irving, H.H., and P.E. Bohm. "A Social Science Approach to Family Dispute Resolution." *Canadian Journal of Family Law* 1 (1978):39–56. C

Isolated Sexual Advances No Ground for Title VII Claim." *United States Law Week*, 14 September 1976, pp. 1039, 2135.   *D,G*

Israel, S. *The Bibliography on Divorce*. New York: Block Publishing Company, 1973.   *B*

Ito, M. "Postmortem Examinations of Japanese Rape Victims." *Victimology* 4 (1979):390–394.   *B,G*

> Findings are derived from postmortem examinations in sixty-one rape/ murder cases in Kanagawa Perfecture, Japan.

"I Was a Battered Wife." *Good Housekeeping* 188 (May 1979):34.   *A*

Jackson, D.D. "The Question of Family Homeostasis." *Psychiatry Quarterly Supplement* 31 (1957):79–90.   *C*

Jackson, S. "In Search of Equal Protection for Battered Wives." Paper presented to the Conference of Mayors on Victimology, 1975.   *A*

———. "Marital Violence in San Francisco." Memorandum to the Women's Litigation Unit, San Francisco Neighborhood Legal Assistance Foundation, January 1975.   *A*

———. "The Social Context of Rape: Sexual Scripts and Motivation." *Women's Studies International Quarterly* 1 (1978):27–38.   *G*

> The social context of rape is examined in terms of sexual scripts, motives, and neutralization. These scripts also provide, in a variety of ways, for the occurrence of rape since implicit in them are techniques of neutralization that a rapist may use to justify his actions in advance and that therefore serve to motivate him.

Jacobs, M. *A Study of Culture Stability and Change: The Moroccan Jewess*. Washington, D.C.: Catholic University of America Press, 1956.   *B*

Jacobson, B. "Battered Women: The Fight to End Wife Beating." *Civil Rights Digest* 9 (Summer 1977):2–11.   *A*

Jacobson, H. "Legal Note on Potiphar's Wife." *Harvard Theological Review* 69 (January/April 1976):177.   *F*

Jacobson, M.B. et al. "The Feminist Attitudes toward Rape Scale." *Catalog of Selected Documents in Psychology*, 1980.   *G*

> The development of the feminist-attitudes-toward-rape scale (FARS) is described. The feminist view of rape is discussed.

Jaffe, A.; P. Papovich; and D. Biers. "Sexual Abuse of Children." *American Journal of Disabled Children* 129 (1975):689–692.   *E*

James, J. "Behavior Trends of Wives of Alcoholics." *Quarterly Journal of Studies on Alcohol* 32 (June 1971):373–381.   *A*

James, J. "A Formal Analysis of Prostitution." Final report. Olympia: Division of Research, State of Washington Department of Social and Health Services, 1971. *A,C*

———. "Early Sexual Experience and Prostitution." *American Journal of Psychiatry*, 1976. *E*

———. "Motivations for Entrance into Prostitution." In *The Female Offender: A Comprehensive Anthology*, edited by L. Crites. University: University of Alabama Press, 1976. *E*

———. "Normal Men and Deviant Women." Unpublished manuscript, 1976. *B*

———. "Self-Destructive Behavior and Adaptive Strategies in Female Prostitutes." In *The Many Faces of Suicide*, edited by N. Farberow. New York: McGraw-Hill, 1980. *E*

The life-style of female prostitutes, some of whom are also drug addicts, is examined in order to evaluate their self-destructive behavior.

James, J., and J. Meyerding. "Early Sexual Experience and Prostitution." *American Journal of Psychology* 134 (December 1977):1381–1385. *E*

James, J; W. Womack; and F. Strauss. "Physician Reporting of Sexual Abuse of Children." *Journal of the American Medical Association* 240 (1978):1145–1146. *E*

The frequency of physician reports of contact with sexually abused children was investigated. Questionnaires concerning frequency of contact with sexually abused children, type of abuse, treatment provided, and reporting procedures were completed.

James, K.L. "Incest: The Teenager's Perspective." *Psychotherapy: Theory, Research, and Practice* 14 (Summer 1977):146–155. *E*

In approximately a three-year period, about 12 percent of the female residents in one treatment unit of a juvenile institution where the author is employed have experienced traumatic incest relationships.

Janoff, B.R. "Characterological versus Behavioral Self Blame: Inquiries into Depression and Rape." *Journal of Personality and Social Psychology* 37 (October 1979):1798–1809. *G*

Distinguishes two types of self-blame: behavioral and characterological.

Janoff, B.R.; L. Lang; and D. Johnston. "Participant Observer Differences in Attributions for an Ambiguous Victimization." *Personality and Social Psychology Bulletin* 5 (1979):335–339. H

Participant-observer differences in attributions were examined in a field setting.

Javorek, F.J., and L.A. Lyon. "Nice Girls Don't Get Raped, or Do They?" *Victimology: An International Journal* 2 (1977):65–66. G

Studies taken to explore the possibility of difference in personality among victims of attempted and completed rapes and a general population of women are reported.

"Jenkins Consents." *Economist* 255 (21 June 1975):19. G

Jensen, R.H. "Battered Women and the Law." *Victimology: An International Journal* 2 (1978):585–590. A,F

The treatment of battered women when they seek help and protection from the criminal-justice system is examined. Reforms in the laws governing spouse abuse are discussed and found to be largely ineffective or unenforced.

———. "New Rape Theory: Just Like Clockwork." Work of Dr. Gene Abel and William Murphy. *Crawdaddy*, May 1978, p. 16. G

Jerrome, D. "Conflict and Collusion in a Nigerian Community Abroad." *Women's Studies International Quarterly* 2 (1979):421–437. E,G

Problems and marital conflicts were examined in IBO women who have migrated to the United Kingdom from Nigeria with their student husbands.

"Joanne Little: America Goes on Trial." *Freedomways* 15 (1975):87–88. F,G

Jobling, M. "Battered Wives: A Survey." *Social Services Quarterly* 47 (1974):142–145. A

Information provided by the National Association of Citizens' Advice bureau shows that husbands were alcoholics, psychotic, psychopathic, or plain bullies. There appeared to be two main types of assault—premeditated and sadistic where care is taken not to leave any visible marks and beatings where the husband loses total control.

Joe, V.C.; S. McGee; and D. Dazey. "Religiousness and Devaluation of a Rape Victim." *Journal of Clinical Psychology* 33 (January 1977):64. G

John, H.W. "Rape and Alcohol Abuse: Is There a Connection?" *Alcohol Health and Research World* 2 (1978):34–37. G

The possible connection between forcible rape and alcohol use and alcoholism in the United States has been studied by researchers who have been divided in their findings.

Johnson, B.D. "Is Crime Really Increasing." *Victimology: An International Journal* 2 (1977):66.   *H*

Evidence is presented to show that crime continues to increase as does pubic concern about crime.

Johnson, C., and M. Kravitz. *Spouse Abuse—A Selected Bibliography*. Washington, D.C.: U.S. Department of Justice, 1978.   *A,B*

This selected bibliography highlights the problem of spouse abuse and the various forms of intervention currently available.

Johnson, E.G. "Evidence/Rape/Trials/Victims' Prior Sexual History." *Baylor Law Review* 27 (1975):222–237.   *F,G*
Johnson, P.R. "The Effects of Rape Education on Male Attitudes toward Rape and Women." *Dissertation Abstracts International* 40(1-B):493, July 1979.   *G*

Discusses Machiavellian attitudes, sex-role identity, rape education, attitudes toward rape and women, and male college students.

Johnson, S. "What about Battered Women?" *Majority Report*, 8 February 1975.   *A*
———. "Abused Wives Strike Back." *Majority Report*, 3 May 1975.   *A*
Johnson, S.D.; L. Gibson; and R. Linden. "Alcohol and Rape in Winnipeg, 1966–1975." *Journal of Studies on Alcohol* 39 (November 1978):1887–1894.   *G*

Examination of data reported by the police department show that alcohol was present in 72 percent of the rapes. Alcohol increased the likelihood of force being used. Evidence shows that the situation of drinking may facilitate rape.

Johnston, T. "When He Stopped Beating His Wife." *City of San Francisco*, 6 July 1975.   *A*
Joint Commission on Mental Health and Illness. *Final Report: Action for Mental Health*. New York: Basic Books, 1961.   *B*
Jones, and Aronson. "Attribution of Fault to a Rape Victim as a Function of Respectability of the Victim." *Journal of Personality and Social Psychology* 26 (1973):415.   *D,G*

Jones, R.A. "Battering Families." *Health and Social Service Journal*, 10
  February 1973.   *A*
Jones, V. "Federal Legislation Concerning Spouse Abuse." *Victimology:*
  An International Journal 2 (1978):623–627.   *A,F*

  Several federal bills concerned with spouse abuse are discussed in an
  attempt to clarity their progress through Congress, to ascertain their current status, and to document their provisions and implications.

————. "Video Tape on Battered Women." Spectra Feminist Media, no
  date.   *A*
Jorne, P.S. "Treating Sexually Abused Children." *Child Abuse and Neglect*
  3 (1979):285–290.   *E*
Joseph, S.P. "The Eighth Amendment, Rape, and Sexual Battery: A
  Study in Methods of Judicial Review." *University of Miami Law Review*
  32 (1978): 690–708.   *B,G,F*

  A new Eighth Amendment test for the constitutionality of punishment that
  may be out of proportion with the severity of a crime is examined.

Josephson, M. "Sexual Harassment on the Job: Why More and More
  Women Are Fighting Back." *Glamour* 78 (May 1980):288–289.   *D*
Jordheim, A.E. "Helping Victims of Rape." *Lutheran* 18 (1980):8–9. *B,G*

  The potential role of the church or other religious groups in helping victims
  of rape and their families to overcome the aftereffects of sexual assault is
  presented.

Joutsen, M. "Victimization and Corruption." *Victimology: An Internation-*
  al Journal 2 (1977):67.   *H*
"Judge Rescinds Court Order to Close Rape Hearing." *Editor and Publish-*
  er, 3 July 1975, p. 33.   *F,G*
Julian, V., and C. Mohr. "Father-Daughter Incest: Profile of the Offender." *Victimology* 4 (1979):348–360.   *E*

  One hundred two cases of father-daughter incest were examined to develop
  an offender profile and to compare incestuous and abusive fathers and
  families.

Jurnovoy, J. "Sex in the Office." *Harper's Bazaar* 113 (August 1980):34. *D*
Justice, B., and R. Justice. *The Broken Taboo: Sex in the Family*. New
  York: Human Sciences, 1979.   *E*

  Incest is examined because of the growth of the problem, the widespread
  miconceptions about it, and the increasing failure of families to assure the
  sexual welfare of both parent and child.

"Justice a Woman?" (Italian Feminists) *Economist* 263 (9 April 1977):38. *F*

Kadushin, A. *Child Welfare Services*. London: Macmillan & Co., 1970. *B*

Kahn, A. "Attribution of Fault to a Rape Victim as a Function Of Respectability of the victim: A Failure to Replicate or Extend." *Representative Research in Social Psychology* 8 (1977):98–107.   *G*

> C. Jones and E. Aronson found that the more respectable the victim of a rape, the more fault attributed to her, and interpreted this relationship in terms of the just-world hypothesis.

Kainz. "*Kinder als Opfer strafbarer handlungen.*" *Kriminalistik* 21 (1967): 605.   *B*

Kalmuss, D. "Attribution of Responsibility in Wife Abuse Context." *Victimology* 4 (1979):284–291.   *A*

> This study investigates one particular attitude toward wife abuse—how individuals attribute responsibility to the participants—and finds that the role-sex configuration is an important determination.

Kamisher, M. "Behind Closed Doors: Battered Women." *Real Paper*, 11 February 1976, pp. 20–22.   *A*

Kanekar, S., and R.B. Ahluwalia. "Perception of an Aggressor as a Function of the Victim's Strength and Retaliation." *European Journal of Social Psychology* 7 (1977):505–507.   *H*

> The hypothesis that an aggressor would be evaluated differently depending on whether the victim was stronger or weaker than the aggressor and whether the victim retaliated or not was investigated.

Kanekar, S., and M.B. Kolsawalla. "Responsibility in Relation to Respectability." *Journal of Social Psychology* 102 (August 1977):183–188. *G*

> Tested the cross-cultural replicability of C. Jones and E. Aronson's finding that the victim of a rape is held more responsible for the crime if she is more respectable. There were no differences in the responsibility attributed to the victim as a function of her respectability.

———. "Responsibility of a Rape Victim in Relation to Her Respectability, Attractiveness, and Provocativeness." *Journal of Social Psychology* 112 (October 1980):153–154.   *G*

> Investigated the interactions of victim's provocativeness with the physical attractiveness and respectability of the victim, and the sex of

Kanin. "Selected Dyadic Aspects of Male Sex Aggression." *Rape Victimology*, 1975.   *H*

Kanin, E. "Sex Aggression by College Men." *Medical Aspects of Human Sexuality* 4 (1970):25–40.   H

Kanowitz, L. *Women and the Law: The Unfinished Revolution.* Albuquerque: University of New Mexico Press, 1969.   F

Kansas City Police Department. Northeast Patrol Division Task Force. "Conflict Management: Analysis/Resolution." Kansas City, 1971–1972.   C

Kanter, J., and M. Zelnik. "Sexual Experience of Young Unmarried Women in the United States." *Family Planning Perspectives* 4 (1972): 9–18.   E

Kaplan, H.B. "Toward a General Theory of Psychosocial Deviance—The Case of Aggressive Behavior." *Social Science and Medicine* 6 (1972). C

Kaplan, P.A. "Attribution of Responsibility to Victims of Rape." *Dissertation Abstracts International* 39(4-B) 1952–1953, October 1977.   H

Kaplan, S.L., and E. Pozanski. "Child Psychiatry Patients Who Share a Bed with a Parent." *Journal of the American Academy of Child Psychiatry* 13 (1974):344–356.   E

Karasic, J. "Analysis of an Adult Who Was an Abused Child." Continuing Medical Education: Syllabus and Proceedings in Summary Form. Washington, D.C.: American Psychiatric Association, 1978.   E

A summary of a paper read at the 131st Annual Meeting of the American Psychiatric Association, held in Atlanta, May 1978, is presented.

Kardener, S.H. "Rape Fantasies." *Journal of Religion and Health* (January 1975):50–57.   G

Presents and Adlerian psychoanalytic interpretation of rape, defining it to include extragenital activities such as oral and anal demeaning.

Karenga, M.R. "In Defense of Sister Joanne: For Ourselves and History." *Black Scholar* 6 (July 1975):37–42.   G

Karl, B.; B. Taylor; L. Frost; N. Channels; and R. Gable. "Evaluation of a Rape Crisis Program: Teaching Police and Volunteer Counselors about Sexual Assault." Final report, NIMH Grant 1R18-MH-29022, Washington, D.C., 1978.   B

The accomplishments of the sexual assault crisis service (SACS), of Hartford, Connecticut, in the areas of police training, volunteer counselor training, and victim counseling services are discussed.

Karl, M.: Refuges in Europe." *Victimology: An International Journal* 2 (1978):657–666.   B

The existence of refuges for battered women in the United Kingdom, the Netherlands, France, Norway, and Switzerland is reported.

Karp, D.J. "Coker versus Georgia: Disproportionate Punishment and the Death Penalty for Rape." *Columbia Law Review* 78 (1978):1714–1730.
F,G

The arguments against the constitutionality of the death penalty for rape offered by the Supreme Court in *Coker* v. *Georgia* are discussed.

Kasinsky, R.G. "Rape: A Normal Act?" *Canada Forum* 55 (1975):18–22.
G

Katan, A. "Children Who Were Raped." *Psychoanalytic Study of the Child* 28 (1973):208–224.
E

Katz, S., and M.A. Mazur. *Understanding the Rape Victim: A Synthesis of Research Findings*. Wiley Series on Personality Processes. New York: Wiley & Sons, 1979.
G

The scientific literature on rape is explored in order to examined environmental, social, and sexual variables; the victim's behavior; the preexisting psychiatry status of the victim; psychological damage to the victim; the psychological interventions; methods of prevention; and present empirically known data to make recommendations for future study.

Kaufman, A. "Impact of a Community Health Approach to Rape." *American Journal of Public Health* 67 (April 1977):365–367.
B

Kaufman, L.I. "The Family Constellation and Overt Incestuous Relations between Father and Daughter." *American Journal of Orthopsychiatry* 8 (1969):606–619.
E

Kaufman, Hilaski; DiVasto; VanderMeer; and Eppler. "Total Health Needs of the Rape Victim." *Journal of Family Practice* 2, (1975).*B,G*

Kaufman, Oransky, and Block. *Off the Beaten Track*. Philadelphia: Women against Abuse, Germantown Women's Center.
A,B

Keefe, and O'Reilly. "Rape: Attitudinal Training for Police and Emergency Room Personnel." *Police Chief*, June 1975.
B,G

———. "Changing Perspectives in Sex Crime Investigation." *Sexual Assault*, 1976.
B,G

Keerdoja, E. "Incest Couple We're Fed Up: Case of V. Pittorino and D. Goddu." *Newsweek*, 12 November 1979, p. 27.
E

Keerdoja, E., and P.E. Simons. "Strong Convictions: Views of Former Judge A. Simonson." *Newsweek*, 11 September 1978, p. 14.
L

Kelber, M. "United Nation's Dirty Little Secret." *Ms.* 6 (November 1977): 51.
D

Kemmer, E.J. *Rape and Rape-Related Issues*. New York: Garland, 1977.
                                                                      F,G
Kemp, M.; B. Knightly; and M. Norton. *Battered Women and the Law*,
     1973.   *A,F*
Kemp, T. *Prostitution: An Investigation of Its Causes, Especially with Re-
     gard to Hereditary Factors*. Copenhagen: Levin and Munskgaard,
     1936.   *C*
Kempe, C.H. "Child Abuse—The Pediatrician's Role in Child Advocacy
     and Preventive Pediatrics." *American Journal of Diseases of Children*
     132 (1978):255–260.   *E*

     Child abuse and neglect and the pediatrician's role are explored historical-
     ly, clinically, and from the standpoint of prediction and prevention.

Kempe, C.H. "Sexual Abuse, Another Hidden Pediatric Problem: The
     1977 C. Anderson Aldrich Lecture." *Pediatrics* 62 (1978):382–389. *E*

     At the Annual Meeting of the American Academy of Pediatrics, held in
     New York, November 1977, the incidence, nature, and treatment of the
     sexual abuse of children and adolescents were discussed.

Kempe, C.H., and R.E. Helfer. *Helping the Battered Child and His Family*.
     Philadelphia: J.B. Lippincott Company, 1972.   *E*
Kempe, C.H.; F.N. Silverman; B.S. Steele; W. Droegemuller; and H.K.
     Silver. "The Battered-Child Syndrome." *Journal of the American Med-
     ical Association* (1962):17–24.   *E*
Kennedy, C.S. *Effects of Marriage on Property and on the Wife's Legal
     Capacity*. London: Reeves and Turner, 1879.   *F*
Kennedy, M.C. "Power and Victimization: The Political Relativity of
     Victims." *Victimology: An International Journal* 2 (1977):67–68. *H*

     In a paper presented at the Second International Symposium on Victim-
     ology, held in Boston, September 1976, war and revolution are examined
     as facets in the theory and practice of victimization.

Kenny, D. *Refuges for Battered Women in London—Provision and Need*.
     Rockville, Md.: NCJRS Microfiche Program, 1978.   *A,B*

     This survey of temporary shelters for battered women and their children
     finds that considerable improvement has been made but that more shelters
     are needed. Changes in local governmental policy are also recommended.

Kent, R. "Should You Sleep with Your Boss?" *Harper's Bazaar* 109 (No-
     vember 1975):147.   *D*

Kercher, G.A., and C.E. Walker. "Reactions of Convicted Rapists to Sexually Explicit Stimuli." *Journal of Abnormal Psychology* 81 (February 1973):46–50.   G

   Describes a study in which twenty-eight convicted rapists and twenty-eight controls convicted of nonsexual crimes were shown a series of slides depicting sexual themes while measures of penile volume, GSR, and subjective ratings were obtained.

Kerr, N.L. "Beautiful and Blameless: Effects of Victim Attractiveness and Responsibility on Mock Jurors' Verdicts." *Personality and Social Psychology Bulletin* 4 (1978):479–482.   H

   The effect of a victim's physical attractiveness and responsibility on judgments of defendant guilt were assessed in a jury simulation of an automobile-theft case in which 268 male and 142 female students served as jurors.

Kerr, N.L., and A.C. Gross. "Situational and Personality Determinants of a Victim's Identification with a Tormentor." *Journal of Research in Personality* 12 (1978):450–468.   H

   The effects of two situational and two personality factors on several reactions of a victim to his tormentor were explored.

Kew, B. Marriages at Risk: Who Should Help. Case University Conference, May 1968.   C
Khan, A.H. "Better Law for Battered Wives." *Solicitors Journal* 122 (16 June 1978):391–392.   A,F
———. "Better Law for Battered Wives." *Solicitors Journal* 122 (23 June 1978):409–412.   A,F

   This two-part article discusses the 1976 domestic violence and matrimonial proceedings act in England and notes the need for crisis centers, refuges, legal services, and law reform to help battered women.

Kiely, M.M. "Rape: The Brownmiller Thesis." *Chronicle and Crisis* 36 (1 March 1976):31–36.   G
Kihss, P. "Women's Wages Fall Even Farther Behind." *The New York Times*, 3 April 1977, p. 35.   D
Kilgour. "Rape: Thoughts for Victims or Intended Ones." *American Association of Registered Nurses News Letters*, April 1975, p. 31.   G,H
"Killing Excuse; Wives' Murdering Husbands Because of Abuse." *Time* 110 (1977):108.   A,H

Kilpatrick, D.G.; L.J. Veronen; and P.A. Resick. "The Aftermath of Rape: Recent Empirical Findings." *American Journal of Orthopsychiatry* 49 (October 1979):658–669.   G

In a longitudinal study of the effects of rape on a woman's subsequent psychological functioning, objective measures of mood state and psychological distress were obtained at four intervals from forty-six recent rape victims and thirty-five nonvictims.

———. "Assessment of the Aftermath of Rape: Changing Patterns of Fear." *Journal of Behavioral Assessment* 1 (1979):133–148.   G

To test a social-learning-theory model that states that fear and anxiety responses are classically conditioned by a terror-inducing rape experience, forty-six recent rape victims and thirty-five nonvictims matched for age, race, and neighborhood of residence were assessed with the 120-item modified-fear survey at four postrape intervals.

Kingham, M. "Squatting in London." *New Society*, 2 May 1974, pp. 254–255.   H

King, H.E.; M.J. Rotter; L.G. Calhoun; and J.W. Selby. "Perceptions of the Rape Incident: Physicians and Volunteer Counselors." *Journal of Community Psychology* 6 (1978):74–77.   B,G

Attitudes toward rape were investigated in a group of physicians and a group of volunteer rape/crisis-center counselors.

King James Bible, Eph. 6:22–24.   B,F
King James Bible, Numbers 5.   F
King's Fund Centre. *Violence in Marriage*. Reprint no. 828. London, 1974.
                                                                                                             B,H
Kinsey, A.; W. Pomeroy; C. Martin; and P. Gebhard. *Sexual Behavior in the Human Female*. Philadelphia: Saunders, 1953.   C
Kinton, E.R. *Family Structures and Roles in Crisis: An Annotated Bibliography*. Aurora, Ill.: Social Science and Sociological Resources, 1973.   C,H
Kirchhoff, G.; C. Kirchhoff; and P. Friday. "A Cross-Cultural Study of the Incidence of Hidden Sexual Victimization and Related Aspects." *Victimology: An International Journal* 2 (1977):68.   B,H

Cross-cultural aspects of sexual victimization and the interrelationship of sex education, victimization, and vita sexualis are discussed.

Kirchner, R.M. *Relationships between Early Pregnancy, Early Marriage, Education and Wife Beating*, 1978.   B

The relationship between wife abuse and early pregnancy, early marriage, and level of education is examined in a study of 600 married women who have applied for legal aid to leave their husbands.

Kirk, S. "Clients as Outsiders: Theoretical Approaches to Deviance." *Social Work*, March 1972, p. 24. **H**
――――. "Four Questions about Sex in Our Society." *Medical Times*, November 1974, p. 68. **H**
――――. "The Sex Offenses of Blacks and Whites." *Archives of Sexual Behavior* 4 (May 1975):295–302. **H**

Presents comparative data on black and white hospitalized sex offenders in terms of the nature of the offense and victim characteristics.

Kirkendall, A.R. "Victim Selection Processes Involved in Rape." *Dissertation Abstracts International* 41(4-B):1567, October 1980. **G,H**
Kirkham, G.L. "Doe Cop." *Human Behavior*, May 1975. **B**
Kiste, R.C., and M.A. Rynkiewich. "Incest and Exogamy: A Comparative Study of Two Marshallese Populations." *Journal of Polynesian Society* 85 (1976):209–226. **E**
Klatt, M.R. "Rape in Marriage: The Law in Texas and the Need for Reform." *Baylor Law Review* 32 (1980):109–121. **A,G**

The need for reform of the Texas law that does not recognize the crime of rape between a husband and wife is examined. At the very least, it is argued, protection should be afforded to women who are no longer living with their spouses or who have instituted legal proceedings for termination of the marriage relationship or who have been the victims of violent sexual attacks by their husbands.

Kleckner, J.H. "Wife Beaters and Beaten Wives: Co-Conspirators in Crimes of Violence." *Psychology* 15 (February 1978):54–56. **A**

Argues that a wife beaten more than once by her husband is a coconspirator who sends him tacit messages that his crimes of violence are legitimate and tolerable activities.

Klein, D. "Can This Marriage Be Saved?—Battery and Sheltering." *Crime and Social Justice* 12 (December 1979):19–33. **A,B**

An examination of wife abuse analyzes factors such as victim blaming, interactionism, the relationship of women and the state, the feminist response, and the antibattering movement.

Klein, D.M.; R. Hill; B. Miller; and J. Schuaneueldt. "Toward a Propositional Theory of Family Problem Solving: Forging Some Integrative Links." Paper presented at the Annual Meeting of the National Council on Family Relations, Toronto, 1973.   C

Klemer, R.R. *Counseling in Marital and Sexual Problems: A Physician's Handbook*. Baltimore: Williams and Wilkins, 1965.   B

Klemmack, and Klemmack. "The Social Definition of Rape." In *Sexual Assault*, edited by M. Walker and S. Brodsky p. 135. Lexington, Mass.: Lexington Books, D.C. Heath and Company, 1976.   G

Klingbeil, K., and D. Stevens. *Alternative Interventions for Sexual Assault Victims*. Final Report. Seattle: University of Washington, 1980.   G

Data are presented to show that it is possible to systematize procedures for agency-initiated intervention services for adolescent and adult victims of rape and to implement these services with a fairly large population.

Klingbeil; Anderson; and Vontver. "Multidisciplinary Care for Sexual Assault Victims." *Nursing Practice*, July/August 1976, p. 21.   G,H

Knopf, O. "Sexual Assault: Victim's Psychology and Related Problems." *Mt. Sinai Journal of Medicine* 45 (1978):1–13.   G,H

The dynamics of guilt in victims of sexual assault/rape are discussed.

Knox, J. *The first Blast of the Trumpet against the Monstrous Regiment of Women*. London: Southgate, 1558.   C

Knudten, R.D. *Victims and Witnesses: Their Experiences with Crime and the Criminal Justice System*. Washington, D.C.: U.S. Government Printing Office, 1977.   F,H

Kobe, P. "The Victim in Judicial Procedure." *Victimology: An International Journal* 2 (1977):68.   F,H

The role of the victim in the legal process is discussed. The question follows whether damages allotted in the criminal process are merely some kind of restitution in the interim or if they constitute a penal measure.

Kobus, E. *Vrij Nederland*, translated by J. Weiss. 19 July 1975.

Koch, K.F. "Incest and Its Punishment in Jale Society." *Journal of the Polynesian Society* 83 (1974):84–91.   B,E,F

Koch, M. "Sexual Abuse in Children." *Adolescence* 15 (1980):643–648. E

Examines recent English language literature on sexual abuse of children, particularly incest.

Koenig, R. "Rape: Most Rapidly Increasing Crime." *McCalls* 100 (July 1973):25.   G

Kohn, M.L. *Class and Conformity: A Study in Values*. Homewood, Ill.:
Dorsey Press, 1969. B

Kolb, T.M., and M.A. Straus. "Marital Power and Marital Happiness in
Relation to Problem Solving Ability." *Journal of Marriage and the
Family* 36 (November 1974):756–766. H

Kole, J. "Rape and What to Do about It." *Harper's Bazaar* 109 (March
1976):118–119. G

Komarovsky, M. *Blue Collar Marriage*. New York: Vintage, 1940. B

Komisar, L. "Violence and the Masculine Mystique." In *The Forty-Nine
Percent Majority: The Male Sex Role*, edited by D.S. David and R.
Brannon, pp. 201–215. Reading, Mass.: Addison-Wesley Publishing,
1976. H

Koos, E.L. *Families in Trouble*. New York: Russell & Russell, 1973. C

Kopernik, L. "The Family as a Breeding Ground of Violence." *Corrective
Psychiatry and Journal of Social Therapy* 8–10 (1962–1964):315–322.
H,C,H

A pilot study was conducted of 100 families of inmates of the Eastern
Penitentiary in Philadelphia. Discussed here is a fragment of a broader
investigation, based on the assumption that violent behavior arises from a
specific background, nurturing a specific individual, who in turn responds
with a specific way of adjustment.

Korengold. "Victims of Rape." *Medical Annals* D.C. 40 (1971):384. G

Korlath, M.J. "Alcoholism in Battered Women—A Report of Advocacy
Services to Clients in a Detoxification Facility." *Victimology* 4 (1979):
292–299. G

Alcoholic and battered women need help in developing positive self-
images and coping skills, according to a client survey of the Hennepin
County Alcoholism Receiving Center of Minneapolis, Minnesota.

Kornblum, C.R. "Report of the Attorney General's Conference on Domestic Violence." *Crime Prevention Review* 6 (October 1978):8–18. H

The California Attorney General's Office sponsored a statewide conference on domestic violence to evaluate the responsiveness of the criminal-
justice system to both victims and law-enforcement officials.

Kosa. "Falsche Beschuldigung zur Verschleierung autoerotischer Handlungen." *Archiv Fur Kriminologie* 148 (1971):106. B

Koslow, S.P. "Are You Crazy-in-Love or Simply Crazy to Be Involved in an
Office Romance?" *Glamour* 77 (September 1979):250. D

Koupernik. "Regression psychotique durable chez une enfante de 4 ans, victime d'un viol." Supplement. *Revue de Neuropsychiatrie Infantile et d'Hygiene Mentale de l'Enfance* (1967):63.   *H*

Koupernik, C.; P.M. Masciangelo; and B.S. Balestra. "A Case of Heller's Dementia Following Sexual Assault in a Four-Year-Old Girl." *Child Psychiatry and Human Development* 2 (Spring 1972):134–144.   *G*

Describes the case of a four-year-old girl who, shortly after an attempted rape and life threat, developed a loss of speech followed by a clinical picture of Heller's Dementia. The major symptom was nocturnal fits of terror, but no evidence of an epileptic nature was established until four years after the onset of these fits.

Kozma, C.L. "An Investigation of Some Hypotheses Concerning Rape and Murder." *Dissertation Abstracts International* 39(3-B):1485., September 1978.   *G*

Personality differences and attitudes toward women and disinhibition and sex roles and sex, male rapists versus murderers in prison.

Krauskopf, J.M. "Partnership Marriage: Legal Reforms Needed." In *Women into Wives: The Legal and Economic Impact of Marriage*, edited by J.R. Chapman and M. Gates, pp. 93–121. Beverly Hills, Calif.: Sage, 1977.   *F*

Krekel, S. "Placement of Women in High Risk Areas." Paper presented at Society on Environmental Health Conference on Women in the Workplace, Washington, D.C. 17–19 June 1976.   *D*

Kremen, E. "The Discovery of Battered Wives: Considerations for the Development of a Social Service Network." Paper presented at the Annual Meeting of the American Sociological Association in New York, 1976.   *A,B*

Kress, J.M. "The Role of the Victim at Sentencing." *Victimology: An International Journal* 2 (1977):69.   *H*

In a paper presented at the Second International Symposium on Victimology, held in Boston, September 1976, a study of the judicial sentencing process is presented with emphasis on the effects of the victim on sentencing variations. The physical injury or financial loss of victim, for example, usually affects gross penal code definitions as well as judicial perceptions of offense seriousness beyond crime code categorization.

Kress, S. "Doubly Abused: The Plight of the Crime Victims in Literature." *Victimology: An International Journal* 2 (1977):69.   *A,H*

In a paper presented at the Second International Symposium on Victimology, held in Boston, September 1976, a study of the victim in popular, serious, and subserious crime fiction is presented. It is reported that the analysis reveals some very disquieting myths circulating in our culture about the nature of crime victims.

Krieger, M.J.; A.A. Rosenfeld; A. Gordon; and M. Bennett. "Problems in the Psychotherapy of Children with Histories of Incest." *American Journal of Psychotherapy* 34 (January 1980):81–88.   E

Discusses two specific issues in the psychotherapy of children with histories of incest. The first issue concerns the child's often seductive initial presentation in therapy. The second issue addresses the more-general difficulties and countertransference reactions experienced by therapists working with such cases.

Krolick, C. "Study Says No Legal Protection from Husband Assault." *Michigan Free Press* 14 April 1975.   F

Kroll, J. "Policeman/Mental Health Worker: In Search of a Common Ground." *Innovations* 2 (Winter 1975):21–26.   B

Describes four programs designed to increase cooperation between mental-health workers and police: (1) The Southern Arizona Mental Health Center that participates in a sex-crimes squad with Tucson police; (2) a New York City program in which police use videotape feedback training for family-crisis situations; (3) a Dayton, Ohio, program where police have a direct referral to mental-health workers combined with feedback to the officer; and (4) a program in Syracuse, New York, where mental-health workers and police form a team that evaluates situations and makes recommendations of the scene.

Kroth, J.A. *Evaluation of the Child Sexual Abuse Demonstration and Treatment Project*. Sacramento: California Department of Health, Office of Child Abuse Prevention, 30 June 1978.   C,E

———. *Child Sexual Abuse: Analysis of a Family Therapy Approach*. Springfield, Ill.: Charles C Thomas, 1979.   C,E

A statistical and methodological analysis of a humanistic family-therapy program for perpetrators and child victims of incest is presented.

———. "Family Therapy Impact on Intrafamilial Child Sexual Abuse." *Child Abuse and Neglect* 3 (1979):297–302.   C,E

A paper read at the Second International Congress on Child Abuse and Neglect, held in London, September 1978, is presented.

Krulewitz, J.E., and J.E. Nash. "Effects of Rape Victim Resistance, As-

sault Outcome, and Sex of Observer on Attributions about Rape."
Journal of Personality 47 (1979):557–574.   *G*

Perceptions of sexual assault were investigated as a function of sex of
observers, nature of victim resistance, and assault outcome with 229 subjects.

Krulewitz, J.E., and E.J. Payne. "Attributions about Rape: Effects of
Rapists Force, Observer and Sex Role Attitudes." *Journal of Applied
Social Psychology*, 8 (1978):291–305.   *G*

Subject's perceptions of a hypothetical rape situation as a function of the
amount of force used in the rape, sex of subject, and subject's attitudes
toward feminism were investigated. Subjects expressed greater certainty
that a rape had actually occurred with increased force on the part of the
assailant.

Kuby, L. "Rape: The Double Standard." *Aphra* 5 (Winter 1973–1974):
31–35.   *G*
Kuhle, S.J. "Rural Perspective on Domestic Violence." *Domestic Violence—Prevention and Services*, 1979, pp. 321–327.   *H*

Nebraska exemplifies problems faced by female victims of domestic violence in rural areas; such victims experience geographical and psychological isolation and pervasive lack of human services.

———. "Domestic Violence in Rural America—Problems and Possible
Solutions." First World Congress of Victimology, Washington D.C.,
August 1980.   *H*

This address by the president of the Nebraska Task Force on Domestic
Violence outlines the particular problems faced by victims of domestic
violence in the rural United States.

Kuhn, M.A. "There's No Place Like Home for Beatings." *Washington Star*,
11 November 1975.   *A*
Labarbera, J.D.; J. Martin; and E. Dozier. "Child Psychiatrists' View of
Father-Daughter Incest." *Child Abuse and Neglect* 4 (1980):147–151.
                                                                               E

Hypotheses of child psychiatrists on the impact of father-daughter incest
were explored. The implications of the present results for future research
are discussed.

Labby, D. "Incest as Cannibalism: The Yapese Analysts." *Journal of the Polynesian Society* 85 (1976):171–180.   E

Labell, L.S. "Wife Abuse—A Sociological Study of Battered Women and Their Mates." *Victimology* 4 (1979):258–267.   A,B

A profile of abused women and their mates is drawn based on information gathered from clients seeking aid from shelters; suggestions are made to reduce abuse.

"Lacked Capacity to Consent to Sex Relations—'Moral Quality' Factor: *People* v. *Earley*." *Mental Health Court Digest* 21 (1978):1.   G

The Court of Appeals of New York in *People* v. *Earley* upheld the conviction of rape in the third degree of a mentally defective seventeen-year-old victim alleged to have been incapable of consenting to the act of sexual intercourse.

Lacy, B. *Domestic Violence Services in Rural Communities—Direct Services and Funding.* Lincoln: Nebraska Task Force on Domestic Violence Rural Domestic Violence Project, 1979.   B

This manual presents guidelines and suggestions for establishing and funding volunteer groups to provide services for battered women or other victims of domestic violence in rural communities.

———. *Nebraska—Domestic Violence Services in Rural Communities— First Steps of Organization.* Washington, D.C.: Action, 1979.   B

This booklet describes five stages—working groups, needs assessment, planning, community education, and community endorsement—for providing services on domestic violence in rural areas.

LaFave, W.R. "Non-Invocation of the Criminal Law by Police." In *Delinquency, Crime and Social Process*, edited by D.R. Cressey and D.A. Ward. New York: Harper & Row, 1969.   H

LaFave, W.R., and A.W. Scott. *Handbook on Criminal Law.* St. Paul, Minn.: West Publishing Company, 1972.   B,F

LaFree, G.D. "Determinants of Police Prosecution and Court Decisions in Forcible Rape Cases." *Dissertation Abstracts International* 40 (4):2281-A, 1979.   F,G

Determinants (victim and offender and offense characteristics) of police prosecution and court decisions were examined in 912 rapes reported to

Indianapolis police between 1970 and 1975. Further research into effects of societal reactions to rape cases on processing decisions/institutional response is recommended.

—————. "The Effect of Sexual Stratification by Race on Official Reaction to Rape." *American Sociological Review* 45 (1980):842–854.   G
—————. "Variables Affecting Guilty Pleas and Convictions in Rape Cases: Toward a Social Theory of Rape Processing." *Social Forces* 58 (1980): 833–850.   G

A social theory of criminal-justice processing of rape cases, which proposes that the likelihood of guilty pleas and convictions will be affected by the extent to which characteristics of cases approximate stereotypes of rape held by criminal-justice personnel, was examined via multiple-regression analysis for 124 rape cases filed in criminal court of a large midwestern city.

Lake, A. "Rape: the Unmentionable Crime." *Good Housekeeping* 173 (November 1971):104–105.   G
—————. "What Women Are Doing about the Ugliest Crime." *Good Housekeeping* 179 (August 1974):84–85.   G
Lalley, T.L. "Some New Research Perspectives on Evaluation of Services to Victims." *Evaluation and Change* Special Issue (1980):90–93.   B,H

Four ongoing research projects concerning programs for victims, supported by the National Institute of Mental Health's Center for Studies of Crime and Delinquency, are assessed with emphasis on the evaluation of services. Findings from the youth study suggest the possibility that more harm than good may be done by providing certain types or durations of services.

Lamborn, L.L. "Crime Victim Compensation: Theory and Practice in the Second Decade." *Victimology: An International Journal* 1 (1976):503.
                                                                                                          B,H
—————. "Developments in the Law Concerning Victims." *Victimology* 4 (1979):173–178.   F,H

Revisions of the New York City Police Department procedures regarding complaints of wife abuse are outlined, in which the department and a group of women, repeatedly battered by their husbands, agreed that police officers will treat complaints of wife abuse like any other cases of assault. The agreement outlines the officer's responsibility to respond to the complaint and to make an arrest.

—————. "Reparation for Victims of Crime: Developments and Direction." *Victimology* 4 (1979):214–228.   H

Reparations for victims of crime as well as theoretical developments concerning crime-victim compensation are reviewed. Acceptance of the concept of crime-victim compensation and expansion of benefits, sources of benefits, and type of benefits are discussed.

Lampley, L., and D.L. Shaw. "Perception of Raped Source and Use of Fact in Stories." *Journalism Quarterly* 54 (Autumn 1977):598–599.   G

Landau. "Rape: The Victim as Defendant." *Trial*, (July/August 1974), p. 19.   G

Landau, L.J. "Volunteers in Rape Prevention." *Police Chief* 47 (1980):32.   B,G

Landau, S. "The Sex Offender's Perception of His Victim: Some Crosscultural Findings." *Victimology: An International Journal* 2 (1977): 69–70.   H

In a paper presented at the Second International Symposium on Victimology held in Boston, September 1976, a cross-cultural investigation of the sex offender's perception of the victim is presented. Findings are discussed in terms of cultural differences and similarities and within the general framework of the victimological literature on this topic.

Landis, J.T. "Experiences of 500 Children with Adult Sexual Deviation." *Psychiatric Quarterly*, Supplement 30 (1956):91–109.   E

Landorf, J. *Tough and Tender: What Every Woman Wants in a Man*. Old Tappan, N.J.: Revell, 1975.   A,B

Landsberg, J. "He Beats Me." *Chatelaine Magazine*, January 1976, pp. 21, 66–70.   A

A lawyer, a psychiatrist, policemen, and a feminist discuss why wife beating happens and what women can do about it.

Langley, R. "Wife Abuse and the Police Response." *FBI Law Enforcement Bulletin* 47 (May 1978):4–9.   A,B

The incidence of wife abuse is examined, together with the typical arrest-avoidance response of police. It is proposed that police intervention be based on a criminal law-enforcement approach.

Langley, R., and R.C. Levy. *Wife Beating: The Silent Crisis*. New York: E.P. Dutton, 1977.   A

Laslett, B. "The Family as a Public and Private Institution: A Historical Perspective." *Journal of Marriage and the Family* 35 (August 1973): 480–492.   B

The Last Taboo. Schiller Park, Ill.: Motorola Teleprograms, Inc. 1977. E

Six women relive their experiences of early sexual molestation. Told with
enormous emotional impact, their stories interweave to form a compelling
public-awareness documentary.

Laszlo, A.T. "Intake Screening as a Concept in Victim Assistance: A
Prosecutorial Model." *Victimology: An International Journal* 2 (1977):
70.   *B,H*

In a paper presented at the Second International Symposium on Victimology, held in Boston, September 1976, the role of the victim specialist in
aiding the victim/witness of crimes is described. The objective of this
project is personalized asssistance to the victim or witness, as well as the
provision of social-service referrals to existing community agencies.

―――. "Court Diversion—an Alternative for Spousal Abuse Cases."
Rockville, Md.: NCJRS Nicrofiche Program, 1978.   *A,B*

Results are reported of a study of spouse-dispute cases processed through a
court-mediation component of the district court of Dorchester, Massachusetts; six other mediation programs are described.

Lauer, B.; E.T. Broek; and M. Grossman. "Battered Child Syndrome:
Review of 130 Patients with Controls." *Pediatrics* 54 (July 1974):67–70.
                                                                                A,B
Laventure, R., and C. May. "The Denial and Displacement of Anger by
Women." Unpublished manuscript, Counseling Center, Southern Illi-
nois University, Carbondale, 1976.   *H*
Laves, R.G. "Self-Report Correlates of Crisis Response to Rape." *Disserta-
tion Abstracts International* 40 (3):1373-B, 1979.   *G*

Self-reported change in anxiety and feelings of control over a crisis period
following sexual assault were assessed in twenty-six voluntary participants
who were adult victims of rape or sexual assault and who reported the
offense to the police rape unit.

Law Commission. *Law-Matrimonial Proceedings in Magistrates Courts.*
Working Paper 53. 1973.   *F*
Laws, J.L. "A Feminist Review of Marital Adjustment Literature: The
Rape of the Locke." *Journal of Marriage and the Family* 33 (August
1971):483–511.   *B,G*
Lawton, E.G. "Persons Who Injure Others: A Study of Criminally As-
saultive Behavior in Philadelphia." *Dissertation Abstracts International*
40(6):3549-A, 1979.   *H*

The contention of Wilkins that general criminality is predictable but that
violent crime cannot be predicted was investigated via analysis of data from

2,118 persons arrested in Philadelphia for the crimes of homicide, rape, robbery, aggravated assault, and simple assault.

Layman, W.A. "Pseudo Incest." *Comprehensive Psychiatry* 13 (July 1972): 385–389.   E

Presents evidence to suggest that in some cases of impotence and frigidity the basic dynamic is a psychophysiological attempt to avoid an act that is perceived as basically incestuous.

Lazarsfeld, P.F.; A.K. Pasanella; and M. Rosenberg, eds. *Continuities in the Language of Social Research*. New York: Free Press, 1972.   B
League of Women Voters. *Challenge of the 70's*. San Francisco, 1975. p. 8.   B
Lear, M.W. "Question: If You Rape a Woman and Steal Her T.V., What Can They Get You for in New York? Answer: Stealing Her T.V." *The New York Times Magazine*, 30 January 1972, pp. 10–11; Discussion, 27 February 1972, p. 24.   G
———. What Can They Say about Laws that Tell a Man: If You Rob a Woman, You Might as Well Rape Her Too?" *Redbook* 139 (September 1972):83.   F,G
Leary, H.R. "Police Response to Family Disputes." Procedural Supplement no. 1. New York City Police Department; Raymond Parnas, 1967.   B
———. "The Police Respond to the Domestic Disturbance." *Wisconsin Law Review*. Morton Bard, 1970, pp. 914–916.   B
"Least Punished Crime." *Newsweek*, 18 December 1972, p. 30.   G
Leavy, D. "Death Penalty for Rape? Case of Coker vs. Georgia." *Ms.* 6 (July 1977):20.   G
Lebeau, J.L. "The Spatial Dynamics of Rape: The San Diego Example." *Dissertation Abstracts International* 40 (4):2281-A, 1979.   G

Four hypotheses related to the spatial dynamics of rape were examined using San Diego police rape data for the period 1971 to 1975. The hypothesis that the spatial order of rape can be explained by the spatial variation of the family life cycle and land-use structure was not confirmed.

Leber, P. "Rape." *New England Journal of Medicine* 298 (1978):167. G

In a letter to the editor, the emotional and physical competence of rapists is discussed. It is maintained that sexual dysfunction cannot be demonstrated in rapists because standards for biological sexual function are based upon acts mutually agreed upon by participants.

Leblanc & Berkman. "Rape and the Community." *Los Angeles Herald-Examiner*, 3 September 1972, *California Living* (magazine).   B,G

LeBourdis. "Rape Victims: The Unpopular Patients." *Dimensions Health Service* 53 (March 1976):12.   G

Lebowitz, B.D. "Research in Status Inconsistency: A Synthesis and Appraisal." Mimeographed. Portland, Or.: Department of Sociology, Portland State University, 1970.   B

Lederer, W. *The Fear of Women.* New York: Harcourt Brace Jovanovich, 1968.   H

Ledray, L.,and M.J. Chaignot. "Services to Sexual Assault Victims in Hennepin County." *Evaluation and Change* Special Issue (1980):131–134.   B

   A new treatment for the victims of sexual assault that keeps the power and
   control in the hands of the woman rather than the counselor is considered.
   The Hennepin County, Minnesota, program has provided over 200 women
   with crisis counseling, long-term follow-up, and linkage to other community services.

Lee, G.R. "The Problem of Universals in Comparative Research: An Attempt at Clarification." *Journal of Comparative Family Studies* 6 (1975):89–100.   B

Leeds, S.J. "Family Offense Cases in the Family Court System—A Statistical Description." New York: Henry Street Settlement, 1978.   B

   Family offenses handled by the family-court system in New York and the
   state's probation department are explored.

Lefkowitz, R. "Help for the Sexually Harassed: The Alliance against Sexual Coercion." *Ms.* 6 (November 1977):49.   D

Leger, G.J. "The Roles of Alcohol in Violence and Aggression: A Critical Review." Non-Medical Use of Drugs Directorate. Ottawa: Treatment Program Development, 1976.   H

   This report summarizes and critically reviews the nature and validity of the
   reputed relationship between the use of alcohol and violence and aggression.

Leghorn, L. "Women's Work." *Houseworker's Handbook*, Spring 1975, p. 11.   B

Legrand. "Rape and Rape Laws: Sexism in Society and Law." *California Law Review* 61 (1973):919.   F,G

Lemasters, E.E. "Parenthood as Crisis." *Marriage and Family Living* 19 (1957):352–355.   C

Lemert, E.M. *Human Deviance, Social Problems, and Social Control.* Englewood Cliffs, N.J.: Prentice-Hall, 1972.   C

Lempp, R. "Psychological Damage to Children as a Result of Sexual Offenses." *Child Abuse and Neglect* 2 (1978):243–245.   E

The psychological harm that results from the nonviolent sexual abuse of a
child is described, and the typical behavioral and mood patterns of an
affected child during a sex-offense trial is discussed.

Lennane, J.K., and R. Lennane. "Alleged Psychogenic Disorders in Wom-
en: A Possible Manifestation of Sexual Prejudice." *New England
Journal of Medicine*, 8 February 1973.   H
Leo, J. "Male dominance Revisited." (views of R. Fox) *Time*, 22 September
1980, p. 76.   H
Leon, C.A. "Unusual Patterns of Crime during 'la Violencia' in Columbia."
American Journal of Psychiatry 125 (1969):1564–1575.   H
Leonieni, and Leszcynski. "Rape Committed with Particular Cruelty."
Palestra (Poland), 1974, p. 27.   G
Lerman, H. "What Happens in Feminist Therapy." In *Female Psychology:
The Emerging Self*, edited by S. Cox. Chicago: Science Research Asso-
ciates, 1976.   B
Lerman, L.G. *Legal Help for Battered Women*. Rockville, Md.: NCJRS
1980.   A,F

Recent developments in the laws affecting battered women and problems
encountered in implementing these new laws are discussed. The legal system and specific remedies are emphasized.

Lernell, L.G. "Victimology: Some General Questions." *Victimology: An
International Journal* 2 (1977):70–71.   H

General questions about the nature of victims, compensation, and punishment in socialist countries are raised.

Lesko, C.M. "Selected Psycho-Socio-Legal Aspects of Rape." *Dissertation
Abstracts International*, Ann Arbor, Michigan University, 1976.   G

The psychological, social, and legal aspects of rape management by law-
enforcement agencies are examined with particular emphasis on those
areas in criminal investigation that have particular impact on the rape
victim.

Leslie, G.R. *The Family in Social Context*. New York: Oxford Press, 1967.
                                                               C
Lesse, S. *Status of Violence against Women—Past, Present and Future
Factors*. New York: Association for the Advancement of Psychothera-
py, 1979.   H

Violence against women is examined in terms of past, present, and future trends, and factors influencing the male/female relationship are reviewed to explain rape and wife beating.

Lester, D. "Incest." *Journal of Sex Research* 8 (November 1972):268– 285.   E

Discusses the following areas concerning incest: prevalence, psychological and physiological effects, characteristics of the participants, and theories of the taboo's origin.

————. "Rape and Social Structure." *Psychological Reports* 35 (August 1974):146.   G

Analyzed the correlation between incidence of rape by state in the United States for 1970 with the male-female ratio indicated in the 1970 U.S. census.

————. "Rape." *The New York Times Magazine*, 26 January 1976, p. 4. G
————. "A Cross-Culture Study of Wife Abuse." *Aggressive Behavior* 6 (1980):361–364.   A

Ratings of wife-beating incidents in seventy-one societies were obtained, as well as ratings of other aggressive behaviors, to test the hypotheses that wife beating should be more common in societies in which other types of aggression were common also and in societies in which women were considered to be inferior.

Levens, B.R. *The Social Service Role of Police: Domestic Crisis Intervention*. Vancouver, B.C.: United Way of Greater Vancouver, 1976. *B,C*

This report, consisting of four research monographs, provides an evaluation of police domestic-crisis intervention in Vancouver, British Columbia.

Levine, K. "Empiricism in Victimological Research: A Critique." *Victimology* 3 (1978):77–90.   B,H

A critical overview of empiricism in victimological research is presented. In an attempt to clarify potential bases of victimological theory, a systematic analysis of types of existing empirical research is presented, the level of explanation implicit in each type is identified, and suggestions for forging connections between levels are presented.

Levine, M.J. "Wife Beaters." *McCalls*, June 1975.   A
Levine, R.A. "Gusii Sex Offenses: A Study in Social Control." *American Anthropologist* 61 (December 1959):965–990.   E

Levine, S. "Crime or Affliction? Rape in an African Community." *Culture, Medicine and Psychiatry* 4 (1980):151–165.				G

The response of families to emotional stress was investigated among the Gusii community in southwestern Kenya, with emphasis on the reaction to rape and sexual assault.

Levinger, G. "Marital Cohesiveness and Dissolution: An Integrative Review." *Journal of Marriage and the Family* 27 (February 1965):19–28.
										B
———. "Sources of Marital Dissatisfaction among Applicants for Divorce." *American Journal of Orthopsychiatry* 36 (1966):803–807.	C

This paper compares marital complaints of husbands versus wives, and of middle-class versus lower-class marriages, in a sample of 600 couples applying for divorce.

———. "Physical Abuse among Applicants for Divorce." In *Violence in the Family*, edited by S. Steinmetz and M. Straus. New York: Dodd, Mead, 1974.								A,C

Lewis, D. "Principles Regarding National Health Insurance and Women's Health Care." Paper presented at the 104th Annual Meeting of the American Public Health Association, Miami Beach, Florida, 18 October 1976.								B
———. "Women and National Health Insurance." *Medical Care* 13 (1977): 549–558.									B

Lewis, D.; S. Shankok; and J. Pincus. "Juvenile Male Sexual Assaulters." *American Journal of Psychiatry* 136 (September 1979):1194–1196.	G

Compared the psychiatric, neurological, and psychoeducational status of seventeen sexually assaultive male juveniles and sixty-one other violent juveniles whose average age was fifteen years. Theoretical and treatment implications are discussed.

Lewis, M.L. "The Initial Contact with Wives of Alcoholics." *Social Casework* 35 (1954):8–14.								A

Although the alcoholic man himself rarely asks for agency help with the social difficulties that his drinking has brought upon himself or his family, his wife often seeks help from family or other social agencies.

Lewis, and Sarrel. "Some Psychological Aspects of Seduction, Incest, and Rape in Childhood." *Journal of American Academy of Child Psychiatry* 8 (1969):606.								E,F

Libai. "The Protection of the Child Victim of a Sexual Offense in the

Criminal Justice System." In *Rape Victimology*, edited by L. Schultz. 1975.   *E*

Libow, J.A. "Self Attributed Responsibility and Self Derogation by Rape Victims from a Social Psychological Perspective." *Dissertation Abstracts International* 39 (7-B):3525, January 1979.   *G*

Libow, J.A., and D.W. Doty. "An Exploratory Approach to Self-Blame and Self-Derogation by Rape Victims." *American Journal of Orthopsychiatry* 49 (October 1979):670–679.   *G*

Studied quantitative and interview data on eighteen rape victims' self-evaluation and attributions of personal responsibility to explore the relevance of theories of defensive attribution and maintenance of belief in a just world.

Lichtenberger, J.P. *Divorce: A Study of Social Causation*. New York: Columbia University Press, 1968. Reprint of 1909 edition.   *C*

Lichtenstein. "Rape Squad: Manhattan Sex Crimes Squad." *The New York Times*, 3 March 1974.   *B,G*

Liddick, B. "The Complex World of Wife Beating." *Los Angeles Times*, 2 January 1977.   *A*

Lieberknecht, K. "Helping the Battered Wife." *American Journal of Nursing* 78 (April 1978):654–656.   *A*

Liebman, D.A., and J.A. Schwartz. "Police Programs in Domestic Disturbance Crisis Intervention: A Review." In *The Urban Policeman in Transition*, edited by J. Snibbe and H. Snibbe. New York: Charles C Thomas, 1972.   *B*

Lief, H.I. "Rape: Is It a Sexual or an Aggressive Act?" *Medical Aspects of Human Sexuality* 12 (1978):55–56.   *G*

The sexual versus aggressive nature of rape is discussed within the context of two empirical studies. Taken together, these studies suggest that both sex and aggression are involved in rape but that the aggressive component predominates.

Lightman, E.S., and H.H. Irving. "Conciliation and Arbitration in Family Disputes." *Conciliation Courts Review* 14 (1976):12–21.   *C*

Lilli, L. "Rape—Italian Style." *New Statesman* 93 (22 August 1977):517–518.   *G*

Lindabury. "Editorial: The Criminal Code and Rape and Sex Offenses." *Canadian Nurse* April 1975, p. 3.   *B,F*

Lindner, H. "Psychogenic Seizure States: A Psychodynamic Study." *International Journal of Clinical and Experimental Hypnosis* 21 (October 1973):261–271.   *B,E*

Defense against overwhelming unconscious incestuous feeling of anxiety and possible reproduction by hypnotic-trance induction, psychogenic seizure states, fifteen-year-old girl and thirty-six-year-old man.

Lindsey, K. "How to Spot It and How to Stop It." *Ms.* (November 1977): 47–48.   G
Lindzey, G. "Some Remarks Concerning Incest, The Incest Taboo, and Psychoanalytic Theory." *American Psychologist* 22 (1967):1051–1059.
     E

Examines the incest taboo, stressing "theories of the origin of the taboo, the implications of the taboo for psychological development, and the relation between these observations and the current status of psychoanalytic theory."

Lion, J.R., and D.J. Madden. *Race, Hate, Assault and Other Forms of Violence.* New York: Spectrum Publications, 1976.   A
Lipton, M.A. "Violence is a Part of the Times." *U.S. News & World Report,* 25 January 1971, pp. 73–74.   H
Lipton, and Roth. "Rape: A Complex Management Problem in the Pediatric Emergency Room." *Journal of Pediatrics,* 1969, p. 75.   G
Lipsha, P. "On Theories of Urban Violence." *Urban Affairs Quarterly* 4 (1969):273–296.   H
Litt, I.F.; S. Edberg; and L. Finberg. "Gonorrhea in Children and Adolescents: A Current Review." *Journal of Pediatrics* 85 (November 1974):595–607.   E
Littner. "The Psychological Study of Sex Offenders: Causes, Treatment, Prognosis." *Police Law Quarterly* 3 (1976):5.   B,C
Litwak, E. "Occupational Mobility and Extended Family Cohesion." *American Sociological Review* 25 (February 1960):9–22.   C
Livingston, N. "Wifebeating Looms as Major City Crime." *St. Paul Sunday Pioneer Press,* 1 December 1974, City Life Section.   A
Lockwood, D. *Prison Sexual Violence.* New York: Elsevier, 1980.   G,H

Observations are offered on the nature and extent of sexual violence in U.S. prisons to highlight the need for prison reforms.

Loew, C. "Acquisition of a Hostile Attitude and Its Relation to an Aggressive Behavior." *Journal of Personality and Social Psychology* 5 (1967): 552–558.   H
Lombroso, C. *The Female Offender.* New York: D. Appleton, 1898.   H
London Boroughs Association. *Battered Women and Their Children.* Avail-

able from D. Clark, Lambeth Town Hall, Brixton Hill, London SW2.
                                                                    H

London, J. "Images of Violence against Women." *Victimology* 2 (1977–
    1978):510–524.   *H*

> Part 1 of this article is a pictorial essay of record-album photos, magazine
> layouts, and other images of women being physically abused. Part 2 de-
> scribes the work of the organization Women against Violence against
> Women, and part 3 lists records promoted with violent, abusive material.

London Sunday Times. "Battered Wives Plea." News Digest, 3 November
    1974.   *A*
Longtain, M. *Family Violence—The Well Kept Secret*. Austin: University of
    Texas Press, 1979.   *H*

> This booklet describes the Austin Center for Battered Women's Program
> and the services it offers to women and children who are victims of family
> violence.

Lopata, H.Z. *Occupation: Housewife*. New York: Oxford University Press,
    1971.   *A*
Lord Chancellor's Office. *Civil Judicial Statistics for England and Wales*.
    Cmnd 5333, 1973.   *B,F*
Lorenz, K. *On Aggression*. New York: Bantam, 1963.   *H*
Los Angeles City Attorney Domestic Violence Program. *Domestic Vio-
    lence—Prevention and Services*, 1979, pp. 367–401.   *C*

> This Los Angeles city attorney domestic-violence-program manual pro-
> vides the operational framework within which a prosecution agency can
> develop an effective response to the problem of domestic violence.

LoSciuto, L. "A Rational Inventory of Television Viewing Behavior." In
    Television and Social Behavior, edited by E. Rubinstein, G. Comstock,
    and J. Murray. Washington, D.C.: U.S. Government Printing Office,
    1972.   *B,H*
Louie. "Rape and Nursing Intervention: Locating Resources." *Imprint*,
    December 1975, p. 32.   *C,G*
Louisville Division of Police. *Police Training in Family Crisis Intervention*.
    Final report. EDRS, 1971.   *C*
Lourie, I.S. "Testimony of Ira S. Lourie on March 8, 1978." *Domestic
    Violence* 1978, pp. 285–294.   *G*

> The testimony of an American Psychiatric Association representative to
> the Senate Subcommittee on Child and Human Development discusses
> legislative needs for curbing domestic violence.

Loving, M., and L. Olson. "Rape and Wife Beating." Conference information packet prepared by Criminal Justice Staff of National League of Cities and U.S. Conference of Mayors. Washington, D.C., 1976. *A,G*

Loving, N. *Responding to Spouse Abuse and Wife Beating—A Guide for Police.* Washington, D.C.: U.S. Department of Justice Law Enforcement Assistance Administration, 1980. *A,B*

> This 1979 study of police response to spouse-abuse calls reveals that the quality of this response varies widely and that the traditional emphasis on reconciling the parties does not deter spouse abuse.

Lowenberg, D.A. "Pima County Services for Battered Women." *Response*, December 1976, pp. 3–4. *A*

———. "Conjugal Assaults: The Incarcerated or Liberated Woman." *Federal Probation* 41 (June 1977):10–13. *A*

Lowenstein, L.F. "The Psychology of Rape." *New Law Journal* 127 (March 1977):201–224. *G*

> Discusses background factors that lead to rape—for example, general factors including hereditary disposition, early traumas, and relationship problems; current tensions; and current environment.

———. "Who Is the Rapist." *Journal of Criminal Law* 162 (April/June 1977):137–146. *G*

> Suggests that the rapist is one who needs or enjoys the forcible or violent taking of another sexually, against the other's wishes.

Ludwig, F.J. *Rape and the Law.* New York: Equal Justice Institute, 1977. *F,G*

Lukianowicz, N. "Incest (I: Paternal Incest); (II: Other Types of Incest)." *British Journal of Psychiatry* 120 (March 1972):301–313. *E*

> Analysis of social factors, family dynamics, and personalities suggests that paternal incest is not necessarily an expression of real sexual deviation but may be a morally and socially accepted type of behavior in some oversexed and underinhibited men.

Lurie, T. "End of Wife-Beating." *San Francisco Chronicle*, 9 May 1975, p. 21. *A*

Lustig, N.; "Incest: A Family Group Survival Pattern." *Archives of General Psychiatry* 14 (1966):31–40. *E*

Luther, M. *Sermons.* Translated and edited by J.W. Doberstein. In *Luther's Works.* Philadelphia, 1959. Cited in J. O'Faolain and L. Martines. *Not in God's Image.* Glasgow: Colling, 1973. *H*

Luther, S. "Child Sexual Abuse: A Review." *Journal of School Health* 50 (1980):161–165.   E

The recent literature dealing with child sexual abuse is reviewed, and the role health educators can play in combatting the problem is discussed.

Lynch, C.G., and T.L. Norris. "Services for Battered Women: Looking for a Perspective." *Victimology: An International Journal* 2 (1978):553–562.   A,B

The problems confronting service programs for battered women are examined.

Lystad, M. *Violence at Home*. Rockville, Md.: National Institute of Mental Health, 1974.   H

A review of empirical research shows clearly that violence in the family is common in all societies including our own.

Lythcott, S. *Powers and Duties of Family Court Commissioners*. Madison: Wisconsin Legislative Council, 1978.   B,F

The family-court commissioner, a parajudicial officer of the court established by Wisconsin law, may issue various temporary orders in domestic cases including orders to abusive spouses to vacate the home.

McBarnet, D. "Victim in the Witness Box: Degradation Techniques and Legal Structures." *Victimology: An International Journal* 2 (1977):72.
                                                                          H

In a paper presented at the Second International Symposium on Victimology, held in Boston, September 1976, the position of the victim in the witness box and techniques of the defense to discredit the victim are examined.

McCabe, S. "Unfinished Business: A Note on the Reports of the Select Committees on Violence in Marriage and Violence in the Family." *British Journal of Criminology* 17 (July 1977):280–285.   H

McCabee, B. "The Tragic Signs of Wifebeating." *Boston Globe*, October 1975.   A

McCahill, T.W.; L.C. Meyer; and A.M. Fischman. *The Aftermath of Rape*. Lexington, Mass.: D.C. Heath and Company, 1979.   G

Problems encountered by rape victims immediately after the rape and the adjustment patterns then and one year later were investigated. The Phila-

delphia Sexual Assault Victim Study, the readjustment of the victim, and
the criminal-justice response are considered.

McCarthy, S.J. "Pornography, Rape, and the Cult of Macho." *Humanist* 40
(1980):11–20, 56.   **G**

The content and effect of pornography on male violence and attitudes
toward women are analyzed. In addition, research on pornography, rape,
aggression, and violence is reviewed.

McCartner, C.F. "Counseling the Husband and Wife after the Woman Has
Been Raped." *Medical Aspects of Human Sexuality* 14 (1980):121–122.
    B,G

A brief guide to office counseling is presented for use by physicians counseling the husband and wife after the woman has been raped.

McClelland, D.C. *Personality, Annual Review of Psychology.* Stanford:
Annual Reviews, Incorporated, 1956.   **B**
McClintock, F.H. *Crimes of Violence.* New York: Saint Martins Press,
1963.   ***G,H***
———. *Criminological Aspects of Family Violence.* New York: Wiley &
Sons, 1978.   ***H***

Data from surveys identifying crimes of violence within families handled by
police are reported for England, Wales, and Scotland, and the processing
of such cases by the criminal-justice system is considered.

McClintock, S. "The Beaten Woman." *Pittsburgh Magazine,* 1975. ***A,H***
Maccoby, E.E., and C.N. Jacklin. *The Psychology of Sex Differences.*
Stanford: Stanford University Press, 1974.   ***B***
McCombie, S.L. "Characteristics of Rape Victims Seen in Crisis Interven-
tion." *Smith College Studies in Social Work* 46 (March 1976):137–158.
    C,G

Seventy female rape victims between the ages of fifteen and twenty-five
years provided interview data on themselves and their traumatic experience.

———. *The Rape Crisis Intervention Handbook: A Guide for Victim Care.*
New York: Plenum, 1980.   ***B,G***

Victim-care strategies for service providers in rape intervention are presented.

McCombie, S.L.; E. Bassuk; R. Savitz; and S. Pell. "Development of a Medical Center Rape Crisis Intervention Program." *American Journal of Psychiatry* 133 (April 1976):418–421.   B

   Discusses a crisis program and its problems of implementation, including staff resistance, funding questions, and varying levels of counseling sophistication and describes how these difficulties have been handled.

McDermott. "California Rape Evidence Reform: An Analysis of Senate Bill 1678." *Hastings Law Journal* 26 (1975):1551.   B,F,G
McDermott, M.J. *Rape Victimization in 26 American Cities. Applications of the National Crime Survey.* Analytic report SD-VAD-6. Washington, D.C.: U.S. Government Printing Office, 1979.   B,G,H

   Victimization survey data are used to examine rape and attempted rape.

MacDonald, A. "Death Penalty and Homicide." *American Journal of Sociology* 16 (1911):96–97.   H
MacDonald, J. "Group Rape." *Medical Aspects of Human Sexuality* 8 (1974):58–88.   G
MacDonald, J.M. "Homicidal Threats." *American Journal of Psychiatry* 124 (1967):475–482.   H
———. *Rape: Offenders and Their Victims.* Springfield, Ill.: Charles C Thomas, 1971.   G,H

   These accurate accounts of rape by offenders and victims contribute to the understanding of the crime and its impact on the victims.

McDonald, W.F. "The Victim's Role in the Prosecutorial and Dispositional Stages of the American Criminal Justice System." *Victimology: An International Journal* 2 (1977):73.   F,H

   In a paper presented at the Second International Symposium on Victimology, held in Boston, September 1976, the victim's role in the prosecutorial and dispositional stages of the U.S. criminal-justice process is examined.

Mace, D., and V. Mace. *Little Girls.* London: Writers and Readers Publishing Cooperative, 1973.   E
———. *Marriage East and West.* Garden City, N.Y.: Doubleday Dolphin Books, Belotti, 1973.   B
MacFarlane, K. *Sexual Abuse of Children. The Victimization of Women.* Beverly Hills, Calif.: Sage Publications, 1978, pp. 81–109.   E
McGeorge, J. "Sexual Assaults on Children." *Medicine, Science, and the Law* 4 (1955):245–253.   E

McGregor, O.R.; L. Blom-Cooper; and C. Gibson. *Separated Spouse.* 1970.   C

McGuire, G.D. "The Measurement of Social Status." Research Paper in Human Development, number 3. Department of Educational Psychology, University of Texas.   B

McGuire, L.S., and M. Stern. "Survey of Incidence of and Physicians' Attitudes toward Sexual Assault." *Public Health Reports* 91 (March/April 1976):103–109.   B

Reports the responses of 458 private physicians in King County, Washington, to a survey dealing with sexual assault.

Machotka, P.; F.S. Pittman; and K. Flomenhaft. "Incest as a Family Affair." *Family Process* 6 (1967):98–116.   E

Three families who revealed a history of past incestuous activity were seen in treatment.

MacInnes. "One Reading of Rape." *New Society*, 33 (1975):147.   G

McKenzie, T. "Sticks and Stones Break More Than Bones." *United States Catholic* 44 (October 1979):34–38.   G

McKinley, D.G. *Social Class and Family Life.* New York: Free Press, 1964.   B

———. "Work and the Family." In *Social Class and Family Life*, edited by McKinley, pp. 118–151. New York: Free Press, 1964.   B

McLaren, L. *The Women's Charter of Rights and Liberties.* London: Grosvenor, 1909.   B

Maclean, C.J., and M.S. Adams. "A Method for the Study of Incest." *Annals of Human Genetics* 36 (1973):323–332.   E

MacLeod, F. *Family Violence—Report of the Task Force on Family Violence.* Vancouver: United Way of the Lower Mainland, 1979.   H

Findings, recommendations, and research materials of the British Columbia task force on family violence that focused on child abuse, wife battering, legal issues, and education are presented.

MacMillan, J. "Rape and Prostitution." *Victimology* 1 (Fall 1976):414–420.   G

Rape and prostitution have been compared and contrasted by many people in order to make various points about these and other issues.

MacNamara, D.E., and E. Sagarin. *Perspectives on Correction.* New York: Crowell, 1971.   B

———. *Sex, Crime, and the Law.* New York: Free Press, 1977.   F

An examination of sexuality and sex-related crime from a legal, sociological, and psychological perspective is presented.

McPherson, M. "Realities and Perceptions of Crime at the Neighborhood Level." *Victimology* 3 (1978):319–328.   B

Responses to three sets of questions that measured individual perceptions and fear of crime on a citizen survey conducted by the Minnesota Crime Prevention Center were analyzed.

McShane, C. "Community Services for Battered Women." *Social Work* 24 (January 1979):34–39.   A, B

A strategy for improving the delivery of services to battered women is discussed, with reference to services such as police protection, legal assistance, financial aid, emergency shelter, and counseling.

———. *Woman Battering*. Milwaukee, Wisconsin University. Region versus Child Abuse and Neglect Resource Center, National Center on Child Abuse and Neglect, Washington, D.C.   A

This annotated bibliography lists materials on spouse battering and family violence in general and on women battering in particular.

MacVicar, K. "Psychotherapeutic Issues in the Treatment of Sexually Abused Girls." *Journal of the American Academy of Child Psychiatry* 18 (1979):342–353.   E

Psychotherapeutic issues in the treatment of sexually abused girls are discussed.

Maerov, A. "Prostitution: A Survey and Review of 20 Cases." *Psychiatric Quarterly* 39 (1965):675–701.   B, E

Maidment, S. *Law's Response to Marital Violence—A Comparison between England and the United States*. Scarborough, Ont.: Butterworth, 1978.   F

The law in England is adequate to handle any degree of violence between husband and wife, but these legal provisions are not used. The informal, coordinated procedures of the United States are urged for England.

Maisch, H., and C. Bearne. *Incest*. New York: Stein & Day, 1972.   E

Makman, R.S. *Some Clinical Aspects of Inter-Spousal Violence*. Scarborough, Ont.: Butterworth, 1978.   B

Interrelationships between marital violence and anxiety, depression, para-
noia, jealousy, sociopathy, and psychosis are examined through case studies. The danger a woman faces when she leaves a marriage is often real.

Malamuth, N.M.; S. Feshbach; and M. Heim. "Ethical Issues and Exposure
to Rape Stimuli: A Reply to Sherif." *Journal of Personality and Social
Psychology* 38 (1980):413–415.   *B,G*

A reply is made to comments on the ethical issues involved in the author's
recent research into norm violations.

Malamuth, N.M., and J.V. Check. "Penile Tumescence and Perceptual
Responses to Rape as a Function of Victim's Perceived Reactions."
Journal of Applied Social Psychology 10 (November/December 1980):
528–547.   *G*

In a study of seventy-five male undergraduates, a rape portrayal in which
the assailant perceived that the victim became sexually aroused was found
to result in high sexual arousal in comparison to a rape emphasizing the
victim's abhorrence of the assault. Further, self-reported possibility of
engaging in rape was found to correlate with callous attitudes to rape and
with self-reported sexual arousal to violent sexuality in a predicted pattern.

———. "Sexual Arousal to Rape and Consenting Depictions: The Importance of the Woman's Arousal." *Journal of Abnormal Psychology* 89
(December 1980):763–766.   *G*

143 male and female undergraduates were randomly assigned to read one
of eight versions of an erotic passage. The independent variables in the
stories were nonconsent versus consent, woman's arousal versus disgust,
and woman's pain versus no pain.

Malamuth, N.M.; M. Heim; and S. Feshbach. "Sexual Responsiveness of
College Students to Rape Depictions: Inhibitory and Disinhibitory
Effects." *Journal of Personality and Social Psychology* 38 (1980):309–
408.   *G*

The dimensions in portrayals of sexual violence that inhibit or disinhibit the
sexual responsiveness of college students were investigated. It is suggested
that arousing stimuli that fuse sexuality and violence may have antisocial
effects.

Malamuth, N.M.; S. Haber; and S. Feshbach. "Testing Hypotheses Regarding Rape: Exposure to Sexual Violence, Sex Differences, and the

'Normality' of Rapists." *Journal of Research in Personality* 14 (1980): 121–137. G

Three hypotheses on the subject of rape were addressed empirically. The association between this self-report and general attitudes toward rape reveals a pattern that bears striking similarity to the callous attitudes often held by convicted rapists.

Malinowski, B. "An Anthropological Analysis of War." *Magic, Science, and Religion.* Glencoe, Ill.: Free Press, 1948. H
Manchester, A.H. "The Legal History of Marital Violence in England and Wales, 1750–1976." Unpublished paper, Faculty of Law, University of Birmingham, England, 1976. B,F
———. "The Law of Incest in England and Wales." *Child Abuse and Neglect* 3 (1979):679–682. B,E

Statutes concerning definitions, legal processes, and sanctions for incest in England and Wales are reviewed.

Mandel, D. "Victims and Witnesses—San Mateo County's Cooperative Solution." *Crime Prevention Review* 5 (January 1978):10–14. B,H

Aid to Victims and Witnesses offers a comprehensive and well-developed program of services for victims of violent crimes and witnesses through a network of public and private community agencies groups.

Mandel, W. *Soviet Women.* Garden City, N.Y.: Anchor, 1975. B
Mander, A., and A. Rush. *Feminism as Therapy.* New York: Random House, 1974. B,C
Mann, D. "Intervening with Convicted Serious Juvenile Offenders." Washington, D.C.: National Institute for Juvenile Justice and Delinquency Prevention, July 1976. C

Some behavior-changing treatments currently in use with serious juvenile offenders are identified and evaluated.

"Man Rapes His Wife—Jailed." *San Francisco Chronicle*, 23 May 1974. A,G
Mantell, D.M. "Doves vs. Hawks: Guess Who Had the Authoritarian Parents?" *Psychology Today*, September 1974, pp. 56–62. C
Marcovitch, A. "Refuges for Battered Women." *Social Work Today* 7 (April 1976):2. A,B

This article discusses how Action Women's Aid tries to help a woman constructively and answers some of the criticisms from social workers who are dubious about the women's aid movement.

Marecek, J. "Power and Women's Psychological Disorders." Unpublished
    manuscript, Swarthmore College, 1975.   H
Marentette, J. "My Sexpot Waitress Uniform Invited Harassment, and
    That's What I Got until I Took My Case to Court." *Glamour* 78
    (October 1980):256.   D
Maretzki, T., and Hatsumi. "Taira: An Okinawan Village." In *Six Cul-
    tures: Studies of Child Rearing*, edited by B. Whiting. New York:
    Wiley & Sons, 1963.   B,E
Margolin. "Rape: The Facts." *Women: A Journal of Liberation*, 3:19.
                                                                 B,G
Marienskind, H. "Restructuring Ob-Gyn." *Social Policy* 6 (1975):48–49.
                                                                   B
Marienskind, H., and B. Ehrenreich. "Toward Socialist Medicine: The
    Women's Health Movement." *Social Policy* 6:34–42.   B
"The Marital Rape Exemption." *New York University Law Review* 52
    (1977):306–323.   B,G
The Marital Rape Exemption: Legal Sanction of Spouse Abuse." *Journal
    of Family Law* 18 (1980):565.   A,B,G
"Marking the Culprit: Use of Sperm Diaphorase in Rape Investigations."
    Family Health 8 (August 1976):26–27.   G
Marks, J. "Incest: Victims Speak Out." *Teen* 24 (February 1980):26.   E
Marmor, J. "Sexual Deviancy, Part I." *Journal of Continuing Education in
    Psychiatry* 39 (1978):23–31.   E,G

    The characteristics, prevalence, psychodynamics, and treatment of various
    sexual deviations are described.

Marquardt, J.A. "Violence against Wives—Expected Effects of Utah
    Spouse Abuse Act." *Journal of Contemporary Law* 5 (Spring 1979):
    272–292.   A

    Utah's Spouse Abuse Act is assessed in relation to the psychological
    dynamics of wife abuse and the legal system's traditional response to such
    abuse.

Marques, J.K. "The Effects of Several Victim Resistance Strategies on the
    Sexual Arousal and Attitudes of Violent Rapists." *Dissertation Ab-
    stracts International* 40 (2-B):926–927, August 1979.   G
Marquez, D.V. "Victims of Crimes in Metropolitan Panama." *Victimology:
    An International Journal* 2 (1977):73.   H

    In a paper presented at the Second International Symposium on Victim-
    ology, held in Boston, September 1976, diverse categories of victims are
    considered with regard to their relationship to the perpetrator of the crime
    and the degree of responsibility that the victim might have in the mechanics
    of the crime.

"Marriage Guidance." *Doctors and Counsellors*, July 1970.   C
Marriage under Stress. Film produced by BBC-TV, London, 1969. Re-
    leased in the United States by Time/Life.   B,C
Marschak, M. "A Puzzling Episode." *Psychiatry* 31 (1968):195–198.   B
Marsden, D. *Mothers Alone*, 2d ed. 1973.   A
———. "Sociological Perspectives on Family Violence." New York:
    Wiley & Sons, 1978.   B

> Patterns of public concern toward family violence in the United Kingdom
> are examined, and various sociological theories that attempt to explain
> family violence are criticized.

Marsden, D., and D. Owens, "The Jekyll and Hyde Marriages." *New
    Society* 32 (8 May 1975):333.   A
Marshall, D.S. "Too Much in Mangaia." *Psychology Today* 4 (February
    1971):43–44.   B
Marshall, M. "Incest and Exogamy on Namoluk Atol." *Journal of the
    Polynesian Society* 85 (1976):181–198.   .   E
Marshall, W., and R. McKnight. "An Integrated Treatment Program
    for Sexual Offenders." *Canadian Psychiatric Association Journal* 20
    (1975):133–138.   B
Martin, D. "Beating Her, Slamming Her, Making Her Cry." *The New York
    Times*, 29, 6 October 1975, p. 29.   A

> Battering is a long-standing tradition. Batterers are of no specific class or
> origin and exhibit a variety of emotional characteristics.

———. *Battered Wives*. New York: Blide Publications, 1976.   A

> From a feminist perspective, the author explores the psychology of the wife
> batterer, the long history and cultural roots of wife battery, and the un-
> willingness of attorneys, policemen, social workers, and psychiatrists to
> help the victim.

———. "Can Society Put a Stop to Wife Beating?" *Washington Star*, 2
    September 1976.   A

> An interview with Del Martin, asking her opinion on a variety of aspects
> connected with wife abuse.

———. "The Economics of Wife Beating." Paper presented at the Annual
    Meeting of the American Sociological Association in New York, 1976.
                                                                    A
———. *Battered Wives*. New York: Simon & Schuster, 1977.   A

This is one of the first major comprehensive books published on spouse abuse. It is an excellent resource on the subject, with contents ranging from analyses of the family, marriage, victim, and abuser to the more-practical considerations of initiating shelters for battered women.

————. "Society's Vindication of the Wife Batterer." *Bulletin of the American Academy of Psychiatry and the Law* 5 (1977):391–401.   A

The need for a new and more-serious approach to the problem of wife beating is discussed, emphasizing that this problem interrelates with other difficulties that women face.

————. *Battered Women—Society's Problem: Victimization of Women.* Beverly Hills, Calif.: Sage Publications, 1978.   A

Presents historical attitudes toward women and wife beating. The lack of legal protection for wives, the inadequacies of social services, the need for changed attitudes among police, and the need for shelters are topics covered.

————. *Scope of the Problem.* Rockville, Md.: NCJRS Microfiche Program, 1978.   A

The extent of wife abuse, the influence of a sexist culture on the causes and handling of wife-abuse cases, and current legislative and therapeutic efforts to deal with the problem are discussed.

Martin, H.S. "Machismo: Latin America's Myth Cult of Male Supremacy." *Unesco Courier*, March 1975, p. 31.   A,H

Martin, J.P. *Family Violence and Social Policy.* New York: Wiley & Sons, 1978.   A,H

The identification of victims of child and wife abuse and the provision of services to victims of domestic violence are discussed and criticized. Development of a service network based on sound research is recommended.

————. *Some Reflections on Violence and the Family.* New York: Wiley & Sons, 1978.   H

Historical and cultural circumstances as factors that determine the legitimacy of force in family relationships are discussed, along with factors in violent personalities and measures to limit violence.

————. *Violence and the Family.* New York: Wiley & Sons, 1978.   H

This collection of papers by psychologists and sociologists in Australia, England, and the United States examines family violence, the state of research on the issue, and social policy directed at family violence.

Marx, E. *Bedouin of the Negev.* Manchester: Manchester University Press, 1967.   B
———. "Some Notes on Violence." *Delinquency and Society* 2 (1967):22–25.   H
———. "Varieties of Individual Violence: Observations in an Immigrant Town in Israel." In Association of Social Anthropologists, Seminar on Conflict Theory, Coniston, 1968.   H
———. "Personal Violence in an Immigrant Town." *Megamot* 17 (1970): 61–77.   H
———. "Coercive Violence in Official Client Relationships." *Israel Studies in Criminology* 2 (1972):24–59.   H
———. "Some Social Contexts of Personal Violence." In *The Allocation of Responsibility*, edited by M. Gluckman. Manchester: Manchester University Press, 1972.   H
Marx, G.T."Issueless Riots." *Annals* 391 (September 1970):21–33.   H
Marx, K. *Critique of Political Economy.* Moscow: Progress Publishers, 1970.   H
———. *Grundrisse: Introduction to the Critique of Political Economy.* Harmondwirth: Penguin, 1973.   H
"Mary Cunningham: So Successful, She Had to Fail." *Mademoiselle* 87 (January 1981):24.   D
"Maryland Court Orders Resentencing of Rape Convict Who Refused Institutionalization." *Mental Disability Law Reporter* 4 (1980):99. F,G

> In *Watson* v. *Maryland*, resentencing of a defendant convicted of second-degree rape and given the maximum twenty-year penalty has been ordered by a Maryland court of appeals.

Mason, E. "How Can a Woman Avoid Rape?" *Intellect* 103 (March 1975): 512–513.   G
Massell, G.J. "Law as an Instrument of Revolutionary Change in a Traditional Milieu: The Case of Soviet Central Asia." *Law and Society Review* 2 (October 1968):179–228.   F
Massey, J.B.; "Management of Sexually Assaulted Females." *Obstetrics and Gynecology* 38 (July 1971):29–36.   H
Masters, W.H., and V.E. Johnson. "Incest: The Ultimate Sexual Taboo." *Redbook*, April 1976.   E
———. "Aftermath of Rape." *Redbook* 147 (June 1976):74.   G
Mastria, M.A. "A Study of Assertiveness as a Function of Training in Rape Prevention and Assertive Training." *Dissertation Abstracts International* 36 (4-B):1923–1924, October 1975.   B,G

Masumara, W.T. "Wife Abuse and Other Forms of Aggression." *Victim-ology* 4 (1979):46–59.   *A,H*

    A sample of eighty-six primitive societies was studied in a cross-cultural survey of wife abuse and other forms of aggression.

"Material on Emergency Housing." *U.S. Family Law Reporter* 1 (22 July 1975):2613–2614.   *B*
Mathiasen. "Rape Victim: A Victim of Society and the Law." *Williamette Law Journal* 11 (1974):36.   *G*
Matland, L. "Hearings Are Held on Battered Wives." *The New York Times*, 15 October 1976.   *A*

    Article reports on hearings held by the New York City Council in which programs were requested to aid battered women.

Matthews, et al. "Two Faces of Sara Jane Moore." *Newsweek*, 22 September 1975, pp. 22–24.   *G*
Mattox, K.L. "Patterns of Reported Rape in a Tri-Ethnic Population in Houston, Texas." *American Journal of Public Health* 69 (1979):480–485.   *B,G*
Matusewitch, E. *"Kyriazi* v. *Western Electric*: Court Fines Five Bosses for Sexual Harassment." *Ms.* 8 (April 1980):27.   *D*
May, M. *Violence in the Family—An Historical Perspective.* New York: Wiley & Sons, 1978.   *H*

    Family violence in the United Kingdom, especially child and wife abuse, is examined from the early nineteenth to the late twentieth centuries; late Victorian and Edwardian period explanations of family violence are discussed.

May, R. *Power and Innocence.* New York: W.W. Norton, 1972.   *H*
"Mayor Vows Quicker Response to Calls from Women's Advocates." *Saint Paul Dispatch*, 18 September 1975.   *B*
Mead, B.T. "'Showing Off' Sexually." *Medical Aspects of Human Sexuality* 12 (1978):44, 49–50.   *C,H*

    The psychological factors involved in sexual showmanship, engaged in to impress or please a partner, are discussed with reference to aspects of the performer's personality that are revealed by the showmanship.

Mead, M. *Male and female.* New York: Dell, 1949.
———. "Proposal: We Need Taboos on Sex at Work." *Redbook* 150 (April 1978):31.   *C,D*
Mechau, D.V. *Alaska—Abused Women's Aid in Crisis—Shelter for Abused*

and Battered Women and Their Children. Final evaluation report. Anchorage.   *A,B*

The evaluation of the first year of the shelter operated by Abused Women's Aid in Crisis (AWAIC), Anchorage, Alaska, is given in this final report.

Medea, A., and K. Thompson. *Against Rape*. New York: Farrar, Straus & Giroux, 1973.   *G*

A survival manual for women: how to avoid entrapment and how to cope with rape physically and emotionally.

―――. "How Much Do You Really Know about a Rapist?" *Ms*. 3 (July 1974):113–114.   *G*
Mediag Med Distributor. *Raised in Anger*. 16 mm film, sound, color, 1979.   *C*

Resource material prepared by the Syracuse, New York, Police Department is provided for use in the area of crisis intervention.

Megargee, E.I. "Assault with Intent to Kill." *Transaction*, September/October 1966, pp. 28–31.   *H*
Mehrotra, R.R. "The Little Secret: Wordsworth's Relationship with Dorothy." *Samiksa* 29 (1975):62–79.   *E*

Considers biographical details of the relationship between W. Wordsworth and his sister, Dorothy, and their relevance to the issue of incest and repression.

Meiselman, K.C. *Incest*. San Francisco: Jossey-Bass, 1978.   *E*
―――. "Personality Characteristics of Incest History Psychotherapy Patients: A Research Note." *Archives of Sexual Behavior* 9 (1980):195–197.   *E*

Discusses personality traits and sexual problems, as well as female patients with versus without history of incest.

Melotti, U. "Towards a New Theory on the Origin of the Family: Some Hypotheses on Monogamy, Polygyny, Incest Taboo, Exogamy, and Genetic Altruism." *Mankind Quarterly* 21 (1980):99–133.   *E*

A new theory based on sociobiological studies of altruism is proposed to explain the emergence of the monogamic family in human societies.

Melville, J. "Some Violent Families." In *Violence and the Family*, edited by J.P. Martin. New York: Wiley & Sons, 1978.   *A,H*

Five battered English wives housed in refuges tell in their own words of their experiences of physical, sexual, and emotional abuse from their husbands.

———. *Women in Refuges*. New York: Wiley & Sons, 1978.   *B*

The history of the development of refuges for battered wives in England is presented, life in a refuge is described, problems encountered are discussed, and the future development of refuges is discussed.

Mendelsohn, B. "Victimology and the Needs of Contemporary Society." *Israel Annals of Psychiatry and Related Disciplines* 11 (September 1973):189–198.   *H*

Discusses the difference between victimology and criminology, the concept of victimity, the environmental factors determining victims, identification of the danger complex, and the further developments needed in victimology.

———. "Victimology and Contemporary Society's Trends." *Victimology* 1 (Spring 1978):9–28.   *H*

Outlines the nature, boundaries, and mission of general victimology.

Menninger, W.C. "Recreation and Mental Health." *Recreation* 42 (1948): 340–346.   *C*

Menzies, K.S. "The Road to Independence: The Role of a Refuge." *Victimology* 3 (1978):141–148.   *B*

The dynamics of the victim/offender relationship and the effectiveness of the refuge for women in helping abused women reestablish their independence was examined in questionnaire data for forty women who lived at the center between January 1976 and April 1977.

Merchant, J.J. "A Model for Police Assistance to Rape Victims." *Journal of Police Science and Administration* 7 (1979):45–52.   *B,G*

A review of the psychological, sociological, and criminal-justice literature, as well as a survey of current criminology texts, is given that reveals an almost singular lack of concern for the way an individual police officer relates to a rape victim.

Mermey. "Rape: Who's on Trial." *Juris Doctor*, December 1974, p. 23. *G*

Merton, R.K. "Manifest and Latent Functions." In *On Theoretical Sociology*, edited by Merton. New York: Free Press, 1967.   *G*

Merton, R.K. and R. Nisbet. *Contemporary Social Problems*. New York: Harcourt, Brace and World, 1966.   *C*

Metzger, D. "It Is Always the Woman Who Is Raped." *American Journal of Psychiatry* 133 (April 1976):405–408.   *G*

> Describes rape as an act of power that is sanctioned by literature, myth, and culture and implies total loss of self—the woman is a function not a person.

Metz-Goeckel, S. "Structural and Personal Violence against Women and the Difficulties of Eliminating Such Violence. In *Verbrechensopfer*, edited by F. Kirchhoff and K. Sessar. 1979.   *H*

> The structural violence inherent in the traditional institution of marriage, reasons for wife beating and for women's tolerance of mistreatment, and existing organizational models for women's shelter houses are explored.

Meulders, M.T. *Domestic Violence—Rough or Judicial Responses in Continental Law*. Scarborough, Ont.: Butterworth, 1978.   *F,H*

> Through information gathered from the departments of justice in Belgium, France, the Netherlands, Great Britain, West Germany, Switzerland, and Italy, analysis is made of statutes regarding conjugal violence.

Meurer, E.M. "Violent Crime Losses: Their Impact on the Victim and Society." *Annals of the American Academy of Political and Social Science* 443 (May 1979):54–62.   *H*

> The changing attitude of society toward victims of violent crime is discussed.

Meyer. "Rape: The Victim's Point of View." *Police Law Quarterly* 3 (1974):38.   *G*

Meyer, A.F.; B. Apfelberg; and C. Sugar "Men Who Kill Women." *Clinical Psychopathology* 7 (1946):441–472, 481–517.   *H*

Meyer, K.E. "Television's Trying Times: *Niemi* v. *NBC* and Chronical Publishing Suit." *Saturday Review* 5 (16 September 1978):19–23.   *H*

Meyer, L.C. *Victims of Rape*. Rockville, Md.: Department of Health, Education, and Welfare, National Institute of Mental Health, 1977. *G*

———. "Rape Cases in Philadelphia: Court Outcome and Victim Response." *Dissertation Abstracts International* 40 (3):1694-A, 1979. *F,G*

Court-outcome and victim-response data for 790 victims reporting a rape in Philadelphia between 1973 and 1975 were analyzed.

Meyers, A.J., and M.A. Jansen. "Assertive Therapy for Battered Women: A Case Illustration." *Journal of Behavior Therapy and Experimental Psychiatry* 11 (1980):301–305. *A,B,C*

A case study is reported of an eighteen-year-old battered woman who took part in assertive group therapy at a battered woman shelter in the Midwest.

Meyers, L. "Battered Wives, Dead Husbands." *Student Lawyer* 6 (1978): 46–51. *A*

The problem of wife beating and the murder of husbands by abused wives are discussed.

Micklewright. "The Law of Rape." *Labour Monthly*, July 1975, p. 314. *G*
Midlarksy, E. "Child Sexual Assault and Incest: A Bibliography." *Catalog of Selected Documents in Psychology* 8 (August 1978):65–66. *E*
Miers, D. *Responses to Victimization.* Nashville, Tenn.: Abingdon Press, 1978. *H*

The proliferation of criminal-injuries-compensation schemes that has been introduced in various jurisdictions since the mid 1960s is considered. While reference is made to many of the thirty-three programs currently in existence, the main focus of the study is a scholarly comparison of the British and Ontario schemes.

Milgram, S. *Obedience to Authority: An Experimental View.* New York: Harper & Row, 1974. *B*
Mill, J.S. *On the Subjection of Women.* New York: Fawcett Premier, 1971. *C*
Miller, B.C. "A Multivariate Development Model of Marital Satisfaction." *Journal of Marriage and the Family* 38 (1976):643–657. *B*
Miller, D.R., and G. Swanson. *The Changing American Parent.* New York: Wiley & Sons, 1958. *C*
Miller, J. et al. "Recidivism among Sex Assault Victims." *American Journal of Psychiatry* 135 (September 1978):1103–1104. *G,H*

Collected demographic data on 341 rape victims seen by a sexual-assault-response team. It was found that 82 (24 percent) of the victims had been assaulted previously.

Miller, M., and J. Hewitt. "Conviction of a Defendant as a Function of

Juror-Victim Racial Similarity." *Journal of Social Psychology* 105 (June 1978):159–160.   *H*

Eighty-three female and fifty male university students saw a videotape of the beginning of an actual court case involving rape.

Miller, M.W. "Rape Consultation and Education." Unpublished paper. National Institute of Mental Health Grant. 1978.   *B,G*

The rape consultation and education process in a rural Arizona poverty catchment area was analyzed, and data regarding the nature and extent of rape in the catchment area were gathered.

Miller, N. *Battered Spouses*. London: G. Bell and Sons, 1975.   *A*

Some aspects of the definition of the problem of battered wives, of explanations of its occurance, and of response to it are examined in this study.

Miller, P.Y., and M.E. Marsden. "Victimization, Norm Violation and Normative Integration." *Victimology: An International Journal* 2 (1977):74.   *H*

In a paper presented at the Second International Symposium on Victimology, held in Boston, September 1976, consequences of juvenile delinquency and juvenile victimization on the formation of attitudes toward criminal justice were examined.

Miller, W.P., and M.E. Seligman. "Depression and Learned Helplessness in Man." *Journal of Abnormal Psychology* 84 (1975):228–238.   *H*

Miller, W.P.; M.E. Seligman; and Kurlander. "Learned Helplessness, Depression, and Anxiety." *Journal of Nervous and Mental Diseases* 161 (1976):347–357.   *H*

Miller, W.R. "Marital Counseling for Rape Victims." Unpublished paper. 1979.   *C,G*

The first systematic examination of the emotional and relationship responses of couples to the rape of the female partner is presented, unique information on the long-term reaction of the male partners of rape victims is provided, and new data regarding the effectiveness of marital therapy for rape victims and their partners are given.

Miller, W.R.; A.M. Williams; and M.H. Bernstein. "The Effects of Rape on Marital and Sexual Adjustment." Unpublished paper. Research report 1979.   *G*

The long-term impact of rape on the victim, her male partner, and her marital relationship was assessed by means of clinicians' ratings and observations and the couples' self-reports.

Millett, K. *Sexual Politics*. Garden City, N.Y.: Doubleday and Company, 1970. **B**

Milling, R.N., and M.R. Johnson. "Changing Attitudes and Procedures in the Crime of Rape." *Journal of the South Carolina Medical Association* 74 (1978):321–328. **G**

Prevailing attitudes toward rape and myths about rapists and their victims are examined. It is asserted that mythical stereotypes of rapists and victims have influenced legal and medical treatment of victims. The stereotypes are considered individually and refuted.

Mills, P., and L. Sachs. *Rape Intervention Resource Manual*. Springfield, Ill.: Charles C Thomas, 1977. **B,G**

A training manual for rape intervention is compiled by surveying U.S. rape-crisis centers and editing existing training manuals.

Milowe, I.D., and R.S. Lourie. "The Child's Role in the Battered Child Syndrome." *Journal of Pediatrics* 65 (1964): 1079–1081. **B,E**

Miner, Q., and P.L. Miner. "Pierre's Sexuality: A Psychoanalytic Interpretation of Herman Melville's Pierre, or The Ambiguities and Roots: A Discussion of an American Literary Heritage from Emerson and Thoreau to Hemingway." *Dissertation Abstracts International* 40 (9-A): 5057, March 1980. **E,G,H**

Minnesota Department of Corrections. "The Sex Offender." St. Paul, 1964. **B,G**

———. "Battered Women—A Hidden Crime." St. Paul, 1978. **A**

This slide/tape show helps to personalize the effects and dynamics of violence toward women and makes specific suggestions to professionals who help battered women.

———. "The Implementation of Minnesota Laws, Chapter 428, 1977; and Minnesota Laws, Chapter 732, 1978 Regarding Programs and Services for Battered Women." Report to the Legislature. St. Paul, 1979. **F**

The progress made by the Minnesota Department of Corrections in implementing provisions of laws on the establishment of programs and services for battered women is outlined.

Minns, R. "Homeless Families and Some Organizational Determinants of Deviancy." *Policy and Politics*, vol. 1, issue 1, p. 1.   *A*

Mintz, M. "University, Firm Sued over DES Tests in Mothers." *Washington Post*, 26 April 1977, p. 1.   *B,C*

Mitchell, A. *Violence in the Family*. Hove, East Sussex: Wayland Publishers Limited, Hove, 1978.   *C,H*

> Focusing on family violence, this volume examines the mechanism of violence in the individual and the larger framework of society and recommends ways to control violent behavior.

Mitchell, H.E.; J.W. Bullard; and E.H. Mudd. "Areas of Marital Conflict in Successful and Unsuccessful Functioning Families." *Journal of Health and Human Behavior* 3 (Summer 1962):88–93.   *C*

Mitchell, J.C. Foreword to *The Politics of Kinship*, by J. van Velson. Manchester: Manchester University Press. 1964.   *B,E,H*

Mitchell, M.H. "Does Wife Abuse Justify Homicide?" *Wayne Law Review* 24 (1978):1705–1731.   *A*

> The battered-wife syndrome and an attempt to discern the trend of justifiable homicide in this area by comparing recently reported cases with traditional defenses to homicide are discussed. Several proposals are made to aid battered wives through the law and law enforcement.

Mithers, C.L."Date Rape: When Nice Guys Won't Take No for an Answer." *Mademoiselle* 86 (November 1980):210–211.   *G*

Moira, A., and A. Rule. "It Happened to Me: I was Raped and Too Ashamed to Tell Anyone." *Good Housekeeping* 186 (May 1978):108.   *G*

"Molested Women: Childhood Traumas Cause Adult Hangups." *Human Behavior* 8 (1979):41.   *E,G*

> Sexual dysfunction in women was studied utilizing 100 women who had been molested as children. It is reported that molested women often only enjoy the penetration phase of intercourse, experience little sexual appetite before having contact or minimal arousal during contact, rarely initiate love making, have great difficulty in touching or caressing their partner or being caressed, experience feelings of disgust and revulsion about their own and partner's body, enjoy sexual contact only when penetration has been effected, and often develop a sexual style restricted to intercourse alone.

Molnar, G., and P. Cameron. "Incest Syndromes: Observations in a General Hospital Psychiatric Unit." *Canadian Psychiatric Association Journal* 20 (August 1975):373–377.   *E*

Reports on ten families in which adolescent fourteen- to seventeen-year-old girls, who had disclosed that their fathers were committing incest with them, had been admitted to a psychiatric ward for treatment.

Monberg, T. "Ungrammatical 'Love' on Bellona." *Journal of the Polynesian Society* 85 (1976):243–246.   *B*

Monochick, R.B. "From Attribution to Labeling: Assessing Blame in Offender-Victim Interactions." *Dissertation Abstracts International* Ann Arbor, Michigan, University, 1978.   *H*

A theory of attributional differentiation is described that explains how resource variables of offenders and victims regulate the decision to label acts and actors as deviant.

Money, J. "The Therapeutic Use of Androgen-Depleting Hormone." In *Sexual Behaviors: Social, Clinical, and Legal Aspects*. Boston: Little, Brown, 1973.   *B,C*

Describes the use of medroxyprogesterone acetate to treat sex offenders whose behaviors have led to a crisis situation. The case of a bisexual male transvestite who had engaged in pedophilic homosexual incest is presented.

Montgomery County Council. "A Report by the Task Force to Study a Haven for Physically Abused Persons." Montgomery County, Md., 1 November 1975.   *A,B*

Moore, D.M., ed. *Battered Women*. Beverly Hills, Calif.: Sage Publications, 1979.   *A*

This collection of essays on battered women consists of an overview of the problem, a consideration of the social context of battering by Del Martin, a description by Lenore Walker of her cycle theory of battering, and two articles on the legal system's relationship to battered women by Eva Jefferson Paterson and Sandra Blair.

Moore, E.C. *Women and Health, United States, 1980*. Public Health Reports. September–October Supplement, pp. 1–84, 1980.   *A,E,F,G*

A broad range of health issues that are either unique to women or of special importance to women are considered, and the roles that women play both as providers and consumers of health care in the United States are noted. The incidence of rape, battering of women, and sexual abuse of children is cited, and services to deal with these problems are described.

Moore, J.B. "Rural Victimization in Texas." *Dissertation Abstracts International* 40 (7):4248-A, 1980.   *H*

The incidence and consequences of criminal victimization were explored in a stratified survey of 2,998 rural Texans. A return rate of 75.7 percent was realized.

Moore, J.G. "Yo-Yo Children—Victims of Matrimonial Violence." *Child Welfare* 34 (September/October 1975):557–566.   E
Moran, R. "Criminal Homicide: External Restraint and Subculture of Violence." *Criminology* 8 (February 1971):357–374.   H
Moran, R., and S. Schafer. "Criminal Victimization of the Elderly in the City of Boston." *Victimology: An International Journal* 2 (1977):75.H

In a paper presented at the Second International Symposium on Victimology, held in Boston, September 1976, characteristics of crimes against 418 victims above the age of 62 were examined.

Morgan, M. *Total Woman*. Old Tappan, N.J.: Revell, 1975.   B
Morgan, R., ed. *Sisterhood Is Powerful*. New York: Vintage, 1970.   B
Morgan, R. *Going too Far*. New York: Random House, 1977.   B
Morgan, S.M. *Conjugal Terrorism: A Psychological and Community Treatment Model of Wife Abuse*. 1982.   A,B

The writer proposes that wife abuse must be understood as a form of political terrorism in which the violent husband systematically employs terror as a means to control and manipulate his wife, the victim.

Morgan, W.K. "The Effect of a Guided Fantasy and Information about Rape on Attitudes toward Rape and victims of Rape." *Dissertation Abstracts International* 40 (9-B):4464, March 1980.   G

Presentation of information about rape and rape victims versus participation in guided rape fantasy and production of positive attitude change toward rape and rape victims, male versus female.

Moriarty's Police Law, 21st ed. 1972.   F
Morris, D. "Status Sex." In *The Human Zoo*, edited by D. Morris. New York: McGraw-Hill, 1969.   B
Moss, C.S.; R.E. Hosford; and W.R. Anderson. "Sexual Assault in a Prison." *Psychological Reports* 44 (June 1979):823–828.   G,H

The fact that only 12 of 1,000 inmates were identified by staff as having sexually assaulted other inmates over a twelve-month period suggests that sexual assault may not be a frequent problem in federal prisons.

"Motive for Murder." *Economist* 255 (12 April 1975):71.   H

Moynihan. "Emergency Medical Technician as First Therapists of the Sexual Assault Victim." *Emergency Medical Services* (May/June 1976):53.
                                                                           C
Moynihan, B.A. "Sexual Assault Victims." *Issues in Mental Health Nursing* 2 (1971):87–101.   C,H

> The nursing care of the sexual assault victim is discussed, and four case studies of rape victims are presented. It is recommended that since sexual assault is a multifaceted problem, a collaborative multidisciplined approach is useful.

Moynihan, D.P. *The Negro Family: The Case for National Action*. Washington, D.C.: Office of Policy Planning and Research, U.S. Department of Labor, 1970.   H
Mueller, K., and M. Leidig. "Women's Anger and Feminist Therapy." Unpublished manuscript. Boulder, Colo.: Boulder Mental Health Center, 1976.   C,H
Mueller, W.R. "I'm a Congregationalist, You Know; List of Incestuous Possibilities Found on an Early Manuscript in Saint Mary's Parish Church, Whitby, England." *Christian Century* 93 (19 May 1976):476–477.   E
Mulligan. "Fight Rape or Do What?" *Girl Talk* (January 1974):56.   G
Mulvihill, D.J.; M.M. Tumin; and L.A. Curtis, eds. *Crimes of Violence*. Staff Report to the National Commission on the Causes and Prevention of Violence, vols. 11, 12, 13. Washington, D.C.: U.S. Government Printing Office, 1969.   H
Mundy, J. "Women in Rage: A Psychological Look at the Helpless Heroine." In *Women: Dependent or Independent Variable*, edited by R. Unger and F. Denmark. New York: Psychological Dimensions, 1975.
                                                                           B
Murphy, G.R. "Statement of Glen R. Murphy on July 17, 1978, Concerning Violence Prevention and Services Act." *Domestic Violence*, 1978, pp. 640–645.   B,H

> A statement of the International Association of Chiefs of Police (IACP) to the Senate Subcommittee on Child and Human Development urges passages of the proposed Domestic Violence Prevention and Services Act.

Murray, C. Letter from C. Murray on the criminal prosecution of violent spouses addressed to Stanley Weiss, director of the San Francisco District Attorney's Bureau of Family Relations, 1974.   H
Murray, L. "Battered Women." *Playgirl*, April 1976, pp. 28–30.   A,H

While there are no statistics on the number of women beaten by men, some authorities think this physical abuse is on the rise. The fact that women are becoming more demanding, feeling they do not have to settle for their lot is a definite factor. The more their expectations are raised, the more likely a man is to resort to force. When a man feels his authority slipping away as a woman asserts her independence and individuality, brute strength is the last arena where he can still prove his superiority.

Mushanga, T. *Criminal Homicide in Uganda.* Nairobi: University of Nairobi, East Africa Literature Bureau, 1974.   H
————. "The Victimization of Wives in East and Central African Communities." *Victimology: An International Journal* 2 (1977):75.   H

In a paper presented at the Second International Symposium on Victimology, held in Boston, September 1976, the incidence of wife abuse in some communities of east and central Africa is explored.

————. "Wife Victimization in East and Central Africa." *Victimology: An International Journal* 2 (1978):479–485.   H

Patterns of wife abuse in east and central African communities are examined. Data collected by several researchers are summarized and analyzed.

————. *Profile of Criminal Homicide.* Nairobi: University of Nairobi, East Africa Bureau, forthcoming.   H
Mussen, P.H., and E. Rutherford. "Effects of Aggressive Cartoons on Children's Aggressive Play." *Journal of Abnormal and Social Psychology* 62 (1961):461–464.   H
"My Boss Wanted More than a Secretary." *Good Housekeeping* 186 (April 1978):28.   D
Mydens, S. "Group Forms to Aid Victims of Wife Beating." *Milwaukee Journal*, 4 August 1975.   A,B
Myers, M.A. "The Effects of Characteristics of the Victim on Case Disposition." *Victimology: An International Journal* 2 (1977):75.   C

In a paper presented at the Second International Symposium on Victimology, held in Boston, September 1976, the way in which victim-related variables affect the treatment of the offender during prosecution, conviction, and sentencing is explored.

Myers, W.A. "The Psychodynamics of a Beating Fantasy." *International Journal of Psychoanalytic Psychotherapy* 8 (1980):623–647.   A

A case history of a woman is presented whose primary conscious masturbatory fantasy from age three until forty was of a paternal beating. Late in her lengthy treatment, the conscious fantasy was seen to screen off the underlying, unconscious fantasy of being beaten by her mother.

"My Husband Was Accused of Rape: Case of Mistaken Identity." *Good Housekeeping* 178 (April 1974):16.   G

Nadelson, C.C. "Rape." *New England Journal of Medicine* 298 (1978):168.
                                                                          G

In a letter to the editor, the author of an article titled "Rapist and Victim" responds to criticism of that article with emphasis on the fabrication of charges of rape.

————. "Healthy Sexual Dysfunctions." *Medical Aspects of Human Sexuality* 13 (1979):106–119.   B

Sexual symptoms that serve a protective function, keeping an manageable distance between partners or preventing further stress or conflict from emerging, are considered.

Nadelson, C.C., and M.T. Notman. "Emotional Repercussions of Rape." *Medical Aspects of Human Sexuality* 11 (1977):16–32.   G

————. "Psychoanalytic Considerations of the Response to Rape." *International Review of Psychoanalysis* 6 (1979):97–103.   G

Nadelson, C.C., and A.A. Rosenfeld. "Sexual Misuse of Children." In *Child Psychiatry and the Law*, edited by D. Schetky. New York: Brunner/Mazel, 1980.   E

The prevalence and nature of sexual misuse of children and treatment/intervention are considered.

Nader, L. "Justice—A Woman Blindfolded?" In *Women in the Courts*, edited by W.L. Hepperle and L. Crites. Williamsburg, Va.: National Center for State Courts, 1978.   F

Several societies are used as models to examine the power of courts to ameliorate or improve women's condition and the ability of social conditions to limit the effectiveness of law and consequence of legal change.

Nagao, D.H., and J.H. Davis. "The Effects of Prior Experience on Mock Juror Case Judgments." *Social Psychology Quarterly* 43 (June 1980): 190–199.   F

The effects of prior experience on case judgments were investigated by asking mock jurors to decide defendants' guilt in either a rape-vandalism or vandalism-rape case presentation order.

Nakashima, I.I. "Incestuous Families." *Pediatric Annals* 8 (1979):300–308.
    E

Nakashima, I.I., and G.E. Zakus. "Incest: Review and Clinical Experience." *Pediatrics* 60 (November 1977):691–670.   *B,E*

"Naming Names: Northern Virginia Sun's Policy of Naming Rape Victims." *Time*, 30 January 1978, p. 61.   *B,G*

Nasjleti, M. "Suffering in Silence: The Male Incest Victim." *Child Welfare* 59 (1980):269.   *E*

Nass, D.R. *The Rape Victim*. New York: Kendall/Hunt, 1977.   *G*

National Center on Child Abuse and Neglect. *Child Abuse and Neglect State Reporting Laws*. Washington, D.C.: U.S. Department of Health and Human Services, December 1979.   *E,F*

National Citizens' Advise Bureaux Council. *Citizens Advise Bureaux Experience of the Problem of Battered Women*. October 1973.   *A*

———. *Survey of Matrimonial Problems and CAB*. May/June 1972.   *A*

National Clearinghouse on Marital Rape. Women's History Research Center, 2325 Oak Street, Berkeley, California 94708.   *B*

> Has a data base that provides information regarding marital rape; includes judicial opinions and legislation, popular magazine articles as well as professional journal articles.

National Commission of the Causes and Prevention of Violence. *Staff Report*. Washington, D.C.: U.S. Government Printing Office, 1969.
    B

National Commission on Observance of International Women's Year (1976–1977). "The Legal Status of Homemakers." A paper has been published for each state and the District of Columbia. Washington, D.C.: U.S. Government Printing Office, 1976.   *B,G*

National Criminal Justice Information and Statistics Service. *Criminal Victimization in the United States*. Rockville, Maryland, 1975.   *G,H*

National Institute of Law Enforcement and Criminal Justice. *Forcible Rape: An Analysis of Legal Issues*. Washington, D.C.: U.S. Government Printing Office, 1978.   *F,G*

> Past attitudes toward rape, current laws, movements toward reform, and problems of enforcement of rape laws are summarized. Special legal problems involved in rape adjudication are discussed, and the major alternative statutory approaches to rape are compared.

National Institute of Mental Health. *Rape and Older Women: A Guide to Prevention and Protection*. Rockville, Md.   *G*

> Guide in recommendations for the adaption of prevention and protection activities for the special needs of older women and for those interested in their welfare.

National Institute of Mental Health. National Center for the Prevention and
    Control of Rape. *Rape: Prevention and Control . . . The Federal Focal
    Point*. DHEW Publication Number (ADM) 79-410. Washington, D.C.,
    1979.   *B,C,G*

    The work of the National Center for the Prevention and Control of Rape,
    established under legislative mandate, is described in a folder containing
    loose-leaf information sheets.

National Organization for Women. *Wife Beating: Counselor Training Man-
    ual #1*. Ann Arbor, Mich.: NOW Domestic Violence Project, Incor-
    porated, 1976.   *A,C*
———. National Task Force on Marriage, Divorce, and Family Relations.
    Newsletter, edited by B. Berry. August 1973.   *A,B*
National Organization for Women Wife Assault Task Force. *A Guide for
    Assaulted Women*. Ann Arbor, Mich.: Ann Arbor-Washtenaw County
    NOW, 1976.   *B*

    Describes wife abuse and help available to victims. Explains NOW's Do-
    mestic Violence/Spouse Assault Project, giving hours available and tele-
    phone numbers.

———. *How to Develop a Wife Assault Task Force and Project*. Ann Arbor,
    Mich.: Ann Arbor-Washtenaw County NOW, 1976.   *B*

    Provides a step-by-step approach to setting up a wife-assault task force and
    project.

National Society for Prevention of Cruelty to Children. *A Study of 23
    Violent Matrimonial Cases*. London: National Society for Prevention
    of Cruelty to Children.   *B*
———. *Yo-Yo Children*. 1974.   *E*
National Women's Aid Federation. *Starting a Refuge*. 51 Chalcot Road,
    Northwest 1, London, England.   *B*
Nauton, E. "Beating of Women Is Major Crime Source." *Miami Herald*, 20
    February 1976.   *A*
Naughton, M.J. *Child Protective Services: A Bibliography with Partial An-
    notation and Cross-Indexing, 1976*. Seattle: Health Sciences Learning
    Resources Center, University of Washington, EDRS, 1976.   *B*
"NBC's First Amendment Rape Case: Controversey over Airing Born
    Innocent." *Esquire* 89 (23 May 1978):12–13.   *G*
Neher, J., and M. Braswell. "Parent Abuse: The Other Side of Child
    Abuse." *Psychiatric Opinion* 15 (1978):39–41.   *A*

    The abusing parent as victim of the punitive rather than rehabilitative
    nature of our service system is examined.

Neiburg, H.L. "Agonistics—Rituals in Conflict." *Annals* 391 (September 1970):56–73.   *A,H*

Neier, A. "Rape at Home." *Nation* 228 (20 January 1979):36–37.   *G*

Nelson, Amir. "The Hitch Hike Victim of Rape: A Research Report." *Victimology: A New Focus*, 1975, p. 47.   *G*

Nelson, S. "How Battered Women Can Get Help." *Readers Digest* 110 (May 1977):21–23.   *A*

Nemy, E. "Women Begin to Speak Out Against Sexual Harassment at Work." *The New York Times*, August 1975, p. 38.   *D*

Neufeld, E. *Ancient Hebrew Marriage Laws*. London: Longmans, Green and Company, 1944.   *F*

Neuhaus, R.H. *Family Crisis*. New York: Bobbs-Merrill, 1974.   *C*

Newfield, N.L. "Crisis Intervention Training for Police: An Innovative Program." *Crisis Intervention* 6 (1975):28–35.   *C*

Describes the training of 202 police officers to be effective caregivers in crisis situations such as rape, suicide, child abuse, and so on.

"New Hope for the Battered Wife: Haven House, Los Angeles." *Good Housekeeping*, August 1976.   *A,B*

Newman, J. "The Wife Beaters." *Parade Magazine*, June 1975, pp. 33, 110, 112.   *A*

———. "How Battered Wives Are Fighting Back." *Parade Magazine*, 11 April 1976, p. 22.   *A*

Newman, J.H. "Differential Reporting Rates of Criminal Victimization." *Dissertation Abstracts International* 39 (8):5158-A, 1979.   *H*

Differential reporting rates of criminal victimization in urban and rural areas were investigated via a five-county victimization survey, wherein urban and rural residents were asked to account for their victimization experiences during 1975.

Newman, P. O. "Wild Man Behavior in New Guinea Highland Community." *American Anthropologist* 66 (1964):1–19.   *H*

New York City Police Department. Press Release no. 30. 31 March 1966. *B*

———. "Police Responses to Family Disputes." Procedural Supplement no. 1. September 1969.   *B*

New York Family Court Act. "Article 8, Family Offenses Proceedings," 1976, pp. 685–719.   *B*

New York Radical Feminists. *Rape: The First Sourcebook for Women*. New York: New American Library, 1974.   *B,G*

New York State Department of Social Services Domestic Violence Program Plan. Albany, 1979.   *B,H*

The domestic-violence program plan adopted by the New York State Department of Social Services is designed to strengthen family units through shelter, community support, counseling, and advocacy services.

Nichols, B.B. "The Abused Wife Problem." *Social Casework* 57 (January 1976):27–32.   A

Contends that the issue of wife abuse has been neglected by conventional family agencies. Caseworkers often take a position that the wife provokes and may even enjoy abusive treatment.

Nichols, W.C. "Wife Abuse." *Parents Magazine* 53 (January 1978):26. A
Nicol, A.R., et al. "The Relationship of Alcoholism to Violent Behavior Resulting in Long Term Imprisonment." *British Journal of Psychiatry* 123 (1973):47–51.   H

This paper explores the relationship between severely violent behavior and alcoholism in a group of long-term prisoners.

Niederhoffer, A. *Behind the Shield: The Police in Urban Society*. Garden City, N.Y.: Doubleday, 1967.   B
Niemi, R.G. *How Family Members Perceive Each Other*. New Haven: Yale University Press, 1974.   C
————. "Rape Replay: Negligence Suit against NBC and the Chronicle Publishing Company." *Time*, 8 May 1978, p. 68.   G
Nisonoff, L., and I. Bitman. "Spouse Abuse: Incidence and Relationship to Selected Demographic Variables." *Victimology* 4 (1979):131–140.
                                                                     A,B

Relationships between demographic variables and spousal violence were investigated in a suburban middle-to-upper-class community.

Nivens, B. "Office Romance: Should You or Shouldn't You?" *Essence* 8 (February 1978):16.   D
Nkpa-Nwokocha, K.U. "The Practice of Restitution to Victims of Crime in a Traditional Society." *Victimology: An International Journal* 2 (1977): 76.   C

Penal actions of the Igbo people in eastern Nigeria before British Colonial rule are examined.

No Exceptions (A Film about Rape). 16 mm film, sound, color, 24 mins. Studio City, Calif.: Film Fair Communications, 1977.   G

Provides suggestions for preventing rape effectively and depicts events in a police department when a woman reports a rape case.

Nordenbrook, R. "Prepared Statement of Ruth Nordenbrook, on July 11, 1979 Concerning HR 2977." *Domestic Violence—Prevention and Services*, 1979.   C,G

The American Bar Association supports H.R. 2977, the Domestic Violence Prevention and Services Act and offers recommendations that could be incorporated in the bill or legislation by states.

"Normal Reaction? Rape." *Economist* 264 (17 September 1977):51–52. G
Norton, C. *English Laws for Women in the Nineteenth Century.* Printed in private circulation. London, 1854.   F
Not Only for Strangers. 16 mm film or videotape, sound, color, 23 mins. Lawrence, Ks.: Centron Films, 1980.   G

Presents advice on what a woman should do after being raped by a man she knows via an interview from a college girl who dated a classmate and later learned of his reputation from police.

Notman, M.T., and C.C. Nadelson. "The Rape Victim: Psychodynamic Considerations." *American Journal of Psychiatry* 133 (April 1976):408–413.   G

Views rape as challenging a woman's ability to maintain her defenses and thus arousing feelings of guilt, anxiety, and inadequacy.

Novak, D.G. "Life Styles and Social Interest Ratings of Battered Women." *Dissertation Abstracts International* 40 (3):1429-B, 1979.   A

Thirty battered women were compared to matched controls in terms of life-style, family constellation, personal history, and intrafamilial violence patterns.

Novak, D.G., and D.T. Meismer. "A Plea for Help: One Community's Response." *Victimology: An International Journal* 2 (3–4):647–653, 1978.   B

The establishment of the Austin Center for Battered Women is described.

Novak, E.R.; G.E. Jones; and H.W. Jones. *Novak's Textbook of Gynecology.* Baltimore: Williams and Wilkens, 1970.   B
Nurse, S.M. "Familial Patterns of Parents Who Abuse Their Children." *Smith College Studies in Social Work* 35 (October 1964):11–25. B,E

Nygreen, G.T. "Interactive Path Analysis." *American Sociologist* 6 (1971): 37–53.   B

Oberlander, M.I.; K.J. Frauenfelder; and H. Heath. "Ordinal Position, Sex of Sibling, Sex, and Personal Preferences in a Group of Eighteen-Year Olds." *Journal of Consulting and Clinical Psychology* 32 (1970):122– 125.   E

O'Brien, J.E. "The Decision to Divorce: A Comparative Study of Family Instability in the Early versus the Later Years of Marriage." Madison: Library of the University of Wisconsin, 1970.   C

———. "Violence in Divorce Prone Families." *Journal of Marriage and the Family* 33 (1971):692–698.   H

> Violent behavior was primarily delivered by husbands who were character-istically underachievers in the work-earner role and who were deficient in certain status characteristics relative to their wives.

O'Brien, K. "Third Party Liability in Civil Actions for Rape." Unpublished paper, no date.   G

Ochberg, F.M. "The Victim of Terrorism." *Practitioner* 220 (1978):293– 302.   H

O'Connor, D. "Domestic Violence Assistance Organizations-Summary Re-port." *Domestic Violence—Prevention and Services*, 1979, pp. 330–336.
                                                                          B

> Results are given of a survey of 400 domestic-violence organizations across the United States and Puerto Rico. The survey included an application for a regional project grant as an incentive for responding.

O'Connor, D.; M. Robert; and J. Robert. *Handbook for Battered Women— Legal Information and Community Resources*. St. Louis, Missouri: Monsanto Foundation, 1979.   A,B

> Practical information explaining the rights of and resources available to the battered woman is presented. The work is geared primarily to victims in the St. Louis, Missouri, area.

Odekunle, F. "Victims of Crime in a Developing Country: A Nigerian Study." *Victimology: An International Journal* 2 (1977):76.   H

> The findings of a pioneering Nigerian victim survey are reported.

O'Donnell, C., and H. Saville. "Sex and Class Inequality and Domestic Violence." In *Violence in the Family—A Collection of Conference Pa-pers*, 79–93, 1980.   H

A study of 145 battered Australian women shows the close link between domestic violence and the inequality of the female sex role.

O'Donnell, T.J. "The Confessions of T.E. Lawrence: The Sadomasochistic Hero." *American Image* 34 (1977):115–132.   H

Descriptions of physically and psychologically painful experiences succeeded by pleasure and detailed descriptions of instruments of punishment in T.E. Lawrence's autobiographical writings.

O'Faolain, J., and L. Martines. *Not in God's Image*. Glasgow: Collins, 1974.   H
"Off the Beaten Track." In *Women against Abuse*, 112 South 16th Street, Philadelphia, Pennsylvania.   A
"Official Aid Is Essential." *Nemesis*, April 1974, p. 1.   B
Offir, C.W. "Don't Take It Lying Down." *Psychology Today* 8 (January 1975):73.   A,G
"Older Rape Victim and Her Assailant." *Journal of Geriatric Psychiatry* 11 (1978):203–217.   G
O'Leary, K.D. "Modification of a Deviant Sibling Interaction Pattern in the Home." *Behavioral Research and Therapy* 5 (1967):113–120.   E
Olive, M.E. "Criminal Law—Rape—Multiple Offenses Severally Punishable." *Tennessee Law Review* 44 (1977):388–400.   F

The problem of extracting the number of punishable offenses arising out of criminal conduct is reviewed as it applies to the crime of rape.

Oliver, J.E., and J. Cox. "A Family Kindred with Ill Used Children: The Burden on the Community." *British Journal of Psychiatry* 123 (July): 81–90.   B,E
Oliver, J.E., and A. Taylor. "Five Generations of Ill Treated Children in One Family Pedigree." *British Journal of Psychiatry* 118 (1971):473–480.   E
Olsen, N.J. "Family Structure and Independence Training in a Taiwanese Village." *Journal of Marriage and the Family* 35 (August 1973):512–519.   B
Olsen, N.J. "Family Structure and Socialization Patterns in Taiwan." Mimeographed. Santa Clara: Department of Sociology and Anthropology.   B
Olson, D.H. "The Measurement of Family Power by Self-Report and Behavioral Methods." *Journal of Marriage and the Family* 31 (August 1969):545–550.   B
Olson, D.H., and C. Rabunsky. "Validity of Four Measures of Family Power." *Journal of Marriage and the Family* 34 (1972):224–234.   B

Olson, L. "Briefing Paper on Victim Compensation." Unpublished paper. Washington, D.C.: National League of Cities/Conference of Mayors, 1975. *H*

O'Neale, R.J. "Court Ordered Psychiatric Examination of a Rape Victim in a Criminal Rape Prosecution—Or How Many Times Must a Woman Be Raped." *Santa Clara Law Review* 18 (1978):119–153. *F,G*

An overview is provided of the present law governing the use of psychiatric evidence in rape cases, focusing on California's experience.

Oneglia, S. "In Her Own Words." Interview conducted by S. Moore, in *People*, 26 April 1976, pp. 35–38. *G*

"Only Lords Can Change Their Minds." *Economist* 267 (18 March 1978): 22–23. *A,B*

"Orange County's (Florida) Spouse Abuse Shelter—Evaluation." Florida East Central Regional Planning Council, Criminal Justice Planning Division, 1978. *B*

A spouse-abuse shelter in Orange County, Florida, is evaluated in its second year of operation.

Orbach, I. "The Victim's Reaction to an Attack as a Function of His Perception of the Attacker Following a Verbal Insult." *European Journal of Social Psychology* 8 (1978):453–465. *H*

The role of perception in determining the behavior of a victim following a verbal attack was studied.

Orford, J., et al. "Self Reported Coping Behavior of Wives of Alcoholics and Its Association with Drinking Outcome." *Journal of Studies on Alcohol* 36 (1975). *A*

Oros, C.J., and D. Elman. "Impact of Judge's Instructions upon Jurors' Decisions: The 'Cautionary Charge' in Rape Trials." *Representative Research in Social Psychology* 10 (1979):28–36. *F*

The impact of nonevidential factors on jury decision making was examined in responses of 359 white male and female simulated jurors to a description of a rape trial in which the nature of the judge's instructions and the defendant's race was varied.

Osgod, C.E., and G.I. Suci. "A Measure of Relation Determined by Both Mean Difference and Profile Information." *Psychological Bulletin* 49 (May 1952):251–262. *C*

O'Shea, J.S., and E.J. Morschauser. "Characteristics of Children Suspected of Being Abused or Neglected." *Rhode Island Medical Journal* 62 (1979):264–269.   *E*

Demographic characteristics of children suspected of being abused or neglected by the pediatric department of a Rhode Island hospital are reported.

Ostrowski, M.V. *Legal Process for Battered Women.* Vancouver: United Way of Lower Mainland, 1979.   *F*

This handbook provides an orientation guide to the legal process in British Columbia, Canada, for women who have decided to invoke its protection against the violence of their husbands or partners.

O'Sullivan, E. "What Has Happened to Rape Crisis Centers? A Look at Their Structures, Members, and Funding." *Victimology* 3 (1978):45–62.   *B,G*

The structures, members, and funding of rape-crisis centers were examined on basis of responses from ninety rape-crisis centers to a mail survey.

Otterbein, K.F. "A Cross Cultural Study of Rape." *Aggressive Behavior* 5 (1979):425–435.   *B,G*

Reports a test of a deterrence theory of rape, using data from a cross-cultural study taken from the human-relations-area files. Fraternal interest-group theory was also tested.

Ottenberg, P. "Violence in the Family: Abused Wives and Children. *Bulletin of the American Academy of Psychiatry and the Law* 5 (1977):380–390.   *H*

Experiences in treating victims of wife and child abuse in Philadelphia are reviewed, and the complexities of social and individual life that have led to an increased incidence of violence in modern society are discussed.

Overmier, J.B. "Interference with Avoidance Behavior: Failure to Avoid Traumatic Shock." *Journal of Experimental Psychology* 78 (1968):340–343.   *C*

Overmier, J.B., and M.E. Seligman. "Effects of Inescapable Shock upon Subsequent Escape and Avoidance Learning." *Journal of Comparative and Physiological Psychology* 63 (1967):23–33.   *C*

Owens, D.J., and M.A. Straus. "Childhood Violence and Adult Approval of Violence." Paper presented to the Annual Meeting of the American Orthopsychiatry Association, 1973.   *E*

———. "Social Structure of Violence in Childhood and Approval of Violence as an Adult." *Aggressive Behavior* 1 (1975):193–211.   E

Ozerkevich, M., and S. Steele. "A Study of the Incidence of Drug and Alcohol Related Problems among Support and Assault Cases Coming to the Attention of Family Court in Kingston, Ontario." Ottawa: Nonmedical Use of Drugs Directorate, Research Bureau.   A

Ozzanna, S. "The Battered Woman's Only Solution." *Majority Report* 21 (7 February 1976):4.   A

———. "What's Red and Black and Harbors Women in Crisis?" *Majority Report* 10, February 27 and March 6, 1976.   B

———. "Women's Crisis Housing Is for Pioneers." *Majority Report*, March 20 and April 3, 1976.   B

Pacht, A. "The Rapist in Treatment: Professional Myths and Psychological Realities." In *Sexual Assault*, edited by M. Walker and S. Brodsky. Lexington, Mass.: D.C. Heath and Company, 1976.   B,G

Pacht, A., and J. Cowden. "An Exploratory Study of Five Hundred Sex Offenders." *Criminal Justice and Behavior* 1 (1974):13–20.   B

Pagan, D., and S.M. Smith. "Homicide: A Medico-Legal Study of Thirty Cases." *Bulletin of the American Academy of Psychiatry and the Law* 7 (1979):275–285.   B,H

Characteristics of the murderer and his victim were examined using medical, neurological, and psychological data for twenty-one men and nine women accused of homicide.

Pagelow, M.D. "Battered Women: A New Perspective." Paper presented at the International Sociological Association Seminar on Sex Roles, Deviance, and Agents of Social Control in Dublin, Ireland, 1977. *A,B*

———. "Blaming the Victim: Parallels in Crimes against Women—Rape and Battering." Paper presented at the Annual Meeting of the Society for the Study of Social Problems, Chicago, 1977.   A,G

———. "Preliminary Report on Battered Women." *Victimology: An International Journal* 2 (1977):76.   A,B

Data provided by fifty battered women in a sociological exploratory study into household violence are presented. Experiences include marriage forced by parents, husband's incestuous relationships, and multiple concubinage.

———. "Secondary Battering: Breaking the Cycle of Violence." Paper presented at the Annual Meeting of the American Sociological Association, Chicago, 1977.   A,B,H

———. "Battered Women—Preliminary Report." *Domestic Violence*, 1978. pp. 555–607.   A,B

The results are reported of a preliminary study of battered women to determine some of the ideas held about battering and the extent to which the ideas are valid conceptions or invalid myths.

————. "Women Battering: Victims of Spouse Abuse and Their Perceptions of Violent Relationships." *Dissertation Abstracts International* 41 (6):2790-A, 1980.   *A,H*

Characteristics of the wife abuser and his victim, the history of violent family relationships, and victims' perceptions of the interactions were investigated, and factors associated with the maintenance of the relationship were examined in a sample of battered women.

Pakula, H., and R. Wood. "Family Violence and the Royal Commission on Human Relationships—Australia." *Crime and the Family*, Proceedings, 1979.   *B,H*

New research on family violence, particularly wife abuse, should consider the multicausal nature of the problem, with preventive and interventionist approaches needed.

Palmer, S. *A Study of Murder*. New York: Thomas Y. Crowell Company, 1960.   *H*
————. *The Psychology of Murder*. New York: Thomas Y. Crowell, 1962.
                                                                                                                          H
————. *The Violent Society*. New Haven: College and University Press, 1972.   *H*
————. "Family Members as Murder Victims." Violence in the Family: 91–97, 1974.   *H*

In this article Palmer summarizes the data on the extent to which murder victims are family members.

————. "Physical Frustration and Murder." Violence in the Family:247–250, 1974.   *H*

The effects of physical punishment on producing tendencies toward violence are in direct proportion to the severity of the punishment.

Pancoast, R.D., and L.M. Weston. *Feminist Psychotherapy: A Method for Fighting Social Control of Women*. Washington, D.C.: Feminist Counseling Collective, February 1974, p. 7.   *B*
"Panel Workshop: Violence, Crime, Sexual Abuse and Addiction." *Contemporary Drug Problems* 5 (Fall 1976):385–440.   *B,H*

Explores the powerlessness of children and women and how this results in their victimization.

Panton, J.H. "Personality Differences Appearing between Rapists of Adults, Rapists of Children and Non-Violent Sexual Molesters of Female Children." *Research Communications in Psychology, Psychiatry, and Behavior*, 1978, pp. 385–393. G,H

Analysis of MMPI test results of thirty adult rapists, twenty child rapists, and twenty-eight nonviolent child molesters (aged 21–49) revealed no significant mean scale differences between the two rapist samples but considerable mean scale differences between the rapist and child-molester samples.

———. "MMPI Profile Configurations Associated with Incestuous and Non-Incestuous Child Molesting." *Psychological Reports* 45 (August 1979):335–338. E

Comparison of MMPI data for thirty-five men (mean age 40.6 years) convicted of incest with those of twenty-eight men (mean age 30.8 years) convicted of nonincestuous sexual molesting of children showed marked similarity between mean MMPI profiles and profile configurations.

Parad, H.J., and G. Caplan. *A Framework for Studying Families in Crisis. Source Book in Marriage and the Family*. Boston: Houghton Mifflin Company, 1963. B

Parcell, S.R., and E.J. Kanin. "Male Sex Aggression: Survey of Victimized College Women." *Victimology: An International Journal* 2 (1977):77. H

In a paper presented at the Second International Symposium on Victimology, held in Boston, September 1976, male-sex-aggression experiences of 282 college coeds were investigated.

Parker, B., and D.N. Schumacher. "Battered Wife Syndrome and Violence in Nuclear Family of Origin: Controlled Pilot Study." *American Journal of Public Health* 67 (1977):760–761. A

Parker, G. "Incest." *Medical Journal of Australia* 1 (1974):488–490. E

Parker, S. "The Precultural Basis of the Incest Taboo: Toward a Biosocial Theory." *American Anthropologist* 78 (June 1976):285–305. E

Argues that the literature on the origins of the incest taboo is characterized by controversy over the nature-nurture issue and fears of reductionism; work emanating from such diverse disciplines as cultural and physical anthropology, ethology, and neuropsychology warrants a new look at this intriguing issue.

Parlee, M.B. "Psychology and Women." *Signs: Journal of Women in Culture and Society* 5 (1979):121–133.   B

An overview of four general areas in research on the psychology of women is presented.

Parnas, R. "The Police Response to the Domestic Disturbance." *Wisconsin Law Review*, Fall 1967, pp. 914–960.   B
———. "The Response of Some Relevant Community Resources to Intra-Family Violence." *Indiana Law Review* 44 (Winter 1969):159–181. B
———. "Judicial Response to Intra-Family Violence." *Minnesota Law Review* 54 (1970):585–644.   F
———. "Police Discretion and Diversion of Incidents of Intra-Family Violence." *Law and Contemporary Problems* 36 (Autumn 1971):54.   B
Parnass, G. "Factors which Denote the Severity of the Crime of Rape. The Disinterment of an Ancient Law: An Eye for an Eye, No Death for Rape." *Brooklyn Law Review* 44 (1978):622–636.   G

The finding by the U.S. Supreme Court that the death penalty is no longer a proportionate or acceptable punishment for rape is examined.

Parsonage, W.H. *Perspectives on Victimology*. Sage Research Progress Series in Criminology, vol. 11. Beverly Hills, Calif.: Sage, 1979.   H

Victimology is examined by exploring the development of reliable crime and victmization data and the methodology to secure it, the characteristics of special types of offenders and victims, and strategies to reveal the social and personal effects of crime and victimization.

Parsons, T. "Aggression in the Social Structures of the Western World." *Psychiatry*, 1947.   H
———. *Certain Primary Sources and Patterns of Aggression in the Social Structure of the Western World. Essays in Sociological Theory*. Glencoe, Ill.: Free Press, 1963.   B,H
Parsons, T., and R.F. Bales. *Family Socialisation and Interaction Process*. 1965.   B
Pascoe, E.J. "Shelters for Battered Wives." *McCalls*, October 1976, p. 51.   B
———. "Wife Beating: A Community to the Rescue: Philadelphia Station KYW-TV." *McCalls*, November 1977, p. 81.   A,B
Pasternack, S.A. *Violence and Victims*. New York: Spectrum, 1975. B,H

Brings together material regarding the clinical evaluation and treatment of violent persons and the victims of violent crime.

Paterson, E.J. "How the Legal System Responds to Battered Women." *Battered Women*, 1979, pp. 79–99.   *A,F*

An overview of how the legal system responds to battered women is presented, together with proposals for how to render the legal system more responsive to and protective of battered women.

Patten, T.G., and D.J. Woods. "Victim Attributions Regarding the Source of Verbal Aggression." *Journal of Psychology* 100 (1978):293–296. *H*

Victims' attributions regarding the source of verbal aggression were examined in 140 male and female undergraduates.

"The Pattern of Rape in Singapore." *Singapore Medical Journal* 15 (1974): 49.   *G*

Patterson, G.R.; J.A. Cobb; and R.S. Ray. "A Social Engineering Technology for Restraining Families of Aggressive Boys." *Issues and Trends in Behavior Therapy*, 1972.   *H*

Paul. "The Medical Examination in Sexual Offenses." *Medical Science and Law* 15 (1975):154.   *B,G*

Paulsen, K. "Attribution of Fault to a Rape Victim as a Function of Locus of Control." *Journal of Social Psychology* 107 (February 1979):131–132.
                                                                      G,H

Thirty-two female undergraduates were administered Rotter's Internal-External Locus of Control Scale (I-E), followed by two irrelevant questionnaires and C. Jones and E. Aronson's (1973) rape report and questionnaire. A significant effect was found, however, in comparing subject samples high and low in I-E. Results suggest an alternative explanation of Jones and Aronson's findings.

Paulsen, M.G. "The Law and Abused Children." In *The Battered Child*, edited by Ray E. Helfer and C. Henry Kempe, pp. 175–200. Chicago: University of Chicago Press, 1968.   *E,F*

Paulson, M.J. "Incest and Sexual Molestation: Clinical and Legal Issues." *Journal of Clinical Child Psychology* 7 (1978):177–180.   *E*

Presents an overview of the clinical and legal issues surrounding incest and sexual abuse of children and discusses a community-based model for intervention. Rights issues in child-abuse intervention are discussed, as well as general legal issues that arise in child-abuse cases.

Paulson, M.J.; A.A. Afifi; M.L. Thomason; and A. Chaleff. "The MMPI: A Descriptive Measure of Psycho-pathology in Abusive Parents." *Journal of Clinical Psychology* 30 (July 1974):387–390.   H

Pear, R. "How the Battered Women Are Stymied in Official Maze." *Washington Star*, 3 January 1976, p. A-1.   *A,F*

> Primarily defines the confusing maze of official problems that beset a victim who confronts an abusive situation. Reviews legal, enforcement, and social aspects.

Pearlin, L. "Parental Discipline." In *Class Context and Family Relations: A Cross-National Study*. Boston: Little, Brown, 1970, pp. 99–122. *B,H*

Pearsall, R. *The Worm in the Bud*. London: Weidenfield and Nicholson, 1969.   *E,G*

Peck, S. "Slighted Orders? Suit Fights Police Policy on Ex-Mates." *Sacramento Bee*, 1 August 1972.   *B,C*

Pellegrino, L. "Victimology in Brazilian Penal Law and Law Reports." *Victimology: An International Journal* 2 (1977):77.   H

> In a paper presented at the Second International Symposium on Victimology, held in Boston, September 1976, the recognition of victimology by Brazilian law is discussed. Although not referred to as such or reduced to a proper system of study, the basic principles of victimology are embodied in the Brazilian code of penal law of 1940 and the new penal code of 1969.

Penhallow, C. "Sexual Assault: Attribution of Fault to Victims and Evaluation of Victims." *Dissertation Abstracts International* 39 (3-B):1547, September 1978.   *G,H*

> Examines victim's level of fault for provoking sexual assault and goodness of character and attribution of fault to, character evaluation of, and sympathy for rape victim, male versus female.

Penland. "NAWL/IBA Program-Rapporteur's Report." *Women Law Journal* 60 (1974):176.   F

Pennsylvania Coalition against Domestic Violence, Harrisburg, Pennsylvania 1977.   H

> Based on the experiences of a Pennsylvania group, this book provides practical information on assisting victims of domestic abuse, including establishment of a hot line and a shelter.

Pennsylvania. General Assembly. Senate. *Protection from Abuse Act*. Session of 1975. Senate bill number 1243.   *A,F*

A bill introduced by Senators Hill, Howard, and Myers, 10 December 1975, and amended 14 June 1976. Eleven sections "relating to abuse of adults and children by a person who resides with them; and providing for remedies and procedures."

————. *Amendment of the Administrative Code of 1929*. Session of 1976, statute number 139. *A,F*

An amendment of the "Administrative Code of 1929" that establishes the Crime Victim's Compensation Board.

Pepitone, R.F. "Patterns of Rape and Approaches to Care." *Journal of Family Practice* 6 (March 1978):521–529. *G*

Focuses on the social and legal definitions of rape as well as the incidence of rape. The rape-trauma syndrome is explained, and normative responses of victims are discussed.

————. "Counseling Women to Be Less Vulnerable to Rape." *Medical Aspects of Human Sexuality* 14 (1980):145–146. *G*

Steps women can take to be less vulnerable to rape are suggested based on findings from a study comparing victims and women who avoided rape.

Perdue, W.C., and D. Lester. "Personality Characteristics of Rapists." *Perceptual and Motor Skills* 35 (October 1972):514. *G*

Compared the Rorschach protocols of fifteen convicted rapists and fifteen men convicted of aggressive nonsexual crimes. No significant differences were found between groups in race, IQ, number of Rorschach responses, or Rorschach factors.

————. "Those Who Murder Kin: A Rorschach Study." *Perceptual and Motor Skills* 35 (April 1973):606–616. *H*

Peretti, P.O., and M. Buchanan. "Psycho-Socio-Behavioral Variables of Enduring Chronic and Acute Battered Wife Roles." *Psychologia* (Kyoto) 21 (1978):63–69. *A*

The existence of behavioral and psychosocial characteristics associated with battered wives was investigated. Interview responses of 184 battered wives revealed eighteen reasons given for enduring the battered-wife role.

Peretti, P.O., and N. Cozzens. "Psycho-Social Variables of Female Rapees Not Reporting and Reporting the First Incidence of Rape." *Acta Psychiatrica Belgica* 79 (1979):332–342. *G*

Psychosocial variables of female rape victims not reporting and reporting the first incidence of rape were analyzed based on structured interviews with women who had contacted a rape-crisis center and/or clergy of various religious institutions.

Perry, C. "Hypnotic Coercion and Compliance to It: A Review of Evidence Presented in a Legal Case." *International Journal of Clinical and Experimental Hypnosis* 27 (July 1979):187–218.   F

Analyzes the court transcript of a case in Australia in which a lay hypnotist was found guilty of three sexual offenses against two female clients.

Perutz, K. *Marriage Is Hell.* New York: William Morrow, 1972.   A
Peterman, P. "Sex and the Working Girl." *Saint Petersburg Times*, 12 September 1975.   D
Peters. "Social, Legal, and Psychological Effects of Rape on the Victim." *Pennsylvania Medicine* 78 (1975):34.   F,G
Peters; Pedigo; Steg; and McKenna. "Group Psychotherapy of the Sex Offender." *Federal Probation* 32 (September 1968):41.   B,G
Peters, E.L. "Some Structural Aspects of the Fued among the Camel-herding Bedouin of Cyrenaica." *Africa* 37 (1967):261–282.   B
Peters, J.J. "Child Rape: Defusing a Psychological Time Bomb." *Hospital Physician* 9 (1973):46–49.   E,G
———. "The Philadelphia Rape Victim Study." In *Victimology: A New Focus. Vol. 111: Crimes, Victims, and Justice*, edited by I. Drapkin and E. Viano, pp. 181–199. Lexington, Mass.: Lexington Books, D.C. Heath and Company, 1975.   B,G
———. "Children Who Are Victims of Sexual Assault and the Psychology of Offenders." American Journal of Psychotherapy 30 (July 1976):398–421.   E,G

Argues on the basis of twenty-one years of experience in private practice and research with both child rape victims and offenders that many Freudian psychiatrists have been too ready to misinterpret real incidents of sexual assault in childhood, ascribing them to fantasy.

———. *Victims of Rape.* Rockville, Md.: DHEW Publication, 1977.   G

The sociological and psychological effects of rape upon female victims are studied and correlated to the circumstances surrounding the rape, the victim's personality and social adaptation prior to rape, and the support available to the victim after the attack, with attention to events as the victim passes through the criminal-justice system.

Peterson, B. "System Frustrates Battered Wives." *Washington Post*, 2 November 1974.   A

————. "Social Class, Social Learning, and Wife Abuse." *Social Service Review* 54 (1980):390–406.   A

Pethick, J. *Battered Wives—A Selected Bibliography*. Columbia: South Carolina Law Enforcement Assistance Program, 1979.   A,B

This annotated bibliography on battered wives includes references to U.S., Australian, British, and Canadian publications of the 1970s dealing with family violence.

Petro, J.A.; P.L. Quann; and W.P. Graham. "Wife Abuse: The Diagnosis and its Implications." *Journal of the American Medical Association* 240 (July 1978):240–241.   A,B

Notes that wife abuse receives widespread attention in the lay press but that its discussion in the medical literature is rare. Identifying a victim of wife abuse is complicated since the women will seldom volunteer that information.

Pfouts, J.H. "The Sibling Relationship: A Forgotten Dimension." *Social Work* 21 (May 1976):200–204.   E

————. "Violent Families—Coping Responses of Abused Wives." *Child Welfare* 57 (February 1978):101–111.   A,H

A theoretical scheme analyzes the responses of abused wives in terms of their cost-benefit analysis of the marriage and its alternatives. It is tested with thirty-five cases for a North Carolina County Welfare Department.

Phelps, S., and N., Austin. *The Assertive Woman*. San Luis Obispo, Calif.: Impact, 1975, p. 1.   B,D

Phillips, A. "Battered Women: How to Use the Law." *Spare Rib* 17:32. Women's Aid, 1973.   A,F

————. *Battered Wives: Report of Women's Aid*. London: Gill, Tess and Coote, 1975.   A,B

Pinsker, W., and E. Doschek. "Courtship and Rape: The Mating Behavior of *Drosophia Subobscura* in Light and in Darkness." *Zeitschrift fur Tierpsychologie* 54 (1980):57–70.   G

The reproductive behavior of *Drosophia Subobscura* was studied in a wild-type strain and in a strain selected for light-independent mating.

Pittman, D.J., and W. Handy. "Patterns in Criminal Aggravated Assault." *Journal of Criminal Law, Criminology, and Police Science* 55 (1964): 462–470.   H

The purpose of this study is to analyze the crime of aggravated assault and to attempt to establish its patterns as Wolfgang did with homicide, by testing where possible Wolfgang's homicide hypotheses against acts of aggravated assaults.

Pittman, F.S. "Counseling Incestuous Families." *Medical Aspects of Human Sexuality* 19 (April 1976):57–58.   E
Pizzey, E. "A Brute Behind that Perfect Bedside Manner." *Manchester Daily Express*, 31 October 1974.   G
———. "The Cultured Graduate Who Became a Thug." *Manchester Daily Express*, 29 October 1974.   H
———. "Violence Begins at Home." *London Spectator*, 23 November 1974.   *A,H*
———. *Scream Quietly or the Neighbors Will Hear*. Short Hills, N.J.: Ridley Enslow, 1977.   *A,H*

> Presents an account of the author's experience as head of a refuge for battered women and discusses the various sociological, legal, and psychological aspects of battered wives and children. Unedited letters from battered women are included, comparisons of situations in England and the United States are discussed, and solutions to the growth of violence in the home are examined.

Pleck, E.H. "Wife Beating in Nineteenth Century America." Paper presented at the American Studies Association, Chicago, 1977.   *A*
Pleck, E.H.; J.H. Pleck; M. Grossman; and P.B. Bart. "The Battered Data Syndrome: A Comment on Steinmetz' Article." *Victimology: An International Journal* 2 (1978):680–683.   *A*

> A critique of Steinmetz' article, which deals with the problem of battered husbands, is presented.

Pleck, J.H., and J. Sawyer. *Men and Masculinity*. Englewood Cliffs, N.J.: Prentice-Hall, 1974.   H
Ploscowe, M. et al. *Family Law: Cases and Materials*, 2d ed. New York: Little, Brown, 1972.   F
Pogash, C. "More Runaway Wives Than Ever Seek Freedom." *San Francisco Sunday Examiner and Chronicle*, 2 March 1975, p. 29, sect. A.
A,B
Pogrebin, L.C. "Do Women Make Men Violent?" Ms., November 1974, pp. 49–50, 52, 55, 80.   *A,H*

> Can it be true that a woman's presence incites male violence? Dotson Rader, in his article, "The Sexual Nature of Violence," asserts that when a woman is present during a hostile confrontation between two men, violence between the men is "ineluctable."

———. "Sex Harassment: Complaints of Working Women." *Ladies Home Journal* 94 (June 1977):24.   D

———. "Lone on the Job." *Ladies Home Journal* 97 (March 1980):10.*D*

Porkorny, A.D. "A Comparison of Homicide, Aggravated Assault, Suicide." *Journal of Criminal Law, Criminology, and Police Science* 15 (December 1965):488–498.   H

Polak. "Social Systems Intervention." *Archives of General Psychiatry* 25 (1971):110.   H

Polendine, R. "Who Knows What About the NMCG? (National Marriage Guidance Council)." *Marriage Guidance*, November 1971, pp. 371–373.   B

Police Experience—'Fear and Anxiety.' 16 mm, optical black and white, 10 min. Babylon, N.Y.: Film Modules Distribution, 1974.   B

Pork County Rape/Sexual Assault Care Center. "A Community Response to Rape." Washington, D.C.: Department of Justice, Law Enforcement and Criminal Justice, Office of Technology Transfer.   B, G

Poma, P.A. "Acute Management of the Sexual Assault Victim." *Journal of the National Medical Association* 71 (1979):589–559.   B, G

> The management of the sexual-assault victim is divided into three main problems: medical, psychological, and legal. The medical problem is comprised of the evaluation of injuries and their management, prophylaxis of venereal disease and pregnancy, and appropriate follow-up.

Poma, P.A., and R.C. Stepto. "Rape: A Community Hospital Study." *Illinois Medical Journal* 154 (1978):25–28.   B, G

> The results of an exploration of the records of women admitted for treatment to the emergency room of a major Chicago hospital in order to determine the number and circumstances surrounding rape are reported.

Pombeiro, B. "Decadence Is Back—in Vogue." *San Francisco Examiner*, 7 December 1975, pp. 1, 28; and *Vogue*, December 1975, p. 149.   B

Pomeroy, W. "Some Aspects of Prostitution." *Journal of Sex Research*, November 1965, 177–187.   H

"Portrait of a Rapist." *Newsweek*, 20 August 1973, p. 67.   B, G

Posner, M. "Rape: The Word May Go, the Violence Remains." *Macleans* 91 (29 May 1979):56–57.   G, H

Potter, J. "Police and the Battered Wife—The Search for Understanding." *Police Magazine* 1 (September 1978):40–50.   A, B

> Procedures for handling the problem of battered wives by police officers are explored, and programs started in some states to deal with the problems are described.

"Power, Sexual Deviation and Crime." *Medicine, Science, and Law* 16 (1976):3.   H

Prescott, J. "Body Pleasure and the Origins of Violence." *The Futurists*, April 1975, pp. 64–74.   H

President's Commission on Law Enforcement and Administration of Justice. "The Challenge of Crime in a Free Society." Washington, D.C., 1967.   B

Press, A. et al. "Abusing Sex at the Office." *Newsweek* 10 March 1980, pp. 81–82.   D

Preston, J. "Rape Issue Unites Mexican Feminists." *Ms.* (December 1978): 21.   B

Price. "Rape Victims—The Invisible Patients." *Canadian Nurse*, April 1975, p. 29.   G

Price, G.M. "A Study of the Wives of Twenty Alcoholics." *Quarterly Journal of Studies of Alcohol* 5 (1945):620–627.   A,B

This paper records the observations of a social-service worker on the role of one of the most important members of the alcoholic's family, the wife. A survey of some relevant data on the wives of twenty alcoholics is presented, with detailed reports of two cases.

Price, J., and J. Armstrong. "Battered Wives: A Controlled Study of Predisposition." *Australian and New Zealand Journal of Psychiatry* 12 (March 1978):43–47.   A

Investigated the possibility that women who were battered by their husbands were predisposed to this abuse by using thirty women who had separated from their husbands for this reason and thirty controls who had separated for other reasons.

Price, J.; N. Brennan; and G. Williams. "Hostility Scores in Australian Women with Special Reference to the Battered Wife." *Australian Psychologist* 15 (July 1980):189–197.   A,B

Administered the hostility and direction-of-hostility questionnaire to 177 Australian women and compared their scores with those of Australian woman who were attempting to escape a battering husband.

"Price of Rape: Awarding of Damages." *Time*, 6 September 1976, p. 32. G

Prince, R., and D. Barrier, eds. *Configurations: Biological and Cultural Factors in Sexuality and Family Life*. Lexington, Mass.: Lexington Books, D.C. Heath and Company, 1974.   B

Prinz, L. "Powerless in the Suburbs: The Battered Wife." *McCalls* 106 (November 1978):63.   A

"Prison Debate—Where Does Abuse End and Coddling Begin?" *Senior Scholastic*, November 1969. H

"Problem of Battered Women." Madison: University of Wisconsin, 1978. A

Samples of documents, articles, and reports from a variety of sources discuss the scope of, causes of attitudes on, and official response to wife beating.

Prosecutor's Responsibility in Spouse Abuse Cases. Superintendent of Documents, Washington, D.C., 1980. A,F

Discussion focuses on the nature and extent of spouse abuse in the United States and the prosecutor's responsibilities in spouse-assault cases.

Proskauer, S. "Oedipal Equivalents in a Clan Culture: Reflections on Navajo Ways." *Psychiatry* 43 (Fall 1980):43–50. B

Describes Navajo culture in which children are brought up within an extended family and the strongest incest taboos are between brothers and sisters rather than parent and child.

Public Affairs Offices. National League of Cities and United States Conference of Mayors. Sample News Coverage: Conference on Women Crime. Washington, D.C., 1976. B

Punch, M., and T. Naylor. "The Police—A Social Service." *New Society* 17 (May 1973):358–361. B

Putnam, J., and D. Fox. "A Program to Help the Victims of Crime." *Police Chief*, March 1976, p. 36. B,H

Puxon, M. "Sexual Violence—Fact and Fantasy." *Medico-Legal Journal* 47 (1979):55–68. G,H

Prevalent myths about rape are reviewed. It is pointed out that sexual assault is not on the increase.

Quenstedt, U. "Survey of 575 Domestic Relations Court Judges, Friends of the Court, and Commissioners of Domestic Relations." Monograph no. 1. Washington, D.C.: Family Law Section, American Bar Association, 1965. F

Quinn, R.E. "On-the-Job Trysts." *Human Behavior* 7 (February 1978):59. D

Quinsey, V.L.; Chaplin, T.C.; and Carrigan, W.F. "Sexual Preferences among Incestuous and Nonincestuous Child Molesters." *Behavior Therapy* 10 (September 1979):562–565. E,H

Qureshi, D.I. "Rape." *New York Stripes*, 1979.   G
"Rx for Rape: The Listening Ear." *Emergency Medicine* 240 (1975).   G
Rabkin, J.G. "The Epidemiology of Forcible Rape." *American Journal of Orthopsychiatry* 49 (October 1979):634–647.   G

> Considers problems of measurement of the incidence of rape and summarizes empirical findings regarding prevalence, demographic and psychiatric characteristics of offenders, spatial and temporal distribution of offenses, victim-offender relationships, and evidence about recidivism and progression of crimes.

Rada, R.T. "Alcoholism and Forcible Rape." *American Journal of Psychiatry* 132 (April 1975):444–446.   G

> Data collected from detailed autobiographies of seventy-seven convicted rapists revealed that 50 percent of them were drinking at the time of the rape and that 35 percent were alcoholics.

———. "Legal Aspects in Treating Rapists." *Criminal Justice and Behavior* 5 (December 1978):369–378.   F,G

> Outlines various legal and ethical problems involved in dealing with rapists and child molesters. The issues of confidentiality, privileged communication, and informed consent are explored to illustrate the potential problems incurred while working with such clients.

Rada, R.T.; R. Kellner; D.R. Laws; and W.W. Winslow. "Drinking, Alcoholism, and the Mentally Disordered Sex Offender." *Bulletin of the American Academy of Psychiatry and Law* 6 (1978):296–300. G,H

> The frequency of alcoholism and the degree of drinking at the time of offense were studied among 382 sex offenders committed to Atascadero State Hospital, California. A history of alcoholism was strongly associated with whether or not the offender was drinking at the time of the offense.

Radcliffe-Brown, A.R. *The Andaman Islanders*. Cambridge: Cambridge University Press, 1922.   B
Rader, C.M. "MMPI Profile Types of Exposers, Rapists and Assaulters in a Court Services Population." *Journal of Consulting and Clinical Psychology* 45 (February 1977):61–69.   G

> Investigated and compared the MMPI profiles of three groups of men—thirty-six exposer, forty-seven rapists, and forty-six assaulters—who had been referred to and tested by a county court service. The scores of individuals either incarcerated or put on probation were compared within each of the three groups.

Radloff, L.S. "Sex Differences in Helplessness with Implications for Depression." In *Career Development and Counseling of Women*, edited
L.S. Hansen and R.S. Raposa. Springfield, Ill.: Charles C Thomas. *H*

Radloff, L.S. "Sex Differences in Depression: The Effects of Occupation
and Marital Status." *Sex Roles* 1:249–265.   *H*

Rafferty, W.J. "Pupillary Activity as a Measure of Sexual Interest in
Pedophiles, Rapists, and Normals." *Dissertation Abstracts Internation-
al* 35 (6-B) 3033–3034, December 1974.   *B,G*

Raft, C. *Rape of the Blindfolded Lady*. Coral Springs, Flor.: Motivational
Methods, Inc., 1979.   *G*

Rainwater, L.; R.P. Coleman; and G. Handel. *Workingman's Wife*. New
York: Oceana Publications, 1959.   *A,D*

Ramsgate, P., producer of Ramsgate Films. *Nobody's Victim II*. 16 mm
film, sound, 24 mins., rental/sale, 1978.   *H*

Using vignettes and instructive commentary, the film offers a positive
impetus for women to accept responsibility for their own safety and gives
suggestions on avoiding danger, confrontations, and rape. Appropriate for
public library, community group, and high school and college program
viewers.

"Rape." Washington, D.C.: Department of Defense, Department of the
Army, Criminal Investigation Command, 1979.   *G*

"Rape." *Medico-Legal Journal* 47 (1979):53–54.   *G*

Difficulties in obtaining convictions in rape trials, the suffering of rape
victims, and the Sexual Offenses (amendment) Act of 1976, enacted to
relieve the distress of rape victims and to improve the course of justice, are
discussed.

"Rape." Washington National Commission on the Observance of International Women's Year. Washington, D.C.: U.S. Government Printing
Office, 1977.   *G*

Rape: A Preventive Inquiry. Schiller Park, Ill.: Motorola Teleprograms,
Inc., 1976–1977.   *G*

This film replaces myth with fact to give practical advice every woman can
use to decrease her chances of being raped and survival alternatives in case
an attack occurs.

"Rape and Culture; Controversial Views of A. Simonson." *Time*, 12 Sep-
tember 1977, p. 41.   *G*

"Rape and Death; Supreme Court Decision of the Death Penalty in Rape
Cases." *Newsweek*, 11 July 1977, p. 48.   *G*

"Rape and Responsibility." *Human Nature* 1 (1978):8.   *G*

Unexpected findings from recent research on the causes of rape and the moral responsibility for it are briefly reviewed. The results indicate that women still accept the notion of raging and uncontrollable male sex drives, while men now acknowledge that this characterization is not true.

Rape and the Rapist. 16 mm film, color, sound, 15 mins. Sale in 1977. Los Angeles: Sid Davis Productions.   G

Examines the psychological makeup of the rapist, including the traditional interpretation of the rapist's personality and basic drives that often help to shape a violence-prone youth. Suggests that the better law-enforcement officers understand the rapist's mentality, the better equipped they are to deal with him.

Rape Culture. Cambridge Documentary Films, Inc., 1976.   G

This film examines popular films, advertising, music and so-called adult entertainment, and records the insights of rapists, victims, rape-crisis workers, authors, and prisoners. The film seeks to establish the connections between sex and normal patterns of male-female behavior.

Rape: Escape without Violence. Cox, JR.-Bart., 1980. Highland Park, Ill.: Perennial Education, Inc.   G

A rape-prevention film to teach women how to stop a rapist in a nonviolent manner.

"Rape: Jenkins Consents." *Economist*, 21 June 1975.   G
"Rape: Motive for Murder." *Economist*, 12 April 1975, p. 71.   G
"Rape: Prevention and Control." Rockville, Md.: National Institute of Mental Health; Department of Health, Education, and Welfare; Public Service; Alcohol, Drug Abuse and Mental Health Administration, 1979.   G
"Rape Prevention Tactics." *Ms.* 3 (July 1974):114–115.   G
"The Rape Problem." *Playboy*, February 1974.   G
"Rape: The Crime against Women." *Ladies Home Journal* 94 (March 1977):69.   G,H
"Rape! These Women Say They Will Stop It!" *National Examiner*, 23 September 1974, p. 103.   G
"Rape: 300 Years On." *Economist*, 16 August 1975, p. 51.   G
"Rape's Traumatic Aftermath." *Human Behavior*, March 1975, p. 47. G
"Rape Treatment Centers Set Up in Two Cities." *Journal of American Medicine*, June 1975, p. 11.   G
"Rape Victim Guidelines." Modern Healthcare, March 1975, p. 74. B,G
Rape: Victim or Victor. 16 mm film. Schiller Park, Ill.: Motorola Tele-programs. Multi-media, 1978.   G

Dramatizes likely instances in which rape occurs and demonstrates the precautionary measures that can reduce the risk of attack. Appropriate for audiences aged fourteen years to adult. Also available in video cassettes and includes a guide.

The Rape Victims. 16 mm film, sound, 23 mins. Solana Beach, Calif.: Media Guild Distributors. Rental/sale, 1978. G

Places rape in the category of violent, rather than sexual, crimes and views rape in the historical perspective of terrorist tactics during wartime. Appropriate for senior high school through adult audiences.

"Rape Victims Need Assistance." *American Association of Registered Nurses News Letter*, March 1975, p. 1. B,G

"Rape Wave: Creation of Rape Investigation and Analysis Section." *Newsweek*, 29 January 1973, p. 59. B,G

Raphling, D.L.; B.L. Carpenter; and A. Davis. "Incest: A Genealogical Study. *Archives of General Psychiatry* 16 (1967):505–511. B,E

Presents a case study documenting multiple patterns of incestuous behavior in a single family.

Rascovsky, A., and M. Rascovsky. "The Prohibition of Incest, Filicide and the Sociocultural Process." *International Journal of Psycho-Analysis* 53 (1972):271–276. E

Presents incestuous craving discussed as the most constant, universal, sexual force in the individual's life.

Raser, H.R. *Simulation and Society: An Exploration of Scientific Gaming*. Boston: Allyn and Bacon, 1969. H

Rasko, G. "The Victim of the Female Killer." *Victimology* 1 (Fall 1976): 396–402. H

Results of a comprehensive study of homicides and attempted homicides perpetrated by 125 women in Hungary since the end of World War II.

"Rather a Wife Than a Mistress Be?" *Economist* (Great Britain), 3 December 1977, p. 23. A,G

Rawlings, E., and D. Carter. *Psychotherapy for Women: Treatment toward Equality*. Springfield, Ill.: Charles C Thomas, 1976. B

Reage, P. *Story of O*. New York: Grove Press, 1965. G

"Really Socking It to Women." *Time*, 7 February 1977. A

Refuge for Battered Women: A Study of the Role of A Women's Centre. London: Her Majesty's Stationery Office, 1978. B

The aim of this study was to monitor the setting up and development of the Canterbury Women's Centre and to evaluate the assistance it offered to the women in the United Kingdom between November 1975 and November 1976.

Registrar-General. *Census Great Britain: Summary Tables*. London: Her Majesty's Stationery Office, 1971.   B
Reich, J.W., and S.E. Gutierres. "Escape/Aggression Incidence in Sexually Abused Juvenile Delinquents." *Criminal Justice and Behavior* 6 (1979): 239–243.   A,H

The relationship between sexual-abuse, escape, and aggressive-crime juvenile-delinquency reports was investigated.

Reid, J.B. "Reciprocity in Family Interaction. *Dissertation Abstracts International* 29 (1):378–379, 1968.   H
Reif, A. "Erich Fromm on Human Aggression." *Psychology Today*, April 1975, p. 22.   H
Reiss, I.L. *The Social Context of Premarital Sexual Permissiveness*. New York: Holt, Reinhart & Winston, 1967.   H
Remick, R., and J.A. Wada. "Couples Partial and Pseudoseizure Disorder." *American Journal of Psychology* 136 (March 1979):320–323. H

Reply with rejoinder J. Goodwin. *American Journal of Psychology* 136: 1231, September 1979.

Rempell, J.P. "Attribution of Responsibility by Police Officers and Mental Health Professionals to Victims and Assailants in Four Paradigmatic Episodes of Rape and Battery." *Dissertation Abstracts International* 40 (5-B): 2384, November 1979.   G,H

Characteristics of victim and assailant and attribution of responsibility in rape and battery cases to police officers and mental-health professionals.

Renick, J.C. "Sexual Harassment at Work: Why It Happens, What to Do about It." *Personnel Journal* 59 (August 1980):658–662.   D

The sexual harassment of women at work, ranging from verbal innuendos to rape, has only recently been brought to public awareness as a significant problem in business, industry, and the military.

Rensbergh, B. *The New York Times*, 5 September 1971, sect. 1, p. 1, col. 4.
                                                                         A,B
Renshaw, D.C., and R.H. Renshaw. "Incest." *Journal of Sex Education and Therapy* 3 (1977):3–7.   E

Various perspectives on incest are explored. Theoretical factors in pro-
moting incest taboos are discussed as are the causes for the breakdown of
powerful incest taboos.

Renvoize, J. *Web of Violence: A Study of Family Violence.* London: Routledge and Kegan Paul, 1978.   *H*

Intergenerational patterns of family violence in which the child victim
becomes the later adult offender are examined using a case-study approach.

Report of the Committee on One-Parent Families (Finer Report). London:
Her Majesty's Stationery Office, 1974.   *B*
"Report of District of Columbia Task Force on Rape." In *Rape Victim-
ology*, edited by L. Schultz. 1975.   *B*
Reppin, H.D., and D.K. Shah. "The Steno Who Said No! A. Tomkins
Sexual Harassment Suit against H.D. Reppin of RSE & G." *Newsweek*,
30 April 1979, p. 72.   *D*
Resnick, J.L.; C.E. Hill; and L. Dutcher. "Rape Crisis Center Training
Manual." *Catalog of Selected Documents in Psychology* 6 (May 1976):
47.   *B,G*

Paraprofessionals rape-crisis telephone-answering training manual.

Resnick, M. *Wife Beating: Counselor Training Manual #1.* Ann Arbor,
Mich.: NOW/Wife Assault, 1976.   *A,B*
———. *Counselor Training Manual #1.* Ann Arbor, Mich.: NOW/Ann
Arbor-Washtenaw County, 1977.   *A,B*
"Resources in the United States and Canada." *Victimology: An Interna-
tional Journal* 2 (1978):666–668.   *B,H*

Resources for the aid of battered women in the United States and Canada
are described.

"Responsibility in Relation to Respectability." *Journal of Social Psycholo-
gy* 102 (August 1977):3–8.   *C*
"Response to Intra-Family Violence and Sexual Assault." Rept. no 1.
Washington, D.C.: Center for Women Policy Studies, October 1976.
                                                                C,E,G
Response of the Judicial System. *Battered Women—An Effective Response
1979.* St. Paul: Minnesota Department of Corrections, 1979.   *B*

Minnesota criminal and civil proceedings bearing upon the circumstances
of battered women are discussed, and recommendations are offered for
providing services to these women in the course of such proceedings.

"Retarded Victim of Rape Charge Could not Give Consent to 'Intercourse':
People vs. O'Neal, 365 N.E.2d 1333, Appellate Court of Illinois. Fourth
District. 25 July 1977." *Mental Health Court Digest* 21 (1978):1. *F,G*

> A conviction for rape of a retarded sixteen-year old was modified to
> conviction for attempted rape by the appellate court of Illinois in *People* v.
> *O'Neal*, the evidence being insufficient to prove penetration beyond a
> reasonable doubt. However, the court ruled that the victim was retarded
> enough to require protection under the mental-deficiency provision of the
> rape statute.

Reubenstein, C. "Self-Blame Can Help (Views of Ronnie Janoff-Bul-
man)." *Psychology Today* 14 (July 1980):111.   *G,H*
Revitz, R. "Retributory Restitution." *Victimology: An International Journal* 2 (1977):78–79.   *H*

> In a paper presented at the Second International Symposium in Victim-
> ology, held in Boston, September 1976, the compatibility of retributive
> justice and the payment of restitution to the victims of crimes is explained.
> It is shown how retribution and restitution may harmoniously and jointly be
> implemented.

"Revolt against Rape." *Time*, 22 July 1974, p. 85.   *G*
"Revolt against Rape." *Time*, 13 October 1975, p. 48.   *G*
Reynolds, R., and E. Seigle. "A Study Casework with Sadomasochistic
Marriage Partners." *Social Casework* 40 (December 1959):545–551.*B*
Rheingold, J.C. *The Fear of Being a Woman*. New York: Grune and
Stratton, 1964.   *C*
Rich, A. *Of Woman Born*. New York: Norton, 1976.   *C*
Richardson, B. "Wife Beating: How Prevalent Is the Problem?" *Dallas
Times-Herald*, 21 September 1975.   *A*
Richardson, D.C., and J.L. Campbell. "Alcohol and Wife Abuse: The
Effect of Alcohol on Attributions of Blame for Wife Abuse." *Personal-
ity and Social Psychology Bulletin* 6 (March 1980):51–56.   *A,G*

> 273 undergraduates read case-history or newspaper accounts of a violent
> incident in which either, both, or neither spouse was intoxicated. In con-
> trast, when the wife was intoxicated, she received more blame than when
> she was sober.

Richardson, D.D. "The Influence of Socioeconomic Status and Reciprocity on Mock Jurors' Verdicts in a Hypothetical Rape Case." *Dissertation
Abstracts International* 40 (1-B):461–462., July 1979.   *F,G*
Ridington, J. "The Transition Process: A Feminist Environment as Reconstitutive Milieu." *Victimology: An International Journal* 2 (1978):
563–575.   *B*

The development and functioning of Vancouver Transition House, a residence for battered women organized on feminist principles, is described. Long-term goals such as preventing batterers from continuing their behavior and improving the position of women that they are not forced to remain in oppressive relationships are discussed.

Rifai, M.A. "The Older Crime Victim and the Criminal Justice System." *Victimology* 2 (1977):79. *F,H*

In a paper presented at the Second International Symposium on Victimology, held in Boston, September 1976, results of a study of victimization and response of the criminal-justice system are presented. A general frustration with the criminal-justice system and feelings that the system was incapable of functioning to meet individual needs are reported.

Riger, S., and M.T. Gordon. "The Structure of Rape Prevention Beliefs." *Personality and Social Psychology Bulletin* 5 (April 1979):186–190. *B,G*

Factor analyses of the responses of random samples of 1,600 men and women from three cities indicate the presence of two relatively independent dimensions of rape-prevention attitudes: (1) Beliefs about measures calling for restrictions in women's behavior and (2) beliefs about measures involving changes in the environment or assertive actions by women.

Rinear, C.E. "An Epidemiological and Attitudinal Analysis of Rape and Other Sexual Assaults among Urban Female Hospital Personnel." *Dissertation Abstracts International* 38 (5-A):2564-2565E, November 1977. *G*

Rinear, C.E., and E.E. Rinear. "Sexual Assault among Hospital Personnel." *Victimology* 4 (1979):140–150. *G,H*

Epidemiological data from 6,807 women employed in urban hospitals were obtained to characterize the experience of being victimized by reported or unreported and completed or attempted sexual assault. The influence of selected interviewing variables on attitudes toward sexual assault and other reactive behavior was also investigated.

Rist, K. "Incest: Theoretical and Clinical Views." *American Journal of Orthopsychiatry* 49 (October 1979):680–691. *E*

Reviews the various theoretical approaches to incest and considers their relationship to the clinical literature. The lack of treatment reports on incest is noted, and directions are suggested for research that will enhance understanding of the phenomenon and guide practitioners in the appropriate therapeutic intervention with participants.

Robbins, K. "Iatrogenic Mother-Daughter Incest." Paper read before the section on Neurology and Psychiatry, New York Academy of Medicine, 11 March 1969.   *E*

Roberts, A.R. *Sheltering Battered Women: A National Study and Service Guide.* New York: Springer, 1980.   *A,B*

Roberts, J. *The Hardships of the English Laws in Relation to Wives.* London: W. Boyer, 1735.   *C,F*

Roberts, W.K., and B.K. Hart. "Technique for Training Paraprofessionals in Rape-Crisis Counseling Procedures." *Catalog of Selected Documents in Psychology* 6 (May 1976):46–47.   *B,C*

Training technique in rape-crisis intervention counseling procedures for paraprofessionals.

Robertson, G. "Slight Case of Rape." *New Statesman*, 9 May 1975, p. 614.
                                                                        G

Robin, B. "A Refuge for Danish Women," *San Francisco Chronicle*, 5 June 1973, p. 21.   *B*

Robin, G.D. "Forcible Rape: Institutionalized Sexism in the Criminal Justice System." *Crime and Delinquency* 23 (April 1977):136–153. *G*

Robinson, Oldham & Sniderman. "Establishment of a Rape Crisis Center." *Canadian Mental Health* 23 (September 1975):10.   *B,G*

Robinson, Sherrod & Malcarney. "Review of Child Molestation and Alleged Rape Cases." *American Journal of Obstetrics and Gynecology* 110 (1971):405.   *B,E,G*

Robitscher, J. "Battered Wives and Battered Children." *Bulletin of the American Academy of Psychiatry and the Law.* 5 (1977):374–379. *A,E*

The complex problems encountered in dealing with battered wives and children are discussed.

Rockford, M. "Courts and Cops: Enemies of Battered Wives?" *Ms.* 5 (April 1977):19.   *A,B,F*

Rod, T. *Marital Murder in Violence in the Family—A Collection of Conference Papers.* 1980, pp. 95–105.   *B,H*

The main characteristics and patterns of marital murders in New South Wales (Australia) are discussed and compared to those of other countries.

Rodman, H. "Marital Power in France, Greece, Yugoslavia, and the United States: A Cross-National Discussion." *Journal of Marriage and the Family* 39 (May 1967):320–324.   *B*

———. "Family and Social Pathology in the Ghetto." *Science* 161 (3 August 1968):762.   *B*

———. "Marital Power and the Theory of Resources in Cultural Context." *Journal of Comparative Family Studies* 3 (Spring 1972):50–70.   B

Rodolfa, E.R. "A Bibliography on Child Sexual Abuse and Incest." *Catalog of Selected Documents in Psychology* 9 (August 1979):55   B,E

Rofsky, M. "Effects of Father-Daughter Incest on the Personality of Daughters." *Dissertation Abstracts International* 40 (5):2386-B, 1979.
    E

The influence of father-daughter incest on the personality development of the daughter was investigated in twenty women.

Rogel, M.J. "Biosocial Aspects of Rape." *Dissertation Abstracts International* 37 (9-B):4763–4764, May 1977.   B,G

Describes distribution of rape over menstrual cycle, mood changes, and energy levels associated with peaks in frequency of rape and analyzes hospital rape reports.

Rogers, C.A. "The Phenomenological Theory of Personality." In *Psychology of Personality: Readings in Theory*, edited by W.S. Sahakian, pp. 473–493. Chicago: Rand McNally, 1965.   B

———. "Sexual Victimization and the Courts: Empirical Findings." Paper presented at American Psychological Association Annual Convention, Montreal, Canada, September 1980.   A,F,H

Rogers, J.G. "The Genetic Consequences of Incest." *Medical Journal of Australia* 2 (1978):362–363.   E

Rogers, L. "Four Years Ago I Was Raped." *Glamour* 76 (September 1978):192.   G

Rogers, M.F. "Instrumental and Infra-Resources: The Bases of Power." *American Journal of Sociology* 79 (May 1974):1418–1433.   B,H

Rogers, M.R. "A Descriptive Study of the Rapist." *Dissertation Abstracts International* 39 (10-B):5084, April 1979.   G

Sociodemographic characteristics and behavioral and attitudinal factors of 19–35-year-old rapists.

Rogovin, S.A. "The Violent Marriage: Investigation of the Battered Woman, Her Parent-Child Relationship and Family Background." *Dissertation Abstracts International* 40 (2):932-B, 1979.   A,H

The parent-child relationship and family background of twenty-five women currently in physically abusive marriages and twenty-seven nonabused women were investigated.

Roiphe, A. "Family War: Can You Win?" *Vogue* 161 (June 1973):105–
106.   H

Rokeach, M. *The Open and Closed Mind.* New York: Basic Books, 1960.
                                                                              B

"Role and Justice Considerations in the Attribution of Responsibility to a
Rape Victim." *Journal of Research in Personality* 10 (September 1976):
346–357.   G

   Conducted a study with 236 male and 241 female undergraduates to assess
   the extent to which social-role and just-world considerations would affect
   perceptions and attributions of responsibility to a rape victim.

Rolph, C.H. "Battered Wives." *New Statesman*, 26 December 1975, pp.
811–812.   A

"Roman Polanski's Tawdry Trouble." *Time*, 28 March 1977, p. 22.   G

Root. "Medical Investigation of Alleged Rape Victims." *Eastern Medical
Journal*, 1974, p. 329.   B,G

Rooth, G. "Exhibitionism, Sexual Violence and Paedophilia." *British Journal of Psychiatry* 122 (June 1973):705–710.   H

   Traditionally, exhibitionists have been considered harmless, but recent
   papers have questioned that view. Thirty cases of persistent exhibitionism
   are reviewed.

Rorty, A.O. "Some Social Uses of the Forbidden." *Psychoanalytic Review*
58 (Winter 1971–1972):497–510.   H

   Discusses the social prohibition of behavior that is also encouraged. The
   restrictions that society places on the expression of aggression are described.

Rose, V.M. "Rape as a Social Problem: A Byproduct of the Feminist
Movement." *Social Problems* 25 (October 1977):75–89.   G

   Analyzes the antirape movement from a theoretical perspective, emphasizing interest-group formation and action and the generation of social problems by social movements. Of these interest groups, the feminist perspective is seen as representing the most active and vocal of antirape interests.

Rosen & Hoffman. "Focal Suicide: Self-Enucleating by Two Young Psychotic Individuals." *American Journal of Psychiatry* 128 (1972):1009.
                                                                              H

Rosenbaum, A. "Wife Abuse: Characteristics of the Participants and Etiological Considerations. *Dissertation Abstracts International* 40 (3-B):
1383, September 1979.   A,B

Discusses characteristics associated with physical abuse and marital violence, effects on children of violent marriage, and abused wives and abusive husbands.

Rosenbaum, D.P. "Victim Blame as a Strategy for Coping with Criminal Victimization: An Analysis of Victim, Community, and Police Reactions." *Dissertation Abstracts International* 41 (3):1165-B, 1980.   H

The importance of victim blame as a mechanism for coping with actual and/or possible criminal victimization was explored using telephone interviews with 240 crime victims and 125 nonvictims. In addition, 77 police officers completed a self-administered questionnaire.

Rosenbaum, M.E., and R. deCharms. "Direct and Vicarious Reduction of Hostility." *Journal of Abnormal and Social Psychology* 60 (1960):105–111.   H

Rosenberg, H.M., and N.L. Thompson, "Attitudes toward Women Dental Students among Male Dental Students and Male Dental Faculty." *Journal of Dental Education* 40 (1976):676–680.   B,C

Rosenberg, R. "A Woman Must Persevere in Battle against Sexism." *Santa Clara Sun*, 20 August 1975, p. 6.   C

Rosenblum, K. "Female Deviance and the Female Sex Role: A Preliminary Investigation." *British Journal of Sociology* 25 (June 1975):69–85.   C

Rosenfeld, A.A. "A Case of Sexual Misuse." *Psychiatric Opinion* 13 (April 1976):35–42.   E

Describes the history and treatment of an 8-year old girl who had been sexually misused by her father from age 2. The parents, both sexually misused as children, were involved with hallucinogenic drugs, preferred sexual involvement with others, and became psychotic.

———. "Sexual Misuse and the Family." *Victimology* 2 (Summer 1977): 226–235.   E

Traces the evolution of psychiatric ideas about incest. In recent years, incest has been conceptualized as a symptom of family dysfunction rather than as etiologic of certain disorders.

———. "A Historical Perspective on the Psychiatric Study of Incest." *American Journal of Forensic Psychiatry* 1 (1978):64–79.   E

———. "Sexual Abuse of Children." *Journal of the American Medical Association* 240 (July 1978):43.   E

Discusses the psychological origins of sexual abuse of children, emphasizing that the situation is more complex than its ordinary characterization as violent acts done by an adult perpetrator to a child victim.

————. "The Clinical Management of Incest and Sexual Abuse of Children." *Journal of the American Medical Association* 242 (1979):1761–1764.   *E*

The role of the primary-care physician in the detection and management of cases of incest and sexual abuse is discussed.

————. "Endogamic Incest and the Victim-Perpetrator Model." *American Journal of Diseases of Children* 133 (1979):406–410.   *E*

The incestuous family situation is discussed, and psychotherapeutic intervention is considered as a first course of action to be taken in incest cases. The traditional view of incest as an aggressive act of a deranged adult perpetrator against a child victim is criticized.

————. "Incidence of a History of Incest among 18 Female Psychiatric Patients." *American Journal of Psychiatry* 136 (June 1979):791–795. *E*

Determined the frequency of reports of a history of incest among eighteen female psychiatric outpatients first evaluated or treated by author in a one-year period; seventeen were randomly assigned to the author by the clinic secretary. Six patients reported a history of incest.

Rosenfeld, A.A.; M.J. Krieger; and C. Nadelson. "The Sexual Misuse of Children: A Brief Survey." *Psychiatric Opinion* 13 (April 1976):6–12.
                                                                                                                          E

Sexual misuse of children, defined as exposure of a child within a given sociocultural context to sexual stimulation inappropriate for its age level of development, forms a continuum from what is clearly abusive to what is merely inappropriate.

Rosenfeld, A.A.; C.C. Nadelson; and M. Krieger. "Fantasy and Reality in Patients' Reports of Incest." *Journal of Clinical Psychiatry* 40 (1979):159–164.   *E*

Some of the complex difficulties facing clinicians trying to assess whether a patient's report of incest is fantasy or reality are discussed. The role of sexualized family interactions, the age of the child, the nature of the act, and the quality of the reports are relevant variables.

Rosenfeld, A.A.; C.C. Nadelson; M.J. Krieger; and J.H. Backman. "Incest and Sexual Abuse of Children." *Journal of the American Academy of Child Psychiatry* 16 (1977):327–339.   *E*

Rosengard, B., ed. *Research, Demonstration, and Evaluation Studies; Fiscal Year 1973*. Washington, D.C.: Children's Bureau, 1974. B

Rosenzweig, S. "Definition and Classification of Aggressive Phenomena." Paper presented at First International Conference on Aggression, Toronto, 1974. H

Rosettis, J. "Vancouver Transition House," Report for the Department of Human Resources. Washington, D.C., January 1975. B

Ross, M.J. "The Legislator's View of the Victim." *Victimology: An International Journal* 2 (1977):79–80. F

In a paper presented at the Second International Symposium on Victimology, held in Boston, September 1976, a typology of the legislator's modes of valuation is offered.

Rossel, J. *Women in Sweden*. Stockholm: Swedish Institute, 1965. B,C

Roth, S., and R.R. Bootzin. "Effects of Experimentally Induced Expectancies of External Control: An Investigation of Learned Helplessness." *Journal of Personality and Social Psychology* 29 (1974):253–264. H

Rounsaville, B.J. "Battered Women—A Medical Problem Requiring Detection." *International Journal of Psychiatry in Medicine* 8 (1977–1978): 191–202. A,C

A one-month study of the surgical and psychiatric service of a university-hospital emergency room was conducted to alert physicians to the magnitude of wife abuse and to identify prevention measures.

———. "Battered Wives: Barriers to Identification and Treatment." *American Journal of Orthopsychiatry* 48 (July 1978):487–494. A,C

Attempted to document the severity and frequency of the wife-abuse problem as it manifested itself in a general emergency room, examined why some are helped and others are not by comparing the characteristics of those who follow through in seeking help and those who do not, and evaluated the treatment implications for these patients.

———. "Theories in Marital Violence: Evidence from a Study of Battered Women." *Victimology* 3 (1978):11–31. A,B

Considers psychological and sociological theories of wife beating in light of data gathered in a study of thirty-one battered women.

———. "Marital Disputes and Treatment Outcome in Depressed Women." *Comprehensive Psychiatry* 20 (1979):483–490. A,H

Rounsaville, B. J., and M. Bieber. "Natural History of Psychotherapy Group for Battered Women." *Psychiatry* 42 (Fall 1979):63–78. B

Psychotherapy with battered women can be useful to those who stay in treatment, and group therapy may be a preferred treatment modality.

Rounsaville, B.; N. Lifton; and M. Bieber. "The Natural History of a Psychotherapy Group for Battered Women." *Psychiatry: Journal for the Study of Interpersonal Processes* 42 (1979):63–78.   *A,B*

A group psychotherapy treatment program for battered women was examined. A group of thirty-one patients was interviewed, and the data gathered were used for assessment.

Rounsaville, B.J.; B.A. Prusoff; and M.M. Weissman. "The Course of Marital Disputes in Depressed Women: A 48-Month Follow-Up Study." *Comprehensive Psychiatry* 21 (March/April 1980):111–118. *H*

In an elaboration of previously published studies by the authors on the efficacy of various treatment methods for depression, the study evaluated the course of marital disputes in sixty-five women forty-eight months after completion of an eight-month treatment program for depression.

Rounsaville, B.J.; M.M. Weissman; B.A. Prusoff; and B.R. Herceg. "Process of Psychotherapy among Depressed Women with Marital Disputes." *American Journal of Orthopsychiatry* 49 (July 1979):505–510.
A,H

Studied the relationship between topics discussed, affects expressed, and quantity of reflectiveness during psychotherapy and improvement in marital disputes in thirty-eight moderately depressed 25–60-year-old women who had been randomly assigned to receive a minimum of one fifty-minute session/week of psychotherapy.

―――. "Marital Disputes and Treatment Outcome in Depressed Women." *Comprehensive Psychiatry* 20 (October 1979):483–490.   *A,H*

Assessed the relationship between reduction of marital disputes and other treatment results in seventy-six women who received eight months of individual psychotherapy as part of a controlled clinical trial to test the efficacy of various outpatient maintenance treatments for depression.

Rowan, C.T., and D.M. Mazie. "Terrible Trauma of Rape." *Readers Digest* 104 (March 1974):198–199.   *G*
Rowland, J.A. "Domestic Violence—The Battered Woman." *San Diego County Law Enforcement Quarterly* 7 (Spring 1978):6–12; and Rockville, Md.: NCJRS Microfiche Program, 1978.   *A,H*

An overview of domestic violence is presented; a victim service program for battered women in Milwaukee County, Wisconsin, is described; and

and efforts to combat domestic violence in San Diego County, California, are discussed.

Roy, M. "Feelings and Attitudes of Raped Women of Bangladesh toward Military Personnel of Pakistan." In *Victimology: A New Focus*, edited by I. Drapkin and E. Viano, Lexington, Mass.: Lexington Books, D.C. Heath and Company, 1975, p. 65. *B,G*
———. *Abused and Battered Wife*. New York: Van Nostrand Reinhold, 1977. *A*
———. *Battered Women: A Psychosociological Study of Domestic Violence*. New York: Van Nostrand Reinhold, 1977. *A,B*

Roy, founder and executive director of Abused Women's Aid in Crisis, Incorporated, has compiled a comprehensive view of the battered-wife syndrome. Her collection includes articles by psychologists, sociologists, law-enforcement officials, and authorities from community programs.

Royal Commission on Medical Education 1968 CMND 3569. *B*
Rubenstein, D.R. *How the Russian Revolution Failed Women*. San Francisco: Socialist Workshop. *B*
Rubenstein, H. "Incest, Effigy Hanging, and Biculturation in a West Indian Village." *American Ethnologist* 3 (November 1976):765–781. *E*

A mock trial followed by the hanging of effigies of the participants in incestuous mating is a ritualized means of punishing sexual deviance in the eastern Caribbean Island of Saint Vincent.

Rubin, D. *Everything You Always Wanted to Know about Sex—But Were Afraid to Ask*. New York: David McKay, 1969; and New York: Bantam Books, 1971. *E,G*
Rubinelli, J. "Incest: It's Time We Face Reality." *Journal of Psychiatric Nursing and Mental Health Services* 18 (1980):17–18. *E*

The phenomenon of incest is discussed, and the need for mental-health professionals to confront their own feelings of revulsion concerning incest is emphasized.

Ruch, L.O.; S.M. Chandler; and R.A. Harter. "Life Change and Rape Impact." *Journal of Health and Social Behavior* 21 (September 1980): 248–260. *G*

Investigated the effects of prior life change on the levels of emotional trauma experienced by 267 adult rape victims.

Ruff, C.F.; D.I. Templer; and J.L. Ayers. "The Intelligence of Rapists." *Archives of Sexual Behavior* 5 (July 1976):327–329. *G*

Compared WAIS IQs of 10 rapists to IQs of 126 nonrapist prisoners convicted of violent and nonviolent crimes.

Ruggiero, G. "Sexual Criminality in the Early Renaissance: Venice." *Journal of Social History*, Summer 1975, pp. 8–37.   E,G
Rumsey, M.G., and J.M. Rumsey. "A Case of Rape: Sentencing Judgments of Males and Females." *Psychological Reports* 41 (October 1977):459–465.   F,G

Judgments made by twenty-four male and twenty-four female undergraduates of defendant guilt and sentencing in a rape case were examined before and after group discussion under two levels each of evidentiary ambiguity and judicial instructions.

Rush, F. "The Sexual Abuse of Children: A Feminist Point of View." *Radical Therapist* 2 (December 1971).   E
Russell, D.E. *The Politics of Rape*. New York: Stein & Day Publishers, 1975.   G
———. "The Necessary Intent in Rape." *Sydney Law Review* 8 (1977): 196–206.   G

The problem of whether rape can be charged against a man who had an honest and reasonable belief that the woman consented to the act is analyzed, and the legal history of the charge is presented and discussed.

Russell, D.E., and D.L. Miller. "The Prevalence of Rape and Sexual Assault." Unpublished paper. Final report of NIMH Grant 289-60, 1979.   G

Data obtained in a study of the incidence and prevalence of rape and attempted rape in San Francisco offer a great deal of information about a previously unknown area.

Russell, D.E., and N. Van de Ven. *Crimes against Women: Proceedings of the International Tribunal*. Millbrae, Calif.: Les Femmes, 1976.
                                                                 B,C,G,H
Russell, G., and J. Zacker. "400 Books on Aggression." Mimeographed. Lethbridge, Canada: Department of Psychology, University of Lethbridge.   B,H
Russell, M. "Rape Victims and Police Reporting." *Canada's Mental Health* 28 (1980):14–16.   B,G

The differential characteristics among rape victims of police reporters from nonreporters were examined through analysis of 403 cases of the Vancouver Rape Relief Center.

Russianoff, P. *Women in Crisis*. New York: Human Sciences Press, 1981.
                                                                                         B,C,H
Rutherford, K. "Why Wives Endure Beating in Silence." *Pittsburgh Press*,
    14 February 1976, p. 9.   *A*
Ryden, R.G. "Communal Life Styles." Paper presented at the Annual
    Meeting of the Groves Conference, San Juan, Puerto Rico. May 1971.
                                                                         B
Sadoff, R.L. "Clinical Observations on Paricide." *Psychiatric Quarterly* 45
    (1971):65–69.   *C*
———. "Treatment and Violent Sex Offenders." *International Journal of
    Offender Therapy and Comparative Criminology* 19 (1975):75–80. *B*
———. *Violence and Responsibility: The Individual, the Family, and Soci-
    ety*. New York: Medical and Scientific Books, 1978.   *H*

     A collection of papers presented at two separate conferences in 1976, one
     entitled "Violence in Families" and the other called "Violence and Re-
     sponsibility," is presented.

Safran, C. "What Men Do to Women on the Job: A Shocking Look at
    Sexual Harassment." *Redbook* 148 (November 1976):149.   *D*
Safilos-Rothschild, C. "Family Sociology of Wives' Family Sociology? A
    Cross-Cultural Examination of Decision-Making." *Journal of Marriage
    and the Family* 31 (1969):290–301.   *C*
———. "The Study of Family Power Structure: A Review 1960–1969."
    Journal of Marriage and the Family 32 (November 1970):539–552. *B*
Sagarin, E. "Forcible Rape and the Problem of the Rights of the Accused."
    Intellect 103 (May 1975):515–520.   *F,G*
———. "Incest: Problems of Definition and Frequency." *Journal of Sex
    Research* 13 (May 1977):126–135.   *B,E*

     Notes that research into factors pertinent to incest is hampered and con-
     fused as a result of the lack of clear-cut definitions. A distinction is made
     between consanguine and affinal relationships, and it is suggested that
     biological consequences as well as psychological problems allegedly result-
     ing from incest could be more clearly determined.

Sagarin, E., and D.E. MacNamara, eds. *Problems of Sex Behavior*. New
    York: Thomas Y. Crowell, 1968.   *B,C*

     Topics include the ambiguity of contemporary sex attitudes, illegitimacy,
     prostitution, male homosexuality, incest, rape, child molestation, and
     pornography.

Saint Louis, A. "The Development of a Statewide Mail Survey of Crime

Victims: Methodology and Preliminary Analysis." *Victimology: An International Journal* 2 (1977):80. B

In a paper presented at the Second International Symposium on Victimology, held in Boston, September 1976, the development of a statewide mail survey of the general public to obtain basic crime data from victims is described.

Salasin, S. "Caring for Victims: An Interview with Steven Sharfstein." *Evaluation and Change* Special Issue (1980):18–20. C

The growing awareness of the difficulties faced by victims of violence and efforts directed at outreach, prevention, and training of professionals are addressed in an interview with the director of the National Institute for Mental Health's Mental Health Services Division.

Salerno. "Violence, Not Sex: What Rapists Really Want." *New York Magazine* 23 June 1975, p. 36. G

Salkin. "The Furman Decision and Current Death Penalty Legislation." *Georgia Journal of Corrections* 3 (1974):10. F

Saltzman, K. "Woman and Victimization—The Aftermath." In *Victimization of Women*, edited by J.R. Chapman and M. Cotes. Beverly Hills, Calif.: Sage Publications, 1978. H

The conditions that must be present before one group can successfully victimize another group are listed, and the socialization process through which women become acceptable targets of criminal abuse is traced.

Samari, C.G., and D. Baskin. "Incest: No Longer a Family Affair." *Child Psychiatry Quarterly* 13 (1980):36–51. E

Samuels, A. "Incest and Omnipotence in the Internal Family." *Journal of Analytical Psychology* 25 (1980):37–57. E

Case material and theoretical concepts are used to demonstrate the link between a certain incestuous style and infantile omnipotence in the internal family.

Sanchez, R., and Dirks. "Reflections on Family Violence." *Alcohol, Health and Research World* 4 (Fall 1979):12–16. H

This paper examines the repetitive cycle from generation to generation of both alcoholism and domestic violence, the similar personalities of all parties involved in these problems, and existing treatment programs dealing with both violence and alcohol abuse.

Sanday, P.R. "The Socio-Cultural Context of Rape." Philadelphia: University of Pennsylvania, unpublished paper. Final report of NIMH Grant, 1979.   *B,G*

A standard cross-cultural sample of 186 tribal societies was studied to determine the meaning of rape by providing a descriptive profile of rape-prone and rape-free societies; analyzing the attitudes, motivations, and sociocultural factors related to the incidence of rape; and presenting a scenario for the evolution of rape-prone versus rape-free cultural configurations.

Sandes. "Sexual Assaults on Children." *British Journal of Clinical Practice* 17 (1963):143.   *C,E*

Sanford, J., and others. "Patterns of Reported Rape in the Triethnic Population: Houston, Texas, 1974–1975." *American Journal of Public Health* 69 (May 1979):480–484.   *G*

Sanford, L.T. *The Silent Children: A Parent's Guide to the Prevention of Child Sexual Abuse.* New York: Doubleday & Company, 1980. *B,E*

Examines the circumstances of child molestation and incest and the motivations of the offenders so that parents can inform and protect children and therefore reduce its incidence.

Sanford, N. "Will Psychologists Study Human Problems?" *American Psychologist* 20 (1965):192–202.   *C*

Sanford, N., and C. Comstock, eds. *Sanctions for Evil.* San Francisco: Jossey-Bass, 1971.   *H*

San Francisco Police Department. Homicide Bureau. Statistics reviewed and evaluated with respect to marital cases by S. Jackson and M. Ashley.   *B*

Sanson, B.E. "Spouse Abuse—A Novel Remedy for a Historic Problem." *Dickinson Law Review* 84 (Fall 1979):147–170.   *A,B*

The historical background of the spouse-abuse problem is discussed, statutory approaches for protecting battered spouses are examined, and Pennsylvania's protection-from-abuse act is analyzed.

Saperstein. "Child Rape Victims and Their Families." In *Rape Victimology*, edited by L. Schultz. 1975.   *G*

Sarafino, E.P. "An Estimate of Nationwide Incidence of Sexual Offenses against Children." *Child Welfare* 58 (1979):127–134.   *B,E*

Extrapolating from studies of the incidence of sexual offenses against children in four geographical areas, a nationwide estimate of 336,200 such offenses annually is presented.

Sarbin, T. "The Dangerous Individual: An Outcome of Social Identity Transformation." *British Journal of Criminology*, July 1967, pp. 285–295.   H

Sargent, D. "Children Who Kill—A Family Conspiracy?" *Social Work* 7 (1962):35–42.   H

Sarles, R.M. "Incest." *Pediatrics Clinics of North America* 22 (August 1975).   E

———. "Symposium on Behavioral Pediatrics: Incest." *Pediatric Clinic of North America* 22 (1975):633–642.   E

Sarrel, L.J., and P.M. Sarrel. "Incest: Why it Is our Last Taboo." *Redbook* 156 (November 1980):83.   E

Satten, J.K. "Murder without Apparent Motive: A Study in Personality Disorganization." *American Journal of Psychiatry* 117 (1960):48–53.   H

Sattin, D.B., and J.K. Miller. "The Ecology of Child Abuse with a Military Community." *American Journal of Orthopsychiatry* 61 (July 1971): 675–678.   E,G

Saturansky, C.H. "A Clinical Study of Rape Victims: An Analysis of the Effects of Rape Experiences on Personality Dynamics and Life Styles." *Dissertation Abstracts International* 37 (9-B):4703–4704, March 1977.   B,G

Analyzes rape experience on ego strength, adjustment, life-styles, and personality dynamics of female rape victims.

Saul, L.J. "Personal and Social Psychopathology and the Primary Prevention of Violence." *American Journal of Psychiatry* 128 (1972):1578–1581.   H

Savage, J.S., and B. Kearney Young. "Community Attitudes: The Issue of Rape." *Journal of Psychiatric Nursing and Mental Health Services* 16 (1978):20–25.   B,C

Whether or not a difference in attitudes about rape existed between the populations of a greater urbanized area and a lesser urbanized area was determined.

Sawyer, S.G. "Lifting the Veil on the Last Taboo." *Family Health* 12 (June 1980):43.   E

Scacco, A.M. *Rape in Prison*. Springfield, Ill.: Charles C Thomas, 1975. G

Scarpitti, F.R., and E.C. Scarpitti. "Victims of Rape." *Society* 14 (July 1977):29–32.   G

"Scarred Lives of Battered Women." *Glamour* 78 (October 1980):56.
                                                                    A,G
Schafer, S. *The Victim and His Criminal*. New York: Random House, 1968.
                                                                    H
Scharer, K.M. "Rescue Fantasies: Professional Impediments in Working
with Abused Families." *American Journal of Nursing* 78 (1978):1483–
1484.   *A,B*

> Professional impediments in working with families where child abuse or
> neglect occurs are discussed, and the need for nurses to be self-searching
> and free from rescue fantasies is emphasized.

Schechner, R. "Incest and Culture: A Reflection on Claude Levi-Strauss."
Psychoanalytic Review 58 (Winter 1971–1972):563–572.   *E*

> Discusses Levi-Strauss's theory that the exchange of commodities is de-
> rived from the exchange of women in marriage, which in turn is based on
> the incest taboo.

Scheff, T.J. *Being Mentally Ill*. Chicago: Aldine, 1966.   *H*
Schenk, R.U. "So Why Do Rapes Occur." *Humanist* 39 (1979):47–50.*G*

> Basic causes of rape are examined, and the role that women play in men's
> attitudes toward rape are discussed.

Scheurell, R.P., and I.D. Rinder. "Social Networks and Deviance: A
Study of Lower Class Incest, Wife Beating, and Nonsupport Offend-
ers." *Wisconsin Sociologist* 10 (1973):56–73.   *E*
Schiff, A.F. "Examining the Sexual Assault Victim." *Journal of the Florida
Medical Association* 56 (September 1969):731–739.   *B,E*
———. "Rape in Other Countries." *Medical Science and the Law* 11 (1971):
139.   *G*
———. "Rape in Foreign Countries." *Medical Trial Technical Quarterly* 20
(1974):66.   *G*
———. "The New Florida Rape Law." *Journal of Florida Medical Associa-
tion* 62 (1975):40.   *F,G*
———. "Attending the Child Rape Victim." *Southern Medical Journal* 72
(1979):906–910.   *E,G*
———. "State of Oregon vs. Rideout—Can Husband Rape Wife." *Medical
Trial Technique Quarterly* 26 (1979):49–56.   *F,G*
Schiff, A.F., and S. Leeds. *New York County Henry Street Settlement's
Family Abuse Project: 1st Year Evaluation, 1978*. Washington, D.C.:
U.S. Department of Justice, Law Enforcement Assistance Administra-
tion, 1978.   *A,B*

A program in New York City to deal with family abuse was evaluated in terms of crisis-oriented and support services for victims, awareness of the abuse problem, needs of family offense victims, and the family court.

Schimel, J.L. *The Parent's Handbook on Adolescence.* New York: World Publishing Company, 1969.   *B,E*

Schindler, S. "Family Constellation and Aggressive Conduct." *Zeitschrift fur Klinische Psychologie und Psychotherapie* 22 (January 1974):180–182.   *C,G,H*

Schlachet, B.C. *Rapid Intervention with Families in Crisis in a Court Setting.* Scarborough, Ontario: Butterworth, 1978.   *G*

The rapid-intervention project of the New York City Family Court is described. This unit provided immediate psychological evaluation of all parties involved in a spouse-abuse or child-abuse case.

Schlesinger, B. "Abused Wives: Canada's Silent Screamers." *Canada's Mental Health* 28 (1980):17–20.   *A,B*

An overview of battered wives in Canada is presented with a summary of research findings on the subject.

Schneck, J.M. "Zooerastry and Incest Fantasy." *International Journal of Clinical and Experimental Hypnosis* 22 (October 1974):299–302.   *E*

Reports specific clinical data on zooerasty revealed in psychotherapy with an intelligent forty-five-year-old man.

Schneider, D.M.; S.B. Jordon, and C.C. Arguedas, "The Meaning of Incest." *Journal of the Polynesian Society* 85 (1976):149–170.   *E*
———. "Sexual Assault Law Reform in Colorado—An Analysis of House Bill 1042." *Denver Law Journal* 53 (1976):349.   *E,F,G*
———. "A Note on Excess Access and Incest." *American Anthropologist* 81 (1979):120.   *E*

Schneider, D.M., et al. "Representation of Women Who Defend Themselves in Response to Physical or Sexual Assault." *Women's Rights Law Reporter* 4 (1978):149–163.   *A,F,G*

The aiding of attorneys representing women who have committed homicides after they have been physically or sexually assaulted or after their children have been molested or abused is discussed from a feminist perspective.

Schoettle, U.C. "Treatment of the Child Pornography Patient." *American Journal of Psychiatry* 137 (1980):1109–1110.   *B,C,E,G*

A case of an early pubescent girl involved in a child pornography ring is reported.

Schonfelder, T. *Die Rolle des Madchens Bei Sexualdelikten*, Stuttgart: 1968.   *A,B,G*

Schram, D.A. *Final Report: Techniques for Improving the Effectiveness of the Criminal Justice Response to Forcible Rape*. Washington, D.C.: National Institute of Law Enforcement and Criminal Justice, 1977. *B*

Schreiber, F.R. *Sybil*. New York: Warner Books, 1973.   *B*

Schreiber, M.D. "The Phenomenological World of the Child Abused Rapist: Six Case Studies." *Dissertation Abstracts International* 39 (5-A): 2762, 1978.   *B,E,G*

Phenomenological study, self-perceptions, and development of integrative typologies and treatment approach and case studies of child-abused rapists.

Schuker, E. "A Treatment Program for Rape Victims." *Alaska Medicine* 20 (1978):48–55.   *B*

The rape-intervention program at St. Luke's Hospital in New York City is described as a prototype hospital-based program for rape victims that can be established as part of the emergency service of a general hospital with high efficiency and minimal cost.

———. "Psychodynamics and Treatment of Sexual Assault Victims." *Journal of the American Academy of Psychoanalysis* 7 (1979):553–573.
                                                                       B,G

The role of psychodynamics in the treatment of sexual-assault victims is discussed.

Schulman, M.A. *Survey of Spousal Violence against Women in Kentucky*. Washington, D.C.: U.S. Superintendent of Documents, 1979. *A,H*

This study attempted to gauge the amount and nature of physical violence and abuse against spouses occurring in Kentucky households.

Schultz, L.G. "The Wife Assaulter." *Journal of Social Therapy* 6 (1960): 103–112.   *A,G,H*

This is a report on a series of cases in each of which a husband was convicted of assaulting his wife with intent to kill.

———. "The Victim Offender Relationship." *Crime and Delinquency* 14 (1968):135–141.   *H*

Victimology is the study of the degree and type of participation of the victim in the genesis or development of the offense.

———. "The Social Worker and the Treatment of Sex Victim." In *Human Sexuality and Social Work*, 174, 1972.   *B,C*
———. "The Child Sex Victim: Social, Psychological and Legal Perspectives." *Child Welfare* 52 (March 1973):147–157.   *B,E*
———. "The Child as a Sex Victim: Socio-Legal Perspectives." In *Rape Victimology*, chapter 15, 1975.   *B,E*
———. "Rape Is a Four Letter Word." *Etcetera*, March 1975, p. 65.   *G*
———. "Rape and Rape Attitudes on a College Campus." In *Rape Victimology*, 1975.   *G*
———. *Rape Victimology*. Springfield, Ill.: Charles C Thomas, 1975. *G,H*

Seventeen reprinted articles and two original pieces by the editor dealing with personal accounts by rape victims; social, legal, and medical aspects of victimization; the child as victim; and policy regarding rape victims.

———. "The Sexual Abuse of Children and Minors: A Bibliography." *Child Welfare* 58 (March 1979):147–163.   *B,E*

Presents a bibliography of works that examined the history of sexual abuse of children, normal sexual development of children and minors, forms of sexual abuse, treatment and prevention of sexual abuse, and the state of treatment of the problem.

Schulz, M.R. "Rape Is a Four Letter Word." *ETC* 32 (March 1975):65–69.
                                                                        G
Schuman, H. "Two Sources of Antiwar Sentiment in America." *American Journal of Sociology* 78 (1972):513–537.   *H*
Schur, E.M. *Labeling Deviant Behavior: Its Sociological Implications*. New York: Harper & Row, 1972.   *C,H*
Schuyler, M. "Battered Wives: An Emerging Social Problem." *Social Work* 21 (November 1976):488–491.   *A,C*

Considers that the isolation of the battered wife is a result of society's failure to assist her and proposes strategies for dealing with wife abuse.

Schwartz, B. "The Effect in Philadelphia of Pennsylvania's Increased Penalties for Rape and Attempted Rape." *Journal of Criminal Law, Criminology and Police Science* 59 (1968):509–515.   *C,G*

Compared rape incidents after increased penalties in Pennsylvania.

Schwartz, M.D., and T.R. Clear. "Feminism and Rape Law Reform." *Bulletin of the American Academy of Psychiatry and Law* 6 (1978):313– 321. F,G

Rape-law reforms are discussed in terms of the efforts of feminists to rewrite legislation so as to increase concern for the female victim.

———. "Toward a New Law on Rape." *Crime and Delinquency* 26 (1980): 129–151. F,G

A number of approaches to removing the unique obstacles in the path of the prosecution of the rapist are discussed.

Schwartz, S., and D.D. Mills. "Wife Beating: Crime and No Punishment." In *Femicide*, edited by C. Orlock. *Seattle Times*, 1975, pp. 6–7. A
Schwartzman, J. "The Individual, Incest, and Exogamy." *Psychiatry* 37 (May 1974):171–180. E

Contends that groups observing the incest taboo and exogamy have a selective advantage by producing more-adaptive individuals than would be the case without such practices.

Schweich, C. "New Protection against Sexual Harassment (Equal Employment Opportunity Commission Guidelines)." *McCalls* 107 (August 1980):60. D,F
Schwendinger. "Rape Myths: In Legal, Theoretical, and Everyday Practice." *Crime and Social Justice* 1 (1974):18. G
Schwing, L. "A Well Placed Kick." *The Furies*, May 1972, p. 5. C
———. "Women: Weak or Strong." *The Furies*, January 1973, p. 3. C
Scott, E.M. "The Sexual Offender." *International Journal of Offender Therapy and Comparative Criminology* 21 (1977):255–263. G,H

Discusses various types of sexual offenses, including exhibitionism, child molestation, incest, and rape.

Scott, J.P. *Aggression*. Chicago: University of Chicago Press, 1958. H
Scott, P.D. "Parents Who Kill Their Children." *Medicine, Science, and the Law* 13 (April 1973):120–126. E,G,H

The annual incidence of filicide by mothers and fathers in England and Wales leads to discussion on classification of the killers with particular emphasis on the difficulties associated with the criteria of motive and depression.

————. "Battered Wives." *British Journal of Psychiatry* 125 (November 1974):433–441.   *A*

Defines the battered wife as a woman who has suffered serious or repeated injury from the man with whom she lives.

————. "Conviction of Secondary Party for Rape Where Principal Acquitted." *Law Quarterly Review* 91 (1975):476.   *F,G*
Scott, R.L. "An Analysis of the Need Structures of Twenty Male Rapists." *Dissertation Abstracts International* 40 (7-B):3421-3422N, January 1980.
                                                                                         G
Scottish Women's Aid Federation. "Battered Women in Scotland: Your Rights and Where to Help." Edinburgh, 1977.   *A,B,F*
Scripcaru, G.H., and T. Pirozynski. "Victimological Incidents in Maladjusted Pathological Behavior." *Victimology: An International Journal* 2 (1977):81.   *H*

In a paper presented at the Second International Symposium on Victimology, held in Boston, September 1976, aspects of maladjusted pathologic behavior affecting the attitude of victims are described. Such an analysis is achieved by clinical examination interpreted through victimological theory.

Scroggs, J.R. "Penalties for Rape as a Function of Victim Provocativeness, Damage, and Resistance." *Journal of Applied Social Psychology* 6 (October/December 1976):360–368.   *G,H*

In two experiments, 235 undergraduates and 222 of their parents and grandparents responded to one of four cases of rape that they read by indicating how many years in prison the rapist should serve as a penalty. Male subjects gave significantly lower penalties when the victim did not resist, while women gave higher penalties when the victim did not resist; this interaction was significant for both crimes.

Scully, D., and P. Bart. "A Funny Thing Happened on the Way to the Orifice: Women in Gynecology Textbooks." In *Changing Women in a Changing Society*, edited by J. Huber, pp. 283–292. Chicago: University of Chicago Press, 1973.   *C,D,G*
Scutt, J.A. "Violence in the Family—A Collection of Conference Papers." 1980.   *B,H*

The contributions of participants at the Seminar on Children and Family Violence that took place in Australia from 26 November to 30 November 1979.

Sealy, A.P., and C.M. Wain. "Person Perception and Jurors' Decisions."
British Journal of Social and Clinical Psychology 19 (February 1980):7–
16. *C,F*

In an experiment on simulated juries, subjects (selected from among
persons eligible for jury service) recorded their impressions of the major
participants in the trial. Results are interpreted in terms of the simulta-
neous operation of the principles of consistency, salience, and postdecision
dissonance.

Search, G. "London: Battered Wives." *Ms.*, June 1974, pp. 24–27. *A*
———. "Scream Quietly." *Ms.*, August 1976, pp. 96–97. *A,F*

Progress report from Great Britain, Pizzey's group, Chiswick Women's
Aid, has taken over a second building to be used as a refuge, set up
twenty-one second-stage homes, received a donation for their own school,
held workshops, and anticipate a home for batterers. They also have produced a ninety-minute movie.

Sears, R.R. "The Relation of Early Socialization Experiences to Aggression
in Middle Childhood." *Journal of Abnormal Social Psychology* 63
(1961):466–492. *H*
Sears, R.E.; E.E. Maccoby; and H. Levin. *Patterns of Child Rearing*.
Evanston, Ill.: Row, Peterson, 1957. *B*
———. "The Sources of Aggression in the Home." In *Violence in the
Family*, edited by S.K. Steinmetz and M.A. Straus, pp. 240–246. *H*

A trait like the tendency to be aggressive or violent can be acquired in many
different ways. The use of physical punishment as a causal factor in producing aggressiveness is particularly interesting because it is so often used with
the intent of controlling the child's behavior and aggressiveness and teaching him not to be aggressive.

Sebba, L. "The Requirement of Corroboration in Sex Offenses." In *Victimology*, edited by I. Drapkin and E. Viano. Lexington, Mass.: Lexington Books, D.C. Heath and Company, 1974. *B*
———. "The Victim's Role in the Penal Process: The Need for a Theoretical Orientation." *Victimology: An International Journal* 2 (1977):81.
H

In a paper presented at the Second International Symposium on Victimology, held in Boston, September 1976, the role of the victim in the penal
process is discussed as a first step toward providing a theoretical framework
that reconciles victimology with prevailing trends in penal philosophy. An
attempt is made to synthesize the historical and contemporary ideologies,

suggesting alternative models of the penal process to take into account the
roles of both offender and victim.

See. "No Woman Is Immune." *Today's Health*, October 1975, p. 30.   *A*
Seebohm Committee. "Local Authority and Allied Social Services." 1968.
                                                                    B
Segal, J. "Violent Men—Embattled Women." *Cosmopolitan*, May 1976,
    pp. 238–241.   *A*

> This article examines the complex emotional dynamics that can lead a man
> to beat his wife. The complex motivations behind a woman's apparent
> acceptance of abuse are discussed.

Segner, L.L. "Two Studies of the Incest Taboo: I. Sexual Activity of Mice
    as a Function of Familiarity. II. A Cross-Cultural Investigation of the
    Correlates of Incest in Myth." *Dissertation Abstracts International* 29
    (2-B), 796, 1968.   *E*
Segovia, A. "Shelters—Short Term Needs." Rockville, Md.: NCJRS Mi-
    crofiche Program, 1978.   *B*

> The history and program of a San Francisco, California, shelter for bat-
> tered wives, primarily serving Mexican-Americans and other minorities,
> are described.

Seiden, A.M. "Expression of Aggression by Women. Continuing Medical
    Education: Syllabus and Proceedings in Summary Form. Washington,
    D.C.: American Psychiatric Association, 1978, p. 172.   *H*

> A summary of a paper read at the 131st Annual Meeting of the American
> Psychiatric Association, held in Atlanta, May 1978, is presented. Ways in
> which inhibition of aggression and sexuality in women are interrelated and
> typically handled by indirect forms of mastery or expression are discussed.

Seidmon, B.L. "Out of My Practice: The Marriage, Family, and Child
    Counselor and Public Education." *Marriage and Family Counselors
    Quarterly* 12 (1978):47–49.   *B,C*

> Ways of gaining public support and recognition for marriage, family, and
> child counselors through participation in public education are discussed. It
> is proposed that counselors create programs of public training and seek a
> place in public education to encourage better mental health for individuals
> and families as a continuing process.

Selby, J.W.; L.G. Calhoun; and T.A. Brock. "Sex Differences in the Social
    Perception of Rape Victims." *Personality and Social Psychology Bulle-
    tin* 3 (Summer 1977):412–415.   *G*

Two investigations examined sex differences in the way rape victims are perceived. Sex differences consistent with the first study were found, with men viewing the victim as playing a greater causal role in the rape episode than women.

Selby, J.W.; L.G. Calhoun; and A. Cann. "Effect of Perceived Motivation on the Assignment of Blame and Punishment to Rapists by Female Respondents." *Journal of Community Psychology* 7 (October 1979): 357–359. *G,H*

Examined the assignment of blame in rape episodes made by eighty-two female undergraduates. Ratings differed because the rape was sexually or aggressively motivated.

Selby, J.W.; L.G. Calhoun; J.M. Jones; and L. Matthews. "Families of Incest—A Collation of Clinical Impressions." *International Journal of Social Psychiatry* 26 (1980):1. *E*

Seligman, C.; J. Brickman; and D. Koulack. "Rape and Physical Attractiveness: Assignment of Responsibility to Victims." *Journal of Personality* 45 (December 1977):554–563. *G*

Investigated the hypothesis that rape might be a situation in which being physically very attractive would not be advantageous to the victim. In the mugging and robbery conditions, attractive and unattractive female victims were not differentially perceived with regard to likelihood of being attacked and of provoking the incident. Results are discussed in terms of attribution theory.

Seligman, M. "Fall into Helplessness." *Psychology Today* 5 (1973):43–48. *C,H*

———. *Helplessness: On Depression, Development, and Death.* San Francisco: W.H. Freeman, 1975. *H*

———. "Submissive Death: Giving Up on Life." *Psychology Today* 6 (1974):80–85. *H*

Seligman, M., and D.S. Hiroto. "Generality of Learned Helplessness in Man." *Journal of Personality and Social Psychology* 31 (1975):311–327. *H*

Seligman, M., and W.P. Miller. "Depression and the Perception of Reinforcement." *Journal of Abnormal Psychology* 82 (1973):62–73. *H*

———. "Depression and Learned Helplessness in Man." *Journal of Abnormal Psychology* 84 (1975):228–238. *H*

Seligman, M., and R.A. Rosellini. "Frustration and Learned Helplessness." *Journal of Experimental Psychology, Animal Behavior Processes* 104 (1975):149–157. *H*

Seligman, M.; R.A. Rosellini; and M.J. Kozak. "Learned Helplessness in

the Rat: Time, Course, Immunization, and Reversibility." *Journal of Comparative and Physiological Psychology* 88 (1975):542–547.   H
————. "Rape." *Psychology Today*, January 1975, p. 71.   G
Selkin, J. "Protecting Personal Space: Victim and Resister Reactions to Assaultive Rape." *Journal of Community Psychology* 6 (1978):263– 268.   H

> Differences in emotional response between rape victims and rape resisters with regard to their retrospective view of how they felt during sexual assault were studied.

Sellitiz, C. et al. *Research Methods in Social Relations*. New York: Holt, Rinehart, & Winston, 1959.   B
Seltman. *Women in Antiquity*. London, 1956.   B
Sendi, I., and P.G. Blomgren. "A Comparative Study of Predictive Criteria in the Predisposition of Homicidal Adolescents." *American Journal of Psychiatry* 32 (1975):423–427.   H
Sennett, R. "The Brutality of Modern Families." In *Marriage and Families*, edited by M.Z. Lopata, pp. 81–90. New York: D. Van Nostrand, 1973.
                                                                      C,H
Separovic, Z. "The Victim and Society: New Problems Posed by the Advancement of Medicine." *Victimology: An International Journal* 2 (1977):81–82.   H

> In a paper presented at the Second International Symposium on Victimology, held in Boston, September 1976, borderline questions between law and medicine are posed from a victimological viewpoint.

Service Guide for Professionals Who Assist Victims of Rape, Child Abuse and Domestic Violence. Chicago: Citizens Committee for Victim Assistance, no date.   B,G

> A service guide is provided by the Illinois Law Enforcement Commission to assist law-enforcement, medical, and social-service professionals in helping victims of rape, child abuse, and domestic violence.

Sewell, E.R. "Attributions about Physical Assault: The Role of Sex of Victim, Victim/Assailant Relationship and Sex of Subject." *Dissertation Abstracts International* 39 (11):5662-B, 1979.   H

> The roles of sex of victim and the victim/assailant relationship in the attribution of responsibility for physical assault were investigated via analysis of responsibility attributions for a fictitious assault of 156 men and 172 women.

"Sexual Abuse (Symposium)." *American Journal of Orthopsychiatry* 49
(October 1979):634–708.   G
Sexual Abuse of Children: Child Victims of Incest. Denver, Colo.: Ameri-
can Humane Association, Children's Division, 1968.   E
Sexual Abuse of Children. Woman. Videocassette, optical, 29 mins. Wash-
ington, D.C.: Public Television Library, 1979.   E

Features social workers Linda Sanford and Florence Rush as they discuss
the incidence of sexual abuse of children by family members and neighbors.
Explains how to inform a child about molestation, and discusses problems
in identifying the abuser. Appropriate for adult audiences.

Sex and Violence. Granada Television Products, Benchmark Films Incorporated Distributors, 1975.   A,E,H

For feminists, defending women against rape has become a major crusade.
Volunteer woman workers in two national organizations—the Feminist
Alliance against Rape and Women Organized against Rape—operate rape-
crisis centers with telephone hot lines for victims and see raped women
admitted to hospitals to support and advise them of their medical and legal
rights.

*Sexual Assault—A Manual for Law Enforcement, Medical, Social Service.
Volunteer and Prosecutorial Personnel and Agencies.* Hennepin County
Attorney, Minneapolis, Minnesota, 1978.   B,G

This manual deals with sexual assault and what has been and can be done
by law-enforcement, medical, social-service, volunteer, and prosecutorial
personnel in Hennepin County, Minnesota, to deter sexual-assault crimes.

"Sexual Assaults on Children." *British Medical Journal* 2 (1963):1146.B,E
"Sexual Crimes and the Medical Examiner: Interview with Milton Hel-
pern." *Medical Aspects of Human Sexuality* 8 (April 1974):161–168.
                                                               E,G,H

Presents the transcript of an interview with the former chief medical
examiner of New York City, who discusses the role of the medical examiner
in handling sex crimes, the relationship between sex and violent crimes, the
types of physical evidence used to determine the intent and nature of the
crime, and possible reasons for increases in attitudes toward relationship
between sex and violent crimes and increase in rape incidence and medical
examiner's role in handling sex crimes.

"Sexual Harassment: How to Handle it on Business Trips." *Glamour* 78
(September 1980):100.   D

"Sexual Harassment Lands Companies in Court." *Business Week*, 1 October 1979, p. 120.   D
"Sexually Assaulted Children." *British Medical Journal* 2 (1962):973.   E
"Sexual Survey #11: Current Thinking on Rape." *Medical Aspects of Human Sexuality* 12 (1978):125–127.   B

> A survey about professional attitude toward various aspects of rape was conducted, and after 500 replies from psychiatrists were received, the results were tabulated in an effort to discover the state of psychiatric knowledge and concern about rape victims.

Seyfert. "Help for the Rape Victim." *Parade*, 26 May 1974, p. 13.   G
Sgroi, S.M. "Sexual Molestation of Children: The Last Frontier in Child Abuse." *Children Today* 4 (May/June 1975):18–21.   E
Shaffer, J.A., ed. *Violence: Award-Winning Essays in the Council for Philosophical Studies Competition*. New York: David McKay, 1971. *B,H*
Shainess, N. "Vulnerability to Violence: Masochism as Process." *American Journal of Psychotherapy* 33 (1979):174–189.   H

> The view that a certain personality trait or psychological difficulty may relate to vulnerability to violence is examined from the standpoint of the female victim. The recent reported increase of violence toward women has elicited much interest among self-help women's groups and the police.

Shamroy, J.A. "A Perspective on Childhood Sexual Abuse." *Social Work* 25 (1980):128–131.   E

> The sharp increases in incidence of childhood sexual abuse reported are discussed, and the procedures used by a children's hospital for identifying these children and the follow-up services necessary for their protection and emotional adjustment are reviewed.

Shanas, E. et al. *Old People in Three Industrial Societies*. New York: Atherton Press, 1968.   H
Shanas, E., and G. Streib. *Proceedings of Symposium on Family Intergeneration Relations and Social Structure*, 1963. London: Tavistock. Reprinted as *Social Structure and the Family: Generational Relations*. Englewood Cliffs, N.J.: Prentice-Hall, 1965.   B
Shatter the Silence. Los Angeles: S-L Film Productions.   *A,H*

> The film tells the story of Marrianne, a teenager who is the victim of incest with her father. It traces her story, the feelings of fear and humiliation she undergoes, and her subsequent fear of male relationships as she grows up.

Shaw, B. "She Killed Her Husband, but Supporters like Valerie Harper Say She was the Real Victim." *People*, 4 August 1980, pp. 66–67.   A

Shaw, D.A. "Family Maintenance Schedules for Deviant Behavior." *Dissertation Abstracts International* 32 (9-13):5459–5460, March 1972. *B*

Shearer. "Defend Yourself with a Whistle." *Parade*, 2 June 1974, p. 10.
A,G

Sheehy, G. "Nice Girls Don't Get into Trouble." *New York*, 15 February 1971, p. 26. *A,G*

Sheldon. "Rape: A Solution." *Women: A Journal of Liberation* 3:22 (n.d.). *B,G*

Sheleff, L. "The Impact of Victimology on Criminal Law." *Victimology: An International Journal* 2 (1977):82. *H*

In a paper presented at the Second International Symposium on Victimology, held in Boston, September 1976, victimological challenges to criminal law and procedure are discussed. The potential diminution of the differentiation between criminal and civil law with the accent not on punishment of the criminal but on reconciliation between criminal and victim is foreseen.

Sheleff, L., and D. Shechor. "Victimological Aspects of Bystander Involvement." *Victimology: An International Journal* 2 (1977):82–83. *H*

In a paper presented at the Second International Symposium on Victimology, held in Boston, September 1976, the role of the bystander in victimology is analyzed. Possibilities by which a bystander can be considered a victim are explored.

Shelley, S. "Why Most Wife-Beaters Escape Punishment." *Detroit Magazine*, 27 August 1972, pp. 6–8. *A*

Shelton, W.R. "A Study of Incest." *International Journal of Offender Therapy and Comparative Criminology* 19 (1979):139–153. *B,E*

Presents four case studies of incest drawn from a total sample of 2,500 seen during the author's thirteen years of experience in correctional settings. The four cases are the only ones from among the 2,500 that involved overt sexual intercourse between a parent and his actual full child.

Shengold, L. "Some Reflections on a Case of Mother/Adolescent Son Incest." *International Journal of Psycho-Analysis* 61 (1980):461–476.
E

A rare case of mother-adolescent-son incest is presented. Reasons why father-daughter incest appears to be more common than mother-son incest are suggested.

Sheperd, M. "Morbid Jealousy: Some Clinical and Social Aspects of a Psychiatric Symptom." *Journal of Mental Science*, July 1961, pp. 687–704. *B*

The clinical features and the concomitant social problems of morbid jealousy are discussed. Illustrative case material is presented separately in the summarized case histories that have been selected from those of patients who have been encountered in the routine practice of one London teaching hospital and a nearby metropolitan observation unit.

Sheppard, Giancinti & Tjaden. "Rape Reduction: A City-Wide Program." In *Sexual Assault*, edited by M. Walker and S. Brodsky, p. 169. 1976.
B,G

Sherif, C.W. "Comment on Ethical Issues in Malamuth, Heim, and Feshbach's Sexual Responsiveness of College Students to Rape Depictions: Inhibitory and Disinhibitory Effects." *Journal of Personality and Social Psychology* 38 (1980):409–412.   *B,G*

> Comments on the ethical issues involved in recent research into norm violations are presented. The research investigated sexual responsiveness of college students to rape depictions and focused on inhibitory and disinhibitory effects.

Sherman, J.A. "The Coatlicue Complex: A Source of Irrational Reactions against Women." *Trans Am Journal* 5 (April 1975).   *B*

Sherman, J.A., and F. Denmark, eds. *Psychology of Women: Future Direction Research*. New York: Psychological Dimensions, forthcoming. *B*

Shinder, D. *Mayhem on Women*. San Francisco: Ombudswoman Press, 1972.   *G,H*

Sholevar, G.P. "A Family Therapist Looks at the Problem of Incest." *Bulletin of the American Academy of Psychiatry and the Law* 3 (March 1975):25–31.   *B,E*

> Discusses the problem of incest from the viewpoint of tradition and of dynamic family interaction. Traditionally, incest between father and daughter has been viewed as a weakness in the father. Investigation of such cases has not included evaluation of the whole family and the possibility of a disordered family system.

Shopper, M. "Psychiatric and Legal Aspects of Statutory Rape, Pregnancy, and Abortion in Juveniles." *Journal of Psychiatry and Law* 1 (Fall 1973):275–295.   *G*

> Considers that although the law recognizes the psychological immaturity of the female minor by passage of statutory-rape laws, it has failed to protect her from the adverse psychological consequences related to unwanted pregnancy.

Shore, B.K. "Examination of Critical Process and Outcome Factors in Rape." Unpublished paper, 1979. Pittsburgh: University of Pittsburgh. *B,G*

Data are presented that suggest that the impact of the rape event must be viewed within the context of the total life experience in order to assess its likely consequences.

Shore, M.F. et al. "Patterns of Masochism: An Empirical Study." *British Journal of Medical Psychology* 44 (1971):59–65.   B

The purpose of this study was to clarify confusion in the literature and in clinical practice about the nature of masochism.

Short, J.F., and M.E. Wolfgang. "On Collective Violence." *Annals* 391 (September 1970):1–8.   H
Shotland, R.L., and M.K. Straw. "Bystander Response to an Assault: When a Man Attacks a Woman." 1976.   G

From newspaper accounts it appears that when women were attacked and bystanders did not intervene, frequently the bystanders justified their inactivity by stating that they thought it was a lover's quarrel.

Shubin, S. "Seductive Psychiatrists." *Today in Psychiatry* 4 (1978):1–4. G

The ethics of the doctor-patient relationship with regard to sexual behavior are discussed in reference to the work of Dr. Virginia Davidson.

Sidel, R. *Women and Cchild Care in China.* New York: Hill and Wang, 1972.   H
Siegel, A.E. "Film-Mediated Fantasy Aggression and Strength of Aggressive Drive." *Child Development* 27 (1956):365–378.   H
"Signs of Rape." *Playboy*, May 1974, p. 50.   G
Silber, A. "Childhood Seduction, Parental Pathology and Hysterical Symptomatology—The Genesis of an Altered State of Consciousness." *International Journal of Psycho-Analysis* 60 (1979):109–116.   E
Silver, B. et al. "Does Violence Breed Violence? Contributions from a Study of the Child Abuse Syndrome." *American Journal of Psychiatry* 126 (September 1969):404–407.   B,H

A longitudinal study and review of family backgrounds over three generations supports the themes that violence breeds violence and that a child who experiences violence as a child has the potential of becoming a violent member of society in the future. The authors believe that the physician has a critical role and responsibility in interrupting this cycle of violence.

Silverman, D.C. "Sexual Harassment: Working Women's Dilemma." *Quest: A Feminist Quarterly* 3 (Winter 1977):15–24.   D
———. "Sharing the Crisis of Rape: Counseling the Mates and Families of

Victims." *American Journal of Orthopsychiatry* 48 (January 1978):166–
173.   G

The involvement of mates and family members in counseling interventions
designed to help victims of rape in their post traumatic reconstitutive efforts
is critical.

Silverman, L.H.; J.S. Kwawer; C. Wolitzky; and M. Coron. "An Experimental Study of Aspects of the Psychoanalytic Theory of Male Homosexuality." *Journal of Abnormal Psychology* 82 (August 1973):178–
188.   H

Tested psychoanalytic dynamic propositions through the subliminal exposure of drive-related stimuli, using two groups of thirty-six male homosexuals and heterosexuals.

Silverman, M.G. "Relations of Production, the Incest and Menstrual
Tabus among Precolonial Barnabans and Gilbertese." *Antropologica*
19 (1977):89–98.   E
Silverman, R.A., and J. Teevan. *Crime in Canadian Society*. Toronto:
Butterworth, 1975.   B

This book brings together a disparate literature of criminological research
and theory as it specifically relates to Canada.

Simari, C.G., and D. Baskin. "Incest—Exploring the Myths." *Cornell
Journal of Social Relations* 14 (1979):155.   E
Simmel, G. *Conflict and the Web of Group Affiliations*. New York: Free
Press, 1955.   C
———. "How Is Society Possible?" In *Essay on Sociology, Philosophy
and Aesthetics*, edited by K.H.Wolff. New York: Harper Torchbooks,
1959.   C
Simon, R.J. "Use of the Semantic Differential in Research on the Jury."
Journalism Quarterly 45 (Winter 1968):670–676.   B

Reports results of the use of the semantic differential to assess the reaction
of jurors to a defendant accused of incest in a criminal trial.

———. "American Women and Crime." *Annals of the American Academy
of Science* 423 (January 1976):31–46.   C
Simpson, K. "Special Cases: Rape Victim's Plight Gets Wide Attention
from Police, Courts." *Wall Street Journal*, 14 July 1975, p. 1.   G
———. *Police—The Investigation of Violence*. Plymouth, England: Mac-
Donald and Evans Limited, 1978.   H

An overview of the investigation of violent crime covers typical injuries, interpreting bloodstains, and investigative considerations for the various types of violence, with reference to forensic medicine.

Singer, J.G., and M Bard. "Community Consultation in the Doctoral Education of Clinical Psychologists." *Clinical Psychologist*, Winter 1969, pp. 79–83.   B

Singer, J.L. *The Control of Aggression and Violence*. New York: Academic Press, 1971.   H

Singer, M. "Perspective on Incest as Child Abuse." *Australian and New Zealand Journal of Criminology* 12 (1979):3–17.   E

Singh, A. "Note on Rape and Social Structure." *Psychological Reports* 41 (August 1977):134.   G

Tested K. Svastloga's hypothesis that rape is more common in communities where the ratio of women to men is relatively low, using data obtained from the publications of the statistics of Canada.

Singh, K. "Why They Fled Pakistan—And Won't Go Back." *The New York Times Magazine*, 1 August 1971, pp. 12–15.   B

Siskind, V. Bias in Estimating the Frequency of Incest. 38 *Annual of Human Genetics* (1975):355–359.   E

Skelton, C.A., and B.R. Burkhart. "Sexual Assault: Determinants of Victim Disclosure." *Criminal Justice and Behavior* 7 (1980):229–236.
                                                                                          A,E,G

The social and attitudinal determinants of victim willingness to define and/or report a sexual assault as a rape to various groups were studied.

Sklar, R.B. "The Criminal Law and the Incest Offender: A Case for Decriminalization." *Bulletin of the American Academy for Psychiatry and the Law* 7 (1979):69–77.   E

Society's rationale for criminalizing incest is examined, and the growing movement for decriminalization is discussed.

Skogan, W.G. *Sample Surveys of the Victims of Crime*. Cambridge, Mass.: Ballinger, 1977.   H

A collection of reports on the value of the sample survey as a research tool in victimology is presented.

Skolnick, A., and J. H. Skolnick. *Intimacy, Family, and Society*. Boston: Little, Brown and Company, 1974.   B,C

Skolnick, J.H. *Justice without Trial: Law Enforcement in Democratic Society*. New York: Wiley & Sons, 1969.   F
Skrocki, M.R. "Sexual Pressure on the Job." *McCalls* 105 (March 1978):43.
                                                                           D
Slaby, A.E. "The Team Approach to the Treatment of the Rape Victim." *Connecticut Medicine* 42 (1978):135–136.   B,G

> The team approach to the treatment of the rape victim is discussed with attention to the varied needs of rape victims and of practitioners dealing with rape.

Slater, C. "Where Can a Battered Wife Run To?" *Detroit News*, 27 July 1975.   A
Sloane, P., and E. Karpinski. "Effects of Incest on the Participants." *American Journal of Orthopsychiatry* 12 (October 1942):66–67.   E
Slovenko, R. "The Marital Rape Exemption." *Victimology* 4 (1979):178–181.   G

> The modification or elimination of the marital-rape exemption, which states that a husband cannot be prosecuted in the case of forced sexual relations with his wife, is examined.

Smale, G.J., and H.L. Spickenheuer. "Feelings of Guilt and Need for Retaliation in Victims of Serious Crimes against Property and Persons." *Victimology* 4 (1979):75–85.   H

> The intensity of feelings of guilt and need for retaliation among victims of violence and serious crimes against property are described.

Smart, C., and B. Smart. *Women, Sexuality and Social Control*. Boston: Routledge and Kegan Paul, 1978.   C

> A collection of papers that is a product of sociolegal work from a feminist perspective is presented.

Smith. "The Rape Victim's Dilemma: How to React?" *Washington Post*, 2 December 1972.   G
Smith, A.C. "Violence." *British Journal of Psychiatry* 134 (May 1979):528–529.   H

> Briefly reviews three papers on violence presented at the Royal College of Psychiatrists.

Smith, A.M. "Complainants Condition in Rape Cases." *Medicine, Science, and the Law* 19 (1979):25–29.   G

Smith, D.L.; R. Durant; and T.J. Carter. "Social Integration, Victimization, and Anomia." *Criminology* 16 (1978):395–402.   H

>   The results of previous victimization research studies suggesting that crimes
>   may cause interaction problems for the victims were tested.

Smith, E.R.; M.M. Feree; and F.D. Miller. "A Short Scale of Attitudes toward Feminism." *Representative Research in Social Psychology*, no. 6 (1975):51–56.   B

Smith, G., and R. Harris. "Ideologies of Need and the Organization of Social Service Departments." *British Journal of Social Work* 2 (1972): 27.   B

Smith, M. "I Was a Married Women with a Boss Who Got Too Friendly." *Ladies Home Journal* 98 (January 1981):28.   D

Smith, S., and S. Noble. "Battered Children and Their Parents." *New Society* 15 (November 1973):393.   C,E,H

Smith, S.M.; R. Hansen; and S. Noble. "Parents of Battered Babies. A Controlled Study." *British Medical Journal* 4 (November 1973):388–391.   C,H

Smith, T. "Early Life Termed Bitter." *The New York Times*, 6 June 1968.
                                                                           E

Smithyman, S.D. "The Undetected Rapist." *Dissertation Abstracts International* 39 (6):3058-B, 1978.   G

>   Male rapists who had escaped contact with the criminal-justice system were
>   interviewed via anonymous telephone contact, and a profile of the un-
>   detected rapist was constructed.

Snell, J.E.; R.J. Rosenwald; and A. Roby. "The Wifebeater's Wife: A Study of Family Interaction." *Archives of General Psychiatry* 11 (August 1964):107–113.   A,B

Snelling. "What Is Non Consent (in Rape)?" In *Rape Victimology*, edited by L. Schultz. 1975.   G

Snelling. "What Is Rape?" In *Rape Victimology*, edited by L. Schultz. 1975.
                                                                           G

Sociological Resources for the Social Studies. *Divorce in the U.S.* Episode in Sociological Inquiry Series. Boston: Allyn and Bacon, 1972.   H

Solomon, T. "History and Demography of Child Abuse." *Pediatrics* 51 (April 1973):773–776.   E

Sommers, T. *The Not So Helpless Female*. New York: David McKay, 1973.   G

Soothill, K.L. "How Rape Is Reported." *New Society* 32 (1975):702.F,G

Soothill, K.L., and T.C. Gibbens. "Recidivism of Sexual Offenders: A Reappraisal." *British Journal of Criminology* 18 (1978):267–276.B,H

The recidivism of sexual offenders is appraised, and the limitations of the knowledge on the subject are emphasized.

Sorel, G. *Reflections on Violence*. New York: Collier, 1961. French original, 1908.   *H*

Sorensen, R. *Adolescent Sexuality in Contemporary America*. New York: World, 1973.   *E*

"Southern Violence. In *Violence in America*, edited by T.R. Gurr. New York: Bantam Books, 1969.   *H*

Southwest Educational Development Lab. *Parenting in 1975: A Listing from PMIC*. Washington, D.C.: National Institute of Education, EDRS, 1975.   *B*

Sparks, C.H. "Program Evaluation of a Community Rape Prevention Program." *Dissertation Abstracts International* 40 (8):4034-B, 1980. *B,G*

Effects of a rape-prevention program on women in the program and on women in the general community were studied over a year.

Spencer, J. "Father-Daughter Incest: A Clinical View from the Corrections Field." *Child Welfare* 57 (November 1978):581–590.   *B,E*

In father-daughter incest, the father is presented as either an extremely religious person, an alcoholic, or insecure in his masculinity.

Spencer, J.C. "Review of the Literature on Multi-Problem Families." In *The Multi-Problem Family*, edited by B. Schleisinger.   *B,C*

Spencer, J.M., and J.P. Zammit. "Family Dispute Services." *Arbitration Journal* 32 (1977):111–122.   *A,B*

Spieker, G. "Family Violence and Alcohol Abuse." Paper presented at the twenty-fourth International Institute on the Prevention and Treatment of Alcoholism, 1978.   *H*

Empirical studies are reviewed in an examination of child abuse and wife abuse in relation to alcohol use and abuse.

Spielberger, C.D. *Current Topics in Clinical and Community Psychology*. New York: Academic Press, 1970.   *B*

Spinnetta, J.J., and D. Rigler. "The Child Abusing Parent: A Psychological Review." *Psychological Bulletin* 77 (April 1972):296–304.   *B,E*

Spitz, R.A. "Hospitalism." In *The Family, Its Structure and Function*, edited by R.L. Coser. New York: St. Martin's Press, 1964.   *B*

Spitzner, J.A., and D.H. McGee. "Family Crisis Intervention Training, Diversion and the Prevention of Violence." *Police Chief*, October 1975, pp. 252–253.   *C*

Spodak, M.K.; A.Z. Fakk; and J.R. Rappeport. "The Hormonal Treatment of Paraphiliacs with Depo-Provera." *Criminal Justice and Behavior* 5 (December 1978):304–314.   H

Reviews a newer and more-reversible form of castration: chemical castration by use of the female hormone medroxyprogesterone acetate (depo-provera) and the new antiandrogen, cyproterone acetate.

"Spouse Abuse: A Special Issue." *Victimology: An International Journal* 2 (1978).   A,B

The sixteen articles included in this special issue of *Victimology* make a significant contribution to the study of domestic violence.

Spouse Abuse in the Legal System—Selected Readings. Washington, D.C.: Center for Women Policy Studies, 1978.   A,B
Sprey, J. "The Family as a System of Conflict." *Journal of Marriage and the Family* 31 (November 1969):699–706.   C
———. "On the Management of Conflict in Families." In *Violence in the Family*, edited by S.K. Steinmetz and M.A. Straus. 1974.   B

In this paper, Sprey applies a number of the findings of ethologists to the analysis of conflict in the human family.

Stachura, J.S., and R.H. Teske. *Spouse Abuse in Texas—A Special Report*. Huntsville, Tex.: Sam Houston State University, 1979.   B

Mail-survey methods were used to examined the scope and nature of spouse abuse in Texas. The study's purpose was to alert citizens and appropriate agencies of the problem.

Stafford, J. "Battered Women and the National Women's Aid Federation." Paper presented at the American Sociological Association Conference, New York, 1976.   A,B
Stahly, G.B. "A Review of Select Literature of Spousal Violence." *Victimology* 2 (1977–1978):591–607.   A,B

Reviews empirical data concerning the frequency, demography, and interpersonal process variables related to spouse violence.

Star, B. "Battered Wives." *Society* 14 (1977):92.   A
———. "Comparing Battered and Non-Battered Women." *Victimology* 3 (1978):32–44.   A

Compares selected psychosocial aspects of fifty-seven battered and non-battered women who sought refuge at Haven House, a shelter in the Los Angeles area.

———. "Family Violence and the Criminal Justice System." Paper presented at Interagency Workshop, Fourteenth Annual Conference, 1979.
C,F

This article discusses family violence and how the criminal-justice system can better deal with the problem.

———. "Patterns in Family Violence." *Social Casework* 61 (June 1980): 339–346.   *H*

A generic approach to the study of family violence reveals similarities among assaulter characteristics, victim characteristics, and family interactions underlying all forms of family violence.

Star, B., and W. Frazier. "Medicine and Patriarchal Violence—The Social Construction of a Private Event." *International Journal of Health Services* 9 (1979):461–493.   *H*

This report describes the pattern of abuse associated with battering and evaluates the contribution of the medical system and broader social forces to this abuse.

Star, B.; "Psychosocial Aspects of Wife Battering." *Social Casework: Journal of Contemporary Socal Work* 60 (1979):479–487.   *A*

Interview, personality, and demographic data were examined in a voluntary sample of fifty-seven women living in shelters for battered women.

Stark, R. *Police Riots: Collective Violence and Law Enforcement.* Belmont, Calif.: Wadsworth Publishing, 1972.   *H*
Stark, R., and J. McEvoy. "Middle Class Violence."*Psychology Today* 4 (1970):107–112.   *H*

The question is raised: How aggressive are we toward each other? Results show the percentages.

State of California. Senate. Health and Welfare Committee. Subcommittee on Nutrition and Human Needs. *Hearing on Marital and Family Violence. Reporter's transcript of Proceedings.* 1975.   *H*
State of California. Senate. Subcommittee on Nutrition and Human Needs. *Testimony of G. Mascone on Family Violence.* 21 July 1975.   *H*

State of California. Senate. Committee on Judicial System and Judicial Process. Subcommittee on Sex Crimes of the Assembly Interim. *Preliminary report no. 26*. 1950. **B**

Stechler, G. "Facing the Problem of the Sexually Abused Child." *New England Journal of Medicine* 302 (1980):348–349. **E**

A brief overview of sexual child abuse is presented.

Stedman, B. "The Right of Husbands to Chastise Wife." *Virginia Law Register* 3 (1917):241. **A**

Steel, R., et al. "The Story of Squeaky." *Newsweek*, 15 September 1975, pp. 18–19. **G**

Steele. "The Strange Case of Inez Garcia." *Majority Reporter*, 8 February 1975, p. 3. **G**

Steele, B.F., and C.B. Pollock. "A Psychiatric Study of Parents Who Abuse Infants and Small Children." In *The Battered Child*, edited by R.E. Helfer and C.H. Kempe. Chicago: University of Chicago Press, 1968. **E**

Stein, M.L. *Lovers, Friends, Slaves*. New York: Putnam's, 1974. **A**

Stein, R. "The Incest Wound." *Spring* 73 (1973):133–141. **E**

Suggests that the split between love and sex is a direct consequence of the incest wound.

———. *Incest and Human Love: The Betrayal of the Soul in Psychotherapy*. Baltimore: Penguin Press, 1974. **E**

Challenges Freud's central assumption that human development depends on the repression of the incestuous drives.

Stein, S. *Other People*. New York: Harcourt Brace Jovanovich, 1978. **G**

A novel is presented that centers around a young woman who was a rape victim and three men who play important roles in her life.

Steinem, G. "But What Do We Do with Our Rage?" *Ms.*, May 1975, p. 51. **C,H**

Steiner, C. "Power." *Issues in Radical Therapy*, Summer 1975, p. 7. **C**

Steinfels, "Rape Reality, Rape Fantasy." *Commonwealth* 102 (1975):554. **G**

Steinmann, A., and D.J. Fox. *The Male Dilemma*. New York: Jason Aronson, 1974. **C**

Steinmetz, S.K. "Occupation and Physical Punishment: A Response to Straus." *Journal of Marriage and the Family* 33 (1971):664–666. **H**

————. "Family Backgrounds of Political Assassins." Paper presented at the American Orthopsychiatric Association Annual Meeting, 1973. *H*
————. "Occupational Environment and Its Relationship to Physical Punishment." In *Violence in the Family*, edited by S.K. Steinmetz and M.A. Straus. New York: Harper & Row, 1974.   *H*
————. "The Sexual Context of Social Research." *American Sociologist* 9 (August 1974):111–116.   *B*
————. "Intra-Familial Patterns of Conflict Resolution: Husband/Wife; Parent/Child; Sibling/Sibling." Ph.D. dissertation, Case Western Reserve University, 1975.   *E,H*
————. *The Cycle of Violence: Assertive, Aggressive and Abusive Family Interaction*. New York: Praeger, 1977.   *H*
————. "The Relationship between Disciplinary Techniques and the Development of Aggressiveness, Dependency and Conscience." In *Contemporary Theories on the Family*, edited by W. Burr. New York: Free Press, 1977.   *H*
————. "The Use of Force for Resolving Family Conflict: The Training Ground for Abuse." *Family Coordinator* 26 (1977):19–26.   *C,H*
————. "Wife Beating, Husband Beating—A Comparison of the Use of Physical Violence between Spouses to Resolve Marital Fights." In *Abused and Battered Wife*, edited by R. Maria. New York: Van Nostrand Reinhold, 1977.   *A,H*
————. Family Violence—The Silent Crime. Contemporary Corrections and the Behavioral Sciences Interagency Workshop, Proceedings of the annual conference, 1978.   *H*

Data indicating the extent of family violence in the United States are cited, some causes are suggested, and means for dealing with it are recommended.

————. "Overlooked Aspects of Family Violence—Battered Husbands, Battered Siblings, and Battered Elderly." Washington, D.C.: U.S. Congress House Committee on Science and Technology, 1978. *C,H*

This paper contends that child abuse and battered women represent only a small part of the problem of family violence. Examination of the problem of family-violence extensiveness may lead to effective societal responses.

————. "Reply to Pleck, Pleck, Grossman and Bart." *Victimology: An International Journal* 2 (1978):683–684.   *H*

A reply to criticism of Steinmetz' article on battered husbands is presented.

————. *Resource Booklet for Families in Crisis*. Wilmington: Delaware
Governor's Commission, 1978.   *B,C*

Dimensions of family violence are discussed in this resource booklet,
followed by a synopsis of Delaware, Pennsylvania, and Maryland law
pertaining to family offenses and lists of these states' family service.

————. "Services to Battered Women: Our Greatest Need. A Reply to
Field and Kirchner." *Victimology* 3 (1978):222–226.   *A,B*

A Reply to the 1978 critique by Field and Kirchner of Steinmetz' article on
the battered husband is presented.

————. "Violence between Family Members—A Review of the Recent
Literature." *Marriage and Family Review* 1 (May/June 1978):3–16. *H*

Recent literature on violence between family members in the United States
is reviewed with emphasis on the scope and nature of such violence and its
causes, prevention, treatment, and future.

————. "Violence in the Family—Testimony Prepared by the Coalition of
Family Organizations." *Domestic Violence*, 1978, 308–327.   *H*

Statistics on family violence and recommendations for its reduction are
presented in testimony to the Senate Subcommittee on Child and Human
Development by a specialist in family-violence issues.

————. Wife Beating: A Critique and Reformulation of Existing Theory."
Bulletin of the American Academy of Psychiatry and Law 6 (1978):322–
334.   *A,B*

The dynamics of wife abuse are examined.

————. "Violence Prone Families." *Annals of the New York Academy of
Sciences*, 20 June 1980, pp. 251–265.   *H*

This paper presents an overview of the characteristics of violence-prone
families. The frequency of domestic violence, sibling violence, child abuse,
and marital abuse are examined in relation to the social and psychological
characteristics of violence.

————. "Women and Violence: Victims and Perpetrators." *American
Journal of Psychotherapy* 34 (1980):334–350.   *A,H*

Women are examined as the victims and the perpetrators of violence, with a focus on violence within the family context.

————. "Fifty-Seven Families: Assertive, Aggressive, and Abusive Inter-action." Unpublished manuscript, University of Delaware, no date.
$\qquad$ A,H
Steinmetz, S.K., and M.A. Straus. "Changing Sex Roles and Their Implica-tions for Measurement of Family Socioeconomic Status." Paper pre-sented at the 1972 meeting of the American Sociological Association, 1973.   B,H
————. "The Family as a Cradle of Violence." *Society* 10 (1973):50–56.
$\qquad$ C,H

Violence seems as typical of family relationships as love, and it would be hard to find a group or institution in U.S. society in which violence is more of an everyday occurrence than it is within the family.

————. "Five Myths about Violence in the Family." *Society* 10 (1973):50–56.   C,H
————. "General Introduction: Social Myth and Social System in the Study of Intra-Family Violence." In *Violence in the Family*, edited by Stein-metz and Straus. New York: Harper & Row, 1974.   H
————. *Violence in the Family*. New York: Harper & Row, 1974.   H

This work is a compilation of thirty-eight papers drawn from a literature review of the subject of violence in the family.

Steinmetz, S.K., and M.A. Straus. "Bibliography for Violence in the Fami-ly." Document no. 02182. New York: American Society of Informa-tion, NAPS.   H
Stelmachers, Z.T. "Evaluations of Victims Services: Is Enough Being Done." *Evaluation and Change* Special Issue (1980):127–130. B,C,H

Program-evaluation methods used in crisis-intervention programs are as-sessed in order to provide guidance for developing better services delivery and evaluations for service programs for victims.

Stencel, S. "Violence in the Family." *Editorial Research Reports* 1 (April 1979):307–324.   H

Focuses on violence in the family. This report examines the severity of child and spouse abuse, violence as a learned pattern of behavior, and new efforts to help abusers.

Stengel, E. "Enquiries into Attempted Suicide." *Proceedings of the Royal Society of Medicine*, 1952, p. 45.   H

———. "The Social Effects of Attempted Suicide." *Canadian Medical Association Journal* 74 (1956):116–120. H

Stephen, B. "Assertiveness—Learning a Kind of Honesty." San Francisco Chronicle, 10 November 1975, p. 20. H

Stern, M.S. "Impacts of Changes in Physician Manpower Sex Ratio." *Journal of Medical Education* 51 (December 1976):1012–1013. C,H

Stern, P. *Battered Wives—A Legacy of Violence*. Falls Church, Va.: Woman's Eye Multimedia Productions, 1978. A

The film explores the historical, social, psychological, and legal complications of the problem of wife abuse. It presents the viewpoints of the therapist, shelter director, director, police, and scholars in the humanities.

Stewart, L.A. "Step by Step Management of Female Victims of Sexual Assault." *Australian Family Physician* 7 (1978):1461–1472. G

Stewart, P. "The Nightmare World of Battered Wives." *Long Island Press*, 28 September 1975. A

This article discusses the little publicized social problem of battered wives.

Still, A. "Police Enquiries in Sexual Offenses." *Journal of Forensic Social Sciences* 15 (1975):183–187. B,G

Stone, K. "The Second Victims: Altruism and the Affective Reactions of Affiliated Males to Their Partner's Rape." *Dissertation Abstracts International* 41 (5):1933-B, 1980. G

The affective states of affiliated men that result from their female partner's rape were investigated.

Stone, L. "The Rise of the Nuclear Family in Early Modern England." In *The Family in History*, edited by C. Rosenberg. Philadelphia: University of Pennsylvania Press, 1975. B

Storaska. "How to Say No to a Rapist and Survive." *Cosmopolitan*, January 1976, p. 122. G

———. "What to Do When You Meet a Rapist." *New Woman*, May/June 1976, p. 34. G

Storck, J.T., and H. Sigall. "Effect of a Harm-Doer's Attractiveness and the Victim's History of Prior Victimization on Punishment of the Harm-Doer." *Personality and Social Psychology Bulletin* 5 (1979):344–347. H

The hypothesis that the influence of prior victimization is moderated by the general attractiveness of the harm doer was tested.

Storen, L. "Hotline for Help Aids Battered Women." *Catholic News*, 1975. A,B

Storr, A. *Human Aggression*. New York: Bantam, 1970.   *H*

Stratman, P.M. "Law Reform and the United Kingdom Domestic Violence and Matrimonial Proceedings Act, 1976." In *Violence in the Family—A Collection of Conference Papers*, 1980.   *B,F*

The British act condemning domestic violence and protecting the victims is discussed, and similar legal reforms are proposed for Australia.

Stratton. "Rape and the Victim: A New Role for Law Enforcement." *FBI Law Enforcement Bulletin*, 1975, p. 3.   *G*

————. "Law Enforcement's Participation in Crisis Counseling for Rape Victims." *Police Chief*, 1976, p. 46.   *C,G*

Straus, M.A. "Measuring Families." In *Handbook of Marriage and the Family*, edited by H.T. Christensen. Chicago: Rand McNally, 1964. *B*

————. "Communication, Creativity, and Problem Solving Ability of Middle- and Working-Class Families in Three Societies." *American Journal of Sociology* 73 (1968):417–430.   *B*

————. "Methodology of a Laboratory Experimental Study of Family in Three Societies." In *Families in East and West*, edited by R. Holl. Paris: Mouton, 1970.   *B*

————. "Social Class and Sex Differences in Socialization for Problem Solving in Bombay, San Juan and Minneapolis." In *Family Problem Solving*, edited by J. Aldous. Hinsdale, Ill.: Dryden, 1971.   *H*

————. "Some Social Antecedents of Physical Punishment: A Linkage Theory Interpretation." *Journal of Marriage and the Family* 33 (1971): 658–663.   *A*

————. "A General Systems Theory Approach to a Theory of Violence between Family Members." *Social Science Information* 12 (June 1973): 105–125.   *H*

————. "Leveling, Civility, and Violence in the Family." *Journal of Marriage and the Family* 36 (1974):13–30.   *H*

The factual basis for therapy and family advice urging leveling in the sense of giving free expression to aggressive feelings is reviewed and the results of a study of 385 couples presented.

————. "Cultural Approval and Structural Necessity or Intra-Assaults in Sexist Societies." Paper presented at the International Institute of Victimology, Bellagio, Italy, 1975.   *H*

————. "Measuring Intrafamily Conflict and Violence." Paper presented at the 1976 meeting of the National Council on Family Relations, 1976. *H*

————. "Societal Morphogenesis and Intrafamily Violence in Cross-Cul-

tural Perspective." *Annals of the New York Academy of Sciences*, 1976.
H

———. "Sexual Inequality, Cultural Norms and Wife Beating." In *Women into Wives*, edited by J.R. Chapman and M. Gates. Beverly Hills, Calif.: Sage Publications, 1977.   *A,C,H*

———. "Social Structure and the Prevention of Wife Beating." In *Battered Women*, edited by M. Roy. New York: Van Nostrand Reinhold, 1977.
A,B

———. "A Sociological Perspective on the Prevention and Treatment of Wife Beating." In *Battered Women*, edited by M. Roy. New York: Van Nostrand Reinhold, 1977.   *A,C*

———. "Wife Beating: How Common and Why." *Victimology* 2 (1977–1978):443–458.   *A*

Administered indexes of severe violence and wife beating to a nationwide sample of 2,143 couples.

———. Normative and Behavioral Aspects of Violence between Spouses Preliminary Data on a Nationally Representative U.S.A. Sample. Rockville, Md.: National Institute of Mental Health, 1978.   *A,H*

The incidence, modes, and patterns of violence between husbands and wives in a nationally representative sample of 2,143 couples are described.

———. Wife Beating—Causes, Treatment, and Research Needs. Rockville, Md.: NCJRS Microfiche Program, 1978.   *A,C*

The extent of wife beating, causes, preventive action appropriate for identified causes, remedial actions that can be taken by a battered wife, and needed research in the area of wife beating are discussed.

———. "Social Stress and Marital Violence in a National Sample of American Families." *Annals of the New York Academy of Sciences* 347 (20 June 1980):229–250.   *B*

This study was designed to determine the extent to which stressful life experiences are associated with assault between husbands and wives and to explore the reasons for such an association.

———. "Some Social Structure Determinants of Inconsistency between Attitudes and Behavior: The Case of Family Violence." *Journal of Marriage and the Family* 42 (Fall 1980):71–80.   *B*

Straus, M.A., and R.J. Gelles. "Physical Violence in Families." In *Families Today—A Research Sampler on Families*, edited by E. Corfman. Washington, D.C.: U.S. Government Printing Office, 1979.   *A,H*

> Child and spouse abuse were investigated in a national survey of the extent of physical violence in U.S. families.

Straus, M.A.,; R.J. Gelles; and S.K. Steinmetz. "Theories, Methods, and Controversies in the Study of Violence between Family Members." Paper presented at the Annual Meeting of the American Sociological Association, 1973.   *B*
————. "Violence in the Family: An Assessment of Knowledge and Research Needs." Paper presented at the American Association for the Advancement of Science meeting, Boston, 1976.   *A,B,H*
Straus, M.A., and G.T. Hotaling. *The Social Causes of Husband-Wife Violence*. Minneapolis: University of Minnesota Press, 1980.   *B*

> Based on the perspective that physical violence between husbands and wives results from the nature of social arrangements and different theories, and methods of investigation are considered to account for this phenomenon.

Straus, M.A., and S.K. Steinmetz. "Violence Research, Violence Control, and the Good Society." In *Violence in the Family*, edited by Steinmetz and Straus. New York: Harper & Row, 1974.   *H*

> From a social-system perspective, Steinmetz and Straus discuss the question of the future of violence in the family.

————. Physical Violence in a Nationally Representative Sample of American Families. Rockville, Md.: NCJRS Microfiche Program, 1978.   *A,H*

> Findings from interviews with 2,143 U.S. couples are given. Of women, 1,145 had one or more children at home. Data cover violence between spouses and between parent and child and children-to-parent violence.

Strentz, T. "Law Enforcement Policy and Ego Defenses of the Hostage." *FBI Law Enforcement Bulletin* 48 (1979):2–12.   *H*

> The Stockholm Syndrome, an automatic, probably unconscious, emotional response to the trauma of being a victim in a hostage situation, is examined.

Strong, B. "Toward a History of the Experimental Family: Sex and Incest in the Nineteenth Century Family." *Journal of Marriage and the Family* 35 (1973):457–466.   *E*

Stucker, C.J. "Story of Mary." *Ms.* 5 (April 1977):66–67. G

"Study Finds Many Indians Sterilized by U.S. Agency without Full Explanation." *The New York Times*, 23 November 1976, p. 16. B

Stumbo. "Rape: Does Justice Turn Its Head?" *Los Angeles Times*, 12 March 1972. G

Suarez, S.D., and G.G. Gallup, Jr. "Tonic Immobility as a Response to Rape in Humans: A Theoretical Note." *Psychological Record* 29 (1979):315–320. G

> The applicability of the designation tonic immobility to special states of behavioral inhibition in humans was investigated with emphasis on the occurrence of rape-induced paralysis.

Subrahmany, B.V.; B.S. Yadwad; and S.M. DasGupta. "Sexual Offences." *Current Medical Practice* (Bombay) 22 (1978):155–164. A,G,H

> Medical and legal aspects of sexual offenses likely to be encountered by medical practitioners are discussed. Guidelines are offered for examination of both victims and accused offenders.

"Suing Her Way Up." *Majority Report*, 5 March 1977. A,B

Sullencer, T.E. *Neglected Areas in Family Living*. Boston: Chris Publishing House, 1960. B

Sullerot, E. *Woman, Society And Change*. New York: McGraw-Hill, 1971, p. 123. C

Summers, S.F.; P.E., Gordon; and J.R. Meagher. "The Impact of Rape on Sexual Satisfaction." *Journal of Abnormal Psychology* 81 (1979):101. G

Summit, R., and J. Kryso. "Sexual Abuse of Children: A Clinical Spectrum." *American Journal of Orthopsychiatry* 48 (April 1978). E

Sussman, M.B. "The Isolated Nuclear Family: Fact or Fiction." *Social Problems* 6 (1959):333–340. B

Sussman, M.B., ed. *Sourcebook in Marriage and the Family*, 4th ed. Boston: Houghton Mifflin, 1973. B

Sutherland, E.H., and D.H. Cressey. *Criminology*. New York: J.B. Lippinscott, 1974. H

Sutherland, and Scherl. "Patterns of Response among Victims of Rape." *American Journal of Orthopsychiatry*, 1970, p. 40. G,H

Sutherlin. "Indiana's Rape Shield Law: Conflict with the Confrontation Clause?" *Indiana Law Review* 9 (1976):418. B,G

Sutton, J. "Battered Women: Another Social Problem?" Paper presented at the Annual Meeting of the American Sociological Association in New York, 1976. A

———. "The Growth of the British Movement for Battered Women." *Victimology: An International Journal* 2 (1978):576–584. A,B

The history of the battered-women movement in the United Kingdom is reviewed. The majority of women's aid groups operates under the principles of the women's liberation movement and is organized as nonhierarchic support groups.

Swank, D.R. "Rape." *New England Journal of Medicine* 298 (1978):168. *G*

In a letter to the editor, the assertion that cases of supposed rape in which the victims fabricate the charges against their assailants are rare is challenged.

Swanson, D.W. "Adult Sexual Abuse of Children (The Man and Circumstances)." *Diseases of the Nervous System* 29 (October 1963):677–683.
E

Swift, C. "Sexual Victimization of Children: An Urban Mental Health Center Survey." *Victimology* 2 (Summer 1977):322–327.   *E,H*

Maintains that while the sexual victimization of children is an old problem, few systematic studies have been conducted, and of the available studies, little focus has been placed on the sexually victimized male child. Results are presented of a survey of twenty clinicians in a midwestern mental-health center regarding the incidence of child sexual abuse over a twelve-month period.

Symonds, A. "Violence against Women: The Myth of Masochism." *American Journal of Psychotherapy* 33 (April 1979):161–173.   *A,H*

Discusses traditional attitudes toward female victims of violence and psychological patterns that operate in people who experience violent acts. Freud's theory of women as unconscious masochists and the characteristics of violence-prone marriages are examined.

Symonds, M. "Victims of Violence: Psychological Effects and Aftereffects." *American Journal of Psychoanalysis* 35 (1975):19.   *H*
———. "The Rape Victim: Psychological Patterns of Response." *American Journal of Psychoanalysis* 36 (Spring 1976):27–34.   *G*

Discusses the behavior of rape victims and compares it with that of the victims of other violent crimes. Rape victims' typical pattern of responses includes shock and disbelief, fright bordering on panic, heightened distortion of perception and judgment, behavior motivated by self-preservation, and traumatic psychological infantilism.

———. "Aggression in the Victim of Aggression. Continuing Medical Education: Syllabus and Proceedings in Summary Form." Washington, D.C.: American Psychiatric Association, 1978.   *H*

A summary of a paper read at the 131st Annual Meeting of the American Psychiatric Association, held in Atlanta, May 1978, is presented. Research and clinical data on women as victims of rape, incest, and wife battering are reviewed.

————. "Acute Responses of Victims to Terror." *Evaluation and Change* Special Issue (1980):39–41.   H

Some acute psychological responses of victims to crimes—for example, rape, kidnapping, or being held hostage—are considered, and particular attention is directed to victim responses as they are exhibited in victims of criminal terrorism and hostage taking.

————. "The 'Second Injury' to Victims." *Evaluation and Change* Special Issue (1980):36–38.   H

Four general phases of response are experienced by victims of violent crimes. The victim's possible perception of rejection and lack of expected support from family, friends, the community, and agencies and the delayed responses of crime victims are considered.

Szasz, T.S. *Law, Liberty and Psychiatry*. New York: Macmillan, 1963. F
————. *The Manufacture of Madness*. New York: Harper & Row, 1970.
                                                                          H
Szumski. "A New Law Shields Rape Victims' Private Lives." *National Observer*, 25 May 1974, p. 15.   F,G
Tahourdin, B. "Battered Wives: Only a Domestic Affair." *International Journal of Offender Therapy and Comparative Criminology* 20 (1976): 86–88.   A
Takakuwa, M.; Y. Matsumato; and T. Sato. "A Psychological Study of Rape." Bulletin of the Criminological Department, Ministry of Justice, Japan, 1971.   B,G
Tan Tjiauw, L., and J. Adlestein. "Management of Psychiatric Emergencies." *Pennsylvania Medicine* 81 (1978):39–42.   B

Basic principles of crisis intervention are described, and the management of specific problems is discussed.

Tanay, E. "Psychiatric Study of Homicide." *American Journal of Psychiatry* 125 (1969):1252, 1258.   H
————. "Reactive Parricide." *Journal of Forensic Sciences*, 1975, pp. 76–82.   H
Tanford, J.A., and A.J. Bocchino. "Rape Victim Shield Laws and the Sixth Amendment." *University of Pennsylvania Law Review* 128 (1980):544–602.   F,G

The contradictions and conflicts between rape-victim shield laws and Sixth Amendment rights are discussed.

Tartler, A.R. "The Dynamics of Abusive Families and Treatment Considerations." *Bulletin of the American Academy of Psychiatry and the Law* 5 (1977):408–414.   *A,H*

Theoretical concepts dealing with child abuse, dynamics of abusive families, and treatment approaches are discussed within the context of the larger society.

Tavris, C. "It's Tough to Nip Sexism in the Bud." *Psychology Today* 58 (December 1975):102.   *E*

Taw, T.E. "The Issue of Reinjury: An Agency Experience." *Child Abuse and Neglect* 3 (1979):591–600.   *B*

The issue of reinjury, as experienced in a specialist child-abuse agency, is examined by both quantitative and qualitative methods.

Taylor. "The Rape Victim: Is She Also the Unintended Victim of the Law?" *The New York Times*, 15 June 1971, p. 52.   *G*

Taylor, D.; P. Walton; and J. Young. *The New Criminology*. Boston: Routledge and Kegan Paul, 1973.   *C,H*

"Techniques of Dispute Intervention." Training Bulletin III-J. Oakland: City of Oakland Police Services, 19 June 1975, pp. 2–3.   *C*

Tedeshi, J.T. "Threats and Promises." In *The Structure of Conflict*, edited by Swingle. New York: Academic Press, 1970.   *C*

"Tell Us What You Think About . . ." Sexual-harassment questionnaire. *Glamour* 78 (November 1980):32.   *B,C,D*

Teoh, S.K. "A Study of Alleged Rape Cases." *Medical Journal of Malaysia* 34 (1979):57–59.   *B,G*

Terry, R.L., and S. Doerge. "Dress, Posture, and Setting as Additive Factors in Subjective Probabilities of Rape." *Perceptual and Motor Skills* 48 (June 1979):903–906.   *G*

Forty undergraduates indicated the likelihood that a woman, photographed in eight situations, would be raped. The situations were created by the Cartesian product of her dress, posture, and setting.

Tessman, L.H., and I. Kaufman. "Variations on a Theme of Incest." In *Family Dynamics and Female Sexual Delinquency*, edited by O. Pollack, pp. 138–150.   *E*

Teutsch, C.K., and J.M. Teutsch. "The Dynamics of Victimization and Devictimization." *Victimology: An International Journal* 2 (1977):83.   *H*

Preconditioning leading to victimization is discussed.

Teutsch, J.M., and C.K. Teutsch. "Victimology: An Effect of Consciousness, Interpersonal Dynamics and Human Physics." *International Journal of Criminology and Penology* 2 (August 1974):249–274.   *H*

Describes a theory that the victim and the victimizer can be shown to be
inseparable components of an interpersonal functional unit occupying the
same unified field based on consciousness factors.

Textor, R.B. *A Cross Cultural Summary*. New Haven: Human Resources
Area Files Press, 1967.   *B*
"That Strict Arab Life." *San Francisco Chronicle*. 2 May 1975, p. 22. *B*
Thibaut, J.W., and J. Coules. "The Role of Communication in the Reduc-
tion of Interpersonal Hostility." *Journal of Abnormal and Social Psy-
chology* 47 (1952):770–777.   *H*
This Film Is about Rape. 16 mm, color, 30 mins. Schiller Park, Ill.: MTI
Teleprograms Incorporated, 1980.   *G*

Features interviews with female rape victims to illustrate the point that rape
happens to women because they are in a particular place and because they
are vulnerable.

"This Is What You Thought about . . . Sexual Harassment." Results of
questionnaire. *Glamour* 79 (January 1981):31.   *B,D*
"This Question of Violence." NET, released by Indiana University A.V.
Center.   *H*
Thomas, R.C., III. "The Forgotten Victim: Sexual Assaults in Penal Insti-
tutions." *Victimology: An International Journal* 2 (1977):83–84. *G,H*

The seriousness of the problem of sexual assault in prison, not only for their
victim but also for the entire society, is discussed.

Thomas, R.M. "The Crisis of Rape and Implications for Counseling: A
Review of the Literature." *Crisis Intervention* 8 (1977):105–116. *B,G*

The crisis reaction, involving an acute phase, followed by a recoil phase in
some cases, and an eventual resolution process, is discussed in terms of
crisis intervention and long-term counseling.

Thompson, G.E. "Attitudes of Police Officers and Rape Service Volunteers
toward Rape and Rape Victims." *Dissertation Abstracts International*
41 (3-B):1167, September 1980.   *G*
Thornton, B. "Effect of Rape Victim's Attractiveness in a Jury Simulation."
Personality and Social Psychology Bulletin 3 (Fall 1977):666–669. *G*

Hypothesized that a rape victim's physical attractiveness would differentially influence the decisions of simulated jurors.

Thornton, B; M.A. Robbins; and J.A. Johnson. "Social Perception of the Rape Victim's Culpability: The Influence of Respondents' Personal Environmental Causal Attribution Tendencies." *Human Relations* 34 (March 1981):225–237.   G

> Investigated the influence of individual differences in attributional tendencies on the perception of a rape victim's causal role in her own victimization.

Thornton, J.W., and P.D. Jacobs. "Learned Helplessness in Human Subjects." *Journal of Experimental Psychology* 87 (1971):367–372.   H
Tidmarsh, M. "Violence in Marriage." *Social Work Today*, 15 April 1976.
                                                                        A,H

> This article deals mainly with factors in the family and social structure that appear to have a bearing on the occurrence of family violence.

Tierney, K.J. "Social Movement Organization, Resource Mobilization, and the Creation of a Social Problem: A Case Study of a Movement for Battered Women." *Dissertation Abstracts International* 40 (8):4756-A, 1980.   *A,B*

> Six social-movement organizations organized around the wife-abuse problem in one local community were studied to investigate organization factors that relate to success of the social-movement organizations.

Tiger, L. "Male Dominance? Yes, Alas, a Sexist Plot? No." *The New York Times Magazine*, 25 October 1970, pp. 35–36.   H
Tilly, C. "Collective Violence in European Perspective." In *Violence in America*, edited by H.D. Graham and T.R. Gurr. New York: Bantam Books, 1969.   H
Tinbergen, N. "On War and Peace in Animals and Man." *Science*, 160 (June 1968):1411–1418.   H
Tinklenberg; Murphy; and Murphy. "Drug Involvement in Criminal Assaults by Adolescents." *Archives of General Psychiatry* 30 (1974):685.
                                                                          H
Tinklenberg, H.R.; and P.G. Bourne. "Alcohol and Violence." In *Alcoholism: Progress in Research and Treatment*, pp. 195–210. New York: Academic Press, 1973.   *A,H*
Tiseo, M. *We Will Not Be Beaten*. Boston: Transition House Films, 1977.
                                                                          A

The experiences of abused women, who have become involved in Transition House, a women's shelter in Massachusetts, are presented in this black-and-white videotape.

Titmuss, R.M. "The Position of Women." In *Essays on the Welfare State*, 1964.   A
Toby, J. "Violence and the Masculine Ideal: Some Qualitative Date." In *Patterns of Violence*, edited by M.E. Wolfgang, pp. 20–27. Philadelphia: Annals of the American Academy of Political and Social Science, 1966.   A,H
Toch, H. *Violent Men: An Inquiry into the Psychology of Violence*. Chicago: Aldine, 1969.   A,H
Tolor, A. "Women's Attitudes toward Forcible Rape." *Community Mental Health Journal* 12 (1978):116–122.   G

The attitudes of women with diverse backgrounds toward possible responses to an attempted sexual assault and their beliefs about how society should handle a convicted rapist were investigated.

Tomalin, C. "Refuge for Battered Women." *Health and Social Science Journal* 84 (1974):1169.   A,B
Tomorug, M.E., and T. Pirozynski. "Victimological Relations in Psycho-Involutive Maladjustment." *Victimology: An International Journal* 2 (1977):84.   H

Victimology is integrated into the concept of relational psychopathology of elderly people.

Tooley, K.M. "The Young Child as Victim of Sibling Attack." *Social Casework* 58 (January 1977):25–28.   E
"Too Many Rapists Get a Second or Third Chance to Rape." *Glamour* 78 (June 1980):56.   G
Toplin, R.B. *Unchallenged Violence: An American Ordeal*. Westport, Conn.: Greenwood Press, 1975.   C,H
Topper, A.B. "Options in Big Brother's Involvment with Incest." *Child Abuse and Neglect* 3 (1979):291–296.   C,E

Options in legal and therapeutic intervention in cases of incest are discussed.

"Touch of Incest: Marriage between Adopted Sister and Brother vs. Pittorino and D. Goddu." *Time*, 2 July 1979, p. 76.   E
Tracy, J.J., and E.H. Clark. "Treatment for Child Abusers." *Social Work* 19 (May 1974):338–342.   B,E

Tracy, R. *Battered Wives*. London: Bow Publications Ltd., 1978.   *A*

Research on wife beating is reviewed, governmental and societal response to the problem in the United Kingdom is assessed, and recommendations for improving that response are offered.

Trainer, R. *Sex and Love among the Poor*. New York: Ballantine Books, 1968.   *A,E*

Traux, C.B., and R. Carkhuff. *Towards Effective Counseling and Psychotherapy*. Chicago: Aldine, 1967.   *C*

Traver, H.H. "The Theory and Practice of Incest." *Dissertation Abstracts International* 34 (9-A, Pt 2):6136–6137, March 1974.   *C,E*

Incest taboo, socialization, family, and social order are discussed.

———. "Offender Reaction, Professional Opinion, and Sentencing." *Criminology* 16 (1978):403–419.   *C,F*

The relationships among the sex offender's reaction to the charges, the probation officer's recommendation, and the court's sentence were studied.

Tsai, M., and N.N. Wagner. "Therapy Groups for Women Sexually Molested as Children." *Archives of Sexual Behavior* 7 (September 1978):417–427.   *B*

Describes therapy groups composed solely of women who were sexually abused in their childhood.

———. "Incest and Molestation: Problems of Childhood Sexuality." *Resident and Staff Physician* 25 (1979):129–131.   *E*

University of Washington statistics on childhood incest and molestation are reported.

———. "Childhood Molestation: Variables Related to Differential Impacts on Psychosexual Functioning in Adult Women." *Journal of Abnormal Psychology* 88 (1979):407–417.   *E*

Trent, D.J. *Wife Beating—A Psycho-Legal Analysis*. Rochester, N.Y.: Lawyers Co-Operative Publishers, 1979.   *A,B*

The laws governing wife beating and the attitudes of law-enforcement personnel in handling these cases are analyzed.

Tripp, H. *Women at Risk*. New York: Macmillan, n.d. *A,G*

Truninger, E. "Marital Violence: The Legal Solutions." *Hastings Law Journal* 23 (November 1971):259–276. *B,F,H*

Tully, M.J. "Funding the Feminists." *Foundation News*, March/April 1975, pp. 26, 28–31. *B*

Turk, J.L., and N.W. Bell. "Measuring Power in Families." *Journal of Marriage and the Family* 34 (May 1972):215–222. *B*

Turner, R.H. *Family Interaction*. New York: Wiley & Sons, 1970. *B*

Tutt. "Washington's Attempt to View Sexual Assault as More Than a Violation of the Moral Woman—The Revision of the Rape Laws." *Gonzaga Law Review* 11 (1975):145. *F,G*

"T.V. Wins a Crucial Case: Dismissal of Suit Blaming NBC for a Rape." *Time*, 21 August 1978, p. 85. *B,F*

Tyra, P.A. "Volunteer Rape Counselors: Selected Characteristics—Empathy, Attribution of Responsibility, and Rape Counselor Syndrome." *Dissertation Abstracts International* 40 (9-B):4209–4210A, 1980. *B,C,G*

Attribution of responsibility to victims with nontraditional behaviors and relationship between empathy and attribution and symptom of rape-counselor syndrome, volunteer rape counselors.

United States. Bureau of the Census. "A Statistical Portrait of Women." Current Population Reports, Series P-23, no. 58. Washington, D.C.: U.S. Government Printing Office, 1976. *B*

United States. Commission on Civil Rights. *Battered Women: Issues of Public Policy*. Consultation sponsored by the U.S. Commission on Civil Rights. Washington, D.C., 1978. *A,B*

Papers on government intervention policies and practices in the area of wife beating, the police and family violence, the question of whether statutory reform is the answer to the battered woman's problem, and alternatives for spouse-abuse cases are presented.

United States. Congress. House. Committee on Education and Labor. Subcommittee on Select Education. *Hearings on H.R. 2977*. July 10 and 11, 1979. *A,B*

Police, medical, and court representatives, together with individuals working in shelters for battered women, offer testimony regarding domestic violence and discuss the Domestic Violence Prevention and Service Act.

United States. Congress. House. Subcommittee on Criminal Justice. *Victims of Crime Compensation Legislation*. 1976.   *F*
United States. Congress. Senate. Committee on Labor and Public Welfare. *Hearings on Alcohol Abuse among Women: Special Problems and Unmet Needs*. 1976.   *F*
———. *Quality of Health Care—Human Experimentation*. 1973.   *B*
United States. Congress. House. Committee on the Judiciary. Subcommittee on Law Statutes. *Privacy of Rape Victims*. 93rd Cong., 1976.   *G*
United States. Congress. House. Committee on Education and Labor. *Displaced Homemakers Act, H.R. 28*. 95th Cong., 1st sess., January 1978, pp. 153–168.   *B,F*
United States. Congress. House. Committee on Education and Labor. *Bill to Establish Programs for the Prevention and Treatment of Family Violence*. 96th Cong., 1st sess., January 1978.   *B,F*

This bill, titled the Family Violence Prevention and Treatment Act, sets up a coordinating council on family violence to coordinate federal programs and a national center for community action against family violence.

United States. Congress. House. Committee on Education and Labor. Subcommittee on Select Education. *Hearings on H.R. 7929 and H.R. 8948*. 95th Cong., 2nd sess. March 16 and 17, 1978.   *B,F*

The two bills under consideration would provide grants for programs to aid battered spouses, set up an information clearinghouse, and support research. The testimony describes the problem and urges passage.

United States. Congress. House. Committee on Education and Labor. Subcommittee on Child and Human Development. *Hearings on Domestic Violence and Legislation with Respect to Domestic Violence*. 95th Cong., 2nd sess., March 4 and 8, 1978.   *B,F*

The text is presented of numerous statements and testimony in hearings before the senate subcommittee on child and human development in March, 1978. They concern domestic violence and legislative proposals for dealing with it.

United States. Congress. House. Committee on Education and Labor. *Monroe County (Indiana) Task Force on Federal Family Violence Legislation*. 95th Cong., 1978.   *B,F*

Surveys conducted at Indiana University, in the town of Bloomington, Indiana, and in Indianapolis, all show a great need for shelter for battered women in Monroe County. Early efforts have failed due to lack of money.

United States. Congress. House. Committee on Science and Technology. *Needs Assessment of Victims of Domestic Violence* by M.D. Pagelow. 95th Cong., 1978.   *B,C*

Determining people most likely to need social services because of domestic violence was the basis for this study. Such data are essential in setting up service programs.

United States. Congress. House. Committee on the Judiciary. Subcommittee on Law Statutes. *Privacy Protection for Rape Victims, Act of 1978.* 95th Cong., 1978.   *F,G*

United States. Congress. House. Domestic Violence Report of the House. Subcommittee on Domestic and International Scientific Planning Analysis. *Research into Violent Behavior.* 95th Cong., 2nd sess., October 1978.   *B*

This report by the house committee on science and technology deals with public hearing on domestic violence including spouse battering.

United States. Congress. House. Committee on Education and Labor. *Statement by Dr. Blandina Cradenas.* 96th Cong., January 1978. *A,E*

As an unforeseen component of their family-oriented aid to abused and neglected children, all twenty child-abuse demonstration-treatment centers provide some services that directly or indirectly assist abused spouses.

United States. Congress. House. Committee on Education and Labor. *Statement by the Honorable Newton I. Steers, Jr., Maryland.* 95th Cong., 1978.   *B*

Legislation addressing the problems of family violence should focus on battered women, because women constitute the largest number of victims. Most federal funding should be earmarked for shelters and training.

United States. Congress. House. Joint Economic Committee. Economic Problems of Women. *Statement of H. Denenberg.* 96th Cong., January 1978, p. 153–168.   *B,F*

United States. Congress. House. Committee on Education and Labor. *Testimony delivered by the Honorable Robert W. Kasten, Jr., Wisconsin* 95th Cong., 1978.   *A,B,F*

Numerous programs and shelters for battered wives have been established in Wisconsin with the rough efforts of volunteer groups. These shelters not only have given a place of refuge, but also have increased public awareness.

United States. Congress. House. Committee on Education and Labor. *Testimony of A. Shero on the Domestic Violence Prevention and Treatment Act (H.R. 7929) and the Family Violence Prevention Treatment Act (H.R. 8948).* 95th Cong., 1978.   H

The plight of battered women in rural areas is made acute by isolation; the state police are many miles away, social services are few, and getting a warrant involves a long trip to the county seat.

United States. Congress. House. Committee on Education and Labor. *Testimony of C.B. Schudson on Criminal Justice System as Family— Trying the Impossible for Battered Women.* 95th Cong., 1978.   *A,B*

Traditionally the extended family contained violence among its members and applied sanctions to prevent it. The criminal-justice system has been asked to assume this function but, due to its structure, cannot.

United States. Congress. House. Committee on Education and Labor. Testimony of C.L. Anderson on the Abused Persons Program, Montgomery County, Maryland. 96th Cong., January 1978.   *A,B*

The Montgomery County program, supported entirely with county funds, gave assistance to 268 families in 1977, its first year of operation. Both emergency aid and long-term support services are offered.

United States. Congress. House. Committee on Education and Labor. *Testimony of James Bannon.* 96th Cong., January 1978.   B

After reviewing statistics that indicate that wife abuse is under-reported by at least 50 percent in Detroit, Michigan, changes are suggested for each point in the criminal-justice system to increase victim confidence.

United States. Congress. House. Committee on Education and Labor. *Testimony of J. Fleming on Family Violence: A Look at the Criminal Justice.* 95th Cong., 1978.   H

Appropriate police intervention, follow-up by prosecutors, and creative sentencing by courts could do much to help the battered wife and change society's attitudes toward the acceptability of domestic violence.

United States. Congress. House. Committee on Science and Technology. *Testimony of A. Flitcraft on Battered Women: an Emergency Room Epidemiology with a Description of a Clinical Syndrome and Critique of Present Therapeutics.* 95th Cong., 1978.   A

The continual interaction of medical care system and battered women is examined in this 1978 study of 481 people who had been patients at the Yale/New Haven Hospital emergency room in December 1975.

United States. Congress. House. Committee on Education and Labor. *Testimony of K. Bellfield*. 96th Cong., January 1978.   A

The Harriet Tubman Women's Shelter, Minneapolis, Minnesota, serves an interracial clientele and focuses on the double problems of racism and sexism faced by minority women who are abused by their spouses.

United States. Congress. House. Committee on Science and Technology. *Testimony by L.A. Kriesbert on Supporting Women's Successful Efforts Against Violence*. 95th Cong., 1978.   A,B

Observations regarding rape crisis centers and battered-wives shelters are highlighted; a recommendation relating to a national commitment to funding these shelters is presented.

United States. Congress. House. Committee on Education and Labor. *Testimony of R.N. Hengesbach on Domestic Violence*. 95th Cong., 1978.   A,B

The women's center, and emergency shelter for battered women run by the Young Women's Christian Association, South Bend, coordinates a network of public and private services to aid the entire family.

United States. Congress. House. Committee on Education and Labor. *Testimony of Susan M. Back for Aid to Battered Women*. 95th Cong., January 1978.   A,B

A series of six recommendations are made for the allocation of funds to programs aiding battered women. The use of grassroots experience and the encouragement of local projects will prove most cost effective.

United States. Congress. House. Committee on Education and Labor. *Testimony Presented by James C. Walsh*. 95th Cong., 1978.   A,B

The victims information bureau is in a middle-to upper-middle-class county of New York. In addition to shelter and advocacy services, it offers a unique counseling service to help abusing husbands change their behavior.

United States. Congress. House. Committee on Science and Technology. *Treatment Alternatives for Battered Spouses* by L.E. Walker. 95th Cong., 1978.   A,B

Using interviews with about 420 women and their helpers, this 1978 congressional testimony shows the three phases that lead to wife beating, using the concept of learned helplessness. Suggestions are offered.

United States. Congress. House. Committee on Education and Labor. *Victimization in the Home—an Overview of Current Research and Community Services with Some Suggestions on Filling Unmet Needs*, by M.D. Pagelow. 95th Cong., 1978.   *A,B,H*

Federal funding to help the victims of violence should be channeled to the grassroots organizations attempting to establish shelters and not to traditional groups that long ignored the needs of battered women.

United States. Congress. House. Committee on Education and Labor. *Women's Center and Shelter of Greater Pittsburgh Pennsylvania: A Model for Sheltering Community*, by G.L. Visser. 95th Cong., 1978.
A,B

Between 1975 and 1977 the Women's Center and Shelter of Greater Pittsburgh gave shelter to 528 women and 311 children, of whom more than half were victims of abuse. The shelter's guidelines are given.

United States. Congress. House. Committee on Education and Labor. *Domestic Violence Prevention and Services Act: H.R. 2977.* 96th Cong., 1st sess., 1979, p. 509–529.   *C*

The Domestic Violence Prevention Service Act, H.R. 2977, is presented. The purpose of the act is to provide federal support and encouragement of state, local, and community domestic-violence prevention activities.

United States Department of Health, Education and Welfare. Public Health Service. Health Resources Administration. National Center for Health Statistics. *Health: United States 1975*. Rockville, Md., 1976.   *B*
———. Public Health Service. Health Resources Administration. National Center for Health Services Research. "Women and Their Health: Research Implications for a New Era." NCHSR Research Proceedings Series. San Francisco, 1–2 August 1977.   *B*
———. *Child Abuse and Family Violence*. Washington, D.C., 1978. *A,E*

The sixty-three items listed in this annotated bibliography place child abuse in the broader context of family violence and explore some of the interrelationships between child abuse and other forms of intrafamily violence.

———. National Institute on Alcohol Abuse and Alcoholism. "Family Violence." *Alcohol Health and Research World* 4 (Fall 1979):complete issue.   *H*

This quarterly publication contains articles dealing with family violence and alcohol abuse, children of alcoholic parents, training program for counselors, and confidentiality of client records.

————. *Rape and Older Women: A Guide to Prevention and Protection.* Rockville, Md.: Alcohol, Drug Abuse, and Mental Health Administration, 1979.   *B,G*
United States. Department of Health and Human Services. Office of Human Development Services. *Monograph on Services to Battered Women.* Washington, D.C.   *A,B*

This monograph presents the results of a national survey on services to battered women in order to help other service providers select a system. The survey covered 163 programs and involved eight site visits.

United States. Department of Justice. *Crimes and Victims: A Report on the Dayton-San Jose pilot Survey of Victimization.* Washington, D.C.: Law Enforcement Assistance Administration, 1974.   *H*

Tested survey methods and instruments in Dayton, Ohio, and San Jose, California, as a part of an effort by the President's Commission on Law Enforcement and Criminal Justice to measure the extent of common theft and assaultive violence in the United States.

————. Law Enforcement Assistance Administration. *Report from the Conference on Intervention Programs for Men Who Batter.* Washington, D.C.: Mott-McDonald Associates, Incorporated.   *C*

This report presents recommendations from participants who attended a two-day conference sponsored by LEAA on issues involved in providing services to battered spouses, particularly in those situations where batterers come under the purview of the justice system.

United States. Department of Labor. Women's Bureau. *Twenty Facts on Women Workers.* Washington, D.C.: U.S. Government Printing Office, 1975.   *B,D*
————. *Women Workers Today.* Washington, D.C.: U.S. Government Printing Office, 1975.   *D*
United States Documents. *Crimes of Violence.* Washington, D.C.: National Commission on Violence, 1969.   *H*
United States Military Police School. "Victims of Sexual Assault." Fort McClellan, Ala.: Department of the Army, 1977.   *G,H*
United States. Work Projects Administration. *The Legal Status of Women.* Des Moines, Iowa: Attorney General's Office, 1938.   *F*

This is an exhaustive translation of laws pertaining to all aspects of womens' lives. Mesopotamian, Chinese, biblical, Hindu, Greek, Roman and medieval major texts and codes are all included. All aspects are covered including under what conditions women could be legitimately chastised and the level of punishment allowed. Also included were punishments to be done to men who overstep these bounds and under what circumstances women could claim unjust treatment. An unexcelled comparative historical survey.

"Up-Date: Sexual Harassment on the Job. Students, Secretaries, Lawyers Fight On." *Ms.* 7 (July 1978):85–88.   D

Urban and Rural Systems Associates. *Exploratory Study of Women in the Health Professions Schools.* San Francisco, 1976.   B,D

Valentine, A. *Fathers to Sons: Advice without Consent.* Norman: University of Oklahoma Press, 1973.   B

Valentine, C.A. *Culture and Poverty.* Chicago: University of Chicago Press, 1968.   C

Van Den Berghe, P.L. *Man In Society*: A Biosocial View. New York: Elsevier, 1975.   C

———. "Incest and Exogamy: A Sociobiological Reconsideration." *Ethology and Sociobiology* 1 (1980):151–162.   E

Incest and exogamy are considered from a sociobiological perspective. Although often confused in the social-science literature, incest and exogamy are two distinct phenomena.

———. "Royal Incest and Inclusive Fitness." *American Ethnologist* 7 (1980):300–317.   E

Vandermeer, J.M. "Psychological Aspects and Family Dynamics of Adolescent Rape Victims." *Dissertation Abstracts International* 37 (5-A):3214–3215, November 1976.   G

Deals with psychological and family profile, identification of high-risk and potential adolescent rape victims, and thirteen- to seventeen-year-old rape victims.

Van Dijk, J.J. "Public Attitudes toward Crime in the Netherlands." *Victimology* 3 (1978):265–273.   B

The status of research on attitudes toward crime in the Netherlands is examined. Numerous surveys conducted there suggest that fear of crime is only loosely connected with actual experiences with crime and that levels of fear are quite high in light of the relatively low crime rate.

Van Dine, S.; J.P. Conrad; and S. Dinitz. *Restraining the Wicked.* Lexington, Mass.: Lexington Books, D.C. Heath and Company, 1979.   H

The costs and benefits of several sentencing policies designed to reduce violent crime were assessed.

VanFossen, B.E. "Intersexual Violence in Monroe County, New York." *Victimology* 4 (1979):299–305. H

Police records were examined and questionnaires were administered to victims of intersexual violence in a rural county in New York.

Van Gelder, L. "Women's War on LP Cover Violence." *Rolling Stone* 237 (1977):32–33. H

Vannoy, R. *Sex without Love: A Philosophical Exploration*. Buffalo, N.Y.: Prometheus Books, 1980. A

Dr. Vannoy endeavors to analyze philosophically the major issues of both sex and love.

Van Stolk, M. "Beaten Women, Battered Children." *Children Today*, March/April 1976, pp. 8–12. A

Wife beating follows the same social, statistical, and cultural patterns that Van Stolk discovered while researching the abuse and battered child in Canada.

Vanzandt, J. *Inquiry into Family Violence in Southern Illinois—Evaluation Report*. Rockville, Md.: NCJRS, 1979. H

Results are reported from a survey designed to determine the extent to which family violence—primarily spouse abuse—is a problem in the greater Egypt criminal-justice region of southern Illinois.

Vaughn, S.R. "Where It All Began." *Do It Now* 9 (June 1976):2. B

Describes services, conditions, and organization of Women's Advocate House, Washington, D.C., 1974. Includes average processing procedure and advocates the establishment of other refuges.

———. "The Last Refuge: Shelter for Battered Women." *Victimology* 4 (1979):113–119. B

Experience in operating two Minnesota shelters for battered women and their children is reviewed and case material is provided.

Vaught, J.A. "Rape-Admissibility of Victim's Prior Sexual Conduct: What Is the Law in Texas." *Baylor Law Review* 31 (1979):317–327. G

The Texas standard of admissibility of rape victims' prior sexual conduct as evidence is evaluated.

Velsen, J. Van. *The Politics of Kinship: A Study in Social Manipulation among the Lakeside Tonga of Nyasaland*. Manchester: Manchester University Press, 1964.   B

Vennard, J. "Victim's Perceptions of Compensation and the Criminal Justice System." *Victimology: An International Journal* 2 (1977):84–85.
                                                                                                   H

Research findings of a study of people who invoked criminal proceedings as a result of having suffered loss or damage to their property or personal injury through an assault are presented.

———. "Compensation by the Offender: The Victim's Perspective." *Victimology* 3 (1978):154–160.   H

Victim's attitudes toward compensation by the offender were examined in a sample of seventy victims of offenses including theft, criminal damage, wounding, and assault occasioning actual bodily harm.

Venward, J., and J. Densen-Gerber. "Incest as a Causative Factor in Antisocial Behavior: An Exploratory Study." *Continuing Drug Problems* 4 (Fall 1975):323–240.   E

Veoist, J. "Quarrels: Family that Fights Together . . . Fights Together." *Redbook* 135 (August 1970):61.   A,H

Vera, H.; G.W. Bernard; and C. Helzer. "The Intelligence of Rapists: New Data." *Archives of Sexual Behavior* 8 (July 1979):375–377.   G

Vernier, C.G. *American Family Laws: A Comparative Study of the Law of the 48 American States, Alaska, D.C., and Hawaii*, 5 vols. London: Oxford University Press, 1971.   F

Veroff, J., and S. Feld. *Marriage and Work in America*. New York: Van Nostrand, 1970.   C

Veronen, L.L. "Fear Response of Rape Victims." *Dissertation Abstracts International* 38 (7–8):3421, January 1978.   G

Veronen, L.L., and D.G. Kilpatrick. "Self Reported Fears of Rape Victims: A Preliminary Investigation." *Behavior Modification* 4 (1980): 383–396.   G

A modified fear survey that contained standard items from the Wolpe and Lang Fear Survey as well as items originating from victim reports of fearful situations was administered to twelve victims of rape and twelve nonvictims to test the hypothesis that rape-victim fears are classically conditioned.

Veronen, L.G.; D.G. Kilpatrick; and P.A. Resick. "Treating Fear and Anxiety in Rape Victims: Implications for the Criminal Justice System." In *Perspectives on Victimology*, edited by W. Parsonage. Beverly Hills, Calif.: Sage, 1979.   G

The rape victim's psychological state and her emotional reactions were explored in order to assess their effect on the process and outcome of her interactions with all parts of the criminal-justice system.

Viano, E. "Rape and the Law in the United States: An Historical and Sociological Analysis." *International Journal of Criminology*, 1974, p. 317.   G
―――. *Victims and Society*. Washington, D.C.: Visage Press, 1975.   H
―――. "Working with Battered Women: A Conversation with Lisa Leghorn." *Victimology* 3 (1978):91–107.   A,B

Aspects of interventions with battered women are discussed, in an interview format, with Lisa Leghorn, author, advocate, and staff member of Transition House in Cambridge, Massachusetts.

"Victim or Criminal?" *Human Behavior*, June 1974, p. 53.   H
Victims of Crime Act. H.R. 3686. 95th Cong., 1st sess., introduced 17 February 1977.   F,H
Victor, J.B. "He Beat Me." *Vogue* 168 (January 1978):177.   A
Vincent, A. "Divorce Tax Helps Battered Spouses." *Ms.* 9 (October 1980): 23.   A
Vinsel, A. "Rape." *Personality and Social Psychology Bulletin* 3 (1977): 183–189.   G
Violence in America. National Broadcasting Corporation, January 1977. H

The program (three hours) contains segments on various forms of common violence.

Violence in the Family. Pleasantville, N.Y.: Human Relations Media, 1978.   H

Presents a comprehensive and sensitive study of the causes, characteristics, and possible solutions to family violence.

"Violence inside the Family." *Washington Star*, 24 February 1976, p. 12.   A,H
Violence in the Home: An American Tragedy. Wilton, Conn.: Current Affairs Films, 1978.   A,H

Battered wives, battered children—neither is a new phenomenon, but until lately neither has received much publicity.

Violent Crime: Homicide, Assault, Rape, Robbery Report. New York: G. Braziller, 1969.   *G,H*

Virkkunen, M. "Incest Offenses and Alcoholism." *Medicine, Science, and the Law* 14 (1974):124–128.   *E*

Visser, G.L. Women's Center and Shelter of Greater Pittsburgh, Pennsylvania: A Model for Sheltering Community. Washington, D.C.: U.S. Congress House Committee on Education and Labor, 1978.   *B*

Between 1975 and 1977 the Women's Center and Shelter of Greater Pittsburgh gave shelter to 528 women and 311 children, of whom more than half were victims of abuse. The shelter's guidelines are given.

Vital Statistics Report (Annual Summary for the United States), vol. 24. Washington, D.C.: National Center for Health Statistics, 1976.   *B*

Vitullo, L.R. "Physical Evidence in Rape Cases." *Journal of Political Science Administration* 2 (June 1974):160–163.   *G*

Vogel, B.F. "The Battered Child Syndrome and Its Management." *Journal of the Mississippi State Medical Association* 19 (1978):23–25.   *A,B*

The battered-child syndrome is discussed as a medical, emotional, and sociological problem.

Vogelmann, S.S. "Implicit Consent and Rape: An Integration Theory Analysis of Female Responses in a Dating Context." *Dissertation Abstracts International* 41 (4-B):1573, October 1980.   *G*

Sex-role stereotypes and judgments of implicit consent to intercourse in dating and rape situations are discussed.

Vogelmann, S.S., et al. "Sex Differences in Feelings Attributed to a Woman in Situations Involving Coercion and Sexual Advances." *Journal of Personality* 47 (September 1979):420–431.   *D,G*

von Hentig, H. *The Criminal and His Victim: Studies in the Sociology of Crime.* New Haven, Conn.: Yale University Press, 1948.   *B*

———. *Der Modus Operandi Beim Verwandtenmord. Archiv fur Kriminologie* 139 (1967):131–143.   *H*

This study shows that one-third of homicide victims are members of the offender's family and that the most frequent victims, in descending order, are wives, male offspring, fathers, mothers, grandmothers, and sisters.

Voss, H.L., and J.R. Hepburn. "Patterns in Criminal Homicide in Chicago." *Journal of Criminal Law, Criminology and Police Science* 59 (1968):499–508.   H

Wachs, E.F. "The Code of Survival: The Crime-Victim Narrative within an Urban Context." *Dissertation Abstracts International* 40 (10):5540-A, 1980.   H

An analysis of 120 crime-victim narratives (verbal reiterations of high-anxiety life-and-death confrontations structured to recount crimiogenic situations) reported by native New Yorkers is presented.

Wahl, C.W. "The Psychodynamics of Consummated Maternal Incest." *Archives of General Psychiatry* 3 (1978):188–193.   E

Waites, E.A. "Female Masochism and the Enforced Restriction of Choice." *Victimology: An International Journal* 2 (1960):535–544.   A

The role of female masochism in the abuse and subjugation of women is examined.

Wake, S.B., et al. "Research Relating to Children." Bulletin no. 27. Urbana, Ill.: Clearinghouse on Early Childhood Education, EDRS, June 1970; February 1971.   B

Walker, C.G. "Rape and the Harlem Woman: 'She Asked for It'—or Did She?" *Majority Report*, 22 August 1974, p. 1.   G

———. "They Beat Their Wives in Rockville." *Washington Newsworks*, 3 March 1976, pp. 9–10.   A

———. "Psycho-Legal Aspects of Rape." *Dissertation Abstracts International* 39 (8-B):4110–4111, February 1979.   C,G

Juror attitudes and group processes and verdicts of rape-trial simulation are examined.

Walker, G. "Rape in Suburbia." *Ladies Home Journal* 97 (July 1980):68.
                                                                       C,G

Walker, H.M., and J. Lev. *Statistical Inference*. New York: Holt, Rinehart & Winston, 1953, pp. 381–382.   B

Walker, K.; C. Baker; J. Barr; and C. Walker. "Fingerprints and Criminal Conviction." *Journal of Community Psychology* 1 (April 1973):192–194.   H

Fingerprint patterns and ridge counts of criminal convicts, sex criminals versus men convicted of violent crimes versus noncriminals.

Walker, L.E. "Battered Women: Hypothesis and Theory Building." Paper presented at American Psychological Association Convention, Washington, D.C., 1976.   A

———. "The Battered Women Syndrome." Symposium presented at the American Psychological Association Convention, Washington, D.C., 1976.   A

———. "The Battered Women Syndrome Study." Grant application submitted to National Institute of Mental Health, Washington, D.C., November 1976.   A

———. "Who Are the Battered Women?" *Frontiers: A Journal of Women's Studies*, May, 1977.   A

———. "Battered Women and Learned Helplessness." *Victimology: An International Journal* 2 (1978):525–534.   A,H

A psychological rationale for why women become and remain victims of battering is advanced.

———. "Feminist Psychotherapy with Victims of Violence." Paper presented at the American Psychological Association, Division 29 Psychotherapy, Midwinter Meeting, March 1978.   C,H

Feminist therapy techniques useful for psychotherapists working with female victims of violence are discussed in this research paper.

———. *Psychotherapy and Counseling with Battered Women*. Washington, D.C.: U.S. Congress House Committee on Science and Technology, 1978.   A.

An examination of data on the psychological dynamics of battered women and their families is undertaken in this 1978 study to determine specific skills and attitudes therapists must use to treat this problem.

———. "Treatment Alternatives for Battered Women." In *Victimization of Women*, edited by J.R. Chapman and M. Gates. Beverly Hills, Calif.: Sage Publications, 1978.   A,C

The three stages of a battering relationship between a husband and wife are presented. Appropriate intervention is given for each stage, and long-term treatments are examined.

———. *The Battered Woman*. New York: Harper & Row, 1979.   A

Walker's work is the first full-volume attempt to describe a psychology of battered women.

———. "A Feminist Perspective on Domestic Violence." Research report. Washington, D.C.: National Institute of Mental Health, 1979. *H*

The incidence and nature of domestic violence are examined from a feminist perspective, focusing on current research and theories specifically related to battered women.

———. "Psychology and Violence against Women—Psychotherapy Issues." Paper presented at the American Psychological Association, Division 29 Psychotherapy, Midwinter Conference, Mexico City, March 1979.
C,E,G

Current psychotherapy theories and practices are examined and found to have sexist biases that interfere with adequate treatment of battered women, especially rape and incest victims.

Walker, L.E., and M.L. Flax. "Psychotherapy with Battered Women and Their Partners." Paper presented at the Conference on Violent Crimes against Women, University of Washington, Seattle, 2 May 1977. *A,C*
Walk In Counseling Center. "No-Red-Tape Counseling for Clients Alienated from Traditional Services." *Hospital and Community Psychiatry* 28 (November 1977):843–845. *B*

Describes the Walk In Counseling Center in Minneapolis that, since 1969, has offered free, no-red-tape counseling to individuals and families alienated from traditional services.

Wallach, M.A.; N. Kogan; and D.J. Bem. "Group Influence on Individual Risk Taking." In *Group Dynamics*, edited by D. Cartwright and A. Zander. London: Tavistock, 1968. *A,C*
Waller, C. "Wife Abuse, Especially as the Problem Is Seen in the District of Columbia." Washington, D.C.: Task Force on Abuse, 1975. *A*
Waller, L. "Victims on Trial: Prosecutions for Rape." *Victimology: An International Journal* 2 (1977):85. *F,G*

The findings of two government inquiries into ameliorating the distress of rape victims confronted by the criminal-justice system are examined and evaluated.

Wallis, J.H. "Matrimonial Problems and the Citizens Advice Bureaux—Reflections on a Sample Survey." *Marriage Guidance*, September 1973, pp. 334–337. *B*
Walter, J.D. "Police in the Middle: A Study of Police Intervention in Domestic Disputes." *Dissertation Abstracts International* 34: (11-A): 7361, May 1974. *C*

Role perception, behavior during police intervention in domestic disputes, policemen and family members.

Walters, R.H.; E.L. Thomas; and C.W. Acker. "Enhancement of Punitive Behavior by Audiovisual Displays." *Science* 136 (1962):872–873. *A, B*
Walther. "Acid Phosphates: Its Significance in the Determination of Human Seminal Traces." *Journal of Forensic Medicine* 18 (1971):15.   *G*
Ward, M.A. "Attribution of Blame in Rape." *Dissertation Abstracts International* 41 (5):1934-B, 1980.   *G*

A study designed to identify the empirical structure of attitudes placing the blame for the occurrence of rape is presented.

Warner, C.G. *Rape and Sexual Assault: Management and Intervention.* Germantown, Md.: Aspen Systems, 1980.   *B, G*

The identification or categorization of rape and sexual-assault victims and approaches for dealing with the persons and circumstances involved are addressed.

Warner, D.B. "Determinants of Bystander Intervention: The Effects of the Verbal Cues of Victims and Others Present." *Dissertation Abstracts International*, Ann Arbor, Michigan: Michigan University, 1977.   *H*

The effects of ambiguity as a situational determinant of help giving were investigated in a three-by-three design in which the content of verbal ambiguity messages by the victim and a confederate bystander were systematically varied.

Warren, C. *Sexuality: Encounters, Identities, and Relationships.* Beverly Hills, Calif.: Sage Publications, 1976.   *B*

The articles included in this volume reflect the sociological diversity of sexuality in Western society.

Warrior, B. *Battered Lives.* Pittsburgh, Pa.: KNOW, Incorporated, 1976.
                                                                        A
———. *Working on Wife Abuse*, 6th rev. ed. Cambridge, Mass.: Bettsy Warrior, 1978.   *A*
Warrior, B., and L. Leghorn. *Houseworker's Handbook.* Cambridge, Mass.: Bettsy Warrior, n.d.   *B*
Washtenaw County Domestic Violence Council. *A Guide to Wife Assault Resources.* Ann Arbor, Mich., n.d.   *B*

Provides a list of alternatives for the victim and the agencies, hospitals, and other crisis-intervention services available in Washtenaw County, Michigan.

Wasoff, F.; R.E. Dobash; and R.P. Dobash. "Current Evidence and Legal Remedies Regarding Battered Women." *Journal of the Law Society of Scotland* 24 (May 1979):178–183.   *A,B,F*

A rejoinder to an article on battered women discusses recent research in Scotland concerning the extent of the problem, causes, and prevention and clarifies misconceptions about domestic abuse.

Wasserman, S. "The Abused Parent of the Abused Child." *Children* 14 (September/October 1967):175–179.   *A,E*

Waterbury, M.K. *Battered Wives: Must We Draw the Curtain and Shut Out the Public Gaze?* Fullerton: California State University, Nursing Department, 1976.   *A*

Waters, C. "Buddy, We Hardly Knew Ya: Alleged Rape by V.A. Cianci." *New Times*, 29 July 1978, pp. 22–29.   *G*

Waters, H. "What TV Does to Kids." *Newsweek*, 1977, pp. 63–70.   *H*

Wathey, R.B., and J. Densen-Gerver. "Incest: An Analysis of the Victim and the Aggressor." Unpublished paper, 1976.   *B,C,E*

Watlenberg, W.W. *The Adolescent Years.* New York: Harcourt Brace Jovanovich, 1973.   *E*

Watzlawick, P.B.; J. Beavin; and D.D. Jackson. *Pragmatics of Human Behavior.* New York: W.W. Norton, 1967.   *H*

Wayne County Sheriff Police Training Academy. "Domestic Complaints Outline." Prepared by Lt. Kurek. International Association of Police Chiefs, 1965.   *B*

Weal, E., and P.F. Kradel. "Rural Rape Brings Special Problems." *Innovations* 6 (1979):36.   *G*

In an attempt to deal with the special problems associated with rape in rural areas, a rape-education program has been developed by the Appalachian Mental Health Center that services a ten-county catchment area in West Virginia.

Webb, A.L. "Social Service Administration—A Typology for Research." *Public Administration*, 1971, pp. 321–341.   *B*

Webb, P.R. "Matrimonial Cruelty—A Lawyer's Guide for the Medical Profession." *Medicine, Science and the Law* 7 (1967):110–116.   *B,F*

This article explains to the medical profession the basic rules applied by the English courts in cruelty cases.

Weber, E. "Incest: Sexual Abuse Begins at Home." *Ms.* 5 (April 1977):64–
67. Discussion. 6 (September 1977):89–92.   E

Weber, M. *The Methodology of the Social Sciences*. New York: Free Press,
1949.   B

———. "Politics as a Vocation." In *From Max Weber: Essays in Sociology*,
edited by H. Gerth and C.W. Mills. London: Routledge and Kegan
Paul, 1948.   C

———. *The Theory of Social and Economic Organization*, translated by
A.M. Henderson and T. Parsons. New York, 1950.   B

———. *Wirtschaft und Gesellschaft: Grundriss der verstehenden Sozio-
logie*. Cologne: Kiepenheuer and Witsch, 1964.   H

Webster, B.D. "An Exploration of Factors Affecting Women's Predictions
about Sexual Assault Reporting and the Prosecution of Assailants."
Dissertation Abstracts International 41 (6):2396-B, 1980.   A, G

The relationship of the factors of respondents' assertiveness, attitudes
toward the law, the circumstances surrounding and the events within assault to 240 women's predictions about a fictionalized victim's postattack
behavior was examined.

Weddington. "Rape Law in Texas." *American Journal of Criminal Law* 4
(1976):1.   F, G

Wegner, E.L. "The Concept of Alienation: A Critique and Some Suggestions for a Context Specific Approach." *Pacific Sociological Review* 18
(April 1975):171–193.   H

Weich, M.J. "The Terms Mother and Father as a Defense against Incest."
Journal of the American Psychoanalytic Association 16 (1968):783–791.
                                                                             E

The terms *mother* and *father* and their equivalents in specific families play a
symbolic part in maintaining and reinforcing the incest taboo in contemporary life.

Weiksnar, M. "To Hire or Fire: The Case of Women in the Workplace."
Technology Review, October/November 1976, pp. 16–18.   D

Weinberg, S.K. *Incest Behavior*. New York: Citadel Press, 1955.   E

Weiner, I.B. "A Clinical Perspective on Incest." *American Journal of
Diseases of Children* 132 (1978):123–124.   E

A clinical perspective on incest is offered in light of speculation about the
origin of the incest taboo and recent openness about incest issues.

Weingourt, R. "Battered Women: The Grieving Process." *Journal of Psychiatric Nursing and Mental Health Services*. 17 (1979):40–42, 45–47.
                                                                             A

The psychodynamics of the wife-abusing relationship are examined, as is the grieving process that must be worked through by the woman who is leaving the abusive relationship.

Weinraub, J. "The Battered Wives of England: A Place to Heal Their Wounds." *The New York Times*, 29 November 1975, p. C-17.   *A*

Weis, K., and S.S. Borges. "Victimology and Rape: The Case of the Legitimate Victim." *Issues in Criminology* 8 (Fall 1973):71–115. *G,H*

Discusses the relationship between victimology and rape and the genesis of the idea of the legitimate victim.

———. "Rape as a Crime without Victims and Offenders? A Methodological Critique." In *Victims and Society*, edited by E.C. Viano. Washington, D.C.: Visage Press, 1976.   *G,H*

Weiss, R.L.; H. Hops; and G.R. Patterson "A Framework for Conceptualizing Marital Conflict, A Technology for Altering It, and Some Data for Evaluating It." In *Behavior Change: Methodology, Concepts and Practices*, edited by L.A. Hamedynak, L.C. Hanty, and E.J. Mash. Champaign, Ill.: Research, 1973.   *A*

Weiss, Taub, and Rosenthal. "The Mental Health Committee: Report of the Subcommittee on the Problem of Rape in the District of Columbia." *Medical Annals D.C.*, 1972, p. 703.   *B*

Weiss, Rogers, Darwin, and Dutton. "A Study of Girl Sex Victims." *Psychiatric Quarterly*, 29 (1955):1.   *B,E,G*

Weisstein, N. "Kinder, kuche, kirche as Scientific Law: Psychology Constructs the Female." In *Sisterhood Is Powerful*, pp. 205–220. New York: Random House, 1970.   *C*

———. "Psychology Constructs the Female." In *Woman in Sexist Society: Studies in Power and Powerlessness*, edited by V. Gornick and B.K. Moran, pp. 207–224. New York: Mentor, 1972.   *C*

Weitzel, W.D.; B.J. Powell; and E.C. Penick. "Clinical Management of Father-Daughter Incest: A Critical Reexamination." *American Journal of Diseases of Children* 132 (1978):127–130.   *B*

Clinical management of father-daughter incest is discussed in the context of four questions.

Weitzman, L. "Legal Regulation of Marriage: Tradition and Change." *California Law Review* 62 (July/September 1974):1170.   *F*

Welch. "Rape and the Trauma of Inadequate Care." Prism, September 1975, p. 17.   *G*

Welsh, D.K. "Derogation of Rape Victims: A Just World and Defensive Attribution Analysis." *Dissertation Abstracts International* 39 (1):451-B, 1978.   *G*

The just-world hypothesis (people have a need to believe that the world around them is a fair and just place to live and that people earn their just rewards) and defensive-attribution theory are examined.

Weninger, R.A. "Factors Affecting the Prosecution of Rape: A Case Study of Travis County, Texas." *Virginia Law Review* 64 (1978):357–397. *G*

A field study of reports, complaints, and prosecutions of forcible rape in Travis County, Texas, during 1970–1976 is presented.

Werber, P. *Battered Wives.* Pleasantville, N.Y.: Human Relations Media Center, 1978.   *A*

The tape cassette and filmstrip, designed for persons from grade eight to college, discuss the causes of wife beating, and case histories indicate the attitudes of battered wives and review possible solutions.

————. *Dynamics of Family Violence.* Pleasantville, N.Y.: Human Relations Media Center, 1978.   *H*

The tape cassette and filmstrip present several reasons for the widespread vioence of U.S. families, including society's fascination with violence and reluctance of non-family members to interfere.

Werber, P.; K. Mayo; and P. Cochran. *Violence in the Family.* Pleasantville, N.Y.: Human Relations Media Center, 1978.   *H*

This kit, containing teachers guide, filmstrip, and tape cassettes, examines the relationship between family intimacy and conflict, emphasizes the seriousness of family violence, and reviews possible solutions.

"We're More Violent Than We Think." *MacLean's Magazine,* August 1970, pp. 25–28.   *H*

Werman, D.S. "On The Occurrence of Incest Fantasies." *Psychoanalytic Quarterly* 46 (April 1977):245–255.   *E*

Contrary to the view that conscious incest fantasies necessarily indicate severe ego or superego distortions, five clinical vignettes are presented to illustrate that such fantasies can occur in nonpsychotic patients before their resistances have been diminished in psychoanalytic treatment.

Werner, A. "Rape: Interruption of the Therapeutic by External Stress." *Psychotherapy: Theory, Research and Practice* 9 (Winter 1972):349–351.   *B,C,G*

Presents a case of rape when psychotherapy was ongoing.

Wesolowski. "Indicia of Consent? A Proposal for Change to the Common Law Rule Admitting Evidence of a Rape Victim's Character for Chastity." *Loyola of Chicago Law Journal* 7 (1976):118.   G

Wessel, P. "Jurisdiction over Family Offenses in New York: A Reconsideration of the Provisions for Choice of Forum." *Syracuse Law Review* 31 (Spring 1980):601–630.   H

> Provisions of the New York Family Court Act (1962), which intended to provide legislative relief to the battered spouse, effects of the legislation, and proposed statutory changes are discussed.

West, D.J. "Rape as Revenge." *New Society* 45 (1978):684–686.   G

> The crime of rape, as being motivated by feelings of masculine inadequacy and a desire to humiliate women, was examined via several case examples of prisoners convicted of rape or sexual assault who were enrolled in an intensive program of psychotherapy.

———. "Study of Rape in Canada." *British Journal of Criminology* 18 (1978):409–411.   B

Westchester County (N.Y.) Domestic Violence Prosecution Program. Washington, D.C.: U.S. Department of Justice.   B,H

> Activites and results are reported for a domestic-violence-prosecution program specializing in the criminal prosecution of domestic-violence cases and the coordination of victim services.

Westermeyer, J. "Incest in Psychiatric Practice: A Description of Patients and Incestuous Relationships." *Journal of Clinical Psychiatry* 39 (1978):643–648.   C,E

> A description of incest encountered in one practitioner's general psychiatric practice was presented.

Westley, W.A. *Violence and the Police: A Sociological Study of Laws*, Customs and Morality. Cambridge, Mass.: MIT Press, 1970.   B,H

We Will Not Be Beaten. 16 mm film, black and white, 41 mins. Boston: Transition House Films, 1979.   A

> Documents the stories of women who have suffered horrible abuse from their husbands.

"What about Battered Wives?" MIND National Association for Mental Health, London, 1974.   A

Whiston, S.K. "Counseling Sexual Assault Victims: A Loss Model." *Personnel and Guidance Journal* 59 (February 1981):363–366.   C

Discusses the psychological consequences of rape for the victim and suggests therapeutic strategies that counselors can use to help such clients deal with the loss of security, control, or sexual identification that may result from an assault.

White, D. "Living with a Family Breakdown." *New Society* 18 (October 1973):137–139.   *B,C*

White, L. "Women Organize to Protect Wives from Abusive Husbands." *Boston Herald-American*, 22 June 1975.   *A,B*

White, M.A., and B. Donadio. "Seven Who Were Raped." *Nursing Outlook* 22 (April 1974):245–247.   G

Whitehurst, R.N. "Violently Jealous Husbands." *Sexual Behavior*, July 1971, p. 41.   *B,H*

———. "Violence Potential in Extra-Marital Sex." *Journal of Marriage and the Family*, November 1971, pp. 683–691.   H

———. "Alternative Family Structures and Violence Reduction." In *Violence in the Family*, pp. 315–319. 1974.   *A,H*

In this article Whitehurst suggests that alternative family structures—that is, families that contain more people than the traditional husband-wife-children combination—might reduce the potential for family violence.

———. "Violence in Husband-Wife Interaction." In *Violence in the Family*, pp. 75–82. 1974.   H

The idea of male superiority is still the dominant ideology in our society.

Whiting, B.B. *Six Cultures: Studies of Child Rearing*. New York: Wiley & Sons, 1963, pp. 363–540.   B

———. "Sex Identity Conflict and Physical Violence: A Comparative Study." *American Anthropologist* 67 (December 1965):123–140. *B,H*

"Who Kills Whom." *Psychology Today* 3 (1969):54–56, 72, 74–75.   H

Analysis of a large number of statistics, associated with homicide, focuses on the intimate relationship that exists between many murderers and victims.

"Why Incest Is Not Nice: Marriage Taboos." *Economist*, 29 September 1979, pp. 272–292.   E

Whyte, W.F. *Street Corner Society*. Chicago: University of Chicago Press, 1943.   C

Whyte, W.H. *Organization Man*. New York: Simon & Schuster, 1956. C

Wickersham, G.W. *Enforcement on Prohibition Laws*. Official Record of the National Commission on Law Observance and Enforcement. Washington, D.C.: U.S. Government Printing Office, 1931.   F

Wieczorek, and Rosner. "The Law, the Nurse, and the Rape Victim."
Journal of New York State Nurses', June 1976, p. 16.   *F,G*
Washington, D.C.: National Commission on the Observance of Interna-
tional Women's Year. 1977.   *B*
"Wife Abuse: Bearing Secret Scars." *Downstate Reporter*, Spring 1978, pp.
21–23.   *A*

Aspects of wife abuse and rape are discussed.

"Wife Abuse: Myths and Stereotypes." *F.A.A.R. Newsletter*, Spring 1976,
p. 2.   *A*

Women's legal defense fund on abused women.

"The Wife Beaters." *Woman's Day Magazine*, March 1976, p. 61.   *A*
"Wife Beating." *Saint Louis Post Dispatch*, 3 August 1975.   *A*
"Wife Beating 'Catch 22' Trauma." *Sun Sentinel*.   .   *A*
Wife Beating and Child Abuse—A Selected Bibliography. Supplement 1977–
1978. Rockville, Md.: NCJRS Microfiche Program, 1978.   *A,B,E*

Approximately fifty English-language entries are included in this bibliography on wife and child abuse.

Williams. "On Sketching the Violent." *Washington Post/Potomac*, 13 Au-
gust 1972, p. 10.   *A,H*
Williams. "Things Your Husband Never Told You about Sex." *New Wo-
man*, April/May 1972, p. 18.   *C,H*
Williams, J.E. "The Neglect of Incest: A Criminologists View." *Medicine,
Science and the Law* 14 (1974):64–67.   *E*
———. "Good Victims and Real Rapes: A Comparison of Anglo, Black
and Mexican American Perspectives." Research report, NIMH Grant
R01-MH-27928, 1978.   *G*

Community attitudes toward rape were surveyed among Anglo-, black,
and Mexican-Americans to determine if any consensus on rape exists across
sex and racial ethnic categories.

———. "Sex Role Stereotypes, Women's Liberation and Rape: A Cross-
Cultural Analysis of Attitudes." Research report, NIMH Grant R01-
MH-27928, 1978.   *G*

Public definitions of rape and the relationship between attitudes about sex
roles and attitudes about rape were surveyed among Anglos, blacks, and
Mexican-Americans.

Williams, J.E., and K.A. Holmes. "Rape: The Public View, the Personal Experience." Final report, NIMH Grant R01-MH-27928, 1979.   G

An exploration of the interplay between society and the personal experience of rape is presented based on a theory of racial/sexual stratification that leads to a view of rape as the convergence of racism and sexism.

Williams, R. "Right Not to Be Beaten: The Problem in Appalachia." *Psychology Today* 11 (June 1977):36.   A
Williamson, J. "I'm Being Sexually Harassed. What Can I Do?" *Working Women* 4 (November 1979):30.   A,D
Willis, J.E. "Compensation for Victims of Domestic Violence." *Violence in the Family—A Collection of Conference Papers*, 1980, pp. 144–155.
B,H

The principal systems of Australian victim compensation and the approaches to compensating victims of criminal domestic violence are discussed.

Wills. "Rape on Trial." *Rolling Stone*, 28 August 1975, p. 80.   G
Wilson, C.F. *Violence against Women—Causes and Prevention*. Madison: University of Wisconsin, Extension Women's Education Resources, 1979.   A,C,H

A report and selective annotated bibliography focusing on crimes of violence against women are presented; topics include the history of violence and subordination of women, statistics, and causes and prevention.

Wilson, E. *The Existing Research into Battered Women*. London: National Women's Aid Federation, 1976.   A,B
Wilson, J. "The Dynamics of Incest: Presentation of One Family in Acute Crisis." *Journal of Family Practice* 7 (August 1978):363–367.   E
Wilson, P.R. *The Other Side of Rape*. Lawrence, Me.: Queensland University Press, 1978.   G
Wilson, S.B."Statement of Susanne B. Wilson on March 8, 1978 Concerning Domestic Violence Legislation." *Domestic Violence*, 1978, pp. 339–345.   F

Actions taken to address the issue of family violence and recommendations for federal legislation action are presented by a representative of the National League of Cities to a Senate subcommittee.

Wilt, G.M., and J. Bannon. "A Comprehensive Analysis of Conflict-Motivated Homicides and Assaults." Unpublished paper, Detroit, Michigan, 1972–1973.   H

Winch, R.F., and L.W. Goodman. *Selected Studies in Marriage and the Family*. New York: Holt, Rinehart and Winston, 1953.   B

Winnik, H.Z. "Victimology and Psychoanalysis." *Israel Annals of Psychiatry and Related Disciplines* 17 (1979):241–254.   H

The development of the science of victimology is reviewed, and the psychodynamic processes underlying this science are considered.

Winslow, R.W., and V. Winslow. *Deviant Reality: Alternative World Views*. Boston: Allyn and Bacon, 1974.   B

Presents an introduction to psychological and sociological theories of deviance.

Winter, G. *Love and Conflict: New Patterns in Family Life*. New York: Doubleday, 1958.   B

Winter, W.D., and A.H. Ferreira. *Research in Family Interaction: Readings and Commentary*. Palo Alto, Calif.: Science and Behavior Books, 1969.   B

Wisan, G. "Reporting on Rape: Study by Gail Wisan." *Human Behavior* 8 (April 1979):48.   G

Wittels, F. *Sex Habits of American Women*. New York: Eton, 1951.   C

Witter, C. "Drugging and Schooling." *Transaction* 8 (July/August 1971): 30–34.   B

Wittles, I., and P.E. Bornstein. "A Note on Stress and Sex Determination." *Journal of Genetic Psychology* 124 (June 1974):333–334.   H

Examined D.H. Schuster and L. Schuster's hypothesis that relative stress of the mother and father is a determinant of the sex of the newborn.

Wobst, H.M. "The Demography of Finite Populations and the Origins of the Incest Taboo." *American Antiquity* 40 (1975):1, 75–81.   E

Wolf, A.P. "Childhood Association and Sexual Attraction: A Further Test of the Westermarch Hypothesis." *American Anthropology* 72 (June 1970):503–515.   E

Wolf, P. "A Comparative Study of Victims of Crimes in Three Scandinavian Countries. (1970–74)." *Victimology: An International Journal* 2 (1977): 86.   H

In a paper presented at the Second International Symposium on Victimology, held in Boston, September 1976, studies of victims of violence, larceny, fraud, and property damage in Finland, Denmark, Norway, and Sweden are compared.

Wolfe, N. "Victim Provocation—The Battered Wife and Legal Definition of Self Defense." *Sociological Symposium*, 25 November 1979, pp. 98–118.   *A,H*

Trends in defense strategies and case dispositions for battered wives charged with murdering their husbands are surveyed, with reference to specific cases.

Wolff, R. "Systematic Desensitization and Negative Practice to Alter the Aftereffects of a Rape Attempt." *Journal of Behavior Therapy and Experimental Psychiatry* 8 (December 1977):423–425.   *G,H*

Seven years after a rape attempt a twenty-year-old woman feared staying alone at night and compulsively checked her apartment when she arrived home.

Wolfgang, M.E. "Husband-Wife Homicides." *Journal of Social Therapy* 2 (1956):263–271.   *A,H*

Homicide is a dynamic phenomenon between two or more persons caught up in a life drama where they operate in a direct, interactional relationship.

————. "Victim Precipitated Criminal Homicide." *Journal of Criminal Law, Criminology, and Police Science* 48 (May/June 1957):1–11.   *H*

Evaluates the relationship of the victim to the offender and describes how the eventual victim's actions escalate violence into homicide.

————. *Patterns in Criminal Homicide*. Philadelphia: University of Pennsylvania, 1958.   *H*

Using the detailed case files of the homicide squad of the police department of the City of Philadelphia, Dr. Wolfgang has produced a valuable study of the 588 cases of criminal homicide, involving a total of 621 offenders, that occurred during the five-year period of 1948–1952.

————. *Studies in Homicide*. New York: Harper & Row, 1967.   *H*

————. "Social Scientist in Court." *Journal of Criminal Law and Criminology* 65 (June 1974):239–247.   *F*

Wolfgang, M.E., and F. Ferracuti. *The Subculture of Violence*. London: Tavistock Publications, 1967.   *H*

Wolfgang, M.E. and M. Riedel. "Rape, Race, and the Death Penalty in Georgia." *American Journal of Orthopsychology* 45 (July 1975):568–68.   *G*

Wolmstrom, L.L., and W. Burgess. "Assessing Trauma in the Rape Victim." *American Journal of Nursing* 75 (August 1975):1288–1291.   *G*

Woman, L.M. "Diary of a Battered Housewife." *Do it Now*, March 1976,
   p. 4.   A
"Women against Rape." *Time*, 23 April 1973, p. 104.   G
Women in Transition, Incorporated. *Women's Survival Manual*. Philadelphia, 1972.   B,C

> Deals with the problems of women in the process of separation or divorce
> and gives advice on how to seek help and survive the transition from
> marriage.

————. *Women in Transition: A Feminist Handbook on Separation and
   Divorce*. Philadelphia, 1975, p. 22.   B,C
Women's Advocate. *Women's Advocates Newsletter*. Saint Paul, Minne-
   sota.   B
Woods, F.B. ".A Community Approach to Working with Battered Wo-
   men." *Dissertation Abstracts International* 40 (3):1435-B, 1979.   A,B

> A model for conceptualizing the problem of woman assault and the steps a
> community may take to aid these victims of domestic violence are pre-
> sented.

Woods, G. "Some Aspects of Group Rape in Sydney." *Australian and New
   Zealand Journal of Criminology* 2 (1969):105–119.   G
Wooten, J.N. "The Effects of Victim/Assailant Familiarity and Victim
   Resistance on Attitudes toward Rape among Law Enforcement Per-
   sonnel and College Students." *Dissertation Abstracts International* 41
   (4-B) 1487-1488V, October 1980.   H
Working Women United Institute. *Sexual Harassment on the Job: Results
   of a Preliminary Survey*. Ithaca, N.Y., 1975.   D
————. "Transcript of Speak Out on Sexual Harassment of Women at Work
   held 4 May 1975." Ithaca, N.Y., 1976.   D
Wright, J. "Wife Beating Not Uncommon: Spouse Assault Doesn't Just
   Happen to Others." *Kalamazoo Gazette*, 5 December 1975.   A
Yankowski, L. "Battered Women: A Study of the Situation in the District
   of Columbia." Unpublished, 1975.   A
Yin, P.P. "Fear of Crime among the Elderly: Some Issues and Sugges-
   tions." *Social Problems* 27 (1980):492–504.   H

> A review of the literature on fear of crime among the elderly and its
> determinants is provided, as well as a conceptual framework within which
> to locate the strengths and weaknesses of these works.

Yorokoglu, A., and J.P. Kemph. "Children Not Severely Damaged by
   Incest with a Parent." *Journal of the American Academy of Child
   Psychiatry* 5 (1966):111–124.   E

Young, L. *Wednesday's Children: A Study of Neglect and Abuse.* New
York: McGraw-Hill, 1967.   *E*
————. "Wife Beating in Britain: A Socio-Historical Analysis, 1850–1914."
Paper presented at the Annual Meeting of the American Sociological
Association in New York, 1976.   *A*
Young, M.E. *Crimes and Crime Prevention*, vol. 2. Springfield, Va.: Na-
tional Technical Information Service, 1979.   *A,G,H*

> Reports are cited on assault, rape, and murder. Crime-prevention systems
> for homes, businesses, and vehicles are described.

Young, M., and P. Willmott. *The Symmetrical Family: A Study of Work
and Leisure in the London Region.* London: Routledge and Kegan
Paul, 1973.   *C*
Zacker, J., and M. Bard. "Further Findings on Assaultiveness and Alcohol
Use in Interpersonal Disputes." *American Journal of Community Psy-
chology* 5 (1977):373–383.   *H*

> In this study, police officers, over a four-month period, employed system-
> atic naturalistic observation during their interventions as third parties in
> disputes between non-family members and between family members.

Zalba, S.R. "The Abused Child: A Survey of the Problem." *Social Work* 2
(October 1966):3–16.   *E*
————. "The Abused Child: II—A Typology for Classification and Treat-
ment." *Social Work* 7 (January 1967):70–80.   *E*
————. "Battered Children." *Trans-Action*, July/August 1971, p. 59.   *E*
Zaphiris, A.G. *Incest: The Family with Two Known Victims.* Englewood,
Colo.: Child Protection, American Humane Association, 1978.   *E*
Zevin, J. *Violence in America: What Is the Alternative?* Englewood Cliffs,
N.J.: Prentice-Hall, 1973.   *H*
Ziegenhagen, E.A. "The Recidivist Victim of Violent Crime." *Victimology*
1 (Winter 1976):538–550.   *H*

> This study investigated types of crime and social context and physical
> setting of crimes, as well as perception of the perpetrator, social back-
> ground, attitudes toward recidivist victimization, and recidivist victims of
> violent crime.

Ziese, P. "Broken Home, Suicide, Complicated by Suicide with Endoge-
nous Depression." *Social Psychiatry* 3 (1968):70–75.   *H*
Zullo, A.A., and R. Fulman. "Wife Beating in Nice Homes." *New Woman*, March/April 1976, pp. 68–69.   *A*

Well in excess of 200,000 American husbands are habitual wife beaters with an increase in the number of professional men who beat their wives of at least 20 percent. In the average pattern of wife beating, the assaults start early in the marriage and the wife endures them for about eight years. These assaults are usually (95 percent of them) the result of the husband's drinking. Only a minority of the husbands beat their wives when they are not drunk. It tends to be a weekend pattern, usually after the husband has gone on a drinking binge.

"Zulu Queen's Custody Case." *San Francisco Chronicle*, 5 May 1975, p. 24.

F

Index

About the Author

Joseph J. Costa is principal of the Shenandoah Valley Junior/Senior High School, Shenandoah, Pennsylvania. He received the B.S. from Bloomsburg State College, the M.S.L.S. from Villanova University, and the M. Ed. (reading specialist) from Kutztown State College. He has had practical experience in elementary, junior-high, and high schools as a teacher, coach, and librarian; and librarian experience at the Schuylkill Campus of The Pennsylvania State University. He coauthored (with Gordon K. Nelson) *Child Abuse and Neglect: Legislation, Reporting, and Prevention*, (Lexington Books, 1978); and authored *A Directory of Library Instruction Programs in Pennsylvania Academic Libraries*, sponsored by the Academic Library Instruction Committee, College and Research Libraries Division, Pennsylvania Library Association, 1980.

DATE DUE